MW01071125

THE GREATNESS OF THE
KINGDOM

THE GREATNESS OF THE KINGDOM

An Inductive Study of the Kingdom of God

by
Alva J. McClain

BMH Books
Winona Lake, Indiana 46590

The Greatness of the Kingdom

Copyright © 1959 by Alva J. McClain

ISBN: 0-88469-011-3

09 08 07 05   14 13 12 11 10

Published by BMH Books
P.O. Box 544, Winona Lake, IN 46590
www.bmhbooks.com

Originally published in 1968 by Moody Press and 1974 by BMH Books
Tenth Printing, BMH Books, March 2005

Cover design: Paul Lewis

Printed in the United States of America

To My Wife

FOREWORD

More than twenty years ago a leading Biblical conservative scholar in this country said to me, "There is a man at Grace Theological Seminary, Dr. Alva J. McClain, who has the finest grasp of the significance of the Biblical teaching about the Kingdom of God of any man of our generation." Other men in whose judgment I have confidence made similar statements to me from time to time. Later, when it was my privilege to become personally acquainted with Dr. McClain, I asked if he were going to publish the results of his research, and he said he was indeed. Heavy responsibilities as the president and guiding genius of Grace Theological Seminary, together with his schedule of teaching, and occasional periods of illness, postponed the completion of this work until now.

When I was a boy, the Biblical Department at the University of Chicago was placing a great deal of emphasis on the subject of the Kingdom of God. Knowing that this school held extremely liberal views, I, living in an ultraconservative atmosphere (for which I have always been grateful), tended to shy away from the entire subject of the Kingdom. However, I was delivered from complete avoidance of the subject, as perhaps many others were, by the magnificent address on the Kingdom by Robert McWatty Russell, delivered at the still-unparalleled prophetic conference held at the Moody Bible Institute in 1914. Since that time, an enormous literature has been developed on the subject, both from conservative and liberal viewpoints; with the result that there is now much confusion in the minds of many Christians about what is meant by "the Kingdom of God." Views range from the extreme left position, where it is made more or less a synonym for democracy, to the extreme right, where it has been identified by some exclusively with a Messianic kingdom to be set up in Palestine at the end of this age. In my judgment, the greater part of this literature has *not* been the result of a close study of the *Biblical* teachings concerning the Kingdom in both Old and New Testaments.

Never having heard Dr. McClain speak on this subject, I approached the reading of his manuscript with an open mind, and, I am afraid, with a slight feeling that probably much of the material in these hundreds of pages would be more or less what I had already read in works of other able authors in years gone by. In this I was greatly mistaken. Many of the truths which the author of *The Greatness of the Kingdom* has here developed, especially in his consideration of Biblical revelation about the Kingdom up to the time of the prophets, has thrown more light upon this theme for me than has any other volume on this difficult subject that has come to my attention. Although I have been teaching English Bible for over twenty years, I must confess that some of the things herein set forth from Pentateuchal passages proved almost embarrassing to me: in reading these pages my frequent reaction was, "Why have I not thought of that?" As I have told Dr. McClain, in my forthcoming manual for the study of the book of Genesis for Sunday school teachers, I intend to include a considerable number of the interpretations he has presented.

My own opinion is that many people, not trained in the intricate nomenclature of modern theology, find many books, even by conservative scholars, difficult to apprehend; and they become somewhat bewildered. They are continually being confronted with names such as Schweitzer, Bultmann, Otto, Dodds, etc., and with such terms as realized eschatology, existentialism, relation of time to eternity, etc.; and often when they have finished reading a volume they do not seem to know any more about the *Biblical* teaching than when they began. Readers will find this work by Dr. McClain a most refreshing exception to this. For he has centered attention on the Biblical teaching about the Kingdom of God, and many passages in the Scripture will now have a new and richer meaning for many of us.

The author was born of parents notably identified with the Brethren movement which originated in Europe in 1708 and came to America in 1719-1729. His mother was a sister of Dr. A. D. Gnagey, an able clergyman and editor who participated in the dissent of 1882 and the organization of "The Brethren Church"; and his father, Walter Scott McClain, was ordained to its ministry in 1890. After studying at the University of Washington, the Bible Institute of Los Angeles, and Antioch College, Dr. McClain graduated from Occidental College with highest honors. His theological education was pursued at Xenia Theological Seminary from which he received the Master of Theology degree. He has been a member of The Brethren Church since 1911, and was ordained to its ministry in 1917. He served as pastor of the First Brethren Church of Philadelphia, Pa., and has been twice elected Moderator of the General Conference of the denomination. He has taught in the Philadelphia School of the Bible, the Bible Institute of Los Angeles, and Ashland College. In 1930 he directed the academic reorganization of Ashland Seminary as a graduate school of the College, and served as Professor of Christian Theology and Apologetics for seven years; also as Associate Dean and Dean successively. He was active in the founding of Grace Theological Seminary in 1937, and since that time has served as its president and Professor of Christian Theology; also as president of Grace College since its organization as a four-year school of Liberal Arts in 1953. The honorary degrees of Doctor of Divinity and Doctor of Laws were conferred upon him by the Bible Institute of Los Angeles and Bob Jones University respectively. Dr. McClain is a member of the honor society of Phi Beta Kappa and is listed in *Who's Who in America.*

Though this volume is Dr. McClain's first major work to appear in published form, his earlier brochure on *Daniel's Prophecy of the Seventy Weeks* (1940), which has gone through seven editions, was at once recognized as the careful work of a Biblical scholar. Also to his credit must be added a number of excellent monographs, among which is *The Doctrine of the Kenosis in Philippians* 2:5-8 (published by "The Biblical Review" in 1928), pronounced by the late Dr. G. Campbell Morgan to be quite the finest treatment of the subject he had ever read.

In my own mind I have often compared Dr. McClain's scholastic record with that of Professor Samuel Harris of Yale Divinity School. With the exception of two or three pamphlets, this great scholar of a former generation published nothing until he was sixty-nine years of age, when he issued his *Philosophical Basis of Theism* (1883), which was immediately recognized as one of the most profound and comprehensive works on theism ever published in this country. When a man does not publish until that time of life, and when the work represents years of teaching and most careful writing and revising, one may expect a notable product.

ix

Foreword

I would like earnestly to commend this work of Dr. McClain's to all Christians who are looking for dependable literature concerning these basic themes of the oracles of God. May our gracious Lord preserve the author for years to come, that he may complete his entire projected series on Christian Theology, of which this is the first published volume.

WILBUR M. SMITH
Professor of English Bible
Fuller Theological Seminary

Pasadena, California

PREFACE

This discussion of the Kingdom of God represents Volume V in a projected series on the general subject of Christian Theology, an area in which I have been lecturing to theological students since 1930; the complete course extending three hours a week for an academic period of three years. The outline of special subjects included in these lectures has been as follows: (1) God and Revelation; (2) The Persons of the Triune God; (3) God and the World; (4) Salvation and the Christian Life; (5) The Kingdom of God; (6) The Christian Church; (7) The Last Things.

In deciding to begin the series with the doctrine of the Kingdom, I have been influenced by encouragement received from my valued friend, Dr. Wilbur M. Smith, whose gracious Foreword appears earlier in the book. For that matter, it is a sound principle of action to undertake the larger and more difficult tasks first. And the Kingdom *is* a difficult theme, not only by reason of its vast extent in the pages of Biblical revelation, but also because of the great variety of opinions which have been expressed about it.

In arriving at the view of the Kingdom of God set forth in this book, I have employed an inductive method of investigation in the Scriptures. It has been a long road, retraced and reviewed often in the course of preparation; yet the personal compensations have been many and richly worthwhile. Certainly, I could not pretend to have divested myself of all presuppositions and predilections in advance of the journey. After all, as someone has truly said, "the posture of impartiality" is generally a very deceptive thing. Nevertheless, I have tried earnestly to weigh the divine testimony honestly and with an open mind. If errors have been made, I shall hope that these may turn out to be what the late Charles F. Kettering once referred to as "informative errors," which at last will lead to something better. But in the main, after some forty years of study of the subject of the Kingdom, I am more firmly than ever convinced that the Premillennial viewpoint is the true doctrine of the Word of God. Furthermore, this view of the Kingdom has the additional merit of mediating reasonably between two unhappy extremes: modern Liberalism, on the one hand, with its dubious and interminable process of "kingdom building"; and a New Orthodoxy with its unresolved tensions and irrational break with history. In the Premillennial view the coming Kingdom becomes the consummating link between history and the eternal order, thus guarding the Church from either illusion or despair as regards the present life. To use the very discriminating words of Lange, in the "Millennial Kingdom" we have "the true mediation of the last metamorphosis of the old world" (On Rev. 21:1).

Since the Kingdom occupies such a large and important place in the area of Biblical eschatology, some readers may feel that more might have been said about certain events in the prophetic program. But the present volume does not purport to be a treatise on eschatology *in general*, a subject reserved for a later volume in the series. By previous definition, the content of the present volume is limited to such material as seemed to be relevant and essential to an intelligible account of the Kingdom of God. Because of the great wealth of Biblical material on the subject, as well as the prevalence of the eschatological element, it has not been easy to draw the lines of limitation. The extent to which I have succeeded, even approximately, will doubtless be a matter of individual opinion.

Because this book is primarily a study of the Kingdom of God as presented in the Scriptures, rather than an account of the *history* of the doctrine, I have not felt it necessary to multiply quotations from the various parties on disputed points. Where disagreement exists in points of Biblical interpretation I have generally sought only to show that the interpretations adopted herein are exegetically possible, and also that they have some support among reputable scholars whose overall views of the Kingdom may not always accord with my own. The documentation of sources will be found at the bottom of each page where quotations or references appear. Biblical quotations are always from the King James Version unless otherwise noted. When the reference extends beyond the text quoted, as in some cases, the purpose has been to show that the context points definitely to the subject of the Kingdom.

In giving literary form to this material I have not been altogether unmindful of the chasm which too often exists between the specialist and the general public. And the theologian, not less than other specialists, has an obligation to *communicate* ideas, not only to those who may have mastered the peculiar terminology of his own craft but also to all men. For this reason, his product should not be disassociated wholly from the contemporary scene; what he has to say must mean something to those who are living here and now. This does not necessarily mean myopic narrowness in a cult of "Today"; but rather a measure of universalism in word and reference which will both speak to the present generation and also exhibit some quality of permanence beyond the restricted interests of the passing moment.

I have ventured to hope, therefore, that the readers of this work may derive some measure of spiritual reassurance and practical guidance in the contemporary situation. We are caught today, as Erich Kahler's title reminds us, between the *Tower* and the *Abyss*. And it has become a serious question whether men can any longer trust themselves with the appalling things they have made. For while these things, on the one hand, offer the promise of a future surpassing the highest dreams of a sinful humanity, it is also true that the same things are warning us of possible catastrophe black as the pit itself. The community of nations is now existing precariously in the delicate balance of what Mendes-France has called an "equilibrium of terror"; and thoughtful men of affairs are not too optimistic about the outcome of human action. The desperate danger of the hour lies in what a few men — perhaps *one* man — may be able to precipitate upon modern civilization involving the possible destruction of all its works. It is becoming clearer that we are not passing through merely another one of those minor crises not uncommon to mankind, but rather that we have reached a cataclysmic junction in the history of the world from which there can be no point of return. As James T. Shotwell,[1] noted historian and internationalist, recently observed, we are now at the last frontier; and, in a sense, history must begin all over again. For it seems quite certain that we shall never again be even measurably safe here on earth until all men without exception have become *good* men, or until God Himself breaks once more into human history supernaturally — this time to establish with divine omnipotence a Kingdom of righteousness and compassion *upon earth*, thus supplanting the misrule and impotence of men. Of the two alternatives, the latter seems by far the most plausible and fraught with better hope

[1] See his article "The Last Frontier" in *Think* magazine for June, 1956 (New York: International Machines Corporation).

for the future. In the meantime, the wise will not forget that above all the uncertainties and tragedy of human action there is a present Universal Kingdom of God which even now "ruleth over all," and that its Invincible King will have the last word in history. "Now unto the King eternal, immortal, invisible, the only wise God, be honour and glory for ever and ever. Amen."

ALVA J. McCLAIN

Grace Theological Seminary
Winona Lake, Indiana

ACKNOWLEDGMENTS

To the Administration and Alumni of Dallas Theological Seminary, and particularly to President John F. Walvoord, I have been greatly indebted for the honor and privilege of presenting in condensed form the main ideas of this volume to the faculty and students as the W. H. Griffith Thomas Memorial Lectures for 1954; and also for the subsequent publication of the lectures in a series of six articles in the *Bibliotheca Sacra*.

The material in Part III, dealing with *The Kingdom in Old Testament Prophecy*, was presented at Western Conservative Baptist Theological Seminary in 1956 under the Frederick Bueerman — John B. Champion Lecture Foundation. Part II, dealing with *The Kingdom in Old Testament History*, was presented at Talbot Theological Seminary in the 1958 Lyman Stewart Memorial Lectures. The final section of the book, under the title of *The Kingdom in the Apocalypse*, was presented to the faculty, students and alumni of Grace Theological Seminary in January, 1959, as the annual Louis S. Bauman Memorial Lectures. For all these valued opportunities, and for the friendly interest so apparent in the various audiences, I am deeply grateful.

I desire also to express my gratitude and obligation to the directing Board of Grace Theological Seminary for their interest and kindness in granting the time necessary for the task of research and writing: to my colleagues in the Administration for their cheerful willingness to assume and perform efficiently many tasks which ordinarily fall to the President: to Dr. Herman A. Hoyt, Dean of the School, with whom important points were often discussed, and who read the manuscript in whole: to other members of the Faculty who read parts of the Manuscript and offered helpful suggestions: to the many students whose enthusiastic interest and provocative "hard questions" were always intellectually stimulating to the teacher: to the Reverend Benjamin A. Hamilton, Research Librarian of the Seminary, for preparing the indexes of Biblical references and authors quoted or referred to: to my former secretary, now Mrs. Charles Lockwood, for typing the final draft, working at times beyond her office hours;

and above all to my wife for her loving encouragement, unfailing patience, and invaluable assistance in the many tedious but important details involved in the preparation and publication of the manuscript.

For written permission to quote from certain publications, I wish to express appreciation as follows: to Abingdon Press, *The Kingdom of God* (1953) by John Bright; to *The American Scholar*, "Wanted: A Sovereign" (Spring, 1957) by F. Lyman Windolph; to Wm. B. Eerdmans Publishing Company, *The Kingdom of God* (1951) by Louis Berkhof; to Intervarsity Fellowship, *Modern Discovery and the Bible* (1952) by A. Rendle Short; to *Interpretation*, "The Israel of God" (July, 1956) by T. F. Torrance; to the Macmillan Company, *The Quest of the Historical Jesus* (1948) by Albert Schweitzer; also *The Kingdom of God* (1931) by Ernest F. Scott; to Oxford University Press, *Christology and Criticism* (1929) by B. B. Warfield; to the Presbyterian and Reformed Publishing Company, *Prophecy and the Church* (1945) by O. T. Allis; also *Revelation Twenty* (1955) by Marcellus Kik; to R. R. Snowden, M.D., *The Coming of the Lord* (1919) by his father, James H. Snowden; and to the *Journal of Bible and Religion*, article by Paul Schubert (August, 1946).

It would be impossible for me to indicate, even in a general way, my obligation to that host of other authors whose writings have made some contribution to my guidance in the study of the Kingdom of God as revealed in the Scriptures, and to the formation of my conclusions. It must suffice to say, I am debtor to all.

ALVA J. McCLAIN

CONTENTS

CONTENTS

PART ONE

INTRODUCTORY CONSIDERATIONS

In a certain sense, every branch of literature may be regarded as auxiliary to the study of the history of the Kingdom of God.

—*John Peter Lange*

PART ONE

INTRODUCTORY CONSIDERATIONS

CHAPTER I

THE GREATNESS OF THE KINGDOM

> The organ of man's religious nature has a wide keyboard. . . . Any
> scientific religious theory which tries to evoke the music by cutting out
> all the octaves but one, will soon be compelled to yield its place to a
> better player.　　　　　　　　　　　　　　*President E. Y. Mullins* [1]

The title chosen for this volume, a phrase found in the seventh
chapter of the Book of Daniel, will indicate the general thesis which
I propose to establish, namely, the *greatness* of the Kingdom of God.
Among many thoughtful students of the Word of God there is a
growing conviction that much of the disagreement about the subject of the Kingdom has arisen out of narrow and one-sided opinions
as to its nature. This situation exists, of course, in many other fields
of intellectual investigation. Men have gone wrong, not so much
in what they have affirmed, but rather in what they have denied
or neglected.

1. *The Danger of Over-Simplification*

This tendency has been given impetus by that natural bent of
the human mind, best exemplified in the systematic philosophers,
which impels men to search for a single principle or idea that will
explain everything else. Although this intellectual motive, held under legitimate restraints, has often led to fruitful results, it nevertheless is always attended by certain hazards. In the first place,
there is the danger of omitting matters of importance which stand
outside our neat little formulas and refuse to yield. [2] In the second
place, thinking now particularly of the field of Christian theology,
this passion for over-simplification may cause men to miss the richness and infinite variety of Christian truth in the interest of a barren
unity. It was William James who once suggested that, considered

[1] *Christianity at the Cross Roads* (New York: George H. Doran, 1924), p. 144.
[2] For a larger discussion of this danger see A. N. Whitehead's *Religion in the
Making* (New York: Macmillan Co., 1926), pp. 76-77. Also my article "Current
Tendencies Which Limit Faith and Life" in *The Biblical Review*, January, 1931.

3

from a certain abstract standpoint, even a masterpiece of violin music might be described as "a scraping of horses' tails over cats' bowels!" Such a definition, of course, has the great merit of simplicity; it gets rid of all the mystery of personality and the nuances of human genius. But the residue is not very interesting.

Now the Biblical doctrine of the Kingdom of God has suffered considerably from this tendency toward over-simplification.[3] Men have overlooked the greatness of this Kingdom, its richness and complexity, its vast sweep through history, and its outreach into the eternal state. Too much has been ignored or explained away in the interest of partial and inadequate definitions. This assertion is underscored by the very small place given to the subject of the Kingdom in certain well-known and honored works by conservative theologians. In some, one looks in vain for even any mention of the term kingdom in their indexes; and their treatment of our Lord's office as King is both regrettably meager and unsatisfactory. When we turn to those books written specifically about the Kingdom, too often they are found to be devoted chiefly to one aspect which is made the "type-phenomenon" of a system which leaves out other important and significant elements.

As examples of this tendency, two authors may be cited. The late Prof. L. Berkhof does recognize the highly complex nature of the Kingdom of God, and he rightly suggests that its many aspects have often given rise to various and diverse interpretations. But Berkhof's own book suffers from the very narrowness he warns against. It is quite astonishing to read a book under the broad title of *The Kingdom of God* without so much as a single chapter dealing with this Kingdom in the Old Testament Scriptures. In the same way, A. B. Bruce's book on *The Kingdom of God* practically ignores the Old Testament which provides both the historical roots of the idea and also the prophetical outline of the Kingdom yet to be realized in eschatological time. More recent books are displaying greater interest in the Old Testament material: for example, John Bright devotes considerably more than half of his *The Kingdom of God* to this particular area of Holy Scripture.

2. *The Centrality of the Kingdom in Scripture*

The Kingdom of God is, in a certain and important sense, the

[3] Cf. Albert Schweitzer who treats with high scorn any interpretation of Christ's Kingdom which goes beyond "a single point of view." *The Quest of the Historical Jesus,* trans. by W. Montgomery from 1st German ed., 1906 (New York: Macmillan Co., 1948), p. 238.

grand central theme of all Holy Scripture. As Dr. Bright has correctly observed, "The concept of the Kingdom of God involves, in a real sense, the total message of the Bible"; and, "Old Testament and New Testament thus stand together as the two acts of a single drama. Act I points to its conclusion in Act II, and without it the play is an incomplete, unsatisfying thing. But Act II must be read in the light of Act I, else its meaning will be missed. For the play is organically one. The Bible is *one book*. Had we to give that book a title, we might with justice call it 'The Book of the Coming Kingdom of God.' That is, indeed, its central theme everywhere."[4] In approving this affirmation we are not forgetting the person and work of our Lord Jesus Christ. For *He* is the King eternal, and there could be no final Kingdom apart from Him and His work as the Lamb slain from the foundation of the world. Surely the primary object of our faith must always be the One who is both Lord and Saviour; but as we contemplate Him and His manifold glories as revealed in the Word of God, we shall inescapably come sooner or later to the Kingdom of which He is the divine center. For it is in this Kingdom that the Father's eternal purpose in the incarnate Son shall be certainly and completely fulfilled. This reign of God arises out of His own sovereign nature, was reflected in the "dominion" bestowed by God upon the first Adam, was forfeited quickly by reason of the sin of man, has been restored judicially in the Last Adam, will be realized on earth in the final age of human history, and reaches out endlessly beyond history where we behold a throne which, as John explains, is "the throne of God and of the Lamb" (Rev. 22:3). Our Lord's inseparable and central relation to the Kingdom may serve to explain, at least in part, the compelling interest and fascination which the subject of the Kingdom of God has exercised upon the greatest minds in the Church, from Augustine with the twenty-two books of his *De Civitate Dei* (426) down to the massive treatise by George N. H. Peters under the title of *The Theocratic Kingdom* (1884). An account of the literature on the subject would include writers of almost every conceivable theological viewpoint.

3. *The Kingdom and Eschatology*

In the Biblical doctrine of the Kingdom of God we have *the* Christian philosophy of history.[5] Hence, to see clearly the many-

[4] John Bright, *The Kingdom of God* (New York: Abingdon-Cokesbury Press, 1953), pp. 7, 197.
[5] See Appendix, chap. XXVIII.

sided nature and vast scope of this Kingdom will not only shed
light on the purposes and ways of God but also give to men a better
"understanding of the times." No adequate system of Biblical eschatology can possibly be constructed apart from the history and
meaning of the concept of the Kingdom of God. Furthermore, it
has been rightly noted that any failure to understand the Kingdom
as set forth in Biblical revelation, with its rich variety and magnificence of design, may actually blur the vision of good men to other
matters of high theological importance to Christian faith. We may
wonder sometimes at Luther's open and determined attitude toward
the Book of Revelation, as he bluntly said, "Even if it were a blessed
thing to believe what is contained in it, no man knows what that is."
But Olshausen puts his finger unerringly on the great Reformer's
blind spot when he remarks that the final book of the Bible was
obscure to Luther simply because "he could not thoroughly apprehend the doctrine of God's Kingdom on earth, which is exhibited
in the Revelation, and forms the proper center of everything contained in it." [6] There have been other scholars who, although fortunately unwilling to follow Luther in his hasty exclusion of the
Apocalypse from the canon of fully inspired Scripture, nevertheless
have not done much better in expounding its glorious visions.

Here again, it should be observed, if men would understand
clearly the future consummation of the Kingdom, they must first
understand the Kingdom in history; if they expect to understand
the Kingdom of which our Lord spoke, they must first consider what
the Old Testament prophets have said about it; if they desire to
expound the Book of Revelation, they must begin with the Book
of Daniel.

    [6] H. Olshausen, *Biblical Commentary on the New Testament,* trans. A. C. Kendrick
(New York: Sheldon and Co., 1861), Vol. I, Intro., p. cxv.

CHAPTER II

VARIOUS INTERPRETATIVE IDEAS ABOUT THE KINGDOM

> No one can make a serious study of the subject without discovering that the Kingdom of God is a many-sided conception, and that its presentation in the Gospels is complex rather than simple. The study of its various aspects leads to a difference of emphasis; and this, in turn, gives birth to a large number of, often disparate, views. —*L. Berkhof*[1]

What follows under this heading is not intended to serve as any strictly chronological account of what men have thought about the Kingdom down through the centuries since the beginning of its revelation in Scripture. Such a task would be enormously complicated, and all attempts to summarize the history in a brief statement must suffer from the defect of over-simplification. Passing over the important period of Old Testament history, Archibald Robertson has stated the matter as follows: "The Kingdom of God has, in the course of Christian History, received three principal interpretations. It has been identified firstly with the perfect reign of God in heaven after the Last Judgment; secondly with a visible reign of Christ on earth between the second coming of Christ and the Last Judgment; thirdly with the Visible Church on earth between the first and the second coming of Christ. Of these three, the first has been the most persistent . . ."[2] Speaking of the various interpretations of the Biblical doctrine of the Kingdom down through the "ages," James Orr says, "The chief are the Patristic Chiliastic [Millennial] idea; the Medieval or Catholic idea . . . ; the Reformation idea, which still identifies the kingdom too exclusively with the Church; and the various modern forms of conception in the Church and schools from Kant downwards."[3]

In the brief space which can be given to this matter here, I have

---

[1] *The Kingdom of God* (Grand Rapids: Eerdmans Publishing Co., 1951), p. 12.
[2] *Regnum Dei*, Bampton Lectures (New York: Macmillan Co., 1901), p. 119.
[3] "Kingdom of God," *Dictionary of the Bible*, ed. James Hastings (New York: Scribner's Sons, 1901), Vol. II, p. 856.

felt it best to restrict my treatment to a bare statement of the various important *ideas* without attempting to trace the ramifications of their history, although the chronological order is not wholly ignored. In reading the statement which follows, it should be remembered that the terms employed do not always designate rigidly defined schools of opinion. Neither are the listed ideas necessarily mutually exclusive; sometimes two or even more of these ideas are held in combination. Furthermore, some ideas have been arrived at by means of a subjectively critical rejection of certain important areas of Biblical testimony; others by a shifting technique of interpretation. It is interesting to note, however, that regardless of how widely men have differed, whether as solidly conservative or radically liberal, all have felt it necessary to find support for their views in the Scriptures. Perhaps it would be best to say that the ideas as stated below represent *emphases* found at various times and places in the long history of the doctrine of the Kingdom. As special or exclusive emphases, a few are early while others are late; some have persisted vigorously; others have been somewhat ephemeral; still others have waned and later have been revived.

1. *The National Kingdom Idea*

This associates the Kingdom with a certain people, the nation of Israel; not in some far-off heavenly state, but in a living nation on the earth. This viewpoint is, of course, pre-Christian in origin and characteristically Jewish. Regardless of the differences between Jewish scholars and their respective religious parties, often so great as to seem utterly irreconcilable, all in some sense or degree have felt that to Israel belongs the Kingdom. Upon this point even the Alexandrian Philo, with all his cosmopolitanism and philosophical speculations, "did not waver."[4] So also the materialistic Sadducee as well as the modern liberal Jew.

2. *The Millennial Kingdom Idea*

Here the Kingdom of God appears as a government of God to be established on earth at the second coming of Christ, who will reign with His risen and glorified saints over the nations in a literal kingdom for "a thousand years." That such was the almost universal belief of the early Church is now generally conceded by scholars who are able to read history with a minimum of theological preju-

---

[4] "Philo of Alexandria," *New Schaff-Herzog Encyclopedia of Religious Knowledge*, ed. E. M. Jackson (New York: Funk and Wagnalls, 1911), Vol. IX, p. 39.

dice. Archibald Robertson says this view "prevailed in the Church generally for two centuries and a half, and in the Western Church for four centuries . . . until the time of Augustine."[5] As a matter of fact, Augustine himself shared this belief at first, but later changed his mind, with momentous consequences to the Christian Church.

3. The Celestial Kingdom Idea

This identifies the Kingdom simply with the reign of God in heaven, and may have been suggested by the term "kingdom of heaven" which occurs so frequently in the Gospel of Matthew. James Stalker says that in early Christian centuries the phrase *kingdom of heaven* was used to "designate heaven itself."[6] At any rate, of all the different ideas, this seems to have been the most popular and persistent.[7] Viewed from the standpoint of time, two variations may be noted: first, a *future* reign of God in eternity after the close of human history; and second, a *present* reign of God in heaven. This second view may be found very widely in the popular mind, to which "entering the Kingdom" means simply "going to heaven" at death. Obviously, this celestial reign of God may also be regarded as both present and future.

4. The Ecclesiastical Kingdom Idea

Here the Kingdom of God is identified with the *Church;* interpreted as the visible hierarchy in Roman Catholicism, and the invisible Church in the Reformation. It must not be overlooked, however, that both Luther and Calvin did regard the external organization of considerable importance, it being "the casket which enshrines the reality," the two being not altogether separable. Augustine may be regarded as the father of this Church-Kingdom idea. His *De Civitate Dei* shifts back and forth between the two conceptions of the Church; sometimes the Church is the visible and external organization; but again it is set forth as an invisible body of the elect known only to God. Thus a theological foundation was provided upon which both Rome and the Reformers would erect respectively two vastly different systems.

5. The Spiritual Kingdom Idea

This finds the Kingdom of God in that inner and therefore unseen rule of God over the hearts of men who yield themselves to

[5] *Op. cit.,* p. 124.

[6] "Kingdom of God," *International Standard Bible Encyclopedia,* ed. James Orr (Chicago: Howard-Severance, 1915), Vol. III, p. 1807.

[7] Archibald Robertson, *op. cit.,* p. 119.

His will. Perhaps the idea has never been better stated than by Bruce: The Kingdom is "not to be sought or found in any existing society, civil or ecclesiastical. It is an inspiration rather than an institution. It possesses the quality of inwardness. It comes not with observation, but has its seat in the heart."[8] It is *a kingdom of grace in order to be a kingdom of holiness.*"[9] Bruce did not think too highly of the Church on earth; in fact, he felt it almost "impossible" to be enthusiastic about its future. But no matter what happens to the Church, we need not despair: "The Kingdom of God will remain"; this much at least "cannot be moved."[10] In developing somewhat the same idea about the Kingdom, Snowden writes: "In the New Testament the material trappings of the kingdom, as prefigured in the Old Testament, . . . are stripped off and it appears in its pure spirituality. It is now clearly brought out that the kingdom has its seat in the heart and consists in the rule of God in the soul or in moral and spiritual dispositions and habits."[11] To Snowden the Church is "the most powerful human agency for the establishing of the Kingdom of God in the world,"[12] but the Church and the Kingdom are not the same thing. "Always the kingdom of heaven is within you."[13]

6. *The Moral Kingdom Idea*

The Kingdom of God, in this view, is pre-eminently a matter of ethics, the reign of the moral law over the lives of men. As conceived by the critical philosopher Immanuel Kant (1724-1804), the "kingdom of God" as a Biblical term was lifted out of its supernatural context and made the semantic framework of a moral kingdom of "ends." This idea has had a strong attraction for those who, for alleged intellectual reasons, have had trouble with the supernatural and even with the question of God's existence, but who at the same time have felt that we must have morality. Hence, as Kant worked out the problem, since without a God it is hard to see how morality could have any valid foundation, we must assume what cannot be rationally proven, namely, that there is a God who rules in some sense through moral law. Thus in a practical way, if not theoretically, the so-called "categorical imperative" of the good life could be validated. Outside of certain intellectual classes,

---

[8] A. B. Bruce, *The Kingdom of God* (4th ed.; New York: Scribner and Welford, 1891), p. 252.

[9] *Ibid.,* p. 54.   [10] *Ibid.,* p. 272.

[11] James H. Snowden, *The Coming of the Lord* (2nd ed., rev.; New York: Macmillan, 1919), p. 55.

[12] *Ibid.,* p. 58.   [13] *Ibid.,* p. 59.

the total scheme has been limited in its influence; although in his day Kant was revered by many almost as a "second Messiah," and his theory of knowledge appears in certain forms of modern theology.

7. The Liberal Social-Kingdom Idea

According to this emphasis, the Kingdom of God is the progressive social organization and improvement of mankind, in which society rather than the individual is given first place. The main task of the Church is, therefore, to establish a Christian Social Order which in turn will actually make "bad men do good things."[14] As a modern movement this notion began with the cult of "Christian Socialism" under the leadership of J. F. D. Maurice and Charles Kingsley. It reached a position of tremendous influence during the first part of our own century with the enthusiastic propagation of liberal scholars and preachers, such as Walter Rauschenbush of Rochester Seminary, R. J. Campbell of London City Temple, Shailer Mathews of Chicago University, H. C. King of Oberlin College, Harry F. Ward of Union Seminary of New York, and Washington Gladden. E. Stanley Jones and J. Bromley Oxnam became its minor, but popular, prophets.

In the long history of special interpretations of the Kingdom of God, there has been none more one-sided or guilty of greater excesses than this Social-Kingdom conception. With fanatical zeal some of its champions have been ready to scrap almost anything in the realm of Christian faith and morals if only the process of "social reconstruction" could be somehow advanced. Gandhi, who never renounced the degraded religion of India, was lauded as the greatest "Christian" of his generation. Opportunist politicians of the worst kind were supported on the ground that they advocated "progressive social principles." Even Russian Communism, its hands bloody with mass murder, was held up as a beneficent forward step in the social progress of mankind. These extreme opinions have shocked many thoughtful observers, yet their logic was inherent in the movement from the very beginning. For it is a fact, though not generally known, that the infamous and now widely publicized dictum about religion being "an opium dose for . . . the people" was originally written by the same Charles Kingsley mentioned above.[15]

---

[14] Walter Rauschenbush, *Christianizing the Social Order* (New York: Macmillan Co., 1912), p. 127.
[15] "Christian Socialism," *Encyclopedia Britannica* (14th ed.; New York: Encyclopedia Britannica, Inc., 1929), Vol. V, p. 639.

As the movement ran its course, the Kingdom of God became a "democracy" in which man and God (if there is a God!) struggled together for the social redemption of mankind. The Social Gospel thus developed may be traced back to a number of religious and philosophical tendencies: First, an unwarranted belief in the inherent goodness of man who, it is assumed, will do right if only given the right kind of social environment. Second, an almost exclusive emphasis on the immanence of God which, following Spinoza, proceeded to strip religion of supernatural elements, and more or less came to identify God with the "social consciousness" of humanity. Third, a politically naive acceptance of Socialism as the best theory of government, with its inevitable regimentation of the individual by means of rigid social controls. Fourth, a critical attitude toward the Bible, highly subjective, by which the material could be reduced to such areas as might more easily lend themselves to a strictly social interpretation. Fifth, the diminishing of essential theology to an alleged universal Fatherhood of God and the Brotherhood of Man.

Although today under attack from many directions, and in spite of its utter failure as an economic theory of government, this Social-Kingdom idea is not dead by any means. For its every failure, its proponents recommend simply a larger dose of the same thing.

8. *The Modern Eschatological-Kingdom Idea*

It is with considerable reluctance that I consent to use the term "eschatological" for the purpose of designating the two modern schools of thought which have thus described their systems. For neither of them employs the term in its original Christian significance. Eschatological things are literally the "last things" (*ta eschata*), that is, the things which are "last" with respect to human history; and among these things the Bible puts the Kingdom. Now both of the modern "eschatological" schools, in complete opposition to the Liberal-Social idea of the Kingdom, argue that our Lord's teaching about the Kingdom must be interpreted "eschatologically." But both schools, strangely enough, are agreed in dogmatically rejecting the realization of any eschatological Kingdom ahead in human history; on totally different grounds, however. The one says that Christ was *mistaken* in His idea of the Kingdom; the other says He put the Kingdom *above and beyond* history.

First, the *Delusion* theory of Albert Schweitzer. His views were first set forth in a remarkable work of immense erudition entitled

The Quest of the Historical Jesus. Dr. Schweitzer's present world fame as musician, philosopher, theologian, medical missionary, and Nobel prize winner, has revived widespread interest in his ideas. According to Schweitzer, our Lord's concept of the Kingdom was based on Daniel and subsequent Jewish Apocalyptic writings. During His earthly ministry Christ made no attempt to establish a kingdom of any sort but taught that He would reappear from heaven and set up the long-expected Kingdom within the lifetime of His disciples. At first He had no expectation of dying but believed that He would be translated like Elijah in order to accomplish His glorious return to establish the Kingdom. This anticipated translation and *parousia* did not take place as He expected.[16] Facing this situation Christ decided to die and took deliberate steps to force the Jewish leaders to kill him.[17] His death demonstrated the folly of expecting an eschatological kingdom and actually put an end to eschatology. In Schweitzer's own terrible words, "the Son of Man lays hold of the wheel of the world to set it moving on that last revolution which is to bring all ordinary history to a close. It refuses to turn, and He throws himself upon it. Then it does turn; and crushes him. Instead of bringing in the eschatological conditions, He has destroyed them. The wheel rolls onward, and the mangled body of the one immeasurably great Man, who was strong enough to think of himself as a spiritual ruler of mankind and to bend history to his purpose, is hanging upon it still."[18] Hence, according to Schweitzer, there will be no future Kingdom of God in human history as conceived by our Lord.

It should go without saying that in no Biblical sense can Dr. Schweitzer be called a Christian, and his conclusion regarding our Lord and His Kingdom is an appalling thing. Our chief interest in his theory is drawn by reason of his terrific attack on the modern liberal interpretations which tried to reconstruct the Biblical material so as to exclude *all* eschatological elements in the interest of a purely social and ethical Kingdom of God. The Jesus of Liberalism and the Kingdom He is supposed to have founded on earth, says Schweitzer, "never had any existence."[19] For the critical methods of modern liberal theology, Schweitzer has little or no respect: "It mixes history with everything and ends by being proud

---

[16] *Quest of the Historical Jesus,* trans. by W. Montgomery from first German ed., 1906. First English ed., 1910 (New York: Macmillan Co., 1948), p. 389.
[17] *Ibid.,* p. 392. [18] *Ibid.,* pp. 370-371. [19] *Ibid.,* p. 398.

of the skill with which it finds its own thoughts . . . in Jesus." [20] Of course, much the same charge might be leveled against Schweitzer who, like the modern Liberals, does not hesitate on alleged critical ground to reconstruct the Biblical records or even throw out relevant parts in order that he may establish his own theories. But his assault against Liberal views of our Lord's teachings about an eschatological Kingdom, for one thing, proves that Premillennial interpreters are not the only "apostles of discord" on the field of theology. And if, in the recorded teaching of our Lord about the Kingdom of God, Schweitzer can find nothing but eschatology, surely we as Premillennialists cannot be totally wrong in thinking that a great deal of that nature can be found there.

One curious aspect of the battle between Schweitzer and his liberal critics is that by different paths they reach the same general conclusions. As Paul Schubert has observed: "Both drop Jesus' faith in the future consummation to the bottom of the ocean of outdated mythology, while they sail on the smooth but treacherous surface of this ocean in the same boat of Jesus' social ethics toward the promised land of a Christian civilization." [21]

Second, let us consider the *Supra-History* theory of the school of Barth, Brunner, and their disciples. With Schweitzer these men have joined battle against the Liberal notion of the Kingdom of God, holding that the teaching of our Lord about the Kingdom must be regarded as eschatological in nature. So emphatic is their stress on this point that they have been referred to as "absolute eschatologists." In their theological system, which is based on the dialectical principle of the paradox, there are some matters not easily understood. But their view of the Kingdom is fairly clear. Taking as a point of departure the presupposition defined by the Danish philosopher Kierkegaard as "the absolute qualitative distinction between time and eternity," they build on this foundation: God belongs to eternity, man belongs to time. God and eternity may intrude or touch human history in time-space, as in the case of the Incarnation, but nothing divine and eternal can ever become an essential part of the time-stream of history. Since the Church is present in history, it cannot be the Kingdom. Neither can the Church bring in the Kingdom, or advance it. The saved can only watch for its coming. All man's attempts to establish the Kingdom must fail, because only God can do this. If the King-

---

[20] *Ibid.,* p. 400.
[21] *Journal of Bible and Religion,* August, 1946, p. 155.

dom is present in the Church in any sense, it is only indirectly and invisibly — it is here *incognito*.

This brings us to the special sense in which the Barth-Brunner school understands the term "eschatology." In the Bible the "last things" come in the future, at the end of history, yet *within* or connected with the historical process. But to these theorists "eschatology" has nothing to do with history; hence it cannot consist of "things" which are "last" *in* history. Eschatology belongs to eternity, not at all to time. Therefore, the Kingdom of God, being wholly eschatological, belongs to eternity; which to them means that the Kingdom does exist now, but above and outside of our time-space history. And, of course, the Kingdom will exist after the brief episode of human history. The attitude of Barth and Brunner toward Scripture, like that of the liberal school, is highly critical; they have no compunction about rearranging the Biblical material or throwing out portions or regarding its history in part mythical. Much of their system seems obscure; in fact, they appear at times to make a virtue of obscurity and irrationality.[22] But they have made one thing crystal clear — they are immovably opposed to the Liberal-Social idea of the Kingdom, holding that it has no foundation whatever in the Biblical records; and they are leading a powerful theological movement which can never make peace with the older Liberalism. What the outcome may be, no one can tell. Theological fashions come and go. But while the Conservatives may be duly grateful that the Liberal position is under vigorous attack, they should never assume that an abandonment of Liberalism necessarily means any genuine return to the Christian faith as set forth in the Word of God.

In summarizing, it may be said that these two modern "eschatological" schools of interpretation, although vastly different in many respects, are nevertheless united upon two important points: first, they are against the Liberal-Social idea of the Kingdom; and second, they are agreed that there will never be any future Millennial Kingdom *in* human history. On this last point, they are in agreement with the modern Amillennial position.

[22] Cf. the pungent remark of Paul King Jewett: "But on Brunner's position it is not clear that we can know anything." *Emil Brunner's Concept of Revelation*: An Evangelical Theological Society publication (London: James Clarke and Co., 1954), p. 185.

CHAPTER III

DEFINITIONS AND DISTINCTIONS

Men take the words they find in use amongst their neighbours; and, that they may not seem ignorant what they stand for, use them confidently, without much troubling their heads about a certain fixed meaning; whereby, besides the ease of it, they obtain this advantage: That, as in such discourses they are seldom in the right, so are they as seldom to be convinced that they are in the wrong; it being all one to go about to draw those men out of their mistakes who have no settled notions, as to dispossess a vagrant of his habitation who has no settled abode. —*John Locke*

1. A Method of Approach

Since the phrase "Kingdom of God" is a Biblical term, it should be clear that no definition can have any authoritative meaning apart from the content assigned to it in the Holy Scriptures. Therefore, passing over for the moment any attempt to evaluate the various ideas enumerated in the previous chapter, our first task will be to establish its meaning and content on the basis of an inductive study of the Biblical material out of which the original idea arose.

In beginning this study it should be held axiomatic that any conception of the Kingdom of God which rests in large part upon a certain interpretation of a single text or passage of the Bible must be regarded with deep suspicion. In this category are the systems built around such passages as, "The kingdom of God is within you" (Luke 17:21), or "I will give unto thee the keys of the kingdom of heaven" (Matt. 16:19), or the parable of the leaven (Matt. 13:33), or the ethical precepts of the Sermon on the Mount (Matt. 5-7), or the 20th chapter of the Book of Revelation. The doctrine of the Kingdom should be determined by an inductive examination of *all* the Biblical material on the subject, and it should not have to stand or fall by the inclusion or exclusion of isolated passages where interpretation may be in serious dispute. To me there is no question as to the general meaning of Revelation 20, but I maintain that the essential outline of the Biblical doctrine of the Kingdom can be established without it. And this doctrine, once

16

established, should be our surest guide in approaching those texts which are under controversy.

The Kingdom of God in Scripture is a concept not easily handled by the conventional method of Systematic Theology. For one thing, it occupies a place in both Biblical history and eschatology. It is so vast in content, and so interminable in its reach both backward and forward, that it resists any attempt to shut it up in one department of theological treatment. Therefore, it is not enough to study a collation of texts on the subject; but the material must be examined in relation to the movement of history and the progress of divine revelation. This means that any adequate treatment must follow basically the method of Biblical Theology. Failure of students at this point has made no small contribution to the rise of the various one-sided notions about the Kingdom.

2. A Tentative Definition

A general survey of the Biblical material indicates that the concept of a "kingdom" envisages a total situation containing at least three essential elements: first, a *ruler* with adequate authority and power; second, a *realm* of subjects to be ruled; and third, the actual exercise of the function of *rulership*.

It is true, of course, that the primary and most important idea is that of the ruler with regal authority. It is also possible that the ruler may withdraw from his realm, and the exercise of his ruling function may be interrupted temporarily. But all three elements are nevertheless present in the Biblical concept of a kingdom; and there can be no kingdom in the total sense without the ruler, the realm, and the reigning function.

I do not think that too much attention need be paid to the efforts to show that the Biblical terms for "kingdom" (Heb. *malkuth*; Greek *basileia*) may refer to a bare divine sovereignty; that is, a royal authority without a realm, or a king without a kingdom. The great ideas of the Bible are concrete rather than abstract; and such terms as the *Kingdom of God* are intended to convey meanings which are pertinent to actual situations in the world of reality with which common men are somewhat familiar. On this point, while recognizing the linguistic basis of the abstract idea, Archibald Robertson is nevertheless careful to add, "We can as little have a reign with no kingdom as a kingdom without one who reigns."[1]

Following Dalman who asserts dogmatically that the Old Testa-

---

[1] *Regnum Dei,* Bampton Lectures (New York: Macmillan Co., 1901), p. 58.

ment *malkuth* when applied to God "means always kingly rule, never the kingdom," Dr. George E. Ladd labors to establish this abstract idea in the usage of the Greek *basileia* in the New Testament; but his selected illustrations are not impressive. For example, in the parable recorded in Luke 19:11-27, the nobleman goes into a far country "to receive for himself a kingdom" (vs. 12; cf. 15). Here Ladd argues that "the *basileia* is clearly neither the domain nor the subjects" but rather only "authority to rule"; and he cites with approval the RSV rendering of "kingly power" in the place of "kingdom."[2] But this seems to be exposition too much controlled by linguistic analysis. Would any average reader of the parable, feeling no urgency to prove something, conclude that when the kingdom was given to the nobleman, he received only an abstract "authority" and not authority over *something*, that is, the actual subjects in the realm over which he was chosen to rule? Consider the rebellion of the people, spoken of as *"his"* citizens even during the absence of the ruler (vs. 14); and also the king's stern judgment on the rebels at his return (vs. 27). Later in his book (p. 83), Dr. Ladd speaks of the Kingdom of God as an "abstract reign" — a contradiction even in English terms — but in the same sentence he surrenders the point at issue by saying that this abstract reign of God is manifested "in various realms." So it turns out at last that the reign of God is associated with very concrete situations. As to Revelation 5:10, another passage cited by Ladd (pp. 79-80) to illustrate the abstract meaning of the word for "kingdom," it can be said that, whatever may be the correct reading of the Greek text, the context of the reference clearly points to a definite realm in which the kingdom operates; it is, as Ladd admits, a *"reign on the earth."*[3]

In an otherwise very excellent discussion of the New Testament term *basileia*, W. E. Vine begins by defining it as "primarily an abstract noun denoting sovereignty" but cites only one textual example, Revelation 17:18, where the literal translation must be "hath a kingdom" instead of "reigneth."[4] Here again the textual example fails to prove the definition, for the kingdom of the Great Harlot is definitely specified as *"over the kings of the earth."* Admitting that

[2] *Crucial Questions about the Kingdom of God* (Grand Rapids: Eerdmans Publishing Co., 1952), p. 79.

[3] On the words "madest us a kingdom" (Rev. 5:10, ASV), A. T. Robertson says that the aorist form of the verb *epoiēsas* is here "a prophetic use anticipating the final result" (*Word Pictures in the New Testament, in loc.*).

[4] *Expository Dictionary of New Testament Words* (London: Oliphants, Ltd., 1940, New Imprint 1944 and 1946), Vol. II, p. 294.

the Hebrew and Greek terms do have an abstract shade of meaning, Dr. Charles L. Feinberg has rightly concluded that "The Semitic frame of mind emphasizes the concrete rather than the abstract," and that the background of the New Testament idea of the Kingdom must be found in the Old Testament.[5] This is in agreement with Ewald's valuable comment on Daniel 7:18, "A kingdom and its sovereign cannot exist without subjects, and in fact, *they* only exist through the latter."

It is true that one may think of regal authority as something possessed but not actually exercised. The New Testament, however, has a word for this. Before His ascension our Lord said, "All power [*exousia*] is given unto me in heaven and in earth" (Matt. 28:18). To be sure, there could be no kingdom without such authority; but the "kingdom" is not synonymous with "power as kings" in Revelation 17:12, as Ladd argues in his discussion of this text where both *basileia* and *exousia* are used.[6] The "power" is essential to the "kingdom," but the kingdom is more than the power. It is easy to slip into the logical fallacy of Composition.

On the basis of the threefold tentative analysis stated at the beginning of this section, the "Kingdom of God" may be defined broadly as *the rule of God over His creation.*

3. *Some Biblical Distinctions*

In a preliminary survey of the very extensive array of Biblical references to the Kingdom of God, especially in the Old Testament, the investigator will be impressed by a series of differences which at first sight may seem to be almost contradictory. Some of the more important of these differences may be stated as follows:

First, certain passages present the Kingdom as something which has *always existed;* yet in other places it seems to have a definite historical *beginning* among men. (Compare Ps. 10:16 with Dan. 2:44.)

Second, the Kingdom is set forth in Scripture as *universal* in its scope, outside of which there is no created thing; yet again the Kingdom is revealed as a *local* rule established on earth. (Compare Ps. 103:19 with Isa. 24:23.)

Third, the Kingdom sometimes appears as the rule of God *directly,* with no intermediary standing between God and man; yet it is also

---

[5] *Premillennialism or Amillennialism* (2nd and enlarged ed.; Wheaton: Van Kampen Press, 1954), p. 296.
[6] *Op. cit.,* p. 79.

pictured as the rule of God through a *mediator* who serves as channel between God and man. (Compare Ps. 59:13 with 2:4-6.)

Fourth, it has been noted that often the Bible describes the Kingdom as something wholly *future;* whereas in other texts the Kingdom is said to be a *present* reality. (Compare Zech. 14:9 with Ps. 29:10.)

Fifth, the Kingdom of God is set forth as an *unconditioned* rule arising out of the sovereign nature of Deity Himself; yet, on the other hand, it sometimes appears as a Kingdom based on a *covenant* made by God with man. (Compare Dan. 4:34-35 with Ps. 89:27-29.)

Some of the above distinctions, if not all, have been noticed by Biblical scholars and attempts have been made to explain them; sometimes by asserting the existence of one kingdom with two aspects or phases; or by the assumption of two kingdoms. For example, Hengstenberg distinguishes between a "kingdom of power" and a "kingdom of grace."[7] Peters speaks of the one as "God's universal, general sovereignty exercised by virtue of his being the creator," and of the other as "a Theocratic rule."[8] In his examination of the Old Testament conception of the Kingdom, Ernest F. Scott finds that "God is already King"; but, on the other hand, it is also true that "God's kingship lies in the future."[9] Likewise John Bright speaks of the kingdom as "a present and victorious reality," but at the same time "it is a thing of the future and far from victorious."[10] Robertson feels that in the writings of Paul there is a distinction between the "kingdom of Christ" and the "kingdom of God," although the difference is never an "absolute."[11]

Many Premillennialists distinguish between the "kingdom of God" and the "kingdom of heaven," not regarding the two as precisely synonymous.[12] In his valuable *Excursus* on the Kingdom of God, E. R. Craven finds two classes of Old Testament passages: "(1) Those which refer to the natural Kingdom of God over the Universe"; and "(2) Those in which the then future Basileia of the Messiah was

[7] E. W. Hengstenberg, *History of the Kingdom of God* (Edinburgh: T. & T. Clark, 1872), Vol. I, p. 1.

[8] George N. H. Peters, *The Theocratic Kingdom* (New York: Funk and Wagnalls, 1884), Vol. I, p. 224.

[9] *The Kingdom of God* (New York: Macmillan Co., 1931), pp. 18, 19.

[10] *The Kingdom of God* (New York: Abingdon-Cokesbury Press, 1953), p. 231.

[11] *Op. cit.,* pp. 53-57.

[12] Lewis Sperry Chafer, *The Kingdom in History and Prophecy* (Chicago: Bible Institute Colportage Ass'n., 1936), pp. 52-55.

predicted."[13] In another passage Craven says, "We must distinguish between a Kingdom *on* earth, and a Kingdom *over* the earth."[14]

These citations, deliberately selected from authors of widely different viewpoints, will be sufficient to show that the distinctions mentioned above are not imaginary. The question is how to explain them. Most of us would not be satisfied with the attitude of one current school of opinion which, apparently rejoicing in religious paradox and tension for their own sake, is content to leave such theological antinomies permanently unresolved. For myself, while recognizing the reality of the problem, I am also convinced that the Scriptures offer a reasonable explanation. In one sense it would not be wholly wrong to speak of *two kingdoms* revealed in the Bible. But we must at the same time guard carefully against the notion that these two kingdoms are absolutely distinct, one from the other. There is value and instruction in thinking of them as *two aspects* or phases of the one rule of our sovereign God. In seeking for terms which might best designate these two things, I can find nothing better than the adjectives "universal" and "mediatorial." These are not exactly commensurate terms, of course, but describe different qualities; the first referring to the *extent* of rule, the latter to the *method* of rule. Nevertheless, in each case the designated quality seems to be the most important for purposes of identification.

As we proceed with the discussion, therefore, the terms used will be the *Universal Kingdom* and the *Mediatorial Kingdom.*

13 *Lange's Commentary, Revelation of John* (New York: Scribner's Sons, 1874), p. 97.
14 *Ibid.,* p. 95.

CHAPTER IV

THE UNIVERSAL KINGDOM OF GOD

There is therefore recognized in Scripture . . . a natural and universal kingdom or dominion of God, embracing all objects, persons, and events, all doings of individuals and nations, all operations and changes of nature and history, absolutely without exception . . . .   —*James Orr*[1]

Since this volume is devoted in large part to the Mediatorial phase of the Kingdom, my treatment of the Universal Kingdom will be quite brief, restricted to one chapter, including not much more than a summary of its chief characteristics. In any conventional system of theology this universal rule or control of God would be dealt with in part under the head of the divine work in Providence. But the Kingdom of God in its universal sense is not a synonym for providence. It is a vastly greater concept as set forth in the Scriptures, especially the Old Testament.

In seeking to establish the existence of such a universal kingdom, as an ever present reality in Biblical history, a problem of interpretation will need to be faced. It will be necessary to distinguish clearly between *history* and *prediction*. The Biblical passages selected, therefore, must contain statements of historical fact, not of predictive prophecy. For example, Psalms 97 and 99 open with the glad announcement, "The LORD reigneth." But a study of the context shows clearly that both speak predictively of a future kingdom. Other psalms, such as 93 and 103, are basically records of historical fact, referring to a rule of God which was existing in the day when these Scriptures were written. Therefore, keeping in mind this selective principle in approaching the Biblical material, we note that the most important characteristics of the Universal Kingdom of God appear as follows.

[1] "Kingdom of God," *Dictionary of the Bible,* ed. James Hastings (New York: Scribner's Sons, 1901), Vol. II, p. 844.

1. *This Universal Kingdom Exists Without Interruption Throughout All Time*

Thy kingdom is an everlasting kingdom. —*Ps. 145:13*

The 29th Psalm has given to us a beautiful and inspired description of the progress of a storm in the land of Israel. It begins with
the rumbling of thunder out over the sea, probably the Mediter-
ranean. It sweeps in across the land breaking the "cedars of Lebanon," making them "skip like a calf." It shakes the wilderness,
causing the frightened animals to bear their young prematurely.
Yet the psalmist wants us to understand that *God* is present in this
violence of nature and is in complete control. More than that—
so intimate and immediate is the relation of Jehovah to the storm
that no less than six times are we told that its manifestations are
"The voice of the LORD." But all this is not to be regarded as something new: looking backward in human history the psalmist declares (vs. 10) that "Jehovah sat at the Deluge."[2] All that happened
there was under the sovereign control of Him who is both the God
of nature and the Judge of men. And, as to the present situation, the
conclusion of the psalm is that "the Lord sitteth King for ever"
(vs. 10).

The prophet Jeremiah bears a similar testimony concerning the
abiding reality and character of the rule of God in his day. With
fine irony he sketches a picture of the vanity and impotence of the
gods of the nations: an object of worship is made of a tree cut from
the forest by the hand of man; it is fastened securely with nails; it is
decorated with silver and gold; it must be carried from place to
place; it cannot move and it cannot speak; it cannot do evil, neither
can it do anything good. Such gods can be ignored. It is otherwise
with the true God who is the LORD of Israel, for He is "the true
God, he is the living God, and an everlasting king" (Jer. 10:2-5, 10).

In the midst of his lamentations, because of the devastation of
Jerusalem and the ruin of the land of Israel by reason of the
Babylonian invasion, Jeremiah finds his comfort and hope in a present
Kingdom of God which is grounded in the eternal nature of God
Himself. The historical situation was dark and terrible (Lam. 4).
The skin of the people was black by reason of the famine; the
women in Zion had been cruelly ravished; the princes were hanged
up by the hands; the crown had fallen from the head of the nation
of Israel; the hearts of the captives were faint and their eyes were

---

[2] Hengstenberg's Translation.

dim. Beyond the terror of darkness and gloom, the prophet has a glimpse of a better day when the enemies of Israel will be punished and the nation will no more be carried away captive (Lam. 4:22). But while they wait in hope for that better day, there is a present consolation found in the eternal God and His abiding Kingdom: "Thou, O LORD, remainest for ever; thy throne from generation to generation" (Lam. 5:19). The historical Kingdom of God in Israel may be interrupted; the nation may abide for many days without a mediatorial king; but there is nevertheless a Kingdom of God which continues without any hiatus or diminution.

2. *The Universal Kingdom Includes All That Exists in Space and Time*

Thou reignest over all.   —*1 Chron. 29:12*

Nothing lies outside its vast reach and scope. It includes all things in space and time; in earth, in heaven, and in hell. The nations of the earth may rebel, follow other gods, even deny the existence of the true God; but all to no avail; Jehovah is still the "King of nations" (Jer. 10:7). Nebuchadnezzar, made the golden head of an ancient world empire by divine appointment, forgets the heavenly source of his authority; and so he is cut down from his throne by the judgment of God in order that "the living may know that the most High ruleth in the kingdom of men, and giveth it to whomsoever he will, and setteth up over it the basest of men." The importance of this divinely given lesson appears in its threefold repetition in the inspired record (Dan. 4:17, 25, 32). Men are not to forget that it is the "God of heaven" who "removeth kings, and setteth up kings" (Dan. 2:19-21).

Witnessing to the present reality of God's universal kingdom in his own day, the psalmist writes, "The LORD hath prepared his throne in the heavens; and his kingdom ruleth over all" (103:19). In this psalm the scope of the Kingdom reaches up into the heavens; the angels are within it and under its rule; the hosts of God are here, and all His works in all places of His dominion. To know this brings blessing and comfort to the souls of men in every generation and in every age (103:19-22).

Neither the underworld of the dead, nor hell itself, lies outside the rule of this Kingdom of God. Even though the enemies of God should "dig into Sheol," He warns, "thence shall my hand take them" (Amos 9:2, ASV). The scornful rulers in Jerusalem may suppose that they have made protective terms "with death and with Sheol," but no such covenants and agreements will be permitted to stand (Isa. 28:15-18, ASV). The fires of divine anger will be found burning even in "lowest Sheol" (Deut. 32:22, ASV). The strange notion that the devil is the king of hell has no basis in divine revelation. *God* is the King of hell, just as He is the King of everything else in time and space. And because this is so, that everlasting prison-house of the lost will not be the noisy and disorderly place that is sometimes imagined by the popular mind. There is no more orderly place than a well-disciplined prison, even under imperfect human government. There will be no riots in hell. For all those who reject the mercy of God in Christ and recognize no final argument but force, there will be force without stint or limit, the force of a divine government from which there can be no escape, either now or hereafter.

As for the Lord's own people in ages past, Sheol could have no terrors for them. With the psalmist they could say, "Whither shall I flee from thy presence? If I ascend up into heaven, thou art there: if I make my bed in Sheol, behold, thou art there. If I take the wings of the morning, and dwell in the uttermost parts of the sea; even there shall thy hand lead me, and thy right hand shall hold me" (Ps. 139:7-10, ASV).

Perhaps the finest and clearest testimony regarding the existence of the Universal Kingdom of God in Old Testament times was uttered by David as he gave his last instructions to his son Solomon and reviewed the goodness of the Lord toward his house and the nation of Israel. No one understood better than David the reality of that divine Kingdom in history of which he had been anointed as the mediatorial king. But above and beyond the limits of the land of Palestine and the city of Jerusalem, David saw another and a greater Kingdom, describing it in these wonderful words: "Thine, O LORD, is the greatness, and the power, and the glory, and the victory, and the majesty: for all that is in the heaven and in the earth is thine; thine is the kingdom, O LORD, and thou art exalted as head above all. . . . and thou reignest over all" (I Chron. 29:11, 12).

3. *The Divine Control in the Universal Kingdom Is Generally Providential*

Fire, and hail; snow, and vapour; stormy wind fulfilling his word.
—*Ps. 148:8*

By the term "providential" we mean control by means of second causes; for example, the accomplishment of God's purpose at the

Red Sea by using a "strong east wind" to sweep aside the waters from the path of Israel (Exod. 14:21). Such a providential method of control applies especially to the operation of the Universal Kingdom with reference to the earth. Because God is in the operations of what men are pleased to call "natural law," He is able to "tip the scales" of nature in ways indiscernible to the eyes of men. For a long time scientists were greatly intrigued with what they called the reign of law in a "closed system" of nature, excluding the possibility of any "divine tinkering" with the system on the part of a sovereign God. Today they are not so sure. To the Bible writers, of course, there is no problem. Since God not only created the system of nature but also sustains the operation of its so-called laws, there can be no question about His ability to manipulate the system from within as well as from without. It is fairly well recognized today by some reputable scientists that, in the system of nature, there is room for "unlawful" events without interfering seriously with the statistical averages which we call "laws." Some investigators, hoping to keep as far as possible from the realm of theology, have named the "outlaw" variant a "cheater"![3] Having no compunctions of this kind, the Bible writers may at times attribute to God directly what happens in the world of nature. Where men would normally say, "*It* thundered," the psalmist does not hesitate to say, "The God of glory thundereth" (Ps. 29:3).

Because in His Universal Kingdom God controls the processes of material nature, He is able by such means to control the circumstances of human existence and thereby direct the stream of history. There are many instances of such divine control. In some cases we are not told what the circumstances were or just how they were divinely used, but are only brought immediately into the presence of the accomplished fact. Thus the Assyrian monarch is spoken of as a "rod" in the hand of Jehovah to be used in the infliction of divine judgment upon Jerusalem, though the king knows nothing about God's purpose and certainly has no intention of serving Him. So complete is God's control in the situation that Isaiah multiplies terms of divine irony to describe it: The Assyrian is not only a mere "rod"; he is also a "staff," an "axe," and a "saw"; all wielded by the hand of a King who is greater than he (10:5-15). Likewise, the king of Babylon is God's chosen "servant" for the accomplishment of His will against the people of Jerusalem (Jer. 25:9). Furthermore, in

[3] Lecomte du Nouy, *Human Destiny* (New York: Longmans, Green and Co., 1947), p. 38.

the long sequence of the rise and fall of world empires, it is Jehovah who raises up and prepares the "kings of the Medes" for the destruction of Babylon (Jer. 51:11, 28-37). And again, long before his birth, the great Cyrus is named prophetically and "anointed" by Jehovah to fulfil His purpose in rebuilding the temple (Isa. 44:28-45:4).

In other Biblical events the veil of providential control is drawn aside and the determining circumstance is openly declared. The Book of Esther dramatically records such an event in the days when the nation of Israel stood in mortal danger of its very existence. Serving in the palace of Ahasuerus, the Persian king, there was a Jew named Mordecai, through whom two important happenings were brought to pass: first, he had counseled his cousin Esther in her conduct leading to her selection by the king as his queen; and second, he had saved the king's life by exposing a plot to kill him (Esther 2:5-23). But there is a villain in the palace, Haman by name, who hated Mordecai because of the latter's stiff-necked refusal to bow before him. And so there was hatched a scheme to destroy not only Mordecai but also the total nation of the Jews throughout the entire Persian kingdom. The decree of destruction had been signed by Ahasuerus, the date had been set, and copies had been sent to all parts of the empire, the king not knowing that his queen was a member of the people thus callously doomed to death. Haman, well satisfied that the thing was as good as done, sat down with the king to "drink" to the success of his nefarious purpose (ch. 3).

For those who have eyes to see, it was one of the most critical points in all human history. At stake, in a very real sense, was the entire divine program for the ages. If Israel perished, there would be no Messiah, no redemption, no Church, no future Kingdom of God among men. With such issues in jeopardy, we might not have been too much surprised to see the arm of Deity breaking forth into the affairs of men with some great supernatural intervention; perhaps something like the deliverance of Israel from the hand of the Egyptian Pharaoh. But nothing of the kind happens. There is not even any mention of God. The writer of the Book of Esther merely records what might be regarded as the master understatement of all time: "On that night could not the king sleep" (6:1). Why he could not sleep, we are not told; but more likely from a troubled indigestion than a troubled conscience. At any rate, turning to the ancient and well-known remedy, the king called for something to read; in this

case the "records of the chronicles" of his kingdom; probably dry
enough in spots (like our own Congressional Record) to induce the
sleep he could not imperiously command. And in the course of the
reading, the attendants came to the record of Mordecai's good deed
in uncovering the plot against the king's life. The remarkable sequel
may be read in the Book of Esther: as the outcome of this fit of regal
insomnia, and also the chance opening of the "chronicles" at exactly
the right place, the nation of Israel is rescued from extermination
and the world was saved from all the irreparable losses which such
a disaster would have entailed (ch. 8).

It may be true, as Cicero once observed, that "kings do not trouble
themselves with insignificant affairs"; which is one reason for the
oft failure of their purposes and plans. It is otherwise in the
Universal Kingdom of God, where things too small to merit human
attention may be used to change the course of history. In fact, "God
must care for the least, or He cannot care for the greatest." Thus He
does concern Himself with small affairs, because the fall of a rain-
drop or the sleeplessness of a king may, under God, have momentous
consequences. As the Book of Proverbs reminds us, "The lot is cast
into the lap, but the whole disposing thereof is of the LORD" (16:33).

It would be hard to think of a simpler event than the fall of a coin
which has been carelessly tossed in the air. The outcome can be
only one of two clean-cut possibilities. Yet the material factors
which contribute to the end-result of such an event are complicated
beyond the understanding of the wisest men. And in this complex
of causation we as Christians must never forget the unseen "finger
of God" whose touch always brings the final decision in the affairs
of the universe. This is the providential factor, for the most part
overlooked or ignored by men, which confounds at last all the
Hamans and the Hitlers and wrecks their well-laid schemes. As the
prophet Isaiah put the matter, it is the LORD who "frustrateth the
tokens of the liars, and maketh diviners mad; that turneth wise men
backward, and maketh their knowledge foolish; that confirmeth the
word of his servant, and performeth the counsel of his messengers;
that saith to Jerusalem, Thou shalt be inhabited" (44:25-26).

4. *The Divine Control in the Universal Kingdom May Be Exercised at Times by Supernatural Means*

He worketh signs and wonders in heaven and in earth.   —*Dan. 6:27*

While it may not be easy to draw a precise line of demarcation
between what is called the natural and the supernatural, neverthe-

less the general difference is clear and absolute. The God of the Bible is said to be both *in* the universe and also *above* it. Therefore at any time He may break into the so-called "closed system" of nature (which He upholds and controls) with great exhibitions of His unveiled power. The writers of Scripture are never conscious of any necessary conflict between the idea of God's rule through the system of nature and that of His rule through the miraculous. In both they recognize the hand of the same sovereign King who is transcendent as well as immanent in His creation. As we have seen above, the method of His divine control in the Universal Kingdom, especially with reference to the earth, is quite generally providential, that is, through second causes: "Fire, and hail; snow, and vapours; stormy wind fulfilling his word" (Ps. 148:8). Yet at certain times and under special circumstances the divine rule may be openly supernatural. Both methods of control are brought together in the 135th Psalm: "Whatsoever the LORD pleased, that did he in heaven, and in earth, in the seas, and all deep places. He causeth the vapours to ascend from the ends of the earth; he maketh lightnings for the rain; he bringeth the wind out of his treasuries. Who smote the firstborn of Egypt, both of man and beast. Who sent tokens and wonders into the midst of thee, O Egypt, upon Pharaoh, and upon all his servants" (vss. 6-9). Here we have clearly both nature and miracle. God rules through the phenomena of nature and also through supernatural "tokens and wonders," such as the terrible plagues which fell upon Egypt and her arrogant king.

The resort to miracles in the rule of the Universal Kingdom does not mean necessarily that God might not be able to accomplish His purposes by other and less spectacular means. The supernatural method is rather for the purpose of demonstrating publicly that there is a true God in heaven who always will have the last word in human affairs. On the one hand, such a miraculous demonstration was needed to answer the insolent challenge of the Egyptian Pharaoh: "Who is the LORD that I should obey his voice to let Israel go? I know not the LORD, neither will I let Israel go" (Exod. 5:2). But on the other hand, the same supernatural demonstration served to confirm the faith of God's own people in the reality of His Universal Kingdom, as Moses reminded them, "Hath God assayed to go and take him a nation from the midst of another nation, by temptations [trials], by signs, and by wonders, and by war, and by a mighty hand, and by a stretched out arm, and by great terrors, according to all that the LORD your God did for you in Egypt before your eyes? Unto thee it was shewed, that thou mightest know that the LORD he is God; there is none else beside him" (Deut. 4:34-35). Furthermore, the inspired record of the historical event stands as a documentary witness to all succeeding generations, that men may have no excuse for any failure to recognize the reality of God's Universal Kingdom, even though His mighty hand may temporarily be hidden beneath the veil of providential control.

5. The Universal Kingdom Always Exists Efficaciously Regardless of the Attitude of Its Subjects

None can stay his hand, or say unto him, What doest thou?—*Dan. 4:35*

Some personal beings have submitted to the rule of this Kingdom. As we might expect, there is no problem in heaven. The King's angels there, we are told, "do his commandments, hearkening unto the voice of his word" (Ps. 103:20). In the same submissive attitude we find the true people of God in all ages. During the period of the theocratic kingdom in the Old Testament, God was indeed the King of the *nation* of Israel in a special sense; but even after the close of the historical kingdom, when God had withdrawn His immediate presence from the nation, when they had been scattered and a "byword among the heathen" with no longer any prophet among them (Ps. 44:14; 74:9), still the remnant of godly individuals acknowledged and claimed a personal relationship to God as King. Several times in the Book of Psalms we read the glad cry in the midst of desolations: "Thou art my King, O God" (44:4). And again, "For God is my King of old" (74:12). Whatever of truth there may be in the asserted "reign of God in the hearts of men," it was something already known and experienced by the saints of the Old Testament. Could anything be any clearer or finer, on this point, than the testimony of the 84th Psalm? "My heart and my flesh crieth out for the living God. . . . O LORD of hosts, my King, and my God" (vss. 2-3). When we come to the New Testament, although our Lord is never called the King of the Church, nevertheless there is no abrogation of the Universal Kingdom of God, and the Church cannot be set outside of it. Nor can there be any dispute about the Church's glad submission to the will of her only Head, who today shares the Father's throne in the Universal Kingdom of God — "He that doeth the will of God abideth for ever" (I John 2:17).

On the other hand, there are many in rebellion against the rule of this Kingdom. The very essence of sin, the Apostle John tells us, is "lawlessness," and "the devil sinneth from the beginning" (I John 3:4, 8, ASV). Thus Satan is described as the primal and original rebel against the control of God's Universal Kingdom; and with him are the "angels that sinned" (II Pet. 2:4). On earth among men there are unnumbered multitudes who, deceived by Satan, are actively opposed to the revealed will of God. Still others, like the Assyrian in the prophecy of Isaiah, may know little or nothing about a sovereign God ruling over the universe. But regardless of the attitudes of men, whether it be indifference or rebellion or submission, the Scriptures declare that the Lord "worketh all things after the counsel of his own will" (Eph. 1:11). Even if in all the universe there were not one solitary personal being not in rebellion against God, whether angel or demon or man; even if there were no heaven of the redeemed but only a hell of the lost — it would still be true of this Universal Kingdom that "The LORD hath prepared his throne in the heavens; and his kingdom ruleth over all" (Ps. 103:19). For this Kingdom is an ever present reality from which there can be no escape. We can be grateful that God has left a place for personal choice and freedom in His dealings with men, but we must understand that there is no room for any freedom with respect to this divine rule. It is not for men to choose whether or not they will be under the rule of the Universal Kingdom. Whether they like it or not, they are already under it (Ps. 75:4-7).

6. *The Rule of the Universal Kingdom Is Administered Through the Eternal Son*

He is before all things, and by him all things consist.   —*Col. 1:17*

The complete Biblical evidence for the deity of our Lord Jesus Christ, and also for the doctrine of the Trinity, must be reserved for another volume in this series. However, any adequate discussion of the Universal Kingdom of God must give some recognition to the high place occupied by the Son of God in relation to that Kingdom. Sometimes men have thought too narrowly of His regal activity, restricting it almost exclusively to His office as the incarnate Ruler of a purely Messianic Kingdom. This is an important idea, of course, as we shall see later in dealing with what I have called the Mediatorial Kingdom. But the kingly function of our Lord appears first in the dateless past, beginning with creation itself.

In this connection several things should be noted. First, the creation of the universe and the establishment of the Universal King dom must be regarded as contemporaneous events. Second, the creation with its divine control was and continues to be a standing revelation of the invisible God. As the Apostle Paul argues, "The invisible things of him from the creation of the world are clearly seen, being understood by the things that are made, even his eternal power and Godhead" (Rom. 1:20). Third, the Son of God is spoken of in the Gospel of John as the eternal "Word" (Grk. *logos*), who is from the beginning both the "life" and the "light" (1:1-5). Now since it is the nature of light to shine and overcome the darkness, we must conclude that the creative and sovereign power of Deity has always been revealed in and through the activity of the eternal Son who in the fulness of time became our incarnate Saviour.

This sovereign activity of our Lord seems to be indicated in the book of Isaiah where the prophet names him the *"Everlasting Father"* (9:6). At first glance, this statement seems to confuse the Persons of the Godhead, calling the Son the Father; but a more literal translation shows that such is not the case. The name may be read as the "Father of the Everlasting" or the "Father of Eternity" (ASV, margin). But we must be careful here not to read into the passage any dialectical notions of time and eternity. In the Bible eternity is not absolutely opposed to time, but is simply (at least in its forward aspect) an unending duration or succession of ages. And the Son of God is the "Father" of this succession of ages. This means not only origination but also Fatherly guidance.[4]

The same idea is found in the first chapter of Hebrews where we are told that through His Son, God *"made the worlds"* (1:2). Now it has often been pointed out that the Greek term here should be rendered "ages." However, it seems clear from the passage in 11:3, where the same word occurs, that the writer is not thinking merely of the flight of time when he declares that God made the "ages" through Christ. As a matter of fact, the writers of the Bible never attempt to deal abstractly with the ideas of time and space in relation to the universe. This world, to them, is a moving world, not a static affair. Thus the writer of Hebrews, in a single term (*aionas*), unites the idea of the world existing in space with the idea of the world moving through time — no mean accomplishment. And the Son of God, we are told, is the Maker of this world, not only viewed from the standpoint of its vast extension in space, but also from the stand-

---

[4] Keil and Delitzsch, *Commentaries* (Grand Rapids: Eerdmans Publishing Co., reprint, 1949), *in loc.*

point of the ages through which the world has passed and is yet to pass.[5]

For a long time men have regarded with deep interest the complex movements of world history, asking the question, What is the meaning of it all? To this some have answered, There is no meaning; lo, we have searched and have found nothing but vanity and a striving after wind. But other men, more thoughtful, have felt deeply that there must be some final significance above and beyond the contradictions of human existence. As the result we have the so-called "Philosophies of History," often the work of earnest and brilliant minds, yet always inadequate and missing the mark. But the philosophers have been right in one respect; that is, in believing that there *is* a philosophy of history. Age does not follow age by a kind of "fortuitous concourse." There is an orderly arrangement, a plan, in the midst of seeming chaos and confusion. The great periods of history were not ushered in by chance, nor are they wound up by the will of men. The Son of God is the Maker of the ages, the Father of the everlasting, the God of history. Because this is so, the man who has found God in Christ has laid his hand upon the key which explains the riddle of cosmic history. And the more we know of Him, the closer we come to the heart of the mystery; for He is indeed the Light of the world, intellectually as well as spiritually and morally. Here is the trouble: men are trying to understand history apart from Christ in whom we have found the God who is described as the "King eternal" (I Tim. 1:17); or better, *King of the Ages.*[6]

It is in this glorious capacity that our Lord Jesus Christ sits today upon the throne of the universe. Not that He ever abdicated for a moment His rightful place there; even during the time of His deepest humiliation and suffering, He was "upholding all things by the word of his power" (Heb. 1:3). Commenting on this remarkable statement, Marcus Dods has rightly said, "The present [tense], *pheron,* seems

[5] On the clause, "By whom also he made the worlds" (Heb. 1:2), Marcus Dods has said, "The writer perhaps has it in his mind that the significant element in creation is not the mass or magnificence of the material spheres but the evolution of God's purposes through the ages. The mind staggers in endeavouring to grasp the vastness of the physical universe, but much more overwhelming is the thought of those times and ages and eons through which the purpose of God is gradually unfolding, unhasting and unresting, in the boundless life He has called into being. He Who is the end and aim, the Heir, of all things is also their creator . . . He only can guide the universe to its fit end . . . ."—*Expositor's Greek Testament* (London: Hodder and Stoughton, 1917), Vol. IV, p. 250.

[6] So Robertson, Olshausen, Meyer, *et al.*

necessarily to involve that during the whole of his earthly career, this function of upholding nature was being discharged. Probably the clause is inserted not merely to illustrate the dignity of the Son, but to suggest that the whole course of nature and history, when rightly interpreted, reveals the Son and therefore the Father."[7] But following His incarnation and death and resurrection, He was exalted *as Man* to sit down "on the right hand of the Majesty on high." This was not the throne of David transferred somehow from earth to heaven, as some have mistakenly supposed, but God the Father's own throne in the Universal Kingdom. The distinction is made very clear by our Lord Himself when, speaking to the Church on earth from His throne in the heavens, He promises, "To him that overcometh will I grant to sit with me in my throne, even as I also overcame, and am set down with my Father in his throne" (Rev. 3:21). These are two thrones, not one. The former is distinctly Messianic; the latter is the throne of God alone upon which "none may sit but God, and the God-Man Jesus Christ."[8]

7. *This Universal Kingdom Is Not Exactly Identical with That Kingdom for Which Our Lord Taught His Disciples to Pray*

His kingdom ruleth over all.   —Ps. 103:19
Thy kingdom come.   —Matt. 6:10

In its universal and providential sense, the Kingdom of God had already come, and the will of God was being done, in every place including even the earth. For, as we have seen above, this Kingdom "ruleth over all" (Ps. 103:19), and its sovereign God "worketh all things after the counsel of his own will" (Eph. 1:11). This rule of God, in fact, had always existed and never had been abrogated or interrupted. The duty of man, in relation to such a Kingdom, was to acknowledge its reality and bow to its sovereignty; not to pray for its coming in any objective sense. There should be no confusion as to this distinction.

What then was the Kingdom for which Christ bade His disciples to pray? The infallible key to the meaning of the petition, "Thy kingdom come," must be found in the clause which follows: "*As in heaven, so on earth*" (Matt. 6:10, ASV). Although this clause is immediately connected with the petition, "Thy will be done," it no doubt qualifies all three of the petitions which precede it.[9] The

---

[7] *Op. cit.*, p. 252.
[8] R. C. Trench, *Epistles to the Seven Churches in Asia* (London: Kegan Paul, Trench, Trubner and Co., 1897), p. 230.
[9] So Alford.

disciples are to pray for the hallowing of God's name, for the coming of God's Kingdom, and for the doing of God's will — all this to be done "*on earth*" as it is being done "*in heaven.*" Although the Kingdom of God was already ruling over all, there was nevertheless a profound difference between the exercise of its rule "in heaven" and "on earth." This difference arises out of the fact that rebellion and sin exist upon the earth, sin which is to be dealt with in a way not known in any other place in the universe, not even among the angels which sinned. It is here that the great purpose of what I have named the *Mediatorial* Kingdom appears: On the basis of mediatorial redemption it must "come" to put down at last all rebellion with its train of evil results, thus finally bringing the Kingdom and will of God *on* earth as it is in heaven. When this purpose has been fully accomplished, the mediatorial phase of the Kingdom will disappear as a separate entity, being merged with the Universal Kingdom of God.

This is substantially the view taken by the discerning Adolph Saphir in his very able and spiritually helpful treatment of *The Lord's Prayer.* Commenting on the clause "Thy kingdom come," he says, "The petition refers primarily and directly to the Messianic kingdom on earth, of which all Scripture testifies. The King of this kingdom is the Lord Jesus, the Son of David; the subjects of it are Israel and the nations, — the chosen people fulfilling the mission which, according to the election of God, is assigned unto them, of being the medium of blessing unto all the nations of the earth; the center of the kingdom is Jerusalem, and the means of its establishment is the coming and visible appearing of our Saviour Jesus Christ. When we pray 'Thy kingdom come,' our true meaning is, 'Come, Lord Jesus, come quickly!' "[10]

Referring to the same petition in the Prayer, Ellicott finds that "Historically, the prayer had its origin in the Messianic expectations embodied in the picture of the ideal king in Isaiah 11:1-6; 42:1-7; Daniel 7:14. It had long been familiar to all who looked for the consolation of Israel. Now the kingdom of God, that in which He manifests His sovereignty more than in the material world or in the common course of history, had been proclaimed as nigh at hand. The Teacher of the prayer knew Himself to be the Head of that

[10] *The Lord's Prayer* (Harrisburg, Pa.: Christian Alliance Publishing Co., no date given), p. 173.

kingdom."[11] Here Ellicott seems to distinguish between the already existing divine kingdom in nature and history and that kingdom for which men are taught to pray.

This distinction is also supported by the Greek text of the Prayer. In each of the petitions concerning God's name, kingdom, and will, the Greek verb is not only in the emphatic position but also aorist imperative in form, thus indicating "single or instantaneous" action.[12] Thus, in harmony with all Old Testament prophecy, the prayer taught by our Lord suggests not only that His kingdom is to be prayed for, but also that its coming to the "earth" will be a definite crisis in history, not a long and gradual process of evolution. This is in sharp contrast with the Universal Kingdom which has always been present in the world, on earth as well as in heaven.

Conclusion

With this rather brief survey of the Universal Kingdom, we shall now turn to a consideration of the mediatorial phase to which the Biblical material gives the great preponderance of attention. And since the Mediatorial Kingdom is a *phase,* we should expect that its characteristics will not be totally unrelated to the larger Kingdom but will shed further light upon the nature of the latter.

The reader should understand that throughout the remainder of this book, to save repetition, the term "Kingdom" will generally refer to the *Mediatorial* phase unless otherwise stated.

11 Charles J. Ellicott, *Commentary on the Whole Bible* (Grand Rapids: Zondervan Publishing House, reprint, 1954), *in loc.*
12 S. G. Green, *Handbook to the Grammar of the Greek Testament* (New York: Fleming H. Revell, 1912), p. 309-310.

PART TWO

THE MEDIATORIAL KINGDOM
IN OLD TESTAMENT HISTORY

Stanley . . . correctly says: "The Theocracy of Moses was not a government of priests as opposed to kings; it was a government *by God Himself*, as opposed to government by priests or kings. It was indeed, in its highest sense, as appeared afterward in the time of David, compatible both with regal and sacerdotal rule." Originally and primarily all civil and religious law proceeded from God; and others in the government were subordinates to carry into execution the supreme will of the King, i.e., God. The Theocracy is something then *very different* from the Divine Sovereignty, and must not be confounded with the same. . . .

— Geo. N. H. Peters[1]

[1] *The Theocratic Kingdom* (New York: Funk & Wagnalls, 1884; Grand Rapids: Kregel, repr. ed.), Vol. I, p. 217.

PART TWO
THE MEDIATORIAL KINGDOM IN OLD TESTAMENT HISTORY

CHAPTER V

THE HISTORICAL BACKGROUND
OF THE MEDIATORIAL IDEA

> Originally this [regal] control was given to man. It was absolute and
> entire. All things were subject to him, and all obeyed. Man was made
> a little lower than the angels, and was the undisputed lord of this lower
> world. He was in a state of innocence. But he rebelled, and this do-
> minion has been in some measure lost. It is found complete only in
> the *second man, the Lord from heaven* (I Cor. 15:47), the Lord Jesus
> to whom this control is absolutely given.   —*Albert Barnes*[1]

The Mediatorial Kingdom may be defined tentatively as: (a)
the rule of God through a divinely chosen representative who not
only speaks and acts for God but also represents the people before
God; (b) a rule which has especial reference to the earth; and (c)
having as its mediatorial ruler one who is always a member of the
human race.

The English term "mediator" does not occur at all in the Old
Testament, and only six times in the New Testament. The nearest
approximation in the Old Testament is the "daysman" of Job 9:33
("umpire," ASV), where the Septuagint translates by the regular
New Testament Greek word *mesitēs*. Yet scholars are quite generally agreed that the *idea* of mediation between God and man per-
meates the entire field of written revelation. In fact, D. Miall
Edwards asserts that in this idea we have the "key to the unity of
the Bible."[2]

The Bible presents the mediatorial idea in connection with three
different functions: that of prophet, of priest, and of ruler. Occasionally two of these functions may be found together in the same
person: Melchizedek was both priest and ruler, while Moses was
both prophet and ruler. And Samuel acted in all three areas in a
limited sense. But only in God's own Messiah can be found truly

---

[1] Albert Barnes, *Notes, Epistle to Hebrews* (New York: Harper and Bros., 1863),
on Heb. 2:6.

[2] "Mediation," *International Standard Bible Encyclopedia* (Chicago: Howard-Severance, 1915), Vol. III, p. 2025.

and fully all three of the mediatorial functions of prophet-priest-king. In Him alone do we have the complete and perfect answer to man's ancient complaint about God: "For he is not a man, as I am, that I should answer him, that we should come together in judgment. There is no umpire betwixt us, that might lay his hand upon us both" (Job 9:32, 33, ASV).

Since this volume is concerned primarily with the idea of mediation in the area of the *divine government,* it will be our task to investigate: (1) the rise and development of the Mediatorial Rule of God as it appears imperfectly realized in *Old Testament history;* (2) its future form as forecast in *Old Testament prophecy;* (3) its character as announced by our Lord and His disciples during the period of *Gospel records;* (4) its place in the history of the apostolic period covered by the *Book of Acts;* (5) the peculiar form in which it appears in the present *Church age;* (6) its visible and established form in the *Millennial age;* and (7) its final mergence in and complete identification with the *Universal and Everlasting Kingdom of God.*

Beginning now with the Mediatorial Kingdom in Old Testament history, we may note that some have tried to erect an absolute separation between the historical kingdom and the future kingdom of prophecy. All such attempts have failed and must fail, for the vital connection between the two will be clear from many passages with which we shall deal in later chapters. Certainly, the future kingdom is to be a genuine revival and continuation of the "throne of David." In a very real sense there is but one Mediatorial Kingdom of God. But where and when did this *idea* of mediatorial divine rule originate?

No attempt here will be made to give any account of the original position of Satan in relation to the earth, nor of his rebellion against God and his consequent fall. There is, of course, considerable revelation dealing with these matters which is of great theological interest as it bears upon man's place in the universe. But since by previous definition the Mediatorial Kingdom of God concerns the human race primarily, our discussion will begin with man.

1. Man's Original Dominion by Creation

Thou . . . didst set him over the works of thy hands.   —*Heb. 2:7*

In the Genesis account of the creation of man, the very first of the divine injunctions laid upon him was regal in character: "Let them have dominion," says the Creator, "over all the earth" and every created thing upon it (Gen. 1:26). The Hebrew word here is *radah*; the same term was used later significantly of the reign of Messiah Himself in His Kingdom: "Rule thou in the midst of thine enemies" (Ps. 110:2). Thus, among other important likenesses to his Creator, man was given a limited sovereignty in relation to the earth. To borrow the fine words of Franz Delitzsch concerning man's original position: "Man is a king, and not a king without a domain; the world around, with all the works of creative wisdom, is his kingdom."[3]

This original dominion over the earth and the animal creation was undoubtedly bestowed on man regarded generically as a race, not merely upon the first man Adam. However, if due consideration be given to the New Testament typical comparison between Adam and Christ as the respective heads of the old and new creations, there must have been some sense in which the first Adam was given dominion not only over the animal world but also over the race of men which would in the process of time issue from him by natural generation. This view of the matter harmonizes with the doctrine of Adamic headship as set forth in the Word of God. (cf. Rom. 5:12-21; I Cor. 15:21-28, 45-49; Heb. 2:5-9). The plural "let them have dominion," on this view, could have some reference to Adam and his wife Eve; for in the antitype the Last Adam also has a "wife" who, though subject to her divine Head, will nevertheless sit regally with Him in His Mediatorial Kingdom (Rev. 19:7; 20:6).

The important point in this history of beginnings, however, is that man's original dominion, being wholly derived and mediatorial in character, was to be exercised under the direction of God. It was just here that the first Adam dismally failed. Setting aside the ultimate sovereignty of his Creator, and arrogating to himself the perilous authority to decide what was good for him and his posterity, Adam lost his immediate contact with God, invalidated his mediatorial position, and brought down a whole train of disasters upon the realm where he might have brought unmeasured blessing. This failure of the first Adam, with reference to his mediatorial dominion, introduced into the stream of human history a hiatus which to the present hour has not at any time been wholly remedied. In the words of the Epistle to the Hebrews, written about A.D. 70, con-

---

[3] Franz Delitzsch, *Commentary on the Psalms*, trans. F. Bolton (Grand Rapids: Eerdmans Publishing Co., reprint, 1952), on 8:7-9.

cerning our Lord as "Son of Man" and His mediatorial dominion, "But now we see not yet all things put under him" (2:8).[4]

We should also observe that in the record of the creation of the physical environment placed under man's dominion, the Creator six times pronounces it "good" (Gen. 1:4, 10, 12, 18, 21, 25); and in the final summary we are told that God saw "everything" that He had made, and it was "very good" (vs. 31). Thus, at the very beginning of man's physical existence on earth, the Word of God declares it to be something eminently worth-while, not something evil *per se* after the platonic tradition.[5] This is an important point, as we shall see later, when we deal with modern theories which decry as "carnal" any doctrine of a genuine Kingdom of God on earth short of the eternal state.

2. From Eden to the Flood

My spirit shall not always strive with man.   —*Gen. 6:3*

The sin of Adam and the loss of his proper dominion not only set the stage for the brutal murder of Abel but also left the race without any *external* divinely mediated controls. And God, for a time, determined to leave the situation so. Only twice in the long period from Eden to the Flood is there any record of divine intervention in human affairs. In the one, Enoch was translated from the earth to be forever in the presence of God (Gen. 5:24). In the other, Cain was shut out of the "presence of the LORD" as manifested upon the earth (Gen. 4:14, 16).

The rather brief record of this era seems to indicate a condition of individual and irresponsible lawlessness so far as any external restraints were concerned. For example, in the case of Cain, strangely enough, instead of leaving this fratricidal killer to the ancient *lex talionis* of a life for a life, God actually protected him from being brought before the bar of any possible human judgment or punishment. And although the Cainite civilization, with its building of a city and development of the arts and crafts, must have led to some degree of voluntary social organization, nevertheless the arrogant and boastful poem of Lamech, probably composed to celebrate the successful outcome of a personal vendetta, suggests a

---

[4] So G. Lunemann, "Epistle to the Hebrews," in *Meyer's Commentary on the New Testament* (New York: Funk and Wagnalls, 1885), *in loc.*

[5] Plato's *Timaeus* does indeed use the most exalted language in describing the creation of the universe, but "there is always lurking about it his besetting inconsistency — the thought of something evil, eternal in itself, and inseparable from matter and from nature." (Cf. Taylor Lewis, trans. of Lange on *Genesis,* 5th ed. rev., footnote *in loc.*).

period in history when men largely followed their own violent impulses without any fear of immediate judicial retribution (Gen. 4:19-24). The period ends, as we might expect, with almost total moral corruption and the earth "filled with violence" (Gen. 6:11).

The words of Genesis 6:3 imply that whatever the restraint upon human conduct may have been during this period, it was *inward* rather than external in nature. "My spirit shall not always strive with man," God says, in pronouncing His verdict upon the entire age. The verb here means to "rule" or "sit in judgment," and this judgment must have been spiritual and moral. Certainly, considering the utter wickedness of that antediluvian world, we cannot think of God's Spirit dwelling within or upon men in any New Testament sense. Some have suggested that the Spirit was striving with these ungodly men through the faithful preaching of Noah; and this may have been true in a limited degree. It would be more in accord with the historical context, however, to regard this work of the Spirit as something wrought through man's *moral nature* or *conscience,* that inward voice which had been implanted within him by original creation (Rom. 2:14, 15). This is the sole avenue of sinful man's immediate contact with his Creator. The conscience may indeed be disobeyed, quenched, wrongly educated, or even seared as with a hot iron; but it remains the voice of God in the soul, telling men that they *ought* to do right and not do wrong.

It is not without some justification, therefore, that by some the period before the Flood has been named the "Age of Conscience." Not that the rule of conscience began and ended with this particular era of human history; but that throughout the period, conscience stood alone as the method of the divine Spirit in judging and restraining the actions of wicked men. The ultimatum of God, "My spirit shall not always strive with man," did not forecast any end of the judging function of conscience, but rather an end of man's probation under its rule as an *exclusive* method of divine restraint. The divine warning is certainly clear: yet "an hundred and twenty years" and judgment will fall; this time not merely the inner judgment of the Spirit's voice in the conscience of man, but a judgment which would be external, visible and supernatural, putting an end to that generation of men which had rejected the moral sovereignty of God (Gen. 6:3-13). The complete failure of mankind under this test should be a sufficient answer to the notion that sinful man needs on earth a kingdom of God which is only spiritual and moral in nature.

3. From the Flood to Babel

The powers that be are ordained of God.   —Rom. 13:1

Following the judgment of the Flood, two events took place which were of great importance in the divine government in relation to the human race. The first of these was a promise on the part of God to the effect that, although recognizing the continuance of man's evil nature and propensities, He never again would smite "every living thing" (Gen. 8:21), as had been done, "by the waters of a flood" (Gen. 9:11). And as a solemn pledge that the covenant thus made would be kept, the "bow in the cloud" was made a token between God and man (Gen. 9:12-17).

The second important event was the divine authorization for the institution of *human government*. Such authorization was a logical sequence of the covenant which God had made with Noah and his family. Since in this covenant God had promised not again to destroy the sinful race by a watery judgment, thereby taking away man's fear of a repetition of such judgment, it became necessary to set up some other form of control upon the lawless impulses of men. It was for this purpose that human government was instituted by divine decree.

Here again the Genesis record is very brief, but the decree laid down very simply and clearly the basic principle of all human law and government: "Whoso sheddeth man's blood, by man shall his blood be shed; for in the image of God made he man" (Gen. 9:6). In this historic text several things should be noted: First, the decree recognizes that fallen man at his best, here exemplified by righteous Noah and his family, still has within his heart unmeasured potentialities for evil which must be curbed. Second, these evil inclinations are now to be restrained by the fear of governmental punishment; and in the case of murder the punishment would be capital. Third, the penalty upon evildoers would be inflicted by *"man"* in the collective or governmental sense; not according to the principle of personal vengeance, as some have supposed. Fourth, the moral justification for the institution of human government, and also its power of capital punishment, is based squarely upon the very argument often used against the latter, namely, the sacredness of human life in God's sight — "for in the image of God made he man."

What we call civil or organized government, whether simple or highly complex, exists for only one reason — the protection, conservation, fostering, and improvement of human life. Genesis 9:6, therefore, becomes one of the most important landmarks in all of human history, for here God not only decrees the beginning of human government in a sinful world but also lays down the moral and social foundation of all such government. As Luther has well said of the text, "This was the first command having reference to the temporal sword. By these words temporal government was established, and the sword placed in its hand by God."

What we have here, then, is something wholly new upon earth; an institution by which God will now mediate His government over the nations through human rulers who, whether they acknowledge Him or not, are nevertheless "ordained of God" as "ministers" of His; and therefore will be held responsible before God for the manner in which they discharge their duties "for good" to mankind in general and to "execute wrath" upon those who do evil (Rom. 13:1-6).

4. *The Confusion of Tongues*
The LORD did there confound the language of all the earth.—*Gen. 11:9*

Following the institution of human government, therefore, it should not be surprising to find next in the order of the Genesis account what has been called "The Table of Nations" in chapter 10. In this remarkable document from the past we are given a glimpse of the birth of nations, the building of cities, and the founding of empires — all of which implies the existence and development of social and governmental organization. The story of the Tower of Babel with its confusion of tongues, which follows in chapter 11, seems to have been introduced at this particular point in the record for the purpose of explaining the existence and wide dispersal of the nations named in the previous chapter.[6]

The implications of the Babel story point to the plurality of nations, in opposition to any central world government, as something definitely in harmony with the purpose of God. The intentions of the builders at Babel are stated in Genesis 11:4 as follows: "Let us build us a city and a tower . . . and let us make us a name, lest we be scattered abroad upon the face of the whole earth." Apparently the city was to provide a world center for the human race, and the monumental tower was to serve as a physical and spectacular symbol of world unification. Having lost in the Fall that *inward* and spiritual

---

[6] So Keil, Kurtz, Ellicott, Candlish, *et al.*

unity of the race which was centered in God, men now resort to the establishment of an *external* unity. We have here the first recorded urge of sinful men toward the "one world" idea of social and governmental organization.

In this connection a question naturally arises: Why would not such a world organization have been a good thing? Would this not, as it is still being argued today, preserve the unity of mankind and thus avoid the confusion and strife which has been historically associated with a multiplicity of nations and governments? Ideally, of course, one world government would seem to furnish the answer to many difficult problems, provided the world was made up of only the *right* kind of people. But the trouble has been that, ever since the fall of Adam, the world has had the *wrong* kind of people — "For all have sinned, and come short of the glory of God" (Rom. 3:23). And in such a world there is mortal danger in a single and total world government. As someone has acutely observed, political power always corrupts and absolute power corrupts absolutely.

The judgment of God upon this first attempt at one world government was not only a clear warning against all such schemes but also an endorsement of what is called "nationalism."[7] Although not the ideal form of human organization, nationalism has proven the *safest* for the preservation of personal liberty in a sinful world. In the world market of political ideas and forms, there will be competition and experiment just as long as there are many nations. And, in the end, such competition and experiment always work out for individual liberty and the development of distinctive cultural values which then may be mutually shared between nations. In a sinful race left to its own devices, one monolithic world state might conceivably put an end to all further political experiment and result in an irreversible totalitarianism.

The nature of the divine judgment upon this first try at a World State is deeply interesting. It is generally conceded that the cement which holds men together in groups and nations is what we call a common culture, and the very core of such a culture is found in language,[8] man's marvelous ability to communicate ideas. It was exactly at this point that the judgment of God struck: the common

---

[7] Cf. Deut. 32:8 and Acts 17:26.

[8] Cf. the observation attributed to Bismarck, that "the most potent factor in human society at the end of the 19th century was the fact that the British and American peoples spoke the same language." And Winston Churchill referred to "this gift of a common tongue" as a "priceless inheritance."

bond of "one language" was supernaturally destroyed, and the multiplication of tongues led to the formation of different groups and, ultimately, nations. For the chief obstacle to the achievement of the one world state of "Internationalism," it has often been recognized, is the barrier of language. The very headphones worn by the delegates of the various member nations at meetings of the United Nations' organization are a witness to the divinely imposed safeguard against the menace of one total world government established by sinful men.

It is true that later the kingdom of Babylon became the golden head of an empire which held authority "wheresoever the children of men dwell" (Dan. 2:38). However, it must not be overlooked that this was an empire established by *divine* sanction, as indicated clearly by the address of Daniel to Nebuchadnezzar: "Thou, O king, art a king of kings; for the God of heaven hath given thee a kingdom, power, and strength, and glory. And wheresoever the children of men dwell . . . hath he given into thine hand, and hath made thee ruler over them all" (Dan. 2:37-38). Furthermore, it is open to serious question whether this universal authority, although conferred by God Himself, was ever actually exercised by Nebuchadnezzar over all peoples in all places. Certainly, the three so-called world empires which followed never completely succeeded in subduing all the different nations on earth; nor were they able to perpetuate their comparatively brief existence without unceasing struggles; and in the end they fell before attacks by peoples of other language areas. In the long history of sinful humanity there will be only one truly universal world empire (called "the kingdom of the world" in Rev. 11:15, ASV), and that will be achieved by superhuman means at the hand of Satan's own ruler, the antichrist, whose brief span of world dominion will be definitely limited by God to exactly 1260 days. Even here, however, this final empire will not be achieved without divine sanction; for his universal authority will be "given unto him" from above (Rev. 13:7).

5. From Abraham to the Exodus

Kings shall come out of thee.   —*Gen. 17:6*

Following the frustration of man's first attempt to establish a world state, and the resultant rise of nationalism through the confusion of language, God turned away from "man" in the collective sense and called out one particular man through whom the divine regal will is to be accomplished on earth (Gen. 12:1-4).

The covenant with Abraham, of course, is essentially prophetical in nature and therefore will be discussed later under the head of "The Mediatorial Kingdom in Prophecy" (ch. 13). But this covenant is also a matter of history, and its fulfillment began incipiently at once to run its course. In Abraham, and later in both Isaac and Jacob, the mediatorial idea began to take concrete form historically in miniature. For Jehovah spoke immediately to these patriarchs, and they in turn mediated the divine will, although often very imperfectly.

The Genesis record indicates that, within the scope of their own families, these great Hebrew men were genuine mediators through whom God ruled in the chosen line of humanity. They were almost absolute rulers in their own household, or clan, which included not only their own progeny but also servants, retainers, and even fighting men (Gen. 14:14). In their hands rested the power of life and death, as may be seen in the seeming callous exposure of Hagar and her child (Gen. 21:9-21), and in the freedom with which Abraham moved to offer up his son (Gen. 22). Furthermore, in his successful military expedition against the allied kings who had ravaged the Jordan Valley and carried away Lot, Abraham unquestionably regarded his slaughter of the kings as an act in harmony with the will of God (Gen. 14). It must not be overlooked, however, that in the exercise of their regal authority, the patriarchs are always held immediately responsible to God for their acts.

It is significantly in connection with Abraham that the strange and interesting figure of Melchizedek appears with tantalizing brevity in the inspired historical record (Gen. 14:17-24). The important point to be noticed is that he is named in Scripture "king of Salem" and "priest of the most high God," and also that Abraham recognized him as a true regal representative of the true God by giving to him a tithe of all the booty taken in the battle. Whether or not Melchizedek stood alone in this capacity outside the Abrahamic line, the record does not state. It is possible that in the era before Abraham there were other kings who held a similar mediatorial authority between their subjects and the true God. At any rate, this one historical example is ample proof that the mediatorial idea was not totally unknown in the period before the call of Abraham. And the citation of this case in the inspired record may be intended to remind us that the God of the Bible is the God of both Jews and Gentiles (Rom. 3:29), and also to point typically to the future

Mediatorial Kingdom when "the one mediator between God and men" (I Tim. 2:5) will reign over all nations, both Jew and Gentile.

The appearance of Melchizedek at this precise point in Biblical history has significance dispensationally. The meeting of these two great figures, Abraham and Melchizedek, marks the end of an era and the beginning of a new order of things. As Westcott has said of the latter, "The lessons of his appearance lie in the appearance itself. Abraham marks a new departure. . . . But before the fresh order is established we have a vision of the old in its superior majesty; and this, on the eve of disappearance, gives its blessing to the new."[9] The "superior majesty" of which Westcott speaks is, of course, a *typical* superiority.

6. *The Sojourn in Egypt*

The people grew and multiplied in Egypt.   —*Acts 7:17*

The departure of Israel from the promised land to go down into Egypt, apparently with divine approval (Gen. 46:1-4), raises the ancient theological problem of the relation between human freedom and divine sovereignty. It will help us here to remember that divine *precept* and *prophecy* are two wholly different matters. The former tells man what he *ought* to do (Gen. 12:1), while the latter foretells what man actually *will* do (Gen. 15:13). In the case of Jacob, once the fateful decision had been made, with all its complicated background of wrongdoing, *then* God graciously came to the patriarch with a reassurance that the promises will hold good in spite of human failure. Israel was responsible for his choices and would certainly suffer for his waywardness, but through all the tangled web of circumstances the providential purpose of God would be carried out.

Thus the sojourn in Egypt, under God, became a providential means of disciplinary training. There the chosen people were brought in contact with a high and well-organized civilization; a great leader was raised up who was learned in all the wisdom of Egypt; yet a sufficient measure of oppression was permitted to weld the tribes into a nation in preparation for the theocratic kingdom soon to be established.

---

[9] B. F. Westcott, *Commentary on the Epistle to the Hebrews* (Grand Rapids: Eerdmans Publishing Co., reprint, 1954), p. 199.

CHAPTER VI

THE ESTABLISHMENT OF THE
MEDIATORIAL KINGDOM IN HISTORY

The history of the exodus, which signifies the birth of Israel as a nation, is fully reported. In this crisis Moses is the prophetical mediator through whom the wonderful deed of God is accomplished . . . . Moses himself had no other authority or power than that which was secured for him through his office as the organ of God. He was the human instrument to bring about the synthesis between Israel and Jehovah for all times . . . . The outcome of these experiences, and at the same time its grandest demonstration, was the conclusion of the covenant at Mt. Sinai. From this time on Jehovah was Israel's God and Israel was the people of Jehovah. This God claimed to be the only and absolute ruler over the tribes that were now inwardly united into one nation.—*C. von Orelli*[1]

Some have tried to distinguish too sharply between the period from Moses to Samuel and the period of the kings, referring to the former as the "theocracy" and the latter as the "kingdom." The terms are used disparately: by "theocracy" they mean the rule of God, and by "kingdom" they mean the rule of men; thus conveying an erroneous contrast when applied to the periods under discussion. For, in an important sense, men were ruling from Moses to Samuel; and God did not cease to rule under the kings. Actually the two periods are *one,* if considered from the standpoint of Jehovah's regal relation to the nation of Israel. For this theocratic kingdom began with Moses, continued under Joshua and the judges, developed and reached its highest degree of extension and prosperity under the first three kings, declined after Solomon and the division of the tribes, and came to a melancholy end with the departure of the Visible Presence at the Captivity. If, in the beginning, it seems strange to have a kingdom without a king, we must not forget that in this kingdom it is *God,* not man, who rules. And this theocratic rule could be, and was historically, mediated through divinely chosen leaders of various

[1] C. von Orelli, "History of Israel," *International Standard Bible Encyclopedia* (Chicago: Howard-Severance, 1915), Vol. III, p. 1515.

types, whether prophets or judges or kings. The important idea is not to be found in the titles these various leaders bore, but rather in their common function of *mediatorial* rule. Considered as individuals, there were vast differences between them both in ability and faithfulness. But all alike were held responsible to God for the manner in which they exercised their divinely appointed mediatorial function in the only kingdom ever established by God Himself on earth over a single nation in human history.

1. *The Supernatural Preparation for the Kingdom*

By signs, and by wonders . . . and by great terrors.   —*Deut. 4:34*

The establishment of a kingdom of God in human history was something so new and important that it was necessary to signalize its appearance on earth by means of a series of great supernatural acts which were designed to compel belief and which could not be misinterpreted by any of the parties involved. These parties were: first, Moses as the mediatorial leader; second, the children of Israel as the chosen nation; third, Egypt and the other Gentile nations.

The first exhibition of divine miraculous power in this connection was addressed to *Moses,* coming in the form of an extraordinary theophany at the *Burning Bush* (Exod. 3:1-10). This event, which constituted the call of Moses to be the first of a long line of mediatorial rulers in the nation of Israel, was properly witnessed by Moses alone. Several aspects of the event are pertinent to this discussion of the Kingdom. First, the miracle occurred at Horeb, "the mountain of God" (3:1), which certainly must be identified with Sinai where later the actual inauguration of the theocratic kingdom would take place. Second, the burning fire points to the judging activity of God, which had become a matter of Fatherly chastening in the case of Israel passing through the furnace of affliction in Egypt, but which would fall upon Pharaoh and his hosts in unrelieved retributory justice. And judgment is a chief function of God ruling as King (Ps. 72:1-2; Isa. 2:4, ASV). Third, upon this important occasion God names Himself as "I AM THAT I AM" (Exod. 3:14). Whatever else may be involved in the use of this remarkable name, certainly one outstanding idea is that of *sovereignty* — "the absolute God of the fathers, acting with unfettered liberty and self-dependence."[2] This is the essential attribute of God in His regal activity. Fourth, it is at the burning bush that God reaffirms His covenant

[2] Keil and Delitzsch, *Commentary on the Old Testament,* trans. James Martin (Grand Rapids: Eerdmans Publishing Co., reprint, 1949), *in loc.*

relation with the people of Israel (Exod. 3:6); and Moses is invested with divine authority to command the elders of Israel, to sound the trumpet of judgment before Pharaoh, to deliver the nation from the oppression of Egypt, and to lead them into the promised land where God would rule over them in mercy and justice. Fifth, it is not without significance that Moses, like Israel's greatest earthly king yet to come, was brought providentially to the place of divine calling as a mediatorial ruler of his people following a long apprenticeship as a shepherd of sheep (Exod. 3:1).

The second demonstration of Jehovah's miraculous power was intended for the *nation of Israel,* and consisted of a group of three miracles: the *rod* which became a serpent, the *hand* healed of leprosy, and the *water* which became blood (Exod. 4:1-9). If the miracle of the burning bush was given to authenticate to Moses the revealed will of God, these three miracles were directed in the same way toward the nation of Israel; "that they may believe" that Moses had been commissioned of God to deliver them from Egyptian bondage and lead them into the promised land of the coming kingdom (4:5). If the people could not be convinced by the miracle of the rod, then Moses was instructed to give them the second sign. But if the two signs failed to produce belief, they were to be given the third sign, namely, the water turned to blood (4:9). The inspired record indicates clearly that all three signs were required to convince the people, for we are told that Moses told Aaron "all the words" and "all the signs" which God had commanded; and, furthermore, that the "signs" were done "in the sight of the people. And the people believed" (4:28-31). Thus Moses was divinely accredited to Israel as the mediatorial leader to stand between God and the nation in bringing them out of Egypt to the place of regal blessing.

The third display of miraculous power was directed toward *Egypt and secondarily toward the surrounding Gentile nations.* It consisted of at least twelve separate acts of power; first, a preliminary sign; second, the ten plagues; third, the Red Sea judgment. The judgment miracles fell directly upon Egypt, but the report of them certainly spread to all the surrounding nations. All these Gentile nations needed to be convinced of three facts: first, the absolute sovereignty of Jehovah over other alleged gods; second, the choice of Israel as the favored nation of Jehovah above all other nations; third, the divine authority of Moses as the accredited mediator of Jehovah's word and will, both to Israel and the other nations.

These were precisely the questions involved in the arrogant challenge of Pharaoh in reply to Moses' simple request to let Israel leave Egypt to worship their God: "Who is the Lord, that I should obey his voice to let Israel go? I know not the Lord, neither will I let Israel go" (Exod. 5:2). This challenge had to be answered in such a way as to leave no further question as to these important matters.

The answer of God to the insolent king began graciously with a preliminary miracle, not judicial in character, but evidently intended as a sign to warn the king of the unequal contest in which he had involved himself. The well-known rod was cast down before Pharaoh and became a serpent. Unconvinced, the king called for his magicians, who apparently were able to duplicate the miracle. But the rod of Jehovah swallowed up the rods of the magicians! Then, instead of seeing in this gracious miracle the clear omen of his ultimate defeat, Pharaoh stubbornly closed his eyes to the evidence. In the language of Scripture, "Pharaoh's heart was hardened" (Exod. 7:13, ASV). The King James Version is certainly wrong here. The verb is intransitive, and "Pharaoh's heart" is its nominative case; the clause therefore might be translated, "Pharaoh's heart hardened itself."[3] In view of later statements to the effect that *God* hardened the king's heart, it is important to note here that the process was initiated by the king himself.

Immediately following the king's scornful rejection of God's gracious warning, given both in word and its authenticating sign, the ten judicial plagues fell upon the land of Egypt with appalling swiftness and progressive severity. The reader should keep in mind that all these judgments were evidential in character and purpose. The very existence and sovereignty of Jehovah had been challenged, and the plagues were God's answer. When at times Pharaoh seemed to weaken and be inclined to give up the contest, his heart was "hardened" by Jehovah in order that the demonstration invited by the king himself might be carried out to the bitter end. Since a kingdom of God was about to be established in history, it was essential that sinful men should be given historic evidence that Jehovah is the true God and sovereign over the nations.

The final blow fell at the Red Sea where, by the word and hand of Jehovah, Israel was delivered and Pharaoh and his armies miserably

[3] George Rawlinson, *Ellicott's Commentary* (Grand Rapids: Zondervan Publishing House, reprint, 1954), *in loc.*

perished. The supernatural demonstration had its immediate effect. The power of Egypt against Israel was temporarily destroyed; the people of Israel "believed the LORD, and his servant Moses" (Exod. 14:31); and the fear of Jehovah spread to all the surrounding Gentile nations (Exod. 15:14-17). That all these great demonstrations of divine power were somehow connected with the Kingdom of God is indicated in the climax of the magnificent paean of deliverance sung by Moses and the children of Israel as they stood victoriously on the shore of the Red Sea and shouted, "The LORD shall reign for ever and ever" (Exod. 15:18).

There is a definite parallel between the supernatural preparation for the kingdom in history under Moses and the supernatural judgments which shall be poured out upon a rebellious world in preparation for the future millennial kingdom of our Lord Jesus Christ at His second advent. There is the same insolent challenge to the true God on the part of the Gentile powers (Ps. 2:1-3). There will be a similar gracious but infinitely greater preliminary miracle — the Rapture of the Church — warning men of the supremacy of Jehovah and the ultimate defeat of all who rebel against Him. There will be the same swift progression in the severity of the divine judgments which follow, and even a striking parallel in the nature of the judgments (cf. Rev. 6 through 18). There will be the same victorious outcome, the destruction of the antichrist and his armies in the judgment of Armageddon, and the deliverance of the people of Israel (Rev. 19). There will be another song of victory, significantly referred to as "the song of Moses . . . and the song of the Lamb" (Rev. 15:1-3).

2. Moses — First Mediatorial Ruler of Israel

This Moses . . . did God send to be a ruler and a deliverer.—*Acts 7:35*

As already suggested above, the mediatorial idea was not unknown before Moses, but until the Exodus there was no *nation* in the political sense. Von Orelli rightly speaks of the Exodus as "the birth of Israel as a nation," a crisis in which Moses appeared as "the prophetical mediator through whom the wonderful deed of God is accomplished." The grand climax of this historic birth was reached at Sinai where the tribes were "inwardly united into one nation"; and the outcome was "that Moses as the recognized organ of God was not only the authority who was to decide in all disputes concerning right, but also the one from whom a new and complete order of legal enactments proceeded."[4] It is true that Moses is never spoken of as a king.[5] But that is also true of more than one great figure in history who have ruled as absolute monarchs over various nations. The difference between Moses and these other rulers is that, in the case of the great law-giver, the regal authority was exercised mediatorially under God and His direct control. Dr. O. T. Allis is right in saying that "Moses exercised the office of a king; he represented the invisible King."[6] And the testimony of Acts 7:35 is decisive.

First, as a mediatorial ruler, Moses *represented Jehovah toward the people*. Because of Moses' slowness of speech and the eloquence of Aaron, the latter is graciously permitted to serve as Moses' spokesman to the people; but it is Moses alone who is authorized to stand before both Aaron and Israel "instead of God" (Exod. 4:16). As for those who might set themselves up as opposers and oppressors of the nation of Israel, they would meet in the person of Moses all the authority and power of the true God Himself: "See," said Jehovah, "I have made thee as God to Pharaoh" (Exod. 7:1, ASV). If there were to be new revelations from God to the people, supernatural signs to be performed, divine laws to be given, decisions to be made between disputing parties, or judgments to be inflicted, Moses had been chosen to be the mediatorial channel. The late Melvin Grove Kyle, in whose classes I had the great privilege of studying Pentateuchal history, has said that the task of Moses was "the most appalling commission ever given to a mere man."

This divinely bestowed authority of Moses was generally recognized among the people of Israel, although upon various occasions they were prone to murmur against their great leader; but only once in his long ruling career did the murmuring break out in open insurrection, and then the divine authority of Moses was underscored in terrible fashion. The rebellion of Korah and his followers seems to have been directed at first against both Moses and Aaron, but doubtless the latter was included because of his relation to Moses as spokesman. At any rate, when the crisis came, the central issue of the opposition and its personal object were quickly isolated by Moses, and stated thus: "Hereby ye shall know that Jehovah hath sent me to do all these works; for I have not done them of

---

[4] C. von Orelli, *op. cit.*

[5] The subject of Deut. 33:5 is Jehovah, not Moses, according to the best authorities. Cf. Lange, *in loc.*

[6] O. T. Allis, *Prophecy and the Church* (Philadelphia: Presbyterian and Reformed Publishing Co., 1945), p. 59.

mine own mind. If these men die the common death of all men . . .
then Jehovah hath not sent me. But if Jehovah make a new thing,
and the ground open its mouth, and swallow them up, with all that
appertain unto them, and they go down alive into Sheol; then ye
shall understand that these men have despised Jehovah" (Num.
16:28-30, ASV). Thus Moses identified rebellion against his leadership as rebellion against *God*, and the awful judgment which fell
upon the rebels clarified once for all the mediatorial authority with
which Moses had been divinely invested.

In the second place, as a mediatorial ruler, Moses also *represented
the people of Israel toward God*. Over and over during the long
wanderings between Egypt and the promised land, Moses appeared
in this aspect of his mediatorial office, pleading the mercy of Jehovah
on behalf of a people which deserved wrath. As he reminded Israel
in one of his final addresses, they had often provoked the LORD to
wrath; "in Horeb"; "at Taberah, and at Massah, and at Kibroth-
hattaavah"; likewise when the LORD had sent them "from Kadesh-
barnea" (Deut. 9:8, 22, 23). In all these crises Moses had faithfully
interceded for his nation: "Ye have been rebellious against the LORD
from the day that I knew you. Thus I fell down before the LORD
forty days and forty nights, as I fell down at the first; because the
LORD had said that he would destroy you. I prayed therefore unto
the LORD, and said, O Lord GOD, destroy not thy people and thine
inheritance, which thou hast redeemed through thy greatness, which
thou hast brought forth out of Egypt with a mighty hand. Remember thy servants, Abraham, Isaac, and Jacob; look not unto the
stubbornness of this people, nor to their wickedness, nor to their
sin . . . they are thy people" (Deut. 9:24-29).

But although the ministry of Moses in mediatorial intercession
for Israel continued faithfully without interruption through all their
terrible lapses into such sins as idolatry and degrading lust, it is
a striking fact that when open rebellion breaks out against Moses
as the divinely authorized mediatorial ruler, there is no record of
intercession on behalf of the rebels. Korah and his followers perished
without mercy under the immediate judgment of God, an event
pointing unmistakably to the great antitypical Prophet like unto
Moses whose blessed intercession is for only those who accept Him
as the one mediator between God and men. "I pray for them," He
says, "I pray not for the world" (John 17:9).

Along with his great mediatorial authority, however, there was laid upon the shoulders of Moses a commensurable *responsibility*. In this capacity Moses must never forget the heavenly source of his power and authority, that his was only a delegated office, that he was never to rule in his own right. Only once did he forget, when, provoked beyond ordinary human endurance by the murmuring of the people at the waters of Meribah, he spoke unadvisedly with his lips. "Must we fetch you water out of this rock?" (Num. 20:10). And for this lapse of memory Moses was held fully responsible; God did not spare him. According to the divine ultimatum, the great mediatorial leader and lawgiver would not be permitted to see the goal of all his faithful ministry — to set his feet upon the good land of promise. He himself records the bitter disappointment: "And I besought the LORD at that time, saying . . . . I pray thee, let me go over, and see the good land that is beyond Jordan . . . . But the LORD was wroth with me for your sakes, and would not hear me: and the LORD said unto me, Let it suffice thee; speak no more unto me of this matter . . . . for thou shalt not go over this Jordan" (Deut. 3:23-27). And the reason is given in Deuteronomy 32:51, "Because ye trespassed against me among the children of Israel at the waters of Meribah-Kadesh."

It is altogether fitting, therefore, that in his official capacity as the first mediatorial ruler in the theocratic kingdom of history, Moses is presented in Scripture as a *type of Christ,* who will be the perfect embodiment of God's mediatorial ruler in the final phase of the mediatorial kingdom on earth. It is true that this future ruler is named a *prophet,* as Moses himself predicted, "The LORD thy God will raise up unto thee a Prophet from the midst of thee, of thy brethren, like unto me" (Deut. 18:15). But the Coming One will be more than a prophet; like Moses He will also be a ruler over His people, and His regal authority will be absolute: "It shall come to pass, that whosoever will not hearken unto my words which he shall speak in my name," God declares, "I will require it of him" (Deut. 18:19). The Apostle Peter applies this very passage to our Lord in the New Testament, connecting its fulfillment with His Second Advent, and emphasizing the absolute nature of His rule: "It shall come to pass, that every soul, which will not hear that prophet, shall be destroyed from among the people" (Acts 3:19-23). By no device of exegesis can the force of this great prophecy, considered in relation to its original context and sense, be watered down to fit the theory of a "kingdom of grace" existing only in the hearts of men. On this point the terrible fate of Korah and his followers, as a swift judgment upon the rebellion against Moses, stands as a clear testimony as to the meaning of the prophecy concerning the regal authority of that coming prophet who will be a greater than Moses. And the writer of Hebrews repeats the warning in unmistakable words: "For if they escaped not who refused him that spake on earth, much more shall not we escape, if we turn away from him that speaketh from heaven" (Heb. 12:25). The verses following indicate: first, that it was the voice of *God* that shook the earth in the days of Moses; second, that the same voice will in the future shake both earth and the heavens; and third, that the coming judgment will be connected with a "kingdom which cannot be shaken" (Heb. 12:28, ASV), out of which, we are assured elsewhere, all forms of rebellion shall be purged by the coming prophet who is also called "the Son of man" (Matt. 13:41-43).

3. The Kingdom-Covenant at Sinai

Ye shall be unto me a kingdom of priests.   —*Exod. 19:6*

The immediate goal of the march from the Red Sea was the mountain of Sinai where, according to previous instructions, Moses understood there was to be a rendezvous with the God of Israel. In the original call Jehovah had said to Moses, "Certainly I will be with thee; and this shall be a token unto thee, that I have sent thee: when thou hast brought forth the people out of Egypt, ye shall serve God upon this mountain" (Exod. 3:12). It should not surprise us, therefore, not only to find that the line of march was directly to Sinai; but also that the first act of Moses upon arrival was to ascend the mountain: "There Israel camped before the mount. And Moses went up unto God" (Exod. 19:2-3). Something was to take place there which would be a "token" to Moses. The expression "serve God," which describes the token, means more than sacrificial or ritual service; it forecasts the willing service of the people in submitting to the covenant which would be set before them at Sinai.[7]

The manifestation of God at Sinai was something uniquely different from all previous appearances. There had been other theophanies: when God had come down to commune with Adam in the Garden; to visit Abraham in his pilgrim tent; to confirm later the divine covenant with the patriarch; and to call Moses to lead the tribes out of the land of Egypt. In these appearances there was a note of gracious and personal intimacy. But at Sinai we have a

---

[7] So Keil and Delitzsch, *op. cit., in loc.*

theophany of unprecedented majesty and grandeur; its attendant phenomena visible to an entire nation; and evidently designed to reveal unforgettably the sovereign character of Jehovah, who is superlatively holy and the King Eternal, now ready to establish a kingdom of His own on earth among men. According to the divine instructions given to Moses, the people must be sanctified for two days and thus be prepared for the third day when the LORD would "come down in the sight of all the people upon mount Sinai" (Exod. 19:10-11). There were thunderings and lightnings, a thick cloud, the smoke of a furnace, a mighty shaking of the mountain, and the increasing tempo of a great trumpet sound. "And the sight of the glory of the LORD was like devouring fire on the top of the mount in the eyes of the children of Israel" (Exod. 24:17). Out of this impressive setting came the voice of Jehovah to Moses who in turn mediated the divine revelation to the people.

The revelation began with the proffer of a covenant which is recorded as follows: "Ye have seen what I did unto the Egyptians, and how I bare you on eagles' wings, and brought you unto myself. Now therefore, if ye will obey my voice indeed, and keep my covenant, then ye shall be a peculiar treasure unto me above all people; for all the earth is mine: And ye shall be unto me a kingdom of priests, and an holy nation. These are the words which thou shalt speak unto the children of Israel" (Exod. 19:4-6). With reference to this covenant several points should be noted.

First, we have here the first occurrence of the word "kingdom" in the Bible, where the idea is directly associated with the rule of God. This is to be no ordinary kingdom where men will rule upon earth in their own right, but rather a kingdom "unto me," that is, unto Jehovah. In other words, whatever else its characteristics may be, it is to be, first of all, *God's* kingdom.

Second, in this proposed covenant the kingdom is to be given to one nation, which is to be lifted up above all other nations in this relationship; and this nation is named "the children of Israel" (vs. 6). There can be no esoteric interpretation of the words used upon this historic occasion. The people here were the descendants of Abraham by natural generation, a literal people standing at that very moment before the literal mountain of Sinai. These facts point to something altogether different from that general rule of God over all the nations which is exercised providentially without interruption.

Third, in the setting up of this new kingdom, which has a definite beginning in the process of history, the other nations of the earth are not ignored. Although Israel is indeed to be set above all other peoples as the LORD's "peculiar treasure" or "possession" (ASV), they are not to forget that the other nations are claimed by Jehovah; for, as He declares, "All the earth is mine" (vs. 5). These words shut out of court the notion advanced by some critical scholars that Jehovah in early Biblical records is conceived of merely as a national or tribal God; and the same words should have guarded the Israelites from the unwarranted and selfish exclusiveness which developed in later history. The Apostle Paul saw this truth clearly as he wrote in the Book of Romans that the God of the Scriptures is not the God of the Jews only, but the God "of the Gentiles also" (3:29).

Fourth, it is only in the light of this universal relation of Jehovah to all nations that a unique feature of the historical kingdom can be properly understood, namely, that the nation of Israel is to be a "kingdom of priests" (vs. 6). Now it is the main function of priests to mediate between God and men. Therefore, since all nations on earth are within the purview of the covenant, in the sense that they are to share somehow as beneficiaries of the act, the divine call of Israel must have had as one of its purposes the idea of one nation acting mediatorially in religious matters between the true God and the nations of the earth. Thus the mediatorial nature of the historical kingdom is broadened: it is not only that God will reign over one nation through a mediatorial ruler, but that through the nation thus ruled there will be mediated the blessings of God to all other nations.

Fifth, because of Israel's favored relation to God, and also because of her exalted regal position as the accredited representative of God to all other nations, Israel must be an "holy nation" (vs. 6). The basic idea of Biblical holiness is *separation;* first, unto God as His own possession; and second, from all that is morally impure. The latter arises out of the first. Thus high privileges and responsibilities carry with them high moral and spiritual requirements. To all in every age who are made the objects of special divine favor, the same word of God must come, "Ye shall be holy; for I am holy" (Lev. 11:44).

A sixth, and very crucial, feature of the kingdom-covenant with Israel was its *conditional* nature. The introductory clause lays down the divine condition: "If ye will obey my voice indeed" (Exod. 19:5). And the central thing thus qualified is stated in the words which follow: "Ye shall be unto me a kingdom of priests" (vs. 6). In this conditional feature we have one great difference between the initial covenant with Abraham and the kingdom-covenant at Sinai, for they are not the same (Deut. 5:3).[8] The latter was made dependent on obedience; and on this ground its continuity could be interrupted, and was historically, by the failure of the people. But the terms of the Abrahamic covenant, being wholly sovereign and unconditioned, hold good in every age. As to the conditionality of the kingdom-covenant at Sinai, it is important to remember that this had to do only with the regal and mediatorial activity of Israel in her own land in relation to Jehovah and the nations. There is no question here of the position of Israel as the elect nation of God. Neither is there here any proposal of an individual salvation based on legal obedience. Although the Law was given to Israel upon this occasion, the covenant does not set forth a way of salvation by means of law-keeping. The conditional clause qualifies the continuance of the nation of Israel in her favored position in the mediatorial kingdom of Old Testament history, functioning as God's "kingdom of priests" among the nations on earth.

Hence, considering precisely what was involved, the response of the people must be regarded generally as evidence of a right attitude. They said, "All that the LORD hath spoken we will do" (Exod. 19:8). If this response deserves any criticism, it should be for its apparent lack of any proper expression of humble insufficiency for the tremendous task of fulfilling the condition of obedience laid upon the nation. In the Book of Deuteronomy there is a review of the transaction which took place at Sinai between Jehovah and Israel; and the record indicates clearly that the LORD not only approved the people's response to the proffered covenant but also regarded with compassionate apprehension the problem of their continuance in the doing of what they had so easily pledged with their lips. The LORD's evaluation of their pledge is thus stated: "They have well said all that they have spoken" (5:28). But this is followed immediately with a divine lament: "O that there were such an heart in them, that they would fear me, and keep all my commandments always, that it might be well with them, and with their children for ever" (5:29). It is one thing to make pledges to God; it is something else to fulfill them. But both records are clear that Jehovah accepted the people's pledge as sincere, although superficially made, and the covenant was thus ratified for the establishment of the mediatorial kingdom in history. The 19th chapter

---

[8] "The covenant at Sinai . . . was essentially distinct from the covenant made with Abraham" (*Keil* and *Delitzsch, op. cit.,* on Deut. 5:3).

of Exodus, therefore, in the words of Lange, "records the establishment of the theocracy, or the typical Kingdom of God."[9]

What had been done at Sinai was later summarized in the final words of Moses just before he died (Deut. 33:1-5). In verse 2 he describes the great theophany at the mountain; the ineffable glory of Jehovah lighting up the entire region where it took place. Verse 3 speaks of Jehovah's tender love for His chosen people. Verse 4 refers briefly to the giving of the Law by the hand of Moses. Verse 5 recalls the great transaction at Sinai between Jehovah and His people in the covenant of the kingdom: "He was king in Jeshurun, when the heads of the people and the tribes of Israel were gathered together." That the pronoun "he" must refer to Jehovah, not to Moses, is the opinion of the best commentators. During the wilderness march to the Land, in Balaam's prophecy, mention was made of the kingdom-covenant established at Mount Sinai between Jehovah and Israel: "The LORD his God is with him, and the shout of a king is among them" (Num. 23:21). And Psalm 114:1-2 looks back to that same grand event: "When Israel went forth out of Egypt, . . . Judah became his sanctuary, Israel his dominion" (ASV).

[9] J. P. Lange, *Commentary on Exodus,* trans. Charles N. Mead (New York: Scribner's Sons, 1876), p. 66, c.

CHAPTER VII

THE CONSTITUTION AND LAWS OF THE KINGDOM IN HISTORY

The statesman-prophet [Moses] framed a *civil government* which illustrated the kingdom of God upon earth. The theocracy did not simulate any government of earth, monarch, republic or socialistic state. It combined the best elements in all of these and set up the most effective checks which have ever been devised against the evils of each . . . . In all the multiform activities of the prophetic career he was *a type of Christ* . . . .   —*Melvin Grove Kyle*[1]

It would be impossible within the limits of this book, and not essential to its main purpose, to examine in detail the Mosaic Code. But there are certain important aspects which are pertinent to our discussion of the mediatorial kingdom.

Perhaps the outstanding characteristic of the Mosaic Code is found in its *indivisible unity,* a point upon which the New Testament and the best commentators agree, as I have shown in a monograph published in 1954.[2] However, within the framework of this unity, there may be found at least three definite elements: religious, moral, and civil. This is as we might expect in a code which is to govern men in a kingdom of God upon the earth. For the total needs of men fall within three general categories: first, since man is a religious being, he needs to be guided in his relation to God; second, since man is a moral being, he needs to be informed as to the basic principles of right and wrong; and third, since he is a social and political being, he needs guidance in the details affecting such relationships. All the various aspects of the Mosaic Code fall within these three general realms; yet never separated into fragmentary and autonomous compartments of human existence, but always finding their indivisible unity in God Himself as man's Creator and Sovereign. An examination of these various aspects of

[1] "Moses," *International Standard Bible Encyclopedia* (Chicago: Howard-Severance, 1915), Vol. III, p. 2091.
[2] Alva J. McClain, *Law and the Christian Believer in Relation to the Doctrine of Grace* (Winona Lake: Brethren Missionary Herald Publishing Co., 1954), pp. 8-10.

the Law will indicate the many-faceted nature of the mediatorial kingdom of God in Old Testament history. Furthermore, it will also be found that the execution of this legal constitution of the historic kingdom is shot through and through with provisions and interventions of supernatural character.

1. *This Historical Kingdom Basically a Spiritual Kingdom*

For they drank of that spiritual Rock that followed them. —*I Cor. 10:4*

This point needs to be asserted with special emphasis in opposition to the popular notion that at His first advent our Lord established a "spiritual kingdom" in contrast to the Jewish kingdom of Old Testament history. The spiritual nature of the Old Testament kingdom can be demonstrated easily by an examination of the Pentateuchal material in the light of the Biblical meaning of the term "spiritual." It is high time that this perfectly good term should be rescued from the abuse it has suffered at the hands of theologians who, either consciously or otherwise, have been under the spell of Platonic philosophy. A discussion of the Biblical use of the term "spiritual" will be found in the Appendix,[3] but this much may be said here: Wherever and whenever we find God establishing a direct and personal relationship between Himself and other personalities, whether as individuals or as a group, regardless of place or conditions, such a relationship must be regarded as basically *spiritual* in nature.

With reference to the spirituality of the Old Testament kingdom, S. D. Press has correctly stated the matter: "It is universally recognized that Israel was a singular community. From the beginning of its existence as a nation it bore the character of a religious and moral community, a theocratic commonwealth, having Jehovah Himself as the Head and Ruler. The theocracy is not to be mistaken for a hierarchy, nor can it be strictly identified with any existent form of political organization. It was rather something over and above, and therefore independent of the political organization. It did not supersede the tribal organization of Israel, but it supplied the centralizing power, constituting Israel as a nation. In lieu of a strong political center, the unifying bond of a common allegiance to Jehovah, i.e., the common faith in Him, the God of Israel, kept the tribes together. The consciousness that Jehovah was Israel's King was deeply rooted, was a national feeling, and the inspiration

[3] See chap. XXVII.

of a true patriotism."[4] It would be absurd in the highest degree to deny to such a relationship, as described so ably by Press, any place within the category of things which may be called spiritual.

It is quite astonishing that the spiritual nature of the Old Testament kingdom should ever have been questioned or overlooked. The relation of the nation of Israel to Jehovah was that of a son, as the king of Egypt was reminded: "Israel is my son, even my firstborn: . . . Let my son go, that he may serve me" (Exod. 4:22-23). Over and over in addressing this historic people, Jehovah reminds them that He is "the LORD your God" (Lev. 19:2, 10, 25, etc.). The entire system of sacrifice, as established in the kingdom-covenant at Sinai, had as a central purpose the maintenance of fellowship between the people and God through the forgiveness of their sins. Compare the oft-repeated promise, "And it shall be forgiven" (Lev. 4:20, 26, 31, 35, etc.). At the tabernacle the LORD promises to "meet" with Moses, and "speak" to him, and "commune" with him (Exod. 25:22; 29:42); and not only with Moses acting in his divinely appointed capacity as the mediatorial ruler, but also with the people themselves: "There will I meet with the children of Israel . . . . And they shall know that I am the LORD their God" (Exod. 29:43-46). Furthermore, the law of the kingdom was not concerned merely with external matters, but also with the "heart" relation of Israel to God: "Thou shalt love the LORD thy God with all thine heart, and with all thy soul, and with all thy might. And these words . . . shall be in thine heart" (Deut. 6:5-6). And as a final word to Israel as the nation was about to enter the land of promise, Moses harks back to the great transaction at Sinai, saying, "And now, Israel, what doth the LORD thy God require of thee, but to fear the LORD thy God, to walk in all his ways, and to love him, and to serve the LORD thy God with all thy heart and with all thy soul" (Deut. 10:12). Of course, it must certainly be acknowledged that, according to the New Testament teaching, the Law made nothing perfect (Heb. 7:19). But we are not to forget, nevertheless, that the law given at Sinai was essentially "spiritual" in character (Rom. 7:14).

It is not too much to say that this spiritual relation of Israel to God was the *foundation* of all other relations existing in the historical kingdom. But we must understand that such a spiritual relation and control is not inconsistent with considerations which are mun-

---

4 "King, Kingdom," *I.S.B.E., op. cit.,* Vol. III, pp. 1799-1800.

dane and material in character. In fact, the spiritual relation produced effects which extended into numerous other realms, as we
shall see.

2. The Political Aspect of the Historical Kingdom

When he sitteth upon the throne of his kingdom . . . he shall write him
a copy of this law.   —Deut. 17:18

From its beginning at Sinai the historic kingdom of Israel was
truly an "organized system of government" with a definite polity, both
internally and externally. It began by taking over the already existing,
rather loose, tribal organization, which consisted of the "heads" of
families and the "elders" of the people. It was to these elders that
Moses was originally sent to report his divine call to lead the nation
out of the bondage of Egypt (Exod. 3:16). And the same group was
assembled by Moses at Sinai to hear from his lips concerning the
kingdom-covenant addressed to Israel by Jehovah (Exod. 19:7). The
"judges" and "officers" of Deuteronomy 16:18, it is thought by
Schürer, were selected from the eldership; the former to exercise
judicial functions, and the latter executive duties. The unifying
feature of the internal political system was the divinely chosen
mediatorial ruler through whom Jehovah ruled the nation. But
Moses, as also in the case of all his successors, was neither a dictator nor a constitutional monarch. He was strictly limited to executive and judicial functions. As a mediatorial ruler, he had no
legislative rights whatsoever (Deut. 17:18-20). All cases, whether
handled by him or lesser officials, were to be decided on the basis
of an objective, written, divine law. If decisions were difficult,
because of problems of evidence and legal interpretation, provision
seems to have been made for immediate access to God (Exod. 22:
8, ASV; Num. 15:32-35), although such access may have been
mediated through special courts of judges whose decisions would
therefore be of God.[5]

The absence of any strong, central, political organization in the
government of Israel had two beneficial effects. First, it left room
for the widest possible freedom among the people to govern them-

---

[5] The so-called "ordeal" for a woman suspected of immorality (Num. 5:11-31)
was no superstitious rite, but rather an appeal to God Himself for decision, "a
symbolic act, to set forth the truth, that God imparted to the water the power to act
injuriously upon a guilty body, though it would do no harm to an innocent one."
In the divinely caused certainty of its effects, it was totally different from the
"ordeals" practiced by other nations (Keil and Delitzsch, *Commentary on Pentateuch*,
trans. James Martin [Grand Rapids: Eerdmans Publishing Co., reprint, 1949], Vol.
III, p. 33-34).

selves at the local level and therefore led to a deep feeling of political liberty, something almost wholly unknown in the rest of the Semitic world, and which has undoubtedly exercised a profound influence upon the growth of the idea of political liberty in the modern world of nations. Second, it tended to prevent the rise of policies which might lead to a struggle to attain the status of a world-empire. In the absence of a strong central government, the problem of finding some unifying factor to hold the nation from falling apart was solved by the immediate presence of Jehovah and His mediatorial relation to the actual conduct of the government.

In this important respect the government of Israel was absolutely unique (Exod. 33:16). Nowhere else in the history of government do we find any comparable solution to the difficult problem of striking a proper balance between national strength on the one hand and political liberty on the other. Always men have been caught between the sharp horns of the historic dilemma: either to sacrifice individual freedom in the interest of national security, or to risk the loss of the latter for the sake of preserving the rights of the individual. It has been suggested by some that the unifying principle should be found in "religion"; but the question immediately arises, What religion? And since modern political freedom means also religious freedom, this carries with it the idea of freedom for all religions without preference or discrimination. Thus, it should be clear that, if there is one true God, religion in general cannot be substituted for God; for this is to put man in the place of God and leaves us exactly where we started, with no final solution to the political dilemma. This humanly irreconcilable conflict need not plunge men into the paralysis of despair, for the sincere efforts of good men are always worth-while; but it should guard them realistically from the snare of all human panaceas which may be proposed as cure-alls for the world's political ills. In the meantime, the people of God will not forget that until the true God breaks supernaturally once more into the stream of history to establish some effective theocratic controls, as He will at the second coming of His Son as the true mediatorial King, the reconciliation of national security and personal liberty must continue to be a matter of political compromise.

Externally, in relation to other nations, Israel was promised a place of both political and economic supremacy: "Thou shalt lend unto many nations, but thou shalt not borrow; and thou shalt reign over many nations, but they shall not reign over thee" (Deut. 15:6). This supremacy, however, was not to be based on the naked force of any political system; but rather on the favor of Jehovah in reward for the people's obedience to His will: "Only if thou carefully hearken unto the voice of the LORD thy God, to observe to do all these commandments . . . thou shalt reign over many nations" (Deut. 15:5). Therefore, if Israel had any general foreign policy, its central feature was reliance upon God with complete independence from all other nations. This was the burden of Balaam's prophecy, uttered under the compulsion of the Spirit of God: "Lo, the people shall dwell alone, and shall not be reckoned among the nations" (Num. 23:8-9, 12).

This distinctive character of Israel was made clear at the very beginning of the historical kingdom, and it was so understood by Moses: "For wherein shall it be known here that I and thy people have found grace in thy sight? Is it not in that thou goest with us? So shall we be separated . . . from all the people that are upon the face of the earth" (Exod. 33:16). With reference to the other nations, Israel was warned again and again of the danger of political leagues with these nations. Such leagues, as later history fully demonstrated, would only lead to religious and moral deterioration, dependence on men rather than upon God, entanglements in useless wars, and finally the loss of the very national security for which such alliances were supposed to be necessary (Isa. 30:1-2; 31:1-3). One of the clearest illustrations of this folly is recorded in the history of King Asa, who first met successfully the military threat to Judah because he was trusting in God's help (II Chron. 14); but later involved himself in unnecessary wars because he had turned to political leagues for national security (II Chron. 16:2-9).

More specifically, in relation to the newly established mediatorial kingdom of Israel, the nations of the ancient world were divided into two different classes: first, there were the Canaanitic nations then in possession of the land of promise; and second, there were the other nations outside the land, designated as those "far off" (Deut. 20:15). As to the first group, Israel is commanded to "make no covenant with them" (Exod. 23:32; Deut. 7:1-2). And the reason for this absolute restriction is given clearly: "lest it be for a snare in the midst of thee" (Exod. 34:12). These nations were to be utterly destroyed (Deut. 20:16-18). If this course of action seems unduly harsh, its justification may be found in the unspeakably degraded practices[6] which are described in horrible detail in the 18th chapter of Leviticus, a chapter to be read and pondered by those who are troubled with the alleged "moral" problem in relation to the character of God. There was indeed a moral problem in the land of Palestine, and it seemed to require what might be called a "surgical operation" on the human race for the sake of its own preservation. And if the nation of Israel was made the divinely chosen instrument in the operation, it should not be forgotten that the same nation was thus preserved from fatal contamination in order to fulfil her destiny as the channel of divine salvation on behalf of all nations.

In their relations to that wider and more numerous class of nations existing outside the promised land, Israel was given certain instructions to provide guidance. These are recorded in the 20th chapter of Deuteronomy, and deal only with the problem of hostility. If any of these nations become "enemies," then Israel is authorized to attack them in battle (vs. 1). However, as they approach any such hostile power, the Israelites must first make an offer of "peace"; and if accepted, the enemy shall be made "tributaries" to Israel (vss. 10-11). But if the offer is rejected, the attack is to proceed until victory is attained; after which the *men only* are to be smitten with the sword, doubtless as a measure of precaution against any further dangerous hostility. Thus the general rule seems to have been that the non-Palestinian nations were to be left alone unless they initiated hostile action; in which case Israel was to begin with an offer of peace; and open warfare could not be pressed until the peace offer had been rejected.

The early so-called "wars" of Israel, in taking over the promised land, were not wars at all in the ordinary sense of that term. Rather they were divinely ordered executions in which the armies of Israel served only as an instrument. The real leader in all these expeditions would be Jehovah Himself (Exod. 23:20, 23, 27, 31; Deut. 7:23-24). The supernatural, and therefore irresistible, character of these "wars" is revealed dramatically in the siege of Jericho (Josh. 6), first city under attack, where the walls fell before the blowing of trumpets instead of the usual military battering rams! Furthermore, whereas in ordinary warfare the hazards of conflict

---

[6] On the moral and religious degradation of these people see W. F. Albright, *From the Stone Age to Christianity* (Baltimore: The Johns Hopkins Press, 1940), pp. 177-178; also his *Archaeology and the Religion of Israel* (Baltimore: The Johns Hopkins Press, 1953), pp. 73, 75-77, 93-94.

overtake both the good and the bad, whether of arrows or bullets or bombs, there is no record of any loss of life in the Israelite armies at Jericho. And the disaster at Ai, where thirty-six men were lost, was wholly due to the sin of Achan (Josh. 7). There is nothing comparable to this in all the long history of the ordinary wars between nations. "For they got not the land in possession by their own sword, neither did their own arm save them" (Ps. 44:3).

As Waller has rightly commented upon these early wars of Israel, Jehovah was present in a special and supernatural way *"not as an ally . . . but as commander-in-chief.* It is not Israel's quarrel, in which they are to ask the Divine assistance. It is the Lord's own quarrel, and Israel and Joshua are but a division in His host. The wars of Israel in Canaan are always presented by the Old Testament as 'the wars of the LORD.' It would be well to remember this aspect of the history. The conquest of Canaan is too often treated as an enterprise of the Israelites, carried out with great cruelties, for which they claimed divine sanction. The Old Testament presents the matter in an entirely different light. The war is a Divine enterprise, in which human instruments are employed, but so as to be entirely subordinate to the Divine will. Jehovah is not for Israel, nor for Israel's foes, He fights for His own right hand, and Israel is but a fragment of His army. 'The sun stood still.' 'The stars in their courses fought against' His foes. 'The treasuries of hail' were opened, which He had 'reserved against the time of trouble, against the day of battle and war.'"[7]

In closing this section of our discussion, it must be emphasized that the mediatorial nation of Israel had been assigned some highly important *international* responsibilities, both spiritual and moral in character. But these responsibilties could be discharged properly only if the nation maintained its divinely ordained position of separation from all entangling connections, either political or religious. Those who are inclined to find fault with the concept of a "chosen nation" in the Kingdom of God sometimes forget that this concept was never intended as an end in itself, but rather a means to a vastly greater end which envisioned the good of all nations of men. Even in the modern world of nations, in spite of the present immense prestige of "internationalism," here and there thoughtful observers are beginning to suspect that isolationism may not be a total evil, but may turn out to be a very salutary policy when pursued with

[7] C. H. Waller, *Ellicott's Commentary* (Grand Rapids: Zondervan Publishing House, reprint, 1954), on Josh. 5:14.

the right kind of motives and goals. In other words, a certain measure of isolationism could become the right kind of internationalism in the long run.

3. *The Ecclesiastical Aspect of the Historical Kingdom*

Ye shall be unto me a kingdom of priests.   —*Exod. 19:6*

The constitution and laws of the mediatorial kingdom provided a definite and large place for religion. I have in mind here religion in the *objective* sense, that is, "the sum of the outward actions in which it is expressed and made manifest."[8] Although in no sense a hierarchy of priestly rulers, it would not be wrong to speak of Israel as in the highest degree a religious state. In fact, the tie between the civil and religious aspects of the government was so vital that neither could exist without the other. The religion thus established in the Jewish state was not something held vaguely as a mere ideal, but a very concrete thing to be embraced and practiced in the everyday life of the people. There was a selected priesthood, a ritual of worship prescribed in minute detail, a central place of assembly; all to be supported by the state and enforced by its authority.

The priests were originally appointed by Moses in his capacity of the mediatorial head of the state, and therefore acting under explicit directions given by Jehovah Himself: "Thou shalt appoint Aaron and his sons, and they shall wait on their priest's office" (Num. 3:10). Once appointed, however, they could not be supplanted or interfered with in the discharge of their duties: "The stranger that cometh nigh shall be put to death." The "stranger" here is not someone from outside the nation, but anyone outside the priestly order. In this sense the priestly function was to be wholly free from interference on the part of the civil rulers, whoever they were. In the later history of the kingdom, one of the greatest and best of the kings of Judah was made to feel the inexorable judgment of God for his violation of this law. Uzziah "transgressed against the LORD his God, and went into the temple of the LORD to burn incense upon the altar of incense. . . . And Uzziah the king was a leper unto the day of his death" (II Chron. 26:16-21). Thus the rights of religion, although established by and in union with the state, were protected from all destructive encroachments on the part of the state. On the other hand, the priests had no civil authority whatsoever. They could indeed be called upon to officiate in certain

---

[8] W. Schmidt, *Origin and Growth of Religion*, trans. H. J. Rose (London: Methuen and Co., 1931), p. 2.

tests; for the determination of guilt in the case of a wife suspected
of adultery (Num. 5:11-31); or for the detection of leprosy (Lev.
13 and 14); but the implementation of their verdicts rested in the
hands of the civil authorities. The union of civil and priestly functions in one person, as in the case of Melchizedek, seems to have
been unauthorized by the legal constitution of Israel. It evidently
was regarded as a dangerous system as long as the rule of God
is mediated through *sinful* men. It will become the ideal system,
however, in the future millennial reign of the sinless Son of God
who is both God and Man.

The religion thus established in the historical kingdom received
the support of the state. The priests and Levites were to own nothing.
Whereas all the other tribes received a definite allotment of the
land, those who exercised the religious offices in Israel got nothing
in a material way: "Thou shalt have no inheritance in their land,
neither shalt thou have any part among them" (Num. 18:20).
In this wise provision at the very beginning of the new kingdom,
there was set up a safeguard against the development of a rich
priestly caste entrenched in the ownership of lands and other
property, such as existed in Egypt and more recently in some modern
religious organizations. In Israel something better is given to the
priests: "I am thy part and thine inheritance," Jehovah says, "among
the children of Israel" (Num. 18:20). And since Jehovah is the
owner of all, their material support would come from tithes and
offerings which were made an obligation upon the tribes which had
received inheritances in the land (Num. 18:21-32).

Under the theocratic government, of course, there could be no
freedom of religion in the modern sense of that term. Since the
state was sternly monotheistic, which meant not merely that Israel
was committed to a general belief in the existence of one God but
also that this one true God was Israel's King in a peculiar sense, the
worship of any other god was forbidden under penalty of death (Deut.
13:1-18). Such a penalty may seem unduly harsh, but the premises
of the mediatorial kingdom of Israel could lead to no other possible
conclusion. For if there is but one true God, and if this God is
Jehovah, and if the welfare of Israel and the world, both here and
hereafter, depends on a proper acknowledgment of this one true
God — then any religious deviation must be regarded as the highest
kind of treason against the theocratic state. The only way to avoid
this conclusion would be to deny its premises.

Furthermore, the Mosaic law against false religion was tested over and over in the crucible of Israel's history. When neglected, the nation went down before its enemies (Judg. 2:11-15). When strictly observed, the nation prospered and was secure (II Kings 18: 1-6).

Various astute rulers in the long history of human government, rightly estimating the tremendous power of religion over the minds of men, have been greatly intrigued with the idea of some kind of union between church and state, in which the government would establish and support some widely accepted religion and this religion in turn would lend its influence to the state. All such alliances thus humanly originated have been based on selfish motives and opportunist policies on both sides, and hence must always break down in the end. Since each side pays a price for the unnatural union, and the price is ever increasing, the break becomes inevitable (cf. Rev. 17). A union between church and state is safe only when inaugurated and controlled by the one true God in a kingdom of His own (Zech. 14:9, 16-21).

4. The Economic Aspect of the Historical Kingdom

Proclaim liberty throughout all the land unto all the inhabitants thereof . . . and ye shall return every man unto his possession.   —Lev. 25:10

The original wealth of the Israelites came from three main sources. First, they had entered Egypt with "flocks" and "herds," which multiplied greatly in Goshen, described as "the best of the land" (Gen. 47:1, 6, 27). Second, they received from the Egyptians great quantities of gold and silver as they were leaving Egypt (Exod. 11:2-3; 12:35-36). This precious metal was not "borrowed" as the King James Version wrongly translates. The Israelites "asked" for it, and the inspired record says the LORD gave their request "favor in the sight of the Egyptians," who doubtless were happy to see them leave because of the plagues. As to the moral problem involved in this curious way of securing the gold and silver, it must be remembered that the Israelites had labored long for the Egyptians under a cruel and murderous corvée system of forced labor which had never been paid for (Exod. 1:8-16). Third, the main source of Israel's wealth came in the form of land acquired by divine grant in Palestine, a point which will be discussed at some length below.

Now the approach of the Mosaic law to the matter of wealth and its distribution is both novel and realistic. It envisioned no perfect Utopia in which all men would be equal in ability and possessions. On the contrary, there was a frank recognition of the perennial nature of the economic problem in a sinful race, even under the beneficent rule of a kingdom of God on earth: "For the poor shall never cease out of the land" (Deut. 15:11). This is not a *laissez faire* form of economic fatalism, but simply one price which a society must pay for human freedom. For, if men are to enjoy any satisfactory measure of personal liberty in economic affairs — men being what they are, widely different in disposition and ability — some will gain and others will lose. Historically, no perfect way has ever been found to reconcile personal liberty with complete economic equality; the reason being that the root of the problem is in the nature of man himself, and consequently individual action is never wholly predictable.[9] The law of the historical kingdom accepted these facts of life and laid down its rule accordingly. Since men could not be left wholly free and at the same time be fully protected from their own economic follies, certain provisions were established to safeguard them in the exercise of their economic rights and also to ameliorate some of the inequalities arising therefrom.

a. To every family in Israel, excepting the Levites, there was given an original allotment of land (Num. 26:52-56, 62); for land is wealth in its most simple and basic form, and this was particularly true of ancient Palestine which was described as "flowing with milk and honey." To these grants of land there were attached some interesting conditions. In the first place, the title to each property came directly from Jehovah Himself as the original owner of all the land and therefore was incontestable. "The land is mine," He said (Lev. 25:23). Second, with each parcel of land thus allotted there was assigned the right of "inheritance," so that the proper heirs were made secure against any future confiscation of the property (Num. 27:6-11). Third, the owner of the grant was guaranteed a large measure of freedom in his use of such land: he could farm it, abandon it, rent it, mortgage it, or even sell it under a reversionist condition which will be discussed later. But, fourth, the one thing the owner could not do was to surrender *permanently* the original title, either for himself or for his descendants, to any other person. The divine command was: "The land shall not be sold for ever: for the land is mine" (Lev. 25:23). This remarkable text must not be construed as a communistic injunction against the ownership of private property, as some have superficially suggested. Actually, it teaches just the opposite view. Inter-

---

[9] This viewpoint is recognized by Ludwig von Mises in his able and definitive book, *Human Action* (Yale University Press, 1949).

preted in the light of the Mosaic Code, the idea is as follows: Since Jehovah is the real and original owner of all the land, He has a sovereign right to parcel it out to the families of Israel; and these allotments may be used freely by the recipients in the inter- play of economic activity, with the one restriction that no one of the human owners can transfer his property title *permanently* to any other party. Thus the right of holding private property was established on a theological foundation, and titles to the land were guaranteed by Jehovah Himself as the original owner, both to the first recipient and to his proper heirs. Perhaps it would be more accurate to speak of this as the right of private *possession* rather than the right of private ownership. However, viewed from a prac- tical human standpoint, the difference is of no consequence.

b. Since the human owner of a parcel of land was free to mort- gage or even sell his property on a temporary basis, it is clear that the problem of impoverishment was certain to arise. In such cases, without inquiring into the matter of possible slothfulness or eco- nomic folly, the Mosaic law required that assistance must be ex- tended to the poor man by those who were able: "For the poor shall never cease out of the land: therefore . . . thou shalt open thine hand wide unto thy brother, to thy poor, and to thy needy, in thy land" (Deut. 15:11). The law of economic freedom could not prevent unwise and foolish action on the part of the individual, but it could ameliorate his situation regardless of its cause. The law granted to every person liberty to lose his property temporarily, but not liberty to starve. However, very wisely, the help extended to the poor demanded some activity on their part if they were able- bodied. Therefore, when crops were being harvested, some portions of the grapes and grains were to be left in the fields where they could be gleaned by those in need (Lev. 19:9-10; Deut. 24:19-22). Thus Ruth the Moabitess, whose husband's inheritance had been lost, gleans in the fields until the inheritance has been restored by the process of redemption. Such procedure might be regarded lightly by some modern authorities. And doubtless it would have been more efficient economically for Boaz with his trained crews to reap the fields completely and then send portions of the grain to the poor. But the Mosaic Code had in mind the welfare of the person as well as the filling of his stomach. The poor must be helped, but in such a way as to maintain his self-respect. If this help took the form of a loan, no interest could be charged (Lev. 25:35-37). Nor was the creditor permitted to hold as security any personal property essential to the welfare of the borrower (Exod. 22:25-27).

c. For the poor there was an added source of help which came periodically every seventh year. This Sabbatical year was set apart primarily to give a period of "rest" for the soil. And what grew up that year "of its own accord" was not to be reaped or gathered by the owner in any regular way (Lev. 25:4-5). This natural increase must be left especially for the "poor" (Exod. 23:11); although others were not excluded from sharing, such as hired servants, the strangers, the owner himself, and even the beasts of the field (Lev. 25:6-7).

d. There was a further provision in the case of impoverishment because of debt. This was a "release" which came automatically to debtors every seven years (Deut. 15:1-3). The best Biblical authorities are agreed that this release was not a complete cancellation of the debt, but rather a whole year of "grace."[10] During this seventh year the creditor could not legally press his claim. The logic of this becomes clear if we remember that the land itself was to be given "rest" in the seventh year, and hence the debtors would have less opportunity to earn wages in that year. In the case of the "foreigner" there was no need for such relief because his ability to pay would not be lessened by the law of the Sabbatic year, which he probably would not observe, and therefore the payment could be required of him.

e. The greatest safeguard against the permanent impoverishment of a family in Israel was the law of the Jubilee Year (Lev. 25). According to this novel and remarkable provision, when seven sabbatic years had passed (i.e., 49 years), the nation was commanded to "hallow the fiftieth year, and proclaim liberty throughout all the land unto all the inhabitants; it shall be a jubilee" (vss. 8-10). Then every slave went free, all debts incurred in connection with real property were cancelled, and every man could freely reclaim his original allotment of land which might have been lost by debt or sale. Dwelling houses in walled cities were excepted, probably because such property represented the product of the builder's own labor and were not an original free grant as in the case of the land. Houses outside the cities were evidently counted as part of the land and therefore included in the jubilee year reversion. Furthermore, both the fiftieth and forty-ninth years were sabbaths of rest for the

10 Keil and Delitzsch, *op. cit.*, on Deut. 15:1-3.

land; there was to be no sowing or reaping of the fields. To supply the needs of the people during these two years, and also for the following year when new crops were being sowed, God promised to bless the increase of the fields in the forty-eighth year sufficiently to provide for the entire three-year period: "It shall bring forth fruit for three years" (Lev. 25:21). Thus it appears that the "liberty" proclaimed in the jubilee year was fourfold in nature: first, liberty from personal bondage; second, liberty from debt; third, liberty from hunger; and fourth, liberty from arduous toil.

It should be carefully noted that no communistic principle was involved in this redistribution of wealth at the jubilee year. There was to be no confiscation of private property for the purpose of indiscriminate public distribution, but simply a *restoration* of all real property to its original *private* owners. Moreover, once the restoration had taken place, the interplay of the normal economic process with its ordinary hazards was resumed immediately. In other words, the re-established liberty from debt and poverty was not something to be guaranteed by a monolithic state regardless of human action, but rather a precious gift which had to be kept for each individual by his own efforts. If he chose the path of indolence and reckless imprudence, he could lose his land and liberty just as quickly and easily as he had regained them. The law of the jubilee year only guaranteed a fresh start for the individual, not economic security irrespective of human folly. Although there may be found traces of plans for land redistribution in other nations, there seems to be nothing precisely comparable to the Mosaic law of the jubilee. It was a notable contribution toward a solution to the age-long problem, how to strike a proper balance between economic liberty and economic security. It allowed, on the one hand, considerable room for the play of individual initiative and energy with their proper rewards. But, at the same time, it guarded against the evils of great concentrations of real wealth in the hands of a few, with the consequent hopeless impoverishment of many others.

Whether or not there is any literary evidence to show that the nation of Israel ever observed the law of the jubilee year except in its breach, although an interesting question, is not essential to the purposes of this discussion of the historical kingdom. It does seem certain, however, that the law of the sabbatical year was observed to some extent. For, since the sabbatical year came only once in seven years, and the seventy years' duration of the Babylonian Captivity was determined by the number of sabbatical years not kept, it is obvious that the total calendar period of non-observance must have been seven times seventy or 490 years (II Chron. 36:21). But this is only a little more than half the entire time the nation had been in the promised land. And since the divine judgment was limited to seventy years, it is a valid assumption that the law of the sabbatical year must have been observed at least half the time for about 800 years. It would be strange, therefore, although possible, if Israel had paid no attention whatever to the most important date in the whole calendar of the nation, namely, the jubilee year which was based on the law of the sabbatical year.[11]

f. For the man who had lost his original land estate, whether through misfortune or economic imprudence, there was always the law of redemption. At any time a near kinsman could exercise the right to redeem the property which had been lost, simply by paying the holder a fair price computed on the basis of the average possible income from the land during the number of years yet remaining before the jubilee year. In fact, it appears that the act of redemption was a duty laid on the poor man's relatives, beginning with the nearest, if any were financially able. If the man was without such relatives, he could exercise the right of redemption for himself whenever he had accumulated sufficient resources (Lev. 25:24-28). The same right of redemption was available to anyone who had sold himself into bond-service (vss. 39-54). Therefore, there was always some hope for the poor man even before the arrival of the jubilee year.

In concluding this discussion of the economic provisions in the laws of the historical kingdom, it must be admitted that the strict application of all these provisions in our modern world is probably impossible, since the original conditions cannot be reproduced by mere human ingenuity, and there is no immediate divinely accredited authority to originate and preside over any plan for the proper distribution of material wealth. Nevertheless, these provisions within the ancient economy of the historical kingdom can be studied with great profit by modern economists, and they should be given the attention which they deserve.[12] From a theological standpoint the

[11] For an opposite opinion, cf. *Hasting's Bible Dictionary*, Vol. IV, p. 326, (iv.).

[12] Although no champion of orthodox Christianity, T. H. Huxley once wrote: "The Bible has been the Magna Charta of the poor, and of the oppressed; down to modern times no state has had a constitution in which the interests of the people are so largely taken into account, in which the duties, so much more than the privileges, of rulers are so insisted upon, as that drawn up for Israel in Deuteronomy and Leviticus."

Mosaic economy furnishes ample proof that within the historical Kingdom of God on earth a very large place was given to the matter of private possessions and the material well-being of all concerned. And this fact should keep us from any theological prejudice against the idea of a similar but more perfect Kingdom of God on earth in the future.

5. *The Physical Aspect of the Historical Kingdom*

> I will rain bread from heaven for you.   —*Exod. 16:4*

It would be difficult, if not impossible, to isolate completely this physical element from the total situation contemplated by the constitution and laws of the kingdom. Furthermore, the physical element presents such a vast mass of material that it cannot be discussed here in detail. But the inspired record makes it clear that the physical well-being of Israel was assigned a very prominent place in the historical kingdom. The clause, "that it may go well with thee," or its equivalent, occurs several times in Deuteronomy and is invariably connected with physical benefits; as in 4:40, "that thou mayest prolong thy days upon the earth"; and again in 6:3, "that ye may increase mightily . . . in the land that floweth with milk and honey." These physical benefits came to Israel in two ways: first, through supernatural acts of power; and second, through divinely ordained natural means.

a. *Physical Benefits Bestowed Supernaturally*

Extraordinary *fruitfulness* would be given to Israel from Jehovah; in the productivity of their fields, in the increase of their flocks and herds, and even in their own progeny of sons and daughters. The astonishing promise was, "There shall not be male or female barren among you, or among your cattle" (Deut. 7:13-14). In the ordinary course of what is called "natural law," nothing like this ever takes place in any nation.

During the emergency of a desert march which lasted for forty years, the nation was given *food from heaven* (Exod. 16:35). And this heavenly manna did not cease until the day of Israel's actual entrance into the promised land (Josh. 5:12). Whatever its precise nature may have been, it was something completely unknown in the earlier history of the nation (Deut. 8:3). It was certainly material food for the physical body, as evidenced by the fact that it bred worms if stored too long! Yet the psalmist refers to it as "angel's food," the "corn of heaven" (78:24-25); and the Apostle Paul calls it "spiritual food," doubtless to indicate its supernatural origin

(I Cor. 10:3, ASV). It came directly from that God who is "spirit," wholly outside of natural causes.

Similarly, when the people were in desperate thirst, *water* was given supernaturally by Jehovah's power. The bitter waters at Marah were made sweet by a miracle (Exod. 15:23-25). At other times, when no water of any kind could be found, Moses was commanded to strike the rock with his rod, with the result that "the water came forth abundantly," sufficient for both men and beasts (Num. 20:2, 7-11; Exod. 17:1-6).

Again, during the long march when the replacement of worn *clothing* must have been practically impossible, the record in Deuteronomy indicates that by one of God's "great miracles" neither the people's clothing nor their shoes had worn out for the space of "forty years" (8:4; 29:3-5). In fact, as Nehemiah later wrote, during the forty years in the wilderness journey "they lacked nothing" (9:21).

Perhaps the most crucial and distressing physical problem of all nations in all ages is that of *disease*. And this problem would be especially acute in the case of thousands of people moving through strange territory under adverse conditions. They had marched only three days into the wilderness when the promise of Jehovah came, "I will put none of these diseases upon thee, which I have brought upon the Egyptians: for I am the Lord that healeth thee" (Exod. 15:26). Later at the foot of Mount Sinai the divine promise was renewed and greatly broadened, "I will take sickness away from the midst of thee" (Exod. 23:25). And at the end of the forty years' march, as the people stood at the border of the promised land, Moses reports again the same promise, this time apparently without limitation, "The Lord will take away from thee all sickness" (Deut. 7:15). By no device of legitimate exegesis can these promises be pushed off into some far-off millennium or heaven; they referred to an immediate situation, and were so understood.

It follows that with supernatural protection from the ordinary ravages of physical disease, the span of *human life could be lengthened*. And this is precisely what Jehovah promised to Israel, "The number of thy days I will fulfil" (Exod. 23:26). That the reference here is no obscure allusion to a future life in heaven is made clear by Deuteronomy 5:16 which specifies that the prolonged days were to be "in the land which the Lord thy God giveth thee," on the border of which Israel was then standing.

b. *Physical Benefits through Divinely Ordained Human Means*

It seems to be God's way, in bestowing His gifts in the form of physical benefits, to require some effort on the part of man. Even in the case of the manna from heaven, a miracle in which man could have no part, he nevertheless must gather and handle it in accordance with certain divine instructions. In other matters, such as protection from disease, much greater responsibility was laid upon the human recipients.

For example, in maintaining the productivity of the land promised by Jehovah, the people must be careful to conserve their *natural resources*. When it might become necessary to lay siege to a city, and trees were needed to supply the means of forcing an entrance through the gates or walls, they were permitted to cut down trees, but not any trees which were food-bearing (Deut. 20:19-20). When hunting fowls the young only could be taken; and the mother must always be spared (Deut. 22:6-7). The law of the sabbatical year, as noted above, required that the land must lay fallow for one year out of every seven in order to gain fresh strength and insure its future fertility (cf. Lev. 25).

Turning now to the matter of public health, there is the factor of *rest and relaxation*. On this point the provisions of the Mosaic law are impressive; for under this code the people were not only to rest one day in seven, but also one *year* in every seven (Lev. 23 and 25). In addition to these regular periods of rest there were also the special sabbaths, appointed feasts, and convocations: all making some contribution toward a beneficial release from the ordinary tensions of human existence which tend to impair health and shorten the span of life. This may help to explain in part why Moses, living under such a system (although not yet fully in force), was able to bear the incredible burdens incident to his mediatorial leadership and yet die at the advanced age of 120 years with no dimness of sight nor diminishing of his physical powers (Deut. 34:7). And it may also help to explain the remarkable vigor of the Jewish nation, even though the laws of rest were never perfectly observed. That these laws were kept in some measure, however, is evidenced by the rather petulant complaint of the Roman Tacitus against the Jews: "For the seventh day they are said to have prescribed rest because this day ended their labors; then, in addition, they also spend the seventh year in laziness" (Hist. V. 4). According to the Mosaic law these periods of rest were not intended to be spent in complete idleness, but at least in part they were to be used for purposes of educational instruction (Deut. 31:10-13). Here the best modern medical authorities agree, not only as to the importance of rest in the maintenance of physical health, but also that ordinarily such rest is better attained by a change of activities rather than by complete idleness.

Consider now the Mosaic laws having to do with *sanitation,* which is invariably a factor of great importance in the prevention and control of disease. These have been lauded as "rules of the highest sagacity" by writers in the field of the history of medicine.[13] For example, the offal from animal sacrifices was to be disposed of by fire outside "the camp" (Lev. 4:11-12). In certain cases where the priest attended to the burning, he must "wash his clothes" and "bathe his flesh" before returning into the camp (Num. 19:5-8). When the armies of Israel went out to battle, the strict provisions for latrine disposal would compare favorably with the specifications for modern military forces engaged in action (Deut. 23:9-14).[14] When the armies returned from battle, every participant was excluded from the camp for a period of seven days during which his body and clothing were to be purified, and any metallic spoil taken had to be passed through the fire (Num. 31:19-24). Furthermore, the commands regarding cleanliness of flesh and clothing, so numerous as to become almost tiresome in the reading, are suggestive of the meticulous procedures taken by the most modern hospital and medical authorities. As to the eating of flesh, the law required the eating of certain offerings on the day they were sacrificed; in other offerings the meat could be eaten on the second day; but any left until the third had to be destroyed by fire; to eat it was "abominable" (Lev. 7:15-18; 19:5-7). Entirely aside from the religious significance of such provisions, they were of great value in a climate where meat quickly reached a state of putrefaction.

The laws concerning *leprosy* are of interest in this connection, for it was a disease endemic from the earliest historical times in the delta and valley of the Nile. The Levitical code gave detailed in-

---

[13] L. T. Townsend, *The Bible and the Nineteenth Century* (New York: Chautauqua Press, 1889), pp. 41-43.

[14] Referring to this remarkable passage, the late Dr. A. Rendle Short, noted English Professor of Surgery, writes: "Water-borne and fly-borne diseases, such as dysentery and enteric fever, have been the scourge of armies in the field even more than of stationary populations. In the South African War the loss of life from these diseases was greater than from wounds. It was not until the Great War of 1914-1918 that effectual precautions were put into practice. Yet all through the centuries the remedy was ready at hand, if the generals had troubled to read their Bibles, and to observe the directions given for the disposal of excreta by burial" [Deut. 23:12-14] (*Modern Discovery and the Bible* [Third edition revised, 1952], pp. 122 ff.).

struction regarding the identification of the disease,[15] and what was to be done with the leper, but no remedy was given for the *cure* of the disease (Lev. 13 and 14). The leprous person was excluded from "the camp"; his appearance must be such as to make him easily identifiable; and he was required to warn others to keep away from contact with him (13:45-46). In short, the problem was handled by a simple plan of segregation; a procedure not generally followed by other ancient nations (cf. II Kings 5:1), but which is still regarded as a very effective precaution against the spread of an infectious disease which at one time became "the greatest disease of medieval Christendom."[16] Now the question may be raised here as to why such a dreadful disease as leprosy should have existed at all among the people of the historical kingdom if, as we have noted above, Jehovah had promised to take away all their diseases. The answer has been given in the Word of God and will be discussed under the following head.

6. *The Moral Aspect of the Historical Kingdom*

Thou shalt do that which is right and good in the sight of the LORD.
—*Deut. 6:18*

The evidence for the moral element contained in the law code of the kingdom is so generally acknowledged and indisputable that it requires no special argument. The very heart of the Sinaitic law appears in the Ten Commandments, and at least six of these are concerned with basic principles of morality. It is true that we now have some archaeological testimony showing that some of the Mosaic statutes were not altogether unknown to the consciences of enlightened men prior to the establishment of the theocratic kingdom at Sinai. Such knowledge may have been derived from primeval revelation (Rom. 1:19), and also from that divine law written in the hearts of men by original creation (Rom. 2:15). The incorporation of material of this kind in the Mosaic law is entirely consistent with the doctrine of a fully inspired record, for the basic principles of moral law are unchangeable and therefore the same in every age. The God who spoke at Sinai was the same God who wrote these principles in the very nature of man created in the divine image (Gen. 1:27). But the revelation at Sinai did several things which have been of inestimable value in the moral realm.

a. Whereas the moral illumination through tradition and con-

---

[15] Probably not exactly the "Hansen's Disease" of modern times.
[16] "Leprosy," *Encyclopedia Britannica* (14th ed.; New York: Encyc. Brit., Inc., 1929), Vol. XIII, p. 957.

science was often dim and distorted, the moral law at Sinai was not only given directly by the God who is the ultimate ground of all moral truth, but it was given to men in a permanent *written record* fully inspired in all its parts and therefore inerrant in its original literary form.

b. The revelation at Sinai joined together inseparably two things which historically have too often been sundered, namely, *religion and morality*. The Mosaic Code therefore struck at two dangerous errors: first, the ancient notion that a true religion can exist apart from morality; and second, the more modern notion that morality is able to stand on its own base without any religious foundation. The well-known failure of the nation of Israel to maintain this vital relation between religion and morals in their historical kingdom is no valid argument against the early date and Mosaic authorship of the record of the Sinaitic law, as critical scholars have sometimes asserted. For it is nothing new to find an appalling discrepancy between the laws of a nation and the everyday conduct of its citizens; as, for example, the lamentable situation in our own nation at this very hour. High moral laws by themselves are unfortunately no guarantee of right conduct.

c. The constitution and laws of the historical kingdom also asserted the vital *connection between human welfare and moral considerations*. In other words, the well-being of men, not only physically but every other way, is morally and spiritually conditioned by a principle confirmed by divinely imposed sanctions. Now this principle holds good generally in all nations in every age. But its operation has often been obscured to human eyes by the time "lag" between the moral breach and the infliction of the sanction. While it is always true that the nation which has "sown the wind" shall also certainly "reap the whirlwind" (Hos. 8:7), the harvest is generally and mercifully long delayed (II Pet. 3:9); and for this very reason men often fail to see the causal connection. Furthermore, in the general history of nations, the divine penalties are inflicted through secondary causes behind the veil of providential control (Jer. 51:28-30). For these reasons the skeptical have been able to question the existence of any divinely ordained moral government in human history, and the LORD's own people at times have been greatly troubled and perplexed by the problem (Hab. 1:1-4).

But in the case of the nation of Israel in her Mediatorial Kingdom of history, the moral government of Jehovah was not only declared at Sinai but also was confirmed spectacularly in the recorded history of that kingdom by means of divine sanctions immediately imposed. And these sanctions were generally supernatural; either by the withdrawal of the promised supernatural protection from the ordinary hazards of human life in a sinful world, or by the positive infliction of supernaturally imposed punishment. Over and over again it is made clear by the Mosaic law that it will "be well" with the chosen nation in the Mediatorial Kingdom of history only if Jehovah is properly honored as King and the people are obedient to His revealed will. But if they dishonor Him and reject His word, the divine judgment will surely fall upon them. This close and immediate connection between the well-being of the chosen nation and their moral and spiritual attitude is most clearly summarized by Moses in his final address to the nation as recorded in Deuteronomy (cf. chaps. 28-30).

The passage begins with a general statement as to the right moral and spiritual attitude on the part of the people, and also the divine blessing which would surely follow: "And it shall come to pass, if thou shalt hearken diligently unto the voice of the LORD thy God, to observe and to do all his commandments which I command thee this day, that the LORD thy God will set thee on high above all nations of the earth: And all these blessings shall come on thee, and overtake thee, if thou shalt hearken unto the voice of the LORD thy God" (Deut. 28:1-2). Then follows a long list of the "blessings," covering almost every conceivable circumstance and situation possible in human existence on earth (vss. 3-14). They will be blessed in children, in material wealth, in their political relation with other nations, in military success against all their enemies; even the operations of nature, over which man has no control, will work for them.

But over against the rich blessings which are attached to a right moral and spiritual attitude, Moses warns the people of the train of disaster which will surely follow moral and spiritual delinquency: "But it shall come to pass, if thou wilt not hearken unto the voice of the LORD thy God, to observe to do all his commandments and his statutes which I command thee this day; that all these curses shall come upon thee, and overtake thee" (vs. 15). Then in terrible detail there is listed a series of calamities so great in number and force that nothing comparable will be found in all the experiences and history of other nations. These divine visitations upon Israel "shall be upon thee for a sign and for a wonder" (vs. 46); and in her apostasy she will become "an astonishment, a proverb, and a byword, among all nations" (vs. 37). If the Jew was given priority in glo-

rious blessings, he also had an appalling priority in moral responsibility (Rom. 2:9-10).

In the light of the Scriptures cited above, it follows that what is
ordinarily called misfortune and calamity could come to Israel in the
days of the historical kingdom only as a direct judgment of God for
rebellion against Him. And this is confirmed by the inspired record of
that kingdom. Although there was a promise of immunity from physical disease, the LORD struck down with plagues the lustful com-
plainers among the people (Num. 11:1, 33); and even the sister
of Moses was made a leper by a miracle of judgment (Num. 12:1, 10).
Although the nation had been promised a lengthened span of physical life, every man of war above twenty years of age at Sinai (Num.
1:45), excepting Joshua and Caleb, died in the desert during the
next forty years because of unbelief (Num. 14:29-33). In the face
of the divine promise of military success, the battle at Ai was lost
because of one man's disobedience (Josh. 7:1-5). Now this is quite
an astonishing thing, utterly unknown in the experience of ordinary
nations in history, and it has not received the attention it deserves.
Admitting that there have been isolated instances of miraculous and
immediate judgments of God in His general providential government
of the world, the striking fact remains that in relation to the chosen
nation within the historical Kingdom of God such instances were
the *rule*.

There is an important theological problem which may be raised
in this connection: Was not the well-being of Israel conditioned
upon their obedience to "all" God's commandments, and therefore
required moral *perfection*? This viewpoint is occasioned by a misunderstanding of the unity of the Mosaic code, in which the moral
and religious elements were indivisibly joined together. For the
law of the historical kingdom not only demanded obedience to "all"
its moral requirements, but in the event of human failure, it also
provided for divine forgiveness through obedience to the law of
sacrifice. See the oft-repeated assurance, "it shall be forgiven him,"
annexed to the Levitical offerings (chaps. 4-6 of Leviticus). These
offerings, prescribed for a redeemed nation, stood continually as a
witness against any theory of absolute moral perfection on the part
of the citizens of the Kingdom of God on earth.

One other point must be noticed: In chapters 28-30 of Deuteronomy there seems to be a clear distinction drawn between the
nation of Israel as such and the *individuals* within the nation.
Chapter 29 begins with a call addressed "unto all Israel" (vs. 2), to

remind them that by the covenant and oath of God they had been established "for a people unto himself" (vss. 12-13). But within this chosen nation there might be some who, trusting for protection in the irrevocable covenant of the national election, might presume they were free to go on sinning with impunity. Therefore Moses turns to warn all such individuals: "Lest there be among you man, or woman, or family, or tribe, whose heart turneth away this day from the LORD our God," saying in his heart, "I shall have peace, though I walk in the imagination of mine heart" (vss. 18-19). Upon any and all such the judgment of God will fall without remedy: "The LORD will not spare him, but then the anger of the LORD and his jealousy shall smoke against that man, and all the curses that are written in this book shall lie upon him, and the LORD shall blot out his name from under heaven" (vs. 20). This was the terrible sin of moral presumption for which in the Mosaic ritual there was no sacrifice (Num. 15:30); and having as its New Testament parallel the sin of "turning the grace of our God into lasciviousness"; or, as Weymouth translates the passage, "who pervert the grace of God into an excuse for immorality" (Jude 4).

In chapter 30 of Deuteronomy Moses returns to a consideration of the *nation* and its distant future. Although divine judgment will certainly fall in the event of moral failure, there is hope for the nation. The original covenant established with Abraham cannot be abrogated or fail. "It shall come to pass, when all these things are come upon thee, the blessing and the curse, which I have set before thee, and thou shalt call them to mind among all the nations, whither the LORD thy God hath driven thee, and shalt return unto the LORD thy God, and shalt obey his voice according to all that I command thee this day, thou and thy children, with all thine heart, and with all thy soul; that then the LORD thy God will turn thy captivity, and have compassion upon thee, and will return and gather thee from all the nations, whither the LORD thy God hath scattered thee. . . . And the LORD thy God will bring thee into the land which thy fathers possessed, and thou shalt possess it; and he will do thee good, and multiply thee above thy fathers" (vss. 1-5). Thus it is clear that while the original covenant with Abraham was not in any sense based on human works (Gal. 3:17-18), nevertheless its fulfilment for Israel's descendants will not be apart from moral considerations. For the nation will "return unto the LORD" (vs. 2), but we are told that this obedient return to the LORD will be wrought by the compassionate grace of the LORD Himself: "The LORD thy God will cir-

cumcise thine heart, and the heart of thy seed, to love the LORD thy
God with all thine heart, and with all thy soul, that thou mayest
live" (vs. 6). If there is any mystery here, it is the mystery of the
grace of God, whose efficacious call can operate as easily in the case
of a sinful nation as in the case of a sinful person.

In conclusion, it may be observed that, especially within the Amillennial school of eschatological opinion, there is high reverence for
the Mosaic law and insistence upon its application to the Church of
the present age. Yet with curious inconsistency the same school is
unalterably opposed to the idea of a coming kingdom of God on the
earth within human history, when the great principles of the Mosaic
code will be made the law of all nations, and enforced by immediate
divine sanctions under the beneficent rule of God Himself in the
Person of His incarnate Son, our Lord Jesus Christ.

CHAPTER VIII

THE MEDIATORIAL RULERS FROM MOSES TO SAUL

> The authority of the Judges was not inferior to that which was afterward
> exercised by *the Kings;* it extended to peace and war. They decided
> cases without appeal, but they had no power to enact new laws or to
> impose new burdens upon the people. They were the protectors of the
> laws, defenders of religion, and avengers of crimes.   —*T. H. Horne*[1]

Because of the literary divisions in the Old Testament, it has been
customary to think of the period of the twelve "judges" separately
from the respective periods of Joshua and Samuel. However, although
the latter two men were incomparably greater than the other twelve,
all alike served in the capacity of leader-judges of Israel between
Moses and the establishment of the monarchial form of the historical
kingdom (Judg. 2:16). Therefore, it will be helpful to regard the
entire time as one period exhibiting certain general characteristics
throughout. The chronology is admittedly difficult, but its exact
duration is not essential to this discussion.

1. *These Leader-Judges Were Directly Chosen of God*

The LORD raised up judges.   —*Judg. 2:16*

With reference to Joshua, as the life of Moses drew to its close,
God said, "Behold, thy days approach that thou must die: call
Joshua, and present yourselves in the tabernacle of the congregation,
that I may give him a charge" (Deut. 31:14). And the divine charge
follows: "Be strong and of a good courage: for thou shalt bring the
children of Israel into the land which I sware unto them: and I
will be with thee" (vs. 23). Later, after the death of Moses, the
charge was renewed and prefaced with divine reassurance: "As I
was with Moses, so I will be with thee: I will not fail thee, nor
forsake thee" (Josh. 1:5).

Of the leaders who came after Joshua, the Word of God declares,
"The LORD raised up judges" (Judg. 2:16). The Hebrew term is

[1] T. H. Horne, *Introduction to the Critical Study and Knowledge of the Holy
Scriptures* (London, 1818), Vol. II, p. 42.

Shophetim which, according to Cassell, is here used for the first time in the special sense which it bears in this period of Israel's history. The ordinary *Shophetim* were nothing new; they existed everywhere in the nation. But these special *Shophetim* of the Book of Judges were different because of "the source, purpose, and extent of their power. . . . They were not regular but extraordinary authorities. Hence, they were not, like the (Punic) suffetes, chosen by the people. God Himself appointed them."[2]

In the case of Samuel, last of the special judges and also the connecting link between them and the period of the kings, both his birth and his commission appear as miracles of divine power. Geden speaks of him as the "greatest of the judges" and "the first of the prophets. . . . occupying the position of a second Moses in relation to the people. . . . like Moses, he closes the old order, and establishes the people with brighter prospects upon more assured foundations of national prosperity and greatness."[3]

2. *These Leader-Judges Were Invested with Regal Functions*

Then the LORD was with the judge.   —*Judg. 2:18*

On this point, the cases of Joshua and Samuel are beyond dispute. To Joshua the divine promise was, "As I was with Moses, so I will be with thee" (Joshua 1:5).[4] Of Samuel it is written, "The LORD was with him, and did let none of his words fall to the ground. . . . And the word of Samuel came to all Israel" (I Sam. 3:19-4:1).

But the *Shophetim* of the Book of Judges are not always regarded as belonging in the same general category. Therefore, the fine words of Cassell as to their regal authority are of interest: "Judicial authority is the chief attribute of the royal dignity. Hence God, the highest King, is also 'the Judge of all the earth' (Gen. 18:25). He judges concerning right and wrong, and makes His awards accordingly. When law and sin ceased to be distinguished in Israel, compassion induced Him to appoint judges again. If these are gifted with heroic qualities, to vanquish the oppressors of Israel, it is nevertheless not this heroism that forms their principal characteristic. That consists in 'judging.' They restore. . . . the authority of law. . . . For this reason, God raises up *Shophetim*, judges, not princes. The title sets forth both their work and the occasion of their appointment. Israel is free

---

[2] Paulus Cassell, Lange's *Commentary on Judges,* trans. P. H. Steenstra (New York: Scribner's Sons, 1875), pp. 61-62.

[3] "Samuel," *International Standard Bible Encyclopedia* (Chicago: Howard-Severance, 1915), Vol. IV, p. 2678.

[4] S. D. Press says "Joshua . . . exercised a royal authority" (*I.S.B.E., op. cit.,* Vol. III, p. 1800)

and powerful when its law is observed throughout the land. Henceforth, (as appears from Deut. 17:14) except *Shophetim,* only kings, *Melakim,* can rule in Israel. The difference between them lies chiefly in the hereditariness of the royal office."[5]

Throughout the record in the Book of Judges, this divinely bestowed judicial authority of the *Shophetim* is underscored by the inexorable catastrophes which always overtook the nation when the people "would not hearken unto their judges" (Judg. 2:16-20).

3. *These Leader-Judges Were Given a Special Enduement of the Spirit*

The Spirit of the Lord came upon him. *Judg. 3:10*

We are told that Joshua was "full of the spirit of wisdom" (Deut. 34:9), an expression used by Isaiah as a title for the Spirit of God (11:2).

Of Othniel, first of the twelve "judges," we read that "The Spirit of the Lord came upon him, and he judged Israel" (Judg. 3:10). Later we find the same general assertion concerning Gideon, "But the Spirit of the Lord came upon Gideon" (6:34). Although the character of Jephthah has been questioned, he apparently enjoyed the same enduement, "Then the Spirit of the Lord came upon Jephthah" (11:29). Of Samson, apparently the last of the twelve "judges," the Word of God four times speaks concerning his spiritual enduement, ranging in force from 13:25, "The Spirit of the Lord began to move him at times," to 15:14, "the Spirit of the Lord came mightily upon him." This special enduement of the Spirit of God continued into the initial period of the kings of Israel (cf. I Sam. 10:1, 6; 16:13).

Three things should be noted about this coming of the Spirit upon the great leaders of the historical kingdom: first, it was not always related to high moral character; second, in certain cases its outstanding effects were seen chiefly in the realm of the purely physical; third, and most important of all, it had to do primarily with the regal functions of those who stood as mediators of the divine government of Israel.

Bright speaks of this spiritual enduement as a *"charisma,"* and rightly asserts that it "well represented the primitive theocracy of Israel; it was the direct rule of God over his people through his designated representative."[6]

[5] Paulus Cassell, *op. cit., in loc.*
[6] John Bright, *The Kingdom of God* (New York: Abingdon-Cokesbury Press, 1953), p. 32.

4. *These Leader-Judges Possessed No Dynastic Rights*

Thus God rendered the wickedness of Abimelech.   —*Judg. 9:56*

The only attempt to establish a dynastic succession during this period came at the hand of one of the many sons of Gideon, Abimelech by name, whose bloody usurpation, lasting only three years, was brought to an ignominious end by the judgment of God through a woman who dropped a millstone upon his head (Judg. 9:1-57).

Commenting on this absence of dynastic succession among the Judges, Cassel says, "The Judge has only a personal commission. His work is to reinspire Israel with divine enthusiasm, and thus make it victorious. He restores things to the condition in which they were on the death of Joshua. No successors were necessary; if without a judge, the nation itself maintained the law, and resisted temptation. Israel has enough in its divinely given law. Rallying about this and the priesthood, it could be free; for God is its King. But it is weak. The Judge is scarcely dead, before the authority of law is shaken. Unity is lost, and the enemy takes advantage of the masterless disorder. Therefore, Judges, raised up by God, and girded with fresh strength succeed each other . . ."[7]

5. *These Leader-Judges Were Genuine Mediators of the Divine Rule*

The LORD your God was your king.   —*I Sam. 12:12*

Here again it must be emphasized that throughout this period there was an established Kingdom of God on earth. Crude as were some of his ideas, Gideon was right in his estimate of the historical situation: "I will not rule over you," he protests to the nation of Israel, "The LORD shall rule over you" (Judg. 8:23). And Samuel, speaking to Israel of that long and remarkable period extending from Moses to Saul, characterizes it as an era "When the LORD your God was your king" (I Sam. 12:12). Therefore, the primary function of the judges was that of mediatorial rulers.

6. *Conditions Were Not Ideal under These Leader-Judges*

Every man did that which was right in his own eyes. —*Judg. 21:25*

It is surely true that conditions under the judges were far from ideal. Yet certain things should not be forgotten. In spite of six major military invasions of the land, long oppressions at the hand of victorious enemies, struggles between the individual tribes, and serious civil war, the nation of Israel came through all these terrible

---

[7] Paulus Cassell, *op. cit.*, p. 62.

dangers with a vigor and a consciousness of divinely ordained destiny unparalleled in recorded history. To those familiar with the international situation of those years, the wonder is that no one of the great world powers reduced the land of Canaan to total subjection, with a consequent destruction of the tiny nation which had as yet no strong centrally organized government. These facts alone point to something above and beyond the ordinary providential control of God; namely, to the existence of a supernaturally ordained and sustained Kingdom of God on earth, in which Israel was the favored nation.

The rather lamentable summary which closes the Book of Judges —"In those days there was no king in Israel: every man did that which was right in his own eyes" — does not necessarily indicate a condition of complete civil and moral anarchy. Such an interpretation would conflict with much contained in the inspired record of those days. The thought connection between the two clauses of this final verse, for one thing, may point to the large measure of individual and local self-government which was exercised in the absence of any strongly centralized government such as would come later under the kings. Furthermore, careful Bible students will always remember that the very beautiful and idyllic story of Ruth and Boaz is located historically "in the days when the judges ruled" (Ruth 1:1). The political situation was not ideal, but it could not have been totally bad.

CHAPTER IX

THE MONARCHIAL FORM OF THE MEDIATORIAL KINGDOM IN HISTORY

> The earthly kingdom was not opposed to the theocracy, i.e., to the rule of Jehovah as King over the people of His possession, provided no one was made king but the person whom Jehovah should choose.[1]

It has been suggested that the setting up of "kings" over the nation of Israel meant not only a popular rejection of the theocratic idea but also its end in Old Testament history. This view has been based on a superficial interpretation of God's words to Samuel when the people asked for a king, "They have not rejected thee, but they have rejected me, that I should not reign over them" (I Sam. 8:7). Such a view cannot be fairly maintained by any careful study of the Biblical records.

1. This Monarchial Form Foreseen in the Plan of God

Kings shall come out of thee.   *—Gen. 17:6*

In the earliest records of the Abrahamic covenant Jehovah had promised to Abraham that "a nation and a company of nations shall be of thee, and kings shall come out of thy loins" (Gen. 35:11). And in Deuteronomy there is the clearest kind of a prediction that when Israel has come into the land of promise, the nation would be ruled by kings (17:14-20). This passage even lays down the guiding rules in the selection of such kings, and also the principles which should characterize their regal conduct, politically, socially, morally, and spiritually.

There are three rules for the selection of any future king: First, he must be an Israelite who is a "brother." Second, the king must not be a "stranger," that is, neither an outsider nor merely a proselyte member of the nation. Third, he must be selected according to God's choosing: "Thou shalt . . . set him king over thee, whom the LORD thy God shall choose" (Deut. 17:15). The historical applica-

---

[1] Keil and Delitzsch, *Commentary on the Pentateuch,* trans. James Martin (Grand Rapids: Eerdmans Publishing Co., reprint, 1949), Vol. III, p. 384.

tion of this third rule is seen in the cases of Saul and David, who were chosen of God, and the choice was then ratified by the people.

As to the king's conduct, there are four rules; three negative, and one positive. First, the king "shall not multiply horses to himself" (Deut. 17:16). There is but one plausible explanation for this restriction. The horses of the Bible are almost exclusively "war-horses," and such horses were either ridden or drew chariots.[2] Therefore the command forbids the building up of a costly type of military forces which might be used for offensive wars conducted *outside* the land, for most of Palestine is unsuited for maneuvering with cavalry or chariots. But the main purpose was to keep Israel from trusting in mere military equipment and power, rather than in Jehovah. The subsequent history of Israel shows that this is precisely what happened when the nation violated this regulation (Isa. 31:1-3). Second, the king shall not "multiply wives to himself" (Deut. 17:17). The growth of the harems in oriental courts always provided fertile soil for palace intrigue and violence. But the chief reason for this restriction is religious: "that his heart turn not away"; for it is a fact that human passion has over and over in history led rulers to do strange things. And the institution of polygamy is always opposed to the Biblical ideal for the home. Third, the king shall not "greatly multiply to himself silver and gold" (vs. 17). The accumulation of great wealth, even apart from personal avarice, not only can blind the minds of rulers to right judgment but also arouse the cupidity of outside foes (cf. Isa. 39).

The fourth command regarding the conduct of future kings reads as follows: "And it shall be, when he sitteth upon the throne of his kingdom, that he shall write him a copy of this law in a book out of that which is before the priests the Levites: And it shall be with him, and he shall read therein all the days of his life: that he may learn to fear the LORD his God, to keep all the words of this law and these statutes, to do them: That his heart be not lifted up above his brethren, and that he turn not aside from the commandment, to the right hand, or to the left: to the end that he may prolong his days in his kingdom, he, and his children, in the midst of Israel" (Deut. 17:18-20). Thus, the king must be God's chosen man, sitting on the earthly throne of God's Kingdom, with God's book constantly before his eyes and in his heart, and ever mindful that as regards the written Word of God he is not above the humblest

[2] *International Standard Bible Encyclopedia* (Chicago: Howard-Severance, 1915), Vol. III, p. 1423.

subject of the realm. It was a government of law, rather than of men.

That the establishment of kings over Israel did not in any sense mean the end of the theocratic rule, is made perfectly clear by the prophet Nathan. Speaking to David concerning Solomon's succession, the word of Jehovah declares, "I will settle him in mine house and in my kingdom for ever" (I Chron. 17:14). Thus the existing kingdom under David and Solomon was not theirs, but God's, just as previously.

2. Events Leading to the Monarchial Form of the Kingdom

When Samuel was old . . . he made his sons judges over Israel.
—*I Sam. 8:1*

In the background of this historical change, some of the conditions may be listed as follows: lack of political unity and stability; recurring defeats by surrounding foes; the moral corruption of the sons of the priest Eli (I Sam. 2:22-25); disappointment in the sons of Samuel because of their perversion of justice (8:1-3); and a strong feeling that only in a powerful monarch could the hopes of the nation be realized. This feeling was not altogether new, for earlier the people had been ready to make Gideon a king with dynastic rights (Judg. 8:22-23). But now the official "elders of Israel" come together to ask Samuel to give them a king: "Behold, thou art old, and thy sons walk not in thy ways; now make us a king to judge us" (I Sam. 8:4-5).

That this demand was regarded with displeasure by Samuel is not too surprising. Even apart from the elders' blunt condemnation of the prophet's own sons, he probably understood that the motives behind the elders' demand were political rather than moral. Instead of recognizing that they themselves were responsible for past failures, they supposed that a change in the external form of government would cure all their troubles. This is the manner of sinful men in all ages, who must learn by bitter experience that "political action" cannot solve problems which are basically moral and spiritual.

In the face of the elders' demand, Samuel resorted to prayer for guidance and the answer of God was, "Hearken unto the voice of the people in all that they say unto thee" (I Sam. 8:6-7). But at the same time Samuel was told to "protest solemnly" as to what this demand would bring upon the nation (vs. 9). Furthermore, in harmony with the directions already laid down in the Mosaic Law (Deut. 17), God Himself would choose the king, which He proceeded to do: first, by having Samuel anoint Saul with oil (I Sam.

10:1); second, by a public confirmation of the divine choice through the ancient casting of the lot (vss. 17-21); and third, by the presentation of Saul to the people for popular ratification (vs. 24).

Later, in an address to all Israel (I Sam. 12), Samuel puts his finger unerringly upon the moral and spiritual root of all their troubles. From Moses to the present moment they had suffered when they forsook Jehovah, and had prospered when they repented and acknowledged their sin (vss. 6-11). Now they have a king, according to their own request, but a man nevertheless chosen of the LORD (vs. 13). They must realize, however, that the mere political change from "judges" to a "king" cannot change the moral conditions of divine blessing. Both the nation and its king must obey the LORD; if not, "ye shall be consumed, both ye and your king" (vs. 25).

3. The Key to the Monarchial Problem

Make us a king . . . like all the nations.   —I Sam. 8:5

Some readers have been disturbed by the apparent problem connected with the inspired record of the change from "judges" to "kings" in the historical kingdom. The elders and the people had asked for a king. Samuel the prophet was greatly displeased with their attitude, speaking of it as "wickedness . . . which ye have done in the sight of the LORD, in asking you a king" (I Sam. 12:17). And Jehovah Himself had characterized their demand as something highly reprehensible, saying, "They have rejected me, that I should not reign over them" (I Sam. 8:7). Moreover, He had warned the nation of the troubles which would come upon them because of the king they wanted (I Sam. 8:10-18). Yet when the people refused to heed His warning, God said to Samuel, "Hearken unto their voice, and make them a king" (I Sam. 8:22). Furthermore, the establishment of kings was quite evidently within the plan of God for the nation of Israel (Gen. 17:6; Deut. 17). Now the problem posed is simply this: If the request for a king was right, why was it called "wickedness"? On the other hand, if the request was wicked, why did God grant it?[3] The answer to this question is twofold.

First, God did not give to the people of Israel exactly what they had asked. For one thing, they were not given the right to set up

[3] Certain critics have sought a *forced literary* solution of the problem of the seeming contradiction, by assuming the existence of three different accounts in chapters 8 to 12 of First Samuel, and then rearranging the chronological sequence to suit their theories (cf. *Hasting's Dictionary of the Bible*, Vol. II, pp. 510-511).

a king of their own choosing, as in the case of other nations. And this brings us, in the second place, to the real key to the problem, which is found in the terms of the original request for a king: "Make us a king to judge us like all the nations" (I Sam. 8:5). The repugnant thing about this demand lies in the qualifying clause, *"like all the nations."* As a matter of fact, the setting up of kings "like all the nations" was wholly unnecessary from the divine standpoint. The rule of God up until this time had been mediated through leaders, judges, and prophets. Even David, the king after God's own heart, could thus have served as head of the state without having all the worldly trappings and material splendor of an Oriental court. Up to this time Israel had had a very simple and unique government, uncomplicated in organization and function. Problems were dealt with as they arose. In wanting a king "like all the nations," Israel would be exchanging the simple theocratic form of government, based on moral principles and dedicated to the general welfare, for something which could become an unwieldy and monstrous governmental structure dedicated mainly to its own perpetuation. Such an arrangement was not only unnecessary but could only add to the burdens of the people and increase the restrictions upon their personal liberties. Therefore, although God assented *in part* to the nation's request, He rebuked them for making it, and at the same time solemnly warned of the perils they were getting into (I Sam. 8:4-18).

The words of Keil are very much to the point here: "The appointment of a king is not *commanded*, like the institution of judges (Deut. 16:18), because Israel could exist under the government of Jehovah, even without an earthly king; it is simply *permitted*, in case the need should arise for a regal government."[4]

4. *The Period of Monarchial Glory*

King Solomon passed all the kings of the earth in riches and wisdom.
—*II Chron. 9:22*

The mediatorial kingdom of Old Testament history reached the pinnacle of its power and glory under its first three kings, each of whom held his throne by the decree and direct appointment of Jehovah. The entire monarchial career of *Saul* is summarized by the prophet Samuel in two brief statements: first, "the LORD anointed thee king over Israel"; and second, "the LORD hath rejected thee from being king over Israel" (I Sam. 15:17, 26). After the failure

[4] Keil and Delitzsch, *op. cit.*, Vol. III, p. 384.

and rejection of Saul, it is Jehovah again who exercises His right of sovereign choice in the case of *David* (I Sam. 16:1, 13). And as his life on earth drew to its close, speaking as a prophet to whom the Word of the LORD had come, David thus indicates the divine choice of succession: "Of all my sons (for the LORD hath given me many sons), he hath chosen Solomon my son to sit upon the throne of the kingdom of the LORD over Israel" (I Chron. 28:5). It is not without significance that *Solomon,* last of the kings directly chosen of God, is also the last king of the united kingdom of Israel.[5]

From Saul to Solomon there was an almost incredible expansion and transformation of the nation of Israel. In the words of Bright, "In one brief generation she had been transformed from a loose, disjointed tribal league, fighting for its life, into a united, self-conscious nation of some importance in the world . . . . Most of the land thought of as 'promised' was now . . . in Israelite hands — a fact she never forgot. Literature and culture flourished as never before, and there was unexampled material prosperity. It was a proud thing to be an Israelite in the tenth century B.C."[6]

The tremendous military achievements of David cleared the way for the more peaceful work of Solomon. The Philistines, perennial and powerful foes of Israel, were decisively defeated and brought under subjection (II Sam. 5:17-25; 8:1). The city of Jerusalem was captured and made the new capital of the nation (II Sam. 5:6-10). The conquest of the Palestinian cities was completed. Across the Jordan the troublesome kingdoms of Moab, Ammon, and Edom were reduced to tributaries. Other kings, watching with concern the progress of this new power, came prudently to seek peace (II Sam. 8:2-15). Occupying a highly strategic geographical location in the ancient world, the kingdom of Israel had swiftly become a compact political factor, which could not be ignored by any of the surrounding nations.

With military security now assured, Solomon proceeded to expand the scope and activities of his kingdom. Certain strategic points were strongly fortified; the cost being defrayed by means of special levies (I Kings 9:15-19). The nation's military forces were increased and a "navy" established (I Kings 9:22, 26). Alli-

---

[5] Dr. John Bright is certainly wrong in seeing nothing more in Solomon's accession than the work of a "palace plot." Is not the testimony of David worth something? (cf. his *Kingdom of God* [New York: Abingdon-Cokesbury Press, 1953], p. 40).

[6] For a very succinct and brilliantly written account of the material glory of the historical kingdom under David and Solomon, see *ibid.,* pp. 35-49.

ances with foreign nations were made, sometimes apparently sealed by diplomatic marriages (I Kings 9:16; 11:1). A special alliance with the king of Tyre brought skillful artisans into the land (I Kings 5:1-18); and also led to a wide expansion of foreign trade (I Kings 9:26-28; 10:22). Recent archaeological discoveries of great and ingeniously constructed copper smelters at Ezion-geber, although not specifically mentioned in the Bible,[7] account for the profusion of this metal and its alloys (I Kings 7:47).[8] The wealth of the nation increased beyond comprehension — "The king made silver to be in Jerusalem as stones" (I Kings 10:27). Gold flowed into the kingdom in great quantity (I Kings 9:27-28; 10:2, 14).

The inspired record of these glories of the historical kingdom is couched in the language of superlatives: "So king Solomon exceeded all the kings of the earth for riches and for wisdom. And all the earth sought to Solomon, to hear his wisdom, which God had put in his heart" (I Kings 10:23-24). Giving all due consideration to the purely natural factors, no one can successfully explain this glorious era apart from the providential and also supernatural workings of God, as some modern critics have sought to do. The testimony of the contemporary queen of Sheba reveals a keener discernment: "The half was not told me . . . . Blessed be the Lord thy God, which delighted in thee, to set thee on the throne of Israel: because the Lord loved Israel for ever, therefore made he thee king, to do judgment and justice" (I Kings 10:7-9).

In concluding on this point, it must be noted that under Solomon we have only a continuation of the same divine kingdom which had been established historically at Sinai with Moses as the mediatorial ruler. There was no change in its original constitution and laws. This is clearly affirmed in David's final charge to his son Solomon: "I go the way of all the earth: be thou strong therefore, and shew thyself a man; and keep the charge of the Lord thy God, to walk in his ways, to keep his statutes, and his commandments, and his judgments, and his testimonies, *as it is written in the law of Moses,* that thou mayest prosper in all that thou doest, and whithersoever thou turnest thyself" (I Kings 2:2-3, italics added). The kingdom under Solomon must continue to operate in conformity with this original constitution and laws, as laid down in the Mosaic code. Furthermore, the identification of Solomon's kingdom as God's

[7] The *place* is named in I Kings 9:26 as the location of Solomon's navy.
[8] The "brass" of the Common Version might better be rendered "bronze," except in Deut. 8:9 where the reference is probably to the natural "copper" ore.

own kingdom was confirmed in no uncertain fashion when, at the dedication of Solomon's temple, "the fire came down from heaven . . . and the glory of the LORD filled the house" (II Chron. 7:1); a striking reminder of what had taken place when this kingdom had originally been established at Sinai (Exod. 40:34). The conventional division between the period of the "judges" and the period of the "kingdom," if not carefully explained, can only be the source of confusion. Viewed from the Biblical standpoint, the one *divine* kingdom of Old Testament history began with Moses, not with Saul.

Chapter X

THE DECLINE OF THE MEDIATORIAL KINGDOM IN OLD TESTAMENT HISTORY

> It is a marvelous fact that it was not because Israel was succeeding in fulfilling its mission, but because it was failing in it, that the spirit of prophecy wrought so powerfully . . . .   —*James Orr*[1]

Without attempting to subtract from David and Solomon any of their excellencies, which were many, it is a striking commentary on the quality of sinful men that in the very period of the historical kingdom's greatest success, there were already present the seeds of political catastrophe. Thus, if we are wise we shall not misunderstand that with reference to salvation, whether spiritual or political, "With men this is impossible" (Matt. 19:26). In such matters there are always things to be done which only God can do.

1. *The Personal Failure of Solomon*

> If he commit iniquity, I will chasten him with the rod of men.
> —*II Sam. 7:14*

Here it must be recorded to the shame of Solomon, this favored king of Israel, that at last he had settled down in open violation of the first three divine rules which had been given by Jehovah to govern the conduct of kings under the constitution of the kingdom (cf. Deut. 17:14-17). First, he multiplied military forces of a kind specifically forbidden in the law of God, gathering together "chariots and horsemen" and "horses brought out of Egypt" (I Kings 10:26, 28). Second, Solomon "loved many foreign women," and he had "seven hundred wives, princesses, and three hundred concubines" (I Kings 11:1, 3-4, ASV). Third, he piled up silver and gold, until the silver became common as stones in Jerusalem and even the vessels of his own house of Lebanon were ordered made of pure gold (I Kings 10:21, 27). And so, along with all this great worldly power and wealth, there came moral deterioration and finally re-

---

[1] "Kingdom of God," *Dictionary of the Bible,* ed. James Hastings (New York: Scribner's Sons, 1901), Vol. II, p. 847.

ligious apostasy — "his wives turned away his heart after other gods: and his heart was not perfect with the LORD his God, as was the heart of David his father" (I Kings 11:4).

But this was not all; economic problems arose. Building projects, military fortifications, ship construction, foreign trade — all these required the labor of men. One source of manpower was found, of course, in the non-Israelites still living in the land and who were pressed into continual bond-service (I Kings 9:15-21). Military service was apparently restricted to Israelites (I Kings 9:22-23), which was doubtless the intent of David in numbering the people (II Sam. 24:1-9); and Solomon may have used this original census for his purposes. But now in addition to this type of service, Solomon proceeded to raise a "levy out of all Israel," amounting to thirty thousand men who were forced to labor in Lebanon one month out of every three (I Kings 5:13-14). This was a revival of the hated *corvée* system remembered by the nation as an intolerable experience in the land of Egypt. It has been estimated that thirty thousand men under forced labor in Israel, compared in terms of the present population of the United States, would equal no less than five million men!

Furthermore, to maintain his far-flung government and the luxury of his own court and household, Solomon required more and more wealth. His father David had been able to enrich the national treasury by means of the spoil taken in his unbroken succession of military victories (II Sam. 8:1-11). But the era of peace under Solomon made it essential to find internal sources of income. This meant taxation, which free men from time immemorial have hated and resisted. The king's plan was thoroughly organized under twelve chief officers whose duty was to see that the court of Solomon was provided for, month by month (I Kings 4:6-19). At the end of twenty years of building, more money had to be raised. And in some kind of a deal made with King Hiram of Tyre, Solomon must have either given away or mortgaged "twenty cities in the land of Galilee" (I Kings 9:10-14). One wonders just how such a business deal appeared in the eyes of the tribes which owned the territory thus handed over cavalierly to an outsider — who was a Canaanite! Grateful as England might feel toward our own country for aid in two world wars, it takes no special imagination to picture what would happen to the current English government if its prime minister would hand over to us twenty cities of the British Isles;

even if these cities were not much to look at, as Hiram seemed to have regarded Solomon's gift![2]

With all this constant drain upon the economic resources and manpower of Israel, which must have stirred up irritation and discontent, it is little wonder that when Solomon's son came to the throne, the first word of the people was, "Thy father made our yoke grievous: now therefore make thou the grievous service of thy father, and his heavy yoke which he put upon us, lighter, and we will serve thee" (I Kings 12:4). But the reply of Rehoboam was a contemptuous "No," an ominous harbinger of worse things yet to come.

Ford C. Ottman has well said, "A king never came to a mighty throne with greater promise than Solomon . . . . Yet Solomon failed. Ascending the throne girded by omnipotence itself, he ended his career shorn of his strength, bereft of his glory, with his heart turned away from Jehovah, and the anger of God kindled against him."[3]

2. The Rupture of the Nation

There was none left but the tribe of Judah only.   —II Kings 17:18

Even before the death of Solomon the sickness of the state was clearly evident. The tribes had always been jealous of their independency and rights. And both David and his son had worked for a genuine political unification of the nation. The undertaking of the magnificent temple at Jerusalem had given definite impetus to a greater centralization of the national worship of Jehovah. Actually, of course, only the true religion of Israel could forge a bond capable of holding the tribes together; and the apostasy of Solomon severed this bond (I Kings 11:1-10). Adversaries began to stir up trouble in various places (I Kings 11:14, 23, 26-28). The final result was the secession of ten tribes under the leadership of Jeroboam, whose outstanding ability had already been recognized by Solomon (I Kings 11:29-43). Since it had been authorized directly by Jehovah through the prophet Ahijah, the secession must be regarded as a divine judgment upon the chosen nation and its mediatorial king, for both had grievously sinned.

[2] There is some question about this transaction. Some think Hiram was so displeased with the twenty cities that he contemptuously turned them back to Solomon. Others suppose that the cities mentioned in II Chron. 8:2 were *Phoenician* cities which Hiram gave to Solomon as a matching gift, after the manner of Oriental potentates. For arguments pro and con, see Lange's *Commentary* on the passage.
[3] *God's Oath* (New York: Geo. H. Doran, 1911), p. 27.

Viewed from the standpoint of Solomon's immediate successor, Rehoboam, the loss of the ten tribes was a perfectly senseless thing. At the death of Solomon, we are told, "all Israel were come to Shechem" to make Rehoboam king; even his rival Jeroboam was among them (I Kings 12:1-3). They offered to serve the heir of Solomon if he would only lighten the heavy burdens which had been imposed by his father. But Rehoboam, impatient with the sage advice of his older counselors, chose to follow the reckless course suggested by his "playboy" associates. To the very moderate and reasonable plea of his people, the king replied roughly, "My father made your yoke heavy, and I will add to your yoke; my father also chastised you with whips, but I will chastise you with scorpions" (I Kings 12:4-14). The hostile reaction of the people was thus made inevitable: "What portion have we in David?" they cried, "to your tents, O Israel." The northern tribes turned to Jeroboam and "there was none that followed the house of David, but the tribe of Judah only" (I Kings 12:16-20). The tribe of Benjamin was probably divided in its allegiance, for we read in the next verse (21) that when Rehoboam assembled his military expedition to force a reunion of the tribes, the "tribe of Benjamin" was represented in the army.

But above and beyond all the political intrigues and the force of armies there was a divine providence which had the last word in this secessionist movement. The prophet Shemaiah was sent of God to Rehoboam to say, "Thus saith the LORD, Ye shall not go up, nor fight against your brethren the children of Israel: return every man to his house; *for this thing is from me*" (I Kings 12:22-25, italics added). This injunction was obeyed for the time being, but evidently the season of peace was very brief, for the Word of God declares that "there was war between Rehoboam and Jeroboam all their days" (I Kings 14:30). But the sword of man could not undo what the judgment of God had decreed, and there was no healing of the rupture of the kingdom.

The catastrophic division of the tribes, however, did not bring an end to the mediatorial kingdom in Old Testament history. Solomon had indeed been fully warned of the impending judgment; but he had also been promised by Jehovah that his kingdom would be perpetuated. "Howbeit I will not rend away all the kingdom," God had said, "but will give one tribe to thy son for David my servant's sake, and for Jerusalem's sake which I have chosen" (I Kings 11:11-13). Hence, Orelli is correct in observing that "The smaller and often overpowered Kingdom of Judah, which faithfully adhered to the royal line of David, passed through many crises and had many unworthy rulers. But the legitimate royal house, which had been selected by Jehovah, constituted spiritually a firm bond which kept the people united, as is seen, e.g., by a glance at the addresses of Isaiah, who is thoroughly filled with the conviction of the importance of the House of David, no matter how unworthy the king who happened to rule appeared to him."[4] As the dying patriarch Jacob had said prophetically, "The sceptre shall not depart from Judah" (Gen. 49:10).

3. Political Disaster Had Been Predicted by Samuel

Ye shall cry out in that day because of your king.   —I Sam. 8:18

It is easy to forget that "we the people" in the long run must always pay for whatever the government does for us. Only fools suppose that by committing a matter to the government, they can get it done for nothing. Still worse, human government not only makes the people pay for everything done for them, but it always makes them pay more than it should cost. For only a part of the wealth taken by the government ever comes back to the people in services. No lesson in human history is taught more clearly than this, yet the lesson apparently is never learned. When, in the days of Samuel, the Jewish people became dissatisfied with the simple and direct rule of Jehovah and demanded a king "like all the nations," they had been plainly warned of the high cost they would pay for being thus governed (I Sam. 8:7-20). The passage reads as follows:

> 7. And the LORD said unto Samuel . . . .
> 9. Now therefore hearken unto their voice: howbeit yet protest solemnly unto them, and shew them the manner of the king that shall reign over them.
> 10. And Samuel told all the words of the LORD unto the people that asked of him a king.
> 11. And he said, This will be the manner of the king that shall reign over you: He will take your sons, and appoint them for himself, for his chariots, and to be his horsemen; and some shall run before his chariots.
> 12. And he will appoint him captains over thousands, and captains over fifties; and will set them to ear his ground, and to reap his harvest, and to make his instruments of war, and instruments of his chariots.
> 13. And he will take your daughters to be confectionaries, and to be cooks, and to be bakers.
> 14. And he will take your fields and your vineyards, and your oliveyards, even the best of them, and give them to his servants.

[4] C. von Orelli, "History of Israel," *International Standard Bible Encyclopedia* (Chicago: Howard-Severance, 1915), Vol. III, p. 1520.

15. And he will take the tenth of your seed, and of your vineyards, and give to his officers, and to his servants.

16. And he will take your menservants, and your maidservants, and your goodliest young men, and your asses, and put them to his work.

17. He will take the tenth of your sheep: and ye shall be his servants.

18. And ye shall cry out in that day because of your king which ye shall have chosen you; and the LORD will not hear you in that day.

19. Nevertheless the people refused to obey the voice of Samuel; and they said, Nay; but we will have a king over us;

20. That we also may be like all the nations; and that our king may judge us, and go out before us, and fight our battles.

This remarkable passage deserves to be studied, not only by theologians and preachers, but also by political scientists and economists. It shows that the needs and problems of human government do not change much from generation to generation. The student will find here, not only an accurate prediction of the trends of government in the historical kingdom of Israel, but also many items which are currently trying the souls of thoughtful men in the field of government. Actually there is not much difference between the various types of political government, as regards their avowed purposes and general tendencies. For all alike start out with the best of professed intentions to give the governed something better than they have had.

In the days of Samuel, Israel had wanted a king to "judge" them and to lead them in their "battles" (vs. 20). We have here a recognition of the two problems of *order* and *power;* the one internal, and the other external. These two have been called "the original and . . . fundamental values of government."[5] It is an axiom of history that no government has ever succeeded, even temporarily, without offering to the people these two values. No dictator or tyrant ever ruled who did not, to some extent, provide for order within the state and protection against external enemies. This, then, is the fundamental good supplied by all government in some measure, regardless of its character or motives.

The real difference between the various kinds of government is found in the *price* people have had to pay for these benefits of internal order and external safety. And the stability of government will vary according to the cost of being governed. This is why a dictatorship in the long run is the most unstable of all governments, because it greatly overestimates the price men will be willing to pay for its benefits.

We may say, therefore, that Israel was right in her desire for

[5] Ralph Barton Perry, *The Moral Economy* (New York: Scribner's Sons, 1909), p. 157.

the benefits of order and power. Her mistake is found in the *kind* of government she asked for. Not that there is anything fundamentally wrong with the *monarchial* form; for the final and perfect government on earth will be centralized in a "King." But Israel asked for a king *like all the nations* (I Sam. 8:19-20). And that kind of a government would cost the people dearly in the long run, as Samuel warned the nation. For, no matter how low the cost at the beginning, the inevitable trend is upward; and the rise is often swift. Compare, for example, the simple requirements of the government under Saul with the gigantic and costly machine under Solomon — all within the brief span of one generation.

Let us now, in the prophecy of First Samuel 8:7-20, observe the tendencies which would arise to plague Israel, and which are inherent in all government under sinful men, i.e., government "like all the nations."

a. *Government service.* Under the contemplated king the government will bring the people into its service: first, into *military* service for "chariots" and "horsemen" (vs. 11); and second, into *civil* service of various kinds — agricultural, manufacturing, and food processing (vss. 12-13). Here we have a beginning of governmental bureaucracy, the growth of which in all recorded history of the nations has never been voluntarily halted.

b. *Job-making.* This will begin in the military department of government where there will be not only "captains over thousands" but also "captains over fifties" (vs. 12). Speaking in modern terms, they make the units smaller so as to create and use more generals! Some men will be employed to "run before" the king's chariots (vs. 11) — a perfectly useless procedure, except for creating public attention. Once launched, men have generally found it impossible to control or dislodge any department of government service. On the contrary, each one invariably tries to expand in scope and numbers.

c. *Labor scarcity.* The Word of God through Samuel warns Israel that the government will take "your sons" and "daughters," "your menservants" and "maidservants" (vss. 11, 13, 16). Thus the unwarranted expansion of the governmental service will take many people out of normally productive pursuits. Sons and daughters who ought to be helping in family activities, as well as other workers needed on farms and in factories, are drawn into the service of the government. The result is labor shortages and serious economic maladjustment.

d. *Government for its own sake.* The state now comes first. As the Bible puts the matter, the ruler sets his employees to doing "his work" (vs. 16), "for himself" (vs. 11), for "his harvest" (vs. 12), and for "his chariots" (vs. 11). Thus the energies of the state are now primarily devoted to the maintenance of the government. For, no matter how idealistically political officials may talk about serving "the people," the ugly fact remains that a government is interested first and last in its own support and perpetuation. Therefore, the average employee must render his first loyalty to the government, which generally means to the "party" or cabal that controls it. In this way the labors of men tend to become nonproductive; personal incentive is diminished; and the vested interests of government operate for their own sake.

e. *Burdensome taxation.* To support all its army of employees and officials takes money. Hence, the state must always be increasing the taxes to keep up with the growth of the bureaucracy. And so, in the words of Samuel, the government will take "a tenth of your seed . . . of your vineyards . . . of your sheep" (vss. 15, 17). Gloomy as the picture seems, it should be noted that this predicted tax would be only one-tenth of one thing, namely, the food production of the governed. In our more enlightened modern times, the cost of government actually exceeds the value of all our expenditure for food! Today a mere ten per cent tax on all production would be hailed as an approach to the Millennium. The curse of heavy taxation has been thus described by a noted modern economist: "For every additional dollar that the government spends, the taxpayers have one dollar less to spend. The situation is worse than this. Taxation erodes the incentives to produce and earn. It penalizes success, and the production of marketable products, often in order to subsidize continued production of unmarketable products. It sets up an army of taxgatherers. In the end it meets fewer real needs than before. *People* spend the money they themselves earn on what they themselves really want. The *government* spends money, not on what the rest of us want, but on what the bureaucrats think is good for us." [6]

f. *Property confiscation.* This is the next logical move of the state. Hence, we read in this eighth chapter of First Samuel that the government, no longer satisfied with a tax on production, begins to take over the basic sources of wealth; i.e., "your fields . . . your

[6] Henry Hazlitt, "The Fourth Dimension," *Newsweek*, Nov. 28, 1955, p. 94.

vineyards . . . your oliveyards, even the best of them" (vs. 14).
Respect for private property diminishes in proportion to the expansion of government and its vast monetary requirements. The
devices of confiscation today are various and often disguised by
high-sounding terms — controlled currency, social legislation, income
taxation, the public good — but underneath them all, the relentless
search goes on to find more sources of income for the state. And
once started on this road, there is humanly speaking no point of
return.

g. *Political corruption.* The ancient prophecy of Samuel warns
further that the government will take the wealth, acquired by taxation and confiscation, and "give to his officers, and to his servants"
(vs. 15). It is an unpleasant fact that a large share of government
income always finds its way into the hands of the partisans of the
ruling party. Of course, politicians will talk grandly about devoting
the "public wealth" to the "common good," but this is never wholly
the case. Often it is taken away from those who produced it and
given to the undeserving. In fact, some modern economists and
state officials have frankly asserted the desirability of thus re-
distributing the wealth of society. But to carry out these "benevolent" purposes, the rulers must keep themselves in power. And
once a government gets enough people working for it, the problem is solved. The formula is simple — spend, tax, elect — as one
cynical official tersely put the matter.

h. *Totalitarian control.* The final word of Samuel's prophecy,
concerning the Gargantuan growth of human government when
left to itself, is addressed to the *whole nation* of Israel, "Ye shall be
his servants" (vs. 17). Thus the end of the vicious circle is reached
when all the people exist and work only for the State, which swal-
lows up the very citizens who created it. It is to the lasting credit
of the founding fathers of our own American system that they regarded all highly centralized government with a deep and cold
suspicion, holding that the less we had of it, the better off we would
be. But strangely enough today, for every failure of highly centralized government, its supporters have no remedy except a larger
dose of the same thing — "the hair of the dog that bit them."

i. *Intolerable oppression.* The overall result of the above tendencies is deep distress for all the subjects of the State. In the words
of Scripture, "Ye shall cry out in that day because of your king
which ye shall have chosen you" (vs. 18). And we must not fail
to note that this oppression has been caused, not by some foreign

power, but by the very government that the people had chosen. Human government is necessary, but people who are wise never let it get too big or powerful. Unless strictly limited, the end is the loss of liberty, economic distress, and political despair.

4. *The Fundamental Political Error*

That we also may be like all the nations.   *—I Sam. 8:20*

The root of all the political problems of Israel, as listed above, was not the *king* demanded by the nation. There is nothing inherently evil about the office of a king. In the Word of God, even the eternal and perfect state of mankind is not described as a soviet, or a republic, or a democracy, but a *kingdom*. The notion that monarchial forms of government are somehow responsible for the world's political ills is a total myth which should have been destroyed by two world wars. In 1917, when America entered the first conflict, it was widely supposed that once we had abolished the kings and emperors, all would be well. So we witnessed the dethronement of the Russian Tzar and the German Kaiser, to say nothing of some lesser breeds. And in their stead we got Stalin and Hitler! Today we look back nostalgically, not too sure that the abolishing of the kings has improved the world political situation over the days prior to 1914.

Actually, basic to Israel's troubles in the historical kingdom was her desire for a government *like all the nations* (I Sam. 8:20). The mention of a "king" in the Biblical context has served to confuse the real issue. But the important point is that Israel was determined to have a government which would be similar to the other nations of the ancient world. She was not satisfied to continue under the system set up at Sinai, uniquely distinct from all other political forms, ancient or modern. She wanted to be in fashion politically. The Constitution of the State, shall we say, must be "reinterpreted" to meet the problems and conditions of the "new day." Instead of seeing that what they already had was infinitely superior to any existing political system, the nation wanted to move with the world. This is a kind of "bastard" internationalism which is recognizable in America today. Instead of seeing that God in His good Providence has given to us a unique system which with all its imperfections has provided a refuge for political liberty unparalleled in the world, there are some voices which call upon the nation to merge its interests in a world organization where all distinct values are likely to be submerged. And we need to be reminded that, as in the case of Israel, there are some political values which can not be preserved, except by what is often scornfully called "isolationism."

It cannot be said too often that the theocratic and mediatorial kingdom of Israel was divinely intended to be *different,* not *like* the other political systems of the world. Here the reader is referred back to the discussion of the Constitution and Laws of the Kingdom established at Sinai (Ch. VII). What a contrast between the early and later history of that kingdom! Think of the ten plagues which brought the proud Egyptian Pharaoh to his knees; or the supernatural passage through the Red Sea; or the bread from heaven and the water from the rock in the wilderness; or the solemn procession of the Israelites around the city of Jericho, its massive walls falling at the blast of trumpets. Recall the simple and unpretentious circumstances of the rule of Moses, Joshua, the Judges, and Samuel; with no worldly pomp or palaces. And then, over against this, consider the proud legions of Solomon with the horsemen and flashing chariots; his royal palace thirteen years in building, his summer house in the forest of Lebanon, the house for Pharaoh's daughter (I Kings 7:1-8), and his great throne of ivory and gold (I Kings 10:18); his stables with 40,000 stalls for the chariot horses alone (I Kings 4:26); his enormous harem of a thousand women (I Kings 11:3); and the groaning table of his court provided daily with all the delicacies of the then known world (I Kings 4:22-24). Even if it be argued that all these riches had been given by Jehovah (I Kings 3:13), certainly the responsibility for their proper use rested upon Solomon who also had been granted divine wisdom above all other rulers (I Kings 3:12). Yet his *use* of these riches reveals no great quality of superior wisdom. In this respect, he became at last like the kings of "all the nations." And Israel had asked for that kind of a king! It was only the mercy of God that Israel was not given *all* that she had asked for, for then her historical situation would have become still more desperate.

5. Role of the Prophets during the Decline

Yet many years didst thou bear with them, and testifiedst against them by thy Spirit through thy prophets.   —*Neh. 9:30, ASV*

A detailed discussion of the years following the secession of the ten tribes is not essential to the main purpose of this volume. It will be enough to say in general that, the seeds of disaster having been sown by Solomon, the political decline of both divisions of the nation became both swift and certain. To be sure, the reigns of Jeroboam II in the north and Uzziah and Josiah at Jerusalem seemed for a time to revive the former glories of the kingdom; but these proved to be only the final rays of a setting sun. After Solomon the kings are no longer chosen *directly* by Jehovah, but take the throne either by inheritance or force. Finally the tide of Jerusalem's fortune fell so low that foreign powers decided who would occupy the throne (II Kings 23:34; 24:17). And, with a few notable exceptions, the line of rulers degenerates. The period is characterized in general by a more indirect rule of God. Prophets become the immediate spokesmen of God, conveying the knowledge of His will to the kings, who sometimes obey, and at other times reject the prophetic counsel.

It is a striking fact that this period of human failure in the historical kingdom is also the period when divine prophecy reaches its greatest volume and highest brilliance. But the prophets of Israel were more than predictors of the things to come, which will be discussed at some length in the next chapter of this book. These prophets were also men of their own times, in the sense that they spoke a message which was immediately relevant to the things present in the historical kingdom.

It should also be noted here that the period of the *writing* prophets parallels the period of the decline and end of the historical kingdom. There had been prophets in Israel before this. But formerly the chief function of the prophet had been to speak the word of the ever-present divine King for the immediate guidance of the nation in its conduct and affairs. For the most part such prophetic utterances were not recorded. But now the historical kingdom is drawing to a close, when the immediate presence of Jehovah will be withdrawn. Thus the need arises for a *written* body of divine prophecy for the guidance and encouragement of Israel during the "many days" the nation will abide "without a king" and "without an ephod"[7] (Hos. 3:4). As S. J. Andrews has well said: "The transition, therefore, from spoken to written prophecy marks an epoch in the history of the elect people."[8]

The ministry of the prophets in the period of the decline of the historical kingdom was at least fivefold:

[7] The "ephod" here seems to have been a symbol of Israel's privilege, under the theocracy, of ascertaining the immediate will of God in every crisis and for every problem not covered by the written Law (I Sam. 23:9-12; 30:7-8).

[8] For a very able discussion of this point, see his *God's Revelations of Himself to Men* (New York: Scribner's Sons, 1886), Chap. XII.

a. The Prophets Probed the Sickness of the Kingdom

Isaiah, first in the canonical order, thus begins his oracle: "The ox knoweth his owner, and the ass his master's crib; but Israel doth not know, my people doth not consider . . . . the whole head is sick, and the whole heart faint. From the sole of the foot even unto the head there is no soundness in it; but wounds, and bruises, and putrifying sores: they have not been closed, neither bound up, neither mollified with ointment" (1:3-6).

There was *moral* sickness: "Woe unto them that call evil good, and good evil; that put darkness for light, and light for darkness; that put bitter for sweet, and sweet for bitter" (Isa. 5:20).

There was *social and economic* sickness: "Hear this, O ye that swallow up the needy, even to make the poor of the land to fail, Saying, When will the new moon be gone, that we may sell corn? and the sabbath, that we may set forth wheat, making the ephah small, and the shekel great, and falsifying the balances by deceit? That we may buy the poor for silver, and the needy for a pair of shoes; yea, and sell the refuse of the wheat?" (Amos 8:4-6).

There was degeneration among the *rulers*: "Thy princes are rebellious, and companions of thieves; every one loveth gifts, and followeth after rewards; they judge not the fatherless, neither doth the cause of the widow come unto them" (Isa. 1:23). "As for my people, children are their oppressors, and women rule over them" (Isa. 3:12).

There was evil among the *spiritual leaders*: "The priest and the prophet have erred through strong drink, they are swallowed up of wine . . . they err in vision, they stumble in judgment" (Isa. 28:7). "Woe be to the shepherds of Israel that do feed themselves! Should not the shepherds feed the flocks?" (Ezek. 34:2). "Woe be unto the pastors that destroy and scatter the sheep of my pasture, saith the LORD . . . they speak a vision of their own heart, and not out of the mouth of the LORD . . . I have not sent these prophets, yet they ran; I have not spoken to them, yet they prophesied. . . . I have heard what the prophets said, that prophesy lies in my name, saying, I have dreamed, I have dreamed. . . . Yea, they are prophets of the deceit of their own heart" (Jer. 23:1, 16, 21, 25, 26).

b. The Prophets Called the Nation Back to Its Original Constitution and Laws

In the face of the desperate sickness of the nation, the first concern of the prophets was not to establish something new in a political way, but rather to call for a return to the ancient Mosaic Code. The prophet Amos set the pattern in his demand for the restoration of the old theocratic ideal. He "was no revolutionary summoning the downtrodden masses to the barricades. He was no humanitarian, moved by the plight of the poor, who advanced a program of social reform designed to cure the national malady. He was — let us not mistake it — no teacher of a new ethic which would ultimately, so the handbooks used to tell us, tame the rough-and-ready morality of the people and lift them to the heights of ethical monotheism. Amos was no innovator, but a man of the ancient ways. His ethical protest was drawn from a well five hundred years deep. His were the ethics of the Decalogue. . . . He advanced no cure for the schism of society save a restoration of the covenant brotherhood which had created Israelite society in the first place."[9]

Isaiah speaks in the same vein, "To the law and to the testimony; if they speak not according to this word, it is because there is no light in them" (8:20). Jeremiah has no other remedy for the sickness of the state: "Stand ye in the ways, and see, and ask for the old paths, where is the good way, and walk therein, and ye shall find rest for your souls" (6:16). And the final word in the Hebrew canon of the prophets only repeats the well-known formula: "Remember ye the law of Moses my servant, which I commanded unto him in Horeb for all Israel, with the statutes and judgments" (Mal. 4:4). These are words which cannot be misunderstood; and although in the case of Malachi they were uttered *after* the close of the mediatorial kingdom in history, they nevertheless call the people back to the ancient ideal revealed in the original constitution and laws given from heaven when the kingdom was established at Sinai. Every revival in Israel was the result of a return to the Law of Moses (cf. II Chron., chaps. 29-31).

c. *The Prophets Warn of Divine Judgment*

The nation of Israel was the elect nation in the Kingdom of God; and the people knew this, as they had a right to know, even in the darkest days of the decline of the kingdom. But, as is always the case, there was a very present danger that the people would fall into the terrible sin of presumption. Some would say, as they said many times in history, "We be Abraham's seed" (John 8:33); therefore, nothing can happen to *us*. Now to their major premise the

---

[9] John Bright, *The Kingdom of God* (New York: Abingdon-Cokesbury Press, 1953), p. 65.

prophet Amos fully assents, as he speaks the Word of Jehovah to
Israel, "You only have I known of all the families of the earth"
(3:2). But the prophet's conclusion is something else: "therefore,
I will punish you for all your iniquities" (3:2). The nation must
learn that election means not only a place of divine favor, but also
a place of divine punishment when favor is presumptuously abused.
The nation of Israel has priority with God — no question about that
— but this is a priority in divine judgment as well as divine favor
(Rom. 1:16; 2:9).

The moral and spiritual responsibility of Israel, the prophets
argue, cannot be abrogated but only heightened by the divine election. And for a people that forgets this, the longed-for day of Jehovah can bring no blessing, but only judgment: "Woe unto you
that desire the day of the LORD! to what end is it for you? the day
of the LORD is darkness, and not light. As if a man did flee from a
lion, and a bear met him; or went into the house, and leaned
his hand on the wall, and a serpent bit him" (Amos 5:18-19). No
mere forms of religion can help: neither their "feast days," nor
their "solemn assemblies," nor their "burnt offerings," nor the
"noise" of their songs. The time has come to "let judgment run
down as waters, and righteousness as a mighty stream" (Amos 5:21-
24).

The judgment of the seventy years' captivity in Babylon should
have taught the chosen nation the lesson that divine election does
not abolish human responsibility. Yet in the days of the Return,
Malachi found many who had forgotten this lesson. While living in
open sin and rebellion against Jehovah, they were nevertheless longing for the coming of the Messiah — "the LORD, whom ye seek . . .
whom ye delight in" (3:1). But here again the prophet warns that
Messiah's coming would bring judgment as well as blessing: "Who
may abide the day of his coming? and who shall stand when he
appeareth? for he is like a refiner's fire, and like fullers' soap. . . .
And I will come near to you to judgment; and I will be a swift witness against the sorcerers, and against the adulterers, and against
false swearers, and against those that oppress the hireling in his
wages, the widow, and the fatherless, and that turn aside the stranger
from his right, and fear not me, saith the LORD of hosts" (Mal.
3:2-5).

But to the voice of the prophets the answer of a rebellious nation
was too often: "Prophesy not unto us right things, speak unto us
smooth things, prophesy deceits" (Isa. 30:10).

d. *The Prophets Reassert the Inviolability of God's Kingdom-Covenant*

Through all the bitter prophecies of judgment uttered against Israel, there is never the slightest intimation that God's covenant with Israel can be broken or ultimately fail. Men may fail, but Jehovah never fails in His purposes: "For I am the LORD," He says, "I change not; therefore ye sons of Jacob are not consumed" (Mal. 3:6).

Concerning the covenant of the kingdom, Jeremiah writes: "For thus saith the LORD; David shall never want a man to sit upon the throne of the house of Israel . . . . If ye can break my covenant of the day, and my covenant of the night, and that there should not be day and night in their season; then may also my covenant be broken with David my servant, that he should not have a son to reign upon his throne" (Jer. 33:17, 20-21).

e. *The Prophets Promise a Future and Better Kingdom*

This important aspect of the ministry of the prophets will be discussed at length in the next chapter. Therefore, it needs only to be noted briefly here in connection with the decline of the historical kingdom. It is the shame of man to bring darkness upon the world by reason of his oft-recurring failure. It is the glory of God to bring light in the midst of the gross darkness. Beyond the night of man's sin there is always the glorious day of God's unfailing grace. To the anxious question of the longing souls in Israel, "Watchman, what of the night?" the answer of the prophet comes back in comforting assurance, "The morning cometh" (Isa. 21:11-12). This note of divine encouragement is never wholly absent from Old Testament prophecy, regardless of its severity. First, the darkness; but afterward there will be light: "It shall come to pass, that at evening time it shall be light. . . . And the LORD shall be king over all the earth; in that day there shall be one LORD, and his name one" (Zech. 14:7, 9).

Chapter XI

THE END OF THE MEDIATORIAL KINGDOM
IN OLD TESTAMENT HISTORY

> Thus saith the Lord GOD; Remove the diadem, and take off the crown
> . . . . I will overturn, overturn, overturn, it: and it shall be no more,
> until he come whose right it is; and I will give it him. —*Ezek. 21:26-27*

As to the exact time of the end of the historical kingdom of God in Israel, there has been some question among various writers. The general opinion seems to be that the end came with the Captivity. Wyngaarden puts it at the beginning of "the New Testament Era."[1] But the answers are often lacking or indefinite and unsatisfying. Certainly, it would seem in the highest degree unlikely that there should be any historical uncertainty as to the *termination* of that kingdom which *began* with such a remarkable show of supernatural power and glory at Sinai. There is in the visions of the prophet Ezekiel a highly dramatic scene which, in my opinion, fixes the time beyond dispute. This is the vision of the departure of the Shekinah-Glory from Jerusalem recorded in chapters 8 through 11.

1. *The Regal Significance of the Shekinah-Glory*

> The pillar of the cloud departed not from them by day, to lead them
> in the way; neither the pillar of fire by night, to shew them light.
> —*Neh. 9:19*

The "glory of Jehovah," often referred to in the Old Testament and named the "Shekinah" in non-Biblical Jewish writings, was more than a mere symbol of God's presence. It was indeed a "sign and manifestation of his presence," but it also described the "form" in which the God of Israel revealed Himself.[2] Doubtless it is correct to find manifestations of this "glory" in such Old Testament phenomena as the Burning Bush and the Pillar of Cloud and Fire, but there can be no question as to its identification on the mount of

---

[1] Martin J. Wyngaarden, *The Future of the Kingdom* (Grand Rapids: Baker Book House, 1955), p. 35.

[2] W. R. Betteridge, "Glory," *International Standard Bible Encyclopedia* (Chicago: Howard-Severance, 1915), Vol. II, p. 1236.

Sinai where, we are told, "The LORD descended upon it in fire" (Exod. 19:18). And when Moses went up by divine command, the inspired record declares that "the glory of the LORD abode upon mount Sinai" (Exod. 24:15, 16). It was here that, as we have already noted, the historical kingdom received its constitution and laws; and when the tabernacle had been completed according to all the divine specifications, we read that "the glory of the LORD filled the tabernacle" (Exod. 40:34). Later in the history of the kingdom, when King Solomon had finished his dedicatory prayer in the magnificent temple he had built, the Word of God records once again that "the fire came down from heaven . . . and the glory of the LORD filled the house" (II Chron. 7:1). Thus the Shekinah-Glory was the visible evidence of Jehovah's personal presence and rule in the Mediatorial Kingdom of Israel throughout its history.

2. *The Historical Situation at the End*

> Hast thou seen this, O son of man?   —*Ezek. 8:17*

His vision of the departure of the "glory of Jehovah" is carefully dated by Ezekiel in "the sixth year" (8:1), a reference to the time of the captivity of King Jehoiachin (1:2). The prophet had been carried away to Babylon and was sitting in his own house there with the elders of Israel assembled before him, when he was suddenly caught up by the hand of God and brought in his "visions" back to the city of Jerusalem (8:1-3). Whether he was actually transported to Jerusalem bodily, or whether, like John in the isle of Patmos, the events at the city were caused supernaturally to pass before his vision, is a question which need not detain us here. The last sentence of 11:24 seems to indicate that Ezekiel remained in Babylon during the vision. But the important point is that the prophet not only saw the vision in the "sixth year" of the captivity, but also that he saw the actual situation there at that particular time. Furthermore, what he saw of the spiritual and moral conditions there fits the historical situation as revealed briefly in other Biblical records (II Kings 24:17-20; Jer. 52:1-3). Following his vision of the events transpiring at Jerusalem, Ezekiel is brought back in his visions to Babylon where he reported to the captives all that the LORD had showed him (11:24-25).

It should be recalled that when the king of Babylon had come against Jerusalem, he had with deliberate astuteness taken back to Babylon King Jehoiachin, his family, his treasures, and also all the people of any consequence, leaving in Jerusalem only "the poorest sort of the people of the land," and setting up Zedekiah as a vassal ruler there (II Kings 24:11-16). Now it might be supposed that such a disaster would have provided an unforgettable lesson to the people left in the land. On the contrary, "they acted like men intoxicated with new power; their accession to property and unwonted position turned their heads."[3] False prophets arose predicting a speedy restoration of what had been lost to Nebuchadnezzar, contrary to the word of Jeremiah (27:14-22). Furthermore, there was an attempt to secure help against Babylon by diplomatic approaches to surrounding nations (Jer. 27:1-7). The consequence was only a deeper plunge into the ways and idolatries of those nations whose friendship was being cultivated. To view this tragic situation, Ezekiel was brought in vision to Jerusalem, and there the unmistakable warning of Jehovah is sounded: "Son of man, seest thou what they do? even the great abominations that the house of Israel committeth here, that I should go far off from my sanctuary?" (8:6). The implication is clear: In the face of the intolerable situation already existing there, God is still in His sanctuary at Jerusalem; *but He may depart.*

Then the prophet, doubtless with an aching heart, was given to see the evidence of Israel's dreadful apostasy as it unfolded in the vision before him. Seventy of the elders of Israel stood in the attitude of worship before the creature-idols, even "creeping things and abominable beasts," which had been painted on the wall of the LORD's temple (8:10). At the north gate of the house Ezekiel saw the "women weeping for Tammuz" (8:14), a heathen god corresponding to the Greek Adonis whose worship was attended by such licentious orgies that the cult was finally suppressed by Constantine the Great. Then the prophet was brought into the "inner court," the court of the priests, where he saw "five and twenty men" with their backs toward the temple of the LORD and facing toward the east while they worshipped the rising sun (8:16). And who were these men? They were the priesthood of the nation, represented here by the presidents of the twenty-four courses with the high priest at their head![4]

In the record of this shocking vision there seems to have been a definitely designed contrast between this situation at the approaching end of the historical kingdom and the situation at its beginning at Sinai. The people of Israel were far from perfect back there. But

---

[3] J. F. Genung, "Zedekiah," *I.S.B.E.,* Vol. V, p. 3141.
[4] So Lange and other expositors (cf. I Chron. 24).

at Sinai "all the people" had together united in a solemn pledge: "All that the Lord hath spoken we will do" (Exod. 19:8). There also we saw the "women" of Israel giving freely of their skill and possessions in the preparation of the tabernacle for Jehovah's dwelling place (Exod. 35:25-26; 38:8). But most impressive of all, at Sinai "seventy of the elders of Israel" with "Aaron, Nadab, and Abihu" of the priesthood actually went up with Moses into the Mount, and there they "saw God, and did eat and drink" in His presence (Exod. 24:9-11). But now in Ezekiel's day the entire picture was changed; the apostasy of Israel had become total in Jerusalem; and it involved the people, the elders, the women, and the priesthood (Ezek. 8:6, 11, 14, 16). And the verdict of Jehovah is rendered in verse 18: "Therefore will I also deal in fury: mine eye shall not spare, neither will I have pity: and though they cry in mine ears with a loud voice, yet will I not hear them." The end had come.

Furthermore, it was the end not only of Israel's political supremacy but also of her *religious* supremacy. For just as the historical kingdom had begun at Sinai with a vital union between the political and religious areas of Israel's national life, so now both were involved in the end, symbolized by the "mitre" of the high priest and the "crown" of the king. Both are mentioned by Ezekiel in his utterance of divine judgment upon the mediatorial nation in the days of Zedekiah: "Thus saith the Lord Jehovah: Remove the mitre, and take off the crown. . . . until he come whose right it is" (21:26-27, ASV).

3. The Vision of the Departing Glory

And the glory of the Lord went up from the midst of the city.
—*Ezek. 11:23*

The total vision of the departure of the Glory must be constructed from references found in chapters 8 through 11. First, the prophet saw the Glory still in the city of David in its proper place in the temple: "Behold, the glory of the God of Israel *was there*" (8:4, italics added). A little later in the vision he notes that "the glory of the God of Israel was gone up . . . to *the threshold* of the house" (9:3, italics added). Then Ezekiel writes, "The glory of the Lord . . . *stood* over the threshold" for a moment, illuminating the inner court with the ineffable "brightness" of Deity (10:4, italics added). Finally, the cherubim lifted up their wings, and the prophet records the tragic end: "The glory of the Lord *went up from the midst of the city,* and stood upon the mountain which is on the east side of

the city" (11:23, italics added). Later, following its destruction by
the Babylonian armies, the city was rebuilt and within its walls
successively two temples were erected; but we read of no Glory
therein. Even Josephus admits the regal absence.[5] The immediate
and personal presence of Israel's divine King was departed.

In this connection, we cannot fail to be impressed with the gracious circumstances of the LORD's withdrawal: not suddenly, but
slowly and gradually by stages, with seeming tender reluctance; as
if He were actually yearning to remain in the place He had chosen
for His dwelling place. But there is no evidence of entreaty or repentance on the part of the nation. The elders bow down to the
idols, the women weep for the god Tammuz, the priests turn their
backs on the Temple and worship the eastern sun. The God of
Israel is forgotten. Although Jehovah had not yet forsaken the
nation, the people in their wishful thinking said, "Jehovah hath forsaken the land" (8:12, ASV). And so at last they got what they
wanted: as God had warned in the days of Hosea, "I will go and
return to my place, till they acknowledge their offence, and seek my
face" (Hos. 5:15).

Samuel J. Andrews has a fine paragraph on the significance of
the departure of the visible Glory: "This departure of Jehovah from
His temple and land . . . marked a change in His theocratic relation
to His people—a change that continues even to this day. They
did not cease to be His covenant people (Lev. 26:44). His purpose
in them was still unfulfilled, His promises respecting the Messiah
and His kingdom were not withdrawn, and He continued to accept
their worship. But He Himself was no more reigning at Jerusalem;
the Visible Glory no more dwelt between the cherubim; the Ark was
not in the Most Holy Place; the holy fire no longer burned upon the
brazen altar; there was no response by Urim and Thummim. The
people might return, as they did from Babylon, the temple be
rebuilt, the worship again set up; yet there was a change. They came
back from their first exile and dispersion, but no more to be an independent nation. To their original standing as the theocratic
people under His immediate rule, they were not restored . . . This
cannot be till the Lord their God again dwells among them, and
rules them through His King of the House of David, in truth and
righteousness."[6]

[5] *The Jewish War*, V, v. 5.
[6] *God's Revelations of Himself to Men* (New York: Scribner's Sons, 1886), pp.
112-113.

4. *The Transfer of Political Supremacy to Gentile Power*

The children of Israel shall abide many days without a king.
—*Hos. 3:4*

A careful comparison of the events closely associated with the departure of the Shekinah-Glory from Jerusalem will show that we have here one of the most important milestones in all of human history. From the initial coming of the Glory at Sinai to its departure from Jerusalem, the Mediatorial Kingdom had endured for approximately eight centuries. During that long period the power and authority of the Theocracy was never in question. No nation, regardless of its size or strength, could stand successfully against Israel as long as that people followed the will of its divine King. Even their defeats because of sin were an evidence of the supernatural supremacy of this tiny nation; something which was never in serious dispute, from the miraculous destruction of the Egyptian armies in the Red Sea down to the disaster suffered by the Assyrian host at the hand of the angel of the Lord. Israel went down in defeat only when she turned aside from the divinely written charter of her kingdom. And even then there was always a gracious restoration of supremacy when the nation came back to the path of God. But now under Zedekiah, last reigning king in Jerusalem, the cup of Israel's iniquity was filled up "till there was no remedy" (II Chron. 36:11-16). The end came quickly, indicated by at least three significantly related events, all occurring in the short space of about ten years. These events, with their approximate dates, are as follows:

First, in 603 B.C. we have the divinely authorized *transfer of world supremacy to Gentile power*. The record of this transfer is found in the second chapter of the Book of Daniel. Here we have the dream of Nebuchadnezzar which, according to the inspired interpretation of Daniel, indicates that political supremacy is being committed to Gentile empire of which Babylon is the first and golden head (vs. 38). After Babylon there will come three other Gentile empires in unbroken succession, the last to endure down to the end when once more the "God of heaven" will establish the Mediatorial Kingdom on earth, never again to be interrupted (vs. 44). This transfer of political supremacy furnishes the immediate background of the next events.

Second, in 597 B.C. the prophet Jeremiah pronounces *the divine ban putting an end to the Solomonic family succession* on the throne of Israel. The record of this important event appears in Jeremiah 22:24-30. It is directed against "Coniah the son of Jehoiakim," who is known in Scripture by two other names: "Jeconiah" (Jer. 24:1) and "Jehoiachin" (II Kings 24:6). Although Zedekiah succeeded this man after he had been carried away captive to Babylon (II Kings 24:11-20), Jehoiachin was very probably the last *living* ex-king of Judah, for he is seen in the court of Babylon thirty-seven years later (Jer. 52:31-34). It was during his brief reign of "three months" in Jerusalem (II Kings 24:8) that Jeremiah was sent to pronounce the doom of his royal family line. It was an utterance of great solemnity and addressed to the entire world as a message of universal interest and concern:

> O earth, earth, earth,
> Hear the word of the LORD.
> Thus saith the LORD,
> Write ye this man childless,
> A man that shall not prosper in his days:
> For no man of his seed shall prosper,
> Sitting upon the throne of David,
> And ruling any more in Judah (22:29-30).

In Jehoiachin the failure of the family of Solomon became complete, and no man of his "seed" shall ever again sit on the throne of David. As a matter of historical fact, Jehoiachin was not "childless." After being carried away into Babylon, he had a son through whom the family line finally culminated in *Joseph,* the husband of the Virgin Mary (Matt. 1:12-16). But our Lord Jesus Christ was not the "seed" of Joseph; He was the seed of Mary, who was descended from David through Nathan (Luke 3:31), not through Solomon. Hence, it is correct to say that Jehoiachin was to be *written* "childless," that is, in the genealogical register of the royal family line.

Finally, following close on the transfer of world supremacy to Gentile power and the divine judgment ending the Solomonic family succession, *the Mediatorial Kingdom of Israel was officially terminated by the departure of the Shekinah-Glory,* dated by Ezekiel in "the sixth year" of the captivity of Jehoiachin (8:1 with 1:2). This was very probably the year 591 B.C. And it should be noted that although the great prophet Jeremiah was in the city of Jerusalem at the time, the vision of the departing Glory was given to a prophet who was a *captive outside* the city and the land of the historical kingdom. It may be significant that immediately following the vision which he recorded in chapter 11, Ezekiel refers to Zedekiah as "the *prince* in Jerusalem" (12:10, italics added). Since the kingdom of the Old Testament was finished, in the mind of the prophet there could be no *king* in Jerusalem until the kingdom would be finally re-established in Millennial glory. In the long interim, political world supremacy has passed by divine decree into the hands of Gentile power, yet never wholly independent of that providential control which is being exercised by the never-ceasing Universal Kingdom of God.

5. A Comforting Prediction of Better Days

> I will sift the house of Israel among all nations . . . yet shall not the least grain fall upon the earth. —*Amos 9:9*

In the midst of the melancholy vision given to Ezekiel concerning the end of the Old Testament kingdom, the prophet was authorized to say that God will be a refuge to Israel even during the long period of her captive and dispersed condition, "Thus saith the Lord God; Although I have cast them far off among the heathen, and although I have scattered them among the countries, yet will I be to them as a *little sanctuary* in the countries where they shall come" (Ezek. 11:16, italics added). The original word rendered "little" in this passage may refer to either time or degree. Against Ellicott and Lange, I feel that the idea of *degree* better fits the context. The temple in Jerusalem is being abandoned by Jehovah, and with the city it will soon be destroyed; but scattered Israel will be compensated to some degree by God's presence and help for the elect remnant through the long centuries of dispersion until the Kingdom is restored and the outcasts are regathered back in the promised land to worship once more in the final temple at Jerusalem (Ezek. 11:17). This comforting promise, however, is not something wholly apart from moral and spiritual considerations. If God will continue to be a "little sanctuary" to scattered Israel, it is also true that He will also be to many in the nation a "stone of stumbling" and a "rock of offence" (Isa. 8:14).

That the blessing of God would in some degree continue to rest upon the nation, even after the end of the Theocratic Kingdom, is evidenced by God's command through Haggai to rebuild the temple (2:1-4). For their encouragement, two motives were set before the people: first, the Mosaic Covenant still holds good (2:5); second, there is the prospect of a future Millennial Temple which will surpass in glory any building in the past (2:6-9).

Furthermore, to the same prophet who saw the departure of the Glory and the end of the Kingdom in Old Testament history, the Lord graciously gave a vision of the future return of the same Glory (Ezek. 43:1-7). Just as Ezekiel had seen the Glory of God leaving by way of "the door of the east gate" (10:19), even so likewise he describes the final return of the Glory: "And the glory of the LORD came into the house by way of the gate whose prospect is toward the east" (43:2,4). As to the general meaning of all this there can be no misunderstanding — the Glory of Jehovah will return to the Jewish temple; the Kingdom of God will again be established on earth; the temple will again be built in the city of Jerusalem. *Here,* the Word of God declares, is "the place of my throne . . . where I will dwell in the midst of the children of Israel for ever" (43:7). And if historically the final glimpse of the departing Glory was "upon the mountain which is on the east side of the city" (11:23), even so the same Glory shall be seen at last returning in the Person of the Messianic King: "His feet shall stand in that day upon the mount of Olives, which is before Jerusalem on the east . . . And the LORD shall be king over all the earth" (Zech. 14:4,9).

Conclusion

In closing this discussion, the question might properly be raised: Why did the Mediatorial Kingdom of history deteriorate and apparently fail? Space will not permit any venture to answer this question fully, but at least two factors can be mentioned:

First, there was a *lack of spiritual preparation on the part of the people.* No government can wholly succeed unless there exists a sufficiently large body of its citizens who are in inward harmony with its constitution and laws. Men are constantly in danger of forgetting the importance of this political principle. To cite a rather recent instance: Many of the American people who helped to pass the 18th Amendment, because they felt sincerely that such a law would be beneficial to the nation, were nevertheless not personally in favor of it for themselves. And so the inevitable result was dismal failure and repeal. Certainly, I am not suggesting any possibility of an ultimate failure of the government of God. But even in the Kingdom of God, the citizens are not all robots to be controlled mechanically and externally by irresistible divine power. There is a better way.

A second defect in the Old Testament Kingdom was *the imperfection of the rulers through whom the government of God was mediated.* It is an axiom of political science that no government in the long run can be more perfect than its rulers. Certainly, it should not be necessary here to review the sorry record of even the best of Israel's rulers: Moses who spoke intemperately and unadvisedly at the waters of Meribah; David with his appalling double crime against society and God; Solomon with his final violation of the most important regulations for the king under the mediatorial economy. And, apart from violent revolution, any lasting reform in government must always start at the top. That is doubtless one reason why the prophet Daniel, who knew a thing or two about government and rulers, thus made his confession for his nation: "O LORD, to us belongeth confusion of face, to our kings, to our princes, and to our fathers, because we have sinned against thee" (9:8).

But over against the darkness of failure on the part of both rulers and the people in the Old Testament kingdom, the prophets spoke of a future and better age when the two defects stated above would be remedied. First, it will be an age when the laws of the Kingdom will be written in the very hearts of its citizens by the Spirit of God (Jer. 31:33); and second, an age when the mediatorial ruler of the Kingdom will be God's own Messianic King; perfect in His character, wisdom, and ways (Isa. 11:1-4).

This means, of course, that the future independence and success of the Jewish State is inseparably bound up with the *divine* re-establishment of the Kingdom of God on earth by supernatural means. The Maccabees made one of the most desperate and heroic attempts in all recorded history to re-establish the independency of the Jewish State, and failed in the end. All other attempts, through political and military means alone, must likewise fail. In its finality and fullness, this must wait for a supernatural intervention on the part of God in human affairs, just as the Kingdom originally began in history with such an intervention in Egypt and at the mount of Sinai. "The children of Israel shall abide many days without a king" (Hos. 3:4). But during the "many days" of waiting, there is always the blessed promise of God through Isaiah: "Say to them that are of a fearful heart, Be strong, fear not: behold, your God will come with vengeance, even God with a recompence; he will come and save you" (35:4).

PART THREE

THE MEDIATORIAL KINGDOM
IN OLD TESTAMENT PROPHECY

I hold for a most infallible rule in expositions of the Sacred Scriptures, that where a literal construction will stand, the furthest from the letter is commonly the worst. There is nothing more dangerous than this licentious and deluding art, which changes the meaning of words, as alchemy doth, or would do, the substance of metals, making it anything what it pleases, and bringing in the end all truth to nothing. —*Richard Hooker*

PART THREE

THE MEDIATORIAL KINGDOM IN OLD TESTAMENT PROPHECY

Chapter XII

INTRODUCTION

A prophet was certainly no fanatic, so that we could say, these are beautiful dreams . . . . The prophet here promises a new age, in which the patriarchal measure of human life will return, in which death will no more break off the life that is just beginning to bloom, and in which the war of man with the animal world will be exchanged for peace without danger. And when is all this to occur? Certainly not in the blessed life beyond the grave, to which it would be both absurd and impossible to refer these promises, since they presuppose a continued mixture of sinners with the righteous, and merely a limitation of the power of death, not its utter destruction. But when then? This question ought to be answered by the antimillenarians . . . . No interpretation of prophecy on sound principles is any longer possible from the standpoint of an orthodox antichiliasm, inasmuch as the antichiliasts twist the word in the mouths of the prophets, and through their perversion of Scripture shake the foundations of all doctrines, every one of which rests upon the simple interpretation of the words of revelation.
                                                        —*Franz Delitzsch*[1]

The field of Old Testament prophecy is not only the largest but also in certain respects the most important area in the entire investigation of the future Mediatorial Kingdom of God. Therefore, by way of introduction, something should be said regarding the nature, interpretation, and extent of Kingdom prophecy.

1. *The Nature of Kingdom Prophecy*

In the third year of Cyrus king of Persia a thing was revealed unto Daniel, whose name was called Belteshazzar; and the thing was true, but the time appointed was long.   —*Dan. 10:1*

a. *Prophecy and History*

Viewed from one standpoint, prophecy arises out of a definite historical situation existing immediately before the eyes of the prophet. There is probably no exception to this rule. No matter how far into the future he was transported in vision, the prophet never lost his contact with history. He never forgot *where* he was, nor the people to whom he was sent to speak on behalf of God. Even in purely predictive prophecy, or what some have called apocalyptic

---

[1] Keil and Delitzsch, *Commentary on Pentateuch,* trans. James Martin (Grand Rapids: Eerdmans Publishing Co., reprint, 1949), Vol. II, p. 492.

vision, although the prophet may say little or nothing about the immediate historical situation, it is nevertheless not forgotten but furnishes the background of all that he has to say with reference to the future. In his vision of the coming Kingdom, the seer never cut loose entirely from the kingdom of history.

Consider, for example, the Book of Daniel which has been called the Apocalypse of the Old Testament. Here all the glorious pictures of the future Kingdom appear against the historical darkness of the Babylonian Captivity. Even when the prophet enters the field of eschatological chronology, measuring the time-distance "unto the Messiah the Prince" in terms of sabbatical years (9:24-27), the chapter begins with a reference to a former prophetic chronology which was even then being fulfilled in God's judgment on the historical kingdom: "In the first year of Darius," the prophet writes, "I Daniel understood by books the number of the years, whereof the word of the LORD came to Jeremiah the prophet, that he would accomplish seventy years in the desolations of Jerusalem" (Dan. 9:1-2). And from this very substantial point in history the prediction looks forward to another measure of "seventy" time-periods which will reach the Messianic Kingdom of the future (9:24).

There is no such thing as Biblical prophecy *totally* unrelated to history. As Murphy has correctly said, "All prophecy . . . starts from present things."[2] Thus Biblical prophecy, rightly understood, furnishes the integrating revelation without which there can be no true philosophy of history. And, apart from such revelation, history falls into a loose aggregation of events which may mean all things to all men, depending on the interpretative principle with which the investigator begins.

b. *Prophecy and Time Perspective*

Sometimes prophecies of the Kingdom have what has been called a "double reference," but which might be more accurately called a "telescopic" character. As Delitzsch has written, "All prophecy is complex, i.e., it sees together what history outrolls as separate: and all prophecy is apotelesmatic, i.e., it sees close behind the nearest-coming, epoch-making turn in history, the summit of the end."[3] In other words, somewhat as a picture lacks the dimension of depth, the prophecy often lacks the dimension of time: events appear together on the screen of prophecy which in their fulfilment may be

---

[2] Francis Murphy, *Commentary on Genesis* (Edinburgh, 1864), p. 507.
[3] Herzog's *Realencyklopädie*, III, p. 226. Quoted from Nathaniel West, *Thousand Years in Both Testaments* (Chicago: Fleming H. Revell, 1889), p. 206.

widely separated in time. Thus the student may find a prophecy having all the external marks of literary unity, yet referring to some event in the *near* future connected with the historical phase of the Kingdom and also to some *far-off* event connected with the Messiah and His Millennial Kingdom. When the first event arrives, it becomes the earnest and divine forecast of the more distant and final event. An excellent example may be found in Isaiah 13:17-14:4, a prediction which begins with the defeat of Babylon by the Medes and moves from that point immediately to a Babylon of the end-time, "in the day" when Israel is finally delivered from "sorrow" and "fear" and "hard bondage" (14:3). The first part of the prediction soon became a fact in ancient history. The latter is even today a future event. The same phenomenon may be observed in prophecies of the coming of the Messianic King, which the New Testament "outrolls" into two advents greatly separated in time. Such a view of prophecy does not mean any abandonment of its literality, as some have argued. The double prediction is literal, and is to be literally fulfilled: The Medes have destroyed historic Babylon, and God will also literally destroy a future Babylon. Christ has come once literally, and He will again break into the stream of history with no less literality.

All this leads to a most crucial point: Although certain areas of the future are definitely clocked as to time sequence and extent, we shall find in Old Testament prophecy *no absolutely continuous and unbroken chronology of the future.* The prophets often saw together on the screen of revelation certain events which in their fulfilment would be greatly separated by centuries of time. This characteristic, so strange to Western minds, was in perfect harmony with the Oriental mind which was not greatly concerned with continuous chronology. And the Bible, humanly speaking, is an Oriental book. The unyielding determination of numerous commentators to pour the events of Old Testament prophecy into a rigid mould of unbroken time, has led to disastrous results. On the one hand, it has opened the way for the date-setters with their endless and often curious attempts to articulate Biblical predictions with historical events. But worse than that, it has led directly to a scheme of interpretations (to be discussed below) which is the main foundation of highly erroneous eschatological systems. Take, for example, the anti-millennial approach to such a passage as Isaiah 9:6-7 which in part reads: "For unto us a child is born, unto us a son is given: and the government shall be upon his shoulder. . . . Of the increase of his govern-

ment and peace there shall be no end, upon the throne of David."
Now the normal and natural sense here should be perfectly obvious:
A Child will be born, and He will reign universally upon the throne
of David. And so we begin our interpretation with a literal child
and a literal birth. But now consider what happens if an unbroken
mould of continuous time is clamped on the prophecy. Because the
regal Child did not *immediately* take the literal throne of David to
rule the world, it is argued that such a thing will *never* come to pass.
And then, to preserve the assumption of unbroken time-sequence
which cannot allow room for any literal fulfilment of the second
part of the prophecy at some future time, the throne of David on
earth is changed into the throne of God in heaven, and Messiah's
reign is reduced to the "influence of the Gospel" or the rule of God
in the "hearts of men."

The prophets sometimes saw future events not only *together;* but
in expanding their description of these events, they seem occasionally
to *reverse* the time sequence in their record of the vision. An example of this may be seen in Isaiah 65:17-25, which opens with a
divine announcement: "For, behold, I create new heavens and a new
earth." Then follows a remarkable picture of millennial bliss which
clearly is *on earth.* Children are born, men plant and build, long
life is restored, and the race is in large measure delivered from the
ordinary hazards of human life. Yet it appears that both sin and
death are still possibilities, even in this glorious age. Now over in
the New Testament, the Apostle John is found using the very words
of Isaiah's prophecy: "And I saw," he writes, "a new heaven and
a new earth" (Rev. 21:1). The description which follows, however,
is unmistakably a record of things in the eternal state where all sin
and death have been abolished (21:3-8). It is apparent, therefore,
that Isaiah saw *together* on the screen of prophecy both the Millennial Kingdom and the Eternal Kingdom; but he expands in detail the
former because it is the "nearest-coming" event and leaves the latter
for fuller description in a later New Testament revelation.

Dunlop Moore, commenting on Isaiah 65:17, supports the viewpoint set forth above: "The proper view then of verse 17 is to
take its prediction literally, and to hold at the same time that in the
following description [which is that of the millennium] future
things are presented to us which are really prior, and not posterior
to the promised complete renovation of heaven and earth. Nor
should this surprise us, as Isaiah and the other prophets place closely
together in their pictures future things which belong to different

times. They do not draw the line sharply between this world and the next. Compare Isaiah's prophecy of the abolition of death (xxv. 8) in connection with other events that must happen long before that state of perfect blessedness."[4]

2. The Interpretation of Kingdom Prophecy

And beginning from Moses and from all the prophets, he interpreted to them in all the scriptures the things concerning himself.
—Luke 24:27, ASV

Without giving room here for the many individual variations, I have reduced the important methods, now current, to three, which I have named the *literal,* the *eclectical,* and the *critical.* I am well aware of the inadequacy and even danger of mere names. At best they can only supply partial meanings, and at their worst they may open semantic paths to total misrepresentations. Therefore, the reader should feel at liberty to improve upon the names suggested. But, as I am in the habit of cautioning my students, let the reader be sure that his are better than mine.

a. The Literal Method

Probably this method has never been stated better than by Ellicott: "The true and honest method of interpreting the Word of God [is] *the literal, historical and grammatical.*"[5] This method, as its adherents have explained times without number, leaves room for all the devices and nuances of language, including the use of figure, metaphor, simile, symbol, and even allegory. In their criticism of this literal method, most of its critics have been guilty of a "crasser literalism" than ever used by any reputable adherent to the method in its application to the Word of God.[6] Certainly the literal method is not without its problems, but these problems are only such as naturally arise out of the nature of human language. Basically the method is extremely simple. For example, the 72nd Psalm speaks of the Messianic King as follows: "He shall come down like rain upon the mown grass" (vs. 6). Here we have a literal coming — the LORD "shall come down." Also the effect of His coming is literal, although in this case it is described by a simile — "*like* rain upon the mown grass" (italics added). Those who

---

[4] Dunlop Moore, trans. and ed. of C. W. E. Naegelsbach's "Isaiah," *Lange's Commentary* (New York: Scribner's Sons, 1878), p. 713.

[5] "Aids to Faith," Essay 9, quoted in G. N. H. Peters' *The Theocratic Kingdom of Our Lord Jesus,* Vol. I, p. 66.

[6] See Wyngaarden's curious obsession with a figurative expression in Isa. 11:14, "fly upon the shoulders of the Philistines," to which he adverts four times in a brief chapter of only twelve pages. *The Future of the Kingdom* (Grand Rapids: Baker Book House, 1955), Ch. VII.

have seen the glorious effect of a summer shower coming down on a field of grass which has been cut will have some idea of what the literal effect of our Lord's coming will be upon a troubled world. Of course, if one wishes to depart from simple common sense, he might say that in this text "grass" stands for the church at Pentecost; "mown" stands for the unsanctified state of the disciples upon that occasion; and the "rain" stands for the gift of the Holy Spirit. Once launched on the sea of conjecture, it is not surprising that interpreters finally arrive at strange ports, as far removed from reality as the popular "beautiful isle of somewhere."

There are many instances of prophetical reference to literal things which are embellished with figurative expressions. In Isaiah 11:1 the coming King of the Kingdom is spoken of as a "rod" and a "Branch," but the King is a very literal person, a descendant of a literal Jewish ancestor, "Jesse." Again, in Isaiah 55:12-13, the hills "break forth . . . into singing," and the "trees . . . clap their hands." Such language, read in its context, can mislead no one with an ordinary amount of intelligence. It pictures the joy of nature over its literal deliverance from a very literal curse imposed by a literal God on a literal earth (Gen. 3:17-19). But. now at last, under the beneficent rule of the "Branch" out of Jesse, "Instead of the thorn shall come up the fir tree, and instead of the brier shall come up the myrtle tree" (Isa. 55:13). That these predictions refer to literal things is confirmed by the Apostle Paul who saw in Jesus the literal "seed of David" (Rom. 1:3) and looked forward to that glad day when even a groaning nature shall be literally delivered from its present unhappy state along with the "redemption of our body" through a literal resurrection (Rom. 8:18-23).

In a comparatively recent book written by Dr. Oswald T. Allis under the title *Prophecy and the Church*,[7] the author in the course of his anti-millennial argument makes a curious attack upon the literal method of prophetical interpretation. First he criticizes severely some premillennial writers for being more concerned about "typical interpretation" than about the Old Testament history from which the alleged types are gathered. This criticism might well be taken to heart by all premillennialists. But then Dr. Allis goes on to complain that, "If Ruth can give 'a foreview of the Church,' if 'the larger interpretation' of the Song of Solomon concerns the Church, why must the Church be absent from the glorious visions

---

[7] (Philadelphia: Presbyterian and Reformed Publishing Co., 1945).

of Isaiah?" (p. 24). Now it is hard for me to believe that the very able and intelligent writer of these words does not know exactly what he is doing, even though a careless reader might miss the point. Reduced to a simple statement, his argument is that if premillennialists are willing to take Old Testament *history* typically, they should not object to the taking of Old Testament *prophecy* typically. "In dealing with prophecy," Dr. Allis writes, the premillennial "treatment is marked by a literalism which refuses to recognize types" (p. 23). This seems to Dr. Allis "strikingly inconsistent" on our part (p. 24).

As a matter of fact, the inconsistency is in Dr. Allis and his fallacious argument. Our answer is as follows: First, premillennialists take *both* history and prophecy literally. We may indeed, within proper limits, find in history certain types and shadows of things to come, but no one among us in his right senses ever questions the literality of the history. But what about the author of *Prophecy and the Church?* Well, Dr. Allis accepts the history as literal, but denies the literality of the *prophecy*, at least in certain areas of the Old Testament, and insists that a typical interpretation is the *only* one! If Dr. Allis were as willing to accept the literality of Old Testament prophecy as he is of its history, I for one would raise no serious objection if he should find some legitimate "types" in both. I would insist, however, that just as in any proper interpretation of Old Testament *history* Joseph is always Joseph and not Christ, even so in *prophecy* Israel is always Israel and never the Church. This does not mean that the preacher may never take a *prophecy* concerning Israel and *apply* it to the Church. But he should always know what he is talking about, and make certain that his hearers know, so that there can be no possible confusion between the history and its typical application, or between a prophecy and any so-called "typical interpretation."

There is, after all, a fundamental difference between Biblical history and prophecy which must not be overlooked. *History* deals with a literal event, which may or may not be a type pointing to some future event. Thus a type seems to be always prophetic in nature. As the late Dr. William G. Moorehead once wrote, "A type always prefigures something future. A Scriptural type and a predictive prophecy are in substance the same, differing only in form."[8]

[8] "Type," *International Standard Bible Encyclopedia* (Chicago: Howard-Severance, 1915), Vol. V, p. 3029.

On the other hand, *prophecy* (predictive) deals directly with the future reality. To talk about a "typical interpretation" of prophecy, therefore, is something like saying that prophecy should be interpreted prophetically, or that types should be interpreted typically! Perhaps it would help to clear the air if we could get rid of all the adjectives and simply use the term "interpretation" alone in its first and original sense, "to give the meaning of." We could then go on from there and talk about other things, such as types and applications. This is what we mean by literal interpretation.

Admitting the homiletical validity of so-called "spiritual application," it should be observed that such applications acquire special force when the basis is found in some *concrete fact which is literally true.* In opposition to this universally accepted pedagogical principle, certain schools of current theology are telling us that the "spiritual" values of early Old Testament history are not impaired even if we regard the recorded events as mythological instead of literal. More than that, they argue, to literalize the stories of Creation and the Fall may largely obscure their spiritual values. Now certainly Dr. Allis and his anti-millennial school would never accept this modern dictum. Yet their own scheme of interpreting certain areas of Old Testament prophecy is crippled with the same hermeneutical infirmity. The literal sense, they argue, is actually detrimental; the sole value in the prophecy is to be found in its "typical" or "spiritual" interpretation. Such a method is both narrow and pedagogically unsound. In opposition to this one-sided anti-millennial scheme, the premillennial method pays some regard to both the *literal* and *typical* (or *symbolical*) values of prophecy. Furthermore, it argues on sound pedagogical principles that literality best preserves and enhances the symbolical values.

b. *The Eclectical Method*

This is sometimes called the "spiritual" method, for the reason that "spiritualizing" is its most distinctive feature. The great Church Father Origen is generally regarded as the originator of this method, although in his better moments he insisted on "an exact grammatical interpretation of the text as the basis of all exegesis."[9] Origen was a Platonist in philosophy, which explains much in his theology. In his hands the spiritualizing method of Biblical interpretaton became a useful tool in opposing the doctrine of a literal millennial rule of

9 "Origen," *New Schaff-Herzog Encyclopedia of Religious Knowledge*, ed. D. M. Jackson (New York: Funk and Wagnalls, 1910), Vol. VIII, p. 272.

Christ on earth, something which no consistent Platonist could possibly accept.

The term "spiritual" should be rejected, I feel strongly, as a proper name for the anti-literal method of interpretation, for at least two reasons: First, the word is much too fine to be surrendered without protest for wrong uses. Second, no one of any consequence was ever known to employ the "spiritualizing" scheme consistently and exclusively. For example, Dr. Shedd speaks disparagingly of what he calls "the blooming age of Millenarianism," and finds that this age was mainly caused by the adoption of "the literal interpretation of the Old Testament prophecies as opposed to the spiritual method."[10] But it must be said to the credit of this able scholar that he himself did not use the "spiritualizing" method exclusively, not even in his approach to Old Testament prophecy. He only resorted to it under the spell of his very narrow and inadequate notions about the Kingdom. At other times in his Biblical interpretations Dr. Shedd became just as literal as the "literalists" whom he criticizes. Doubtless we should thank God that not all men are logically consistent in holding their erroneous opinions. What can happen when men cut loose from literality may be seen in Gregory the Great's exposition of the Book of Job, where we learn that the patriarch's three friends denote the heretics; his seven sons are the twelve apostles; his seven thousand sheep are God's faithful people; and his three thousand hump-backed camels are the depraved Gentiles![11]

As a matter of fact, in contrasting the anti-millennial and premillennial methods of Biblical interpretation, the term "literal" is in some respects about as unsatisfactory as is the term "spiritual." For even spiritual things are literal; actually, they are the most literal of all facts in the entire realm of reality. But these terms have become so embedded in the discussion of Biblical interpretation, that any effort to get rid of them would be in vain. In this connection, I know of nothing more pertinent than the suggestions made by E. R. Craven, able editor of Lange's *Commentary on Revelation*:

> No terms could have been chosen more unfit to designate the two great schools of prophetical exegetes than *literal* and *spiritual*. These terms are not antithetical, nor are they in any proper sense significant

[10] W. G. Shedd, *A History of Christian Doctrine* (Edinburgh: T. and T. Clark, 1872), Vol. II, p. 392.

[11] Even the spiritualizers have their doubts at times; e.g., G. Vos: "It is possible to go too far. . . . We may not dissolve everything into inward processes and mental states, as modern theologians do when they say that heaven and hell are in the hearts of men" (*The Kingdom and the Church* [Grand Rapids: Eerdmans Publishing Co., 1951], p. 43).

of the peculiarities of the respective systems they are employed to characterize. They are positively misleading and confusing. *Literal* is opposed not to *spiritual* but to *figurative; spiritual* is in antithesis on the one hand to *material,* on the other to *carnal* (in a bad sense). The *Literalist* (so called) is not one who denies that *figurative* language, that *symbols,* are used in prophecy, nor does he deny that great *spiritual* truths are set forth therein; his position is, simply, that the prophecies are to be *normally* interpreted (i.e. according to the received laws of language) as any other utterances are interpreted—that which is manifestly literal being regarded as literal, that which is manifestly figurative being so regarded. The position of the Spiritualist (so called) is not that which is properly indicated by the term. He is one who holds that whilst certain portions of the prophecies are to be *normally* interpreted, other portions are to be regarded as having a *mystical* (i.e., involving some secret meaning) sense. Thus, for instance, Spiritualists (so called) do not deny that when the Messiah is spoken of as "a man of sorrows and acquainted with grief," the prophecy is to be *normally* interpreted; they affirm, however, that when He is spoken of as coming "in the clouds of heaven" the language is to be "spiritually" (mystically) interpreted . . . . The terms properly expressive of the schools are *normal* and *mystical.*[12]

It should be clear, however, that regardless of the terms chosen to designate the anti-millenarian scheme of prophetical interpretation, it is a combination of two different systems, shifting back and forth between the spiritualizing and literal methods. The hermeneutical plow is pulled by "an ox and an ass." For this reason, the scheme may appropriately be called *eclectical.*

c. *The Critical Method*

Adherents of this method regard the Bible for the most part as a collection of human writings setting forth the religious experiences of men in their search for God. Since it was written by men, they argue, the Bible should be treated somewhat like other books written by men. Feeling no compulsion to defend any particular doctrine of Biblical inspiration or infallibility, they move through the Biblical literature dropping burning matches anywhere and everywhere regardless of what may be burned up. The one good thing in this attitude is that *the Bible is permitted to speak for itself literally.* But if the Bible says something which to these men seems to contradict history or science, so much the worse for the Bible. They simply reject what it says.

This rejection was accomplished in two ways. The more radical critics, on the *a priori* assumption that true prediction is impossible, arbitrarily rearranged the historical order of Biblical authorship. According to this scheme, the "prophecy" was always written after the event. The actual writer (generally unknown) simply made a

[12] Lange's *Commentary on Revelation,* trans. E. Moore (New York: Scribner's Sons, 1874), p. 98, footnote.

literary record of what had already taken place; and, by putting out his writing under the name of some earlier known prophet, the record was given the pseudo character of a prediction. By this device, the critics could accept what the "prophet" wrote as literal history, but at the same time reject it as literal prediction.

A second critical method of rejection is to admit the literal meaning of the prophets but deny, at least in part, its present validity. Among the more moderate adherents to this school of interpretation is the late Dr. A. B. Davidson. He leaves no question whatever about his attitude toward the Old Testament predictions concerning Israel and the coming Kingdom. The problem of interpretation here, he argues, is a "double one." The first question is, What did the prophets mean? "And to this question there can be but one answer," writes Davidson, "*Their meaning is the literal sense of their words*" (italics added). The second question has to do with the fulfilment of this literal meaning. Again, let Dr. Davidson answer in his own words: "There is no question as to the meaning of the Old Testament prophecies; *the question is how far this meaning is now valid*" (italics added).[13] In seeking to determine an answer to this question of present validity, although Davidson feels that the testimony of the Apostle Paul should be considered, it is quite clear that he is not greatly concerned to maintain the complete harmony between the Old and New Testaments. In substance, Davidson seems to reach much the same goal that appears in the "spiritualizing" school of Dr. Allis, only by a different and more forthright road. Although we may regret his lack of concern with reference to Biblical inspiration, at least Davidson's candor is to be commended.

3. The Extent of Kingdom Prophecy

> . . . which God hath spoken by the mouth of all his holy prophets since the world began.   —*Acts* 3:21

In a very real sense, all Messianic prophecy in the Old Testament is Kingdom prophecy. Even those predictions which deal with Messiah's humiliation and sufferings cannot be separated from the context of regal glory. As Archibald M'Caig has rightfully observed concerning the great prophetic period in Old Testament history, "The prophecies all more or less have a regal tint, and the coming one is pre-eminently the coming king."[14]

Generally we may say that Old Testament prophecy of the future

---

[13] "Eschatology," *Dictionary of the Bible*, ed. James Hastings (New York: Scribner's Sons, 1901), Vol. I, p. 737.

[14] "Christ as King," *I.S.B.E., op. cit.*, Vol. III, p. 1802.

Mediatorial Kingdom of God begins with a few scattered references in the Pentateuch; opens up clearly in the records of the historical kingdom, grows in volume and brilliance as the historical kingdom declines, and comes to its close in Malachi.

This material is so extensive that no pretense can be made in this volume to present an exhaustive list of references; nor have I tried to deal with the ideas always in the order of their historical utterance. The plan is to set forth in very much condensed form a series of generalizations, supported by selected but representative material from the inspired text, as space permits. The question before us is, therefore: What do the Old Testament prophets say about the future Kingdom? Whether their conception is identical or not with the Kingdom announced in the Gospel records is a question to be dealt with in a following section of this book.

But it is highly relevant here to observe that perhaps the most important guiding principle suggested by an examination of the Old Testament material is that the Mediatorial Kingdom of the prophets is *one* Kingdom, not two kingdoms. This one Kingdom has various aspects, as we shall see, but these aspects must not be pluralized into different kingdoms, the one *spiritual* and the other *earthly*. There are indeed some references by the prophets to what I have designated the Universal Kingdom of God, as already shown in chapter IV above; but in their predictions of a future *Mediatorial* Kingdom of God, which is the main burden of their message, they contemplate but one indivisible Kingdom.

CHAPTER XIII

THE PROPHETIC KINGDOM AS RELATED TO HISTORY

> Unto thee shall it come, yea, the former dominion shall come, the
> kingdom of the daughter of Jerusalem. —*Micah 4:8, ASV*

According to the Old Testament prophets, the Messianic Kingdom will not only be established in future history but its roots are
anchored in history past. The historical theocracy is to be restored
in a more perfect theocratic kingdom. Although greatly separated in
time, between the two there is no necessary Platonic disconnection, as
some interpreters seem to demand. It is true that the prophets picture the future Kingdom as something which comes down from
heaven, but this does not involve any complete break with what is
historically past. For those whose minds are under the spell of
philosophic dualism this may be a hard saying, but the mystery is no
greater than that of the Person and career of the One who will rule
in the coming Kingdom.

1. *Its Coming King Will Be Related to History*

> In that day will I raise up the tabernacle of David that is fallen.
> —*Amos 9:11*

As to His origin, according to the prophets, the ruler of the future
Mediatorial Kingdom will be a member of the human race (Gen.
3:15); the "seed" of Abraham (Gen. 17:8); of the tribe of Judah
(Gen. 49:10); a "rod" from the family of Jesse (Isa. 11:1); a
"branch" out of the royal line of David (Jer. 23:5); born at the
village of Bethlehem in the land of Palestine (Mic. 5:2); of a
mother who is a Jewish virgin (Isa. 7:14). Thus, on His human
side, the coming King cannot be dissociated from historical persons,
places, and processes. And He will be a person, not merely an
"event."

Furthermore, the dynastic rights of the coming King reach back
into history. He will sit on "the throne of David" (Isa. 9:7), ex-
ecuting "judgment and righteousness in the land" (Jer. 33:15). And
these dynastic rights which attach to the house of David are in-

violable; they cannot be abrogated or transferred: "Thus saith the
LORD; If ye can break my covenant of the day, and my covenant of
the night, and that there should not be day and night in their season;
then may also my covenant be broken with David my servant, that
he should not have a son to reign upon his throne" (Jer. 33:20-21).

Moreover, lest there be some question raised as to the historical
connection between the kingdom of David and the future Kingdom,
the prophet Amos is meticulously careful to establish this very connection: "In that day," saith the LORD, "will I raise up the tabernacle
of David that is fallen . . . and I will raise up his ruins, and I will
build it as in the days of old" (Amos 9:11). Therefore, the dynastic
rights of the future King will constitute a restoration of certain historic rights which in their exercise have been temporarily interrupted
but not extinguished. The rule of Messiah, while something wholly
new and without parallel in all human history, will nevertheless display and maintain an unbroken historic connection with a kingdom
which once existed "in the days of old." This is a Biblical fact
beyond dispute which must be taken into account as a guiding principle in all attempts to understand the Kingdom set forth in Old
Testament prophecy.

2. Its Establishment Will Be Within the Arena of Human History
The LORD of hosts shall reign . . . in Jerusalem.   —Isa. 24:23

The Kingdom will be on *earth*. In the vision of Isaiah the coming
King is seen judging on behalf of the meek of "the earth," smiting
"the earth" with the rod of His mouth; and "the earth" is filled with
the knowledge of the LORD, as the waters cover the sea (11:4, 9).

Its geographical center will be the land of *Palestine*. In the day
when the Messianic King is present and His Kingdom established on
earth, the historic nation of Israel will enjoy the divine promise:
"And they shall dwell in the land that I have given unto Jacob my
servant, wherein your fathers have dwelt; and they shall dwell
therein, even they, and their children, and their children's children
for ever; and my servant David shall be their prince for ever" (Ezek.
37:25).

Its capital will be the city of *Jerusalem*. The divine King "shall
reign in mount Zion, and in Jerusalem" (Isa. 24:23). There the
eyes of men shall see "the king in his beauty" (Isa. 33:17). This
ancient city of hallowed memories will be called "the throne of the
LORD" (Jer. 3:17). As Lange observes on this text, "What the
ark has hitherto been to Jerusalem . . . Jerusalem is now to be to the

nations." In that day of the reign of Messiah, "Out of Zion shall go forth the law, and the word of the LORD from Jerusalem" (Isa. 2:3).

Out of a heart and mind saturated with the writings of the ancient prophets, our Lord formulated the matchless prayer in which the disciples were taught to pray for the coming of God's Kingdom, and this blessed Kingdom would be *"on earth"* (Matt. 6:10, ASV). Commenting on this petition, the late Adolph Saphir, godly and learned Christian Jew, rightly observed that the Kingdom of God must come "On earth, where God has been denied and forgotten; where His honor has been disregarded and His commandments have been transgressed; where nations and kingdoms, instead of seeking His glory and showing forth His praise — have not bowed to His authority and reverenced His law; it is on earth that the Lord shall reign; injustice, cruelty and war shall be banished; and instead of idolatry, selfishness and sin, the fear and love and beauty of God will be manifest. . . . We may not be able clearly to conceive the fulfilment of the predictions concerning this earth during the Christocracy, but our danger does not lie in believing too implicitly or too literally what is written."[1]

3. *Its Favored Nation Will Be the Israel of History*

He that scattereth Israel will gather him.   —*Jer. 31:10*

The prophecies of the future Mediatorial Kingdom are replete with glowing promises made to the Old Testament people of Israel. They are to be made the head over all other nations, both religiously and politically. All their enemies are to be put down. Through them the glorious blessings of the Kingdom will flow out to all the world. As to the existence and reality of these promises, there can be no dispute.

Attempts have been made, however, to deny the historical continuity of the Israel of the future Kingdom with the Israel of Old Testament history. Two hermeneutical schemes have been devised to implement this denial: first, certain of the Old Testament promises to Israel are treated as having been fulfilled in the historic return of the exiles from the Babylonian captivity; and second, those prophetic promises which cannot be thus handled are stripped down to a tenuous "spiritual" content and transferred to another "Israel" having no genuine nexus with the historical nation. Such attempts to

---

[1] *The Lord's Prayer* (Harrisburg: Christian Alliance Publishing Company, no date), p. 193.

eviscerate the promises of God to the Israel of history cannot be sustained in the face of the Biblical testimony. What are the facts?

First, all the prophets unite in a solemn warning that the people of Israel are to be punished for their sins, and that this punishment will involve defeat by their enemies, the loss of their place in the promised land, and dispersal among all the Gentile nations. "Ye shall be plucked from off the land whither thou goest to possess it. And the LORD shall scatter thee among all people, from the one end of the earth even unto the other. . . . And among these nations shalt thou find no ease" (Deut. 28:63-65). Here there can be no question as to identity — this is the Israel of Old Testament history.

Second, during this divinely imposed and world-wide dispersal of Israel, according to the prophets, there will be no absolute break in the historical continuity of the nation. "For I am with thee, saith the LORD, to save thee: though I make a full end of all nations whither I have scattered thee, *yet will I not make a full end of thee:* but I will correct thee in measure, and will not leave thee altogether unpunished" (Jer. 30:11, italics added). "Behold, the eyes of the Lord GOD are upon the sinful kingdom, and I will destroy it from off the face of the earth; *saving that I will not utterly destroy the house of Jacob,* saith the LORD" (Amos 9:8, italics added).

Third, the prophets promise specifically that there will be a restoration of the nation which was once cast off. "For I have mercy upon them," Jehovah declares, "and they shall be as though I had not cast them off; for I am the LORD their God, and will hear them" (Zech. 10:6). "And it shall come to pass, that like as I have watched over them, to pluck up, and to break down, and to throw down, and to destroy, and to afflict; so will I watch over them, to build, and to plant, saith the LORD" (Jer. 31:28).

Fourth, the prophets assert that the promised restoration of historic Israel will involve a regathering of the dispersed nation back into the land from which they were cast out. The Word of God is that He "shall set up an ensign for the nations, and shall assemble the *outcasts* of Israel, and gather together the *dispersed* of Judah from the four corners of the earth" (Isa. 11:12, italics added). "He that scattered Israel will gather him, and keep him, as a shepherd doth his flock" (Jer. 31:10). "The LORD thy God will . . . gather thee from all the nations, whither the LORD thy God hath scattered thee. . . . And the LORD thy God will bring thee into the land which thy fathers possessed, and thou shalt possess it" (Deut. 30: 3, 5).

Fifth, to this same historic nation of Israel, regathered from its world-wide dispersion, there will come a restoration of ancient privileges and rights. In the day of their regathering in the land, to "her that was cast far off," God will speak, "And thou, O tower of the flock, the strong hold of the daughter of Zion, unto thee shall it come, *even the first dominion;* the kingdom shall come to the daughter of Jerusalem" (Mic. 4:7-8, italics added). More than that, the future dominion will surpass all the glories of the past: "I will settle you after your old estates," Jehovah promises, "and will do better unto you than at your beginnings" (Ezek. 36:11).

Sixth, all this will come to pass in what the prophets call *the last days.* This is clearly indicated by the fourth chapter of Micah. The first five verses describe the glories of the LORD's Kingdom which will be established in "the last days," and verse six fixes definitely the regathering and restoration of Israel at that time. Since the phrase "in the last days," as used in the context of Micah 4, certainly refers to eschatological time, the prophecies of Israel's restoration cannot be regarded as fulfilled by any partial restorations in the past.

Seventh, all the prophetic descriptions of historic Israel's future restoration indicate that the restored relation to Jehovah's favor will be something permanent, never again to be interrupted. "The LORD shall reign over them in mount Zion from henceforth, even for ever" (Mic. 4:7). Of this chosen people, finally restored, it is said by the prophet Isaiah, "Thy sun shall no more go down; neither shall thy moon withdraw itself: for the LORD shall be thine everlasting light, and the days of thy mourning shall be ended" (60:20).

The 37th chapter of Ezekiel may well be used to summarize the entire point under discussion. Here the prophet is set down in a valley filled with dry bones and commanded to prophesy to these dead bones. And as he spoke the word of the LORD, the bones came together, flesh and sinew appeared upon them, they stood up a great army, breath came into them, and they lived. The vision is explained by the LORD thus: "These bones are the whole house of Israel," who are to be brought up out of their graves and back into their own historic land (vss. 1-11). Thus the people of Israel, long dispersed and with waning hopes as to the future, will again be made a nation. But this is not enough. The divided people must become *one* nation. To impress upon the prophet this lesson, the LORD commands him to take two sticks, one for Ephraim and one for Judah, and "make them one stick" before the eyes of the people. Then Ezekiel is told to explain the meaning of the symbol: "Thus saith the Lord GOD; Behold, I will take the children of Israel from among the heathen, whither they be gone, and will gather them on every side, and bring them into their own land: And I will make them one nation in the land upon the mountains of Israel; and one king shall be king to them all: and they shall be no more two nations, neither shall they be divided into two kingdoms any more at all" (vss. 21-22). Certainly, in no place throughout this remarkable chapter is there any point where the historical continuity may be broken. To use a modern figure: if anyone should wish to take off on some hermeneutical flight of fancy, he will find himself compelled to land exactly where he took off, or not come down at all. The Old Testament nation of Israel, historically ruptured and scattered among the nations, is the nation which in the prophets is again restored and reunited in the future Kingdom of God.[2]

4. It Will Destroy and Supplant Historical Powers

It shall break in pieces and consume all these kingdoms.—*Dan. 2:44*

In the second and seventh chapters of Daniel there is given a preview of the coming of God's Kingdom in its relation to the governments of men. Although the symbols used are totally different — a great image in chapter 2 and four beasts in chapter 7 — the two visions have certain striking similarities. In each there is presented a succession of four world empires; and in each the fourth empire in its final development consists of a coalition of ten lesser powers. The vision of chapter 7 carries the political development one step further: among the ten powers a notable world ruler emerges who will embody the consummation of all sinful men's efforts at political organization apart from and opposed to God (Dan. 7:20-25).

Now without entering into the arguments about the complete identification of these empires, states, and ruler, at least three things are perfectly clear: first, the symbols employed are intended to represent a succession of political organizations which will appear

---

[2] Some, while flatly denying any historical continuity between the ancient Jewish nation and the Israel of the future Kingdom of God, at the same time feel compelled to admit that, in the Old Testament prophets, there is unmistakable evidence for "belief" in the eternal continuity of the historic royal line (John Bright, *Kingdom of God;* New York: Abingdon-Cokesbury Press, 1953; pp. 87-89). Such an admission, of course, sweeps away all a priori objections to a similar continuance for David's *nation.*

on the stage of *human history;* second, this succession began with the Babylonian Empire, already existing historically when the prophetic visions were given to Daniel. The divine word to King Nebuchadnezzar was: "Thou art this head of gold" (2:38); third, it is in the final stage of this succession of political organizations and rulers that "the God of heaven" will "set up a kingdom, which shall never be destroyed" (2:44).

Now it is deeply significant that in these visions the heavenly Kingdom comes down and destroys and supplants *existing* political powers. By no stretch of hermeneutical imagination can these powers be idealized or reduced to mere intangible evil tendencies. If the first empire is on earth, so are the others. In the succession of powers, beginning with historical Babylon, there is no point where a shift can be made from earth to heaven, from things seen to things unseen. The express language of the passage forbids any such attempt. After allowing the widest possible latitude for the symbolic frame of representation, no fair and consistent interpretation can ignore the unqualified similarity in the descriptions of the rise of these world powers. It is not merely that the divine Kingdom is a fifth and the last in the historical succession beginning with Babylon. But, we are told, just as the fourth power shall *"break in pieces"* the political power it displaces, even so the heavenly Kingdom will *"break in pieces"* the powers which it supplants (Dan. 2:40, 44).[3]

That the force employed by the heavenly Kingdom will be supernatural in origin instead of human, does not alter in the least its tangible effects on the stage of history. Babylon went down before the force of the Medo-Persian armies, and the fourth empire will likewise go down before the force of a heavenly power. If this idea were something wholly new in Biblical history, it might give pause to the interpreter of prophecy concerning the future Kingdom of God. But the historical theocratic kingdom is replete with similar intrusions of supernatural power. The ancient kings of Egypt and Assyria could bear no uncertain testimony as to the reality and effectiveness of the heavy hand of God in the "power politics" of their day. Let the reader recall what happened to Pharaoh and his armies in the Red Sea — "there remained not so much as one of them. . . . and Israel saw the Egyptians dead upon the sea shore." "Thus the LORD saved Israel that day" (Exod. 14:28-30). Or consider the fate of the arrogant Assyrians at a later date — "The angel

---

[3] The verbs are identical in the original.

of the LORD went out, and smote in the camp of the Assyrians an hundred fourscore and five thousand: . . . behold, they were all dead corpses" (II Kings 19:35). In the clear light of history, why should it seem incredible and unworthy for God to do once more — this time universally and permanently — what He has so often done in the past?

5. Its Beneficiaries Will Include Nations of History

In that day . . . . Blessed be Egypt . . . and Assyria . . . and Israel.
—Isa. 19:24-25

As an added argument for the place of the coming Mediatorial Kingdom in human history, it should be observed that the judgment and destruction of existing political powers at the hand of the heavenly King does not necessarily mean the annihilation of the nations involved. Recent history has witnessed in two world wars the destruction of German political forms and military power, but the German *nation* continues under new political forms.

Likewise, the prophets indicate, "many nations" will survive the holocaust of divine judgment on their political systems, but under new and happier forms. There will be humble submission to the "God of Jacob," in whose ways they will walk, and political forms based on military force will be abandoned as of no longer any effective purpose in the face of authority enforced by supernatural power (Mic. 4:1-3). Very significantly, among the nations to be thus favored, special mention is given to Egypt and Assyria, historical foes of the Mediatorial Kingdom of Old Testament history. Of these the divine King will say, "Blessed be Egypt my people, and Assyria the work of my hands, and Israel mine inheritance" (Isa. 19:25).[4] The mention of these nations along with Israel lifts the Old Testament conception of the future Kingdom infinitely above the narrow confines of Jewish rabbinism. What the coming King will be able to do for Egypt and Assyria is a token of the unimaginable reach of His Kingdom, not only in spiritual blessings but also in political and social benefits for a needy and confused world.

6. Its Covenant Basis Is Grounded in History

Then will I remember my covenant with Jacob, . . . with Isaac . . . with Abraham.   —Lev. 26:42

The covenants to be examined here briefly are the Abrahamic, the Mosaic, the Davidic, and the New. The first three are peculiar in

---

[4] Rather strangely, Wyngaarden finds in this favor extended to Egypt and Assyria an evidence that the prophetic Kingdom is wholly "spiritual," and cannot be literal! *Future of the Kingdom* (Grand Rapids: Baker Book House, 1955), pp. 151-153.

that they deal with both history and eschatology. However, since eschatology means simply "last things," and these "things" in Biblical thought are only "last" with reference to human history, it may be clearer to say that the above-named three covenants deal with *both* the Kingdom in Old Testament history and also the Kingdom promised by the prophets in eschatological history. In this respect they differ radically from the "New Covenant" of Jeremiah's prophecy, which is wholly eschatological in its regal sense, having no existence in the Kingdom of Old Testament history.

In considering the three historical covenants I shall depart somewhat from the chronological order, dealing with the Mosaic covenant last because it exhibits one radical difference from the covenants with Abraham and David. Notice will be given only to those features of these covenants which are pertinent to the future Mediatorial Kingdom of God.

a. *The Abrahamic Covenant*

Under the terms of this covenant Abraham was promised certain regal rights and privileges, involving: first, an innumerable progeny through natural generation (Gen. 12:2; 13:16; 15:3-5); second, a guarantee of historical continuity by means of divine protection (Gen. 12:3); third, an everlasting and irrevocable title to a definite land area on earth (Gen. 13:14-17; 15:18; 17:7-8); and, fourth, a final world supremacy through which "great" divine blessings would flow out to all mankind (Gen. 12:2-3).

This Abrahamic covenant was *unconditional* in character. That is, the promises originated wholly in God and were not conditioned upon any meritorious acts on the part of Abraham but were received by him simply by faith. The inspired record states that Abraham "believed in the LORD" and the LORD "counted it to him for righteousness" (Gen. 15:6). This does not mean that *every* individual descended from Abraham will personally share in *all* the blessings promised under the covenant, apart from moral and spiritual considerations. But it does mean that the fulfilment of the promises to *Abraham* is in no sense dependent upon human character or action, but rests upon divine grace and sovereignty, and therefore cannot fail. No matter how bad conditions may become in Israel, and the situation was terrible in the days of Micah, the prophet can bid the nation to remember that Jehovah will "perform the truth to Jacob, and the mercy to Abraham" which He had "sworn unto our fathers from the days of old" (7:18-20).

b. *The Davidic Covenant*

This covenant consisted of a reaffirmation of the regal terms of the original Abrahamic covenant; with the further provision that these covenanted rights will now attach permanently to the historic house and succession of David; and also that by God's grace these rights, even if historically interrupted for a season, will at last in a *future kingdom* be restored to the nation in perpetuity with no further possibility of interruption (II Sam. 7:1-16; 23:1-5; I Chron. 17:1-14).

Here again, as in the case of Abraham, the Davidic covenant is both unconditional and irrevocable, for the one is simply a more detailed extension of certain features of the other. According to the words of the Holy Spirit spoken through King David, who was also a prophet, the divine covenant with him was "an everlasting covenant, ordered in all things, and sure" (II Sam. 23:1-5). It was this historic assurance that, in the face of national failure and calamity, kept the light of hope burning in Israel; so that Isaiah could look back to the "everlasting covenant" given by a sovereign God, "even the sure mercies of David" (55:1-3). The "children" of David might indeed "forsake" the law of God, as they did subsequently over and over — and in that case God would "visit their transgression with the rod" of chastisement — but God's covenant with David "shall stand fast." God has sworn by His own holiness, "I will not lie unto David. His seed shall endure for ever, and his throne as the sun before me" (Ps. 89:20-37). Let the student read Jeremiah 33:15-26 and observe that this irrevocable covenant with David is linked historically to the promises made to the people of "Abraham, Isaac, and Jacob" (vs. 26).

c. *The Mosaic Covenant*

According to the terms of this covenant, the nation of Israel would be established in the promised land, and her regal rights under the Abrahamic covenant would be *exercised there as long as the nation obeyed* the voice of God as expressed in the Mosaic Code of laws (Exod. 19:5-6 ff.). Thus it is clear that we have here a covenant which is *conditional,* that is, dependent for its fulfilment upon the actions of the people. In this respect, the Mosaic covenant is radically different from both the Abrahamic covenant which preceded it and the Davidic covenant which followed it. The terrible curses of divine judgment attached to the Mosaic covenant are wholly absent from the other two.

By no device of interpretation can this Mosaic covenant be precisely equated with the earlier covenant with Abraham. In fact, Moses himself is careful to distinguish between the two: in Deut. 5:2-3 where, referring to the covenant made at "Horeb" (Sinai), he says emphatically, "The LORD made not this covenant with our fathers."[5] In this distinction the whole of New Testament revelation concurs. The Mosaic Law was something "added because of transgressions"; and it cannot "disannul" the promise of the Abrahamic covenant made 430 years before the Mosaic covenant (Gal. 3:17-19). Furthermore, according to the writer of Hebrews, the Mosaic covenant was "ready to vanish away" (8:13). But the Abrahamic covenant will never pass away.

It was precisely this conditional nature of the Mosaic covenant that led to its failure. Since its fulfilment depended on man's complete obedience (Deut. 27:26), it could not succeed. Although its legal requirements were holy and good (Rom. 7:12), it was "weak through the flesh" (Rom. 8:3). That is, the root of the failure was not in the Law but in man. For this reason there had to be a "new covenant" to replace it.

d. *The New Covenant*

Among the several Old Testament passages in which reference is made to this covenant, the most complete account appears in the prophecy of Jeremiah (Chap. 31). A study of this passage reveals a number of things about the New Covenant which are relevant to our study of the Mediatorial Kingdom.

First, the future covenant is "new" only in relation to the Mosaic covenant. In an earlier chapter Jeremiah shows that he is fully aware of the character and the weakness of the latter covenant (11:1-8). It is against this background that the prophet describes the "new covenant." It will not be, God says, "according to the covenant that I made with their fathers in the day that I took them by the hand to bring them out of the land of Egypt" (31:31-32). The New Covenant is never thus set over against the Abrahamic and Davidic covenants, as if they needed to be replaced by something better.

Second, the New Covenant arises out of, and is based on, Jehovah's everlasting love and grace. The announcement of this covenant is

[5] This important text is ignored by some: Dr. Allis, who argues that the two covenants are one and the same, nevertheless does not even list it in his Index to *Prophecy and the Church.* Others pervert its meaning: as Waller in Ellicott's *Commentary.* Keil and Delitzsch rightly say that the two covenants are "essentially distinct" from one another (*in loc.*).

prefaced by these words: "The Lord hath appeared of old unto me, saying, Yea, I have loved thee with an everlasting love: therefore, with lovingkindness have I drawn thee" (Jer. 31:3). This is asserted in the face of Israel's deplorable condition (Jer. 30:12-15), which absolutely precluded any divine favor based on meritorious character or deeds on her part.

Third, the moral problem posed by the failure of the Mosaic covenant will under the New Covenant be met by God's own sovereign grace and power. The regal benefits promised by the Mosaic covenant had been lost because the nation had broken it. But now a "new covenant" will secure these benefits by means which are no longer legally conditioned. The solution of the problem is this, God says, "I will put my law in their inward parts, and write it in their hearts" (Jer. 31:33). By these means the benefits of the Mosaic covenant will be attained, and at the same time its moral requirements will be secured; not as a legal condition of blessing but as its divinely caused result. And the issue will be a new manner of life (vs. 34).[6]

Fourth, the New Covenant, therefore, is in the gracious spirit of the earlier Abrahamic covenant, rather than in the legalistic spirit of the Mosaic covenant which it supplants. It is true that under the latter there was promised divine forgiveness in the case of Israel's failure. But here it is deeply significant that when the sin has been confessed and pardon has been granted, it is not on the basis of any surviving rights in the broken covenant of Sinai but simply because Jehovah remembers His earlier "covenant with Jacob, . . . with Isaac, and . . . with Abraham" (Lev. 26:42). It is on this basis, He reminds the nation, that in spite of all they have done, "neither will I abhor them, to destroy them utterly, and to break my covenant with them: for I am the Lord their God" (Lev. 26:44). Exactly the same idea is expressed by Ezekiel in his reference to the New Covenant: Although the nation had broken the Mosaic covenant, "Nevertheless," God says, "I will remember my covenant with thee in the

---

[6] In his effort to show that all Old Testament covenants are "in reality one and the same covenant," and that under all of them the condition of divine favor is always "obedience," Dr. O. T. Allis seems to put salvation at times on a legal basis. Certainly, obedience is an important matter; there can be no argument on this point. But the real question is, In what theological category shall obedience be placed? Is obedience the essential *result* of salvation, or is it the *procuring* requirement for its reception? In one place Dr. Allis answers this important question as it should be answered—obedience is not a "means" of salvation, but its proper "fruit." But later, in his determination to establish an absolute covenantal unity throughout the Bible, and also to attach the stigma of Antinomianism to his opponents, he becomes theologically confusing, to put the matter as kindly as possible (see his *Prophecy and the Church*, pp. 42, 59).

days of thy youth, and I will establish unto thee an everlasting covenant" (Ezek. 16:59-60). The expression "days of thy youth" fixes definitely the reference to the earlier covenant.

The law of Moses, by sacrifice and Messianic prediction, had indeed "witnessed" (Rom. 3:21) to the future compassion of God extended to a sinful people who deserved nothing; but this mercy goes back for its ultimate ground to Jehovah's sovereign grace as expressed in His covenant with Abraham. In this respect, the New Covenant is totally different from the Mosaic covenant at Sinai. As Dr. C. W. E. Naegelsbach has written: "It is true no legal enactment of the Old Covenant is declared false in the New (Matt. 5: 17-19); it is true that men knew even under the Old Covenant that the law, in order to be fulfilled . . . must be in the heart (Deut. 30:6; Ps. 40:8; Prov. 3:1). But this . . . is quite a different thing from that which Jeremiah means in this passage."[7]

Fifth, the New Covenant and its benefits will be guaranteed by the very order and stability of the created universe. "Thus saith the LORD, which giveth the sun for a light by day, and the ordinances of the moon and of the stars for a light by night. . . . If these ordinances depart from before me. . . . If heaven above can be measured, and the foundations of the earth searched out beneath, I will also cast off all the seed of Israel for all that they have done, saith the LORD" (Jer. 31:35-37). The creation and preservation of order in the universe are matters wholly beyond the control of men, depending on God alone. Even so, the New Covenant rests on what God is and does.

Sixth, according to Jeremiah 31, the New Covenant is *solidly embedded in a historical context.* The people involved is the Israel of history, which had been "scattered" (vs. 10), and whose children shall be gathered again "from the uttermost parts of the earth" (vs. 8, ASV). The *land* to which they are gathered is identified as the ancient "land of Judah" (vs. 23) and the "mountains of Samaria" (vs. 5). The *city* is historic Jerusalem which shall be "built to the LORD from the tower of Hananeel unto the gate of the corner" (vss. 38-40). There is reference also to *other cities* of the historic land which shall exist and be inhabited by worshipers of Jehovah (vss. 23-24). There the chosen people will enjoy once more their historic blessings of "the goodness of the LORD" in "wheat'" and "wine" and "oil" and the "young of the flock" (vss. 12-14).

---

[7] Lange's *Commentary on Jeremiah,* trans. S. R. Asbury (New York: Scribner's Sons, 1870), on 31:33, p. 275.

In concluding our discussion of the relation of the future Mediatorial Kingdom to historical considerations, it should be said that this indubitable relationship goes far toward establishing the literality of the Kingdom of Old Testament prophecy. Although in a real sense an embodiment of the finest ideals and aspirations of men, it is not merely an "ideal" kingdom like the Kantian "kingdom of ends" toward which man must ever strive but never wholly attain. On the contrary, the coming Kingdom will be as concrete and literal in the realm of sense experience as the historical kingdom of Israel or the kingdom of Great Britain today. All prophecy from first to last asserts and implies this genuine tangibility: "Thine eyes shall see the king . . . they shall behold the land" (Isa. 33:17); and "all flesh shall see it together" (Isa. 40:5). While it is true that only the pure in heart will ever see God in a moral and spiritual sense (Matt. 5:8), and there are some things which must by their very nature remain forever invisible even to the pure in heart (I Tim. 6:16), it is nevertheless also true that some of the "invisible things" of God can be made tangibly manifest to the eyes of men, regardless of their moral condition. Because of the derangement caused by sin, men may become vain in their reasonings and arrive at false conclusions, but this cannot erase the tangible facts of divine revelation which "are clearly seen" (Rom. 1:20-22). It is wrong, therefore, in the interest of a purely philosophic "spirituality," to close our eyes to what the Scriptures so unmistakably assert about the future Kingdom of Old Testament prophecy.

Chapter XIV

THE MEDIATORIAL RULER
IN THE PROPHETIC KINGDOM

A Kingdom of God without a King; a Theocracy without the rule of God; a perpetual Davidic Kingdom without a 'Son of David'— these are *antinomies* (to borrow the term of *Kant*) of which neither the Old Testament, the Apocrypha, the Pseudepigraphic writings, nor Rabbinism were guilty.   —*Alfred Edersheim*[1]

In their description of the coming Kingdom, the prophets give first place to its Ruler Himself. This might be otherwise if this Kingdom were merely the consummation of human attempts at social improvement and political organization; for in that case the most important things would be principles, laws, and systems. In all purely mundane schemes we have reached nothing higher and finer than the ideal of government by laws, not by men. For here and now, as Kipling once intimated, "the captains and the kings" are not the most important factors. There is, we like to think, no "indispensable man." It is not so in that future government portrayed by the prophets: There the Ruler Himself *is* the indispensable figure. For this is God's *mediatorial* government, and hence there must be a personal ruler — not merely an organization to stand between God and men. What the world needs, as the prophets saw clearly, is not primarily a better philosophy of government or a more perfect system of legislation, but a *Person* who has the character, wisdom, and power needed to rule for God among men. This is the central theme of prophecy from first to last. The restoration of man's lost dominion must come through a Person — He shall bruise the usurper's head (Gen. 3:15, ASV). It is not to some impersonal organization, but to the "King," that the judgments of God will be committed (Ps. 72:1). "On his shoulder" the government of God must rest (Isa. 9:6). His features are so clearly and completely delineated by the prophets that, although some notable attempts have been made, not one has suc-

[1] Alfred Edersheim, *Life and Times of Jesus the Messiah* (New York: Longmans, Green, and Co., 8th ed., rev., 1912), Vol. I, p. 265.

ceeded in reducing this Messianic ruler to a mere nation, church, principle, movement, or ideal. It would not be wrong to say that, if the coming Biblical Kingdom has any chief glory, its luster is a "borrowed ray" derived from the glorious person of its wondrous King. He is indeed "an *ideal* person": but more than that; He is a "*real* person, in whom all that had been foretold of the Davidic family should, at some future period, find its full realization."[2]

1. The Nature of the Coming Ruler

> A child is born . . . and his name shall be called . . . the mighty God.
> —*Isa. 9:6*

Certain names and titles applied to this future Ruler indicate that He will be both human and divine in nature. Isaiah sees Him reigning in righteousness and names Him "a man" (32:1-2). Daniel, given a vision of the ineffable splendor of the coming Kingdom, describes the King's appearance as "like unto a son of man" (7:13, ASV). Furthermore, many of His experiences, as outlined particularly in Isaiah 53 and Psalm 22, are those which are common to mankind. He is taken "out of the womb" and feeds at His mother's "breasts." He is "acquainted with grief," "wounded" and "bruised": suffers from thirst; and at last comes down "into the dust of death." He is truly a *human* king.

On the other hand, it is equally certain that the coming King is more than a man. In the prophecies of Isaiah He is named "Immanuel," that is, "God with us" (7:14; cf. Matt. 1:23). And in his 9th chapter the prophet crowns Him with an aggregate of titles which, taken together, cannot possibly be emptied of the unmistakable effulgence of divinity: "His name shall be called Wonderful counsellor, Mighty God, Everlasting Father, Prince of Peace" (9:6, ASV margin). In a later chapter, devoted wholly to a description of idyllic conditions which will exist under the future Kingdom, the people who with fearful hearts have waited so long for its coming are assured that One who is "your God will come . . . he will come and save you" (35:4). In that glad day the nation of Israel is called upon to shout and sing because "the King of Israel, even Jehovah, is in the midst of thee; thou shalt not fear evil any more" (Zeph. 3:15, ASV). And Zechariah, in a magnificent description of the Mediatorial Kingdom as it concerns the nations of the earth, affirms that these nations will come up to Jerusalem to "worship the King" whose name is "Jehovah of hosts" (14:16-17, ASV). As to His

[2] E. W. Hengstenberg, *Christology of the Old Testament* (Edinburgh: T. and T. Clark, 1854), New Series, Vol. I, p. 145.

self-identification there can be no question: "Thus saith the LORD the King of Israel, and his redeemer the LORD of hosts; I am the first, and I am the last; and beside me there is no God" (Isa. 44:6).

2. The Origin of the Coming Ruler

> The second man is the Lord from heaven.   —I Cor. 15:47

As might be expected, the paradox of a Ruler who is both human and divine will inevitably present a further paradox in the description of His origin, where we find elements which are both natural and supernatural.

On the one side, He is out of the "womb" of a human mother (Isa. 49:1; cf. vs. 6) and "born" as a child (9:6). The place of His birth is Bethlehem, a minor Judean village (Mic. 5:2). He grows up before the LORD as a "tender plant" (Isa. 53:2). In these respects we have phenomena which might be affirmed of any other child called to a special ministry under God. But in the case of this particular child the so-called "natural" phenomena are produced by supernatural means: as a hopeful "sign" given to the house of David, which was then standing under the threat of historical extinction, the conception of this child will take place in the womb of a woman who is a "virgin" (Isa. 7:14).[3] And Jeremiah, in the central context of a chapter presenting one of the clearest pictures of the Kingdom found in all of Old Testament prophecy, has recorded a prediction which the Christian Church Fathers almost unanimously regarded as a reference to the supernatural origin of the Messianic King: "For the LORD hath created a new thing in the earth, A woman shall compass a man" (31:22).[4]

But above and beyond all the human context of His divinely caused origin on earth, the prophets picture the King as coming gloriously from above. The One to be born in Bethlehem is also the One "whose goings forth have been from of old, from everlasting" (Mic. 5:2). Likewise, in Daniel's vision, He comes "with the clouds of heaven" to receive a kingdom both universal and everlasting (7:13-14). Again and again in the prophetic picture, the King is presented on the stage of human history with no mention whatever of any humanly conditioned origin on earth. Compare such chapters

---

[3] For a brilliant exegetical defense of the traditional Christian interpretation of this text, see Dr. E. J. Young's *Studies in Isaiah* (Grand Rapids: Eerdmans Publishing Co., 1954) pp. 143-198.

[4] For the exegetical arguments, see A. R. Fausset in *Commentary on the Bible* by Jamieson, Fausset and Brown (New York: Geo. H. Doran, no date), p. 539.

as Psalms 2, 45, 72, 110; Joel 3; Micah 4; Zechariah 14; Malachi 3 and 4.

No theological account of the Messianic King, as He is presented in the Old Testament prophets, can be true which fails to give due place to both the human and divine elements in His nature, and also to both the earthly and heavenly aspects of His origination. And in any *seeming* rational conflict between the two ideas, the human and earthly must be controlled by the divine and the heavenly. The Apostle Paul, no superficial scholar in matters of Old Testament prophecy, summarizes the doctrine of its Messianic King in a single pregnant sentence — He is indeed the "second man," the "last Adam"; but above all, this glorious Man is "the Lord from heaven"[5] (I Cor. 15:45-47). Thus the regal Man, who in Pauline theology reveals humanity and Deity indissolubly united in His own Person, must be one who comes down "from heaven."

3. The Character of the Coming Ruler

Behold my servant . . . in whom my soul delighteth.   —*Isa. 42:1*

As we have already noted, at the center of the failure of the Kingdom in Old Testament history the Scriptures place the imperfect character of its mediatorial rulers. Over against this background, dismal at its best, the prophets picture the coming King in sharp contrast. "Righteousness shall be the girdle of his loins, and faithfulness the girdle of his reins" (Isa. 11:5). In the glad day of His arrival, the inhabitants of Zion will sing and shout because "the Holy One" of Israel is in the midst of them (Isa. 12:6). He will be the "servant" of Jehovah, revealing in His character and leadership all the perfections[6] which were so sadly lacking in even the best of former rulers in the historical kingdom.

David in prophetic vision sees this glorious Ruler and describes Him as "the King of glory," ascending the "hill of the LORD," entering through the "everlasting doors," standing in the "holy place." And in distinction from all previous rulers, His regal rights stem not only from the covenants of a God of grace but also from a personal character in which no flaw can be found: He has "clean hands" and a "pure heart"; He has never "sworn deceitfully" (Ps. 24). He loves righteousness and hates wickedness; His chief majesty consists of

---

[5] The words "The Lord" do not appear in the best extant Greek mss., but their omission does not affect the argument. The preposition is *ek*, used here in the sense of "originating from" (T. T. Shore in *Ellicott's Commentary* [Grand Rapids: Zondervan Publishing House, reprint, 1954], *in loc.*).

[6] For these perfections the student should consult chapters 42 through 53 of Isaiah.

"truth and meekness and righteousness" (Ps. 45). If He is hated, it is "without a cause" (Ps. 69:4), for He has "done no violence" and there is no "deceit in his mouth" (Isa. 53:9). Unlike all other kings, He arrives as one needing no salvation for Himself, but "having salvation" for others, sufficient for every need of humanity, whether spiritual or material (Zech. 9:9-11). As Keil interprets the passage: The Messianic King will be "endowed with salvation."[7]

4. The Ability of the Coming Ruler

> He shall not fail. —Isa. 42:4

In matters of government it is never enough to have rulers with high character, good will, and noble intentions. There must be intelligence and wisdom so that men may know *what* needs to be done; also a commensurate ability to carry out the clear mandates of righteousness and wisdom. During those few and very brief seasons when the world of nations has enjoyed some measure of release from serious political and economic problems, the people may be satisfied with rulers who are weak. But in the face of internal distress and external danger, there is always a demand for leaders who are strong. Unhappily at such times, if a choice must be made between righteousness and strength, people may not inquire too closely into the higher virtues of personal character. They are likely to say: give us a man who can get things done. But in the prophetic picture of the coming Kingdom, there is never any compromise in things that matter. There the divine government always represents a perfect balance between righteousness, wisdom, and power. Its Mediatorial Ruler is not only wise and good; He is also *strong*.

On the one hand, He will be great in knowledge, understanding, wisdom, counsel, and the fear of Jehovah; not judging after "the sight of his eyes" nor making decisions "after the hearing of his ears." But with "righteousness shall he judge the poor, and decide with equity for the meek of the earth" (Isa. 11:1-4, ASV). Micah sees Him as a ruler who will stand and rule as a shepherd "in the strength of Jehovah" and be "great unto the ends of the earth" (5:4, ASV).

As for His ability and power, Isaiah pictures Him in figure as a foundation "stone" which is "tried," "precious," and "sure" (28:16). Coming to a world in dire need of strong deeds as well as strong words, He will "speak peace" to the nations and the weapons of

---

[7] Translation by C. F. Keil, *Commentary on Minor Prophets* (Grand Rapids: Eerdmans Publishing Co., reprint, 1951), Vol. II, p. 332.

warfare shall be "cut off" (Zech. 9:10). No longer will the art of governing be the art of compromise between what *ought* to be done and what *can* be done. Furthermore, in sharp contrast with all previous rulers, this King "shall not fail nor be discouraged, till he have set judgment in the earth" (Isa. 42:1-4).

5. *The Functions of the Coming Ruler*

I will raise them up a Prophet.	—*Deut. 18:18*
He shall be a priest upon his throne.	—*Zech. 6:13*

In the historical commonwealth of Israel there were three main functions of leadership: the regal, the sacerdotal, and the prophetical. With notable exceptions, these functions were kept strictly separate. In the cases of Moses and David we have mediatorial rulers who also exercised the prophetic gift (Deut. 18:15; Acts 2:29-30). But this arrangement was unusual. Because of the imperfection of the political leaders, there was generally need for a class of prophets who were free to correct and rebuke, apart from the entanglements of political responsibility. King David, although himself a prophet, had to be rebuked by another prophet (II Sam. 12:1-14). In relation to the sacerdotal area, there is no instance where the political ruler was permitted to usurp the functions of the priesthood, death being the penalty for such usurpation (Num. 18:7; II Chron. 26: 16-21). Apparent exceptions may be explained on the basis of that *personal* liberty of worship allowed in the Old Testament theocracy (Exod. 20:24). Nor were the priests allowed to rule the state. As W. G. Moorehead has said, "They had no political power conferred upon them. . . . Their services . . . precluded them from exercising any undue influence in the affairs of the nation."[8] Among sinful men, the rule of a priestly hierarchy has generally resulted in the corruption of both functions, political as well as sacerdotal. This was a glaring characteristic of one of the darkest periods in the entire history of the Jewish state. It was under the presidency of a high priest that the Great Council of Israel, in an appalling travesty of justice, condemned to death her own Messianic King.

In contrast to this historical separation of functions, Old Testament prophecy looks forward to a kingdom when the Mediatorial Ruler will unite in His own Person all the functions of prophet, priest, and king.

First, He will perfectly combine the functions of *prophet and king*: speaking faithfully to the people all the words of God, and

---

[8] "Priest," *International Standard Bible Encyclopedia* (Chicago: Howard-Severance, 1915), Vol. IV, p. 2440.

also invested with complete regal authority to enforce what is commanded under penalty of divine judgment. In this respect the coming King will be the perfect antitype of Moses, first of Israel's mediatorial rulers (Deut. 18:15-19; Acts 3:22-23).

Second, He will also perfectly combine the functions of *priest and king:* fully able to stand between God and men in the office of sacerdotal mediation, and at the same time having the requisite regal authority to "judge" among the nations and to execute the awful sanctions of divine wrath upon the rebellious kings of the earth. In this respect He does not follow the Aaronic succession but rather the "order of Melchizedek," whose dual office was not acquired by genealogical descent nor did he pass the office on to any successors (Ps. 110:1-7; Heb. 5 and 7).

In the Person of the final mediatorial Ruler in the coming Kingdom, it will be safe to concentrate all the functions which appear in relation to the historical kingdom. For He will minister for God among men as the perfect Servant of Jehovah in whose service there will be nothing lacking or out of balance. In Him, for the first time in human history, the world will find a King who will rule as a "servant" and who will perfectly blend the demands of mercy and justice. Of Him alone will God be able to say, "Behold my servant, whom I uphold; mine elect, in whom my soul delighteth" (Isa. 42:1). "And men shall be blessed in him: all nations shall call him blessed" (Ps. 72:17).

6. The Mystery of the King's Career

Who hath believed our report?   —Isa. 53:1

Along with His clearly revealed regal glory, as indicated above, there is a deep note of mystery in the career of the coming King. He is presented in Old Testament prophecy not only as the Servant of Jehovah but as a *suffering* servant; a man of sorrows, despised and rejected of men; an alien to His mother's children, and hated without a cause; wounded, bruised, afflicted, and dying for the iniquities of men (Ps. 69; Isa. 53). He is the great and good Shepherd of Israel (Isa. 40:9-11); yet when the sheep in their sinful waywardness wander from the paths of righteousness, it is not the sheep but the Shepherd Himself who is smitten by the sword of God (Zech. 13:7). He restores that which He took not away; yet when He looks for pity and comforters, there are none (Ps. 69). He comes at the appointed time as the long-awaited "Messiah the Prince" of Israel; yet He is "cut off" and has nothing which belongs to His regal glory (Dan. 9:25-26, ASV). And the mystery must have deepened to the Old Testament saint as he read that "it pleased the LORD to bruise him" (Isa. 53:10). In the face of this mystery, therefore, it should not be surprising to find Isaiah opening his 53rd chapter with the exclamation, "Who hath believed our report?" i.e., the report of a Messianic King who must suffer and die under the hand of Jehovah.

How shall these two apparently conflicting elements — the glory and the suffering — be reconciled? How can chapters 2 and 53 of Isaiah be joined together? What is the unifying factor between Psalms 22 and 72? This mysterious problem did not go altogether unnoticed by the Jewish rabbins. Some thought there might be two Messiahs; one, the "son of Joseph," who would suffer and die; the other, a "son of David," who would come and reign in glory. Other Jewish scholars applied the prophecies of suffering to the nation of Israel personified; a view favored by modern Jewish interpretation. These proposed solutions, however, seem to be definitely post-Christian in origin, and were probably motivated by Jewish antagonism toward the Christian interpretation of Old Testament prophecy.[9] It is highly doubtful whether anyone, having only the Old Testament writings and with no knowledge of Christian history, could or ever did arrive at a correct solution of the problem; that is, not two Messiahs, but one Messiah with two comings separated by a vast gulf in time. Dr. Keil speaks too strongly, however, when he says, "The prophets of the Old Testament throughout make no allusion to any second coming of our Lord to His people."[10] It is certainly there by implication in many predictions of the Messianic Kingdom, but it could not be discerned clearly until after the first coming of the King.

We do know, however, that the problem was given serious consideration in pre-Christian times by the Old Testament prophets themselves. These men saw clearly the sufferings and glory of Messiah. It is fairly certain also that they understood the *sequence* of events: the suffering would come first, and the glory would "follow." But the time *extent* between the two was an unsolved problem to the prophets, although they searched their own writings to discover, if possible, "what time or what manner of time" was signified by the Spirit of Christ (I Pet. 1:9-11, ASV). If this time

<hr>

[9] The learned Alfred Edersheim refers to the first theory as "the fiction of two Messiahs" (*op. cit.,* Vol. I, p. 79).
[10] C. F. Keil, *op. cit.,* Vol. II, p. 474.

relationship was ever revealed exactly to the prophets, Old Testament Scripture is wholly silent as to any such revelation. Furthermore, the absence of any evident attempt to present some rational explanation on the part of the Old Testament writers, who were deeply conscious of the problem, should clearly indicate that we have here a silence designed by inspiration. And this silence will become a fact of high significance when we come later to the gospel records and inquire, Was the Kingdom in any sense postponed? For it cannot be argued, by those who believe in any kind of genuine inspiration, that attention to detail is unworthy of divine revelation. If the Spirit of God is careful to identify the exact geographical spot where the King is to be born, we are not wrong in asking why the *time* problem of His career has not been given some explanation. And the answer ought to be somewhat commensurate to the importance of the problem.

Chapter XV

THE COMING OF THE PROPHETIC KINGDOM

Thy kingdom come . . . . in earth, as it is in heaven. —*Matt. 6:10*

Centuries before the first Christian disciples were taught to pray, "Thy kingdom come," this petition had been often upon the hearts of godly men and women in Old Testament days. In fact, apart from the great prophecies of the Old Testament, there could have been no basis or inspiration for such a prayer. For in this hope for the coming of the Kingdom were gathered all the best and highest aspirations of that elect people, who historically had been made the channel of divine revelation. It was in the spirit of the Old Testament prophets, therefore, that the ancient petition was laid in a new way upon the lips of the men who by grace would become members of the royal family of the Mediatorial King. To them He said, "Think not that I am come to destroy the law, or the prophets: I am not come to destroy, but to fulfil" (Matt. 5:17). And later when His chosen apostle to the Gentiles had been brought before King Agrippa to answer the charge of apostasy from Old Testament revelation, his reply was, "I continue unto this day, witnessing both to small and great, saying none other things than those which the prophets and Moses did say should come" (Acts 26:22). Whatever light has been shed upon the coming of God's Kingdom, in its original source, has come from the prophets of the Old Testament.

1. *The Time of Its Coming*

The vision is yet for an appointed time . . . though it tarry, wait for it; because it will surely come. —*Hab. 2:3*

a. *The Chronological Question*

This was not born out of mere curiosity. Considering the dark background of divine judgment on the historical kingdom, over against the glowing promises of better things to come, it is not surprising that the words "How long?" were often on the lips of the people of God. The prophet Isaiah, with hopes for his nation re-

170

vived by reason of the magnificent accomplishments of King Uzziah, had seen these hopes fail when the king was suddenly struck down by the wrath of God (II Chron. 26:20-21). And as if this blow were not enough, "In the year that king Uzziah died" (Isa. 6:1) there was laid upon the prophet a terrible commission: to proclaim against his own nation a further judgment of spiritual blindness and estrangement from God. And although Isaiah's submission is unreserved — "Here am I; send me" — we cannot fail to sense the heaviness of his heart in his cry, "LORD, how long?" (6:8-11).

Yet this was not a cry of despair, but rather an expression of unyielding hope on the part of one who knew that ahead somewhere down the long corridors of time there would surely be a Kingdom of God on earth for the rectification of ancient wrongs and the establishment of righteousness. We hear it again in the 74th Psalm where the afflicted nation complains: "We see not our signs: there is no more any prophet: neither is there among us any that knoweth how long. O God, how long shall the adversary reproach? Shall the enemy blaspheme thy name for ever?" (vss. 9-10). "Arise, O God, plead thine own cause" (vs. 22). The same question is uttered in the 89th Psalm, perhaps the greatest of all the Kingdom songs, where the writer describes the heartbreaking disparity between the glorious promise of the future Kingdom and the present devastation in Israel (vss. 27-45). For, concerning David and his kingdom, had not God promised that "His seed shall endure for ever, and his throne as the sun before me" (vs. 36)? Yet now the judging hand of God had "cast his throne down to the ground" (vs. 44). And once again we hear the expectant cry, "How long, LORD?" (vs. 46).

b. *The Appointed Time*

On the one hand, in Old Testament prophecy, sometimes it seems that the coming of the Kingdom must be very near at hand. Haggai says it will come in "a little while" (2:6-9). And Isaiah specifies the extension of time as "a very little while" (29:17-18). But other predictions indicate that the Kingdom is far distant in the future, after the lapse of "many days" (Hos. 3:4-5), and in the "last days" (Isa. 2:2). The proper reconciliation of these forecasts, doubtless, may be found in the difference between the divine Mind and man's ideas. For our "many days" may be only a "very little while" to that eternal God in whose sight a thousand years are but "as yesterday when it is past" (Ps. 90:4).

But the time of the coming Kingdom is lifted out of the realm of total ambiguity in other prophetic utterances. Speaking in the midst of national affliction, the psalmist is confident that Israel's God will "arise, and have mercy upon Zion"; and he refers to that future season of divine blessing as *"the set time"* (Ps. 102:12-13). The context here goes far beyond any event in Biblical history. This "set time" will arrive when the LORD Himself "shall appear in his glory," when the nations and kings of the earth are gathered together to "serve the LORD" (vss. 16-22). Also in the prophecy of Habakkuk there is a reference to a specific time. Beyond the disturbing moral contradictions of his own day, Habukkuk saw a vision of better things when "the earth shall be filled with the knowledge of the glory of the LORD, as the waters cover the sea" (2:14). And if the arrival of this blessed time seems long delayed, the prophet is assured that the vision will not fail; its fulfilment will "surely come" at God's own "appointed time" (2:1-3).

c. *The Intervening Events*

In looking forward to the establishment of the coming Kingdom, the prophets agree that this grand event will *follow* certain preliminary circumstances and conditions, which will be rather fully discussed later in the next chapter (XVI). It will be sufficient here to notice that the Kingdom will not come "until" after a period of complete devastation in the land of Palestine (Isa. 6:11-12; 32:13-18); until after a period of world-wide dispersion of the nation of Israel (Amos 9:8-10); until after a prolonged period when Israel will be "without a king, and without a prince, and without a sacrifice" (Hos. 3:4-5); until after a long succession of four world empires culminating in a world dictator whose terrible persecution will mark the end of Jewish suffering (Dan. 7:17-27); and until after a resurrection of godly Israelites (Dan. 12:1-3). The totality of these events, even apart from others yet to be mentioned, cannot be equated with anything in the known history of the world.

d. *The King's Arrival Is Dated*

When we come to the visions of the Book of Daniel, the prophetic calendar becomes more specific, actually now a matter of historical chronology. Standing near the end of seventy years of Babylonian captivity foretold by Jeremiah (Dan. 9:1-2; Jer. 25:12), Daniel prayed for light as to the future of his people and city in relation to the coming Kingdom (9:16-19). The answer came swiftly by the hand of the angel Gabriel: "Seventy weeks" (of years) are determined upon Israel and Jerusalem to bring in the long predicted blessings of the Mediatorial Kingdom (9:24). These seventy weeks of years will begin with "the commandment to restore and to build Jerusalem"; and the end of the first sixty-nine of the weeks will mark the arrival of "Messiah the Prince" (9:25). Passing over for the moment the problem of the seventieth week and any events which may intervene between the first sixty-nine and the final week, the reader should note that in these sixty-nine weeks we have one stretch of prophetic time which is definitely clocked, not only in length but also as to its beginning and its end. The official "commandment"[1] authorizing the rebuilding of Jerusalem was issued to Nehemiah by the Persian king, Artaxerxes, in "the twentieth year" of his reign, which happens to be one of the best authenticated dates in ancient history — 445 B.C.[2] From this date to the arrival of the Messianic King, according to Daniel, will be 69 weeks or 483 prophetic years. After allowing all due consideration for the various differences in computing these years, the prophecy remains unshaken. Its *terminus ad quem,* within close limits, is fixed and must fall somewhere within the earthly career of Jesus of Nazareth. If He is not the Messianic King of Old Testament prophecy, then prophecy has failed, and we can have no certain hope that there will ever be any such king.

e. *The Kingdom's Establishment Is Left Undated*

From the prophecy of the seventy weeks itself (Dan. 9:24-27), even when read apart from the light of New Testament history, interpreters should have been cautioned against any dogmatic attempt to identify chronologically the *establishment* of the Kingdom with the initial arrival of its King. Certain features of the prophecy are definitely opposed to any such identification. For instance, when the King arrives, according to verse 26, He will be "cut off and shall have nothing" (ASV).[3] Certainly, the meaning of "shall have nothing" must be limited by the context: that is, the Messianic King

[1] Against the argument that this "commandment" was *wholly of God,* and therefore either uncertain or unascertainable in exact time, Keil has well said that "the 'going forth of the commandment to restore,' etc., must be a *factum* coming into visibility, the time of which could without difficulty be known—a word from God regarding the restoration of Jerusalem, which went forth by means of a man at a definite time, and received an observable historical execution" (*Commentary on Daniel* [Grand Rapids: Eerdmans Publishing Co., reprint, 1949], p. 352). This view is supported by James Strong against Otto Zockler in Lange's *Commentary, in loc.*

[2] See my *Daniel's Prophecy of the Seventy Weeks* (7th ed.; Grand Rapids: Zondervan Publishing House, 1940), pp. 17-19 with note 3.

[3] This rendering is supported by Hengstenberg, Barnes, Ellicott, *et al.*

will have none of the blessings named in verse 24, for these attach specifically to Daniel's historic "people" and "city" when the Kingdom shall have been established on earth in accordance with other Old Testament predictions. And it should be carefully observed that, in the literary sequence of the prophecy, both the cutting off of the King and a subsequent destruction of Jerusalem are placed *before* the seventieth week, the end of which will bring in the Kingdom's blessings for Israel as described in verse 24. The time which may intervene between the sixty-ninth and the seventieth weeks is left indefinite and obscure for a divine purpose, which will become apparent when we consider the New Testament material. Thus, in Daniel's prophecy, while the King's arrival is definitely clocked, the establishment of His Kingdom is left uncertain chronologically.[4]

2. *The Manner of the Kingdom's Coming*

> Jehovah saith unto my Lord, Sit thou at my right hand, Until I make thine enemies thy footstool . . . . The Lord at thy right hand will strike through kings in the day of his wrath. He will judge among the nations, He will fill the places with dead bodies; He will strike through the head in many countries.   —*Ps. 110:1, 5, 6, ASV*

a. *It Will Be Sudden and Catastrophic*

There is a current and popular idea that the coming of the Kingdom of God to earth is a process, long and gradual; at times so imperceptible that sceptics may be able to dispute seriously whether there be such a thing as the reign of God. Such a notion has no foundation in the writings of the Old Testament prophets. Malachi declares the Lord of the Kingdom for whom Israel had long been waiting "shall suddenly come to his temple," to be a "swift witness" against all who practice immorality, oppression, and false religion (3:1-5). Again, in chapter 4, the same prophet sees that day coming as a *fire* which quickly consumes the "stubble" of the field; and the Lord of the harvest arrives as the "Sun" rising in the morning (vss. 1-2). In that "day of the Lord's wrath," there will be a "speedy riddance" of all those in Jerusalem who, because of God's long delay in openly manifesting His righteous rule upon earth, will be arguing that there never will be any such reign (cf. Zeph. 1:18 with 1:12). In the case of those Gentile nations which have contemptuously scattered and afflicted the chosen nation of Israel, there will come divine retribution "swiftly and speedily" (Joel 3:1-4). And in the visions of Daniel the Kingdom of God comes down from heaven

---

[4] For the best discussion of this prophecy, see *The Coming Prince* by Sir Robert Anderson (11th ed.; Edinburgh: Pickering and Inglis, no date).

to earth after the manner of a stone falling from a mountain to crush the political world systems (2:45). Such descriptions as these can never be reconciled with the notion of any long, drawn-out evolutionary development of the divine Kingdom on earth.

b. *It Will Be Supernatural*

During the present age the control of God's Universal Kingdom over earthly affairs has been largely providential.[5] Therefore this divine control has been veiled from the eyes of all, except those who have been enlightened spiritually from above. And even the people of God have been deeply perplexed at times about the long silence of God, so far as any apparent supernatural intrusions of power on earth are concerned (cf. Ps. 73:11-17). In referring to these matters, the prophets use two striking figures of speech: the *face* of God and the *arm,* or *hand,* of God. The Old Testament usage of both figures would richly repay a more careful examination than can be given in this study. But the connection is clearly shown in Psalm 44 where the writer looks back to those great supernatural acts of divine power which brought the chosen nation into the promised land: "They got not the land in possession by their own sword, neither did their own arm save them; but thy right hand, and thine arm, and the light of thy countenance, because thou hadst a favor unto them. Thou art my King, O God" (vss. 1-4). Later in the history of Israel, when there was a period of divine silence with reference to exhibitions of God's regal and supernatural power, the "face" of God is spoken of as hidden: "Wherefore hidest thou thy face? . . . Arise for our help" (Ps. 44:24-26). And Jehovah Himself, speaking through Isaiah of this period of His silence, says to Israel: "In a little wrath I hid my face from thee" (Isa. 54:8). The same prophet recognizes both the nature of this divine silence and also that it someday will come to an end: "I will wait upon the LORD, that hideth his face from the house of Jacob, and I will look for him." In the meantime the people of God are enjoined not to seek spurious signs of supernatural power, but to rest in the written word of God (Isa. 8:17-20).

It is especially in connection with the coming of God's Kingdom on earth that the prophets speak of the "arm" of God, which will then be "made bare" and "stretched out." In that coming day when men shall say to Zion, "Thy God reigneth," Isaiah describes it as a time when "the LORD hath made bare his holy arm" in comforting Israel

[5] See Chap. IV, Sec. 3.

and redeeming Jerusalem (52:7-10). It will be a day of wrath upon the enemies of God when the amazing Ruler comes "glorious in his apparel," and saying, "the day of vengeance is in mine heart . . . . Therefore mine own arm brought salvation unto me" (63:1-5). What is done in that coming day will be the work of God alone, in which human effort will have no place. Certainly the context of the chapter forbids any attempt to limit this "salvation" to spiritual matters alone. For the God who comes to deliver His people is the same God who in history led them supernaturally through the sea "with his glorious arm, dividing the water before them" (vss. 11-12). In his picture of the coming Kingdom, Ezekiel also emphasizes the supernatural aspect of its coming: "As I live, saith the Lord Jehovah, surely with a mighty hand, and with an outstretched arm . . . will I be king over you" (20:33, ASV). And the regathering of scattered Israel will be accomplished by supernatural means: The Lord "will gather you out of the countries wherein ye are scattered, with a mighty hand, and with an outstretched arm" (vs. 34).

In sharp contrast to these overwhelming manifestations of supernatural power at the *establishment* of the Mediatorial Kingdom, Isaiah speaks of the lowly career of the King on His first arrival. Although mighty works of divine power would not be wholly absent, they would be restricted in number, duration, and extent, so that the prophet describes thus the scepticism of that day: "Who hath believed our report? And to whom is the arm of the Lord revealed?" (53:1).

c. *It Will Be Tangible*

In the day of the coming Kingdom, it will not be necessary to write endless volumes on Christian "evidences" and "apologetics." Debates on the existence of God will become absurd and obsolete, suited only to be classed with arguments over the existence of sunlight. Eschatological systems which define the Kingdom of God wholly in terms of the invisible will need to be revised. For the supernatural evidences of the existence of God, and of His Christ, and of His Kingdom, will be open to all men. "The glory of the Lord shall be revealed, and all flesh shall see it together: for the mouth of the Lord hath spoken it" (Isa. 40:5). In that day it can be said truly that "The Lord hath made bare his holy arm in the eyes of all the nations; and all the ends of the earth shall see the salvation of our God" (Isa. 52:7-10).

The same prophet who, writing by divine inspiration, solemnly affirms, "In the year that king Uzziah died I saw also the Lord sitting upon a throne" (Isa. 6:1), also declares that at the coming Kingdom "Thine eyes shall see the king in his beauty" (33:17): For those who may be inclined to limit these texts to subjectively perceived visions, the parallel of Isaiah 53:2 may be cited. For the latter passage refers to the first coming of the King in humiliation, asserting what has already been historically fulfilled, "When we shall see him, there is no beauty[6] that we should desire him." Here there can be no question about literality, for the men who saw Him failed to see anything desirable in Him. Hence, the aspect of spirituality is excluded. Likewise, the eyes of all, even of the unsaved, shall *see* the King when He comes to establish His glorious Kingdom on earth.

It is true that Daniel speaks of the coming of the Kingdom as a stone which is cut out of the mountain "without hands" (2:34, 45). But in the symbolic dream of the Babylonian king, as confirmed by the prophet, the *stone* was seen; the *cutting* act was seen; also its *fall* and the consequent *destruction* of the image. The words "without hands" are intended to indicate the supernatural origin of both the King and His Kingdom. Although tangible to men, no human or natural means have any part in the ushering in of this Kingdom.

The coming of the Kingdom, attended by a supernaturalism fully tangible to all, will put an end to the rationalistic taunts of men like G. E. Lessing who once wrote, "I do not deny at all that prophecies were fulfilled in Christ; I do not deny at all that Christ wrought miracles; but I do deny that these miracles, since their truth has altogether ceased to be evinced by miracles which are still accessible today, since there exist nothing but accounts of miracles (no matter how undenied, how undeniable, they may be supposed to be), can or ought to bind me to the least faith in any other teachings of Christ."[7]

[6] The Hebrew words rendered "beauty" in Isa. 33:17 and 53:2 are different, but that does not affect the argument. Both imply visibility.

[7] Quoted by B. B. Warfield in his *Christology and Criticism* (New York: Oxford University Press, 1929), p. 319.

CHAPTER XVI

THE ESTABLISHMENT OF THE PROPHETIC KINGDOM

And in the days of these kings shall the God of heaven set up a
kingdom.
—*Dan. 2:44*

The tremendous actions and events attending the establishment
of the Mediatorial Kingdom on earth are so numerous and complex that some attempt should be made to organize the material in
general outline form. One useful key to the problem is provided in
what the prophets name the *Day of Jehovah,* a period which is always
associated with the Kingdom of Old Testament prophecy. Although
it is a period of unrevealed and indefinite length, the descriptions
of its general character suggest that the prophets must have had in
mind a form somewhat parallel to the ordinary day in the Jewish
calendar. This latter was a solar day which began at sunset and extended to the next sunset (Lev. 23:32), consisting of a period of
darkness followed by a period of light. Similarly, the great Day of
the Lord is pictured as a period composed of both darkness and light;
and the sequence is the same: first, the night, and then the light of
the rising sun. As Isaiah states the order: "Behold, the darkness
shall cover the earth . . . but the LORD shall arise upon thee" (60:2).
In the prophets that Day always begins with the darkness of divine
wrath (Isa. 34:8, cf. context); and then moves on to the light of
divine blessing (Isa. 35).

Furthermore, to this twofold division of the Day of the LORD, the
prophets add a third category, namely, those events which take place
"before" that great Day (Mal. 4:5; Joel 2:31). Finally, there are
a few important events which seem to belong to the *dawning* period
between the darkness and the light. Following this outline we get a
fourfold division of events associated with the establishment of the
Mediatorial Kingdom on earth: first, events which take place *before*
the Day; second, events during the *darkness* of the Day; third, events
at the *dawn* of the Day; and fourth, events during the *light* of the
Day. In determining the proper category of the various events, it will

178

be necessary to examine not only the stated time sequence (if any) but also the nature of the event. Some are clearly preparatory in character; others are penal; still others are transitional; and the final events are constitutive. In our treatment, therefore, the statement and order of the four divisions will be as follows:

1. *Preparatory Events — Before the Day of the Lord*
2. *Penal Events — During the Darkness of the Day of the Lord*
3. *Transitional Events — at the Dawn of the Day of the Lord*
4. *Constitutive Events — During the Light of the Day of the Lord*

Within each of these categories the order of the series of events can be established in a general way by observing the interrelationships which they display in the prophetic writings; but the reader should be cautioned not to presume that the order followed below is asserted with any unalterable dogmatism.

1. *Preparatory Events — Before the Day of the Lord*
   Before the great and the terrible day of the Lord.   —*Joel* 2:31
a. *A Court of Judgment Will Be Set in Heaven*
   The judgment was set.   —*Dan.* 7:10

In the seventh chapter of Daniel's prophecy there is a scene which has no parallel in other Old Testament forecasts of the Kingdom. The prophet describes the vision as follows: "I beheld till thrones were placed, and one that was ancient of days did sit; his raiment was white as snow, and the hair of his head like pure wool; his throne was fiery flames, and the wheels thereof burning fire. A fiery stream issued and came forth from before him: thousands of thousands ministered unto him, and ten thousand times ten thousand stood before him: the judgment was set, and the books were opened" (7:9-10, ASV). Several points here should be noted.

First, the scene is unquestionably *judicial* in character. The solemn atmosphere is that of a high court. There is a central throne surrounded by other thrones. Books are opened. There are attendants waiting to carry out the decisions of the court. The words, "the judgment was set" (vs. 10), have been rather freely rendered by the RSV, "the court sat in judgment"; but this idea is in harmony with the general context.

Second, these activities take place *in heaven,* not on earth. This is made clear by the various contextual details: the presence of the Ancient of Days, the description of His fiery throne, the myriads of angelic ministers, the opening of the books — all point to that which is above. There will be subsequent judgments on the earth, but these will only carry out the prior decrees of this heavenly assize. By some, the language of verse 13 is used to rule out the location in heaven. But the words, "came with the clouds of heaven" are just as appropriate to picture the Son of man's coming *to* the heavenly throne of God as to describe His descent *from* heaven to earth. "Clouds" in Scripture are often made the distinctive environment of Deity. As a matter of fact, our Lord's ascension is thus described — "he was taken up; and a cloud received him out of their sight" (Acts 1:9).

Third, in the vision this session of the heavenly court is placed immediately at the *end of Gentile dominion*, represented by the four successive world empires and their final subdivisions as indicated by ten kings, among which the "little horn" begins his brief career. Thus the convening of the high court in heaven is made the *first* important event in Daniel's vision of the establishment of the Kingdom. For it is in the days of these ten kings that the God of heaven will set up His indestructible Kingdom (cf. Dan. 2:44; 7:24-27).

Fourth, although in the record of Daniel's vision there is no mention of certain other important events which will attend the setting up of the divine Kingdom, it is both reasonable and Biblically sound to regard the heavenly judgment scene as the *first great preparatory event*. For the day of God's Kingdom on earth will be initially a day of *judgment*. And the court must first be officially convened before its judicial work can begin.

Fifth, the plurality of "thrones" in Daniel 7:9 certainly suggests the *presence of associate judges* in the judgments which are about to proceed from the celestial court. The occupants of these thrones are not named, but they cannot be angels as Keil wrongly insists.[1] Only the saints of God are ever thus associated with the divine judgment of the world. Angels are but servants who stand before the throne of God (Dan. 7:10). Only when we come over into the New Testament do we find a clear identification of the occupants of these thrones (cf. I Cor. 6:1-3). And even the most careless reader could hardly miss the striking parallel between Daniel 7:9-10 and the scene pictured in Revelation 4 and 5.

b. *The Voice of a Prophetic Messenger Will Be Heard on Earth*

I will send you Elijah the prophet.   —*Mal. 4:5*

Three important Old Testament passages speak of the career and ministry of this messenger. In Isaiah 40:1-11 there is a "voice"

[1] C. F. Keil, *Commentary on Daniel*, trans. M. G. Easton (Grand Rapids: Eerdmans Publishing Co., reprint, 1949), p. 229.

heard crying in the wilderness. In Malachi 3:1 God speaks of one called "my messenger." And in 4:4-6 he is definitely named "Elijah the prophet." An examination of these passages presents the following features with reference to this messenger.

First, he is divinely commissioned to do a work of *preparation* in the nation of Israel: "Prepare ye the way of the LORD," will be the burden of his message (Isa. 40:3); and it will sound to the nation a note both of comfort and of warning. He will announce the end of Jewish affliction, certain judgments of God, and the good news of the coming Kingdom (Isa. 40:1-2, 9-11).

Second, the ministry of this divinely sent messenger in Israel will in some measure be *effective*: He "shall turn the heart of the fathers to the children, and the heart of the children to their fathers" (Mal. 4:6). The meaning here is that a reconciliation will be effected between the godly fathers of Israel and their ungodly descendants. Abraham is ashamed of the sinful generation to which God's messenger will speak; and they are ashamed of their great patriarchal ancestors.[2] But the barrier will be broken down. Except for this great accomplishment in Israel, the earth would be smitten by the curse of God (Mal. 4:6). Thus the fate of the world is in a real sense bound up with the future work of the messenger in turning Israel back to God.

Third, the messenger will also have something to say *to all men* concerning the frailty of human life and the evanescence of all its "goodliness," in comparison with the glory of the coming Kingdom (Isa. 40:6-9). He will also warn men of the impending judgments of God by which the mountains shall be made low and crooked things shall be made straight (vs. 4).

Fourth, as to the *identity* of this messenger of Jehovah there should be little question. The coming "voice" will be that of a man, and he is named "Elijah the prophet" (Mal. 4:5). Whether or not there may be some secondary reference in the Old Testament passages to John the Baptist is a matter reserved for discussion in connection with the New Testament material. But certainly some attention should be given to the testimony of John himself who, when asked by the Pharisees, "Art thou Elijah?", replied, "I am not" (John 1:21, ASV). And our Lord, after the death of John, said to the disciples, "Elijah indeed cometh, and shall restore all things" (Matt. 17:11, ASV).

---

[2] So Hengstenberg and Keil.

Fifth, as to *time,* it is definitely stated that the messenger will appear "before the coming of the great and dreadful day of the LORD" (Mal. 4:5). This means that he will begin his ministry, not only before the establishment of the Kingdom, but also before the awful judgments which immediately precede the Kingdom. The context of the Isaiah passage is in harmony with this: for the messenger here comes to warn of the leveling judgments of God (40:4), as well as to announce the good news of the Kingdom (40:9-11).

c. *Internecine Warfare and Chaos Will Sweep the World*

The ambassadors of peace shall weep bitterly.   —*Isa. 33:7*

Warfare is nothing unusual among the nations of the earth. The seasons of peace, in the recorded history of the world, have been very few and disconcertingly brief. Viewed from the vantage point of Old Testament prophecy, Daniel saw no relief short of the Kingdom: "Unto the end shall be war" (9:26, ASV). And, considering the sinful nature of men, nothing else could be reasonably expected: "There is no peace, saith the LORD, unto the wicked" (Isa. 48:22; 57:21). This must be an axiom in a moral universe. But at the end of man's long misrule on earth, there will come a special outbreak of wars with all the attendant disastrous results. From the many references, three are selected for consideration.

First, in the 25th chapter of Jeremiah this evil of international conflict is set forth under the figure of a "cup" of divine "fury" which the prophet is commanded to take and make "all the nations to drink" (vss. 15-17). If they refuse, the dictum of the LORD of hosts is: "Ye shall certainly drink" (vs. 28). The "cup" is interpreted as a "sword" sent of God among all nations (vss. 16, 27, 31). The chosen nation and Jerusalem must drink first (vss. 18, 29). But this monstrous "evil shall go forth from nation to nation" until the whole world is involved (vs. 32). The devastating effects are pictured in verse 33: even the proper burial of the dead will finally become a task beyond the power of the living. And all this is related to man's failure to recognize and obey the true God, who therefore "hath a controversy with the nations" (vs. 31).

The chaos, which always attends great and prolonged seasons of warfare, seems to be pictured in Isaiah 24:1-13. The earth is made "empty" and "waste" (vs. 1). In the cities there is "desolation" (vs. 12); the houses are closed (vs. 10). An atmosphere of gloom and despair envelops the world; even the pleasures of ordinary social life no longer seem worth-while (vss. 7-11). The decimation of populations is beyond comprehension: "few men left" (vs. 6); the situation is compared with the few olives and grapes left after the harvest (vs. 13). No class of people escapes the terrible scourge; whether master or slave, rich or poor, priest or people: there are no protected places (vs. 2). And again we are reminded that, at bottom, the cause of all these disasters is moral and spiritual: "The earth also is defiled under the inhabitants thereof; because they have transgressed the laws . . . broken the everlasting covenant. Therefore hath the curse devoured the earth, and they that dwell therein are desolate" (vss. 5-6).

In the face of this spreading evil of international conflict at the end-time, all the efforts of men to bring about a condition of world peace will utterly fail. This is suggested in chapter 33 of Isaiah. Although the historical background of this chapter is set in the reign of King Hezekiah, its predictions certainly reach far into the future (cf. vss. 17-24). Viewing the desolations which will precede the coming of the Kingdom, the prophet says, "Behold, their valiant ones shall cry without: the ambassadors of peace shall weep bitterly" (vs. 7). All the earnest efforts of sincere men to bring in a permanent condition of world peace without the presence of the "Prince of peace" will come to nothing. The world must learn its lesson: "Without me ye can do nothing" (John 15:5); a lesson that even the people of God are sometimes in danger of forgetting, when dealing with mundane problems.

d. A Blasphemous Political Ruler Will Rise to World Power

> The man that made the earth to tremble, that did shake kingdoms.
> —Isa. 14:16

To all those familiar with the relation of cause and effect in the stream of political world history, it is nothing new to find the chaos and disorganization of widespread military conflict furnishing the soil out of which the tyrants and dictators grow. The picture drawn in the last book of the Bible is amazingly accurate in this respect: Along with the dreadful horsemen of war and famine and death, there rides the Conquering Hero, whose white horse speaks symbolically of fair hope to nations desperately weary and discouraged before the prospect of endless conflict (Rev. 6:1-8). And once again, in the days just prior to the coming of Mediatorial Kingdom, history will re-enact the agelong drama. Out of the welter of international warfare and its dismal aftermath, there will emerge the great political leader of the end, a gigantic figure when measured by any human estimate, whose panaceas will receive the applause of the world.

Although mentioned in other books of the Old Testament, the sharpest outline of his person and career is given in the prophecies of Daniel.

As to his *political origin,* this great leader will begin as a rather minor figure somewhere among the final subdivisions of the Roman Empire. In the visions of Daniel he is described as a "little horn" coming up in the midst of the "ten horns" on the "fourth beast," and whose first act is one of violence: by his hand three of the ten horns are "plucked up by the roots" (Dan. 7:7-8).

The time *sequence of events* must not be overlooked here. The divine court is set in heaven, not at the end of the little horn's career, nor at its height, but at its *beginning.* The order in Daniel 7:8-9 is unmistakable: The little horn rises on earth and opens his mouth to speak "great things"[3] — and at this precise moment the prophet looks up to behold the high court of divine justice set in heaven. This cannot be mere literary coincidence; for the little horn is Satan's man, and the start of his mad career is apparently the signal for heavenly judicial action. Neither is there any abatement of the action until this evil genius has been utterly defeated and the Kingdom of God's Man is fully established on earth.

Therefore, although the political *origin* of the little horn precedes the establishment of the judgment throne in heaven, his actual *rise to world domination* follows that high and holy event. And the succeeding steps of his terrible march come swiftly: his seven-year covenant or treaty with the people of Israel and its speedy violation (Dan. 9:26-27); the exaltation of himself above every god (11:36); his military successes against the great powers of the north and south (11:40-43); and his persecution of the saints of God on earth (7:25). In all these events, for those who have eyes to see, the great rebel is acting only under the permission of the heavenly court. If he has power over the saints, it is because they have been "given into his hand"; even the extreme limit of his career is inflexibly set by divine decree — "until a time and times and the dividing of time" (7:25).

e. *There Will Be Great Geological and Cosmic Disturbances*

The earth shall reel to and fro like a drunkard.   —*Isa. 24:20*

By scientific observation it has been established that many changes are constantly taking place in both the earth and other cosmic bodies.

---

[3] These "great things" may be either *blasphemous* things (Lange), or *presumptuous* things (Keil); probably boastful promises of what *he* can do for a world facing problems too great for human solution.

Most of these changes are so slight that men ordinarily are not even aware of their occurrence. Beyond the estimated 4000 earthquakes that are *felt* somewhere on the earth daily, there are many other thousands wholly imperceptible except by means of scientific instruments. But in the history of the universe, as recorded by immediate observation and scientific deduction, it is generally agreed that there have been particular seasons when numerous and catastrophic changes have taken place in a comparatively brief space of time. Such a season, according to the Old Testament prophets, will come in the days preceding the coming of God's Kingdom to earth.

As to the character of these coming changes, the Word of God in Joel's prophecies gives a short yet comprehensive account: "And I will shew wonders in the heavens and in earth, blood, and fire, and pillars of smoke. The sun shall be turned into darkness, and the moon into blood, before the great and the terrible day of the LORD come" (2:30-31). We should notice here, first, that the "earth" will be affected. Second, that on earth there will be "fire" and "pillars of smoke," evidences of volcanic eruptions which have often accompanied great geological shifts in the earth's surface. Third, at the same time there will be disturbances in the "heavens." It is altogether possible, judged by the past, that some of these changes in the earth and other planetary bodies may be causally related. Fourth, the mention of "blood" in connection with the "earth" suggests the great destruction of life always involved in major geological disturbances.

Fifth, all this will take place "before" the Day of the Lord, a fact which harmonizes with the nature of that day. For, by sceptics who reject the idea of the supernatural, all the above described disturbances up to this point might possibly be attributed wholly to natural causes. But the chief events of the coming Day of the Lord will be indisputably supernatural in their origin. In that terrible Day there will be further convulsions in the world of nature which will far surpass in intensity the preliminary "wonders" described by Joel; for the latter are only harbingers of that Day, and are intended to warn the world of its proximity. As a matter of fact, excepting the judgment court in heaven (invisible to the world), all the tangible events mentioned above — the proclamation of the divinely sent messenger, the military conflicts, the rise of the little horn, and the disturbances in the natural world — will be largely providential in character and therefore not completely demonstrable as supernaturally caused events.

Finally, in connection with these devastating events preliminary to the establishment of the Kingdom, Joel holds forth bright hope for all who turn to the Lord — "whosoever shall call on the name of the Lord shall be delivered" (2:32). This gracious provision, as we shall see later, will be in force during *all* the judgments associated with the setting up of the Kingdom on earth; a fact which demonstrates that these judgments cannot be placed in the category of *final* judgment, for then the day of salvation will be past.

2. *Penal Events — During the Darkness of the Day of the Lord*

The great day of the Lord is near . . . . That day is a day of wrath, a day of trouble and distress, a day of wasteness and desolation, a day of darkness and gloominess, a day of clouds and thick darkness.
                                                                    —*Zeph. 1:14-15*

The arrival of this Day of the Lord will first bring darkness, not light; for initially it is a "day of wrath." Therefore, the events of this period of darkness will be *penal* in nature — "behold, the Lord cometh out of his place to punish the inhabitants of the earth for their iniquity" (Isa. 26:21). The wrath of God will fall progressively upon different segments of sinful humanity until at last the infliction becomes universal in extent.

a. *Wrath Will Fall Upon a Great Northern Power*

I will call for a sword against him . . . saith the Lord God.
                                                                    —*Ezek. 38:21*

Chapters 38 and 39 of Ezekiel are given to a description of this northern power and its place in the events of the end. No attempt can be made here to deal with the prophecy in detail, but the following analysis will indicate its general features.

First, the *time* of its fulfilment is undoubtedly eschatological. Ezekiel places it in "the latter years" and "the latter days" (38:8, 16). The time is further specified as coming before the final regathering and conversion of Israel (39:22-29).

Second, the great northern power involved is named "Gog, of the land of Magog, the prince of Rosh" (Ezek. 38:2-3, ASV). As to the identity of Rosh, Gesenius has said that "it can scarcely be doubtful that the first trace of the Russians is here given."[4] Apart from any linguistic considerations, however, this identification is confirmed by the geographical *location* as given by the prophet: "in the uttermost parts of the north" (38:6, 15, ASV). Since the directional standpoint of the prophet was always in relation to Pales-

---

[4] Cf. W. J. Schröder, Lange's *Commentary on Ezekiel*, trans. by S. Manson (New York: Scribner's Sons, 1899), p. 361.

tine, a glance at any map of the world will make it evident that there is no other great power on earth except Russia which could possibly answer to Ezekiel's description.

Third, this great northern power will lead a coalition of satellite nations against Palestine for the purpose of plundering the people of Israel who at the end-time will again be living there in great prosperity, but apparently without adequate military resources of their own (Ezek. 38:8-16). It is possible that for protection Israel will be depending on the great Roman prince of Daniel 9:26-27 with whom they will have made a treaty (vs. 27).

Fourth, the invasion will be frustrated by the hand of Jehovah Himself (Ezek. 38:19-22), whose wrath is described in superlative terms, falling upon the invading hordes in a fivefold manner: a fearful shaking of the earth centered in the land of Palestine (vss. 18-20); fratricidal fighting between the allied invaders (vs. 21); an epidemic of pestilential disease; violent storms of rainfall and hailstones; and eruptions of fire and brimstone (vs. 22). The resulting loss of life will be so great that the burial of the dead will require "seven months" (39:11-16).

Fifth, this prophecy of Ezekiel concerning Gog and Magog cannot be identified with the prophecy in Revelation 20:7-10 for three reasons. The former takes place *before* the Kingdom is established on earth; the latter *after* this Kingdom. Also, in Ezekiel the invasion comes only from the north, but in Revelation it comes from the "four quarters of the earth." Furthermore, the rebellion of Gog and Magog and their destruction in Revelation 20:7-10 marks the ushering in of the eternal state (20:11-15); but in Ezekiel it is preliminary to the Millennial Kingdom on earth.

Finally, it should be observed that if Russia should prove to be the *first* object of God's penal wrath at the end-time, the divine justification can be found in two facts: first, Russia is the only great political power in recorded history with an openly avowed policy to abolish God completely and everything connected with Him; second, it is this northern power, according to Ezekiel, which will launch the final and worst period of anti-Semitic persecution in the history of the world.

b. Wrath Will Fall Upon the Nation of Israel

But I . . . will not leave thee altogether unpunished.   —Jer. 30:11

Persecution and suffering are nothing new in the history of the chosen nation. Because of their elect position, they have always

borne a primary moral responsibility before God. Through the
centuries of their existence the suffering of this people has been
proverbial. All this was forecast in the very Scriptures which they
treasured. Chapter 28 of Deuteronomy describes in harrowing detail
what they would suffer — so great that they would "become an
astonishment, a proverb, and a byword among all nations" (vs. 37).
But great as these sufferings have been historically, there is ahead
something which is far worse. It will come with the Day of the Lord:
"Alas! for that day is great, so that none is like it; it is even the
time of Jacob's trouble" — thus the terrible day is described by
Jeremiah (30:7).

In that day when Jehovah rises up to do His "strange work" —
the execution of wrath upon His own elect people (Isa. 28:21) —
that nation shall be as "burnings of lime" and as thorns "burned
in the fire" (Isa. 33:10-14). As a result of these terrible visitations
both the luxuries and necessities of civilization, held in such high
regard by apostate members of the nation, will be taken away. All
the devices of bodily ornamentation will disappear; clothing will be
in rags; even decent cleanliness for the body will be impossible.
"Instead of well set hair, baldness; and instead of a robe, a girding of
sackcloth" (Isa. 3:16-24, ASV). Because of involvement in wars of
the last days, the men will be so greatly reduced in number that
"seven women shall take hold of one man, saying, We will eat our
own bread, and wear our own apparel; only let us be called by thy
name; to take away our reproach" (Isa. 3:25-4:1).

The climax of these end-time sufferings for Israel will be reached
at the hand of the blasphemous "little horn" who, having risen to
world power and callously broken his seven-year covenant with
the nation, will inaugurate a season of persecution so violent and
destructive that it will have no parallel, either in the past or the
future. According to Daniel, he not only makes war with God's
people, but he *prevails* "against them" (7:21), and shall wear them
out (7:25). Concerning these sufferings, the prophet is careful to
point out two extraordinary things: first, it is not the Jewish apos-
tates, but the "saints," who are the primary object of persecution;
second, the suffering is a visitation of God Himself who delivers the
saints into the hand of the great blasphemer (7:25). But they will
suffer in hope.

As for the hypocrites in Israel who think the Day of the Lord
can bring any final blessing for them, the Word of God is clear:
"Woe unto you that desire the day of the LORD! To what end is

it for you? The day of the LORD is darkness, and not light. As if a man did flee from a lion, and a bear met him; or went into the house, and leaned his hand on the wall, and a serpent bit him" (Amos 5:18-19). Beyond the darkness there will be light for the godly in Israel in that day; but for the ungodly it will bring only darkness, with "no brightness in it" (vs. 20). Not even membership in the elect nation can give any hope apart from moral considerations: "Seek good, and not evil, that ye may live: and so the LORD, the God of hosts, shall be with you, as ye have spoken" (vs. 14). Mere forms of religion, no matter how correct, will not be accepted as a substitute for a change of heart (vss. 21-24).

c. *Wrath Will Fall Also on All the Gentile Nations*

> The LORD cometh out of his place to punish the inhabitants of the
> earth for their iniquity.   —*Isa. 26:21*

When the Day of the Lord comes, "cruel both with wrath and fierce anger," no nation on earth will escape its force. "I will punish the world for their evil," is the ultimatum of Jehovah (Isa. 13:9-11). This infliction of divine wrath will be directed primarily against two characteristic world sins: *human pride* and *false religion*. "For the day of the LORD of hosts shall be upon every one that is proud and lofty, and upon every one that is lifted up; and he shall be brought low" (Isa. 2:12). "In that day a man shall cast his idols of silver, and his idols of gold, which they made each one for himself to worship, to the moles and to the bats" (Isa. 2:20). The utter impotence of all false religion will be demonstrated before the eyes of all men. What a spectacle!—the proud adherents of the great world religions and cults casting away as worthless all the precious symbols of their misplaced faith, and crawling into "holes" and "caves" for refuge when the true God rises up to "shake terribly the earth" (Isa. 2:19, 21). All the great achievements of mankind, which have ministered to human pride and self-sufficiency, will be forgotten; and "the LORD alone shall be exalted in that day" (Isa. 2:12-17). The account in this chapter of Isaiah is notable in that not one of the grosser sins of humanity is even mentioned—human pride and human religion stand here alone as the immediate objects of divine wrath.

But in addition to these sins, the Old Testament prophets present the nations of the earth in deliberate *rebellion* against the true God and His appointed King. Human religions may indeed become very tolerant of one another, but they can never tolerate the one true faith of God. And thus, at the end-time, we find nations and peoples, their kings and rulers, all raging in rebellion "against the LORD, and against his anointed," and saying, "Let us break their bands asunder, and cast away their cords from us" (Ps. 2:1-3). There seems to be a reference to this same rebellion in Psalm 83:1-2 where the writer calls upon Jehovah to break His silence: "For, lo, thine enemies make a tumult; and they that hate thee have lifted up the head." There can never be any neutrality in relation to the true God. If men do not love Him, they will hate Him; as our Lord warned, "He that is not with me is against me" (Matt. 12:30).

The immediate answer of Jehovah to all these insolent ragings of rebellious nations is derisive laughter: "He that sitteth in the heavens shall laugh" (Ps. 2:4). But there will also be divine *action*: "Therefore wait ye upon me, saith the LORD, until the day that I rise up to the prey: for my determination is to gather the nations, that I may assemble the kingdoms, to pour upon them mine indignation, even all my fierce anger: for all the earth shall be devoured with the fire of my jealousy" (Zeph. 3:8).

The climax of this rebellion against the God of heaven will be reached when the armies of the nations, under the leadership of the great evil genius of the end-time, will march against Jerusalem and its chosen people. The prophet Zechariah, speaking of this military movement against Jerusalem, affirms that "all the nations of the earth shall be gathered together against it" (12:2-3, ASV). And Daniel refers to their wicked leader when, among the final exploits of his terrible career, he is pictured as invading "the glorious land" and with great fury pitching his royal tent "between the sea and the glorious holy mountain" (11:41-45, ASV).[5]

But the providential hand of God is in this arrogant march against the holy city of Jerusalem. For it is God's own determination thus to use the wrath of man to assemble the kingdoms of the world into the place of judgment where they shall be dealt with as they deserve (Zeph. 3:8). "I will gather all nations against Jerusalem to battle," says Jehovah (Zech. 14:2). In accents of great irony the divine call will go forth, "Proclaim ye this among the Gentiles; Prepare war, wake up the mighty men, let all the men of war draw near; let them come up: Beat your plowshares into swords, and your pruning-hooks into spears: let the weak say, I am strong. Assemble yourselves, and come, all ye heathen . . . . Multitudes, multitudes in the valley of decision" (Joel 3:9-11, 14).

[5] Keil remarks that Daniel 11:40-45 can "refer only to the final enemy of the people of God, the Antichrist" (*Commentary on Daniel, op. cit.,* p. 469).

Rather strangely, according to Zechariah, the attack upon Jerusalem is initially successful: "the city shall be taken, and the houses rifled, and the women ravished; and half of the city shall go forth into captivity, and the residue of the people shall not be cut off from the city" (14:2). In this apparent victory of the anti-God rebellion, the world comes to its darkest hour in the long night of Satanic power, and the dawn is about to break.

3. Transitional Events — at the Dawn of the Day of the Lord

But it shall be one day which shall be known to the LORD, not day, nor night: but it shall come to pass, that at evening time it shall be light.
—Zech. 14:7

Up to this point, in the sequence of events of the end-time, the judgments of God have issued from His throne in the heavens (Dan. 7:9-10). But now there will be something new: the incarnate Mediatorial King who sits at the right hand of God on high will rise from the throne and come down personally from heaven to put an end to the darkness and usher in the light of God's Day. Although the area of time will be short, and the divine action will be swift, at least three events must be placed in this transitional category.

a. The Glorious Arrival of the Mediatorial King

Lo, this is our God; we have waited for him. —Isa. 25:9

In the hour of deepest darkness for Israel and Jerusalem, when it seems that total defeat is certain, "Then shall the LORD go forth, and fight against those nations, as when he fought in the day of battle" (Zech. 14:3). And lest these words might be misunderstood as referring to some spiritual or providential coming of the LORD, the next verse adds a note of literality: "his feet shall stand in that day upon the mount of Olives, which is before Jerusalem on the east" (vs. 4). For those who may have some reluctance in accepting the literality of these details, a parallel may be cited in the same prophetic book where the lowly first coming of the King is described as follows: "behold, thy King cometh unto thee: he is just, and having salvation; lowly, and riding upon an ass, and upon a colt the foal of an ass" (Zech. 9:9). Since this has been literally fulfilled, why should the other be rejected as unreasonable? As far as plausibility is concerned, what is the difference between the King riding in humiliation upon an ass and the King standing gloriously on a mountain? — especially since it is the same King and both events occur on the same mountain (cf. Luke 19:37).

To the people of God on earth the glorious coming of the King will bring unspeakable comfort and joy. The prophets recur again and again to this glad theme. "And it shall be said in that day, Lo, this is our God; we have waited for him, and he will save us: this is the LORD; we have waited for him, we will be glad and rejoice in his salvation" (Isa. 25:9). "O Jerusalem, that bringest good tidings, lift up thy voice with strength; lift it up, be not afraid; say unto the cities of Judah, Behold your God! Behold, the LORD God will come with strong hand" (Isa. 40:9-10). "This is the day which the LORD hath made; we will rejoice and be glad in it. . . . Blessed be he that cometh in the name of the LORD" (Ps. 118:24, 26). For other references to this glad day, see Isaiah 63:1; and Psalms 96:13, 98:9, 102:16, and 110:1-2.

The importance of this grand event cannot be overemphasized. For the arrival of the divine King from heaven to take over the kingdoms of the world will mark the most crucial turning point in human history since Calvary. From this point onward nothing will ever be the same again. The deep darkness of man's "day" will now pass into the glorious light of God's "Day." Through the long night of man's misgovernment, the godly had often complained, "We wait for light, but behold obscurity; for brightness, but we walk in darkness. . . . We stumble at noon day as in the night" (Isa. 59:9-10). But now the King who descends from heaven is the LORD who Himself is the "everlasting light" (Isa. 60:19). And under His strong hand the action will be swift, with no more heartbreaking delays to try the faith of God's elect. Best of all, the change from darkness into light will be irreversible, leaving no room for any point of return back to the dismal failures of man's attempts to govern himself. The "Sun of righteousness" will have risen upon the world, and it will not set again (Mal. 4:2; cf. Isa. 60:20).

b. *The Destruction of the Hostile Armies*

> I will seek to destroy all the nations that come against Jerusalem.
> —Zech. 12:9

Against all the devices of interpreters who seek to show that God is finished with the historic people of Israel and with their beloved city of Jerusalem, the prophetic ultimatum stands firm: "He that toucheth you toucheth the apple of his eye" (Zech. 2:8; cf. vss. 4-7). In this city the Theocratic Kingdom of history was once centered, and it is reserved as the place where the Kingdom shall again be established. Therefore, those who are wise have never ceased to "Pray for the peace of Jerusalem" (Ps. 122:6). For all the hopes of a future Kingdom of God on earth are in a certain sense bound up with the future of this city.

As an evidence of God's continued and loving interest in Jerusalem, it should be observed that the final assault against the city by the armies of the world, under the leadership of the blasphemous "little horn," will bring swift destruction upon these military forces. In fact, it is precisely this presumptuous assault that will bring the divine King down from heaven, and His first action on earth will be the defense of Jerusalem: "In that day shall the LORD defend the inhabitants of Jerusalem" (Zech. 12:8). What may seem to the attackers only a routine and rather minor military project will turn out to be a veritable Waterloo of catastrophe: "in that day," God warns, "will I make Jerusalem a burdensome stone for all people: all that burden themselves with it shall be cut in pieces, though all the people of the earth be gathered together against it" (Zech. 12:3). "I will seek to destroy all the nations that come against Jerusalem" (Zech. 12:9).

The crushing of the attacking forces will be supernaturally accomplished, and this power will be manifested in three ways. First, the human defenders left in the besieged city will be endowed with superhuman power. "In that day will I make the governors of Judah like an hearth of fire among the wood, and like a torch of fire in a sheaf; and they shall devour all the people round about. . . . he that is feeble among them at that day shall be as David; and the house of David shall be as God, as the angel of the LORD before them" (Zech. 12:6, 8). Second, a heavenly reserve, in the person of Michael the archangel, will be sent into the action on behalf of the besieged Israelites. Through the centuries the chief ministry of this great angel has been to defend the interests of the chosen nation (Dan. 12:1). Third, there will be supernatural visitations of wrath which will fall directly on the attackers. Every horse will be smitten with "terror" and "blindness" while the riders will be seized with "madness" (Zech. 12:4, ASV). In this condition of mental confusion and derangement, the attackers will begin fighting each other (Zech. 14:13). And added to all these blows there will come a supernatural "plague" upon the armies, so that the eyes and tongues and flesh of men shall suddenly "consume away while they stand on their feet" (Zech. 14:12).

The prophet Isaiah has given a vivid description of this terrible judgment of God upon a wicked and rebellious world: "For, behold, Jehovah will come with fire, and his chariots shall be like the whirlwind; to render his anger with fierceness, and his rebuke with flames of fire. For by fire will Jehovah execute judgment, and by his sword, upon all flesh; and the slain of Jehovah shall be many" (Isa. 66:15-16, ASV). So staggering will be the loss of life under the divine "indignation" that in the days of the coming Kingdom men will look back to this terrible occasion as "the day of the great slaughter" (Isa. 30:25).

If such a judgment seems to run beyond the requirements of justice, it should not be forgotten that the devilish intent here is the same as that which always has motivated the great historic attacks on this chosen city of God: "And now many nations are assembled against thee, that say, Let her be defiled, and let our eye see our desire upon Zion" (Mic. 4:11, ASV). Thus the eyes that look with eager desire for evil upon Jerusalem shall be made to feel the inflexible *lex talionis* of God (Exod. 21:23-25).

c. The Doom of the Blasphemous "Little Horn"

Yet he shall come to his end, and none shall help him.
—*Dan. 11:45*

Various means — supernaturally enabled, as we have already seen — may be used to destroy the armies of the nations. But it is altogether fitting that the doom of their wicked leader should be reserved for the personal hand of the Mediatorial King Himself. For this "man of sin" has dared presumptuously to match his strength against "the Prince of princes" (Dan. 8:25). And therefore his destruction will be accomplished by the immediate and invisible power of Deity apart from all human means — "he shall be broken without hand" (Dan. 8:25).

In that hour all his vast "dominion" shall be taken away (Dan. 7:26). The prophet Haggai speaks of this final universal concentration of political power as "the throne of kingdoms" and affirms that it shall be overthrown (2:22). Stripped of all his satanic power and authority, his vast empire crumbling under the force of the Stone from heaven, he comes to his "end"; and among all his once powerful allies "none shall help him" (Dan. 11:45).

In the hearts of most of the world's great tyrants, even in the hour of defeat and death, there has often seemed to be a deep concern about the proper disposal of their physical remains. The mausoleums of the Egyptian kings bear historical witness to this concern. In this respect the end of this final world dictator is particularly ignominious. Daniel says, "I beheld even till the beast was slain, and his body destroyed, and given to the burning flame" (7:11). In still greater detail his end is described by Isaiah: "All the kings of the nations, even all of them, lie in glory, every one in his own house. But thou art cast out of thy grave like an abominable branch . . . as a carcase trodden under feet. Thou shalt not be joined with them in burial" (14:18-20).

The defeat and doom of the beast produces a reaction which will reach even to the underworld of the dead. On earth there will be relief; men will shout with joy: "How hath the oppressor ceased! . . . The LORD hath broken the staff of the wicked, and the sceptre of the rulers. . . . The whole earth is at rest, and is quiet; they break forth into singing" (Isa. 14:3-8). And as the naked soul of this once great world dictator descends into the underworld, the reaction becomes still more impressive: "Hell from beneath is moved for thee to meet thee at thy coming. . . . All they shall speak and say unto thee, Art thou also become weak as we? Art thou become like unto us?" (Isa. 14:9-10). "Is this the man that made the earth to tremble, that did shake kingdoms; that made the world as a wilderness, and destroyed the cities thereof . . . ?" (Isa. 14:16-17). The king of Babylon described in this chapter cannot be the king of historic Babylon, for the shout of joy over his downfall comes from Israel "in the day" when they are given rest from all their agelong sorrow and fear and bondage, as indicated in verses 1-4. He is the final king of the world system which began in the Babylon of history and which will end in a future and greater Babylon.

4. Constitutive Events — During the Light of the Day of the Lord

> Arise, shine; for thy light is come, and the glory of the LORD is risen upon thee. . . . Thy sun shall no more go down; neither shall thy moon withdraw itself: for the LORD shall be thine everlasting light, and the days of thy mourning shall be ended.   —Isa. 60:1, 20

With the doom of the beast and his armies, the penal and destructive actions of the Day of the Lord are finished and the transition from the darkness to the light is accomplished. The way is now cleared for what I have termed the *constitutive* events of the Day. In the establishment of the Kingdom there are certain constructive acts of the King by which He will deal judicially with humanity, separate the righteous from the unrighteous, effect the organization of His government, make right the things which are wrong — in short, do the things necessary to bring in the wondrous benefits and conditions of the long awaited Kingdom.

a. *There Will Be a Resurrection*

Thy dead men shall live.   —*Isa. 26:19*

The chief Old Testament passage is Daniel 12:1-3, which reads as follows: "And at that time shall Michael stand up, the great prince which standeth for the children of thy people: and there shall be a time of trouble, such as never was since there was a nation even to that same time: and at that time thy people shall be delivered, every one that shall be found written in the book. And many of them that sleep in the dust of the earth shall awake, some to everlasting life, and some to shame and everlasting contempt. And they that be wise shall shine as the brightness of the firmament; and they that turn many to righteousness as the stars for ever and ever." Several things here are of interest.

First, this is a *physical* resurrection. The people involved are those "that sleep in the dust of the earth" (vs. 2). These words could only refer to the physical body.

Second, it is a resurrection of *Israelites*. As the angelic messenger clearly indicated to Daniel, the primary subject of the passage is "thy people" (vs. 1). It is Daniel's historic people who will suffer the terrible time of trouble, and the same people are to be the subjects of this resurrection.

Third, even among the Israelites it will be a *selective* resurrection. Not all, but only *"many"* of them that sleep in the dust of the earth shall awake. By no reasonable device of interpretation can "many" be turned into *all*. Furthermore, the resurrection does not include both good and bad, as the King James version seems to indicate. Verse 2 may be rendered as follows: "Many *from among* the sleepers . . . *these* shall be unto everlasting life; but *those* [the rest of the sleepers who do not awake at this time] shall be unto shame."[6] Thus, just as there is a selective deliverance among the *living* Israelites, restricted to those "found written in the book" (vs. 1); even so there is a selective resurrection among the *dead,* restricted to those who shall be awakened to everlasting life. Scripture knows nothing of a general resurrection, either of Israelites or of all men, both good and bad, simultaneously.

Finally, Daniel's prophecy places this resurrection as the first event

[6] So Tregelles reads the passage, and A. R. Fausset says the Jewish commentators support him (Jamieson, Fausset, and Brown *Commentary on the Bible* [New York: Geo. H. Doran, no date], *in loc.*).

at the terrible "time of trouble" which Israel will suffer at the end (vss. 1-2). This order is supported by other considerations. For centuries the godly of the nation had been praying and longing for the promised Kingdom. And since the ordeal of death seemed to extinguish the hope of a personal sharing in that Kingdom, the doctrine of a physical resurrection became the solution of this distressing problem. It is wholly appropriate, therefore, to find that the first constitutive act of the King is a resurrection of godly Israelites who, like Joseph of Arimathaea, throughout all their days on earth had "waited for the kingdom of God" (Luke 23:51).

Whether or not there may be a resurrection hope for godly Gentiles at this time is a matter of which Daniel says nothing. But Isaiah seems to indicate a wider scope in his words, "Thy dead men shall live . . . Awake and sing, ye that dwell in the dust" (26:19). For this resurrection of God's "men" is associated with the glorious coming of the Lord to punish the inhabitants of the earth (vs. 21). New Testament revelation will shed further light on this point.

b. *There Will Be a Repentance of Israelites in the Land*

They shall call on my name, and I will hear them.   —Zech. 13:9

Among the numerous passages in the Old Testament which speak of a great spiritual change yet to be wrought in the nation of Israel in the last days, the most vivid picture is given by Zechariah (12:10-13:2). In this passage some important facts about this great turning of Israel are revealed.

First, the *time* is definitely stated. It follows immediately after the judgment upon the nations which come against Jerusalem (Zech. 12:9-10).

Second, the *cause* of Israel's repentance is twofold. Basically this is the work of *God:* "I will pour upon the house of David, and upon the inhabitants of Jerusalem, the spirit of grace and supplications" (vs. 10). It is Jehovah, not man, who always must initiate the work of grace. But, on the other hand, the divine work is wrought through tangible means; in this case, a vision of the King of Glory as the One who had been slain: "They shall look upon me," says Jehovah, "whom they have pierced" (vs. 10). And the sudden realization that the great Deliverer in their hour of peril is none other than the historic Jesus of Nazareth will start the flood of tears.

Third, Israel's repentance will be *genuine,* not superficial. The tears are bitter; they mourn "as one mourneth for his only son . . . his firstborn" (vs. 10). So deep is the grief of Israel, as they stand now in the presence of the One whom they had crucified, that it can only be compared to the memorable grief of Israel over the death of good King Josiah "in the valley of Megiddon" (vs. 11; cf. II Chron. 35:24-26).

Fourth, as to its *extent,* the tearful repentance will begin in Jerusalem and move throughout "the land" (Zech. 12:11-12). Every family will mourn, beginning with the "house of David" and spreading to "all the families that remain" (vss. 12-13). From other passages to be considered later, we shall find here the beginning of a turning to God which will spread through all the world.

Fifth, the *results* of this repentance appear immediately: there is spiritual cleansing for sin and uncleanness (Zech. 13:1); and the false prophets and false gods are forsaken (13:2). Other texts indicate comfort for the grief-stricken nation: "As one whom his mother comforteth, so will I comfort you; and ye shall be comforted in Jerusalem" (Isa. 66:13).

Finally, in this repentance of Israel we have the preliminary condition for her spiritual ministry to all the nations of the earth. The promise of Psalm 67:7 states the divine order with infallible accuracy: "God shall bless us" — the blessing of Israel must be first. Then the world-wide blessing follows: "and all the ends of the earth shall fear him." The long obduracy of the chosen nation will at last be ended: "Thy people shall be willing in the day of thy power" (Ps. 110:3).

c. *There Will Be a Regathering of Dispersed Israelites*

I will gather you from all the nations.   —*Jer. 29:14*

The regathering of historic Israel is one of the major themes of prophetic Scripture, beginning in the writings of Moses (Deut. 30: 1-3) and reaching its climax in the minor prophets. Yet the sole notice given to it in many theological works is a *denial* that it will ever be fulfilled. Such an attitude is hard to understand. For the same inspired Word which affirmed that the nation would be scattered throughout the world also predicted that the nation shall again be assembled. There is certainly no historical uncertainty about the literality of the dispersion, and there should be no question about the regathering. "Hear the word of the LORD, O ye nations, and declare it in the isles afar off, and say, He that scattered Israel will gather him, and keep him, as a shepherd doth his flock" (Jer. 31:10). "Behold, I will gather them out of all countries, whither I have driven them in mine anger . . . and I will bring them again unto this place. . . . For thus saith the LORD: Like as I have brought all this great evil upon this people, so will I bring upon them all the good that I have promised them" (Jer. 32:37, 42). An unbiased examination of these and numerous other passages on the regathering of Israel will lead to several general conclusions.

First, the regathering will be both a *divine* and a *human* accomplishment. Primarily the work is God's; but, although there are intimations which point to supernatural means, certain texts indicate that human instrumentalities will also be used: "And the peoples shall take them, and bring them to their place" (Isa. 14:2, ASV). Using a beautiful figure, Isaiah describes the ships speeding to carry the Israelites back to their own promised land. They come as "doves" homing to "their windows," led by the "ships of Tarshish," bringing not only the "sons" of Israel but also "their silver and their gold with them" (Isa. 60:8-9).[7]

Second, the regathering of Israel will be *international* in its scope. God will bring them out of "all countries" wherever they have been scattered in His anger (Jer. 32:37). They will come from east, west, north, and south (Isa. 43:5-6). No matter how far removed from the promised land they may have been driven, God will find them and fetch them back (Deut. 30:4). The blind and the lame, and those who weep, will not be forgotten by the Great Shepherd of the sheep (Jer. 31:8-10). He will leave "none of them any more there" among the nations (Ezek. 39:28). The work will be thorough: "Behold, I will send for many fishers, saith Jehovah, and they shall fish them up; and afterward I will send for many hunters, and they shall hunt them from every mountain, and from every hill, and out of the clefts of the rocks" (Jer. 16:16, ASV). The next verse (17) suggests that among those gathered will be some whose ways are evil. Even today there are many Jewish people who care little or nothing about the ancient promises of Jehovah to Israel; as one wealthy Jew in southern California once expressed himself: "Los Angeles is good enough for me." Such members of the nation will be gathered out of the lands where they dwell and be dealt with judicially (cf. point 4 below).

Third, this regathering of Israel will be accompanied with a great *spiritual revival* among the people. We have already seen the won-

[7] The linguistic explanation of Franz Delitzsch here is very helpful until he slips into the semantic confusion of Israel with the Church. However, he correctly asserts that "the distinction between Israel and the Gentiles" is maintained in Scripture, "even in the New Jerusalem" (*Commentary on Isaiah* [Grand Rapids: Eerdmans Publishing Co., reprint, 1950], Vol. II, pp. 415, 414).

derful work of God among those in the land when the King arrives. The same thing will take place among those still scattered
among the nations. This is foretold in the great Deuteronomy passage (30:1-6). In fact, here the revival precedes the regathering:
"And it shall come to pass, when all these things are come upon thee,
the blessing and the curse, which I have set before thee, and thou
shalt call them to mind among all the nations, whither the LORD thy
God hath driven thee, and shalt return unto the LORD thy God . . .
with all thine heart, and with all thy soul; that then the LORD thy
God shall turn thy captivity. . . . And the LORD thy God will bring
thee into the land which thy fathers possessed." In words almost without parallel, Ezekiel (34:10-16) pictures the gracious work of the
regal Shepherd who will tenderly gather the sheep who have been
neglected and abused by their human shepherds: "I will feed my
flock, and I will cause them to lie down, saith the LORD God. I will
seek that which was lost, and bring again that which was driven
away, and will bind up that which was broken, and will strengthen
that which was sick" (vss. 15-16).

Fourth, this regathering of Israel and restoration to their own land
will be *permanent*. There have been other regatherings recorded in
history.[8] But those have been only partial and never permanent. On
the contrary, the regathering at the time of the Kingdom's establishment will bring a full end to the wanderings of this ancient people.
In that day they will never again defile themselves with idols or de-
testable things, they shall dwell in the land forever, and God's sanctuary will be in their midst for evermore (Ezek. 37:21-28). Never
again will the face of God be hidden from them, "for I have poured
out my spirit upon the house of Israel, saith the Lord GOD" (Ezek.
39:29). "I will plant them upon their own land, and they shall no
more be pulled up out of their land which I have given them,
saith the LORD thy God" (Amos 9:15). The long wanderings of
Israel, their persecutions, their disasters, their sufferings, their estrangement from God, even their present uncertainties and deadly
perils — all these things add up to one unanswerable argument that
the Old Testament prophecies of Israel's regathering have never been
fulfilled. The Amillennial reply is too easy and glib; in fact, no
answer at all. For those who accept it, the hermeneutical price is immeasurable; for in the interest of a rigid philosophic unity, it actually
blots out many of the richest pages of Holy Writ. All it can say in

8 See the records in Ezra and Nehemiah.

the face of these wonderful pages is to repeat monotonously, "These things cannot be literally fulfilled."

d. *There Will Be a Judgment of Living Israelites*

I will purge out from among you the rebels. —*Ezek. 20:38*

The main passage is Ezekiel 20:33-38, which is reproduced here in full as it appears in the American Standard Version: "As I live, saith the Lord Jehovah, surely with a mighty hand, and with an outstretched arm, and with wrath poured out, will I be king over you. And I will bring you out from the peoples, and will gather you out of the countries wherein ye are scattered, with a mighty hand, and with an outstretched arm, and with wrath poured out; and I will bring you into the wilderness of the peoples, and there will I enter into judgment with you face to face. Like as I entered into judgment with your fathers in the wilderness of the land of Egypt, so will I enter into judgment with you, saith the Lord Jehovah. And I will cause you to pass under the rod, and I will bring you into the bond of the covenant; and I will purge out from among you the rebels, and them that transgress against me; I will bring them forth out of the land where they sojourn, but they shall not enter into the land of Israel: and ye shall know that I am Jehovah."

First, the *time* of the event here described is set very definitely. It will immediately follow the regathering of Israel out of the countries unto which they have been dispersed (cf. vss. 34 and 35). And the context clearly shows that the judgment will precede the actual entrance of Israel back into the land.

Second, the *place* is specified as "the wilderness of the peoples" (vs. 35). Certain of the commentators argue that this wilderness is a "spiritual" description of the Jews' present condition where they are now among the nations. But this introduces a flat contradiction into the prophecy. How can God gather Israel "out of the countries" and bring them into the "wilderness," if the latter is merely another name for the former? The comparison drawn between this event and that which took place during the historical march from Egypt to Palestine, fixes beyond question the geographical location. It is the well-known wilderness of the Sinaitic peninsula, which to this day is occupied by various "peoples" (vs. 35, ASV).

Third, the action of God here is *judicial* in character. He will "enter into judgment" with regathered Israel "face to face" (vs. 35). And the comparison with the historic events which occurred "in the wilderness" (vs. 36) is highly significant. For there, after God had established the Mediatorial Kingdom of Old Testament history at Sinai, organizing it as a true theocratic government, He proceeded to purge out all dissidents. Even so, in the establishment of the future Kingdom, God will renew His "face to face" dealings with Israel (cf. Deut. 5:4).

Fourth, the *results* of this judicial event are clearly indicated. The rebels will be purged out from the regathered nation. They shall be brought out of whatever country where they reside, but they "shall not enter into the land of Israel" (Ezek. 20:38, ASV). These rebels may desire to submerge their identity by full integration with other nations and their idolatrous ways (vs. 32), but all such attempts will be suppressed by the "mighty hand" of God (vs. 33). On the other hand, out of this judicial separation will come a cleansed remnant who will humbly and joyfully submit to the King, and these shall enter the land as the people of God (cf. vss. 40-44).

Finally, throughout this divine action, it should be observed that the Lord is acting in His *regal* capacity. His judicial work in the regathered nation is based on His determination to be their King. "As I live," He declares, "will I be king over you" (vs. 33). To this end, nothing essential will be left undone. And judgment must begin with the chosen nation.

e. *There Will Also Be a Judgment of Living Gentile Nations*

I will gather all nations and . . . execute judgment upon them.
                                                        —*Joel 3:2, ASV*

In the formal judgment of a court, whether of God or of man, there are always two distinct factors: first, there is the *judicial* action, a determination of the law and the facts, issuing in a verdict; second, there is an *execution* of the verdict, consisting in the proper awards to the parties involved. Although in Biblical prophecy it is not always easy to distinguish sharply between these two factors, it should be admitted by all that there can be no execution of awards without a prior judicial examination of parties and the facts. The penal wrath of God already poured out on the Gentile nations, as we have seen above, has issued from a court set *in heaven* (cf. above: a. under 1.). But now the Mediatorial King has come down from heaven and set up His throne of judgment *on the earth*, and from the vantage of this throne He will now deal with the living nations there. In the words of Isaiah: "He shall judge among the nations" (2:4).

For this purpose there shall be a gathering together of the living nations left on earth following the world-wide inflictions of divine wrath. Concerning these God has forewarned: "I know their works and their thoughts: the time cometh, that I will gather all nations and tongues; and they shall come, and shall see my glory" (Isa. 66:18, ASV). The nations of the world have seen the King coming in humiliation, the lowly Carpenter of Nazareth; a Man of sorrows and acquainted with grief; despised and rejected of men. They have seen Him standing thorn-crowned at Pilate's bar of judgment. Now they must see Him coming in regal glory; and they must stand before His throne of judgment. Having thus dealt with the living nation of Israel, the King will now bring the living Gentile nations into a like ordeal of judgment.

The outstanding Old Testament passage on this subject is Joel 3:1-3 (ASV), which reads as follows: "For, behold, in those days, and in that time, when I shall bring back the captivity of Judah and Jerusalem, I will gather all nations, and will bring them down into the valley of Jehoshaphat; and I will execute judgment upon them there for my people and for my heritage Israel, whom they have scattered among the nations: and they have parted my land, and have cast lots for my people, and have given a boy for a harlot, and sold a girl for wine, that they may drink." Several ideas here should be noted.

First, the *time* of this judgment is stated precisely as "in that time" when God will "bring back the captivity of Judah and Jerusalem" (vs. 1). Therefore, it must follow the great destruction of the attacking armies described in verses 9-16. The literary order of prediction does not always follow the chronological order of events. The assault upon Jerusalem is introduced after the announcement of divine judgment for the very good reason that this supreme crime of the nations will form the main subject for judicial examination.

Second, the *place* of judgment is specified as "the valley of Jehoshaphat" (vss. 2, 12). The identification of this place has been a matter of some controversy. However, Keil concludes that "the tradition of the church . . . has correctly assigned it to the valley of the Kidron, on the eastern side of Jerusalem."[9] Whether or not this opinion is correct, it is significant that the judgment will be held *in the place where the high crime was committed*. In the valley where the nations assemble for their assault against God's city, there He will "sit to judge" them. This is a procedure not unknown to human jurisprudence. The trials of the so-called "war criminals" of the Hitler

[9] C. F. Keil, *Commentary on Minor Prophets,* trans. J. Martin (Grand Rapids: Eerdmans Publishing Co., reprint, 1951), on Joel 3:2.

regime, which sought to annihilate the Jewish people, were held in Germany, not in London or Washington. And, since the supreme crime of human government was its treatment of Israel's King, no more appropriate place for the judgment could be found than the valley of Kidron. On this point nothing finer could be written than the words of Dr. Pusey:

> There was the garden whither Jesus oftentimes resorted with His disciples; there was His agony and Bloody Sweat; there Judas betrayed Him; thence He was dragged by the rude officers of the High Priest. The Temple, the token of His accepting their sacrifices which could only be offered there, overhung it on the one side. There, under the rock on which that temple stood, they dragged Jesus, as a lamb to the slaughter. On the other side, it was overhung by the Mount of Olives, whence He beheld the city and wept over it, because it knew not in that its day, the things which belong to its peace; whence, after His precious Death and Resurrection, Jesus ascended into Heaven. There the Angels foretold His return, "This same Jesus which is taken up from you into heaven shall so come in like manner as ye have seen Him go into heaven." It has been a current opinion, that our Lord should descend to judgment, not only in like manner, and in the like Form of Man, but in the same place, over this valley of Jehoshaphat. Certainly, if so it be, it were appropriate, that He should appear in His Majesty, where, for us, He bore the extremest shame; that He should judge there, where for us, He submitted to be judged.[10]

To the objection that this limited space is not adequate for the assembling of all the nations, the answer is twofold: (a) Since there is no direct assertion that all are brought here at one time, the period of judgment may be prolonged.[11] (b) The population of the world will have been greatly reduced by reason of the preceding world-wide judgments of God.

Third, the *main indictment* in the judgment of the nations will be their crimes against the chosen people of Israel. "I will execute judgment upon them there for my people and for my heritage Israel," is the declaration of the regal Judge (Joel 3:2, ASV). Listed among these crimes are the forced dispersions of Israel, the division and plundering of the Holy Land, and the contemptuous evaluation and callous treatment of even the children: a Jewish boy is the price of a harlot, and a girl goes for a drink of wine! And our Lord, for whose raiment the Roman soldiers cast lots, was a Jew! For these agelong crimes the existing governments of the world will now be brought into a judgment long delayed. Nor will the judgment be confined to matters of *Jewish* ill-treatment. It has sometimes been asked whether

[10] E. B. Pusey, *Commentary on the Minor Prophets,* (New York: Funk and Wagnalls, 1886), Vol. I, p. 201.
[11] See the very interesting discussion of this point by Dr. Merrill C. Tenney, under the title, "The Importance and Exegesis of Rev. 20:1-8," *Bibliotheca Sacra,* April, 1954, pp. 146-148.

God is concerned only with the injustices done to Israel. The answer is found in Isaiah 2:4, "He will judge between the nations" (ASV). Surely this must involve an inquiry into many a wrong committed against the innocent and defenseless of *all* nations.

Fourth, this judgment of the nations will involve *persons* as well as governments. In any judgment of this nature the problem of moral responsibility cannot be side-stepped. In the crimes of nations, do the people share to any extent in the guilt of their rulers? Does the minor official escape responsibility in obeying the orders of his superiors? May the chief of state enjoy an immunity not vouchsafed to an ordinary criminal? These problems have never been satisfactorily solved in the history of human government; but they will be solved in the coming divine judgment of the nations. It will be found in that day that the citizens of the state, as well as its rulers, will bear a certain measure of moral responsibility for national crimes. To say it is *always* the duty of the citizen to obey the state, as some have carelessly argued, is to forget that there are times when *God* should be obeyed rather than men (Acts 5:29). The truth is that *morally* there can be no absolute divorce between personal and governmental responsibility. For a government, apart from its rulers and citizens, is wholly an abstraction.

Finally, it must be observed that this is not a general judgment of all men, but only of *living Gentile nations* on earth at the beginning of the Mediatorial Kingdom. There is no resurrection of the dead, as would be required in any such an alleged general judgment. But for the living men involved, as well as for existing governments, it will be a *final* judgment. At the inauguration of the Kingdom on earth the judgment of God will make an absolute and final separation between the righteous and the unrighteous, between those who rebel and those who submit to the King. Rebellious governments will be abolished; rebellious men will be destroyed. "For the nation and kingdom that will not serve thee shall perish" (Isa. 60:12). In this respect the Millennial Kingdom will begin with a clean slate.

CHAPTER XVII

THE GOVERNMENT IN THE KINGDOM OF OLD TESTAMENT PROPHECY

> Thus there is during the Kingdom period a well-ordered system of government, embracing the whole earth, administered by Christ, through those whom He appoints; a system adapted to meet the needs of all its inhabitants in all their varied conditions and degrees of intellectual development. —*Samuel J. Andrews*[1]

It is generally conceded that however lofty and good our basic principles may be in the field of political science, they cannot become effective in human life except by implementation through concrete forms and organization. Even the so-called "leavening" process, according to those who insist upon an exclusively "spiritual" Kingdom of God, could not operate in a vacuum. It had to have the "three measures of meal" as a physical structure in which to accomplish its work. Thus, as is becoming clearer in modern times, the reformers of government must become interested in organization and forms, which are the body through which principles and ideals are realized in human life. And if the body apart from the spirit is dead, it is likewise true that the human spirit apart from the body can produce no effective results in the world of sense experience. Hence, as far as the present life and world are concerned, there can be no longer any valid argument about the importance of perceptible forms for the realization of political ideals. The only questions are: first, are the people of God, in their present state on earth, wholly competent to produce these essential forms and organizations? And, second, may they legitimately look for some supernatural reinforcement from above, for the purpose of establishing such forms on earth among men? In their visions of the future Mediatorial Kingdom of God, the Old Testament prophets devote considerable space to these matters.

1. *The Form of Mediatorial Government*

> Behold, a king shall reign.   —*Isa. 32:1*

Concerning this there can be no question. The Mediatorial King-

[1] S. J. Andrews, *God's Revelations of Himself to Men* (New York: Scribner's Sons, 1886), p. 323.

dom of Old Testament prophecy is *monarchial* in form. Its ruler is a King, who will sit upon a "throne"; and the government will be "upon his shoulder" (Isa. 9:6-7). He receives regal authority and exercises it by divine grant: He is God's King, established upon His throne on earth by the supernatural power of "the God of heaven" (Ps. 2:6; Dan. 2:44, 7:14).

All the functions of government are centered in the glorious Person of this Mediatorial King. The prophet Isaiah paints a vivid picture of the political situation in the days of the established Kingdom: Then the eyes of men "shall see the king in his beauty" ruling upon the earth as a "judge," "lawgiver," and "king" (Isa. 33:17, 22) — a remarkable forecast of the conventional divisions of modern government: judicial, legislative, and executive.

The chief problem in the operation of government has always been to keep these necessary functions in a state of proper balance, and at the same time to provide some center of unification. This problem has never been wholly solved. Human government, therefore, always swings between the two opposite poles of regimentation and fragmentation: the former leading to a sacrifice of liberty in the interest of strength; the latter to a sacrifice of strength in the interest of liberty. And the head of the state tends to become either a dictator or a mere symbol.

The founding fathers of our own American state, approaching their task with a deep suspicion of human nature, designed an ingenious system of checks and balances to separate these three functions into departments and keep any one of them from usurping too much power. Although it seems clumsy and inefficient at times, lacking both in unity and economy, nevertheless our government has furnished a welcome refuge for political liberty in a sinful world, and will continue to do so — if we can keep it.

But this precarious balance of powers is not the most ideal political form. When God's own glorious King takes over the kingdoms of earth, it will be safe at last to concentrate all the functions of the state in one Person. This does not mean that He will do everything; but rather that He will be the directing head and final authority; thus providing a unifying center, both infinitely wise and good, for all the activities of government; something which no state on earth has ever enjoyed. Under His beneficent rule, it will no longer be necessary to sacrifice political unity and strength in the interest of political liberty. "If the Son therefore shall make you free, ye shall

be free indeed" (John 8:36) — this principle is true in every department of human life, whether spiritual or political.

2. The Nature of the Mediatorial Government

Righteousness and justice are the foundation of thy throne.
—Ps. 89:14, ASV

It will be a rule based on *moral principles*. In the prophets four
great words are used to indicate these principles: truth, holiness,
righteousness, and justice. Under the reign of the coming King the
earth will rejoice and the isles will be glad because "righteousness and
justice are the foundation of his throne" (Ps. 97:1-2, ASV). His
Kingdom will prosper because He will "execute justice and righteousness in the land" (Jer. 23:5, ASV). As the visible center of His
government, Jerusalem shall be called "the city of truth" and "the
holy mountain" (Zech. 8:3, ASV). The Hebrew terms used in Isaiah
16:5 suggest the moral character of the King's reign: He will not
only keep to the *forms* of the law ("judging"); but He will also
interest Himself to find the *substantial* right in every case ("seeking
judgment"); and then He will *promptly execute* the verdict ("hasting righteousness").[2] As to the desperate need of the world for the
establishment of such a government, there is clear evidence on every
hand. Even in the most enlightened of modern states, too often the
tragic confession of ancient Israel could be written over its gates:
"Justice is turned away backward, and righteousness standeth afar off;
for truth is fallen in the street, and uprightness cannot enter" (Isa.
59:14, ASV).

These great moral principles of the mediatorial government will be
enforced by *sanctions of supernatural power*. The answer of God
to all people and kings who venture to set themselves against the
beneficent rule of the coming Kingdom is a solemn commission to
His anointed King: "Thou art my son. . . . Ask of me, and I shall
give thee the heathen [nations] for thine inheritance. . . . Thou shalt
break them with a rod of iron; thou shalt dash them in pieces like a
potter's vessel" (Ps. 2:7-9). No longer will the wicked oppressor of
the poor be able to utter his cynical judgment: "God hath forgotten;
he hideth his face; he will never see it" (Ps. 10:9-11). No longer will
the righteous be troubled about the ways of God in a world where
things seem to be upside down (Ps. 73:2-16). The question as to
whether or not we live in a "moral universe" will no longer be a

[2] C. W. E. Naegelsbach, Lange's *Commentary on Isaiah*, trans. S. T. Lowrie
(New York: Scribner's Sons, 1878), on 16:5.

subject for philosophic debate. For in the coming Kingdom the judgments of God will be immediate and tangible to all men (Zech. 14:17-19; Isa. 66:24). The long period of God's judicial silence, which men have perversely construed as an evidence of moral indifference instead of long-suffering mercy on the part of God, will come to an end (Ps. 50:21). And with the judgments of a holy God once more manifest in the earth, "the inhabitants of the world will learn righteousness" (Isa. 26:9).

But moral government is more than an infallible determination of what is right and its inflexible enforcement. There must be a place for *mercy and tenderness* in dealing with the ignorant and the erring. Therefore we read in Isaiah 16:5 that "in mercy shall the throne be established." The King who comes to rule "with strong hand" will at the same time "feed his flock like a shepherd: he shall gather the lambs with his arm, and carry them in his bosom, and shall gently lead those that are with young" (Isa. 40:9-11). And if there will be swift and terrible justice for all who rebel, it is also true that "Blessed are all they that put their trust in him" (Ps. 2:9, 12). To maintain a perfect balance between mercy and justice is never an easy achievement. Historically, governments have been prone to swing between the two opposite poles of legal harshness on the one hand or sentimental laxness on the other. And the end is disaster in either case. But under the coming Mediatorial Kingdom the perfect equilibrium shall be reached. Its happy subjects will be able to say, "Mercy and truth are met together; righteousness and peace have kissed each other" (Ps. 85:10).

3. The External Organization of Mediatorial Government

Behold, a king shall reign . . . and princes shall rule. —*Isa. 32:1*

Here it must be said that in any government involving the participation of finite persons there must be some structural form. As S. J. Andrews has said, "There is during the Kingdom period a well-ordered system of government." This is true even in the Universal Kingdom with its divine throne in heaven. Among the angelic ministers of God there is organization — Michael is named as "one of the chief princes," who in his relation to earthly matters is "the great prince" with special responsibilities to the nation of Israel (Dan. 10:13; 12:1). There are "armies . . . in heaven" (Rev. 19:14), from which our Lord could have called "twelve legions of angels" (Matt. 26:53). And however deep the mystery may be, even some measure of protocol seems to be carefully observed in the heavenly organization of principalities and powers (Jude 9). Those who accept the inspired description of the *heavenly* Kingdom can hardly with any degree of consistency reject the idea of organization in God's Kingdom on *earth*, as set forth by the Old Testament prophets. Rather strangely, some of the most determined opponents of the idea of an organized Millennial Kingdom on earth, are at the same time the most insatiable organizers of the Christian Church, which they consider to be God's present "spiritual kingdom" on earth!

First, at the head of this Mediatorial Kingdom, of course, there is *"a king"* (Isa. 32:1). In the covenant with Abraham it was promised that "kings shall come out of thee" (Gen. 17:6); but among these kings there is One who is above all: He is "the LORD," who shall be "king over all the earth" — "one LORD, and his name one" (Zech. 14:9). The gracious New Testament promise, "we shall . . . reign with him" (II Tim. 2:12), should never blind our eyes to the un-bridgeable gulf between Him and us. He is infinite; we are finite. He is perfect in holiness; we are sinners saved by grace. In Him alone resides that regal authority which is final and complete, and which cannot be equally shared by even the highest and best of His creatures.

Second, in the structure of mediatorial government the prophets put the *"saints."* Following his vision of the sequence of world empires, which is consummated by the coming of the King "like unto a son of man" to establish an everlasting kingdom on earth, Daniel observes that "the saints of the Most High shall receive the kingdom, and possess the kingdom for ever, even for ever and ever" (7:13, 18, ASV). This important fact is asserted three times within the space of a single chapter (vss. 18, 22, 27). As to the identification of these saints, it will be sufficient to say that they are the saved of God, doubtless glorified, for there is a resurrection set at this time of con-summations (Dan. 12:1-3).[3] Perhaps these are the "princes" of Isaiah 32:1 who will "rule in judgment." In Ezekiel's visions of the coming Kingdom, David is named a "prince" who will resume his shepherdly care and reign in the midst of Israel "for ever" (37:24-25; cf. 34:23-24). If the "saints" are to possess the Kingdom, there can be no sound hermeneutical reason for denying to David a regal position in that Kingdom. The antimillennial use of these references to David as an argument against literal interpretation seems rather absurd. Even if the passages refer to Messiah, might not the name

---

[3] The place of the New Testament saints in the Mediatorial Kingdom will be discussed in later chapters.

be a patronymic properly applied to the greater "son of David"? But there can be no insuperable objection to a reference here to the historical king of Israel. Certainly David will be among the "saints" who will "possess the kingdom." The same can be said of Zerubbabel (Hag. 2:23). These Old Testament leaders may indeed be typical of the future Messianic King, but there is no sound reason for denying to them a place of honor in Messiah's Kingdom (cf. Matt. 8:11).

Third, at the next level in the governmental structure, the prophets all agree in presenting the *living nation of Israel*. In the future Kingdom this historic people will at last realize fully that international supremacy implied in the Abrahamic covenant. They are the chosen seed of Abraham, the friend of God; and therefore all attempts to destroy them must fail. For God will uphold them with His own right hand and fulfil His promises to them (Isa. 41:8-16). The restoration and supremacy of this nation will be accomplished by the Messianic King who is God's "servant" to do this very thing (Isa. 49:6). There can be no question here about their identity, for the prophet carefully distinguishes "Israel" from the "Gentiles." If this people in their long history of persecution and afflictions should feel that they are cast off and forgotten, the answer of God is, "Behold, I have graven thee upon the palms of my hands; thy walls are continually before me" (Isa. 49:16). A mother may forget the child at her breast, God says, "yet will I not forget thee" (vs. 15).

Nothing in the whole field of Old Testament prophecy could possibly surpass the brilliance and grandeur of the 60th chapter of Isaiah; and its central theme is the restoration and world supremacy of the nation of Israel. According to all the principles of sensible interpretation, the people under consideration in Isaiah 60 are the same as in chapter 59. It can only be theological prejudice which sees in chapter 59 "the sins of the Jews" and in chapter 60 "the glory of the church."[4] The prophet begins with a dramatic address to this people: "Arise, shine; for thy light is come, and the glory of the LORD is risen upon thee" (Isa. 60:1). Then he sees them as they return from their world-wide dispersion back to their own land and city (vss. 4-9). The nations which had afflicted them now come to pay homage to them as the chosen people of God (vs. 14). Foreign kings shall minister to them (vs. 10). The wealth of the nations will be devoted to their prosperity and the beautification of the sanctuary of their God (vss. 11, 13, 16, 17). The days of their mourning will be

4 See these chapter headings in certain editions of the King James Version.

ended (vs. 20). Violence and destruction will no more invade their borders (vs. 18). Their political supremacy will be guaranteed by the edict of Jehovah: "For the nation and kingdom that will not serve thee shall perish; yea, those nations shall be utterly wasted" (vs. 12).

But this world supremacy of Israel, as set forth in the prophets, is never an end in itself. Its grand purpose is the welfare of all nations, as asserted in the original covenant, "In thee shall all families of the earth be blessed" (Gen. 12:3). All the hard discipline of the centuries has had only one divine intention — the preparation of a nation to be the channel of divine blessing to a world unable to solve its own problems. To see this clearly sweeps away all objections to the idea of a "chosen nation." For along with the divine election of Israel to a place of world supremacy, there was attached a solemn responsibility. The nation of Israel has been chosen above all other nations to be the "servant" of God to bring good to those very nations (Isa. 41:8-9). All anti-Semitic prejudice (as well as narrow Semitic pride) arises out of blindness to the benevolent purpose of God. Once the eyes of men are opened to this divine purpose, the world must rejoice in the favor of God to Israel (Isa. 49:13).

The 47th Psalm presents a rather strange prophetic picture of all "people" clapping their hands for joy in the day when Jehovah will bring these very peoples and nations under the feet of Israel (vss. 1-3). Yet such an attitude is not so strange in the light of the unimaginable blessing to be brought to the world through the supremacy of Israel. Furthermore, the prayer of Israel in Psalm 67 may seem rather selfish at first sight: "God be merciful unto *us*, and bless *us*; and cause his face to shine upon *us*" (vs. 1, italics added). But the next verse lifts the prayer infinitely above all selfish considerations, for the purpose of God's blessing upon Israel is plainly stated: "That thy way may be known upon earth, thy saving health among all nations." In the light of this good purpose of God, the nations will "be glad and sing for joy" (vs. 4). For the nation of Israel, repentant and reconciled to God, shall be a "crown of glory in the hand of the LORD, and a royal diadem in the hand of thy God" (Isa. 62:3).

Fourth, at the lowest level, but definitely within the political framework of the mediatorial government, we find *the Gentile nations.* As we have already seen, the prophetic picture includes Gentile nations and rulers. The peculiar cultural values of the various nations, in so far as they may be used to contribute to the good of all, will not be abolished. In this respect, there will be no reduction of human society to one dull and faceless mediocrity, as it appears in the "one world" of Marxism. "Many nations" will be found within the structure of the coming Kingdom, their values and substance consecrated to "the LORD of the whole earth" (Mic. 4:2, 11-13). In that day "the princes of the peoples are gathered together to be the people of the God of Abraham" (Ps. 47:9, ASV). And these nations will be owned of Jehovah as "nations that are called by my name" (Amos 9:12, ASV). Even those peoples which were once enemies of Israel and her God may find a place of favor within the future Mediatorial Kingdom (Isa. 19:23-25). For, as the New Testament reminds us, God is the God of all men, whether Jews or Gentiles (Rom. 3:29).

The placing of the great Gentile nations at a lower political level in the coming Kingdom may seem, to some, to be a humiliating arrangement. But this feeling is only a manifestation of that ancient national pride which arises out of superior size and strength rather than superior contributions to the general welfare of the world. In that coming Kingdom it will be true of nations, as well as men, that "whosoever will be chief among you, let him be your servant" (Matt. 20:27). For that matter, it is recognized even today, at least in theory, that the ablest should occupy the highest echelons of human government; and also that it is no necessary disgrace for others to concur in such a disposition of talent.[5]

4. The Extent and Duration of This Mediatorial Government

All nations shall serve him . . . . His name shall endure for ever.
—Ps. 72:11, 17

First, it will be *universal in extent.* "In that day," the prophet Zechariah writes, "the LORD shall be king over all the earth" (14:9). The Kingdom will include "all nations" (Isa. 2:2). In his vision of the future Kingdom, Daniel sees it as a "stone" which smites the current political systems and then becomes a great mountain which fills "the whole earth" (2:34-35). In a later vision, the Kingdom is revealed as one which will include "all people, nations, and languages" (7:14). And the psalmist describes in still greater detail the universal scope of the reign of God's Mediatorial King: "He shall have dominion also from sea to sea, and from the river unto the ends of the earth. They that dwell in the wilderness shall bow before him; and his enemies shall lick the dust. . . . Yea, all kings shall fall down before him; all nations shall serve him" (72:8-11).

Instead of regarding government as a necessary evil — the less of it,

[5] Upon the entire point of these *gradations* within the future Kingdom, see the apt words of S. J. Andrews, *op. cit.,* p. 323.

the better — the beneficent rule of this Kingdom will extend to every department of human life and affect in some way its every detail; "In that day shall there be upon the bells of the horses, *HOLINESS UNTO THE LORD*. . . . Yea, every pot in Jerusalem and in Judah shall be holiness unto the LORD of hosts" (Zech. 14:20-21). It would be hard to imagine anything in human life more trivial than the tinkling bells with which men have decorated their horses; yet even on such things the prophet sees the sacred words which appeared on the golden plate of the diadem of Israel's high priest without which he could not minister on pain of death (Exod. 28:36, 43). Thus the agelong distinction between sacred and secular things, still so dear to the hearts of many who insist that Zechariah's prophecy must be fulfilled in the present Christian Church, will at last disappear in the immediate presence of the great King who is the giver and sustainer of all that exists. Everything, both small and great, will become holy by the touch of His rule.

In his comment on the final two verses of Zechariah's book of prophecy, Talbot W. Chambers describes conditions under the future commonwealth in words which deserve to be quoted in this connection:

> . . . the ordinary conditions of human life are not to be reversed; but on the contrary the infusion of grace will be so large and general that every rank and class will feel it, and its effects will be seen in all the relations of life, purifying and elevating without upturning or destroying. In business, in recreation, in politics, in art, in literature, in social life, in the domestic circle, there will be a distinct and cordial recognition of the claims of God and of the supremacy of his law. There will be no divorce anywhere between religion and morality, no demand that any department of human activity shall be deemed beyond the domain of conscience. When even the bells on the horses bear the same sacred inscription which once flashed from the diadem of the High Priest, nothing can be found too small or too familiar to be consecrated to the Lord. The religious spirit will prevail everywhere, securing justice, truth, kindness, and courtesy among men; doing away with wars, contentions, jealousies, and competitions; hallowing trades and handicrafts; softening the inevitable contrasts of ranks, gifts, conditions; binding men to one another by their devotion to a common master in heaven; and thus introducing the true city of God on earth for which all saints long with an ever increasing desire. The idea of such a commonwealth originated in the scriptures, and it can be realized only in the way they point out. All schemes of political, social, or even moral reform, apart from the principles of the Word, are the merest chimeras. They are impossible of accomplishment, and if accomplished, would disappoint their projectors.[6]

Although the writer of these words has accurately and beautifully described world conditions which are yet to be realized in the future,

---

[6] T. W. Chambers, Lange's *Commentary on Zechariah* (New York: Scribner's Sons, 1898; copyright 1874), p. 114.

he makes the mistake of supposing that all this will be accomplished by *men* in the exercise of "true religion." Written nearly a century ago, one wonders whether Dr. Chambers would express such optimism in the face of the present world situation.

Second, the Kingdom will be *everlasting in duration*. Unlike the greatest of earthly rulers, whose days at best are only a handbreadth of time and then they die like men, God's King "shall live" and "His name shall endure for ever" (Ps. 72:15, 17). Because He ever lives with the power of an endless life, His Kingdom will live as an "everlasting dominion" (Dan. 7:14). Its authority and power will never suffer any diminution or reverses, such as are common to the governments of men: "Of the increase of his government and peace there shall be no end, upon the throne of David, and upon his kingdom, to order it, and to establish it with judgment and with justice from henceforth even for ever." And this continuity is assured because its foundation is not in man but in God: "The zeal of the LORD of hosts will perform this" (Isa. 9:7).

The regal civilizations established by men and nations in the past, according to Spengler's gloomy philosophy of history,[7] have all had their mornings, their high noons, and then the twilight of oblivion. But God will put an end to this dreary cycle of history when He sets up a kingdom and culture of which it can be said: "Thy sun shall no more go down" (Isa. 60:20). In a remarkable description of its enduring quality, the prophet Daniel seems to pile up verbal absolutes: It is a "kingdom, which shall never be destroyed"; which "shall not be left to other people"; and which "shall stand for ever" (2:44). All this is guaranteed by the covenant and oath of a holy God who "will not lie" (Ps. 89:34-37).

The seeming chronological discrepancy between the everlasting character of the Old Testament prophetic Kingdom and the thousand-year reign described in Revelation 20 will be discussed in a later chapter. The method of prophecy must be kept in mind, i.e., the bringing of things together in the vision, which history will separate in their fulfilment. There are intimations in the Old Testament Prophets, however, which suggest a time limitation in Messiah's Kingdom on earth prior to the final judgment. The prophet Isaiah speaks of certain rebels among "the high ones that are on high" (angelic beings) and "the kings of the earth" (24:21). The next

[7] Oswald Spengler, *Decline of the West*, trans. C. F. Atkinson (New York: Alfred A. Knopf, 1926).

verse (22) says, "And they shall be gathered together, as prisoners are gathered in the pit, and shall be shut up in the prison, and after many days shall they be visited [punished]." The "many days" here correspond to the "thousand years" of Revelation 20. Both begin with the imprisonment of Satanic and human rebels, and end with the final judgment of the prisoners (cf. Rev. 19:20-20:3 with 20:11-15). During the "many days" the LORD of hosts "shall reign . . . in Jerusalem . . . gloriously" (Isa. 24:23).[8]

The reconciliation of the "many days" with the idea of "everlasting" will be found in the fact that, at the close of human history, the Mediatorial Kingdom of our Lord will be merged into the Universal Kingdom and thus perpetuated forever (I Cor. 15:24-28).

[8] On this point see *The Thousand Years in Both Testaments* by Nathaniel West (Chicago: Fleming H. Revell, 1889), pp. 35-49.

CHAPTER XVIII

THE BLESSINGS OF THE PROPHETIC KINGDOM

The Kingdom period will be the true golden age of the world, for
which the lofty-minded and pure-hearted of all generations have longed;
a time in which all that is noblest and holiest in man will be called
forth, and all that is evil will be repressed. Now is brought into
strongest contrast the two conditions of humanity, the natural and the
spiritual, the mortal and the immortal, the life of the first Adam
and the life of the Second. Between the disembodied and those in
the body God has set a gulf that we may not pass over, and a natural
repulsion; but between those in the immortal body and those in the
mortal, there is no gulf and no repulsion. Both coexist in the Kingdom period; and those still in mortal bodies, seeing in Christ and the
Church what the perfected condition of humanity is, are lifted up
with the hope of attaining to the same condition of immortality.
                                                  —*Samuel J. Andrews*[1]

The establishment of the Mediatorial Kingdom on earth will bring
about sweeping and radical changes in every department of human
activity; so far reaching that Isaiah speaks of its arena as "a new earth"
(65:17). Every need of humanity will be anticipated and provided
for: "Before they call," God says, "I will answer" (Isa. 65:24). The
King and His Kingdom will come down upon the world "like rain
upon the mown grass," healing the arid and devastated areas of human
life (Ps. 72:6). Under His divine government there will be made
a "feast of fat things," and the beneficiaries will be "all people" (Isa.
25:6). Working through the chosen nation, God will "fill the face of
the world with fruit" (Isa. 27:6). There will be an "abundance of
salvation" (literally, "salvations"), so that no legitimate aspect of
human life will be left without the regal saving activity (Isa. 33:6,
ASV).

It is precisely at this point that most of the current views of the
Kingdom become woefully inadequate. The hermeneutical beds are
too short, and the covering is too narrow. In concentrating upon certain of its aspects, men have missed the richness and greatness of the
Kingdom. Especially is this true concerning the treatment of the regal

---

[1] S. J. Andrews, *God's Revelations of Himself to Men* (New York: Scribner's
Sons, 1886), p. 324.

blessings set forth in Old Testament prophecy. Some have almost wholly ignored this Biblical area, while others have omitted the parts which could not be fitted into the confines of their narrowly rigid systems. Yet nowhere in Scripture does the rich variety of the Kingdom appear so clearly as in the Old Testament prophets. They saw the future Kingdom penetrating and functioning in all the important realms of human life: spiritual, ethical, social, political, ecclesiastical, and physical. An examination of these activities will reveal the many-sided nature of the Mediatorial Kingdom.

1. *The Coming Kingdom Will Be Basically Spiritual*

It shall come to pass afterward, that I will pour out my Spirit upon all flesh.   —*Joel 2:28, ASV*

a. The establishment of the Kingdom will bring spiritual *salvation* from the hand of God; with joy men will draw water from the "wells of salvation" (Isa. 12:1-6). They shall be clothed with the "garments of salvation" (Isa. 61:10). The very walls of the capital city of the Kingdom will be called "Salvation" (Isa. 60:18). The same watchmen who will shout, "Thy God reigneth," will also publish salvation, saying, "The LORD hath made bare his holy arm in the eyes of all the nations; and all the ends of the earth shall see the salvation of our God" (Isa. 52:7-10).

b. And this salvation will be by the *grace* of God. The age in which we are living today has been called "the Age of Grace," which it is, in a certain peculiar sense; but the coming of the Kingdom age will see no end to God's saving grace. The 45th Psalm describes the coming of the Mediatorial King in all the glory and majesty of Deity, but the opening word about Him is very precious and reassuring: "Grace is poured into thy lips" (vs. 2). Even amid the terrible judgments of His arrival, we are told, He will begin the great millennial outpouring of "the spirit of grace" (Zech. 12:10). And throughout all the days of His Kingdom on earth He will give both "grace and glory" (Ps. 84:11). As a matter of fact, apart from the grace of God there could be no Kingdom of God on earth. In one of the most terrible chapters of the Old Testament (Ezek. 16) the damning record of Israel is outlined without reserve. The nation had begun as a "beautiful" kingdom and ended in the wickedness of "Sodom" (vss. 13, 49). But over against the undeserving character of the nation, the promise of grace is written: "Nevertheless I will remember my covenant with thee in the days of thy youth, and I will establish unto thee an everlasting covenant" (vs. 60). Wherever and whenever the Kingdom of God is manifested, whether in history or in prophecy, the God of that Kingdom remains the Changeless One: He is "gracious, and full of compassion; slow to anger, and of great mercy" (Ps. 145:8 with 13).

c. *All the spiritual elements* of salvation will be present during the Kingdom age. There will be true *repentance.* for sin, wrought by God Himself (Jer. 31:19). For the contrite soul there will be *forgiveness*: "let him return unto the LORD, . . . for he will abundantly pardon" (Isa. 55:4-7). The sins of the saved shall be cast "into the depths of the sea" (Mic. 7:19). The very name of the coming King is a promise of *justification* for sinners: "This is his name whereby he shall be called, THE LORD OUR RIGHTEOUSNESS" (Jer. 23:6). As for the great blessing of *regeneration,* this belongs preeminently to the future age of the established Kingdom when Israel is regathered back into her own land (Ezek. 36:24-38). Along with the new birth, the *Holy Spirit* of God will be poured out upon Israel and also upon "all flesh" (Joel 2:27-28). As a result, there will be a new and more complete *sanctification* of human life (Zeph. 3:11-13). The "incurable" wounds of sin shall be healed in all who come to the King (Jer. 30:11-12, 17-18). The people of God "shall be all righteous," the work of God's hands, that He may be glorified (Isa. 60:21). And these blessings will be *secure* to all the Lord's people: "I will not turn away from following them, to do them good," He says, "I will put my fear in their hearts, that they may not depart from me" (Jer. 32:40, ASV).

d. All these spiritual blessings will be *centered in the royal Man*: "Behold, a king shall reign in righteousness. . . . And a man shall be as an hiding place from the wind, and a covert from the tempest; as rivers of water in a dry place, as the shadow of a great rock in a weary land" (Isa. 32:1-2). And since He will be King over all the nations, His spiritual blessings will be extended to all men. The 98th Psalm gives a picture of the universality of these blessings in the days of His reign: "The LORD hath made known his salvation: his righteousness hath he openly shewed in the sight of the heathen. . . . All the ends of the earth have seen the salvation of our God" (vss. 2-3). Speaking of these saving activities of the King, Isaiah tells us that they are for all — "Ho, every one that thirsteth, come"; that they are free — "without money and without price"; and best of all, they cannot fail — for the mercies of David are "sure" (Isa. 55:1-3).

e. The regal outpouring of spiritual blessings upon the world

in the coming Kingdom will be so profuse that it will bring an unparalleled experience of *joy throughout the world*. Although joy is
something which manifests itself visibly, at bottom it is spiritual as
to its source and nature. That is why, apart from God, "even in
laughter the heart is sorrowful; and the end of that mirth is heaviness"
(Prov. 14:13). It is true that the people of God in every age have
known in their hearts the joy of the Lord; but all their rejoicings have
been tempered by a somber note, as they faced the uncertainties and
problems inevitably present in human life this side of the Kingdom.
At the coming of the King all this will be changed: He will come
to "comfort all that mourn . . . to give unto them beauty for ashes,
the oil of joy for mourning, the garment of praise for the spirit of
heaviness" (Isa. 61:2-3). In those days, the prophet Jeremiah writes
of the redeemed, "They shall come and sing . . . their soul shall be
as a watered garden; and they shall not sorrow any more at all"
(31:12). In all the literary masterpieces of the world there is probably nothing comparable for beauty to a single verse in Isaiah's
picture of the joy which will prevail in the coming Kingdom of our
Lord: "Therefore the redeemed of the LORD shall return, and come
with singing unto Zion; and everlasting joy shall be upon their head:
they shall obtain gladness and joy; and sorrow and mourning shall
flee away" (51:11).

f. It must be observed that the spiritual blessings described in
the Old Testament are set firmly in a *context of sense experience*.
They are not blessings confined exclusively to an immaterial and far-
off heaven somewhere in the skies. On the contrary, they are inseparably united with other blessings which are social, physical, and
even political in nature. What is spiritual is joined to the sensible
and perceptible. To find this, the student has only to read any of the
great Old Testament chapters dealing with the prophetic Kingdom.

Consider, for example, the 36th chapter of Ezekiel where the
variegated threads of the divine tapestry are woven together into one
glorious whole: Here we have a regathering of Israel back into their
own land (vs. 24); divine cleansing from sin (vs. 25); a new heart
(vs. 26); the gift of God's Spirit (vs. 27); a great increase in agricultural production with no more famines (vss. 29-30); genuine
repentance for sin (vs. 31); a work of divine grace (vs. 32); waste
land shall be reclaimed and ruined cities rebuilt (vss. 34-35); the
nations shall see that *God* is doing all this (vs. 36); and a great increase in population shall fill the devastated cities (vss. 37-38).

No interpreter can separate the threads of this tapestry, nor reduce the many colors to a single one, without destroying in part the inspired beauty of the total picture. If the spiritual thread is genuine, so are the others. We can have no quarrel with the dictum of writers who insist that the Kingdom is a "spiritual" matter, unless they insist upon a definition which is exclusively Platonic, or if they are so foolish as to deny that a spiritual kingdom can function tangibly in a world of sense experience. As a matter of fact, it would not be wrong to say that the Kingdom of Old Testament prophecy is *basically "spiritual,"* yet a Kingdom producing tangible effects in every area of human life.[2]

2. The Coming Kingdom Will Be Ethical in Its Effects

And the crooked shall be made straight.   —Isa. 40:4

a. There will be a much needed *readjustment of moral values.* In Isaiah's day, he writes, there were men who called evil good, and good evil; who put darkness for light, and light for darkness (5:20). This has always been a problem of deep concern to thoughtful men; and today the moral confusion is evident on every hand. In many cases the perversion seems to be deliberate: covert sneers at fixed standards of goodness, and a glorification of evil. In other cases, the popular attitude is one of lofty indifference. Men in the highest levels of education and government have thrown the weight of their influence on the side of moral agnosticism.[3] But in the days of the future Kingdom, the prophet declares, "the crooked shall be made straight" (Isa. 40:4). A realistic appraisal of moral values will permeate the whole of human life.

b. Moral values will be measured by an *objective standard.* The final word of Malachi with reference to the coming Kingdom is to point the eyes of men to the law of God (4:4). In that day these matters will not be left to the conclusions of discussion panels. The written Word of God will be the lamp to guide the thinking and actions of men (Ps. 119:105). Furthermore, in the city of Jerusalem the Master Teacher will sit as King, and from that world center the Word of God shall go forth (Isa. 2:3). All questions of right and wrong will be settled by the one infallible standard (Isa. 8:20). Although in the personal presence of the King there will no longer be any necessity for didactic arguments for His existence (Jer. 31:34),

---

[2] See Appendix, chap. XXVII, for a larger discussion of this important point.
[3] A late chief justice of the United States Supreme Court has said that there are no "absolutes."

there are intimations that the nations will still need to be taught in matters of faith and morals. Thus we read of "teachers" who will provide instruction, saying, "This is the way, walk ye in it" (Isa. 30:20-21). In that day there will be moral instruction at every educational level, and it will not be divorced from the one true religion: "All thy children shall be taught of the LORD" (Isa. 54:13). By such means the consciences of men will be educated and reinforced.

c. With the establishment of objective standards, there will come a more *accurate appraisal of moral worth*. "The vile person shall be no more called liberal [noble], nor the churl [crafty] said to be bountiful" (Isa. 32:5). Not only things and ideas, but also persons, will be called by their right names. No longer will wicked men be called "great" merely because they have written charming poetry, painted beautiful pictures, produced useful inventions, achieved high intellectual eminence, or won important military engagements.[4] Too often our human estimates are a stench in the nostrils of a holy God, when we have said that men who do evil are "good" (Mal. 2:17). In the days of the Kingdom there will be clarity in these matters: "Then shall ye return, and discern between the righteous and the wicked, between him that serveth God and him that serveth him not" (Mal. 3:18).

Even Plato, who was not always wrong, saw that some very highly respected things could not be tolerated under a genuinely moral government. Concerning the poet who might write like the angels but violate good morals, the philosopher wrote rather ironically: "We will fall down and worship him as a sweet and holy and wonderful being; but we must also inform him that there is no place for such as he in our State — the law will not allow them. And so when we have anointed him with myrrh, and set a garland of wool upon his head, we shall send him away to another city."[5]

Of course, in the Millennial Kingdom, such poets will neither be worshiped nor garlanded — but they will be *sent away*, forever.

d. The moral virtue of *truth* will be exalted in every phase of the Kingdom. In contrast to the average ruler of today — who is able to justify almost any sort of an untruth on the ground of "political expediency" — the coming King will "bring forth justice in truth" (Isa. 42:3, ASV). According to Scripture, there is no deeper form of immorality than untruth. The great originator of sin in the universe is

---

[4] Contrast the laudation of Shelley, whose actions were often contemptible, and the fame of Rousseau, whose personal life was hardly fit for public discussion.
[5] *Republic*, trans. B. Jowett, Book III, p. 398.

called a "liar" and a "murderer" (John 8:44); and the lie came first (Gen. 3:1-3). And since Satan is the deceiver of the nations, it is not surprising to find governments often using deceit as a deliberate policy in relation both to their own citizens and toward each other. Like the kings of Daniel 11, when diplomats gather in conference, too often they "speak lies at one table" (vs. 27). This is why the cause of international peace always fails: it has no firm foundation in truth. It is utterly false to say, Peace, peace, when there is no peace. Rather recently we have had in our nation the shocking spectacle of rulers who, while preparing for war, have promised peace to the voters. And then, worst of all, these officials have been defended by presumably responsible historians on the ground that the lie was politically necessary and served a good purpose in the end.[6] From such immoral expediencies we turn with relief to the prophetic descriptions of the moral atmosphere of the coming Kingdom. Its world center, in contrast to the present capitals of the nations with their propaganda mills, is called the "city of truth" (Zech. 8:3).

e. Retribution for wrongdoing will become an exclusively *personal* matter. There was a proverb often used in the land of Israel which ran like this: "The fathers have eaten sour grapes, and the children's teeth are set on edge" (Ezek. 18:2). In the days of Ezekiel the proverb had been wrongly used by that generation to escape personal responsibility for their sins, and by implication to charge God with injustice in His dealings with men. At considerable length the prophet corrects the false opinions of the people. Each man must bear his own moral responsibility for what he deliberately chooses to do (Ezek. 18:3-29). The people should have known this, for it had been taught clearly in the Mosaic Law (Deut. 24:16).

However, as in the case of most proverbs, this one did contain a grain of truth. Within certain limits, the sins of the fathers are visited upon the children (Exod. 20:5). More than one child is born diseased and deformed because of parental sin. More than one family has lived in poverty because of the prodigal actions of the father. These are facts of human life here and now which cannot be gainsaid. And they are recognized as such by Jeremiah who shows that

---

[6] Such cynical argument is nothing new under the sun. Over 23 centuries ago Plato stated it baldly as follows: "Then if any one at all is to have the privilege of lying, the rulers of the state should be the persons; and they, in their dealings either with enemies or with their own citizens, may be allowed to lie for the public good. But nobody else should meddle with anything of the kind; and although the rulers have this privilege, for a private man to lie to them [the rulers] in return is to be deemed a more heinous fault . . ." (*The Republic*, Book III).

in the coming Kingdom things will be different, for the ancient proverb will then have no justification whatever. "In those days. . . . everyone shall die for his own iniquity: every man that eateth the sour grape, *his* teeth shall be set on edge" (31:29-30, italics added). No innocent child will die because the parents sinned. No father will be able to involve an unborn child in future disaster and suffering. This will mark a revolutionary change and will take away what some have regarded as the greatest of all hindrances to a rational belief in a moral universe.

f. Thus, in the coming Kingdom, the existence and reality of a divine moral economy will be *openly demonstrated*. God will establish *visibly* an unbroken and immediate relationship between moral character and human well-being. There will be no interminable and heartbreaking delays between human action and its proper awards.

No one can deny that at present the moral question can be raised; and it *has* been raised even by the Lord's own people. The student should read Psalms 72 and 73 in this connection. In Psalm 73 the writer describes his perplexity and discouragement over the visible "prosperity of the wicked" and the sufferings of the righteous (vss. 2-14). And the solution of the moral problem took time and required a divine revelation of the future adjudication of these inequalities (vss. 16-24). In sharp contrast to the present situation, Psalm 72 paints a picture of the situation as it will be under the coming King. Then all moral contradictions will be resolved: "In his days shall the righteous flourish" and the "oppressor" shall be broken to pieces (vss. 7, 4), which is as it should be.

In that Kingdom no room will be left for the cynical interrogation, "Where is the God of justice?" (Mal. 2:17, ASV). And moral scepticism will be dealt with for the deep sin that it is: "It shall come to pass at that time," God warns, "that I will search Jerusalem with candles, and punish the men that are settled on their lees: that say in their heart, The LORD will not do good, neither will he do evil" (Zeph. 1:12).

3. *The Coming Kingdom Will Have Social Effects*

They shall not labour in vain . . . . They shall not hurt nor destroy in all my holy mountain, saith the LORD.   —*Isa. 65:23, 25*

a. *All Military Warfare Will Be Abolished*

The 46th Psalm speaks of the raging of the nations at the end-time and the arrival of the King and His Kingdom to rescue Israel in the hour of peril. Following the divine judgments on a rebellious world, we read that "He maketh wars to cease unto the end of the earth; he breaketh the bow, and cutteth the spear in sunder; he burneth the chariot in the fire" (vs. 9). And Hosea, picturing the coming day when the nation of Israel will be rescued from all her troubles and married to her divine King forever, recognizes that there can be no Millennial Kingdom for the people of God until the problem of war is solved. Therefore, we have the Word of the Lord: "I will break the bow and the sword and the battle out of the earth." Only then can the righteous "lie down safely" (Hos. 2:18). Military science and training, which today occupy so large a place in our educational system, will no longer have any justification: "Neither shall they learn war any more" (Mic. 4:3). An era of world-wide peace will be ushered in, never to end again (Isa. 9:6-7). How the elimination of warfare will be accomplished will be discussed in the following section (pp. 228-9). Just now it will be sufficient for our purpose to observe that there can be no thorough and permanent social reform until the basic problem of war has been solved.

The social benefits resulting from the abolishing of war will be immediately evident. First, an incalculable wastage of wealth and life will be saved. Second, all this treasure, together with the labors of science which today are contributing to the horrors and destruction of military action, will be turned to economic uses: the swords will become plowshares, and instead of spears we shall have pruninghooks (Mic. 4:3). In more modern terms: the stuff of the atomic bomb, instead of hanging over mankind as a deadly threat to human existence, will bring light and power and healing to a needy world. Third, the end benefit to society will be freedom from want and fear: "They shall sit every man under his vine and under his fig tree; and none shall make them afraid" (Mic. 4:4).

b. *Complete Social Justice Will Become a Reality*

Even if it were possible for men without God to put an end to the staggering economic waste of war, there would still remain two obstacles to the realization of social justice: First, the experts must know *what* to do. Economic experiments may work immeasurable disaster to society. Recently the leaders of Communist Russia have been confessing with great fanfare that many of their policies under the long leadership of Stalin were wrong. But in their glib statement of penitence there is no mention of the untold human suffering and destruction which was the awful price of their economic "mistakes." But, second, even if the experts had the infallible answers to all our

social problems, there would still be needed some higher and beneficent power to enforce the remedies without leaving the patient in
worse condition than before.

There is nothing inherently wrong with the central thesis of classical Socialism. No intelligent man of goodwill would wish to deny
that every person on earth ought to have at least as much as he
produces. But the twin errors of Socialism are: first, that they have
left the true God out of their panaceas; and, second, they have had an
unwarranted confidence in the alleged "goodness" of sinful men.
Even professed Christians have supposed that the social ideals of the
Kingdom of God could be fully realized without the wisdom and
power of the divine King personally and visibly manifested on earth.
Yet the Word of God is unmistakable on this point: nowhere short
of the established Kingdom under the personal control of Christ will
complete social justice *rule* on earth.

In Old Testament prophecy of the Kingdom a large place is given
to social justice. In that day, Isaiah writes very specifically, "They
shall build houses, and inhabit them; and they shall plant vineyards,
and eat the fruit of them. They shall not build, and another inhabit;
they shall not plant, and another eat" (65:21-22). The same idea is
asserted by Amos. Looking ahead to the day when the historic "tabernacle of David" is re-established on earth and Israel is finally restored to their own land, the prophet declares not only that men shall
"build . . . cities," "plant vineyards," and "make gardens"; but also
that the people who do the work shall enjoy the benefits (Amos
9:11, 14). The wastrels and parasites will not be living at the ex-
pense of others, and labor will acquire a new dignity and worth.

But social justice in the prophetic Kingdom will be something more
than an exact *quid pro quo*. As long as men live in the flesh on earth,
there will be differences in abilities and needs. Even with the Kingdom established on earth there may be attempts on the part of selfish
men to deprive the less able of their rights. Hence we read that
under the gracious rule of the coming King, the "poor" and the
"needy" will be given a special protective care, which will extend
beyond all mere legal considerations (Ps. 72:4, 12, 13). We are at
present finding it very difficult, even with all our advanced social laws,
to preserve a proper balance between strict justice and the virtue of
benevolence. In the administration of social benefits, government
agencies tend to swing either toward legalistic harshness or toward
sentimental laxness. Under the all-wise rule of the coming King

such problems will be solved with unerring skill. In Him the world at last will find a perfect balance between the "strong hand" of the law and the gentle arm of the One who is the great Shepherd of the sheep (Isa. 40:10-11).

c. *Social "Wastes" in Human Life Will Be Reclaimed*

Wherever human civilization has gone, certain great evils have marched in the rear. The great material resources of the earth have been profligately wasted; and where beauty once reigned, there is often left nothing but ugliness and desolation. Nations are at last awakening to the perilous nature of these losses, but the work of repair is often slow and ineffectual. The prophet Isaiah writes of a better day when "they shall build the old wastes, they shall raise up the former desolations, and they shall repair the waste cities, the desolations of many generations" (61:4). The open sore of city "slum areas" will be healed: "they of the city shall flourish like the grass of the earth" (Ps. 72:16).

d. *Everything Worthwhile in Human Life Will Be Tenderly Fostered*

The hopeless cripple and the diseased will not be consigned to the tragic comfort of euthanasia; neither will the backward child be rigidly classified at a certain capacity level: "A bruised reed will he not break, and a dimly burning wick will he not quench" (Isa. 42:3, ASV).

Too often the theoreticians of social progress have been careless of personal values in their struggles toward a better world. They have been willing to ride roughshod over the individual for the good of "society." Callously and coldly, millions of persons have been treated like guinea pigs, starved and executed, in the interest of economic policies which were admittedly "experimental" and sometimes later had to be revised or even abandoned. Such things were regarded as the inevitable price of social progress. It will be otherwise in the coming Kingdom. There will be social progress, but there will be no abridgement of the infinite value of human personality. Not a single soul will ever be needlessly sacrificed on the altar of economic "progress." Of the compassionate interest of the great King it is written: "Precious shall their blood be in his sight" (Ps. 72:14).

e. *Every Legitimate Interest of Human Life Will Receive Its Due*

Marriage and the home, too often at present made desolate by human violence or degraded below the level of the beasts, will be restored to its pristine honor and joy. Where desolation had once reigned there will be again heard "The voice of joy, and the voice of gladness, the voice of the bridegroom, and the voice of the bride, the voice of them that shall say, Praise the LORD of hosts: for the LORD is good; for his mercy endureth for ever" (Jer. 33:10-11 with 15). The aged will have a place of respect and dignity; and for the children there will be joyous and safe recreation. "Thus saith the LORD of hosts; There shall yet old men and old women dwell [lit. "sit"] in the streets of Jerusalem. . . . and the streets of the city shall be full of boys and girls playing in the streets thereof" (Zech. 8:4-5).

This is no kingdom of asceticism where the normal impulses of humanity, implanted by divine creation, will be rigorously suppressed. The coming of God's Kingdom will bring glad release to all who submit to its blessed King. The change will be so great that, at first, men will be "like them that dream." Then, as they realize that what is happening is no illusion, their mouths will be "filled with laughter" and their "tongue with singing" (Ps. 126:1-2).

4. *The Coming Kingdom Will Be Political in Its Effects*

For out of Zion shall go forth the law, and the word of the LORD from Jerusalem. And he shall judge among the nations, and shall rebuke many people . . . neither shall they learn war any more.
—*Isa. 2:3-4*

It is generally agreed today that there can be no absolute divorce between social reform and political considerations. No matter how good our ideals may be, there must be some machinery for their realization. And the implementation of high principles cannot be safely committed to political leaders who are ignorant, weak, or selfish. In short, human life being what it is, the best of principles cannot operate in a political vacuum. In this respect, there is a great deal of blunt realism in the predictions of the Old Testament prophets. What they had to say about the Kingdom, as Delitzsch has rightly affirmed, was not composed of merely "beautiful dreams." The prophets were deeply interested in the political aspects of the future Kingdom; and they spoke with great definiteness on these matters.

a. *An International Authority*

A central authority in international affairs will be established. By all men of intelligence and goodwill, it is admitted that in such an arrangement we have a *possible* key to most of the political problems of the world. But the difficulty always has been to find or create such an authority which is both competent and just. To commit the future of the nations to any central body composed of fallible and sinful men, however well intentioned, would entail mortal risk. This is especially true today when a small group, in control of our present fantastically destructive weapons of war, could impose controls which might conceivably put an end to all liberty and progress. For this reason, sensible political leaders approach the idea of a world government with great caution and even scepticism. Others, more recklessly idealistic, argue that the risk must be taken because the choice is now between a central world government and the possible destruction of the human race.

Long ago the Old Testament prophets saw clearly the problem and under divine inspiration laid down the final solution. In the coming Kingdom there will be a central authority for the purpose of adjudicating and settling international disputes. And since this authority will be centered in the divine King Himself, personally present on earth, the decisions will not only be wise, impartial and good, but there will also be the necessary benevolent power to enforce them: "And it shall come to pass in the latter days, . . . he will judge between the nations, and will decide concerning many peoples" (Isa. 2:2, 4, ASV). Hence, because there can be no appeal from His decisions, which will be enforced with divine sanctions, resort to human warfare will become both unnecessary and useless. All military science will become obsolete — "Neither shall they learn war any more" (Isa. 2:4). The same wonderful prediction appears also in the fourth chapter of Micah, but with certain significant additions: Among the powers dealt with, there will be some "strong nations afar off" (4:3). Thus, in the face of divine power, the factors of military strength and geographical distance, which are of such great importance today, will no longer be of any consequence. National security will be guaranteed to all nations.

b. A World Capital

A capital city will be set up as a tangible symbol of this centralized divine authority. Scornful criticisms of this idea, often indulged in by anti-millennial writers, are not only in conflict with Scriptures but also with psychological realism. These very critics are often the most enthusiastic builders of denominational centers; and also many times have been incorrigible supporters of world political centers; first at the Hague, then in Geneva, and now in New York. In this attitude they have been able at least to recognize the impressive value of the visible symbol of an ideal, however wrong they may have been in their theological and political opinions.

The Old Testament prophets are not bound by any such unrealistic inhibitions. In the days of the coming Kingdom, they affirm,

"Out of Zion shall go forth the law, and the word of the LORD from Jerusalem" (Isa. 2:3). Ezekiel, given a vision of the future re-entrance of the divine Glory into the millennial temple at Jerusalem, hears the voice of God saying that here will be "the place of my throne . . . where I will dwell in the midst of the children of Israel for ever" (43:1-7). As to the precise identification of this place, Delitzsch has well written, "Zion is mentioned as the royal seat of the Anointed One; there He is installed, that He may reign there, and rule from thence (Ps. 110:2). It is the hill of the city of David (II Sam. 5:7,9; I Kings 8:1), including Moriah, that is intended. That hill of holiness, i.e., holy hill, which is the resting-place of the divine presence and therefore excels all the heights of the earth, is assigned to Him as the seat of His throne."[7]

Certainly, if there is ever to be a Kingdom of God on earth, no more appropriate place for its world center could be found than the place hallowed by the sacred memories of the One who there suffered and died for the sins of the world. Furthermore, in this ancient city we have literally the crossroads of the world, joining the three great continents of Africa, Asia, and Europe. Ezekiel speaks appropriately of the location as the "navel of the earth" (38:12, ASV margin).

To the objection that Jerusalem is hardly fitted in geographical features and area to serve the grand prophetic purpose, it need only be said that the prophets envisage an enlargement of the city with its various adjoining areas, which, on the basis of measures given in Ezekiel, would yield an immense metropolis entirely worthy in size to serve the divine purposes. As he approaches the material in chapters 40 to 48 of Ezekiel, Gardiner complains that the prophet's predictions regarding the city and temple and land could not possibly be fulfilled literally "without changes in the surface of the earth."[8] Well, of course, this is exactly what the Old Testament prophets declare shall be done. Zechariah speaks of a great geological disturbance centered in this area (14:4); and one result is that apparently the surrounding land is levelled down to a "plain" while the city proper is "lifted up" into a conspicuous elevation (vs. 10). On this latter point the learned Hebrew Christian, David Baron, has written: "As the 'city of the great King' (Ps. 48:2), whose dominion extends to earth's utmost bounds, and as the center whence God's

---

7 Franz Delitzsch, *Commentary on the Psalms,* trans. F. Bolton (Grand Rapids: Eerdmans Publishing Co., reprint, 1952), on Ps. 2:6.

8 F. Gardiner, Ellicott's *Commentary on Ezekiel* (Grand Rapids: Zondervan Publishing House, reprint, 1954), p. 315.

light and truth shall go forth among all the nations, Jerusalem is also to be physically exalted above the hills by which she has hitherto been surrounded and overshadowed."[9]

In this historic city will be focused the interest and hopes of a needy world. Into it will flow the wealth of nations; strangers will build up its walls; kings will contribute to its beautification (Isa. 60:10, 13, 17). So great are the issues involved that God Himself calls upon men to pray "and give him no rest, till he establish, and till he make Jerusalem a praise in the earth" (Isa. 62:6-7). The words of the 48th Psalm give us a remarkable picture of the unimaginable glory of the coming city:

> Great is Jehovah, and greatly to be praised, In the city of our God, in his holy mountain. Beautiful in elevation, the joy of the whole earth, Is mount Zion, on the sides of the north, The city of the great King (vss. 1-2, ASV).

c. The Jewish Problem

One of the first acts of the divine government will be a settlement of the Jewish problem. It is utterly unrealistic to deny that there is such a problem, and has been ever since the end of the historical Theocracy and the world-wide dispersion of the chosen nation. The frequent anti-Semitic outbursts, from Haman to Hitler, represent the attempts of wicked men to solve this problem by irrational and cruel means. Even the Jewish people themselves bear witness as to the existence of the problem, for they cannot even agree among themselves on what ought to be done. Bitter disputes exist among them: as, for example, the conflict between the Zionistic and anti-Zionistic parties and between the religious and irreligious groups. And this Jewish problem, however much the fact may be cloaked by denial or palliatives, is related vitally to the political problems of the world. It is not that the Jew is worse or better than other men. But this nation, in the good purpose of God, is an appointed means for the future well-being of the world: "In thee shall all families of the earth be blessed" (Gen. 12:3). Therefore, until Israel is where he ought to be, both religiously and politically, there can be no thorough and permanent solution of the international problems.

Historically, the people of Israel have not been wholly without friends. Moved by widely different motives, various governments have come to their aid. Recent attempts to help them, on the part of England and the United States, have raised a storm of irreconcil-

---

[9] David Baron, *Visions and Prophecies of Zechariah* (4th impression; London: Hebrew Testimony to Israel, 1951), pp. 510-513.

able protest from the Arab nations and brought into the Near East a fresh and ominous interest of Russian Communism, which is always fishing in troubled waters. At present no solution of the political problem is in sight. Yet without some solution the cause of world peace will remain in constant jeopardy.

For these reasons the Old Testament prophets give a prominent place to the political welfare of Israel. In the coming Kingdom, the dispersed of the nation will not only be gathered back into their own land and spiritually cleansed, but the ancient internal rupture will be healed. God promises, "I will make them one nation in the land upon the mountains of Israel, and one king shall be king to them all: and they shall be no more two nations, neither shall they be divided into two kingdoms any more at all" (Ezek. 37:21-22). Apart from the fulfilment of these divine conditions, the nation of Israel cannot fully serve the divine purpose. There is also a frank recognition of the problem and its solution in Zechariah: "And it shall come to pass, that as ye were a *curse* among the heathen [nations], O house of Judah, and house of Israel; so will I save you, and ye shall be a *blessing*" (8:13, italics added). Furthermore, in that day, when the political unification and supremacy of Israel have been firmly established by divine power, all nations will gladly recognize the benefits of such an arrangement: "In those days it shall come to pass, that ten men shall take hold out of all languages of the nations, even shall take hold of the skirt of him that is a Jew, saying, We will go with you: for we have heard that God is with you" (Zech. 8:23).

d. A Righting of Political Wrongs

With the covenant rights of Israel established, there will also be a rectification of other ancient political wrongs. The great pledge recorded in Isaiah and Micah certainly warrants this conclusion. The King "will judge between the nations, and decide concerning many peoples" (Isa. 2:4, ASV).

One of the tragedies of international relations is the willingness of governments to accept the *status quo* and forget the crimes of the past. It has been a general policy of the various nations, in dealing with new governments, to extend diplomatic recognition once they are firmly established, without enquiring too closely into the morality of their rise. Thus, finally, recognition was given to the bloody communistic government of Russia; England has done likewise with Red China; and loud voices in our own nation are being raised for similar action. The motive behind this policy of recognition has been that of political expediency. The world being what it is, the nations have realistically seen that to police the morality of other governments would involve endless military action all over the globe. And so, caught between the moral and political horns of the dilemma, nations have chosen what they regard as the lesser evil. To be sure, moral idealism raises its head occasionally in world affairs. Morally enlightened governments do go to war to keep their covenants and defend the "self-determination of nations." But in the end, brutal political expediency has generally had the last word. Who would ever have supposed that the conscienceless killers of the Kremlin would be given seats of honor in a world organization of "peace-loving nations" located in New York City? Who would have dreamed that leading pacifists, viewing with abhorrence *any* violent shedding of blood, would have become the chief advocates of diplomatic recognition of communistic tyrants with hands still bloody with mass murder?

But, however forgetful men may become in the interest of political expediency, there is a God who does not forget. In the days of His Kingdom there will be an examination of the political crimes of the past in the light of divine justice, and a correction of ancient wrongs which have been too easily accepted even by the best of statesmen. "He . . . shall break in pieces the oppressor" (Ps. 72:4). If, as some theologians have argued, the Church is now God's Kingdom on earth, then in the interest of ordinary morality they should be advocating some "holy wars" for the purpose of setting right the wrongs of history. There is plenty to be done.

e. *The Barrier of Language*

In the coming Kingdom every obstacle to human understanding and international accord will be taken away. Among these obstacles, perhaps the most stubborn is the barrier of diverse languages. Other things being equal, the most successful diplomats are those who speak and understand the tongues of the nations to which they are accredited. Recognizing the great value of some *lingua franca*, more than one effort has been made to produce something to fill the void. But the problem here is the jealousy of the various nations for the preservation of their own distinctive cultures.

In Zephaniah we seem to have a recognition of this language difficulty. In the days of the Kingdom, God says, "Then will I turn to the peoples a pure language, that they may all call upon the name of Jehovah, to serve him with one consent" (3:9, ASV). As to the meaning of this prediction, Jennings has said, "The discord of Babel shall, as it were, give place to the unity of language."[10] This meaning is disputed by Keil who argues that the Hebrew word rendered "pure" means purity from sin rather than linguistic *clarity,* and also that the Hebrew noun means *lip* and "does not stand for language."[11] But Keil seems to ignore the fact that in Genesis 11:1-9 this noun is so used no less than four times in connection with the confusion of tongues at Babel. As for the idea of *moral* purity, it is admitted that this is the correct meaning. But this only adds to the force of the idea of linguistic unity, for the curse of language multiplicity came because of the sinful *speech* of man upon that occasion. And therefore the removal of this curse, in the Millennial Kingdom, would certainly involve a recognition of its moral implication. Purity does not exclude unity. As Pusey has said, "Before the dispersion of Babel the world was *of one lip,* and that, impure, for it was in rebellion against God. Now it shall be again of *one lip,* and that, purified."[12]

5. *The Coming Kingdom Will Have Physical Effects*

> Therefore take no thought, saying, What shall we eat? or, What shall we drink? or, Wherewithal shall we be clothed? . . . But seek ye first the kingdom of God and his righteousness; and all these things shall be added unto you.   —*Matt. 6:31-33*

Rather strangely, among "orthodox" anti-millennarians, there is a strong feeling that there is something theologically disreputable about the idea of a future Kingdom in which God will effect great changes in man's physical environment by supernatural means. Such an idea is stigmatized as a "carnal" view of the Kingdom. In their antipathy they seem to forget that man was created a perfect physical being and placed in a physical environment which God Himself called "very good" (Gen. 1:31). This is to say nothing of those great supernatural intrusions of divine power recorded in connection with the Old Testament Kingdom; and also the miracles of Christ Himself which operated in the physical realm. Furthermore, those very theologians who insist upon an exclusively "spiritual Kingdom" now present on earth, argue that it is the duty of all members of that Kingdom to join in every effort to bring about beneficent changes in man's physical environment. They see nothing incongruous or inconsistent, for example, between a present "spiritual" Kingdom and

---

[10] A. C. Jennings, Ellicott's *Commentary on Zephaniah* (*op. cit.*) *in loc.* So also Hofman; and Jamieson, Fausset and Brown.

[11] C. F. Keil, *Commentary on Minor Prophets,* trans. J. Martin (Grand Rapids: Eerdmans Publishing Co., reprint, 1951), *in loc.*

[12] E. B. Pusey, *Commentary on Minor Prophets* (New York: Funk and Wagnalls, 1886), *in loc.*

human efforts to prevent and eliminate physical disease. But if we preach a coming Kingdom in which God will *supernaturally* put an end to physical diseases, then the Kingdom suddenly becomes a "carnal" Kingdom! Such an attitude, even apart from Biblical consideration, seems decidedly less than rational. Moreover, it indicates the ease with which anti-millennialism slips into an attitude of anti-supernaturalism in the physical realm. The Old Testament prophets were not hampered by any such dualistic prejudices. Recognizing the hand of God everywhere present in the processes of nature, they saw nothing incredible in the idea of a spiritual Kingdom where intrusions of supernatural power would become the rule instead of the exception.

a. *Beneficial Climatic Changes*

The alleged remark of Mark Twain — "Everybody talks about the weather, but no one ever does anything about it" — contains more truth than humor. As a matter of fact, beyond the not-always-accurate predictions of the weather bureau, there is little that man *can* do about it, except to alleviate somewhat its effects by such means as heating and cooling devices, the building of stormproof shelters, the prevention of deforestation, and the damming of rivers for irrigation and flood-control purposes. The factors involved in climatic conditions are immensely complicated, and nothing in our physical environment is more closely related to the preservation and sustenance of human life. Nowhere does man's weakness appear more vividly than against the harsh phenomena of climatic violence.

It should not be surprising, therefore, to find considerable attention devoted to this matter in predictions of the coming Kingdom. Viewed from the standpoint of the system of nature, the climate of the earth is an effect of *cosmic* and *geological* causes; and both are mentioned in prophecy. Isaiah says that in the coming day "the light of the moon shall be as the light of the sun, and the light of the sun shall be sevenfold, as the light of seven days" (30:26). Whatever these cosmic changes may be, it is interesting to note that they are associated with climatic changes on earth (cf. vss. 23-25). Nor is the language merely figurative, according to Delitzsch: "This also is not meant figuratively . . . it is not of the new heaven that the prophet is speaking, but of the glorification of nature, which is promised by both Old Testament prophecy and by that of the New at the closing period of the world's history. . . . No other miracles will be needed for this than that wonder-working power of God, which even now produces those changes of weather, the laws of which no researches of natural science have enabled us to calculate, and which will then give the greatest brilliancy and most unchangeable duration to what is now comparatively rare; namely, a perfectly unclouded day, with sun or moon shining in all its brilliancy, yet without scorching from the one, or injurious effects from the other. Heaven and earth will then put on their sabbath dress, for it will be the Sabbath of the world's history."[13]

Climatic conditions are also inseparable from geological factors. The upheaval of a mountain range can turn a garden spot into a desert waste, or the reverse. It is not strange, therefore, to have the prophets speaking of violent and widespread geological changes in connection with the coming of the Kingdom and its salubrious climatic conditions. The earth will be shaken "terribly" (Isa. 2:19-21). It will "reel to and fro like a drunkard" (Isa. 24:20). The mountains will be "thrown down" and "every wall shall fall to the ground" (Ezek. 38:19-20). The land of Palestine, which has a definite history of geological disturbances, will experience great changes at the end-time (Zech. 14:4, 8).

It is true that modern scientists regard geological change for the most part as something almost interminably slow and gradual. But it is admitted that there is also evidence for changes which have been sudden and catastrophic. However, the fulfilment of inspired prediction rests upon the supernatural power of God, not on the history of the past.

b. *Waste Places Become Fruitful*

The waste areas of the earth's surface are enormous in comparison with the fractional part suited for cultivation. And this small arable part is being destroyed by various agents at a frightening rate. Some progress has been made in scientific conservation and restoration in places, and the total food-producing area has been enlarged somewhat by irrigation. But the problem in relation to population increase is causing serious concern. A recent book entitled *The Challenge of Mans' Future* by Dr. Harrison Brown, a brilliant geochemist at the California Institute of Technology, underscores anew the terrifying nature of the problem. This scientist is pessimistic regarding man's scientific remedies, such as chemical fertilization, algae farms, atomic resources, and birth control. Even if we knew what to do, Dr. Brown

[13] Franz Delitzsch, *Commentary on Isaiah*, trans. J. Martin (Grand Rapids: Eerdmans Publishing Co., reprint, 1950), Vol. II, p. 39.

wonders whether mankind would have the will to do it. The editors of *Newsweek,* reviewing the book, conclude that "Such a society may be as impossibly utopian as a world without sin. . . . The world's margin of subsistence is paper-thin already. Every cry of a newborn child brings nearer the ultimate crisis."[14]

The Old Testament prophecies of the Kingdom recognize this problem and present a future solution. First, there is a promise of that abundant rainfall necessary for the production of agricultural resources (Joel 2:21-24); and it will come at the proper times: "I will cause the shower to come down in his season" (Ezek. 34:26). Second, as a result there will be profuse streams of water in new and unlikely places. "There shall be upon every high mountain, and upon every high hill, rivers and streams of waters" (Isa. 30:25). "In the wilderness shall waters break out, and streams in the desert. And the parched ground[15] shall become a pool, and the thirsty land springs of water" (Isa. 35:6-7). "I will open rivers in high places," God promises, "and fountains in the midst of the valleys" (Isa. 41:18).

In addition to these natural results which must follow properly controlled rainfall, there may also be streams continually flowing by *miraculous* causation, such as the marvelous stream pictured by Ezekiel (47:1-12). Its issue from the temple, its immense size, the beneficial qualities of its fruit, its perennial flow "in summer and in winter" (Zech. 14:8) — all emphasize the supernatural nature of the stream. There is nothing at all inherently impossible in such a phenomenon. Why should anyone stumble at the idea of a beautiful stream springing up at the geographical center of our Lord's blessed Kingdom on earth, with healing in both its waters and the fruit which grows beside it? Is there anything incredible here, if we remember that the coming King is the One who once turned water into wine and sent the sightless man to wash away his blindness in the waters of Siloam (John 9:11)? What a visible symbol this will be to remind the nations of the unfailing blessings which will flow from the throne of the Son of David! And from *this* shrine none will go away in heartbreaking disappointment because no help has been found.

c. *Increased Fertility and Productiveness*

With beneficial changes in climate and controlled rainfall, the earth will begin to yield a commensurate increase of products. In-

---

[14] *Newsweek,* Sept. 13, 1954, p. 73.
[15] The Hebrew term doubtless refers to that common desert phenomenon, called a "mirage." So Lange, Barnes, J. A. Alexander, and ASV margin.

stead of "thorns and briers" the wilderness will become a "fruitful field" (Isa. 32:13-15). "The wilderness and the dry land shall be glad; and the desert shall rejoice, and blossom as the rose. It shall blossom abundantly" — comparable to the richness of Lebanon and Carmel and Sharon (Isa. 35:1-2, ASV). As a result there will be no more devastating famines (Ezek. 34:29, ASV). The mountains and hills, as well as the valleys, will be restored to their productiveness (Ezek. 36:4-11). Even in the most unlikely places the earth will bring forth in astonishing measure: "There shall be an handful of corn in the earth upon the top of the mountains; the fruit thereof shall shake like Lebanon" (Ps. 72:16). Drawing a prophetic picture of these glorious days, Amos writes that "the plowman shall overtake the reaper, and the treader of grapes him that soweth seed" (9:13).

But beyond the increase flowing naturally from changes in climate and rainfall, we cannot be wrong in seeing in these prophetic descriptions a *supernatural* restoration of ground fertility. In a remarkable but often overlooked passage, the Word of God attributes the ordinary yet complicated process of soil fertilization to the work of the Holy Spirit in nature (Ps. 104:29-30). And it is significant that the millennial renovation of the earth is connected directly with the special outpouring of God's Spirit; when He shall be "poured upon us from on high, and the wilderness be a fruitful field" (Isa. 32:15).

d. Changes in the Animal World

There is nothing in our physical environment more fascinating than its various forms of animal life. Brilliant minds have been willing to devote an entire lifetime to investigations of only small segments of this world. And wholly apart from any scientific interest, the pleasure of simply looking at this rich area of life is universal. One serious hindrance to both the pleasure of contemplation and investigation, however, is the danger which is often present.

The prophets devote some attention to this matter. For the safety of mankind, God promises, "In that day will I make a covenant for them with the beasts of the field, and with the fowls of heaven, and with the creeping things of the ground . . . and will make them to lie down safely" (Hos. 2:18). Ezekiel pictures the safety still more definitely: "They shall dwell safely in the wilderness, and sleep in the woods" (34:25). It is obvious that such a condition could not exist apart from a change in the very nature of animal disposition. And this is definitely asserted in the well-known passage from Isaiah which pictures a beautiful harmony in nature, not only between man and the animals, but also between the various animals themselves: "The wolf also shall dwell with the lamb, and the leopard shall lie down with the kid, . . . and a little child shall lead them. . . . And the suckling child shall play on the hole of the asp" (Isa. 11:6-8). Even the eating habits of dangerous beasts will be modified: "the lion shall eat straw like the ox" (v. 7). This great prophecy has often been treated with both incredulity and ridicule. But those who accept as inspired the Genesis account of man's original state in Eden (2:19) will have no difficulty in believing that God is able to restore these conditions in the coming Kingdom of His Son.

e. *The Disappearance of Physical Disease and Deformity*

In spite of all man's progress in the science of medicine and surgery — and it has been very great — the fact remains that we still live in a world of suffering and death. As we ride past endless miles of homes, to say nothing of hospitals and sanitariums, most of us cannot possibly form any conception of the total pain and heartbreak shut up behind their walls. Only those who minister constantly to the ills of mankind can have any idea of the bulk of this problem. Most of us are mercifully shielded from it, except as we ourselves or those close to us are touched by the hand of hopeless disease or death. And while we should be deeply grateful for all that has been done to alleviate, somewhat, the problem, the present situation is still utterly. irreconcilable with the idea of a Kingdom of God upon earth.

As to conditions in the coming Kingdom, it should be noted: first, that the prophets envision human life as continuing through the natural processes of procreation, birth, and growth. The rejoicing of the bride and bridegroom is heard (Jer. 33:11); the children play in the streets of the cities (Zech. 8:5); the little one shall become "a thousand" (Isa. 60:22).

But the accidents and deviations of nature, often so appalling in character, will be dealt with by divine power. All physical infirmity and deformity will be rectified: "Then the eyes of the blind shall be opened, and the ears of the deaf shall be unstopped. Then shall the lame man leap as an hart, and the tongue of the dumb sing" (Isa. 35:5-6). Disease, which is distinguished from deformity (Mal. 1:8), will likewise be controlled by divine power, perhaps through both prevention and cure. At any rate, "The inhabitant shall not say, I am sick" (Isa. 33:24). The manner in which these happy results will be accomplished is not precisely stated; but, as we have suggested above, there are intimations that in some cases tangible means may be used; "the fruit thereof shall be for food, and the leaf thereof for healing" (Ezek. 47:12, ASV). For any who may regard such prophecies as wholly implausible, a sufficient answer may be found in the amazing progress in the chemistry of food and medicine. Investigators of high eminence are even seriously suggesting today that the final answer to the scourge of cancer may be found in the field of internal medicine rather than in surgery.

With physical ills under divine control, it follows that long life will again become the rule: "For as the days of a tree shall be the days of my people, and my chosen shall long enjoy the work of their hands" (Isa. 65:22, ASV). For longevity no more appropriate comparison could be suggested than a "tree." Infancy will be measured by years instead of days, and there will be no more "an old man that hath not filled his days." In fact, Isaiah suggests that the crisis of physical death will be experienced only by those incorrigible individualists who rebel against the laws of the Kingdom; and even in such cases the gracious probation will be a century in length (Isa. 65:20).

f. Freedom from Ordinary Hazards

Beyond the problem of disease and its train of liabilities, there still remain what are called the "ordinary" hazards of human existence. Among these one of the most glaring is the risk of travel. In spite of all the safety regulations covering vehicle construction and traffic control, we are now in this country killing about 40,000 people annually in automobile accidents, to say nothing of the crippled millions and the consequent economic losses, which are enormous. Even with the most advanced devices of automation, assuming no failure of the machine, there is always the human factor which is fallible at its best. Yet to stay at home is not without danger. Students of the accident problem have pointed out that one of the most dangerous places in the world is the bathroom of your own home! Even if scientific research could eventually find a remedy for every disease, the accident problem would still remain a terrible liability in human life for which there is no complete remedy in sight. The inventions of man have outrun his ability to cope with their attendant risks. To turn back the clock from our highly mechanized civilization to a more simple life of nature would not solve the problem. For, with all her beauty and magnificence, Nature herself may be very cruel and merciless. We drown in the sea, mountains fall on us, earthquakes shake our houses to rubble, our children fall into the fire, the bugs bite us — there is no end to the hazards in the world of nature.

Now this humanly insoluble problem has received attention in the Old Testament prophecies of the Kingdom. In Ezekiel 34:23-31 we have a glimpse of a condition when the hazards of wild beasts, weather, famine, and warfare are gone — "they shall dwell safely" (vs. 25), and "none shall make them afraid" (vs. 28). In that day such hazards will be under divine control; therefore, the blessed promise of Psalm 91 will become fully and literally true: "There shall no evil befall thee, neither shall any plague come nigh thy dwelling. For he shall give his angels charge over thee, to keep thee in all thy ways. They shall bear thee up in their hands, lest thou dash thy foot against a stone" (vss. 10-12). These are not merely "beautiful dreams," never to be realized in human society. The day is coming when "They shall not hurt nor destroy in all my holy mountain, saith the LORD" (Isa. 11:9; 65:25).

In the days of the coming Kingdom some books on ethics will become obsolete. For example, Durant Drake has written, "When we have done our best we are still at the mercy of fortune. . . . If all men were perfectly righteous, we should still be at the mercy of flood and lightning, poisonous snakes, icebergs and fog at sea, a thousand forms of accident and disease, old age and death. The millennium will not bring pure happiness to man; he is too feeble a creature in the presence of forces with which he cannot cope."[16] The answer of the Old Testament prophets to all such naturalistic systems of morality is that in the future Kingdom men "shall not labor in vain, nor bring forth for calamity" (Isa. 65:23, ASV). For the environment of nature then will be under the supernatural and immediate control of One whose voice even the "winds and the waves obey." Those who can believe in the account of our Lord's power and ministry within the realm of nature, as recorded in the four Gospels, should have no difficulty in accepting the predictions of a vast and permanent extension of the same blessed ministry in a coming Kingdom on earth.

6. The Coming Kingdom Will Have Ecclesiastical Effects

For mine house shall be called an house of prayer for all people.
—Isa. 56:7

Excepting within those philosophic circles which are purely materialistic in outlook, it is now generally agreed that religion is something essential to human welfare. But religion — certainly in Christianity — is both a personal and social matter: "Thou shalt love the

---

[16] *Problems of Conduct* (rev. ed.; Boston: Houghton Mifflin, 1921), p. 168.

Lord thy God. . . . and thy neighbour" (Matt. 22:37-39) — "Not for-
saking the assembling of ourselves together" (Heb. 10:25) — "Go
ye therefore, and teach all nations" (Matt. 28:19). Hence, although
religion is primarily an inward and personal relationship to God, it
finds external expression in human life through forms of worship,
organization, government, and propaganda. I am here using the
term "ecclesiastical" to designate these externals.

Considering now the proper place of religion in any model form of
human society this side of an eternal heaven, there are certain
questions which cannot be avoided. What would be the ideal form
of religion in such a society? Who are to be its leaders? How shall it
be externally organized? What relation should it sustain to the
political State? Can freedom be allowed for various types of religions? How shall the matter of dissent be handled? These are some
of the crucial problems touched by the Old Testament prophets in
their outline of the future Kingdom of God on earth.

a. A Priest-King

Theoretically, there are some very obvious advantages in the idea
of an organization of all religious activities under one supreme head
who would be also the political ruler of the state. And this is the
ecclesiastical picture presented in Old Testament predictions of the
Kingdom. Its Ruler will exercise the functions of both King and
Priest: "Behold, the man whose name is the BRANCH; . . . he
shall bear the glory, and shall sit and rule upon his throne; and he
shall be a priest upon his throne"[17] (Zech. 6:12-13). In the 110th
Psalm, Jehovah speaks to the "LORD" at His right hand, saying,
"Thou art a priest for ever after the order of Melchizedek" (vs. 4).
The entire context of this psalm is Messianic and regal. Today
Messiah sits at the right hand of God on the Father's throne. In the
coming Kingdom He will sit as King and Priest upon His *own*
throne. In principle, the Roman Catholic theory of an ecclesiastical
State is correct; but its tragic error has been an attempt to establish
the Kingdom of God on earth in the absence of the King and under
an ecclesiastical hierarchy ruled by a succession of sinful and fallible
popes. It represents the logical and practical development of the erroneous Church-Kingdom idea; and it is like a number of other

---

17 The rendering of vs. 13 by RSV, which makes the "priest" a different person
from the King, is rejected by Keil who says it is "precluded by the simple structure
of the sentences, and still more by the strangeness of the thought which it expresses" (*Commentary on Minor Prophets, op. cit., in loc.*).

excellent human ideals which, for their realization, require the intervention of supernatural wisdom and power on the part of God.

b. Israel — the Religious Leader

In the days of the coming Kingdom the living nation of Israel, converted and cleansed, will be restored to her original ministry in the good purpose of God. In the establishment of the historical Theocracy at Sinai, the word of Jehovah came to Israel, saying, "Ye shall be unto me a kingdom of priests" (Exod. 19:6). And, although the nation failed through unbelief and disobedience, the purpose of God will not fail. In the dark days of Israel's failure, Isaiah looked forward to a better time when "ye shall be named the Priests of the LORD: men shall call you the Ministers of our God" (61:6). And here, lest there be any confusion as to the identity of the people in view, the prophet carefully distinguishes between them and the Gentile world: "Ye shall eat the riches of the Gentiles." Thus the blessing of God promised through the seed of Abraham, although already realized in part even in the present age, will receive its ultimate fulfilment in the future Millennial Kingdom of God on earth. Then the religious ministry of Israel shall be fully recognized: "Their seed shall be known among the Gentiles, and their offspring among the people: all that see them shall acknowledge them, that they are the seed which the LORD hath blessed" (Isa. 61:9). To prepare the nation for a world-wide mission among the Gentile nations, God will give to the people of Israel faithful "shepherds" to feed them (Jer. 23:4). In this important ministry the tribe of Levi will again have a definite place (Jer. 33:17-22). "At that time," the Lord promises to Israel, "I will make you a name and a praise among all the people of the earth" (Zeph. 3:20).

In this connection an objection has been raised that in the Messianic Kingdom, according to Jeremiah, religious instruction will no longer be needed because all will "know" the LORD "from the least of them unto the greatest of them" (Jer. 31:34). But this prediction is limited by its context. When the new covenant is fully realized in the nation of Israel, it is true that all will *know* the Lord in the sense of glad and willing recognition of His right to rule over them, but this will not make unnecessary the ministry of instruction in the ways and will of the Lord. Certainly, the new covenant is operative even now in the lives of God's people; yet there is need for teaching. Thus we read of "pastors" and "teachers" placed in the Church (Eph.

4:11); and the same ministry will be exercised in the future under more perfect conditions.

c. Jerusalem — the Religious Center

In Holy Scripture there are two Jerusalems: the one is on earth in the land of Palestine; the other is "above," in heaven (Gal. 4:25-26; Heb. 12:22). Now the Old Testament prophets speak of a city which, in the coming Kingdom, shall be reclaimed from Gentile power, rebuilt, restored to the historic nation of Israel, and made the religious center of the world. This Jerusalem cannot be the "heavenly Jerusalem," for that city is impeccably holy, the eternal dwelling of the true God, and has never been defiled or marred by human sin and rebellion. Any such notion is to the highest degree impossible and absurd. All predictions of a restored and rebuilt Jerusalem must therefore refer to the historical city of David on earth.

In Isaiah it is written that this city which in history had "become an harlot" would in the future be called "The city of righteousness, the faithful city" (1:21, 26). The nations which once "despised" Jerusalem shall call her, "The city of the LORD, The Zion of the Holy One of Israel" (Isa. 60:14). Her walls will be called "Salvation" and her gates "Praise" (Isa. 60:18). This very city is to be "a crown of glory in the hand of the LORD, and a royal diadem in the hand of thy God" (Isa. 62:3). It shall be made "a praise in the earth," not in heaven (Isa. 62:7). Here, according to the prophets, the covenant God of Israel in the person of the Mediatorial King will be present: "Thus saith the LORD; I am returned unto Zion, and will dwell in the midst of Jerusalem" (Zech. 8:3). Along with the political reunion of the nation, centered in Jerusalem, there will come also *religious* unity: Ephraim will say, "Let us go up to Zion unto the LORD our God" (Jer. 31:6).

From this world center, enlarged and rebuilt in regal magnificence, the divine Word will go forth to all nations in a way never before seen: "Out of Zion shall go forth the law, and the word of the LORD from Jerusalem" (Isa. 2:3). And to this city the nations will go "from year to year to worship the King, the LORD of hosts" (Zech. 14:16). With both religious and political activities centered in one city and under one King, the world will at last see a successful and beneficial union of religion and government.

d. The Problem of Religious Freedom

It must be evident that the final and perfect union of church and state in the coming Kingdom will also put an end to what we call "freedom of religion." The American policy of complete separation of church and state, which most sensible men fully approve under present conditions, is not however the ideal policy. It is rather a policy of *precaution* in a sinful world, where political and ecclesiastical power too often get into the wrong hands, and the result is intolerable oppression. But under the personal rule of the Messianic King the union of church and state will not only be safe; it will also be the highest possible good. For, if religion is of any essential value in human life, and if there is some one true religion, and if there is coming a time when both political and religious authority will be exercised by a wise and loving God acting supernaturally in human affairs — it follows logically that in that day what we call "religious freedom" must come to an end. Today men are allowed to rebel against the true God, but there is no freedom to rebel against the State! In the days of the coming Kingdom, *both* political and religious rebellion will become high treason against God and humanity.

Therefore, as we might expect, the prophets take cognizance of this problem. After asserting that in the Kingdom the various nations shall come up to Jerusalem to worship the Mediatorial King, Zechariah discusses the possibility of dissent. "And it shall be, that whoso will not come up of all the families of the earth unto Jerusalem to worship the King, the LORD of hosts, even upon them shall be no rain" (Zech. 14:17). In the case of lands like Egypt, there will be a "plague" to smite the nation (Zech. 14:17-19).[18] In other words, the divine procedure will simply be to deprive the dissenters of the Kingdom blessings of food and health. The divine King who controls all the factors of physical environment will need no armies to rule the nations. The sanction of hunger alone would be a sufficient deterrent to all rebellion.

The idea of sin and rebellion in the future Messianic Kingdom has been severely criticized by anti-millennial writers. How account for

[18] The Hebrew construction in verse 18 is somewhat obscure. Keil (*op. cit.*) thinks that the "plague" in the case of rebellion in Egypt is, in fact, the withholding of rainfall threatened in verse 17. But this ignores the general Old Testament usage of the word for "plague"—something Keil does not even discuss— which points definitely to some form of *disease*. Furthermore, since the only rain needed by Egypt was that which fell upon the upper sources of the Nile, such a punishment would injure the peoples there as well as in Egypt. Such an interpretation commits the prophet to absurd and unjust ideas. Did Zechariah know nothing of the connection between rainfall and irrigation? Instead of trying to find reasonable solutions for some of these difficulties, commentators sometimes seem content to let them stand as a welcome argument against the literal interpretation of certain areas of Kingdom prophecy.

such things in an otherwise perfect millennial state? The answer should be obvious: Since human life will proceed under the natural laws of procreation, children will be born with a sinful nature and with sinful tendencies. Such a state of affairs should not trouble the anti-millennial theologians who believe that Messiah's Kingdom is already *now* established on earth! And if, according to the premillennial view, the same sinful tendencies continue to exist in the future Kingdom, there will be one great advantage: Such tendencies will then be under divine and supernatural control. For that matter, even in the eternal state when God will rule over *all*, sinners will continue to exist in the eternal prison-house of the lost. The curious objections raised by some anti-millennialists against the idea of sin present in the coming Kingdom might make one wonder whether they believe in the reality and eternity of hell. If a loving God can tolerate hell in the *eternal* future, is there anything irrational in the divine toleration and strict control of sinful tendencies for a thousand years in Messïah's Kingdom on earth? Or do they suppose that there can be sinners in hell without sin? [19]

Some have objected to such a method of control, arguing that in God's Kingdom He rules by love and spiritual influences; that the use of *force* is the mark of "carnal" ideas of the Kingdom. A sufficient reply to such objections is (1) the heavy hand of God in the material world where there is no forgiveness for violators of its laws; and (2) the reality of a future and final place of punishment for the lost. For hell is a place where the naked force of Deity will be applied without reserve to all incorrigible rebels against the goodness of God. If the doctrine of hell is consistent with the idea of divine goodness, then there can be nothing unreasonable about a kingdom *on earth* where righteousness is enforced among the nations. And in the latter case there will still be mercy available for all, but in hell there will be no mercy.

There is a great deal of intellectual confusion regarding the place of religious freedom in the Kingdom of God. Some of this is the result of wrong notions about the nature of the Kingdom itself. Several years ago the Baptist World Alliance, meeting in London, adopted a five-point statement on the subject of religious freedom. With much of this statement, in its application to the present age, all religiously inclined men of goodwill should agree, regardless of their affiliations. Religious freedom is properly defined as "not only

[19] As an example of confused argument, see *The Future of the Kingdom* by Martin J. Wyngaarden (Grand Rapids: Baker Book House, 1955), p. 75 ff.

freedom to worship privately and publicly, but the right to teach, preach, publish, and advocate, openly and without hindrances, the Gospel of Christ or other religious convictions." But the statement concludes with an irreconcilable conflict of ideas: "We will not rest content until we witness the achievement of religious freedom and individual liberty throughout the world. We believe this is an essential part of our contribution to the thought of the church, as well as to the establishment of Christ's reign on the earth." Certainly these churchmen are right in battling for complete religious liberty on behalf of all men here and now. On the other hand, according to both Scripture and reason, the establishment of the Kingdom of Christ on earth could never make room for liberty on the part of false and degraded religions to propagate and practice their iniquitous delusions. If it is the business of the Christian Church to establish "Christ's reign" on earth, as the Baptist World Alliance seems to assume, then it ought logically to enter the field of religious preferentialism and suppression. But if the Church of the present age finds its greatest good under the political rule of full religious liberty, as it indubitably does, then such liberty must be an *interim* policy, useful only until the Kingdom of Biblical prophecy arrives; and that Kingdom will not be realized on earth until God in Christ comes to set it up.

e. *The Future Temple*

Considering all the profuse and magnificent predictions concerning the nation of Israel, their land, their city, and their divine mission to the Gentile nations, it would be almost inconceivable to find no word concerning the temple where historically all the interests of the ancient theocracy were centered. In the Old Testament prophets there is evidence that the people of Israel were deeply concerned over the destruction of God's house by the Babylonian armies: "Our holy and our beautiful house, where our fathers praised thee, is burned up with fire" (Isa. 64:11).

Not only so, but Jehovah Himself was concerned over this loss. When a remnant of the dispersed nation had come back from the Captivity, and the people's interest had turned from the Lord's house to building homes for themselves, they began to say, "The time is not come, the time that the LORD's house should be built" (Hag. 1:2). To this apathetic attitude a stern reply is uttered by the prophet: "Is it a time for you yourselves to dwell in your ceiled houses, while this house lieth waste? . . . Consider your ways" (Hag. 1:4-5, ASV).

Later, as the rebuilding of the new temple proceeded, there was deep discouragement on the part of the elders who had seen the glory of the former temple: "Who is left among you that saw this house in her first glory? and how do ye see it now? is it not in your eyes in comparison of it as nothing?" (Hag. 2:3). In Ezra we learn that, during the rebuilding, many of the "old men that had seen the first house . . . wept with a loud voice" (3:12, ASV).

Yet the builders were offered divine encouragement to "be strong" (Hag. 2:4), for God was with them. And if any are disappointed in the rebuilt temple of Zerubbabel, there is set before them a prophetic picture of the superlatively glorious temple in the future Kingdom, a structure which will far exceed anything in the past: "For thus saith Jehovah of hosts: Yet once, it is a little while, and I will shake the heavens, and the earth, and the sea, and the dry land; and I will shake all nations; and the precious things of all nations shall come; and I will fill this house with glory, saith Jehovah of hosts. The silver is mine, and the gold is mine, saith Jehovah of hosts. The latter glory of this house shall be greater than the former, saith Jehovah of hosts; and in this place will I give peace, saith Jehovah of hosts" (Hag. 2:6-9, ASV).

This future temple of the Lord, with the organization of its ritual, is outlined in great detail by the prophet Ezekiel in the final section of his book, chapters 40-48, where the magnificent building described is spoken of as a "house" (40:5) and a "temple" (42:8), terms which in the Hebrew original are used of the historic temples of Solomon and Zerubbabel. As to the general character of Ezekiel's prophetic temple, several points may be noted: First, it is generally admitted by all interpreters that there is nothing in the known history of Israel corresponding to the prophet's architectural description. No attempt was ever made to undertake the construction of such a building. This fact should indicate that the Jewish readers of Ezekiel properly placed the fulfilment of his prophecy in the Messianic future.

Second, the prophecy itself indicates that the temple in view belongs to the future Kingdom of Messiah on earth. Ezekiel was given a vision of the return of the Shekinah-Glory to this temple, and identifies it specifically with the "Glory" he had seen departing from the historic temple (43:1-3 with 11:23). Furthermore, as the Glory enters the future temple in his vision, the prophet hears the voice of Jehovah saying, "Son of man, this is the place of my throne. . . .

where I will dwell in the midst of the children of Israel for ever" (43:7, ASV). Nothing in past or current history can be equated with this prediction. There was no Shekinah-Glory in the second and third temples.

Third, as to the general interpretation of Ezekiel's prophecy, an astonishing amount of labor has been expended to show that no *literal* fulfilment can ever be expected.[20] For example, F. Gardiner in *Ellicott's Commentary* argues against literality on the ground that Ezekiel introduces certain details which are impossible. Yet the same commentator offers drawings of the temple gate, the court, the altar, and its location on the map of Palestine! All of which leads to the observation that if an uninspired commentator can make some sense out of the architectural plan, doubtless the future builders working under divine guidance should have no trouble putting up the building. C. von Orelli says that Ezekiel's plan and arrangement "are so clear that one can as easily make a sketch of Ezekiel's as of Solomon's temple."[21] Other problems raised by Gardiner are: (1) that such a building as described, with its various accessories, would require great "physical changes" in the land area as well as a perpetual miracle to feed the river flowing from under its altar; and (2) that the builders of the second temple paid no attention whatever to certain changes in the Mosaic ritual required by Ezekiel's prophecy.

In reply to these objections, it may be said (1) that the Word of God declares specifically that there will be physical changes in the area, wrought by supernatural power (Zech. 14:4); and (2) the fact that the builders in Ezra's day made no attempt to carry out Ezekiel's plan only shows they properly understood his prophecy as referring to the future age of the Messianic Kingdom.

f. *Problem of Animal Sacrifices*

The association of animal sacrifices with Ezekiel's temple has been declared utterly incompatible with any literal fulfilment of the prophecy. On this point, Dr. Gardiner speaks for the objectors as follows: "For it is impossible to conceive, in view of the whole relation between the old and the new dispensations, as set forth in Scripture, that animal sacrifices can ever again be restored by divine command."[22] Here it must be admitted that a future renewal of animal sacrifices raises some very serious problems, but most of these

---

[20] For the various views, see Lange, Ellicott, Keil, Fairbairn, *et al.*
[21] C. von Orelli, "Ezekiel," *New Schaff-Herzog Encyclopedia of Religious Knowledge* (New York: Funk and Wagnalls, 1909), Vol. IV, p. 255.
[22] F. Gardiner, *op. cit.*, p. 314.

have been answered satisfactorily by premillennial writers.[23] Only two problems will be discussed here briefly:

First, to the objection that a renewal of "expiatory" animal sacrifices is unthinkable and would deny the complete efficacy of our Lord's atoning death, the reply is very simple: no animal sacrifice in the Bible has ever had any expiatory efficacy. Yet Dr. Allis says that such sacrifices were "expiatory" and "efficacious in the days of Moses and David."[24] This is a deplorable misuse of words into which he seems to have been inadvertently led by his zeal to refute any literal interpretation of Ezekiel's prophecy. Such terms as "expiatory" and "efficacious" should never have been used as descriptive of sacrifices which, according to the New Testament, could not take away human sin (Heb. 10:4). As to the future, Dr. Allis says, "There is not the slightest hint in Ezekiel's description of these sacrifices that they will be simply memorial."[25] But why should Ezekiel have discussed the point at all? This prophet doubtless understood, as the Epistle to the Hebrews plainly states, that the Old Testament sacrifices were only "a shadow of the good things to come" and "a remembrance made of sins year by year" (10:1-3, ASV). The word "remembrance" here represents the same Greek word (*anamnēsis*) used by our Lord when He said, "This do in remembrance of me" (Luke 22:19; I Cor. 11:24-25). Certainly no evangelical interpretation of the Christian Eucharist would attach to it any expiatory efficacy. Likewise, there was nothing of this kind attached to the Old Testament sacrifices. These sacrifices were simply a "remembrance" of the sins committed, and pointed forward to the one sacrifice which would take them away. What could be wrong, therefore, with a pattern of symbols in the future to remind the worshipper not only of his sin but also of an expiation which at Calvary was accomplished once for all, for all who believe? As the godly H. Bonar once wrote: "Why should not the *temple*, the *worship*, the *rites*, the *sacrifices*, be allowed to point to the Lamb that was slain, in the Millennial age, if such be the purpose of the Father. . . . And if God should have yet a wider circle of truth to open up to us out of His word concerning His Son, why should He not construct a new apparatus for the illustration of that truth?"[26]

[23] See the very able monograph, "The Question of Millennial Sacrifices," by John L. Mitchell, *Bibliotheca Sacra,* issues of July and October, 1953.

[24] O. T. Allis, *Prophecy and the Church* (Philadelphia: Presbyterian and Reformed Pub. Co., 1945), p. 247. On the same page Dr. Allis quotes the very text (Heb. 10:4) which should have cautioned him against his misuse of terms.

[25] *Ibid.*   [26] Quoted by John L. Mitchell, *op. cit.,* July, p. 267.

Second, the idea of a renewal of any animal sacrifices has been denounced as "carnal" and "Judaistic" in origin. In reply it may be said that not a few things in Christianity are derived from Judaism. There is nothing necessarily invidious about such an origin. Consider, for example, some of the forms and special days observed in the Christian Church. The practice of water baptism, all authorities agree, has a definite background in historical Jewish practices.[27] The same can be said of the Lord's Supper or *agape*, and the Eucharist which attended it. The Day of Pentecost on which the Christian Church was founded, and which in Christian history has been celebrated almost universally, was the second of the great Jewish national festivals. To condemn in advance any practice which may have had a "Judaistic" background is dubious business, and smacks of that anti-Jewish prejudice which has too often marked the course of Church history.

In closing on this point, it must not be forgotten that Ezekiel is not alone in his affirmation of a revival of a temple ritual in the coming Kingdom. As Reeve says, "The great prophets all speak of a sacrificial system in full vogue in the Messianic Age."[28] No matter how great the hermeneutical difficulties may seem to be involved in such predictions, we do well to hold fast to their integrity and wait for the divine fulfilment to clear up the problems. Dr. Fausset suggests the proper Christian attitude in such matters when, after outlining frankly the problems connected with a literal fulfilment of Ezekiel's prophecy, he writes: "These difficulties, however, may be all *seeming*, not real. Faith accepts God's Word as it is, waits for the event, sure that it will clear up all such difficulties."[29]

g. A World Center of Worship

We have already noted that in the visions of the Old Testament prophets, all nations are seen going up to a millennial Jerusalem for purposes of worship (Zech. 8:20-23; 14:16). Here again certain problems have been raised in relation to the idea of a world center of worship. For one thing, there is the problem of *distance*, which David Baron, writing as late as 1918, mentioned and answered as follows: "But we do not yet know what the facilities of travel will

---

[27] "Baptism," *International Standard Bible Encyclopedia* (Chicago: Howard-Severance, 1915), Vol. I, p. 386.

[28] J. J. Reeve, "Sacrifice," *I. S. B. E., op. cit.*, Vol. IV, p. 2651.

[29] A. R. Fausset, Jamieson, Fausset and Brown, *Commentary* (New York: Geo. H. Doran), pp. 613-614.

be in the Millennium."[30] Of course, the whole problem has since become obsolete by modern developments in the field of travel.

Furthermore, it has been argued that neither in Jerusalem nor its temple would there be available space for "all nations" to come for purposes of worship. But this is to forget that the prophets predict a vast enlargement of both city and temple. And the borders of the land itself will at last be established as originally promised: "From the river of Egypt unto the great river, the river Euphrates" (Gen. 15:18). Moreover, the prophets do not say that all will come to Jerusalem at the same time, but rather at stated times: "from year to year" (Zech. 14:16); "from one new moon to another, and from one sabbath to another" (Isa. 66:23). Even today churches care for the problem of building space by holding a repetition of services. Also the worship of the nations could be rendered through chosen representatives.[31]

But the most widely cited objection to a world center of worship is that this would constitute a backward step, reversing the important spiritual and universal principle laid down by our Lord when He said to the Samaritan woman, "The hour cometh, when ye shall neither in this mountain, nor yet at Jerusalem, worship the Father. . . . They that worship him must worship him in spirit and in truth" (John 4:21-24). But the objectors (carelessly, I think) miss the point of the passage entirely. Our Lord was not abolishing the worship of God in the city of Jerusalem (there are bodies of believers there today). But to the historical idea of localized worship He added the spiritual idea of *universality*. It is not a question of either/or. All sensible men ought to know that there is no necessary conflict between spiritual worship and a localized place of worship. And the re-establishment of a central sanctuary in Jerusalem for international worship will no more detract from the principle of universality than the going of any one of us to the church of his choice next Sunday morning. The assumption that universality and localization in worship are mutually exclusive ideas is certainly unwarranted, either in revelation or reason. Such objections arise out of prejudice, not logic. For example, recently an author actually argued against a literal interpretation of the prophets because Zechariah says all nations will come to *"Jerusalem"* to worship (14:17), while Malachi says that *"in every place"* worship will be offered to the Lord

[30] David Baron, *op. cit.*, p. 512.
[31] In our own times, to say that people worship in their respective localities does not mean necessarily that they never worship at any other places!

(1:11).[32] This is certainly a remarkable *tour de force!* Has it ever occurred to this author that men today may and do worship in solitude, and also with their families, in a local church building, or even in the present city of Jerusalem on Easter morning? As a matter of fact, some of the most incorrigible opponents of a millennial religious center in Jerusalem, at the same time have an untiring enthusiasm for "trips" to the Holy Land here and now. And, surely, it is a great privilege to walk where the Son of God once lived, suffered, and died. If this be so, how much more wonderful it will be to go there when He is once more there in visible manifestation and glory.

CONCLUSION

Such is the extensive nature of the Mediatorial Kingdom as presented in Old Testament prophecy. For those who have considered seriously the great wealth of material found there, it is scarcely necessary to suggest that, if accepted, the prophetic picture satisfies and reconciles all legitimate viewpoints. The Kingdom is spiritual, but with effects which extend into areas of life which are ethical, social, economic, political, physical, and ecclesiastical. To single out any one of these important aspects and deny validity to the others, is to narrow unwisely the vast breadth of the inspired vision of the future, and also to set limits upon the possibilities of human life under God here and now.

Furthermore, the manifestation of a spiritual Kingdom of God through supernatural and visible effects in human life will have a distinct pedagogical value. Even today there is a general recognition of the value of the sensible and concrete in the teaching of unseen values. The visible effects of the coming Kingdom will be great benefits in themselves, but they will also serve as symbols of greater things which are invisible. In the words of B. W. Newton:

> We read in many parts of the Scripture that the land of Israel will in that day teem with evidences of the miraculous power of God in dispensing blessings. On the sides of Zion, for example, the wolf and the lamb, the leopard and the kid, shall be seen together, and a little child shall lead them. Nothing shall hurt or destroy throughout God's holy mountain. These will be sights that no one will deny to be in themselves blessed. But they are *symbols also, living symbols,* speaking of higher blessings; for they indicate the peace and harmony and love that shall pervade all hearts and all peoples whom the power of Zion shall effectually reach. And if God has appointed

[32] Martin J. Wyngaarden, *op. cit.,* p. 73b.

that the spiritual influence of which I have spoken above should go forth from His forgiven and privileged nation in Jerusalem, we might expect to find some outward symbol of this, its relation. And, accordingly, a symbol is given in the perennial flow of those streams which, going forth from the sanctuary in Jerusalem, shall heal waters, which, like the Dead Sea, have been accursed, and spread life and refreshment in the midst of desolation.[33]

[33] Quoted by David Baron, *op. cit.,* pp. 504-505.

PART FOUR

THE MEDIATORIAL KINGDOM
IN THE FOUR GOSPELS

And, behold, thou shalt conceive in thy womb, and bring forth a son, and shalt call him JESUS. He shall be great, and shall be called the Son of the Highest; and the Lord God shall give unto him the throne of his father David: and he shall reign over the house of Jacob for ever; and of his kingdom there shall be no end.

—Luke 1:31-33

––––––

The throne of David should not be taken here as the emblem of the throne of God, nor the house of Jacob as a figurative designation of the Church. These expressions in the mouth of the angel keep their natural and literal sense. It is, indeed, the theocratic royalty and the Israelitish people, neither more nor less, that are in question here; Mary could have understood these expressions in no other way. It is true that, for the promise to be realized in this sense, Israel must have consented to welcome Jesus as their Messiah. In that case, the transformed theocracy would have opened its bosom to the heathen; and the empire of Israel would have assumed, by the very fact of this incorporation, the character of a universal monarchy. The unbelief of Israel foiled this plan, and subverted the regular course of history; so that at the present day the fulfillment of these promises is still postponed to the future. *— Frederick L. Godet*

CHAPTER XIX

INTRODUCTION: THE INTERPRETATIVE RELATION
BETWEEN THE TWO TESTAMENTS

Again, the example of Christ and His disciples in their treatment of
the Old Testament teaches the principle that the *ipse dixit* of a Scriptural passage is to be interpreted as decisive as to its meaning. In the
about 400 citations from the Old Testament found in the New Testament, there is not one in which the mere "It is written" is not regarded as settling its meaning . . . . It is one of the characteristic
and instructive features of the New Testament writers that they absolutely refrain from the allegorical method of interpretation current
in those times, particularly in the writings of Philo. Not even Gala-
tians 4:22, correctly understood, is an exception, since this, if an allegorical interpretation at all, is an *argumentum ad hominem*. The
sober and grammatical method of interpretation in the New Testament
writers stands out, too, in bold and creditable contrast to that of the
early Christian exegetes, even of Origen.   —*G. H. Schodde*[1]

In moving from the Old to the New Testament material, something
should be said about the hermeneutical relation between these two
bodies of divine revelation. This becomes a matter of special importance with reference to our subject of the Messianic Kingdom. Concerning the King Himself, His person, and His redeeming work in
saving men from sin, as delineated in both Testaments, there is
general agreement among believing scholars. According to Old Testament prophecy, Messiah would be the divine Son of God; yet also
a descendant of David, born of a virgin, in the village of Bethlehem;
who would present Himself as the King of Israel riding on the foal
of an ass. He would be rejected, suffer, die, and rise again from the
grave. In such details as these it is acknowledged that there is clear
and literal correspondence between the Old Testament prophecies and
their historical fulfilment as recorded in the New Testament.

But when we come to the subject of Messiah's glorious Kingdom
and its establishment among men, although the Old Testament material is both voluminous and set in the same prophetical context, the
anti-millennialists begin to hedge and balk, insisting that what the

[1] G. H. Schodde, "Interpretation," *International Standard Bible Encyclopedia*
(Chicago: Howard-Severance, 1915), Vol. III, p. 1490.

prophets say about these matters must be given special interpretative treatment. By such means they arrive at conclusions which are often arbitrary, mystical, and far-fetched. According to such schemes, in order to get at the hidden sense of prophecy it is alleged that we must find some "key" which will unlock the mystery of Scripture. And almost always this "key" turns out to be some exclusive theological emphasis or some New Testament text, the meaning of which may itself be in serious dispute. Then the interpreter insists that everything must be read according to this "key." Or, to vary the figure, the key text or special emphasis becomes a set of colored spectacles through which Old Testament prophecy is read, distorting some things and filtering out completely other things.[2] Against such procedures the weight of Biblical testimony is both clear and convincing.

1. *The Authority and Clarity of the Old Testament*

First, for many centuries and until the Christian era, the sole written divine revelation available to men was *Old Testament* Scripture; and this body of truth was the final court of appeal. This is attested many times by the prophets, by our Lord, by His chosen apostles, and by the Early Church (cf. Luke 24:44; Acts 28:23, etc.).

Second, early New Testament preaching in the Apostolic Church was tested by its agreement with the Old Testament writings. Thus we find the Berean Jews commended because, after hearing Paul and Silas, they "searched the scriptures daily, whether those things were so"; and as a result many were convinced and "believed" (Acts 17:11-12). Furthermore, while defending himself before King Agrippa against the Jewish charges of religious heresy, the Apostle Paul de-

---

[2] As a recent example of this sort of thing, the reader is referred to a paper by Henry R. Van Til published in the *Journal of the American Scientific Affiliation*, September, 1955, page 9. After writing with considerable erudition about the subject of Biblical hermeneutics, and having properly asserted that any Old Testament meanings which are not clear must be settled by the New Testament, Van Til then abruptly says that "James tells the first Synod at Jerusalem that the conversion of the Gentiles as attested by Paul and Barnabas is the fulfilment of the promise of God to David that His tabernacle would be built and that His kingdom would be sure, *thus cutting off in one stroke any physical, material, worldly kingdom in the future for David's heirs*" (p. 13, italics supplied). For the writer, this one text (Acts 15:13-18), interpreted privately by himself, settles everything. He makes no attempt to exegete the text in question; he gives no recognition of any possible alternate view; he makes no examination of the many other New Testament passages bearing on the subject at issue; he offers no explanation of the great body of Old Testament prophecy which has led millions of devout and intelligent Christians to believe in a literal future Kingdom for the Son of David and the nation of Israel—he leaves the reader with nothing but a sweeping and dogmatic *ipse dixit*. Furthermore, he begs the entire theological question by tacitly assuming that a literal Kingdom on earth for David's heirs could not also be a spiritual kingdom. And this goes by the name of "Biblical Hermeneutics."

clares that he had said "none other things than those which the prophets and Moses did say should come" (Acts 26:22).

Third, it was an invariable assumption on the part of our Lord and His Apostles that the Old Testament Scriptures could be understood, at least sufficiently to make their readers and hearers morally responsible for believing their essential demands. Men were commanded to "search" these Scriptures because they testified of Christ (John 5:39). And the Jews' failure to believe on Him is traced back to a failure to believe the Old Testament: "For had ye believed Moses, ye would have believed me: for he wrote of me. But if ye believe not his writings, how shall ye believe my words?" (John 5:46-47). Again, in a remarkable story recorded in Luke 16:20-31, Abraham is heard saying, in answer to the rich man's plea for some warning to his five brothers, that "They have Moses and the prophets; let them hear them" (vs. 29). If they refuse to hear the prophets, they would not believe, even though one were sent from the world of the dead (vs. 31).

Fourth, there is no intimation that the Old Testament writings in general were esoteric in character, incapable of being understood except by the use of some "key" given or discovered centuries after their composition. This does not mean that there were no problems of interpretation in the Old Testament, for the prophets sometimes searched their own writings for meanings. But such problems involved mainly the matter of *time* in relation to morally conditioned prophecies (cf. I Pet. 1:10-11). And this particular problem could only be solved by the historical fulfilment of Messiah's career at His first coming.[3] Furthermore, this coming provided a pattern of literal fulfilment to guard the reader against any misinterpretation of unfulfilled prophecy.

Fifth, it is true that the New Testament must always have the last word in deciding problems of Old Testament interpretation. But it should not be forgotten that even the New Testament has its passages which are "hard to be understood" (II Pet. 3:16). And no New Testament text under question should ever be used to "wrest" or invalidate the clear utterances of the Old Testament prophets. Moreover, where Old Testament problems are settled by an appeal

---

[3] Geerhardus Vos seems to admit this *principle* when he says that "owing to the appearance of the Messiah and the only partial fulfilment of the prophecies for the present, that which the Old Testament depicted as one synchronous movement is now seen to divide into two stages" ("Eschatology of the New Testament," *International Standard Bible Encyclopedia*, Vol. II, p. 979).

to the New Testament, the deciding voice must be that of the *totality* of Scripture on the point in question.

Sixth, if there is difficulty connected with the understanding of the essential doctrines of Scripture — and surely the *Kingdom* is one such doctrine — the problem must be found in man rather than in the revelation. As Schodde has correctly observed, "The Bible is written for men . . . and accordingly there is no specifically Biblical logic, or rhetoric, or grammar."[4] This is why God can hold all men responsible for believing and meeting the essential demands of the written Word at every stage of revelation. If it is possible for human authors to make what they write sufficiently clear for the understanding of those who read, shall we say that God cannot do as much? The answer is given by the Apostle John: "If we receive the witness of men, the witness of God is greater" (I John 5:9). What is wrong, then, that men fail to understand the great essential truths of Scripture?

2. Some Problems Connected with Human Understanding

a. The Problem of Ignorance

Peter speaks of this problem in his second epistle where, with special reference to the writings of Paul, he says, "in which are some things hard to be understood, which they that are unlearned and unstable wrest, as they do also the other scriptures, unto their own destruction" (II Pet. 3:15-16). Instead of "unlearned," Weymouth has "ill-taught," and the American Standard Version has "ignorant." Evidently this particular ignorance is somehow connected with teaching, or the lack of it. And it is a fact that large and important areas of the Word of God are comparatively unknown to many people because they are either given no place in the pulpit or wrongly taught. As a result, other parts of Scripture are wrested or "tortured" to the destruction of men's souls.

But ignorance may also be something deliberate, a path upon which men set their feet with wilful intent. Peter describes certain scoffers of the last days as men who "willingly are ignorant" of things they should have known. And it is a matter of significant interest that the object of this deliberate ignorance is eschatological in nature, having to do with the question of the promise of the Lord's second coming (cf. II Pet. 3:1-5). Furthermore, the revelation to which these "scoffers" deliberately shut their eyes is found for the most part in the Old Testament (vss. 5, 6, 10). The remedy for such igno-

---

4 G. H. Schodde, *op cit.,* Vol. III, p. 1489.

rance, of course, is to receive and read the whole Word of God with an open mind under the guidance of the Spirit of God.

b. *The Problem of Unbelief*

It is possible for men to know and yet to draw back in unbelief. This is true even of the saved, who may believe one part of the Word of God and at the same time hesitate at another part which is just as clear. There is an instructive case of this recorded in Luke 24. Following His death and resurrection, our Lord met two disciples on their way to Emmaus, who in the face of His death and burial were wondering whether or not their hopes in Him as the Messiah-Redeemer of Israel were well founded. In reply, Christ goes straight to the heart of the problem: "O fools, and slow of heart to believe *all* that the prophets have spoken" (Luke 24:25, italics supplied). The context shows clearly that these disciples believed in the Old Testament prophecies concerning the glory of Messiah, but had not accepted literally what the same prophets had said about His suffering and death. As a result these men were actually wavering in their belief in *Jesus* as the Messiah. It is never safe to reject anything in the Scriptures, no matter how unlikely it may seem to mere human reason. And any scheme of interpretation which empties any part of Scripture of its normal meaning is essentially a form of unbelief and can lead to disastrous results all along the line. For example, the Unitarian and Arian views of our Lord accept the Biblical testimony regarding His true humanity, but "interpret" away the testimony concerning His true Deity. The only safe attitude is to accept the totality of Scripture on all its various subjects, whether on the Person of Christ or His Kingdom, and to accept it all at its normal or face value.

c. *The Problem of Limited Discernment*

This seems to have been a handicap under which the Corinthian church was laboring; for to them Paul wrote, "I have fed you with milk, and not with meat: for hitherto ye were not able to bear it, neither yet now are ye able" (I Cor. 3:2). The cause of this limitation was found in their lack of spiritual growth. They were yet "babes in Christ" (I Cor. 3:1), and had to be treated accordingly. Paul even calls them "carnal" (vs. 3), for there is a certain carnality of childhood. The child's mind is unable to judge correctly as to the comparative value or importance of things, being susceptible to attraction by things which are near and can be seen rather than by the things less spectacular and far-off. Still further, the evidence of spiritual childishness among the Corinthian believers was their dependence on, and partisanship for, individual human leaders: "one saith, I am of Paul; and another, I am of Apollos" (I Cor. 3:4). Both were great men, but at their best they were only "ministers by whom ye believed" (I Cor. 3:5). And no mere man, not even the Apostle Paul, has ever been made the divine channel of *all* divine truth. Therefore, for any believer to feed on the Pauline Scriptures alone, or the Four Gospels alone, or to lean wholly upon any one human teacher of the Scriptures, or to restrict the total significance of a Biblical doctrine to the measure of a one-sided selection of texts, indicates spiritual immaturity and the limited discernment which always attends it. The remedy, of course, is to "grow in grace, and in the knowledge of our Lord and Saviour Jesus Christ" (II Pet. 3:18). And since the Scriptures testify concerning Him, there will be spiritual growth as we read, study, and feed upon the *whole* Word of God.

d. *The Problem of Spiritual Blindness*

This is the condition of the whole unsaved world, so that we cannot expect anything but confusion in the ideas of unregenerated men regarding the essential truths of Scripture, no matter how great their scholarship. This blindness has a threefold aspect: First, it is something inherent in the sinful nature of fallen men: "The natural man receiveth not the things of the Spirit of God . . . neither can he know them" (I Cor. 2:14). Second, it is manifested and deepened by the personal sins of the unsaved: "He that hateth his brother is in darkness, and walketh in darkness, and knoweth not whither he goeth, because that darkness hath blinded his eyes" (I John 2:11). Third, it is also induced by the work of Satan who as "the god of this world hath blinded the minds of them which believe not" (II Cor. 4:4). In this verse it is worthy of notice that the particular object of Satan's venomous hatred is "the gospel of the glory of Christ, who is the image of God" (ASV). This is a matter of high importance in relation to the Kingdom, for it is in the establishment of that Kingdom at the second coming of our Lord that His "glory" shall be so fully manifested that "every eye shall see him" (Rev. 1:7). The reality of this glory, unseen today, is part of the Good News set forth in the written Word, and which we accept by *faith*. But the minds of the unbelieving are blinded to this glorious light by the devices of Satan.

Now the remedy for this blindness is very simple. In II Corinthians 3, verses 14 and 15, Paul describes the blindness of those who read the "old testament" without seeing the glory of Christ: "even unto this day," he says, "the veil is upon their heart." The "veil" here is certainly human sin. And how can we be rid of it so that we may see? The answer is very clear: "When it [the heart] shall turn to the Lord, the veil shall be taken away" (II Cor. 3:16).

e. *The Problem of the Finiteness of the Human Mind*

With reference to all that has been said above, it must never be forgotten that in the Scriptures we have a revelation coming down from an Infinite Mind, expressed in the vehicle of human language; and therefore, as Alford has well said, "Its simplest saying has in it a depth which the human mind cannot fathom . . ."[5] But this does not mean that men here and now cannot know the *essential* truths of Scripture. It only means that in relation to these truths "new lights will ever be thrown upon God's Word, by passing events, by the toil of thought, by the discoveries of historical research and of scientific inquiry."[5] For instance, there is no insoluble difficulty in learning from the written Word of God that Jesus Christ is both God and man; and no amount of research or discovery can ever reverse these facts of divine revelation. But through all time and eternity these truths will be seen in fresh brilliance and with new glories as we shall pursue our contemplation of the written Word; and this pursuit will never be wholly done. There is no end to God.

In summarizing this introductory discussion, two things should be emphasized: first, the crucial problems of understanding the written revelation of God are found in man, not in the revelation; and second, excepting man's finitude, these problems are all basically moral and spiritual in nature. If men cannot see, it is not that they have lost their minds, but they have lost their holiness. If men do not believe, it is not that they are incapable of the intellectual act of assent, but that they *will* not believe. To say that the simple act of belief, considered psychologically, is beyond the power of man, is nonsense. Every day, men show clearly by their actions that they *can* believe in each other, in themselves, even in the lies of the propaganda mills. But men of themselves will not believe *God*. If there is an impossibility somewhere — and there is — it is not to be found in any alleged esoteric meaning of Scripture; nor can it be located in some defect of the human intellect. The impossibility is moral and spiritual.

[5] Henry Alford, *New Testament for English Readers* (new ed.; Boston: Lee and Shepherd, 1872), Intro., p. 4.

Man can not believe and understand what God says because he *will* not. That is why fallen men are "ever learning," yet never, without the saving operation of the Holy Spirit, "able to come to the knowledge of the truth" as revealed in Jesus Christ and recorded in Scripture (II Tim. 3:7). And that is why, in the last analysis, it is *God* who must open the "understanding" of men that they might "understand the scriptures" (Luke 24:45).

CHAPTER XX

THE ANNOUNCEMENT OF THE KINGDOM

It is, perhaps, not always appreciated how great a popular excitement was roused when, as Mark puts it . . . "Jesus came into Galilee, preaching the Gospel of God, and saying, The time is fulfilled, and the Kingdom of God is at hand" (1:14-15). It is not the fault of the Evangelists if it is not fully understood.

— Benjamin Breckinridge Warfield[1]

I have in mind here, of course, primarily the teaching and deeds of our Lord during the historical period covered by the gospel records. In approaching this important body of Biblical material, it is possible for interpreters to forget that the stream of history never stands still, not even in the comparatively brief time-span of Christ's public ministry. His teaching about the Kingdom, therefore, cannot be read with understanding apart from the constantly changing historical situation. This principle has been rightly stressed by scholars in connection with the great expanse of Old Testament history. It is no less important in dealing with the gospel records, when the very narrowness of the time increased the swiftness of the current. Hence we shall do well, not only to heed exactly *what* the incarnate King said about His Kingdom, but also to give careful attention to the time and circumstances *when* He said what He did. At least twice in the record of Matthew — both marked by a definite historical crisis — we read that *"From that time"* Jesus began to speak a message distinctly framed by the purpose of God in relation to the historical circumstances peculiar to the hour (4:17; 16:21). To miss the meaning of such changes will plunge the interpreter into endless misunderstanding and confusion.

It is not that God changes in His eternal purposes; but *men* may change. In the dealings of God with men, there come times when they are called upon to make decisions which are moral and spiritual in character. And, although such decisions do not ultimately control

[1] B. B. Warfield, *Christology and Criticism* (New York: Oxford University Press, 1929), p. 53.

the stream of history, they are nevertheless *genuine* and constitute a part of the stream. Our Lord clearly recognized the reality of human decision and its possible tragic consequences, when He wept over the city of Jerusalem, saying, "How often would I have gathered thy children together, even as a hen gathereth her chickens under her wings, *and ye would not*" (Matt. 23:37, italics supplied). But once man's decision has become a fact in human history, it is always met by the infinite, and sometimes hitherto unrevealed, resources of God's eternal purpose in Christ, which never fail.

1. *The New Testament period opens with several verbal announcements of a kingdom.*

It was spoken of by angels: to Zacharias (Luke 1:11-17); to the virgin Mary (Luke 1:26-35); to Mary's husband Joseph (Matt. 1:20-25); and to shepherds of Judea (Luke 2:8-15). It was anticipated by the Magi from the east (Matt. 2:1-6). It was celebrated by the song of Elisabeth (Luke 1:39-45), by the Magnificat of Mary (Luke 1:46-55), and by the prophetic utterance of Zacharias (Luke 1:67-79). This announcement of the Kingdom was called "gospel" or good news (Mark 1:14); and this good news was preached by John the Baptist (Matt. 3:1-2), by our Lord Himself (Matt. 4:17), by the twelve disciples (Matt. 10:5-7), and later by the appointed seventy (Luke 10:1, 9, 11).

This Kingdom is spoken of variously as the "kingdom of heaven" (Matt. 3:2); as the "kingdom of God" (Matt. 12:28); as "Thy kingdom," the pronoun here referring to the Father (Matt. 6:9-10); and also as "my kingdom," indicating that our Lord Jesus Christ regarded the Kingdom as His (Luke 22:30).

2. *The Gospels present Jesus as the King of this Kingdom.*

The very first word about Him recorded in the first of the four Gospels deals with His descent from the royal line in Israel; and thus the written record is named "The book of the generation of Jesus Christ, the son of David, the son of Abraham" (Matt. 1:1). To emphasize His royal character, Matthew reverses the historical sequence, putting David before Abraham. At His birth in Bethlehem the Magi came from the east, asking, "Where is he that is born King of the Jews?" (Matt. 2:1-2). And when the politically-minded Herod, troubled at the news, called together the religious authorities of the nation to inquire where the Messianic King would be born, they answered with no disagreement or hesitation, "In Bethlehem of Judaea: for thus it is written by the prophet, . . . for out of thee shall come a Governor, that shall rule my people Israel" (Matt. 2:4-6). Both Mary, His virgin mother, and Joseph, His legal father, were descendants of the royal house of David. Joseph is addressed as "thou son of David," through the line of Solomon (Matt. 1:20 with 1:6). And to Mary, who was informed that the royal Child would have no *natural* father, the angel Gabriel announced that the Child would sit on the throne of "his father David" (Luke 1:32), thus placing Mary in the family of David apparently through the line of Nathan (Luke 3:31).[2] Early in His ministry, Nathanael expresses his faith in Jesus as follows: "thou art the Son of God; thou art the King of Israel." And our Lord does not repudiate the title, but on the contrary graciously commends Nathanael for what he had come to believe: "Because I said unto thee, I saw thee under the fig tree, believest thou? thou shalt see greater things than these" (John 1:48-50). The very term *Christ*, which is the Greek equivalent of the Hebrew *Messiah* (John 4:25), points to our Lord's royal character, because "It designates Jesus as the fulfiller of the Messianic hopes of the Old Testament and of the Jewish people."[3]

3. *The announcement of the Kingdom was supported by miraculous works.*

These miracles were remarkable both for their nature and extent; and they begin with the ministry of the King Himself, for His forerunner John "did no miracle" (John 10:41). Merely to read in consecutive order the inspired records of our Lord's supernatural works cannot fail to produce a powerful impression. "And Jesus went about all Galilee, teaching in their synagogues, and preaching the gospel of the kingdom, and healing all manner of sickness and all manner of disease among the people. And his fame went throughout all Syria: and they brought unto him all sick people that were taken with divers diseases and torments, and those which were possessed with devils, and those which were lunatick, and those that had the palsy; and he healed them" (Matt. 4:23-24). "When the even was come, they brought unto him many that were possessed with devils: and he cast out the spirits with his word, and healed all that were sick" (Matt. 8:16). "And Jesus went about all the cities and villages,

---

[2] S. J. Andrews says, "We conclude that the two [genealogical] tables given by Matthew and Luke are to be regarded as those of Joseph and Mary" (*Life of Our Lord* [Grand Rapids: Zondervan Publishing House, reprint, 1954], p. 65). So also Orr, Lange, Auberlen, Alexander, Van Oosterzee, Godet, Keil, *et al.*

[3] James Orr, "Jesus Christ," *International Standard Bible Encyclopedia* (Chicago: Howard-Severance, 1915), Vol. III, p. 1626.

teaching in their synagogues, and preaching the gospel of the kingdom, and healing every sickness and every disease among the people" (Matt. 9:35). "But when Jesus knew it, he withdrew himself from thence: and great multitudes followed him, and he healed them all" (Matt. 12:15). "And great multitudes came unto him, having with them those that were lame, blind, dumb, maimed, and many others, and cast them down at Jesus' feet; and he healed them" (Matt. 15:30).

Divine authority to perform similar miracles was also given by our Lord to His twelve disciples who were sent to announce the good news of the Kingdom: "And when he had called unto him his twelve disciples, he gave them power against unclean spirits, to cast them out, and to heal all manner of sickness and all manner of disease. . . . These twelve Jesus sent forth, and commanded them, saying, . . . And as ye go, preach, saying, The kingdom of heaven is at hand. Heal the sick, cleanse the lepers, raise the dead, cast out devils: freely ye have received, freely give" (Matt. 10:1-8). The same authority was apparently extended later to another group of "seventy" specially appointed messengers to go before Him, to whom He said, "And into whatsoever city ye enter, and they receive you, eat such things as are set before you: And heal the sick that are therein, and say unto them, The kingdom of God is come nigh unto you" (Luke 10:1, 8-9).

4. *The impact of these miracles upon the people of Israel was tremendous.*

The early part of the Gospel of Mark gives the clearest testimony as to the instant yet cumulative effect upon the nation in the vast enthusiasm aroused by our Lord's message and its attendant miracles. "And immediately his fame spread abroad throughout all the region round about Galilee" (1:28). "And at even, when the sun did set, they brought unto him all that were diseased, and them that were possessed with devils. And all the city was gathered together at the door" (1:32-33). When He sought a "solitary place" to pray, the disciples found Him and said, "All men seek for thee" (1:35-37). As He entered Capernaum and the report of His presence was spread, "straightway many were gathered together, insomuch that there was no room to receive them, no, not so much as about the door: . . . And when they could not come nigh unto him for the press, they uncovered the roof where he was," in order to bring a palsied man to His attention (2:1-4). "But Jesus withdrew himself with his disciples to the sea: and a great multitude from Galilee followed him, and from Judaea, and from Jerusalem, and from Idumaea, and from beyond Jordan; and they about Tyre and Sidon, a great multitude, when they had heard what great things he did, came unto him. And he spake to his disciples, that a small ship should wait on him because of the multitude, lest they should throng him. For he had healed many; insomuch that they pressed upon him for to touch him, as many as had plagues" (3:7-10). Commenting on this remarkable phenomenon, Dr. B. B. Warfield says, "Disease and death must have been almost eliminated for a brief season from Capernaum and the region which lay immediately around Capernaum as a center. No wonder the public mind was thrown into a state of profound perturbation, and, the enthusiasm spreading, men flocked from every quarter to see this great thing."[4]

5. *The genuineness and import of Christ's miracles were widely acknowledged.*

This was true even on the part of His enemies among the religious leaders of Israel. Following the raising of Lazarus from the dead, the Apostle John informs us, "Then gathered the chief priests and the Pharisees a council, and said, What do we? for this man doeth many miracles. If we let him thus alone, all men will believe on him" (John 11:47-48). The Greek term *sēmeion* used here by the Lord's enemies to designate His "miracles" means literally a "sign"; that is, a miracle which authenticates both a messenger and the truth of his message.[5] Although they rejected *Him,* they could not deny the reality of His miracles; nor would they wish to deny that such miracles, according to the prophets, would be the authenticating signs of Messiah and His Kingdom. After His triumphal entry into Jerusalem and His cleansing of the temple, the chief priests and scribes "saw the wonderful things that he did" in the temple, healing the blind and the lame; yet they were "sore displeased" when they heard even the children there crying, "Hosanna to the son of David," in recognition of His regal claims and signs. So they put the crucial question to Jesus Himself: "Hearest thou what these say?" And our Lord indicates beyond dispute His full approval and acceptance of the Messianic title upon the children's lips, as He replies with a quotation from their own Scriptures show-

[4] B. B. Warfield, *op. cit.,* p. 54.
[5] J. H. Thayer, *Lexicon of the New Testament* (cor. ed.; New York: Harper and Bros., 1889) p. 573, 2b.

ing that even "babes" are sometimes wiser than the most learned of men (Matt. 21:12-16).

6. *The announced Kingdom was near at hand.*

In announcing the coming Kingdom several strong expressions were used to indicate its nearness. First, as to its supernatural *powers,* the Kingdom had "come upon" those who heard its proclamation and witnessed its signs. As our Lord warned His hearers, "But if I by the finger of God cast out demons, then is the kingdom of God come upon[6] you" (Luke 11:20, ASV).

Second, as to the personal presence of its *King,* the Kingdom was actually "in the midst" of men. Answering the query of the Pharisees as to "when" the Kingdom of God would come, Christ said, "The kingdom of God is in the midst[7] of you" (Luke 17:21, ASV margin). The King James rendering, by *"within,"* cannot be true; for surely in no sense could the Kingdom of God have been "within" the hearts of the Pharisees to whom our Lord was speaking, and who had charged blasphemously that His miracles were being accomplished through the power of the devil (Matt. 12:24). But in the Person of its divinely appointed King, visibly present in incarnate form on earth where He must eventually reign, the Kingdom was in that sense already "in the midst of" men regardless of their attitude, whether for or against Him. For it is a sound political principle that the government of any realm in a genuine sense attaches to the person of its sovereign wherever he may be, but especially when he is present in his own realm, as our Lord was, even though it be occupied by hostile forces. That Christ so regarded the

[6] The Greek preposition is *epi* with the accusative case; which by some authorities is taken to mean "movement toward a place" in distinction from the idea of actual arrival, the latter being expressed by the genitive case. By others, however, the two constructions are regarded as almost identical in meaning. Certainly, on the basis of Luke 11:20, no conclusive argument can be built for a *present* establishment of the Kingdom. See J. H. Thayer, *op. cit.* Moreover, according to A. T. Robertson, the aorist indicative form of the verb is "timeless" (*Word Pictures in New Testament, in loc.*).

[7] The Greek adverb *entos* may be translated either "within" or "among" in the sense of "in the midst of." But the context of Luke 17:21 is decisively against "within." As Dean Alford has said, "The misunderstanding which rendered these words *'within you'* meaning this in a spiritual sense, *'in your hearts,'* should have been prevented by reflecting that they are addressed to the *Pharisees,* in whose hearts it [the Kingdom] certainly *was* not" (*New Testament for English Readers* on Luke 17:21). With this opinion H. A. W. Meyer agrees, adding that the entire idea of a kingdom existing in the heart or soul of man is *"modern,* not historico-biblical" (*Commentary on the New Testament,* Luke 17:21). So also J. J. Van Oosterzee in Lange's *Commentary on Luke.* M. R. Vincent renders *entos* by the phrase "in the midst of," quoting Trench as follows: "The whole language of the kingdom of heaven being within men, rather than men being within the kingdom, is modern" (*Word Studies in the New Testament,* Vol. I, p. 401).

historical situation is strongly supported by His words to the disciples which immediately follow: "The days will come, when ye shall desire to see one of the days of the Son of man, and ye shall not see it" (Luke 17:22).

Third, as to the actual *establishment* of its government on earth, the Kingdom had "come nigh" unto men (Luke 10:9, 11). The same Greek verb *eggizo* is used in recording John the Baptist's announcement of the Kingdom as something "at hand" (Matt. 3:2). The tense of the verb is a perfect which A. T. Robertson explains as meaning "has drawn near."[8] In truth, the long-awaited Kingdom of Old Testament prophecy had come so near to the men of that generation that they had actually seen the face of the King and also had witnessed the supernatural works, which were the predicted harbingers of His Kingdom.

[8] *Word Pictures in New Testament* (New York: Harper and Bros., 1930), Vol. I, p. 24.

Chapter XXI

THE IDENTITY OF THIS ANNOUNCED KINGDOM

> But this Kingdom is either essentially the same as that predicted by
> the prophets, or it is not.   —*L. Berkhof*[1]
> In announcing the approaching advent of "the kingdom of heaven,"
> Jesus had in view the very kingdom which the prophets had foretold.
>   —*James Orr*[2]

To the ordinary devout reader of the Scriptures it may come as a surprise to learn that any question should ever have been raised concerning the identity of the Kingdom announced as at hand in the beginning of our Lord's ministry on earth. But the question has been raised: Was this Kingdom identical with the Kingdom of Old Testament prophecy? Or was it something different? To these questions the various current answers can be summarized under five heads:

First, the *Liberal-Social* view: that Christ took over from the Old Testament prophets their ethical and social ideals of the kingdom, excluding almost wholly the eschatological element, and made these ideals the program of a present kingdom which it is the responsibility of His followers to establish in human society on earth here and now.[3] By this school, unwelcome Biblical material was disposed of by a subjectively determined critical method.

Second, the *Critical-Eschatological* view: that Jesus at first embraced fully the eschatological ideas of the Old Testament prophets regarding the Kingdom, and to some extent the current Jewish ideas; but later in the face of opposition He changed His message; or, at least, there are conflicting elements in the gospel records. As to the precise nature and extent of this change, or the alleged conflicts, the critics are not agreed.[4] The critical attitude here differs essentially

---

[1] L. Berkhof, *The Kingdom of God* (Grand Rapids: Eerdmans Publishing Co., 1951), p. 167.

[2] James Orr, "Kingdom of God," *Dictionary of the Bible*, ed. James Hastings (New York: Scribner's Sons, 1901), Vol. II, p. 849.

[3] See works by Walter Rauschenbush, R. J. Campbell, Shailer Mathews, Henry C. King, *et al.*

[4] See works by Johannes Weiss, Albert Schweitzer, Carl Barth, Emil Brunner, *et al.*

from the Liberal-Social school only in the type of Biblical material rejected or retained on alleged critical grounds.

Third, the *Spiritualizing-Anti-millennial* view: that our Lord appropriated certain spiritual elements from the Old Testament prophetical picture, either omitted or spiritualized the physical elements (excepting the physical details involved in the Messiah's first coming!), and then added some original ideas of His own.[5] Bruce thus defines the attitude of our Lord: "His spiritual nature determined the form of the Messianic idea, gathering up as by elective affinity the congenial elements of Old Testament prophecy."[6]

Fourth, the *Dual-Kingdom* view: that Christ at His first coming offered to Israel and established on earth a purely spiritual kingdom; and that at His second coming He will establish on earth a literal Millennial Kingdom.[7] In opposition to this theory it should be said that, while the Bible does make a clear distinction between the Universal Kingdom which is everlasting and the Mediatorial Kingdom which is limited in both location and time, neither the Old Testament prophets nor our Lord knew anything about two Mediatorial Kingdoms, the one "spiritual" and the other "earthly."

Fifth, the *One-Kingdom Millennial* view: that the Kingdom announced by our Lord and offered to the nation of Israel at His first coming was identical with the Mediatorial Kingdom of Old Testament prophecy, and will be established on earth at the second coming of the King. This might well be called the *Biblical* view because

---

[5] See works by A. B. Bruce, L. Berkhof, G. Vos, O. T. Allis, *et al.*

[6] A. B. Bruce, *The Kingdom of God* (4th ed.; New York: Scribner and Welford, 1891), p. 150.

[7] George E. Ladd, *Crucial Questions about the Kingdom* (Grand Rapids: Eerdmans Publishing Co., 1952), Chaps. V and VI. Although Dr. Ladd insists on the over-all unity of the divine Kingdom, and also that his distinction is between two phases or realms of the same kingdom, he nevertheless slips continually into the terminology of *two* kingdoms. No less than ten times in Chap. V he calls his future Millennial Kingdom "the earthly, Davidic Kingdom" in contrast to his present "spiritual" kingdom; and on page 125 he refers to the one as "the present spiritual kingdom" and to the other as "the future glorious kingdom." Concerning the former he says, "The Jewish people rejected this kingdom" (p. 131); and concerning the latter, "Had He offered them the earthly, Davidic kingdom, they would have accepted it . . ." (p. 113). He even draws a parallel between the Messianic Advent and the Messianic Kingdom: Since there are two *comings* of Messiah, he argues, likewise there are two "realms" of His reign, one established at His first coming, the other to be at His second coming (pp. 114, 131). If there is any true parallel here, as Ladd asserts, then there must be two kingdoms. For there are certainly two distinct and separate comings. What Dr. Ladd seems to be doing is to abstract two elements or aspects from the *one* Mediatorial Kingdom and make of them two kingdoms to be established respectively at two separate times on earth, and occupying two separate ages.

it is supported by the material in both Testaments taken at its normal or face value.[8] Without intending to imply that the late Dr. James Orr would have endorsed in every detail this viewpoint, it is not unfair to say that his words do support its central thesis: "In announcing the approaching advent of 'the Kingdom of heaven,' Jesus had in view the very kingdom which the prophets had foretold."[9]

We shall now examine the gospel records of the New Testament for the purpose of inquiring whether or not there is a genuine and complete correspondence between the Kingdom predicted by the Old Testament prophets and that Kingdom which was announced by our Lord at the beginning of His earthly ministry. What are the facts?

1. *The absence of any formal definition of the Kingdom in its initial announcement indicates that the Jewish hearers were expected to know exactly what Kingdom was meant.*

In the gospel records, the announcement of the Kingdom is impressively abrupt. "In those days came John the Baptist, preaching in the wilderness of Judaea, and saying, Repent ye: for the kingdom of heaven is at hand" (Matt. 3:1-2). "From that time Jesus began to preach, and to say, Repent: for the kingdom of heaven is at hand" (Matt. 4:17). "Now after that John was put in prison, Jesus came into Galilee, preaching the gospel of the kingdom of God, and saying, The time is fulfilled, and the kingdom of God is at hand: repent ye and believe the gospel" (Mark 1:14-15). Although doubtless our Lord said a great deal about the Kingdom of which there is no record in Scripture, we can be sure that the Biblical writers have not omitted any essential elements of His message. And, since there is no record of any formal definition in these initial announcements of the Kingdom, it is highly improbable that any was given. Obviously, such a definition would have been absolutely necessary if Christ had entertained a radically novel conception of the Kingdom of God.

The complete absence of any formal explanation has puzzled more than one interpreter, resulting in not a little speculation and guesswork regarding the nature of the Kingdom preached by our Lord. This problem is today receiving more of the attention that it deserves. Among liberal scholars, Scott has stated the problem as fol-

[8] See works by G. N. H. Peters, W. G. Moorehead, Nathaniel West, A. J. Gordon, J. H. Brookes, S. J. Andrews, David Baron, James M. Gray, C. I. Scofield, G. Campbell Morgan, Sir Robert Anderson, L. S. Chafer, Wilbur M. Smith, John F. Walvoord, Chas. L. Feinberg, H. C. Theissen, *et al.*

[9] James Orr, Kingdom of God," *op. cit.,* Vol. II, p. 849.

lows: "Our Gospels are full of sayings and parables about the Kingdom of God. We are told what it is like, how it will be manifested, who will inherit it, on what conditions it will be entered. But when all this has been learnt, we are still left inquiring, 'What *is* the Kingdom?' "[10] Now, although we cannot agree with the total content of Scott's answer, it is a matter of interest that he points in the right direction when he insists that our Lord's message cannot be explained apart from the Old Testament. In short, the very lack of any formal definition in the teaching of Christ, instead of raising conjectures, should have sent the investigators to the prophets of the Old Testament.

Among the Jewish people in our Lord's day there were different parties, each holding their own views regarding the nature of God's rule over the earth in relation to Israel. And the widespread interest and public excitement aroused by the Lord's preaching of the Kingdom raised the inevitable inquiries as to its nature. Thus in one of the earliest incidents of His ministry we have Nicodemus coming to talk with the new Prophet. When Nicodemus is perplexed about the way of entrance into the Kingdom, the reply of Jesus is not a definition but a rebuke: "Art thou the teacher of Israel, and understandest not these things?" (John 3:10, ASV). This rebuke makes no sense at all apart from the assumption that the Kingdom announced by our Lord was in all respects the Kingdom of Old Testament prophecy; and consequently Nicodemus, by virtue of his position as an authorized teacher in Israel, could properly be held fully responsible for understanding exactly the nature and various aspects of that Kingdom.

2. *Our Lord never intimated that His conception of the Kingdom differed in any respect or degree from that presented by the Old Testament prophets.*

If, as some argue, the prophets were wrong in any respect, or if our Lord intended to purge out the alleged "carnal elements" of the Old Testament prophetic Kingdom, or if He came to establish on earth a purely "spiritual kingdom," how simple it would have been for Him to say so. But the closest scrutiny of His teaching about the Kingdom has never disclosed any break with the composite Old Testament prophetic picture. On the contrary, from the beginning of His public ministry to the end of it, His evaluation of the pro

[10] Ernest F. Scott, *The Kingdom of God* (New York: Macmillan Co., 1931), p. 48.

phetic Scriptures remains the same. In the Sermon on the Mount, which is concerned specifically with the things of the "kingdom of heaven," He cautions the disciples that He has not come to "destroy the law, or the prophets: . . . but to fulfil." Therefore, although heaven and earth may pass away, "one jot or one tittle shall in no wise pass from the law, till all be fulfilled" (Matt. 5:17-18).

Furthermore, His rejection and death at the hands of the chosen nation effected no change in His attitude. After His resurrection, walking with two disciples who were deeply troubled over the seeming conflict between what had happened and the Old Testament picture of the Kingdom, He reassures them in these words: "All things must be fulfilled, which were written in the law of Moses, and in the prophets, and in the psalms, concerning me" (Luke 24:44). Thus the problem did not arise from any discrepancy between our Lord's views and those of the Old Testament prophets, but rather from a failure on the part of Israel to see the total picture of the coming Kingdom as presented in the prophets.

All the elaborate attempts to explain Christ's strict adherence to the Old Testament Scriptures by resorting to certain *kenotic* and *accommodation* theories have utterly failed. For if He did not know the difference between the true and the false ideas concerning the Kingdom, then we can trust Him in nothing. But if He knew and did not speak for fear of giving offense, then His moral integrity is hopelessly compromised and He descends to the level of a second-rate politician.

As a matter of fact, instead of acquiescing in the errors of His contemporaries, Christ never hesitated to rebuke and correct them. Hear Him as He denounces the Sadducees: "Ye do err, not knowing the scriptures, nor the power of God" (Matt. 22:29). And again as He supports the Old Testament Scriptures against the traditions of the Pharisees: "Full well ye reject the commandment of God, that ye may keep your own tradition" (Mark 7:9). Surely in a doctrine so important as that of the Kingdom of God, if there were in the Old Testament prophets anything false or out of line with His own doctrine, He was morally responsible to say so. Although spoken in another connection, we cannot be wrong in quoting and applying His own words to the point at issue: "if it were not so, I would have told you" (John 14:2). No teacher of the things of God, least of all the infallible Teacher, can evade this solemn responsibility by taking refuge in silence.

3. *The terms "kingdom of heaven" and "Son of man," used by Christ in preaching the Kingdom, acquire their significance solely in relation to the Old Testament prophetic concept.*

The most cherished self-designation of our Lord was "Son of man." In the four Gospels it occurs at least eighty-two times, always on His own lips except once when the bystanders ask what He means by this title (John 12:34). Outside the gospel records it is found once in Acts (7:56) and twice in Revelation (1:13; 14:14). In the Gospel of Matthew, which is chiefly concerned with the regal character of Christ, the generally used name of His Kingdom is "the kingdom of heaven." Since it was used first by John the Baptist (Matt. 3:2), it cannot be said to have been originated by our Lord.

As to the derivation of these two expressions, some very ingenious attempts have been made to explain them apart from their obvious Old Testament prophetic context. But for the most part such explanations may be regarded as "ghosts which appear for an hour on the stage of learning, attracting attention and admiration, but have no permanent connection with the world of reality." By the best conservative scholars, the use of these terms is traced back to the Book of Daniel, where the association of their underlying ideas with the Messianic Kingdom is so obvious and striking that it cannot be fairly denied.[11]

In the second chapter of Daniel there is set forth a series of world empires, symbolized by a great image, which are followed by a divine Kingdom. The latter is described as follows: "In the days of those kings shall the God of heaven set up a kingdom, which shall never be destroyed" (2:44, ASV). Since this divine Kingdom comes from "heaven" to destroy and supplant kingdoms existing on earth, it is apparent that we have here a clear correspondence of ideas between Daniel's prophecy and Matthew's terminology. This correspondence becomes still more certain in the vision of Daniel 7. Here we have the same succession of earthly empires, now symbolized by four beasts, followed by the same divine Kingdom which is described as follows: "I saw in the night-visions, and, behold, there came with the clouds of heaven one like unto a son of man, and he came even to the ancient of days, and they brought him near before him. And there was given him dominion, and glory, and a kingdom, that all the peoples, nations, and languages should serve him: his dominion is an everlasting dominion, which shall not pass away, and his kingdom

[11] So Alford, Ellicott, Stalker, Orr, *et al.*

that which shall not be destroyed" (7:13-14, ASV). Here the divine King comes *"with the clouds of heaven"* to set up this Kingdom over all nations forever, and He is like unto *"a son of man."*

It should be observed that we have here, not only a parallel of language and concept between Daniel's prophecy and the New Testament terms, but also a significant political context. Both the Kingdom which is from "heaven" and its regal "son of man" come to judge and supplant political rulers and realms. The deliberate choice of such terms as "son of man" and "kingdom of heaven" cannot be explained apart from a genuine identity between the Kingdom in our Lord's thought and the Kingdom of the Old Testament prophets.

Thus, read in the light of its evident Old Testament context, the phrase "kingdom of heaven" does not refer to a kingdom *located* in heaven as opposed to the earth, but rather to the coming to earth of a kingdom which is heavenly as to its origin and character.[12]

4. *Our Lord constantly appealed to the Old Testament prophets in support of His regal claims and His message of the Kingdom.*

The Biblical material here is so voluminous that only a few selected specimens can be examined. As our Lord began His preaching in his home town of Nazareth, He identifies Himself and justifies His ministry by reading a passage from Isaiah: "The Spirit of the Lord is upon me, because he hath anointed me to preach the gospel to the poor; he hath sent me to heal the brokenhearted, to preach deliverance to the captives, and recovering of sight to the blind, to set at liberty them that are bruised, to preach the acceptable year of the Lord." Having closed the book, He declares that "This day is this scripture fulfilled in your ears" (Luke 4:18-21), thus indicating that He is Jehovah's Anointed One who will bring in the Kingdom pictured in the last section of Isaiah's prophecies, chapters 40 through 66. Even if we limit the context to chapter 61, it is clear that we have here the Messianic Kingdom promised to the nation of Israel, which will be established over all nations, in its great splendor and richness.

Again, referring to the ministry of John the Baptist as His forerunner, Christ connects it with the prophecy of Malachi (Luke 7:24-27 with Mal. 3:1). But Malachi 3:1 cannot be disconnected from the context in which it appears, where the regal "messenger of the covenant" comes to His temple to sit in judgment upon the nation of Israel, purifying the "sons of Levi," making the "offering of

---

[12] Cf. M. R. Vincent, *Word Studies in the New Testament* (New York: Scribner's Sons, 1924), Vol. I. pp. 23-24.

Judah and Jerusalem [to] be pleasant unto the Lord, as in the days of old, and as in former years"; and adjudicating the social wrongs common to a sinful race (Mal. 3:1-6).

Later in His earthly ministry, after meeting with great wisdom the interrogatory attacks of His enemies, He reverses the situation and becomes the questioner: "How say they that Christ is David's son? And David himself saith in the book of Psalms, The LORD said unto my Lord, Sit thou on my right hand, till I make thine enemies thy footstool. David therefore calleth him Lord, how is he then his son?" (Luke 20:41-44). Here we have clearly stated our Lord's doctrine as to the person of Messiah: He is both "Son" and "Lord" of David, both human and divine. And significantly this doctrine is found by Christ in one of the greatest Kingdom passages of the Old Testament, the 110th Psalm, where Messiah is pictured as the divine King-Priest, ruling in the midst of His enemies, striking through kings in the day of His wrath, judging among the nations, and filling the places with dead bodies in His overthrow of the satanic "head" over many countries (Ps. 110:6, ASV).

Following His death and resurrection, Christ spent a period of at least forty days giving instruction to His chosen disciples. The main subjects of this special teaching were two: first, "concerning himself" (Luke 24:27, 44); and second, "the things pertaining to the kingdom of God" (Acts 1:3). The source materials used were the Old Testament Scriptures: "all things . . . which were written in the law of Moses, and in the prophets, and in the psalms" — the customary threefold division of the Old Testament books (Luke 24:44). Thus, in this post-resurrection school of instruction, we have both the King and His Kingdom brought together as the one central theme of Old Testament prophecy, upon which our Lord rested His regal claims as the King of God's Kingdom on earth.[13]

5. *The gospel records always connect the Kingdom proclaimed by our Lord with the Kingdom of Old Testament prophecy.*

This connection is very striking in the *nativity accounts*. John, the child of the aged Zacharias and Elisabeth, will go before the Son of Mary "in the spirit and power of Elijah" to make ready for

---

[13] Yet Dr. O. T. Allis makes the astonishing statement: "To prove his Messiahship Jesus did not appeal to the kingdom prophecies, but rather to his works of mercy and healing" (*Prophecy and the Church*, p. 70). Even if we were to limit ourselves to our Lord's "works of mercy and healing" (an entirely unwarranted limitation), these very works were precisely the things predicted by the Old Testament in connection with Messiah's Kingdom. In proof of this we need only to read Matthew 11:1-6, a passage to be discussed later.

the Messianic Kingdom a prepared people, in accordance with Malachi's prophecy of the Kingdom (Luke 1:17 with Mal. 3:1). The word of the angel Gabriel to the virgin Mary is that her Son "shall be great, and shall be called the Son of the Highest: and the Lord God shall give unto him the throne of his father David: and he shall reign over the house of Jacob for ever; and of his kingdom there shall be no end" (Luke 1:32,33). The "throne of David" here is not God's throne in heaven, nor is the "house of Jacob" a reference to the Christian Church. As Godet has rightly observed: "These expressions in the mouth of the angel keep their natural and literal sense. It is, indeed, the theocratic royalty and the Israelitish people, neither more nor less, that are in question here; Mary could have understood these expressions in no other way."[14] This is confirmed by the Magnificat of Mary in which she celebrates the coming birth by referring back to God's promise of help to "his servant Israel, in remembrance of his mercy; as he spake to our fathers, to Abraham, and to his seed for ever" (Luke 1:54-55). The birth of John the Baptist and his naming opens the mouth of his father Zacharias in a remarkable prophetic utterance concerning the child as the forerunner of Messiah and His regal work (Luke 1:67-79). In this prophecy Zacharias speaks of "the Lord God of Israel" (cf. Ps. 72:18), of God's redemption of "his people" (cf. Isa. 43:1), of the "house of his servant David" (cf. Ps. 89:20-36), of God's "holy prophets" of Old Testament days who promised that Israel would be "saved" from their "enemies" (cf. Isa. 60:14), of God's "holy covenant" (cf. Ps. 105:7-11), of the "oath" sworn to Abraham (Gen. 22:16-18), and of the visitation of the "dayspring [sunrising] from on high" (cf. Mal. 4:2). An examination of the above Old Testament references will show that all are set in the context of Kingdom prophecy.

Likewise Luke tells us of Simeon, who was among those who waited "for the consolation of Israel," giving thanks to God because he had lived to see the One who was to be "A light to lighten the Gentiles, and the glory of thy people Israel" (Luke 2:25-33). Here the words of Simeon take us back to Isaiah 42:6 and 49:6, both passages set in a regal context. In Luke's account we come next to the testimony of the prophetess Anna who speaks of the divine Child to "all them that were looking for the redemption of Jerusalem" (Luke 2:36-38, ASV). These expressions, "the consolation of

14 F. Godet, *Commentary on Luke* (New York: Funk and Wagnalls, 1886) *in loc.*

Israel" and "the redemption of Jerusalem," represent ideas which are so firmly embedded in the doctrine of the Kingdom of Old Testament prophecy that no exposition can be valid which leaves out the historic nation of Israel and its historic city.

The same connection appears in the ministry of Christ. When He takes up His great Galilean ministry, preaching that the "kingdom of heaven is at hand," Matthew connects it with a prophecy in Isaiah: "Galilee of the Gentiles; the people which sat in darkness saw great light; and to them which sat in the region and shadow of death light is sprung up" (Matt. 4:12-17; cf. Isa. 9:1-2). It takes only a glance at this particular prophecy in Isaiah to see that it forms an introductory yet integral part of that great Kingdom prediction containing the well-known words, "For unto us a child is born, unto us a son is given: and the government shall be upon his shoulder: and his name shall be called Wonderful, Counsellor, The mighty God, The everlasting Father, The Prince of Peace. Of the increase of his government and peace there shall be no end, upon the throne of David, and upon his kingdom, to order it, and to establish it with judgment and with justice from henceforth even for ever. The zeal of the LORD of hosts will perform this" (Isa. 9:1-7).

If we are puzzled by our Lord's expressed opposition ·to undue publicity for His great miracles (Matt. 12:15-16), Matthew finds the explanation in another prophecy of Isaiah: "He will not wrangle or raise his voice, nor will his voice be heard in the broad ways" (Matt. 12:17-19, Weymouth trans.). Here again the original prophetic context is regal; for this King who is God's "servant" will not reach His rightful place of eminence by any of the usual human means of carnal force or political demagoguery; yet by means of the supernatural forces at His command, "He shall not fail nor be discouraged, till he have set judgment in the earth: and the isles shall wait for his law" (Isa. 42:4).

Later in His Galilean ministry, the disciples of John and the Pharisees came to Jesus asking why His disciples did not fast. His answer is to point out the utter incongruity of fasting while "the bridegroom is with them." So important was this incident that it is given a place in each of the Synoptic Gospels (Matt. 9:14-17; Mark 2:18-22; Luke 5:33-39). Now the idea of a divine Bridegroom was nothing new to the Jewish people, for it held a central place in Old Testament prophecies concerning the relation of God to Israel in the days of the coming Kingdom. The figure of the divine Bridegroom appears in Isaiah 61 and 62, both chapters dealing with the Kingdom in which Israel will again be married to the Lord. In those days, we read, "as the bridegroom rejoiceth over the bride, so shall thy God rejoice over thee" (Isa. 62:5). The same idea appears in the prophecy of Hosea. To the nation of Israel, cast off because of unfaithfulness, Jehovah speaks in tender love: "I will betroth thee unto me for ever; . . . and thou shalt know the LORD (2:19-20). And in chapter 3 the personal experience of the prophet is made the occasion and figure of what God will do for Israel. Just as Hosea was commanded to take to himself an unfaithful woman, so God will take to Himself a faithless people. As to this people's identity there can be no question: "For the children of Israel shall abide many days without a king, . . . Afterward shall the children of Israel return, and seek the LORD their God, and David their king; and shall fear the LORD and his goodness in the latter days" (Hos. 3:4-5). It is the Israel of history.

Now it is both startling and highly significant that Christ, fully acquainted with the Old Testament meaning and prophetic setting of this figure of the divine Bridegroom in relation to a repentant Israel in the coming Kingdom, *assumes for Himself the place of the Bridegroom*. Hence, while He is on earth with His people, there can be no mourning nor fasting. It is rather a time for eating and drinking and rejoicing (John 3:28-30). It should be unnecessary to remind the reader that by no possible device of interpretation can this eating and drinking and fasting be emptied of their literality. In the divine Person of the regal Bridegroom, the long-promised Kingdom was at hand; and in His presence, for those who had acknowledged Him, it was a time for great rejoicing and feasting. In this connection a careful reading of the entire 54th chapter of Isaiah will illumine our Lord's reference to His presence as the regal Bridegroom of Israel. Instead of fasting, His people must "break forth into singing" (54:1).

6. *The events attending the appearance of the Messianic King indicate a literal identity between the Kingdom preached in the Gospels and that of Old Testament prophecy.*

Concerning the earthly origin of Messiah, the prophet Micah had written: "But thou, Bethlehem Ephratah, though thou be little among the thousands of Judah, yet out of thee shall he come forth unto me that is to be ruler in Israel; whose goings forth have been from old, from everlasting" (5:2). But when the virgin Mary is about to give birth to her Child, she is still living in *Nazareth* of Galilee. And Luke is very careful to give the chain of providential events which took both Joseph and Mary to the village of Bethlehem at the right moment for the exact fulfilment of Micah's prophecy (Luke 2:1-7). Of course, it might be argued by some that the point is of little consequence, whether He was born at Nazareth or at Bethlehem; that the important fact is that He came into the world. But this is not the attitude of the writers of Scripture. Upon the fulfillment of the jots and tittles rests the veracity of God (Matt. 5:18). And since Micah 5:2 must be fulfilled to the letter, the devout student of Scripture will not be easily led to surrender the literality of other details found in Micah's predictions of the Messianic Kingdom. See especially the great events described in chapter 4, which are closely connected with the Bethlehem prophecy in chapter 5.

As another instructive case of literal correspondence, the historic triumphal entry of Christ may be cited (Matt. 21:1-9). Toward the close of His earthly ministry He approached the city of His rejection and death. At the Mount of Olives He sends two disciples into a village to get a colt, the foal of an ass, which had never been ridden. If anyone interferes, they are to say simply, "The Lord hath need of them" (vs. 3), i.e., both the colt and its mother. The question as to why the Lord needed these *two* animals has led to all sorts of speculation, from the coarse jest of the unbelieving Strauss, who has our Lord riding *both* animals, to the devout but far-fetched suggestion of Lange that "the old theocracy runs idly and instinctively by the side of the young church, which has become the true bearer of the Kingdom of Christ"! Such guesswork is both idle and unnecessary. Matthew tells us exactly why the Lord needed the animals: because an ancient Messianic prophecy must be fulfilled: "All this was done, that it might be fulfilled which was spoken by the prophet, saying, Tell ye the daughter of Sion, Behold, thy King cometh unto thee, meek, and sitting upon an ass, and [even] a colt the foal of an ass" (cf. Matt. 21:4-5 with Zech. 9:9). Two animals appear in the prophecy; and both are present in its fulfillment. Thus, in His solemn march to rejection and death at the hands of His own nation, the divine King is meticulously careful to omit no physical detail of the Old Testament forecast of the long-awaited Kingdom.

It should be unnecessary to remind the reader, not only that these things came to pass exactly as predicted, but also that the gospel writers were fully aware of the connection between the Old Testament prophecy and the gospel history; and that no legitimate Biblical criticism has been able to dislodge the relevant passages from the literary and historical records. Furthermore, as Ottman has well said, "This measured conformity with prophecy, so repeatedly and so strikingly set before us in Matthew's Gospel, should warn us against the spiritual application to which so many, in order to escape from presumed difficulties, have fled for refuge." [15]

7. *In our Lord's message of the Kingdom and His evidential works there appear all the essential aspects of the Old Testament prophetical Kingdom.*

While it must be admitted that our Lord gave more space and emphasis to some things and less to others (for reasons to be discussed below), it is a fact that any careful and unbiased examination of the gospel records will discover that no essential element of the Old Testament prophetic picture is missing.

a. *The Spiritual Element*

In harmony with the Old Testament prophets, our Lord insisted upon a *spiritual* basis for His Kingdom. In preparation for this Kingdom which was at hand, men must "repent" of their sins (Matt. 3:2; 9:13); and also "believe" the Good News of its imminence (Mark 1:15). For all those who comply with these demands there is promised a divine "remission of sins" (Luke 3:3). Furthermore, there can be no entrance into the Kingdom, except as men are "born again" (John 3:3). Important though it is, mere physical descent from Abraham is not enough (Matt. 3:8-10). Those who would enter must "become as little children" (Matt. 18: 1-4). According to the laws of the Kingdom, only the "pure in heart" will see its God (Matt. 5:8). And the supreme requirement of the citizens of the Kingdom is that they shall "love the Lord" in their entire being with no reservation nor division of allegiance (Mark 12:30). As to their daily needs, they are called to a life of continual trust and dependence upon God through sincere and believing prayer (Matt. 6:1-7:11).

When by a great physical miracle He used five loaves of bread and two small fishes to feed five thousand men, and the people rightly saw in the miracles the evidence that Jesus was in truth the Messianic prophet foretold in Deuteronomy 18:15 (cf. John 6:14), we read that the people were about to "take him by force, to make him a king" (John 6:15). And yet, although He was born

15 Ford C. Ottman, *God's Oath* (New York: Geo. H. Doran, 1911), p. 71.

"King of the Jews," He shuns this path to the royal throne. His action here was not motivated wholly by an abhorrence of the use of "force," as many have supposed, for He clearly declares elsewhere that force will be used when He comes to establish His Kingdom on earth (Luke 19:27). But the force then will be that of divine omnipotence, not that of sinful men. Furthermore, His refusal to exert the necessary force at this particular time in His ministry is explained in His own words: "Ye seek me, not because ye saw the miracles, but because ye did eat of the loaves, and were filled" (John 6:26). The miracle was indeed a sign that should have identified Him as the Messiah of prophecy in His *total* work, within which the *spiritual* aspect was supreme and the foundation of everything else. But his audience was only concerned with the fact that their bellies were filled. The discourse which follows, dealing with Himself as the Bread of Life, was not intended to be a denial of the importance of physical life and its needs, but rather to indicate the supremacy of spiritual matters above everything else in the Kingdom of Messiah. The sermon accomplished its purpose for when it was finished, we read that "From that time many of his disciples went back, and walked no more with him" (John 6:66).

Now it must not be forgotten that these spiritual demands and blessings of the Kingdom are not novel; they are not exclusively New Testament revelations. But all of them had been forecast in the Old Testament prophecies of the Kingdom. That is, for example, why Nicodemus, learned teacher in Israel, could be rebuked for not understanding the new birth; for a comparison of John 3:5 with Ezekiel 36:25-27 demonstrates beyond dispute the Old Testament derivation of our Lord's doctrine of regeneration. In John 3:5 there are three things: a new birth, and the two indispensable factors which produce it; i.e., "water" and "spirit." In Ezekiel's prophecy we find the same three ideas: the "new heart" which then is related to "clean water" and God's "spirit." That this water is not *material* in nature should be apparent from the context.[16] Such water can never cleanse the human heart from sin and idolatry. But the Word of God speaks of another kind of water (cf. Isa. 55:1; Eph. 5:26), which is able to accomplish this great thing.

b. *The Moral Element*

In harmony with the Old Testament prophets, there is also a

---

[16] Certainly, since our Lord's word in John 3:5 is without doubt derived from Ezekiel 36:25-26, there are many Christians who would hesitate to apply the reference to water baptism, for the water in Ezekiel's prophecy is "sprinkled"!

moral element in our Lord's message of the Kingdom. In its ethical
principles there is no relaxation of the divine laws with reference
to human action. The great categorical imperatives of the ancient
theocracy are to remain unchanged: "Thou shalt do no murder,
Thou shalt not commit adultery, Thou shalt not steal, Thou shalt
not bear false witness" (Matt. 19:18). But there is a fresh and
added emphasis on the inward aspect of the moral life. Our Lord
is concerned with the unseen springs of human conduct. Therefore, to look upon a woman with lust in the heart, or to harbor
malicious anger and hate, must be equated with the overt acts of
murder and adultery, even though never actually carried out (Matt.
5:21-22, 27-28). Moreover, a passive attitude of goodness is not
enough; not only are men not to resist evil done to them personally,
but they are to return good for evil (Matt. 5:39-44). As to its
foundation, the moral life in our Lord's Kingdom does not rest on
its own base; it is undergirded by God Himself in whose being and
character man is to find the perfect moral pattern and the motiva-
tion for all his actions (Matt. 5:45, 48). Furthermore, the moral
life in the Kingdom is safeguarded by divine sanctions of rewards
and penalties; some present and temporal; others future and eternal
(Matt. 5:22; 6:4, 33). Recognizing that moral justice is never
perfectly realized in this present world, our Lord envisions a future
day of judgment when, with Himself as the Judge, the crooked
shall be made straight and all moral inequalities and contradictions
shall be resolved (Matt. 7:21-23; 25:31-46).

It should be observed that in all this there is nothing absolutely
new. For the main features of this Kingdom of *good* may be found,
at least in germ, in the Mosaic theocracy, and also in the prophets
who not only called their contemporaries back to its moral principles
but also at the same time predicted a future and more perfect re-
establishment of the Kingdom on earth. Even in those places where
Christ seemed to break with certain things allowed in the historical
Kingdom, He only goes back to an original code which had been
breached temporarily by divine permission because of "the hardness" of men's hearts (Matt. 19:7-9). And thus what is sometimes
called Christ's "new" law of monogamy turns out to be almost the
oldest moral principle in all of written revelation (Gen. 2:24).

It is true that when He finished His Sermon on the Mount as
recorded by Matthew, we read that the people were "astonished at
his teaching" (7:28, ASV). But this astonishment was provoked
more by the *manner* of His teaching than by its content, as Matthew

tells us in the next verse: "for he taught them as one having authority" (vs. 29). He had not come to abolish what already had been revealed concerning the Kingdom, but to interpret its meaning by a new divine and regal authority.

By practical-minded men it has sometimes been argued that Christ's moral principles are so idealistic that they are not only impossible of realization, but that even to attempt to follow them may prove dangerous in the present world of reality. And such objections are not altogether without justification. It was the late Dr. J. Gresham Machen who rightly pointed out that the Golden Rule, apart from a society of regenerated men whose desires are morally right, is never wholly workable and may actually prove to be a perilous mode of action.[17] And it is possible that, had not Dr. Machen's amillennial views kept him from following the logic of his own argument to the end, he might also have observed that, even in the regenerated members of the Church on earth, there are still many selfish and sinful desires. And the conclusion seems inescapable that, short of heaven and the eternal state, only in a Kingdom of God on earth, where the outworking of the wrong desires of men is under external and immediate control, can the Golden Rule become *fully* a practical principle for all human action.

c. *The Social Element*

In harmony with the Old Testament prophets, there was a social element in our Lord's message of the Kingdom. He had a great deal to say about the principles which should govern men in their relations to each other in the Kingdom. In His Sermon on the Mount, He repeats the ancient laws which safeguarded human life and its basic institution of marriage; at the same time deepening immensely their scope and meaning (Matt. 5:21-28, 32). He was genuinely concerned for those who mourned and for those who were being persecuted unjustly (Matt. 5:4, 11). There would be a special blessing for those who showed mercy to the needy and for those who labored to resolve the conflicts indigenous to a sinful society (Matt. 5:7, 9). In their personal disputes and contentions, He offers to men practical instruction as to the principles and rules which should guide their conduct (Matt. 5:23-25, 39-48; 18:15-17). He shows a tender regard for little children (Mark 10:13-16); for the widow and the poor (Mark 12:40-44; Luke 14:13). He denounces un-

---

[17] J. Gresham Machen, *Christianity and Liberalism* (New York: Macmillan & Co., reprint 1940), pp. 37-38.

sparingly the social injustices of His day and does not hesitate to single out by name the offenders (Matt. 23:14, 26; Luke 11:46). The classic story of the Good Samaritan is our Lord's answer to the perennial question, "Who is my neighbor?" (Luke 10:29-37), and stands as an unanswerable indictment of all those mere religionists who are indifferent to human needs. A large part of His ministry was given to the healing of disease and the relief of human suffering, thus revealing not only His awareness of what is still today a major social problem but also His understanding that there could be no Kingdom of God on earth apart from its solution. He finds no fault with the external forms of religion, but where any conflict arises between these things and the relief of human need, the former must yield (Matt. 12:1-13).

If at times He seems somewhat indifferent to the physical needs of human existence (Matt. 6:25-31), it is only because He is anxious to put first things first. When men have made the Kingdom of God a matter of primary concern, all these other temporal benefits shall be added unto them (Matt. 6:33). If He consorts with publicans, it is not because He acquiesces in their often unscrupulous ways of collecting taxes, but rather because He has come as the divine Physician to heal the sin-sick and to call the offenders to repentance (Matt. 9:10-13). While it is true that in His doctrine eating and drinking are not the most important things in life, and man cannot live by bread alone, yet He Himself comes not as an ascetic but "eating and drinking" (Matt. 11:19); and He is careful to feed the five thousand before telling them not to be overanxious about "the meat that perisheth" but rather to labor for the "bread of God," which endureth unto everlasting life (John 6:10-13, 27-33). In the greatly misunderstood incident of the rich young ruler, it is striking that every commandment quoted by our Lord is from the Second Table of the Law; not because in the observance of these social laws men could earn eternal life, but in order that the young man might be tested by his own claims of moral perfection and come to see himself as a sinner whose only hope is in what God can do (Matt. 19:19-26).

As to the social implications in the *establishment* of the Kingdom on earth, our Lord's teaching is in complete harmony with the Old Testament prophets. There will be a judgment of the nations at the inauguration of the Kingdom in which certain social considerations are given a prominent place: ministering to the sick, clothing the naked, and feeding the hungry (Matt. 25:32-46). And attending this divine adjudication of social inequalities, there will be effective action: The regal Son of man will send forth His angels to "gather out" of His Kingdom "all things that offend, and them which do iniquity" (Matt. 13:41-43). Our Lord's parable of the rich fool, sometimes used in attempts to show that our Lord's rule has nothing to do with the divine enforcement of social justice in a Kingdom on earth, was intended rather to indicate the supremacy of spiritual things over that which is only temporal and physical in that Kingdom. When Christ said to His questioner, "Man, who made me a judge or a divider over you?", He was not disclaiming the reality of His authority in mundane matters. He was rather asserting that the great social benefits of the Kingdom could be had only on a spiritual and moral basis (Luke 12:13-20). Like the rich fool, it is easy to be more concerned about our own personal rights than about a kingdom in which social justice will prevail for *all*. Furthermore, it must not be overlooked that the Kingdom had not yet been established, and therefore the time had not arrived for Him to begin His regal work of judging.

It has sometimes been objected that certain features of Christ's teaching, as outlined above, seem intended to ameliorate social conditions which will not exist in the future Millennial Kingdom. Is it possible, they argue, that in that glad day the righteous will be persecuted and slandered wrongfully? (Matt. 5:10-11). In reply, we may say that when the Kingdom breaks into human history from above, it must begin with things *as they are*. For the Kingdom will come to set right the things that *are* wrong. And even the Beatitudes carry the savor of eschatological judgment. Furthermore, under the rule of the coming Kingdom there will still be present upon earth a humanity with a sinful nature out of which all wrong action springs. And the essential moral difference between our present age and the coming age of the Kingdom must be found chiefly in the *immediate* character of divine justice. Whereas at present unrighteous conduct and its social consequences are not adjudicated at once, in the Kingdom there will be no time lag: both the offense and its consequences will be dealt with without delay.

d. *The Ecclesiastical Element*

In harmony with the Old Testament prophetic picture, there was an ecclesiastical element in our Lord's message of the Kingdom. As already indicated in my discussion of the Kingdom of Old Testament prophecy, I am using the term "ecclesiastical" here to designate the externals of religion, such as forms of worship, its organization, and control; but not to suggest that the Church of the present age is an established Kingdom of Christ on earth, as some believe.

Excepting for certain changes, abrogations, additions, and wider interpretations (which He as the divine Lawgiver had authority to make), the religious laws of the Kingdom of Christ are those of the ancient Mosaic Theocracy. Whoever violates even "one of these least commandments," or teaches others to do so, "shall be called the least in the kingdom of heaven" [18] (Matt. 5:17-19). Our Lord was born under the law and kept it from His childhood (Luke 2: 21-24, 41-42). Certainly, any open breach of this law would have given His enemies the very legal basis for which they sought in vain to justify His death (Mark 14:55-59). As to the minutiae of the law — such as "tithe of mint and anise and cummin" — our Lord has no rebuke for the Pharisees' insistence upon these matters: "these ought ye to have done," He says; but the weightier matters of judgment and mercy should not be left undone (Matt. 23:23). In the law there is nothing unimportant, but some things are more important than others. When He heals a leper, the man is directed to carry out the rather complicated ritual of priestly examination and sacrifice "that Moses commanded" (Matt. 8:2-4). The Passover, that greatest of all the historical "holy convocations" of Israel, is graced by the presence of Christ (John 2:13, 23). Not only so, but in the final drama of His life on earth, although knowing that He Himself would not eat the last passover, yet He directed the disciples to carry out in detail the ritual of its preparation (Luke 22: 7-16, ASV).

As suggested above, our Lord asserted on more than one occasion His divine authority over the Law. In the interest of mercy He does not hesitate to breach technically the Sabbatic law, for "the Son of man is Lord even of the sabbath day" (Matt. 12:8; Lev. 23:3). And in the much discussed passage in Mark 7:18-19, according to eminent authorities including the ASV, the final clause should read: "This he said, making all meats clean." [19] See also our Lord's assertion of His authority over the law in the Sermon on the Mount (Matt. 5:33-34, 38-42). We do well to remember this principle in thinking of the establishment of the Mosaic Code as the law of

---

[18] Alford refers "these least commandments" to the things of the Mosaic law, (*Commentary, in loc.*).
[19] Cf. Ellicott (*Commentary*) and A. T. Robertson (*Word Pictures*), *in loc.*

the future Millennial Kingdom. What modifications and changes may be made by the divine Lawgiver at that time, we do not know. But they may be far-reaching in ceremonial areas. And we can be sure that whatever is done will be for the glory of God and the good of mankind. In such matters the divine principle is clear: "The sabbath was made for man, and not man for the sabbath" (Mark 2:27).

As to the ecclesiastical position of the nation of Israel in the future Kingdom of heaven, our Lord follows the clear doctrine of the Old Testament prophets. Gentiles will not be denied the benefits of the Kingdom, but Israel will hold the place of primacy: "for salvation is of the Jews" (John 4:22). And, in this context, the term *salvation* must not be restricted to the spiritual salvation of the individual soul. It means all that the Kingdom of Messiah includes, both temporarily and eternally. The nation of Israel remains the divinely ordained channel of blessing for the world. Hence, when the regal Saviour arrives, He says to a Gentile woman, "I am not sent but unto the lost sheep of the house of Israel," for they are the covenant "children" and to them first therefore must come the "bread" which belongs to them (Matt 15:22-28). If the woman obtains some of this bread, it is only because in humble faith she concedes that her blessing comes from the table of Israel. This religious primacy of Israel appears in the formal announcement of the Kingdom as at hand. When the Twelve had been chosen and commissioned, they were rigidly circumscribed as to the field of their ministry: "Go not into the way of the Gentiles, and into any city of the Samaritans enter ye not: But go rather to the lost sheep of the house of Israel" (Matt. 10:5-6). Although physical descent from Abraham *per se* is no guarantee of membership in the Kingdom (Matt. 3:9), it is nevertheless true that all those called into the Kingdom from other nations will sit down at a table which by divine covenant belongs primarily to "Abraham, and Isaac, and Jacob" (Matt. 8:10-11).

Although true worship cannot be tied to any particular geographical place, yet in the coming Kingdom the city of Jerusalem will be "the city of the great King" (Matt. 5:35); and our Lord speaks of its temple as "my Father's house" (John 2:16). And though He was infinitely greater than the temple, being Himself free therefore from its monetary exactments, nevertheless by a miracle He provides for Peter and Himself the tax money required for its support by the Mosaic law (Matt. 17:24-27; cf. Exod. 30:11-16). Neither is there any change in His attitude as, on the way to His death, once more He drives the moneychangers out of the temple. Why not simply ignore this temple if, as some argue, because of her sin God is done with the nation of Israel and the Old Testament theocratic idea? On the contrary, as the Messianic Priest-King of Israel, our Lord in His final word lays claim to the existing Jewish temple, citing an Old Testament prophecy in defense of His action: "My house shall be called a house of prayer for all the nations" (Mark 11:15-17, ASV; cf. Isa. 56:7-8).

e. *The Political Element*

In harmony with the Old Testament prophets, there was a political aspect in our Lord's message of the Kingdom. The term "political" is here used in its best sense as referring to that which is concerned with government, its organization and functions. According to Luke's account of the angelic announcement of His birth, doubtless derived from the virgin Mary, our Lord was born to sit upon "the throne of his father David" and "reign over the house of Jacob for ever" (Luke 1:31-33) — predictions which were never qualified or repudiated by Him. This throne and reign cannot be limited to an exclusively spiritual control over the hearts of men, but they have unmistakable political connotations when read in the context of the Old Testament from which they are derived. John the Baptist, acclaimed by our Lord as the equal of any prophet born of women, was certainly not mistaken in demanding of a political ruler conformity to the moral principles of the Kingdom of which Christ came to be the King (Matt. 14:1-5). When our Lord lays down rules for the settlement of disputes between men, He speaks in terms of political government — a court, a judge, an officer, a penalty, and a prison (Matt. 5:23-26). In His divinely ordained experience of temptation, the kingdoms offered Him were existing political realms — "the kingdoms of the world" (Matt. 4:8-9). Whether or not Satan could have made good his boast is quite beside the point. In the Kingdom which Christ proclaimed," the city of the great King" is the historic city of Jerusalem (Matt. 5:35), in literal harmony with a well-known Messianic Psalm (48:2).

When the Kingdom has been established on earth, He will "sit upon the throne of his glory," judging "all nations," admitting some and excluding others from that Kingdom (Matt. 25:31-46). As a reward for faithful service, some servants will be given "authority over ten cities," and others over "five cities" (Luke 19:11-19). For those who hate the King and rebel against His reign there will be no mercy. Here are the words of Christ Himself: "But those mine enemies, which would not that I should reign over them, bring hither, and slay them before me" (Luke 19:27). The hosts of angels, who might have been called to save Him from death (Matt. 26:53), will then be called upon to clean up the world in preparation for the establishment of His Kingdom (Matt. 13:41). Although rejected by the human kingdom "builders," He will come at the appointed time as the regal "stone . . . cut out . . . without hands" to smite the empires of men and replace their misrule with a reign characterized by inflexible divine justice: "Whosoever shall fall upon that stone shall be broken; but on whomsoever it shall fall, it will grind him to powder" (cf. Luke 20:13-18 with Dan. 2:31-45). It should go without saying that, under the immediate and personal reign of the divine Mediatorial King, what is called "freedom of religion" will properly come to an end.

The divine order in our Lord's doctrine of the Kingdom is not essentially different from that in the Old Testament prophets. In two notable passages (Matt. 19:28 and Luke 22:30) the order appears as follows: first, seated upon the throne of His glory is the divine "Son of man"; second, seated upon "twelve thrones" are the twelve apostles; third, the nation of Israel appears, in both passages identified specifically as composed of "the twelve tribes of Israel," being judged by the twelve apostles, a proper and essential function of government. In neither passage are the Gentiles even mentioned. Apparently, viewing the world as a group of nations, Israel holds the central place of interest. However, other texts make clear that the Gentile nations will have a place in the Kingdom. "Many shall come from the east and west, and shall sit down with Abraham, and Isaac, and Jacob, in the kingdom of heaven" (Matt. 8:11). Although the announcement of the coming Kingdom was initially restricted to the nation of Israel (Matt. 10:5-6), yet the preaching of the Kingdom made clear that the Gentiles would share in its benefits: God's chosen King would "shew judgment to the Gentiles," and "in his name shall the Gentiles trust" (Matt. 12:17-21).

But the nation of Israel, as well as the Gentile nations, must be purged by judgment in preparation for the Kingdom. This is the true meaning of certain texts which have been used to teach erroneously that the historic nation has wholly lost her original place of supremacy in the governmental structure of the Kingdom. The text upon which the greatest weight of this theory has rested is Matthew 21:43 where our Lord speaks as follows: "Therefore say I unto you, The kingdom of God shall be taken from you, and given to a nation bringing forth the fruits thereof."[20]

This text does not affirm that the Kingdom will be taken from the nation of *Israel* and given to a nation which is *another* nation racially and politically. When our Lord said the Kingdom would be taken away *"from you,"* He was speaking to the "chief priests and the elders" (Matt. 21:23), in whom civil and religious authority was vested and who were determined to destroy Him, as distinguished from the "multitude" who on the previous day had actually acclaimed Him as the Messianic "son of David" (Matt. 21:45-46; cf. 21:9). Even the priests and Pharisees understood clearly that Christ's words were not to be construed as an irrevocable indictment of the Jewish nation as a whole, for "they perceived that he spake of them" (Matt. 21:45). Therefore, the correct sense of the passage must be found in the historical situation: The nation as represented by its then existing rulers had rejected the King; therefore, the Kingdom is taken from *them*.

But this Kingdom, as foreseen by the prophets and announced by our Lord, is not therefore metamorphosed into something else. The same Kingdom shall yet be "given to a nation bringing forth the fruits thereof" (Matt. 21:43). Now the question is, What nation? Here the Greek noun *ethnos* must not be pressed to mean *Gentile,* for the same term is often used by John and Paul in referring to the nation of Israel (John 11:51; Acts 24:17). And according to the uniform testimony of Scripture, the covenants and rights of this people are irrevocable (Jer. 33:24-26; Rom. 9:3-5). The fulfilment of these divine promises may indeed be interrupted temporarily, and certain individuals or even a whole generation may be cut off from the benefits, but the promises to Israel cannot be abrogated. And although God cannot bestow His covenanted blessing upon "a disobedient and gainsaying people" (Rom. 10:21), He can and will purge and purify this very people so that it may once more be a *nation* before Him. There is to be a future restoration (Rom. 11:11-15), a new birth for this nation (Isa. 66:5-13). Just as the resurrection body is in one sense a new body and yet in another sense the same body, even so the Israel to whom the Kingdom shall be given will be a *new* nation spiritually but also the same nation historically which

[20] On this text A. T. Robertson has written what seems an unjustifiable dogmatic comment: "It was the death knell of the Jewish nation with their hopes of political and world leadership" (*Word Pictures in New Testament, in loc.*). And the anti-millennialists use the same text to sweep away the covenant rights of historic Israel, against the total testimony of Old Testament prophecy, to say nothing of the clear assertions of Christ and the Apostle Paul.

came from the loins of Abraham. This is nothing unusual in the manner of human speech. We may and do speak of the German nation today as something radically different from the nation of Hitler's terrible years, yet the historical and vital connection between the two has never been broken.

The prophet Hosea gave a divinely inspired forecast of this very situation in Israel's relation to God. God had pronounced His judgment upon a wicked nation of Israel: "Ye are not my people, and I will not be your God" — but the promise of mercy comes in the same context: "Yet the number of the children of Israel shall be as the sand of the sea, which cannot be measured nor numbered; and it shall come to pass, that in the place where it was said unto them, Ye are not my people, there it shall be said unto them, Ye are the sons of the living God" (1:9-10). And again, "I will say to them which were not my people, Thou art my people; and they shall say, Thou art my God" (2:23). As for the alleged mistake of the Apostle Paul in his use of the Hosea prophecy in Romans 9:25-26, it is not unfair to say that the commentators were misled, not the Apostle, in supposing that he took a prophecy originally spoken of Israel and applied it to Gentiles. Nowhere in verses 25 and 26 does Paul affirm any such application, nor does the occurrence of the term "Gentiles," last word in verse 24, necessarily prove such a connection. As a matter of fact, all of the Old Testament quotations in verses 25-29 are brought in to support the entire foregoing argument of Romans 9, namely, a divine election within the historical nation of Israel based on sovereign grace. That Paul is thinking of Israel, not Gentiles, is shown by the first clause of verse 27, "Esaias also crieth concerning Israel."[21]

To summarize: the Kingdom was taken from a nation of our Lord's day because of its sin; and it shall be given to a nation which brings forth proper fruit. The difference between the two nations is spiritual and moral, not racial. That nation on which the Kingdom is bestowed will be the nation of *Israel*, in harmony with all Old Testament prophecy; but an Israel repentant and regenerated. Just as in the case of a regenerated *individual*, it is wholly proper to contrast the *new* man with the *old* man without any implication of two separate persons; even so the nation which shall receive the Kingdom will be *spiritually* a new nation but, at the same time, racially and politically the Israel of history. For those acquainted with the language of

---

[21] The conjunction *de* may indicate an *addition* rather than a *contrast* to what has been said before. Cf. S. G. Green, *Handbook to Grammar of New Testament*, p. 344.

divine revelation, there is here no conflict of ideas. The confusion is wholly semantic in character, an attempt to press into a physical and political mold language which describes a change which is exclusively moral and spiritual.[22]

This explanation is supported by numerous texts, notably Micah 4:6-8: "In that day, saith the LORD, will I assemble her that halteth, and I will gather her that is driven out, and her that I have afflicted; and I will make her that halted a remnant, and her that was cast far off a strong nation: and the LORD shall reign over them in mount Zion from henceforth, even for ever. And thou, O tower of the flock, the strong hold of the daughter of Zion, unto thee shall it come, even the first dominion; the kingdom shall come to the daughter of Jerusalem." The nation which was historically afflicted and driven out of its land shall once more be gathered. This divinely recovered "remnant" of historical Israel shall be made "a strong nation," and the "kingdom shall come" to this nation in likeness to "the first dominion." The political supremacy of Israel will be restored, this time to be exercised by a regenerated nation over Gentile nations which are willing to submit to the rule of Israel's regal Messiah in the coming days of His power and Kingdom (Mic. 4:1-4).

f. *The Physical Element*

In harmony with the Old Testament prophets, considerable attention was given to physical matters in our Lord's activities in relation to the Kingdom. No one can read the gospel records, even carelessly, without being impressed with the large place given by Christ to problems which were distinctively physical in nature. In fact, for those who insist upon the exclusively "spiritual" nature of His Kingdom as opposed to what they deride as the "carnal" kingdom of premillennialism, the interest of Christ in physical problems and the large amount of His time given to their relief become almost embarrassing.

This discussion should begin by calling attention to the patent but sometimes overlooked fact that what is termed miracle in the New Testament is essentially a phenomenon which always occurs in the *physical* area of the world. Thus, in Archbishop Trench's classic work, he lists for treatment thirty-three miracles, and all of them are in this physical category, from the turning of water into wine to the last great draught of fishes.[23] For that matter, the entire period

---

[22] It is also true, of course, that the future nation of Israel will be different even in a *physical* sense, too, because it will be composed wholly of a new generation of persons.

[23] R. C. Trench, *Notes on the Miracles of our Lord* (London: Routledge and Sons, no date), pp. vii-viii.

of our Lord's life upon earth, to say nothing of His ministry, began and ended with stupendous miracles: the virgin birth and the resurrection and ascension, each one occurring within a physical context.

But beyond these miracles of our Lord's life and ministry, which are singled out for special description by the gospel writers, there is a vastly wider area of miraculous activity of which we know practically nothing, except that what was done took place in the physical realm. Matthew says, "Jesus went about all the cities and villages, . . . healing every sickness and every disease among the people" (9:35). Commenting on this activity of Christ in only one district of the land, Warfield says, "Disease and death must have been almost eliminated for a brief season from Capernaum and the region which lay immediately around Capernaum as a center."[24] Describing this miraculous activity of our Lord, the Apostle John speaks even more sweepingly: "And many other signs truly did Jesus in the presence of his disciples, which are not written in this book: But these are written, that ye might believe that Jesus is the Christ, the Son of God; and that believing ye might have life through his name" (John 20: 30-31). "And there are also many other things which Jesus did, the which, if they should be written every one, I suppose that even the world itself could not contain the books that should be written" (John 21:25). It is quite evident that in the comparatively few miracles described in the Gospels, we have only touched the hem of the garment of our Lord's power and activity in dealing with the physical side of human existence.

But consider now the wide sweep of our Lord's miraculous activity within the physical world in connection with His proclamation of the Kingdom. First, if we may judge from the space given in the gospel records, the miracles of Christ were concerned chiefly with the healing of physical *disease and infirmity*. Although demon-possession is never confused with physical disease, nevertheless the former had a physical aspect in that the casting out of the demons often brought relief for certain physical disorders caused by them. Second, in some cases where illness had issued in physical *death*, the Lord exercised His miraculous power by raising them back to physical life. Third, in recognition of the basic needs of physical existence, we have His miracles for the purpose of providing *food* so that hungry men might eat. Fourth, touching the *economic* aspect of human life, there are the miraculous catches of fish provided for men who had labored

[24] B. B. Warfield, *Christology and Criticism* (New York: Oxford University Press, 1929), p. 54.

without any reward; and also the gold in the fish's mouth to pay the required tax. Fifth, as to man's *social* life, at a wedding He provides wine by a miracle, not to sustain mere physical existence, but in order that men might have the physical means for their social enjoyment. Sixth, by the miracle of cursing the fig tree, He shows Himself in regal control over the factors of growth and *production* in the world of nature. Seventh, when He passes unscathed through the midst of enemies determined to kill Him (Luke 4:29-30), walks upon the water, and calms the storm (Matt. 14:24-32), He demonstrates as man His complete safety from, and control over, the ordinary *hazards* of man's physical environment.

Furthermore, it should be observed that, although our Lord's death and resurrection ushered Him into a higher and different plane of existence, He does not therein lose His interest and concern in the physical needs of men. Thus John tells of the miraculous catch of fish taken after a night of profitless labor and also of the breakfast lovingly prepared for the tired and hungry disciples (John 21:1-11). And as He stood in the shadow of Calvary, He looked beyond the hour of His suffering to a kingdom where His own disciples would eat and drink at the table of the King (Luke 22:15-18, 29-30). In that day, as He had promised, those who are "poor" and hungry shall "be filled" (Luke 6:20-21). Since the "poor" of this text are contrasted with those who are "rich" (vs. 24), it is clear that the words of Christ here cannot be wholly disassociated from a physical and economic context.

The same thing must be said of our Lord's astonishing promise found in John 14:12, "He that believeth on me, the works that I do shall he do also; and greater works than these shall he do; because I go unto my Father." If we take this promise in its full strict sense without evasion (as Alford thinks we should), certain conclusions must follow: first, the promise includes the works such as Christ actually performed while on earth, both physical and spiritual in nature; second, the promise is made to all those who *believe*, not merely to a few chosen apostles. Viewing the matter thus, and allowing room for all the great works recorded in the Book of Acts and subsequent history, it must still be said that the complete fulfilment of the promise must be found in a future Kingdom such as we find described by the Old Testament prophets. On the basis of the words, "because I go unto my Father," it has been argued that the possibility of the "greater works" depends on Christ's presence in heaven rather than reigning upon earth as the Messianic King. But these words of our Lord include much more than a reference merely to His ascension. They speak of His entire passion and its blessed result. It was His way of saying that the promise of the "greater works" could not be realized until He had gone to the Father *by the path of Calvary and the Resurrection.* And while we must be deeply grateful for the great spiritual accomplishments of the true Church during the past nineteen centuries, it should be apparent to all that the physical and social problems of humanity are still today distressingly far from any adequate solution. The world is still sick unto death. This is to say nothing of the fact that, considered from the standpoint of a total humanity, even the *spiritual* needs of the world are today greater than when the Church began on Pentecost. In other words, we still need on earth the complete fulfilment of the promised "greater works" as they shall be ministered in the coming Kingdom by those who will be reigning with its King.

Any consideration of Christ's great miracles in the physical realm raises the question as to whether these works had some purpose above and beyond the relief of human need and suffering. And the answer is clear: "If I cast out devils [demons] by the Spirit of God," He says, "then the kingdom of God is come unto you" (Matt. 12:28). His great miracles were therefore the divine authentication of His regal Messiahship and the imminency of the Kingdom which He had announced. In this connection there is one passage in Matthew (11:2-5) so important that it should be given special attention. The historical situation was as follows: John the Baptist was in prison about to lose his head for rebuking the unlawful conduct of an earthly ruler, a strange predicament for the herald of the great King who, according to the prophets, would correct all such injustices. Under the circumstances, we may well wonder whether John's faith did not begin to waver. And it may have been so, for he sent messengers to Jesus, asking wistfully, "Art thou he that should come [*ho erchomenos* — 'the coming one'], or do we look for another?" Now the answer of Christ to John not only furnishes an infallible guide to the interpretation of the Old Testament prophets but also clarifies the exact relation of His own message to their vision of the Kingdom: "Go and shew John again those things which ye do hear and see: The blind receive their sight, and the lame walk, the lepers are cleansed, and the deaf hear, the dead are raised up, and the poor have the gospel preached to them."

Such an answer was worth a thousand mere verbal affirmations.

To John it was intended to show that he had not been mistaken about the identification of Jesus with the promised Mediatorial King of Old Testament prophecy, nor about the nature of His Kingdom. And to us Christ's words should prove what to John needed no proof; namely, that when the Kingdom is established on earth, it will be a literal Kingdom, exhibiting all the varied aspects revealed by the Old Testament prophets. Certainly, if John had been mistaken in his views of the Kingdom (as some theologians seem to think), this would have been the time for our Lord to enlighten him. On the contrary, John is directed to contemplate the great miracles of Christ as described in the very words of Old Testament prophecy (Isa. 35:5-6). And it is worthy of note that, of the six items mentioned in Christ's answer to John, no less than five are concerned with human needs which are purely *physical*. Only one, i.e., the preaching of the Gospel, can be regarded as something *spiritual*, and even this has a *social* aspect — the "poor" are hearing it.

But to this official answer sent back to John in the Roman prison, our Lord added a very special and personal word, an assurance intended to guard John's mind against all future contingencies and doubts: "Blessed is he," said Jesus, "whosoever shall find no occasion of stumbling in me" (Matt. 11:6, ASV). How tender and gracious! For the rising tide of Jewish opposition had already demonstrated historically that the King would be rejected and the complete establishment of His Kingdom delayed — and John must die. He walked bravely, I am sure, into the valley of the shadow with this last precious assurance from his Lord, the King.

In connection with this discussion of the great physical miracles of Christ in relation to the Kingdom, two questions might be asked of those who insist upon the exclusively spiritual nature of our Lord's Kingdom: First, if the Kingdom announced by the Lord was thus narrowly spiritual, why all these physical miracles so great in both kind and number during the ministry of Christ on earth? But, on the other hand, if such miracles properly belong to a spiritual kingdom, allegedly established at His first coming, why then are they not present today? They are not less needed than nineteen centuries ago. These are questions that ought to be faced, and the answers should be somewhat commensurate with the importance of the issues involved.

In summarizing the argument under point 7 above, I repeat that the message and activities of Christ in relation to the Kingdom display all the essential aspects of the Kingdom predicted by the Old Testament prophets. That not one of these elements can be omitted without seriously narrowing or distorting Christ's conception of the Kingdom, is being admitted even by critical and liberal scholars. "Nothing has so obscured Jesus' conception as the attempt to sum it up in a single formula. It has been assumed that since he took up the apocalyptic tradition his thought must all be construed apocalyptically; since his teaching is mainly ethical he had nothing in mind but an ethical ideal; since he dealt so largely with social relations his interest was in the building of a new society. All one-sided interpretation of this kind means a narrowing and distortion of the idea of Jesus."[25]

In affirming the precise identification of Christ's announced Kingdom with that predicted in the Prophets, it should be explained that, while our Lord always follows closely the Old Testament prophetic pattern, there is never any mere slavish repetition of words, phrases, and texts. Rather He unfolds and interprets the utterances of the prophets, so that meanings become deeper and richer. "In His doctrine of the righteousness of the kingdom, Jesus declares that He is not introducing anything absolutely new, but only unfolding the deepest spirit and teaching of law and prophets."[26] Furthermore, it is quite evident that our Lord did lay special emphasis upon the spiritual and ethical aspects of the Old Testament vision, not only because these were important in themselves, but also because the Jewish teachers had neglected these matters and were concentrating mainly upon the political and national aspects. And, like all the great preachers of the Word, Christ fought many of His battles over *neglected* truth. It is possible today, were He standing in some pulpits, that He might stress other aspects of the Kingdom which are currently ignored and even denied. We may also add that if the Kingdom, announced as "at hand" by the Lord, had been exclusively a "spiritual kingdom," or as some have defined it, "the rule of God in the heart," such an announcement would have had no special significance whatever to Israel, for such a rule of God had *always* been recognized among the people of God. Compare the psalmist's affirmation concerning the righteous, "The law of his God is in his heart" (37:31). Any denial of this would certainly be a new kind of dispensationalism.

25 Ernest F. Scott, *op. cit.,* p. 186.
26 James Orr, *op. cit.,* Vol. II, p. 853.

CHAPTER XXII

THE REJECTION OF THE KING AND HIS KINGDOM

The reader is reminded that this preaching of the nighness of the Kingdom, this offer of the Kingdom to the Jews at the First Advent on condition of repentance, is the *key* to the commingling of the Advents of Christ. It could not be otherwise. It being predetermined as eminently suitable to tender this Kingdom at the First Advent of Jesus, the Messiah, and it being also foreknown that it would be rejected, the matter is so guardedly presented as not to interfere with the free moral agency of the nation, and as not to be opposed to foreknown fact.
—*George N. H. Peters*[1]

1. *In the gospel records the proclamation of the Kingdom was inseparably connected with its King.*

The Kingdom was "at hand" because the Mediatorial King had arrived. Without such a King there could be no kingdom established on earth in the Biblical sense. It follows, therefore, that to reject its King would be to reject the Kingdom. Now, as shown in Part I of this book, there is a Universal Kingdom of God which has always existed unconditionally regardless of the attitudes of angels, devils, or men. But the existence of God's Mediatorial Kingdom on earth has always been *conditioned*. It was received as a promise by Abraham through faith; it was established in history at Sinai subject to Israel's willingness to obey God; it was terminated on earth because of Israel's sin; its restoration on earth is foretold by the prophets in connection with Israel's repentance; and the initial demand of its announcement in the gospel period was, "The kingdom of God is at hand: repent ye, and believe the gospel" (Mark 1:15). In this demand, no room was left for any separation of the Kingdom from its King; although this is precisely what the religious leaders of our Lord's day (and also some today) have thought to do.

The late Prof. Berkhof has rightly said that "In the preaching of Jesus the Kingdom of God and the Person of the Messiah go hand in hand. The two are inseparable corollaries." And also "that its future perfect manifestation would depend on his coming in glory."

[1] G. N. H. Peters, *The Theocratic Kingdom* (New York: Funk and Wagnalls, 1884), Vol. I pp. 364-365.

But he seems to temper this excellent statement by suggesting that Christ is the "principle" of the Kingdom, apparently in the interest of his theory of "the Church as a visible manifestation of the Kingdom" today during the absence of its King.[2] If when our Lord was on earth He proclaimed the Kingdom and His Person as inseparable, and if the future manifestation of the Kingdom will depend on His personal presence, it is not easy to understand how there could be today any genuine Kingdom of God on earth in the Mediatorial sense. We cannot admit the propriety of substituting a "principle" for the Person of the Messianic King.

2. *The good news of the Kingdom was announced to Israel alone.*

The Apostle John describes thus the mission of Christ: "He came unto his own" (John 1:11), i.e., the people of Israel.[3] In the great mission of the Twelve, they were expressly forbidden by the Lord to go into any way of the Gentiles or to enter into any city of the Samaritans; but to go only "to the lost sheep of the house of Israel" (Matt. 10:5-6). And although these restrictions are not verbally repeated in the later commission to the Seventy, Christ did send them "before his face into every city and place, whither he himself would come" (Luke 10:1). These words, as well as their general context, indicate clearly that the scope of the ministry of the Seventy was also limited to Israel. For, in His word to the Syro-Phoenician woman, our Lord defined sharply His own original ministry with reference to the Kingdom: "I am not sent," He says, "but unto the lost sheep of the house of Israel" (Matt. 15:24). This dictum of Christ, which has so troubled some commentators,[4] was no harsh denial of help for this Gentile mother on behalf of her demon-possessed daughter. As a matter of fact, the Old Testament prophets often spoke of benefits from the Kingdom flowing out to Gentile peoples. But our Lord's words did underscore two things: first, that to Israel alone belonged the special covenanted rights of the Davidic kingdom; and, second, if the Gentiles received any of its blessings, these must be acknowledged in humble faith as having fallen from the table appointed by God for the "children" of Israel.

This restriction which appears in the original preaching of the gospel of the Kingdom surely indicates that we have here something

---

[2] L. Berkhof, *Kingdom of God* (Grand Rapids: Eerdmans Publishing Co., 1951), p. 19, footnote.

[3] So Lange, *Commentary on John, in loc.*

[4] David Smith says, "There is no incident in our Lord's earthly ministry more puzzling than this" (*In the Days of His Flesh* [8th ed.; New York: Geo. H. Doran, no date], p. 248).

extraordinary, quite different from the usual program of evangelism in the Christian Church.

3. *This preaching of the Kingdom to Israel laid upon that chosen nation the demand for a decision.*

This demand was openly present in all the early preaching of the gospel of the Kingdom. The imperatives were "repent," "believe," "receive," "confess," and "follow." No room was left for neutrality: those who heard the message must either be *for* the Messianic King or *against* Him (Matt. 12:30). "No man can serve two masters: for either he will hate the one, and love the other; or else he will hold to the one, and despise the other" (Matt. 6:24). The same demand was implicit in all His mighty works: were they from God or from Satan? For the nation of Israel, hearing and seeing these things, there could be no escape from the dilemma of decision. And the demand was both immediate and urgent, because the regal feast of good things was ready and there could be no acceptable excuse for delay (Luke 14:15-24). Even the ordeal of death could not be permitted to temper the high urgency of the hour (Luke 9:57-62). The accredited messengers of the Kingdom brought into every village and home the crisis of swift decision. If received, the messengers brought blessings; if rejected, the very dust of that place was to be shaken off in token of certain judgment (Luke 10:8-12).

In the face of this uniform testimony of the gospel records, it is difficult to understand how anyone could ask (as some have), Where did Jesus ever *offer* the Kingdom to Israel? Such an objection would seem to be little more than strife "about words to no profit." Certainly, Jesus offered *Himself* to Israel as the *Christ*, the Messiah of Old Testament prophecy. But this title had no meaning apart from that prophetic Kingdom over which Messiah was divinely ordained to reign as King.

Furthermore, in the last analysis, this demand for a decision was laid upon Israel as a *nation*. In the words of Samuel J. Andrews:

> As the covenant of God with the Jews was a national one, so must also Christ's acceptance or rejection be. From the beginning of their history, God had dealt with the people as a corporate body. Their blessings were national blessings, their punishments national punishments. All their institutions, ecclesiastical and civil, were so devised as to deepen the feeling of national unity—one high priest, one temple, one altar, one royal family, one central city. What was done by the heads of the nation was regarded as the act of all, and involving common responsibility. Only in this way could the purpose of God, in their election to be His peculiar people, be carried out. Hence, in this greatest and highest act, the acceptance or rejection of His Son, the act must be a national one.

It must be done in the name of the whole people by those who acted as their rightful representatives. If those who sat in Moses' seat should discern and receive Him, the way for the further prosecution of His work was at once opened, and under His divine instruction the nation might be purified and made ready for the glorious Kingdom, so often sung by the psalmists and foretold by the prophets. But if, on the other hand, He was rejected by the nation acting through its lawfully constituted heads, this national crime must be followed by national punishment. Individuals might be saved amid the general overthrow, but the people, as such, failing to fulfill God's purpose in their election, must be scattered abroad, and a new people be gathered out of all nations.

It was under the conditions imposed by these great historic facts that the Lord began His ministry among the Jews. He came to a people in covenant with God; a people that God desired to save, and that must, as a people, accept or reject Him. All the details that are given us of that ministry by the Evangelists must, therefore, be viewed in the light of these facts.[5]

4. The ministry of Christ and His message of the Kingdom met with opposition from the very beginning.

There was never any question as to the attitude of the religious and political *rulers* of Israel. The lines of the battle were drawn early when, in His initial cleansing of the temple, our Lord made the first great public assertion of His Messianic rights (John 2:13-25). One of the curious things about this event is that apparently there was no attempt on the part of the officials to resist forcibly an astounding action which publicly humiliated these religious traffickers as they were scourged out of the temple along with their own sheep and oxen. Edersheim is doubtless right in saying that "behind Him was gathered the wondering multitude, that could not but sympathize with such bold, right royal, and Messianic vindication of temple sanctity from the nefarious traffic of a hated, corrupt, and avaricious Priesthood."[6] Although no restraining hand was laid upon the angry Lord of the temple, its officials did have the cunning foresight to demand of Him a "sign" of authority to do what He had done. And His notable answer was never forgotten, for at His final trial it was recalled by the same ecclesiastical hucksters and made the ground of their false charge that He was worthy of death (Matt. 26:61). Thus, in the very beginning, the stage was set for the vindictive opposition of the Jewish rulers which pursued His steps until He came to His death upon the Cross.

This opposition of the ruling classes should not be too surprising, since Christ was never diplomatically cautious in what He said and

[5] S. J. Andrews, *Life of Our Lord* (1891 ed.; Grand Rapids: Zondervan Publishing House, reprint, 1954), pp. 127-128.

[6] Alfred Edersheim, *Life and Times of Jesus* (8th ed., rev.; New York: Longmans, Green and Co., 1912), Vol. I, p. 374.

did. Not only does He deliberately precipitate the battle by driving them out of the temple precincts, but later He does not hesitate to breach publicly their legalistic traditions by healing an impotent man on the Sabbath (John 5:16). When He defended His compassionate act by saying, "My Father worketh hitherto, and I work" (vs. 17), His enemies renewed their efforts to destroy Him on the added charge of blasphemy, rightly interpreting His defense as a claim of divine prerogative — "making himself equal with God" (vs. 18). Over and over He characterizes these ruling classes in ways that could only deepen the chasm between them and Himself. They are "hypocrites," a "wicked and adulterous generation" (Matt. 16:3-4). "The publicans and the harlots" will go into the Kingdom ahead of them (Matt. 21:31). They are children of "hell," "blind guides" who strain at gnats and swallow camels, "full of extortion and excess," "whited sepulchres" filled with dead men's bones, a "generation of vipers" (Matt. 23:15, 24, 25, 27, 33). Instead of being truly children of Abraham, they are of their "father the devil" (John 8:39-44). And the reaction to such language is only what might have been expected from these proud men who sat in Moses' seat.

It is true that upon occasion the ministry of Christ seems to have been received with high favor by *the general public*. The early narrative of Mark indicates that His ministry attracted a tremendous interest and following, so that the disciples could report, "All men seek for thee" (Mark 1:37). But this following was due mainly to the great physical benefits bestowed upon the people; and our Lord was never under any illusions as to the superficial and evanescent nature of this initial popularity. As a result of His first great sign, we are told, "many believed in his name, when they saw the miracles which he did." But John adds that "Jesus did not commit himself unto them, because he knew all men" (John 2:23-25). And the fickle attitude of the people is unmistakable when He comes to Nazareth early in His great Galilean ministry (Luke 4:16-30). The first reaction seemed auspicious: As He spoke in the synagogue there on a Sabbath day, "all bare him witness, and wondered at the gracious words which proceeded out of his mouth" (vs. 22). But the question quickly raised as to His origin, "Is not this Joseph's son?", must be regarded as anything but friendly if read in connection with His sharp reply, "No prophet is accepted in his own country" (vs. 24). The outcome of this initial ministry in His own home town, when He exercises His sovereign right to bestow greater benefits upon one city than upon another, is swift and shocking: "And all they in the synagogue, when they heard these things, were filled with wrath, and rose up, and thrust him out of the city, and led him unto the brow of the hill whereon their city was built, that they might cast him down headlong" (vss. 28-29). Accounts of the tremendous enthusiasm shown at times by the multitudes must always be read in the light of our Lord's own words: "Ye seek me, not because ye saw the miracles [signs], but because ye did eat of the loaves, and were filled" (John 6:26); and again, "Ye also have seen me, and believe not" (John 6:36). At heart, the common people were no more ready for the Kingdom of Christ than their rulers. The main difference was that in the case of the rulers there were certain vested rights at stake, while the people in general thought they had nothing much to lose in any event.

5. *This tide of opposition toward our Lord's good news of the Kingdom grew steadily to a definite crisis.*

This historical crisis[7] with its attendant events is recorded in Matthew's Gospel, chapters 11 and 12, and also the parallel passages in Mark 3:19-35 and Luke 7:18-8:39. The time is definitely pinpointed as one of the most remarkable days in all the ministry of our Lord. So many important events took place that it has been called "The Busy Day."[8] But from the standpoint of historical significance the central event is the blasphemy against the Holy Spirit and our Lord's reaction to it. The opposition which forms the immediate background of this crisis arose from three widely different sources.

First, reference is made to those who were *nearest to Him*: His family and possibly some close friends. Mark 3:21 refers to the group as "his friends." The Greek phrase is *hoi par' autou*. Robertson thinks it is an idiom referring to the kinspeople or family of Jesus but admits that it could include a circle of close disciples.[9] Warfield, who has written an extended treatment of the passage, says, "We might think, in the varying circumstances which would render each natural, of His clansmen, of His fellow townsmen, of His responsible friends, of His blood kinsmen, of His household, of

---

[7] Cf. an excellent article, "The Argument by Matthew," by S. Lewis Johnson in *Bibliotheca Sacra*, April, 1955, pp. 148-149.

[8] A. T. Robertson, *Harmony of the Gospels* (New York: Geo. H. Doran, 1922), p. 61.

[9] A. T. Robertson, *Word Pictures in the New Testament* (New York: Harper and Bros., 1930), Vol. I, p. 281.

His family, of His parents, of His brothers."[10] Certainly, when read in connection with verses 31-35 of Mark 3, it is clear that at the center of the group were the members of His immediate family, "his brethren and his mother" (vs. 31).

Consider now what they were doing and saying: "They went out to lay hold on him: for they said, He is beside himself" (Mark 3:21). The same charge was evidently made later against the Apostle Paul (II Cor. 5:13). Although the Greek verb may refer to insanity in its extreme form, it is undoubtedly used of Jesus in the well-known sense of the loss of self-control in religious ecstacy.[11] As Warfield has written, "We need not imagine, then, that Jesus' friends saw in Him a maniac; we need only understand — what surely would not be unnatural in men who had as yet at least no sense of the nature of His mission — that they were led by the reports which had come to them to believe that He was in a state of exaltation which endangered His health and safety and needed some soothing hand to guard Him from Himself. That they felt His condition to be serious, may be inferred from the fact that they were prepared 'to lay hold on him.'"[12] Granting what is certainly true, that the charge cannot possibly be equated with the terrible charge of His enemies (John 10:20), still it is a "mournful spectacle" to find those closest to Him uniting in the unfavorable judgment, "He is beside himself." But this judgment concurs with the sorry record in John 7:1-5 which concludes, "For neither did his brethren believe in him."

Second, the attitude of the *people in general* is described in the eleventh chapter of Matthew (cf. also Luke 7:18-35). The group here is identified as "the multitudes," and "this generation" (Matt. 11:7, 16). The terrible denunciation of verses 20-24 is not addressed to any special class but to "the cities wherein most of his mighty works were done" (vs. 20). As to this particular "generation" of Israelites, our Lord likens them to "children sitting in the markets" who can be pleased by nothing. Concerning John who lived and ministered among them in ascetic self-denial, they had said, "He hath a devil." But when the regal Son of man came eating and drinking, they said, "Behold, a man gluttonous, and a winebibber, a friend of publicans and sinners" (Matt. 11:18-19). It was a generation of people capricious, unpredictable, and indifferent to the great spir-

---

[10] B. B. Warfield, *Christology and Criticism* (New York: Oxford University Press, 1929), p. 60.

[11] Cf. Lange's *Commentary on Mark* (rev. by Shedd; New York: Scribner's Sons, 1899), on 3:21.

[12] B. B. Warfield, *op cit.*, pp. 65-66.

itual issues of the hour. As Philip Schaff has paraphrased the Lord's words, "Ye are like a band of wayward children, who go on with their own game, at one time gay, at another grave, and give no heed to anyone else, and expect that everyone should conform to them. You were angry with John, because he would not dance to your piping; and with Me, because I will not weep to your dirge. John censored your licentiousness, I your hypocrisy; you, therefore, vilify both. . . ."[13] But the worst thing about them was that they had not "repented" in preparation for the Kingdom at hand. This in spite of the fact that they had witnessed the "mighty works," foretold in Old Testament prophecy, which had infallibly both identified the Messianic King and confirmed His announcement of the Kingdom (Matt. 11:20). So impressive and convincing had been these indubitable *signs* of the Kingdom that if they had been done in Tyre and Sidon, or even in Sodom, there would have been a turning to God in repentance (vss. 21-23). In the face of such an attitude, nothing but judgment remained for these highly favored cities of Israel. And in this judgment it would be more tolerable for the ancient cities of wickedness than for these Jewish cities in whose streets the great King had walked, worked, and taught. For theirs is the worst of all sin, the rejection of God's King in the face of unparalleled light (vss. 23-24). And the sin is not less culpable in that it was foreseen and made a part of the plan of God (Matt. 11:25-27). Even so, although the nation of Israel is moving toward the ordeal of divine judgment, the King in His final word throws open wide the door of personal salvation: "Come unto me, all ye that labour and are heavy laden, and I will give you rest" (Matt. 11:28-30). And thus He proves that He is a God of grace, even on the threshold of judgment.

In the Gospel of Luke, two verses appear for which there is no parallel material in Matthew's account of Christ's parable of the children in the market place. These verses read: "And all the people that heard him, and the publicans, justified God, being baptized with the baptism of John. But the Pharisees and lawyers rejected the counsel of God against themselves, being not baptized of him" (Luke 7:29-30). This passage seems to express a more favorable opinion of the "people" in their attitude toward the Kingdom at this particular time. But the verses in question are a continuation of the discourse of Christ regarding John and the general reaction of Israel

---

[13] In Lange's *Commentary on Matthew*, trans. with additions by Philip Schaff (12th ed., rev.; New York: Scribner's Sons 1893), on 11:16.

to his preaching; they are not Luke's description of current events taking place in the historical context of chapter seven.[14] And the current situation described in the parable which follows, in contrast to the people's original response to John's preaching, only proves the main point of the parable, i.e., the fickleness of the crowd. The same thing must be said about Matthew 12:22-23, which records the people's wonder at the miracle of healing and the question it provoked, "Is not this the son of David?" Regarding the attitude of the people, as indicated by this question, Schaff has pointed out that the interrogative adverb *meti*, "both in the N.T. and in classic Greek, always implies some doubt and the expectation or the wish of a *negative* answer."[15] And the original English translation of the question in the editions of 1611 and 1613 was properly, "Is this the son of David?" Certainly the question falls far short of any genuine confession of faith in Jesus as the Messiah.

Third, and most important, there came a definite crisis of opposition on the part of *the religious leaders* of Israel. These men, as our Lord pointed out to His disciples, sat in "Moses' seat" (Matt. 23:2) — a place of great authority and responsibility. The crisis came when Christ had cast a demon out of the man who was both dumb and blind, an act which provoked from the scribes and Pharisees an ascription of His miraculous ability to devilish power. The two main passages are Matthew 12:23-33 and Mark 3:22-30.[16] The accusation against Him is substantially the same in both of the records. Matthew gives it as phrased by the Pharisees: "This man doth not cast out demons, but by Beelzebub the prince of the demons" (Matt. 12:24, ASV). It should be recalled here that at an earlier time John the Baptist had been charged with being demon-possessed, and upon later occasions the same charge would be leveled against Christ Himself (John 7:20; 8:48, 52; 10:20). There is, however, a vast difference in Scripture between a victim of demon-possession and one who deliberately consorts with evil spirits. The former was treated with great compassion (Matt. 8:16-17), while the latter under the law was to be stoned to death (Lev. 20:6, 27).

The incident recorded in Matthew 12:24 marked the first open assertion that Christ was in league with the demonic world, perform-

---

[14] For a discussion of the literary problem, see J. J. Van Oosterzee in Lange's *Commentary on Luke, in loc.*

[15] In Lange's *Commentary, op cit., in loc.*

[16] A similar passage in Luke (11:14-22; cf. 12:10) seems to refer to a later incident. Cf. A. T. Robertson's note in his *Harmony, op cit.,* p. 123.

ing His miraculous signs by means of satanic power.[17] In this charge
the vindictive opposition of the religious rulers of Israel reached a
new plateau beyond which it could not go. It was bad enough to regard Him as a religious enthusiast "beside Himself," or to put Him
on a level with earlier prophets (Matt. 16:13-14), or to reject Him as
a law-breaking imposter (John 5:16), or even the unfortunate victim of demon-possession. But to admit the genuineness of His miracles, which had been foretold in their own Scriptures, and then to
charge Him with having done these things by the powers of hell,
thus ascribing wickedness to their own incarnate Messiah — this was
something new and terrible among the many sins of the chosen nation. And the charge provoked from the Son of God an ultimatum
of such unparalleled severity that it stands alone in the gospel
records as an appropriate witness to the awful possibilities of human
sin in the face of the light of God's grace.

6. *The charge uttered by the rulers involved blasphemy against
the Holy Spirit.*

In the many able discussions of this particular sin, it has generally
been treated as a phase of the general doctrine of sin or of the Holy
Spirit; which, of course, is not an improper approach. But, too often,
little or no attention has been paid to the historical setting and significance of the sin as it appeared and was first identified by our
Lord in His earthly ministry. We shall examine the Biblical record
with this especially in mind.

First, this particular instance of blasphemy was definitely related to
the *Kingdom of God.* The concept of a kingdom runs throughout the
passage. The people had in mind the Kingdom of Old Testament
prophecy when, viewing our Lord's great miracle, they raised the
question, "Is this the son of David?" (Matt. 12:23, KJV, 1611
edition). Over against this idea the Pharisees were thinking of a
kingdom of evil when they averred that Jesus cast out demons by
the *prince* of demons (12:24). The reply of Jesus was also couched
in the concept of a kingdom: "If Satan cast out Satan, . . . how
then shall his kingdom stand?" (12:25-26). At the center of the
entire controversy was the Kingdom which John the Baptist and our
Lord had proclaimed at hand: "But if I by the Spirit of God cast
out demons, then is the kingdom of God come upon you" (12:28,
ASV). The Greek construction of the conditional clause in this

---

[17] The similar accusations referred to in Matthew 9:34 and 10:25 belong to *later*
incidents. Cf. A. T. Robertson in his *Harmony;* James Orr, "Jesus Christ," in
I. S. B. E.; and S. J. Andrews in his *Life of our Lord.*

sentence does not leave the question in any doubt, as the English translation might seem to suggest. It is as if He had said, But if I cast out demons by the Spirit of God, *and I do!* Thus the historical issue was sharply drawn. Was the Messianic Kingdom of Old Testament prophecy actually impending in the person and works of Jesus of Nazareth? He avers that it is and points to His miracles, accomplished by the power of the Spirit of God, as the indubitable evidence before the eyes of Israel.

Second, the blasphemy of the Pharisees, therefore, involved a question regarding the *regal credentials of Christ.* According to the Old Testament prophets when Messiah came to establish the Kingdom, He would perform great miraculous signs: the eyes of the blind would be opened, and the tongue of the dumb would sing (Isa. 35:5-6). Our Lord had already pointed to His own mighty works as the prophetic credentials of His regal authority (Matt. 11: 2-5). Now in the presence of both Pharisees and people, by casting out a demon, He heals a man both blind and dumb. As in the case of many of His earlier works, no one could dispute the genuineness of the miracle. The evidence was before the eyes of all. Hemmed in by only two possible alternatives, either to accept Him as their King or to charge that His works were not of God, they chose the latter, saying that the miracle was done "by Beelzebub the prince of the demons" (Matt. 12:24, ASV).

Third, this sinful opposition to the claims of Jesus as the Messianic King reached its climax in open *blasphemy against the Spirit of God.* How are these two things related? When the pre-existent and eternal Son became incarnate in flesh and blood, we are told, He "emptied himself, taking the form of a servant" (Phil. 2:7, ASV). During the days of His flesh He was the perfect Servant of Jehovah, doing nothing of Himself but always speaking and acting under the direction and power of the Holy Spirit. All this was in perfect accord with Old Testament prophecy: "Behold my servant, . . ." said Jehovah, "I have put my spirit upon him: . . . He shall not fail nor be discouraged, till he have set judgment in the earth: and the isles shall wait for his law" (Isa. 42:1, 4). Therefore, knowing Himself to be this Spirit-anointed regal Servant of the Father, our Lord could take upon His lips the words of Isaiah's great prophecy of the Messianic King, "The Spirit of the Lord is upon me, because he hath anointed me. . . ." And then His self-identification was completed by the words, "This day is this scripture fulfilled in your ears" (Luke

4:18,21; cf. Isa. 61:1). Thus the great miracles of our Lord, which attested to His person and Messiahship, were actually the direct testimony of the Holy Spirit. It follows, therefore, that the ascription of these works to the kingdom of evil meant that the speakers had identified the Third Person of the Godhead with Satan, the prince of demons! Now much as they hated Jesus, they had never called *Him* that. They could charge Him with being *possessed* of a demon, but to His enemies He was only a man, and nothing more.

Fourth, this brings us to the ultimatum of our Lord that such blasphemy against the Holy Spirit is *unpardonable*. "All manner of sin and blasphemy shall be forgiven unto men," He says, "but the blasphemy against the Holy Ghost shall not be forgiven unto men. And whosoever speaketh a word against the Son of man, it shall be forgiven him: but whosoever speaketh against the Holy Ghost, it shall not be forgiven him, neither in this world, neither in the world to come" (Matt. 12:31-32). In Mark's account we have a still more terrible word: "Whosoever shall blaspheme against the Holy Spirit . . . is guilty of an eternal sin" (3:29, ASV). Now this infinite difference between the sin of blasphemy against the Son and that against the Spirit is not based upon any difference in the sanctity of their respective persons, but rather upon the difference between their respective ministries. The Father sent the Son to be the Saviour of men, and therefore *in Him* any and all sin can be forgiven without limitations. But outside of Him nothing can be forgiven. Now it is the peculiar ministry of the Spirit to testify to the Son and thus bring sinners into the only place where sin can be forgiven. And such pardon for repentant sinners was basic in the Kingdom of our Lord. It follows therefore that sinful resistance to the Holy Spirit, in the exercise of this peculiar ministry, must logically belong to a category of sin which is unpardonable. It is not that God ever ceases to be a God of grace; but that it is morally impossible for God to forgive sin outside of Christ, and a hardened resistance to the witness of the Spirit will keep the sinner outside of Christ forever.

Fifth, it is important now to observe, in the historical situation, exactly *who were involved* in this sin against the Holy Spirit. In the foreground, as the inspired records make clear, are the religious leaders of Israel. Mark mentions the "scribes" (3:22). Matthew speaks of the "Pharisees" (12:24), and later names both classes (12:38). The context of this last cited passage makes clear that the blasphemous utterance of verse 24 was no inadvertent remark made thoughtlessly on the spur of the moment. For immediately following

His denunciation of their blasphemy, the scribes and Pharisees answered Him with these words, "Master, we would see a sign from thee" (Matt. 12:38). And our Lord's response, "An evil and adulterous generation seeketh after a sign" (vs. 39), has led many expositors to suppose there was something wrong with this desire for a sign. But this is to miss the point entirely. For the Old Testament prophets had foretold in great detail the exact signs which would be credentials of Messiah and His Kingdom. Hence it was a solemn duty on the part of the religious leaders of Israel to demand of any self-designated Messiah the appropriate signs of his identity. Now it is sometimes forgotten that these Jewish leaders of our Lord's day had already been given many such "signs," but they had wilfully shut their eyes to them all. And now, with insolent audacity, they come asking for a sign! It is the irony of this historical moment that, having already pronounced His previous miracles to be satanic in origin, these leaders should now ask for another sign! And their demand demonstrates that the verbal blasphemy was only the climax of a long sinful resistance to the Spirit's testimony through the works of Christ; that they had reached the point of no return in a self-imposed blindness which had now taken on the character of divinely imposed retribution.

Sixth, it is also clear from the Biblical record that the *nation of Israel* must be held responsible in a measure for the blasphemy of its leaders. For it is a sound political and ecclesiastical principle that the people of a church or a nation in the long run get the kind of leaders that they deserve. And in the judgment pronounced by the regal Son of man for the blasphemy uttered by its leaders, the nation does not escape. For in their selfish interest in the mere physical benefits of the impending Kingdom, in their apathy to the great moral and spiritual issues of the hour, and in their fluctuating and unpredictable attitudes, the fickle populace showed themselves little better than the arrogant leaders they often resented and despised. Even the worst of tyrants, it is well known, cannot demand too great a price for their dictatorships. There is always *some* deference which must be paid to the opinions of the people who are being ruled. In the gospel records there are numerous references to this fact (cf. Matt. 21:26; Mark 11:18, 32; 12:12; 15:11, 15; Luke 20:19). Furthermore, if the people of Israel had read and believed their own prophets, they would have known that the Messiah at the establishment of His Kingdom would visit judgment upon the false shepherds who fed themselves instead of caring for the sheep (Ezek. 34:

1-10). This corporate responsibility of the *people* of Israel is made clear by the words of our Lord. Four times in His discourse immediately following the blasphemy, He uses the term "generation" (Greek, *genea*) in assessing the responsibility for His rejection (Matt. 12:39, 41, 42, 45). The Greek term may refer either to a race or class, or to a whole people during a period of time. The latter idea is certainly present in verse 41 where Christ declares that "The men of Nineveh shall rise in judgment with this generation, and shall condemn it: because they repented at the preaching of Jonas; and behold, a greater than Jonas is here." And this meaning is confirmed in chapter 13 of Matthew where Christ speaks to the "great multitudes" in parables (vs. 2), later telling His disciples that in these people is fulfilled the prophecy of Isaiah, "For this people's heart is waxed gross, and their ears are dull of hearing, and their eyes they have closed; lest at any time they should see with their eyes, and hear with their ears, and should understand with their heart, and should be converted, and I should heal them" (vss. 14-15).

Seventh, the historical importance of this particular hour in the gospel narratives is underlined by the *judgments* pronounced upon the Israelites who had failed to accept Jesus as the Messianic Saviour and King. For the individual persons guilty of uttering the words of blasphemy, there will be no forgiveness. The words here are "whosoever" and "never" (Matt. 12:32; Mk. 3:29). As to the "generation" involved, an ominous sign is given, "the sign of the prophet Jonah," which will now speak typically of the death of the Messianic King by the determination and consent of His own nation (Matt. 12:39-40). Furthermore, in the final day of judgment both Nineveh and the queen of the south will rise up as witnesses against this unrepentant "generation," because what it had heard and seen incomparably surpassed any previously given divine revelation to the sons of men (Matt. 12:41-42). But the penalty for the sin of Israel will not be wholly reserved for the final day of divine adjudication: for there is to come an *immediate* judgment within the history of that particular generation. To make this clear, our Lord speaks a parable peculiarly appropriate to the circumstances of the hour. Obviously having in mind the case of the man out of whom He had just cast the demon, the very incident which had precipitated the conflict (12:22), He draws a parabolic picture of the contemporary generation: it is like a man out of whom an unclean spirit has gone. The unclean spirit wanders about seeking rest but finds none. Returning to the former dwelling place, he finds the place swept and garnished, but empty.

Then, joining with seven other spirits, more evil than himself, they enter the man; and his last state is worse than the first. "Even so," Christ declares, "shall it be also unto this wicked generation" (Matt. 12:43-45). That this terrible warning was not limited to the religious leaders is clear from the words of verse 46 which affirm that Christ was also talking "to the people."

As to the general application of the parable, there is little question. A very genuine and widespread moral cleansing had been experienced in the nation through the great preparatory ministry of John the Baptist. But the house of Israel remained empty: there was no national reception of its incarnate King. Not only did the people of that generation accept the responsibility for His crucifixion (Matt. 27:25), but within the lifetime of those concerned, among all the enemies of the Gospel of salvation through the Cross of Christ, the people of Israel would become the bitterest. The last state would become worse than the first. Recorded in the Book of Acts, which covers the years of a single generation, the lamentable story may be found. And the account derived from noninspired sources is not better. As Ellicott has said, "We must turn to the picture drawn by the Jewish historian of the crimes, frenzies, insanities of the final struggle that ended in the destruction of Jerusalem, if we would take an adequate measure of the 'last state' of that 'wicked generation.' "[18]

It is not to be overlooked, however, that the judgment pronounced by our Lord was in a sense both eternal and temporal. For the *persons* of that generation who were guilty of blasphemy and rejection, there could be no recovery. But for the *nation* represented historically by that generation, the judgment was temporal. The very term "generation" suggests temporality. And in A.D. 70, within the time-span of a single generation, judgment fell in the destruction of Jerusalem and the world-wide dispersion of the nation. But while an entire generation had lost its historical opportunity, and with dire results for many succeeding generations, the *nation* itself nevertheless could not irrevocably lose those ancient rights which had been guaranteed by the God of Israel.

If any doubts remain as to the responsibility of the "people" for the adverse historic decision recorded in Matthew 12, these must be dissolved by our Lord's dictum in verse 30: "He that is not with me is against me." In the face of the crucial issue of the hour, there was left for no Israelite any room for apathetic indifference or cal-

18 C. J. Ellicott, *Commentary*, on Matt. 12:45.

culated neutralism. To make no decision was to make the wrong decision. And so in this manner, although a scattered few members of the nation had believed on Jesus as the Messianic King, the nation as such came ingloriously to its great hour of opportunity and decision. From this point onward, in the gospel narratives, we shall see the concomitants of Israel's decision as it became effective, under the overruling Providence of God, in the history of both the chosen nation and the Gentile world.

7. *What has been said above, of course, will raise the problem of contingency.*

To put the matter briefly: The *immediate* establishment of the Kingdom on earth was contingent upon the attitude of Israel toward her Messianic King, for to that nation pertained the divine promises and covenants (Rom. 9:4). It is not that the favor of God would terminate upon this elect nation, but rather that through them all the blessings of the Mediatorial Kingdom would flow to the world of nations. It should be clearly understood, however, that in speaking of contingency here, we refer to the *human* factor in history. Certainly our Lord was not caught by something unexpected. There are evidences in His earliest teaching (recalled and recorded by the latest gospel writer, as we might expect, knowing the historical sequence) that indicate at least a veiled reference to His rejection and death (John 2:18-22). But there are also evidences that He believed in the reality of human responsibility and moral decision, which pose the problem of historical contingency.

To take one example, consider His evaluation of John the Baptist and his career. Every intelligent Jew knew that the final word of the final Old Testament prophet predicted the appearance of Elijah as the precursor of the established kingdom (Mal. 4:5-6). And Christ had declared concerning John the Baptist, "If ye are willing to receive him, this is Elijah, that is to come" (Matt. 11:14, ASV margin).[19] Later, when the events recorded in Matthew 12 have demonstrated the certainty of His rejection and death at the hands of the Jewish nation, our Lord again refers to John; but now the historical situation has changed, the decision has been made, and the die is cast. "Elijah indeed cometh, and shall restore all things," he assures His disciples; but then He quickly adds, "I say unto you, that Elijah is come already, and they knew him not" (Matt. 17:11-12, ASV).[19]

[19] Cf. Alford on both passages.

We have here a key to one of the most puzzling problems of New Testament eschatology in relation to the Kingdom: How could the Kingdom be "at hand," and yet *not* near at hand? (Mark 1:15 with Luke 19:11). The true answer is to be found in the word "contingency." The very first announcement of the Kingdom as "at hand" had called upon the nation of Israel to make a decision (Mark 1:15), a genuine decision, a moral and spiritual decision; and they made it, tragically, the wrong way. The fact that all this was "by the determinate counsel and foreknowledge of God" (Acts 2:23) does not in the least detract from its moral and historical reality. Those who fail to see this can make nothing out of certain portions of our Lord's prophetic teaching. There still remains the philosophical problem, of course, but this is nothing new; it being only an aspect of the wider problem of Divine Sovereignty and Moral Responsibility. And for this there is no completely rational solution which does not end by affirming one and denying the other. But the Word of God teaches the reality of both. And if perhaps we shall never wish to give up the search for an answer to the problem, a Christian attitude of intellectual humility will help in some degree to alleviate our uneasiness as we continue the quest.

Chapter XXIII

CHRIST'S MINISTRY IN PREPARATION FOR THE INTERREGNUM

> A comparison of the Evangelists justifies us in saying broadly that a new epoch in our Lord's ministry had now begun.   *—James Denny*[1]

We come now to a large and important body of Biblical material which may be described as our Lord's acts and teaching in view of His final rejection by the nation of Israel, a prospect now become evidently certain in the movement of Biblical history. In this ministry the death of the King and His second coming will hold the central place. And the chief purpose of the new phase of teaching will be to prepare the disciples for His rejection and also for the interregnum which will intervene between His death and His return from heaven in glory to establish the Kingdom on earth in accordance with Old Testament prophecy. We shall now consider this new ministry in its progression.

1. *In a new series of parables, Christ sets forth the mystery form which the Kingdom will assume during the interregnum.*

   Why speakest thou unto them in parables?   *—Matt. 13:10*

As to the general purport and use of New Testament parables, scholars are not wholly agreed. For example, A. T. Robertson defines parable in the broad etymological sense, as a *simile;* and consequently finds that our Lord employed this method from the beginning of His ministry (cf. Matt. 5:13-16; 7:3-5, 17-19, 24-27, etc.). But Schodde doubtless has a narrower definition in mind when he says that Christ did not use the parabolic device at first, but introduced it later in teaching the "mysteries of the kingdom," as recorded in Matthew 13 and Mark 4.[2] An examination of these Biblical records will point to a solution of the problem as something historical as well as linguistic; and that too little attention has been paid to the former.

---

[1] James Denny, *The Death of Christ* (3rd ed.; New York: Armstrong and Son, 1903), p. 26.

[2] J. H. Schodde, "Parable," *International Standard Bible Encyclopedia* (Chicago: Howard-Severance, 1915), Vol. IV, p. 2243.

First, it should be observed that the initial five of these special parables about the Kingdom (four in Matt. 13 and one in Mark 4) were addressed primarily to *the general public* in Israel, not to the disciples. All three of the Synoptics place the hearers in this category. Mark says, "There was gathered unto him a great multitude. . . . And he taught them many things by parables" (4:1-2). Matthew says, "And great multitudes were gathered together unto him, so that he went into a ship, and sat; and the whole multitude stood on the shore. And he spake many things unto them in parables" (13: 2-3). Although present, the disciples apparently did not feel that these parables were addressed to them primarily. This is clear from their question, "Why speakest thou unto them in parables?" (13:10). And this distinction is confirmed by Mark's comment at the end of the first five of these parables: "And with many such parables spake he the word unto them, . . . and without a parable spake he not unto them: but privately to his own disciples he expounded all things" (4:33-34, ASV). It is true that the last four of the new series of parables were spoken to the disciples in the house after the multitudes had been dismissed (Matt. 13:36-53). But it is equally true that we have here two distinct pedagogical methods used in teaching respectively two different groups: parables to the general public; exposition to the disciples.

Second, consider the *stated purpose* of these parables about the "mysteries of the kingdom of heaven." Here we should recall that ordinarily the use of such similes and comparisons was intended to aid in the understanding of something (cf. Luke 6:39). But the parables about the mysteries of the Kingdom were not primarily so intended. On the contrary, we are informed by the Lord Himself, their purpose was to *hide* rather than to reveal.[3] In reply to the disciples' question as to why He spoke to the multitudes in parables, the Lord explained that it was "Because . . . to them it is not given" to know the mysteries of the kingdom (Matt. 13:10-11).

The giving of these parables, therefore, must be regarded as a *divine judgment* upon the nation of Israel. Because they had not received the simple announcement of the Kingdom, they now are given something they cannot understand. This judicial significance of the mystery parables is confirmed by the quotation of a well-known passage from Isaiah. Jesus said, "Therefore speak I to them in parables: because they seeing see not; and hearing they hear not, neither

[3] *Ibid.*, p. 2244.

do they understand. And in them is fulfilled the prophecy of Esaias, which saith, By hearing ye shall hear, and shall not understand; and seeing ye shall see, and shall not perceive: For this people's heart is waxed gross, and their ears are dull of hearing, and their eyes they have closed; lest at any time they should see with their eyes, and hear with their ears, and should understand with their heart, and should be converted, and I should heal them" (Matt. 13:13-15).

This remarkable passage, originally given in Isaiah 6:9-10, is referred to five times in the New Testament, always in connection with Israel's rejection of her King (Matt. 13:13-15; Mark 4:11-12; Luke 8:10; John 12:39-40; Acts 28:25-27). Arguments over the meaning of the conjunctive particles *hina* and *hoti,* whether the parables were given to produce blindness, or as the result of blindness, cannot change the judicial nature of our Lord's words. The context of the passage, both in its original Old Testament utterance and its quotation in the New Testament, should be decisive on this point. And S. G. Green argues ably for the judicial meaning on grammatical grounds: "We believe that the former [purposive] interpretation is the only one admissible. The blindness is represented as judicial — a punishment inflicted by God on disobedience and hardness of heart."[4] On the contrary, Bruce is so violently opposed to the judicial meaning of this series of Kingdom parables that he is willing to impute error to the New Testament writers rather than to admit it, saying, "It is much better to impute a mistake to them than an inhuman purpose to Christ."[5] As if it were "inhuman" for God to judge men for their wicked unbelief!

Third, all this does not deny that these mystery parables of the Kingdom had a *beneficent* purpose. As a matter of fact, for those who had already accepted the simple facts about the Kingdom, these parables would give further enlightenment. The principle of double purpose, both beneficent and penal, is stated succinctly by our Lord while He was giving the parables: "For whosoever hath, to him shall be given, . . . but whosoever hath not, from him shall be taken away even that he hath" (Matt. 13:12).[6] It should be observed, however, that even in the case of those already willingly enlightened, the parables had to be explained. To the disciples, whose eyes and ears

---

[4] S. G. Green, *Handbook to the Grammar of the New Testament* (new rev.; New York: Fleming H. Revell, 1912), pp. 321-322.

[5] A. B. Bruce, *Expositor's Greek New Testament,* ed. W. R. Nicoll (New York: Hodder and Stoughton, 1917), Vol. I, p. 196.

[6] Thus Alford refers to the "revealing and concealing properties" of these parables (*Commentary on Matthew, in loc.*)

had been opened, Christ felt it necessary to interpret the first two of the series, the parables of the sower and the wheat and the tares (Matt. 13:10, 16-23, 36-43). In these two recorded interpretations we have the key to much contained in the entire series. And we may assume that the other parables also were explained by the Lord, for Mark says that privately to His own disciples He "expounded all things" (4:34, ASV). Furthermore, at the end of the entire series, when Jesus asked the disciples, "Have ye understood all these things?" they answered, "Yea, Lord" (Matt. 13:51). Allowing for some naive overestimation of their understanding, nevertheless we cannot miss the note of approval in our Lord's final word in verse 52 concerning the one who has been "instructed" about the Kingdom, and is therefore able to bring forth out of his treasure "things new and old."

The point to be emphasized in all this is that these parables of the Kingdom, even for the saved, must be divinely interpreted in order to serve any beneficial purpose. In no area of the Word of God is there greater need for caution on the part of interpreters than in the parables, and especially in those concerned with the "mysteries of the kingdom of heaven." Even the most spiritual and well-taught among students of the Word may go astray here; and many an error has found its basis in some parabolic detail, e.g., the gradual and ultimate triumph of the Church in converting the world through the "leavening process" of the Gospel. It is never safe to use either a type or parable to teach something not elsewhere taught directly and clearly in the Word of God.[7]

Fourth, this particular series of parables is not only concerned with "the kingdom of heaven," or "of God," but more specifically with the "*mysteries*" of that Kingdom (Matt. 13:11; Mark 4:11; Luke 8:10). The Greek term is *mustērion* which, in the three parallel passages, appears for the first time in the New Testament, and the only time in the Gospels. It refers to that which is hidden and secret, what can be known only to those who are specially initiated or taught. The word does not necessarily mean something incomprehensible to the human mind, but rather that which has hitherto been unrevealed. Thus it would seem that we have here something new in *content* as well as *method* in Christ's teaching to Israel about the Kingdom.

Now, without attempting any detailed exposition of these parables,

---

[7] Schodde correctly says, "The interpreters of former generations laid down the rule, *theologia parabolica non est argumentativa; i.e.,* the parables, very rich in mission thoughts, do not furnish a basis for doctrinal argument . . . . They illustrate truth but they do not prove or demonstrate truth" (*op, cit.,* Vol. IV, p. 2244).

it does appear that, among the mysteries of the Kingdom revealed here privately to the disciples by the Lord, the most important has to do with the mystery of an *interregnum* which is to follow the arrival of the King and continue until His second coming. Though implicit there, this is something not revealed in Old Testament prophecy, and it could not be made known clearly until the King's rejection had become historically certain. But now, in the progress of events, the time has come for its revelation to the disciples, and this is done in the Lord's explanation of the parable of the "tares of the field" (Matt. 13:36-43).

This parable speaks of a seed-sowing, a period of growth, and a harvest. The harvest is definitely set at "the end of the age"[8] (vs. 39, lit.), or "the end of this age"[8] (vs. 40, lit.). The period of sowing and growth, therefore, must be the present age,[9] during which our Lord is creating and developing a body called "children [lit. *sons*] of the kingdom" (vs. 38). And this age will be brought to a close when the Son of man comes to establish His Kingdom on earth by means of a harvest-judgment, in which the lawless will be taken away and the righteous will be made to "shine forth as the sun" in that Kingdom (vss. 41-43). Thus, after the interregnum caused by Israel's rejection of her King, the Kingdom will finally come, in full accordance with Old Testament prophecy. The length of the interregnum is not revealed in the parable, whether long or short.

> 2. *Our Lord next announces the building of a new thing—His Church—a body of believers invested with special authority in the future Kingdom of heaven.*
>
> It is difficult to conceive how the idea of the identity of the Kingdom of God with the Church could have originated.   —*Alfred Edersheim*[10]

In the immediate background of this announcement was the disciples' gloomy report of their recent ministry in Israel (Matt. 16:13-14). They had been sent out, two by two (Mark 6:7), to announce to the "house of Israel" that the long-awaited kingdom of heaven was at hand (Matt. 10:1-7). Now, as they return to Him, Christ asks for a report. The question is, "Whom do men say that I the Son of man am?" (Matt. 16:13). This question involves, first, a clear assertion of Messiahship. He, the questioner, *is* "the Son of man." The title stems directly from Daniel's great prophecy of Messiah and

---

[8] The Greek term is *aionos* in both verses, not the *kosmos* of verse 38.
[9] So Ellicott and H. A. W. Meyer.
[10] Alfred Edersheim, *Life and Times of Jesus* (8th ed., rev.; New York: Longmans, Green, and Co., 1912), Vol. I, p. 269.

His Kingdom (7:13-14), and was our Lord's favorite self-designation, used upon the most solemn occasions (Matt. 24:30; 26:64). As Canon Liddon has declared, "In these passages there is absolutely no room for doubting either His distinct reference to the vision in Daniel, or the claim which the title Son of Man was intended to assert."[11] Actually, therefore, our Lord is asking for a report as to the attitude of Israel toward Him as the regal Messiah of Old Testament prophecy. And the opinions as reported, which to superficial readers might seem highly complimentary, were nevertheless infinitely below the truth. To equate Jesus with John the Baptist or any of the Old Testament prophets, however great, was not enough; for He is the divine Son of Man, the Lord from heaven. Therefore, any failure to confess Him as such is nothing but unbelief.

In the face of this blind attitude on the part of the nation, our Lord turns to the small circle of His disciples with the same searching question, "But whom say ye that I am?" And Peter, speaking doubtless for the group as well as for himself, answers, "Thou art the Christ, the son of the living God" (Matt. 16:15-16). It is a confession of both Messiahship and Deity, one which receives full approval and acceptance from Jesus in the words that follow: "Blessed art thou, Simon Bar-jona: for flesh and blood hath not revealed it unto thee, but my Father which is in heaven" (vs. 17). And then, significantly choosing this great moment of heavenly inspired confession shining with glory against the darkness of national unbelief, our Lord reveals the new thing that He will build, "And I say also unto thee, That thou art Peter, and upon this rock I will build my church; and the gates of hell [hades] shall not prevail against it" (16:18).

The full development of the doctrine of the Church is reserved for Volume VI of this series, but some things should be said here regarding its nature and place in relation to the Kingdom.

a. Christ speaks of the Church in terms of the *future*: His word is not "I am building" but "I will build." And the time of its beginning can be definitely identified. In later passages this Church will be described as a "body" (I Cor. 12:12, 13), also a "building" (Eph. 2:20-22); and in both references the Spirit of God is directly associated with the building process: "by one Spirit are we all baptized into one body," and "ye also are builded together . . . through the Spirit." This points definitely to the Day of Pentecost as the historical

11 H. P. Liddon, *Divinity of our Lord* (9th ed., rev.; London: Rivingtons, 1882), p. 7.

beginning of the Church, for upon that day the Spirit of God came upon the waiting disciples to build them into one body of Christ where all distinctions of race and nation would be cancelled (Gal. 3:28). No other date fits either the Biblical doctrine of the Church or its history.

b. The Greek word is *ekklēsia*, occurring here (Matt. 16:18) for the first time in the New Testament. Etymologically, the term is a compound of the preposition *ek*, meaning "out," and the verb *kaleo*, to "call" or "summon." Thus the general meaning is any group of people called out of their places to form an assembly, the nature and purpose of which must always be ascertained from its usage. In the Book of Acts, the word is often used of the *Christian churches* (9: 31); once of the Old Testament congregation or *assembly of Israel*[12] (7:38); once of a *riotous mob* (19:32); and once of a lawful *governmental assembly* at Ephesus (19:39). It should be clear, therefore, that linguistically there is no more reason for identifying the New Testament Church with the Old Testament Jewish assembly than with the political assembly in the city of Ephesus. Although each one was truly an *ekklēsia*, they were widely different in character and purpose.

However, although wholly different in identity, it is significant that the Jewish *ekklēsia* of the Old Testament and the political *ekklēsia* at Ephesus had one thing in common: both exercised governing powers. Of the former, Kuenen has written, "In very weighty matters the decision even rested with the whole community, which was summoned to Jerusalem for that purpose."[13] The entire congregation of Israel was held responsible for the execution of the divine laws (Num. 15:36; Josh. 7:25). And in the reign of Hezekiah both king and congregation unite in establishing a "decree" (II Chron. 30:1-5). Concerning the political *ekklēsia* at Ephesus at the time of Paul's visit (Acts 19:39), Ramsay has stated that in spite of the limitations imposed by Rome, "the assembly was still, in name at least, the supreme and final authority in the city."[14] Thus our Lord's choice of the Greek term *ekklēsia* to designate His Church points at least in the direction of governmental powers, a matter to be discussed more fully below.

[12] The Septuagint of the Old Testament frequently uses *ekklēsia* to translate the Hebrew *qahal;* the latter being generally rendered *congregation* in the Common Version.

[13] "Congregation," *Dictionary of the Bible*, ed. James Hastings (New York: Scribner's Sons, 1901), Vol. I, p. 467.

[14] W. M. Ramsay, "Ephesus," *Dictionary of the Bible, op. cit.*, Vol. I, p. 723.

c. As to the *foundation* of the Church, as set forth in Matthew 16:18, there are four main interpretations of Christ's words, "Upon this rock I will build my church." (1) That it was founded upon Peter himself as the primate of the apostles — the Roman Catholic theory. (2) That it was founded upon Peter's confession. (3) That the foundation is Christ Himself as the true Rock. (4) That the church was established upon "the foundation of the apostles and prophets, Jesus Christ himself being the chief corner stone" (Eph. 2:20); and that Peter is addressed by our Lord only as the first to make the great confession, being therefore only representative of the whole apostolic foundation. The argument for this last view has been stated convincingly by M. R. Vincent as follows:

> The word refers neither to *Christ* as a *rock*, distinguished from *Simon*, a *stone*, nor to *Peter's confession*, but to *Peter himself*, in a sense defined by his previous confession, and as enlightened by the "Father in Heaven."
>
> The reference of *petra* to Christ is forced and unnatural. The obvious reference of the word is to Peter. The emphatic *this* naturally refers to the nearest antecedent; and besides, the metaphor is thus weakened, since Christ appears here, not as the *foundation*, but as the *architect:* "On this rock *will I build.*" Again, Christ is the great foundation, the "chief corner-stone," but the New Testament writers recognize no impropriety in applying to the members of Christ's church certain terms which are applied to him. For instance, Peter himself (I Pet. ii 4), calls Christ a *living stone*, and, in ver. 5, addresses the church as *living stones*. In Apoc. xxi, 14, the names of the twelve apostles appear in the twelve foundation-stones of the heavenly city; and in Eph. ii 20, it is said, "Ye are built upon the foundation of *the apostles and prophets* (i.e., *laid* by the apostles and prophets), Jesus Christ himself being the chief corner-stone."
>
> Equally untenable is the explanation which refers *petra* to Simon's confession. Both the play upon the words and the natural reading of the passage are against it, and besides, it does not conform to the fact, since the church is built, not on *confessions*, but on *confessors* —living men.[15]

The Church here in Matthew 16 is viewed in its totality as the one universal body. Therefore, against it the "gates of hell shall not prevail" (vs. 18). In Matthew 18:17-18 the reference is obviously to the church in its local and visible character, with full disciplinary authority over its own membership. But to such a local *ekklēsia* there is no guarantee of perpetuity and final victory. Its candlestick may be taken away (Rev. 2:5).

d. *The relation of this new ekklēsia to the Kingdom* is set forth in the words of Matthew 16:19, "And I will give unto thee the keys of the kingdom of heaven: and whatsoever thou shalt bind on earth shall be bound in heaven: and whatsoever thou shalt loose on earth

---

[15] M. R. Vincent, *Word Studies in the New Testament* (New York: Scribner's Sons, 1924), Vol. I, pp. 91-92. See also Edersheim, *op. cit.*, Vol. II, pp. 81-84.

shall be loosed in heaven." In the voluminous discussions of this passage, some very important matters have not received the attention they deserve.

First, the language here is clearly the language of *authority*. The conferring and power of the "keys" speaks of stewardship, an authoritative control over the treasures of a house (Gen. 43:19; Matt. 20: 8). The terms "bind" and "loose" carry the idea still further, especially in the light of the heavenly concurrence.

Second, this authority is given to the *whole* Church. The words of Matthew 16:19 were addressed to Peter merely as the first, but only one, of the many who would utter the great confession and be builded as "living stones" into that glorious temple which is the true *ekklēsia* of the Lord. As Meyer has well said, Peter is "simply to be looked upon as first among his equals," and "as far as the *ekklēsia* is concerned, it is to be understood as meaning the *congregation of believers, including the apostles*." And with this interpretation the American editor of Meyer fully agrees: "Whatever the contents of this power, therefore, they pertain not to Peter exclusively, as chief of the apostles, nor to the body of apostles exclusively, but to the Church."[16]

Third, this authority given the Church is to be exercised in *the Kingdom of heaven*, and therefore belongs to the future[17] when this Kingdom shall have been established on earth. The word of our Lord is very specific: the keys are those "of the kingdom of heaven," and the things to be bound or loosed are "on earth" (Matt. 16:19). This is in complete accord with the eschatological promises of the New Testament. The Kingdom and reign of the saints are said to be in the future "on the earth" (Rev. 5:10; see also Matt. 13:41-43; Luke 19:12, 17, 19, etc.). The error of identifying the Kingdom with the Church, followed by the logical attempt of certain ecclesiastical organizations to exercise during the present age a regal authority which belongs to the true Church in a *future* Kingdom, has been the source of untold evil and disaster. Such authority and power could never be safely committed to sinful men, even though redeemed and members of the body of Christ. To this lamentable fact we have the clear witness of nineteen centuries of church history. The Church

---

[16] H. A. W. Meyer, *Commentary on Matthew*, ed. Geo. R. Crooks (New York: Funk and Wagnalls, 1884), on 18:18ff., pp. 331 and 305. See also M. R. Vincent, *op. cit.*, on Matt. 16:19, pp. 96-97.

[17] H. A. W. Meyer, *Ibid.*, on Matt. 16:19, p. 299.

must be perfected in order to reign with Christ over the nations in the coming Kingdom (Rom. 8:17-23).

It is true that the promise of binding and loosing is repeated in Matthew 18:18, but here the context definitely limits the authority in three respects: first, it is obviously conferred on the *local* church; second, it delegates to such a church only the power to discipline its own membership and is therefore limited to its own affairs (cf. vss. 15-17); and third, there is no mention whatever of the power of the keys of the Kingdom of heaven, as described in 16:19.

The opinion that the "keys" under discussion are for the opening or shutting of the "door of salvation" to men, although advanced by some great names, should be rejected as utterly out of harmony with the doctrine of Scripture. This is a matter subject to divine control alone, for only God can forgive sin. The idea of men having authority to dispense the Grace of God in saving the soul should be left to the Dark Ages of theology where it belongs.

The place of honor to be occupied by the Church in the future Messianic Kingdom seems to be taught in a subsequent discourse of Christ (Luke 13:28-30). Here we have two groups in the Kingdom: first, the Jewish patriarchs and prophets of Old Testament history (vs. 28); and second, a company coming from all parts of the world (vs. 29), a possible reference to the universality of the Church. The expression, "sit down [lit. recline] in the kingdom of God," certainly speaks of high privilege and intimacy. Those who are "thrust out" (vs. 28) are the Jewish "adversaries" of Christ (vs. 17). On this expression Van Oosterzee says it means "the *temporal* exclusion of the Jews from the blessings of the Messianic Kingdom" (italics added).[18]

> 3. *Our Lord now begins definitely to instruct the disciples about the necessity of His death and resurrection.*
>
> From this time the teaching of Jesus to His disciples, and also to the people at large . . . assumed a new character.   —*S. J. Andrews*[19]

Earlier in the gospel records there had been a few allusions to His death and resurrection; recorded for the most part by John the latest writer, as we might expect, knowing the historical sequence. But these references had been indirect, not much more than veiled intimations which could be read with understanding only in the clear light of the accomplished facts. For example, when John the Baptist

---

[18] J. J. Van Oosterzee, Lange's *Commentary, in loc.*
[19] S. J. Andrews, *Life of Our Lord* (Grand Rapids: Zondervan Publishing House, reprint, 1954), p. 355.

first caught sight of Jesus, he names Him "the Lamb of God, which taketh away the sin of the world" (John 1:29), an implication of death, for, in the Jewish ritual, a lamb could symbolize the taking away of sin only by dying. Again, very early in His ministry, when asked for a sign, He answers, "Destroy this temple, and in three days I will raise it up." But John, who recorded the prophecy long after its fulfillment, explains that it was recalled and understood only after "he was risen from the dead" (John 2:18-22). It is in John's Gospel also that we have from the lips of Christ the great imperative: "And as Moses lifted up the serpent in the wilderness, even so must the Son of man be lifted up," an act He describes in verse 16 as a divine giving of the only-begotten Son that men might have eternal life (John 3:14-16).[20] In the Synoptics also there are intimations of death: in our Lord's baptism, in His word about the bridegroom being taken away (Mark 2:19-20), and in the ominous sign of Jonah (Matt. 12:38-40).

But following the crisis marked by the blasphemy against the Holy Spirit and the announcement of an *interregnum* and the building of a new *ekklēsia,* we come to a new epoch in the teaching of Christ. His death and resurrection are now openly revealed as a divine imperative. The key phrase is given by Matthew: *"From that time forth began Jesus to shew unto his disciples, how that he must go unto Jerusalem, and suffer many things of the elders and chief priests and scribes, and be killed, and be raised again the third day"* (16:21, italics added). Mark and Luke give substantially the same material, except that both add the verb "be rejected"; and Mark recalls that the new teaching is now given "openly," i.e., plainly and without ambiguity (Mark 8:31-32; Luke 9:22). Later passages indicate that this *open* teaching about the necessity of His passion was continued up to the very end (cf. Matt. 17:23; 20:17-19, 28; Mark 9:31; 10:33-34; Luke 18:31-33). Mark uses the vivid imperfect form of the Greek verbs, suggesting that what Christ "taught" and "said" about this matter was done repeatedly (9:31). References to this teaching appear in John's later record, in which our Lord speaks of Himself as the bread of life whose flesh and blood will bring eternal life to men (6:51-56); as the good Shepherd who lays down His life for the sheep, with power to take it up again (10:11, 18); and as the corn of wheat which must fall into the ground and die in order to

---

[20] The theory that the words beginning at John 3:16 are John's rather than Christ's, adopted by the Revised Standard Version, is emphatically and justly opposed by Schaff, Alford, Lange, Meyer, Stier, *et al.*

bring forth fruit (12:24). The same teaching was given clearly in parabolic forms, in which Jesus appears as the "beloved son" who is killed by wicked husbandmen, and also as the rejected stone which is subsequently made the "head of the corner" (Matt. 21:33-42; Mark 12:1-11; Luke 20:9-17). The Bread and the Cup at the last supper also spoke plainly of His death for His people (Luke 22:19-20).

Now these facts, as presented in Scripture, raise some very serious problems of interpretation which involve both history and theology. In the history of the Church, as set forth in Acts and especially in the epistolary writings of the New Testament, no one can deny the centrality of the Cross and the Resurrection. Viewed from this standpoint, the Son of God came not to live but to die: He was the Lamb of God "slain from the foundation of the world" (Rev. 13:8). It is no exaggeration to say that we have here the fundamental of all the fundamentals in the Christian Church. But, since this is so, how can we explain why from the very start of His ministry Christ did not make His death and resurrection the spear-point of all His teaching? Why was it that through the whole of His initial preaching of the Gospel of the Kingdom and up to the sharp crisis of Jewish rejection, so little was taught about these important matters, and even that little was not left unveiled by any recorded clear explanation? If the Church and the Kingdom of Heaven are virtually identical, and if this Kingdom is exclusively *spiritual* (as some affirm), how then shall we account for the comparative silence of the Lord and His chosen apostles about things without which there could have been no Church which is the body of Christ? Furthermore, if the "gospel of the kingdom" (Mark 1:14), as preached by our Lord and His chosen disciples early in His ministry, is identical with the Gospel proclaimed after the Resurrection, why was the Cross not proclaimed as its central feature from the beginning? And if the content was not exactly the same, wherein was the difference? These are important questions which ought to be answered. The very clash of widely divergent opinions shows that the problem is genuine, not something to be shrugged off as of little consequence. Nor can we accept any explanation which ignores or mishandles the historic facts as recorded in the inspired Word of God.

Furthermore, without denying there are certain theological aspects of the problem which probably will never be fully resolved, it is fair to say that no answer can be received as valid unless it recognizes that in the preaching of the Kingdom, our Lord actually offered to men *something* which it was their moral duty to accept.

Therefore, although He was delivered up to death by the "determinate counsel and foreknowledge of God" (Acts 2:23), it could not have been a divinely imposed duty on Israel to reject and kill their own Messiah! Nor did our Lord, according to the horrible theory of Albert Schweitzer, grow discouraged over the apparent failure of His early ministry and set out deliberately to force the Jews to kill Him. The truth is that Jesus offered Himself as the Messianic King of Israel, that the offer was genuine, and therefore the nation *should* have accepted Him. To argue otherwise is to forget the demands of moral obligation and to set up a façade of forced theological unity which obscures the reality of the movements of history.

It is true that all kinds of questions may be raised at this point in the discussion; e.g., What would have happened if Israel had accepted Jesus as their Messianic King? Could there have been any true kingdom on earth without the death of Christ as its spiritual foundation? This is like asking what would have happened if Adam had not sinned. These are speculative questions to which the Christian interpreter need not attempt a final answer.[21] It is our duty rather to hold fast the recorded facts of Biblical history and the reality of man's responsibility within its processes. To concede the irrevocable nature of predictive prophecy does not relieve man in any respect of his moral responsibility. For divine prophecy is not in itself the efficacious *cause* of human action. The few passages which seem to teach otherwise must be read in the light of the total doctrine of Scripture. For example, on John 12:39 — "Therefore they could not believe because Isaiah said" — Lange wisely comments regarding Israel's fate, "But their divinely decreed destiny, as a judicial infliction, presupposes their guilt in choosing unbelief." [22]

This raises the problem of the disciples' failure to understand the teaching of Christ about the necessity of His death and resurrection. For although the recorded teaching seems perfectly clear to us today, it is a fact that they did not understand. Almost immediately following the Transfiguration, we read that He "taught his disciples" about His approaching death and resurrection (Mark 9:31), urging their high importance, "Let these sayings sink down into

---

[21] The objector might well be reminded, however, that there was once in Old Testament history a Theocratic Kingdom on earth *before* Messiah died, and therefore the possibility need not be rejected on *a priori* grounds.

[22] J. P. Lange, *Commentary on John, in loc.*

your ears" (Luke 9:44). But Mark records their undiscerning attitude: "But they understood not that saying, and were afraid to ask him" (9:32). The tense is an imperfect, suggesting that they *continued* to be afraid to ask. Why this fear? Possibly they recalled with bitter memories an earlier occasion when Peter had questioned the necessity of His death, and Christ had laid upon that erring disciple the terrible name of "Satan" (Matt. 16:21-23). There is also the psychological tendency to suppress in thought and discussion the things we fear may happen; and the disciples were very human. Luke's explanation of their lack of understanding about Christ's death is that "it was hid from them, that they perceived it not" (9:45). Whether this failure to understand is wholly chargeable to the disciples, or whether there is to be found here evidence of divine purpose and causation, is a question not easily answered. Certainly the disciples were intelligent men capable of understanding human language; and they might have asked for an explanation, but there is no record that they did. It seems equally certain that the factor of divine purpose is present, as urged by Alford, who renders the clause in Luke 9:45 *"that they might not"* perceive.[23] This idea of divine purpose and restraint seems to be present also in a later and striking passage of Luke where the Lord speaks very clearly of His death in fulfillment of Old Testament prophecy; yet the disciples "understood none of these things: and this saying was hid from them, neither knew they the things which were spoken" (18:31-34). While the theologian may never be able to put his finger upon the exact point at which the divine purpose meets the human responsibility, we can at least affirm two certainties: first, men are always held responsible for their unbelief; and second, God may use this very unbelief in the fulfillment of His purposes and predictions.

> 4. *Christ also reassures the disciples that His impending death will not mean any abandonment of the Kingdom; and now indicates explicitly that its establishment will be connected with a second coming of the King.*
>
> The *Basileia* cannot be supposed to come without the *Basileus*.
> —H. A. W. Meyer[24]

Following the open revelation of the necessity of His death, our Lord immediately promises that He will come again, this time in

---

[23] Henry Alford, *Commentary, in loc.* So also A. T. Robertson, who nevertheless calls it a "hard problem" (*Word Pictures in the New Testament, in loc.*).
[24] H. A. W. Meyer, *op cit.,* on Matt. 16:28.

the full glory they had expected on the basis of Old Testament prophecy: "For the Son of man shall come in the glory of his Father with his angels" (Matt. 16:27). Here we have for the first time in the gospel narrative an explicit reference to the *second* advent.[25] And the second advent is associated with the coming of the Kingdom: for the Son of man will come "in his kingdom" (Matt. 16:28). Furthermore, the promise in verse 27, that "then he shall reward every man according to his works," confirms the identification of the coming of the Kingdom *in time* with the second coming of Messiah. For this judicial work of Messiah clearly appears in Old Testament prophecy of the Kingdom, and it certainly was not accomplished at His first coming to earth. The testimony of the New Testament writers as to this synchronism is both clear and consistent: The judging work of Christ will begin at His second coming (Matt. 25:31 ff.; I Cor. 4:5; II Tim. 4:1).

Actually, of course, the rejection and death of Messiah introduced nothing new into the concept of the Kingdom, except to clarify the puzzling element of *time*. The Old Testament prophets had already pictured Messiah as both a glorious and a suffering person. But the idea of two separate comings of Messiah could not be clearly revealed until His first arrival on earth and His rejection had become historically certain in the movement of events. Only then could the certainty of a second coming be fully unveiled; and this future coming is now made the focal point for the hopes of men regarding the establishment of God's Kingdom on earth. Nothing is clearer, according to Old Testament prophecy, than that the great goal of the Lord's people was centered in the arrival of God's Kingdom on earth. But if that Kingdom was established at the first coming of our Lord, as some affirm, it becomes impossible to explain why following His rejection by Israel all New Testament Scripture agrees in setting the goal, not in the present world order, but in the future at His second coming. The interpretative dilemma is very simple: either the Kingdom has not yet been established in the Old Testament prophetic sense, or the reality of Christ's second advent must somehow be explained away.

---

[25] Even if Matt. 10:23 refers to the second advent, which is disputed by Lange and others, the events of chap. 10 follow those in chaps. 12 and 13; and therefore in the progress of revelation the full disclosure of a second advent did not come until after the crisis of Jewish rejection. (See A. T. Robertson's *Harmony* and S. J. Andrews' *Life of Our Lord.*)

In order to indicate certain aspects of its nature, Christ gives to three of His disciples a *prevision, in miniature,* of His coming in the Kingdom. Following the promise of a second coming in glory, He had made the following prediction: "Verily I say unto you, There be some standing here, which shall not taste of death, till they see the Son of man coming in his kingdom" (Matt. 16:28). To identify the coming event to which our Lord referred in these words, at least half a dozen different views have been proposed. The most natural reference is to the Transfiguration which occurred a few days later. The connection between the prediction and its fulfillment has been obscured in Matthew by an unfortunate chapter division. But the conjunction with which chapter 17 begins clearly establishes the unbroken continuity of thought between 16: 28 and 17:1, as also in the accounts of Mark and Luke where no chapter division occurs. This is the view of Andrews who says, "The promise that some then standing before Him should not taste death till they had seen 'the Son of man coming in his kingdom' . . . was fulfilled when, after six days, He took Peter, James, and John into a high mountain apart, and was transfigured before them. . . . These apostles now saw Him as He should appear when, risen from the dead and glorified, He should come again from heaven to take His great power and to reign. They saw in the ineffable glory of His Person and in the brightness around them, a foreshadowing of the Kingdom of God as it should come with power, and were for a moment 'eyewitnesses of his majesty' (II Pet. 1:16)."[26]

Any doubts regarding the correctness of this interpretation should be settled by the word of the Apostle Peter himself who, writing by divine inspiration, has explained the significance of our Lord's Transfiguration (II Pet. 1:16-18). In this passage, Peter first speaks of "the power and coming" of Christ, a reference certainly to His second coming in power. Then, in support of the reality and glory of this event, Peter cites the personal experience of himself with James and John, when they were on "the holy mount" (vs. 18). There, he insists, they "were eyewitnesses of his majesty," and they

---

[26] S. J. Andrews, *op cit.,* p. 356. Andrews also cites Trench on the point as follows: "Nearly all the early expositors, the fathers, and the mediaeval interpreters, find in the glory of the Transfiguration the fulfillment of the promise" (*Studies in the Gospels,* p. 188).

"heard" the heavenly voice saying, "This is my beloved Son, in whom I am well pleased" (vss. 16-17).

If the reader will observe carefully the order of events recorded in Matthew 16:21 - 17:8, it will become increasingly clear that against the dark background of our Lord's open announcement of His rejection and death, there was need for some reassurance as to the reality and nature of the Kingdom which the apostles had been preaching to the nation of Israel. And this reassurance was given to them on the Mount of Transfiguration. In this prevision of "the Son of man coming in his kingdom," certain things were made crystal clear. First, when the Kingdom comes at the second advent of Christ, it will be tangibly evident to sense experience: men will see the "majesty" of the King and "hear" His voice. Second, the arrival of the Kingdom will be attended by great supernatural events, as suggested by the details of the Transfiguration scene. Third, the presence of Moses, under whose mediatorial rule the ancient Theocratic Kingdom was established at Sinai, speaks strongly of the reality of its future re-establishment. Fourth, the appearance of Elijah, whose coming was promised prior to the establishment of the Kingdom, witnesses to the literal fulfilment of Old Testament prophecies concerning the Kingdom. Fifth, the Transfiguration experience suggests that at the coming of Christ in His Kingdom, His presence will supersede all other authority: the heavenly voice commands, "Hear ye him," and even Moses and Elijah are no longer seen. In their place there will be One who is both Mediatorial *Ruler* and *Prophet*.

The question of the disciples, probably uttered sometime later (cf. Mark 9:10-11), is interesting. Evidently assuming that the appearance of Elijah on the Mount had fulfilled the Old Testament prophecy concerning His coming (Mal. 4:5), the disciples ask, "Why then say the scribes that Elijah must first come?" (Matt. 17: 10). But the Lord's reply set them right: In this matter the scribes had not been wrong; for "Elijah truly shall first come, and restore all things" (Matt. 17:11). This does not deny to John the Baptist a place in divine prophecy. For as S. J. Andrews has pointed out, since there were to be "two comings" of Messiah, so also there must be "two forerunners."[27] John the Baptist was the forerunner of Messiah at His first coming when He *offered* to Israel the Kingdom.

[27] *Ibid.,* p. 360.

Elijah will be the forerunner of Messiah when He comes a second time to *establish* His Kingdom. But the mystery of these two forerunners could not be cleared up until Messiah arrived for the first time and had revealed that there would be a second coming.

> 5. *Furthermore, in unmistakable words our Lord also declares that His disciples will yet have their promised share in the Kingdom when established on earth.*
>
> To affirm that mortal and sinful men are already admitted to have part in His functions of universal rule, and are empowered by Him to govern the nations, is a proud and presumptuous ante-dating of the Kingdom. His kings must first be made like Him, immortal and incorruptible . . . then can they exercise His heavenly authority.
> —*Samuel J. Andrews*[28]

It was only natural that the new emphasis upon the necessity of His death should have raised questions in the disciples' minds about the promised Kingdom and their own part in it. On this point, therefore, Christ hastens to reassure them. They are not to be afraid, for it is the Father's good pleasure to give them the Kingdom (Luke 12:32). Hence, there is no need for preoccupation about material possessions. The important and immediate duty is to lay up treasure in heaven, and to be watching for the Lord's return from heaven with their reward. At that time the faithful will participate in the rulership over the King's household (Luke 12:33-44).

This teaching is substantially repeated a little later in reply to a question which arose out of our Lord's attitude toward material wealth in the case of the rich young ruler. The question was voiced by Peter: "Behold, we have forsaken all, and followed thee; what shall we have therefore?" (Matt. 19:27). And the Lord's answer is categorical: "Verily I say unto you, That ye which have followed me, in the regeneration when the Son of man shall sit in the throne of his glory, ye also shall sit upon twelve thrones, judging the twelve tribes of Israel" (vs. 28). This comforting promise of reward to the Twelve, moreover, is extended generally in verse 29 to "every one" who has made sacrifices and suffered loss for His "name's sake." All such shall "receive an hundredfold." The immediate and close connection with verse 28 places the time of their recompense at the future "regeneration" of the world to be effected by the establishment of the Kingdom. Meyer remarks that verse 29 "can certainly have no other reference but to the recompense *in the future*

---

[28] S. J. Andrews, *God's Revelations of Himself to Men* (New York: Charles Scribner's Sons, 1886), p. 293.

kingdom of the Messiah." [29] But as to the exact position of each one in the coming Kingdom, they are to remember that "many that are first shall be last; and the last shall be first" (Matt. 19:30). The explanation of this seeming paradox is to be found in the principle of divine grace which will be operative even in the bestowal of rewards. To illustrate this, our Lord adds a parable about the "kingdom of heaven," the chief point of which is that its King is always sovereign in the giving of His rewards (Matt. 20:1-16).

The reaction of the disciples to these promises about their place in the Kingdom was very characteristic of sinful men. Earlier there had been some disputing as to which of them should be the greatest (Luke 9:46-48). And following the promise of Matthew 19:28, the dispute was again precipitated by the request of James and John, supported by their mother, that they might be given the highest places in the Kingdom, an action which aroused great indignation among the other ten (Mark 10:35-38, 41; Matt. 20:20-21, 24). In dealing with this situation, our Lord qualifies in no respect His promise that the disciples shall rule with Him in the Kingdom. But He shows them that the path to a throne is the path of service. If men would sit as kings in the Kingdom, they must also stoop to minister, even as the Messianic King Himself "came not to be ministered unto, but to minister, and to give his life a ransom for many" (Matt. 20:25-28).

Weak, selfish, and vacillating as the disciples showed themselves to be, yet the Lord graciously renewed His promise to them in a very solemn moment at the Last Supper. "Ye are they which have continued with me in my temptations. And I appoint unto you a kingdom, as my Father hath appointed unto me; that ye may eat and drink at my table in my kingdom, and sit on thrones judging the twelves tribes of Israel" (Luke 22:28-30). Here the attendant circumstances of the hour — the words concerning His sufferings, the bread and the cup as symbols of His death, the reference to His betrayer, the irrevocable direction of His path to Calvary (Luke 22:

---

[29] Mark and Luke seem to differ from Matthew's account, in setting the period of divine recompense "now in this time" instead of in the future Kingdom of Messiah (Mark 10:30; Luke 18:30). Meyer (p. 348) supposes that the variation may have been due to "exegetical reflection" on the part of Mark and Luke! But it is to be noted that neither of these writers mentions the "regeneration" which dates the fulfilment of the promise in Matthew 19:28-29. And since all three accounts purport to be the quoted words of Christ Himself, the explanation may well be that He promised both a *future* recompense in the Messianic Kingdom and also a present recompense. Furthermore, the recompense in Mark is "with persecutions," which points to the present order of things. And there is a sense, of course, in which the divine recompense for our sacrifices begins at once.

15-22) — all combine to give peculiar force to His promise about the Kingdom. But to the disciples, their eyes not yet enlightened as to the meaning of what was transpiring, the prospect of His death must have seemed to sound the knell of failure to all their hopes. Therefore, against the darkness of that hour, He reaffirms the certainty of the coming Kingdom and the regal part His disciples shall have within it. Nothing can fail. By His grace the weakest of men can be made strong and given the regal character essential in the royalty of the coming Kingdom. For its great King is also a great priest; and as He prayed for Peter in the hour of his weakness and failure (Luke 22:31-32), even so He prays for all who have believed on Him (John 17:20).

> 6. *To correct a current expectation that the Kingdom would come immediately, Christ outlines in parabolic form the facts of its present rejection, the interval of its delay, and its future arrival.*
>
> Subordinate kings went to Rome to receive the investiture to their kingdoms from the Roman Emperor, and then returned to occupy them and reign. So Christ received from his Father, after his ascension, the investiture to his kingdom; *but with the intention not to occupy it, till his return at his second coming.* In token of this investiture he takes his seat as the Lamb on the divine throne.   —E. B. Elliott [30]

The main passage on this point is the parable of the pounds found in Luke 19:11-28, for which there is no parallel account in the other Gospels. The parable of the talents (Matt. 25:14-30), although similar in some details, was certainly given later and lacks the specific design found in the parable recorded by Luke. As Alford strongly insists, *"The whole structure and incidents of the two are essentially different."* [31] The parable of the pounds is so distinctive and important in connection with the Kingdom that it deserves special attention here.

The *circumstances* attending the utterance of the parable were all highly pertinent to the subject of the Kingdom. First, as the Lord approached the city of Jericho, where the parable was spoken, He had healed a blind man — one of the great miracles predicted by Isaiah in connection with the Kingdom (35:5), and wrought in response to the man's appeal to Him as the regal "Son of David" (Luke 18:35-43). Second, while passing through [32] Jericho (Luke 19:1), He meets and becomes a guest in the home of a rich and notoriously dishonest Jewish tax collector (Luke 19:1-10). The

---

[30] E. B. Elliott, *Horae Apocalypticae*, on Rev. 5:6-8 (italics added).
[31] Henry Alford, *Commentary for English Readers* (2nd ed.; Boston: Lee and Shepard, 1872) on Luke 19:11-28.
[32] Greek imperfect tense.

meeting brings about the remarkable conversion of Zacchaeus, and this "son of Abraham" at once, in accordance with the law of the ancient Theocratic Kingdom (cf. Exod. 22:1), proceeds to restore "fourfold" all that he had wrongfully extorted. At the same time he promises to give to the poor half of what he had rightfully acquired — an impressive reminder of Old Testament prophecies of the Kingdom when social wrongs shall be set right and "the crooked shall be made straight" (Isa. 40:4).

The *audience* to which the parable was spoken is a matter of importance. Who were the persons that "heard these things"? Probably both the *multitude* and the *disciples*. The healing of the blind had attracted a crowd: Luke 18:43 speaks of "all the people." Luke 19:3 speaks of "the press" which compelled Zacchaeus to climb into the tree in order to see Jesus; and verse 7 says, "they all murmured" when they saw He had accepted the hospitality of the despised publican. But the disciples also were undoubtedly present, for they were with Him when He came from Jericho to Jerusalem (Luke 18:31). And the parable itself indirectly suggests the presence of two classes of persons in the distinction made between the "servants" of the nobleman and his "citizens" (vss. 13-14).

The *imagery* of the parable was undoubtedly drawn from actual events in the political history of the times. It was a regular procedure for native princes to journey to Rome to receive their right to rule. For this purpose, during our Lord's youth at Nazareth, the son of Herod the Great, Archelaus, went to Rome. He was so hated of the Jews that they sent a delegation after him to protest against his enthronement, but to no avail. And upon his return Archelaus rewarded his supporters with certain cities and took vengeance on his enemies. Josephus says that his great palace was built at Jericho, perhaps not far from the home of Zacchaeus where the parable was first spoken.

The *purpose* and *occasion* of the parable are stated in verse 11, "And as they heard these things, he added and spake a parable, because he was nigh to Jerusalem, and because they thought that the kingdom of God should immediately appear." The reference to His nearness to Jerusalem is intended to remind the reader of Christ's intention to enter on the morrow into the city of Jerusalem as its Messianic King, in accordance with Old Testament prophecy. And it is hardly possible that the disciples or the crowd (or both) knew nothing of His intention. In fact, the next clause indicates that they did know, and therefore "thought that the kingdom of God should immediately appear." Such an expectation was not unnatural, as Alford remarks on the passage, "They imagined that the present journey to Jerusalem, undertaken as it had been with such publicity, and accompanied with such wonderful miracles, was for the purpose of revealing and establishing the Messiah's Kingdom."[33] As a matter of fact, as Van Oosterzee admits with some reservation, the people were not wrong in looking for a very genuine appearing or manifestation of the Messianic Kingdom; but the error of which they needed to be cured was the supposition that the Kingdom could come at once without first a departure and a return on the part of the King.[34] To set them right on this point, the parable of the pounds was given. To cite the fine statement of Ellicott: the parable was given to "safeguard against the prevalent expectations of the immediate coming of the Kingdom, and, we may add, against the thought which sprang up afterwards in men's minds, that there was no kingdom to be received, and that the King would never return."[35]

Let us consider now some of the parabolic details as our Lord used them to set forth certain aspects of His own relation to the Kingdom of God (Luke 19:11-27).

First, the nobleman (Christ) goes into a far country (heaven) for a twofold purpose: to receive for himself a kingdom, and to return (vs. 12).

Second, two classes of people appear in the parable: those called "servants" and others called "citizens"; and although both are said to be "his," i.e., Christ's (vss. 13, 14), yet their relationship to Him is quite different.

Third, to each of the ten servants He gives an equal amount of money and commands them to "occupy," or more literally, "trade," until He returns (vs. 13); and they accept the responsibility.

Fourth, the "citizens" of the nobleman "hated" him and officially repudiated his regal claims, saying, "We will not have this man to reign over us" (vs. 14); an accurate forecast of Christ's rejection by Israel and their cry, "We have no king but Caesar" (John 19:15).

Fifth, having received His Kingdom rights in heaven, Christ will bring that Kingdom to earth at His second coming; at which time

[33] Alford, *op, cit., in loc.*
[34] J. J. Van Oosterzee, Lange's *Commentary,* on Luke 19:11.
[35] Ellicott's *Commentary* (Grand Rapids: Zondervan Publishing House, reprint, 1954), *in loc.*

His first regal action will be to reward His servants according to their services during the period of His absence (vss. 15-24).

Sixth, also at the return of Christ and His assumption of the throne, He will execute judgment upon the citizens who rejected Him at His first coming (vs. 27). The implication is very clear: the nation of Israel will maintain officially its enmity until the return of Christ.

Seventh, the parable gives "the definite assurance that the interval between the departure and the return of the Lord is only an *interim*."[36] The length of the interim is not here given, though in the similar parable of the talents the same interval is stated as "a long time" (Matt. 25:19). But there is no warrant for pressing this expression into a definite revelation of the nineteen centuries of our present era. For, according to the imagery of both parables, the Lord returns *within* the lifetime of the same servants to whom He had committed the money.[37] And therefore, while the interval of time is left indeterminate, the language seems intended to keep every generation expectant and watchful for the coming of the Lord and His predicted Kingdom.

Finally, it is of the utmost importance to observe that neither this parable nor the parable of the talents was given until *after* the rejection and death of Christ had become historically certain, and also *after* the revelation that there would be a second coming of the King. In the progress of revelation there is perfect synchronization with the movement of history.

7. *Although His rejection had now become historically certain, our Lord nevertheless proceeds to Jerusalem, there to offer Himself officially and finally as the King of the Messianic Kingdom in exact fulfilment of prophecy.*

> It was no common pageantry; and Christ's public Entry into Jerusalem seems so altogether different from—we had almost said, inconsistent with—His previous mode of appearance. Evidently, the time for the silence so long enjoined had passed, and that for public declaration had come. And such, indeed, this Entry was. From the moment of His sending forth of the two disciples to His acceptance of the homage of the multitude, and His rebuke of the Pharisees' attempt to arrest it, all must be regarded as designed or approved by Him; not only a public assertion of His Messiahship, but a claim to its national acknowledgement.   —*Alfred Edersheim*[38]

a. *The Journey to Jerusalem*

If there was to be such an offer, it is unimaginable that it could be

36 J. J. Van Oosterzee in Lange's *Commentary, in loc.*
37 Cf. H. A. W. Meyer, *op cit.*, on Luke 19:12-13.
38 Alfred Edersheim, *op. cit.*, Vol. II, p. 370.

made anywhere except in the capital city of the nation. And the first reference to this fateful journey came almost at once following the blasphemous rejection of His Messianic signs: "From that time forth began Jesus to shew unto his disciples, how that he must go unto Jerusalem" (Matt. 16:21). The beginning of that journey, shortly afterwards, is recorded by Luke: "And it came to pass, when the time was come that he should be received up, he steadfastly set his face to go to Jerusalem, and sent messengers before his face" (9:51-52).[39]

The purposes and results of the last journey to Jerusalem had been clearly stated by the Lord Himself: "the Son of man must suffer many things, and be rejected of the elders, and of the chief priests, and scribes, and be killed, and after three days rise again" (Mark 8:31). Now, while the civil and religious leaders of Israel had already made known their rejection of His claims, and in terms which could not be misunderstood (Matt. 12:24; Mark 3:22), there had been as yet no *official* decision on the part of the nation. And to secure such a decision, our Lord now sets His face toward Jerusalem, there to make the official *offer*. Those who cavil at the idea of an offer which is certain to be rejected, betray an ignorance, not only of Biblical history (cf. Isa. 6:8-10 and Ezek. 2:3-7), but also of the important place of the legal proffer in the realm of jurisprudence.

b. *Preparation for His Arrival*

Furthermore, if there was to be a final and official offer, it was essential that the nation should be largely represented. And the actions of Christ seem designed specifically to serve this important end. Thus, in striking preparation for His advance upon Jerusalem, which will be circuitous, deliberate, and unhurried, possibly extending over a period of five months, the Lord now appoints a band of seventy[40] messengers who are sent ahead of Him to act as heralds of both the Kingdom and the coming of its King. "After these things the Lord appointed other seventy also, and sent them two and two

---

[39] While opinions vary as to the exact identity and order of our Lord's intervening movements, eminent authorities agree that here we have the start of that solemn march which would lead at last to the city of His death. Edersheim concludes that "all—from the moment of His finally quitting Galilee to His final Entry into Jerusalem—formed, in the highest sense, only one journey" (*Life and Times of Jesus the Messiah*, Vol. II, p. 128). See also H. A. W. Meyer and S. J. Andrews.

[40] Whether so designed or not, it seems hardly possible for the populace of Israel, familiar with the seventy elders of the ancient theocracy (Num. 11:16) and also with the numerical composition of the Sanhedrin, not to attribute some significance to this number in relation to the expected Kingdom.

before his face into every city and place, whither he himself would come" (Luke 10:1). The ministry of the Seventy, therefore, was more narrowly limited than that of the Twelve who earlier had been sent to all "the lost sheep of the house of Israel" (Matt. 10:6). The Seventy are sent only where the King Himself will come on the last journey to Jerusalem. Lightfoot makes the distinction as follows: "The Twelve apostles were sent to declare the coming of the Kingdom, these (the Seventy) the coming of the King." And S. J. Andrews says, "They were to give notice that the Messiah was coming, and that in those places only which He had chosen."[41] Their commission was very simple: in the cities which received them, they were to heal the sick and say, "The kingdom of God is come nigh unto you" (Luke 10:9). Where they were not received, there was to be no miraculous sign, but they were nevertheless to warn that "the kingdom of God is come nigh," with the ominous omission of the words "unto you" (vs. 11).[42]

The impact of the ministry of the Seventy, followed by that of our Lord personally, must have been tremendous and would account in part for the large crowds on the way when He entered Jerusalem. Matthew says, "Great multitudes followed him" (19:2). Mark says, "And multitudes come together unto him again" (10:1, ASV). Luke says, "The people were gathered thick together" (11:29); and again, "There were gathered together an innumerable multitude of people, insomuch that they trode one upon another" (12:1); and again, "And there went great multitudes with him" (14:25).

Another reason for the presence of large numbers of people when He entered Jerusalem was the spectacular miracle of raising Lazarus from the dead. This immediately became a matter of high public interest. John says, "Much people" had come "that they might see Lazarus also, whom he had raised from the dead" (John 12:9). All this public furor greatly disturbed the religious officials in Israel, for Lazarus *alive* made it impossible to deny the reality of the miracle. Therefore, with practical astuteness they laid plans to kill the risen man (vs. 10) and thus put an end to the public excitement and the consequent increase of the Lord's following. But there is no evidence in the record that there was any actual attempt to carry out this cold-blooded proposal. And the crowds grew until the Pharisees in despair said to one another, "Perceive ye how ye prevail nothing? behold, the world is gone after him" (John 12:17-19).

[41] S. J. Andrews, *op. cit.*, p. 381.
[42] The best Greek text of Luke 10:11 omits "unto you."

Furthermore, it must not be forgotten that the celebration of the annual Passover was at hand, an event that normally brought large numbers of Jews to Jerusalem. Though perhaps somewhat exaggerated, Josephus relates that at one celebration over 250,000 lambs were sacrificed, which, estimating ten men to each, would mean a total of two and a half million people. Many of these Jews would come from all parts of the ancient world (Acts 2:5), where some had acquired great wealth and high position.

The combination of all these circumstances — the important word of the Seventy, the personal follow-up ministry of our Lord, the raising of Lazarus, the Passover celebration, and a general expectation that some kind of an announcement would be made about the coming of the Kingdom (Luke 19:11) — both by conscious design and providentially, worked together to assemble in Jerusalem an impressively large and important section of the nation to witness the regal entrance of Christ into the city to offer Himself as the King of Israel (Luke 19:38-40).

c. *The Royal Entrance into Jerusalem*

The triumphal entry, celebrated by Christendom for the most part with little understanding of its relation to the history of the Kingdom of God, was an event of tremendous import. Even its timing was something accomplished with exact precision. Each of the gospel writers gives the event a conspicuous place of importance in his record, all four agreeing as to the main circumstances attending it. Luke gives the most complete account, including some material which shows how crucial our Lord Himself regarded the event in relation to Old Testament prophecies of the Kingdom and the future of the nation of Israel. Some of the circumstances will now be considered.

First, as He drew near to Jerusalem, our Lord pauses to send two disciples to a nearby village to get *the colt of an ass,* with its mother, which in His omniscience He perceived tied in a certain spot. If the owners protest, the disciples are to explain their action simply by saying, "The Lord hath need of them." As a result, the two animals are released and brought to Christ (Matt. 21:1-3). Here we may properly ask, Why did the Lord need these two animals? Certainly not because He had any physical need for some means of transportation on the short distance into the city! But Matthew explains the matter as a *prophetical* necessity. In the prophecy of Zechariah, the precise manner of the arrival of the Messianic King had been foretold five hundred years in advance: He would come riding upon the foal of an ass. And Matthew declares that Jesus did what He did in order that Zechariah's prediction "might be fulfilled" (Matt. 21:4-5 with Zech. 9:9). This does not mean, surely, that to ride into Jerusalem on the colt of an ass would by itself prove Jesus to be the Messianic King; for any impostor might have thus come into the city. But it does mean that Jesus, who had already by undeniably miraculous signs proven His Messiahship, was careful to fulfil down to the last physical detail all the predictions concerning His arrival in Jerusalem as the King of Israel.

It is noteworthy that Matthew, in explaining the need of a literal colt for the King's entry, is careful to restrict his quotation to only the first part of Zechariah's prophecy. Verses 9-10 of Zechariah 9 form one continuous prophecy joined by the conjunction "and." Verse 9 tells the manner of the King's arrival, while verse 10 tells what the King will do when His beneficent reign is established. Then the "chariot," the "battle bow" and the war "horse" will be cut off; He will "speak peace unto the nations: and his dominion shall be from sea to sea, and from the River to the ends of the earth" (ASV). Not one of these details of Messiah's *reign* in verse 10 is even mentioned by Matthew. Writing both by divine inspiration and from the vantage point of known history, Matthew knew that the King had arrived and also that the King had *not* occupied His Messianic throne. If the colt ridden by the King upon His arrival had to be literal, so also must the warfare be literal which will be abolished when He reigns. If Matthew had believed in a "present Messianic reign" ushered in by the first coming of the King, here would have been the time and place to cite in full the details of Zechariah 9:9-10, but He says not a word about the wondrous things of verse 10.

It has been said by anti-millennial writers that the animal ridden by our Lord was intended to show humility and indicate that the Kingdom He came to found would accomplish its purposes by "peaceable" means and wholly without the use of force. But this is to forget that Deity may exercise forcible control effectively without any carnal means (cf. Acts 5:1-10). The absence of all military pomp, of which the war horse would have been a fitting symbol, only demonstrated that as the Messianic King our Lord would need none of the conventional weapons of this cosmos in order to rule the nations with a rod of iron. He needs only to speak, and the thing will be done.[43] If Christ had wished merely to display His humility, as Marcus Dods has reminded us,[44] He would not have ridden at all, for it would have been humbler to *walk* with the disciples!

Second, the *actions and praises of the people* indicate an awareness of the regal meaning of our Lord's entry into Jerusalem. As He rode, Matthew says, "a very great multitude spread their garments in the way" (21:8), an act reserved only for those of the highest rank (cf. II Kings 9:13). As Edersheim says, "They 'unwrapped their loose cloaks from their shoulders and stretched them along the rough path, to form a momentary carpet as He approached.'" To this carpet of raiment they added the further tribute of strewing His path with branches of trees — in John's record identified as palm branches (12:13) — a common demonstration in the East to welcome "a king, a conqueror, or a deliverer." Branches of palm trees were also associated with the ritual of the Feast of Tabernacles as a symbol of Israel's prosperity dwelling in the land of Palestine (Lev. 23:39-40). In this connection, we must not fail to notice the occasion of the people's praise: "And when he was come nigh, even now at the descent of the mount of Olives, the whole multitude of the disciples began to rejoice and praise God with a loud voice for all the mighty works that they had seen" (Luke 19:37). And what were these works? The miraculous feeding of hungry men; the healing of the blind, the deaf, the lame, and the diseased; the raising of the dead — all of which had been predicted in the prophets in connection with the coming of the Messianic King (Isa. 35:5-6; 26:19).

Third, there is deep significance in the very *language* with which the multitude expressed their joy. As reported by the four gospel writers, they cried, "Hosanna to the son of David; blessed is he that cometh in the name of the Lord; Hosanna in the highest" (Matt. 21:9). "Blessed be the Kingdom of our father David, that cometh in the name of the Lord" (Mark 11:10). "Blessed be the King that cometh in the name of the Lord: peace in heaven, and glory in the highest" (Luke 19:38). "Blessed is the King of Israel that cometh in the name of the Lord" (John 12:13). All these joyous cries, it is evident, arose out of the 118th Psalm which was recognized by the ancient Jewish Rabbins and early Christian writers as one of the

[43] On Zech. 9:9, Lowe says that the use of an ass by the Messianic King cannot be proved to "symbolize either peace or humility" (In Ellicott's *commentary*).

[44] Marcus Dods, *The Gospel of John* (New York: Geo. H. Doran Co., no date), Vol. II, p. 22.

greatest of all the Messianic Psalms.[45] The Lord Jesus Himself put its Messianic reference beyond all dispute when, immediately after His Triumphal Entry and in the face of the opposition from the Jewish leaders, He quoted from this psalm and applied its prophetic words to His own career: "Did ye never read in the scriptures, The stone which the builders rejected, the same is become the head of the corner: this is the Lord's doing, and it is marvellous in our eyes?" (Matt. 21:42 with Ps. 118:22-23). And again, later, as He pronounced the judgment of desolation upon the rebellious nation, He graciously quoted from the same psalm to indicate the joyous words which will be spoken sincerely by a future repentant Israel in the day when He will come back from heaven to establish and reign in His glorious Kingdom: "Behold, your house is left unto you desolate. For I say unto you, Ye shall not see me henceforth, till ye shall say, Blessed is he that cometh in the name of the Lord" (Matt. 23:38-39 with Ps. 118:26).

Fourth, the very *protest of the Pharisees,* against the acclamations of the multitude, shows that in the triumphal entry something wholly new had come in the ministry of Christ. Some of these leaders said, "Master, rebuke thy disciples" (Luke 19:39). By the commentators in general, almost no attention has been given to the implications of this Pharisaic protest. These jealous and sharp-eyed religious leaders of Israel had long been watching every action of the popular Galilean Prophet and marking His every utterance. They must have known that upon former occasions our Lord had strictly enjoined silence upon His disciples with reference to public acclamation of His regal claims (Matt. 16:20; Luke 9:21); and also that He had steadfastly resisted the popular movement to "make him a king" (John 6:15). But *now,* as He rides into the city, they hear the shouts of the people acclaiming Him openly as the "King of Israel"; and they must have wondered that there was no rebuke from the lips of Jesus as previously.

Fifth, the *answer of Christ* shows clearly that a radically new junction has arrived in His career upon earth, something without any previous parallel. Up to this time, the witness to His regal Person

---

[45] Godet says, "Every Israelite knew these words by heart: they were sung at the Feast of Tabernacles, in the procession which was made around the altar, and at the Passover in the chant of the great Hallel during the Paschal supper. *Hosanna* . . . is a prayer addressed to God by the theocratic people on behalf of His Messiah-King; it is, if we may venture to use the expression, the Israelitish *God save the King"* (*Commentary on John* [New York: Funk and Wagnalls, 1886], p. 213).

and Messianic office had been left largely to His mighty works and the prophetic Scriptures (John 5:36-39). But now the time has come when there can be no longer any place for verbal silence: "I tell you," He replies to the Pharisees' demand, "that, if these should hold their peace, the stones would immediately cry out" (Luke 19:40). To express with some adequacy the greatness of this unique moment, I can find nothing better than the fine words of Van Oosterzee:

> Once in His life He grants to His own publicly to proclaim what lies so deeply at their heart, and He fulfils intentionally a prophecy which at His time was unanimously interpreted of the Messiah. If He has previously considered the declaration of His dignity as dangerous, He now counts silence inconceivable . . . . It was hereafter never possible to say that He had never declared Himself in a wholly unequivocal manner. When Jerusalem afterwards was accused of the murder of the Messiah, it should not be able to say that the Messiah had omitted to give a sign intelligible for all alike. Our Lord will prove that He is more than a prophet mighty in word and deed; that He is King in the full force of the word.[46]

Sixth, the moving *lament of our Lord,* as He beheld the city, and the judgment He pronounced upon it, prove that a crisis-point is reached here in the history of Israel in relation to the Kingdom. Weeping over Jerusalem, because in His omniscience He knew that the acclamation of the fickle multitude would within a few hours be turned into a savage demand for His death, He indicated the irrecoverable passing of Israel's present opportunity, and also the consequent judgment to fall upon the city and the generation which would reject Him. Speaking to the nation, so fully represented upon that solemn occasion, He said, "If thou hadst known, even thou, at least in this thy day, the things which belong unto thy peace! but now they are hid from thine eyes" (Luke 19:41-42). Then follows the prediction of the destruction of the city and the sufferings of its people, to be fulfilled in A.D. 70, all of which will come, our Lord says, "because thou knewest not the time of thy visitation" (vss. 43-44).

The *time* element set forth in these words is very precise. Verse 42 speaks of *"this thy day,"* i.e., Israel's day. And verse 44 refers to the *"time of thy visitation."* Because the nation of Israel was blind to the *"day"* of opportunity, certain "things" which could have brought "peace" to the nation would now be "hid" from her eyes, and there would be judgment instead of peace. The Old Testament prophets had spoken in great detail of the "things which belong" to the peace

---

[46] J. J. Van Oosterzee, Lange's *Commentary, op. cit.,* p. 295.

of Israel in the future Kingdom. And the prophet Daniel had spoken
of the "day" when "Messiah the Prince" would arrive: "from the
going forth of the commandment to restore and to build Jerusalem
unto the Messiah the Prince shall be seven weeks: and threescore and
two weeks" (9:25). These 69 weeks of prophetic years of 360 days
each add up to 173,880 days, and on the final one of these days our
Lord rode into Jerusalem as the Messianic King of Israel.[47] The
nature of the circumstances attending this great event add to the
impression that we have here no random day, but rather a "day" set
by divine knowledge and decree in fulfilment of Biblical prophecy.
And when the figures are given so exactly, as Daniel states them, we
cannot be wrong in expecting that the fulfilment will likewise be
exact. The closest scrutiny of the gospel narrative will fail to discover
any other day in the earthly career of our Lord which is comparable
to the day of His triumphal entry into Jerusalem. Viewed from the
standpoint of His kingly rights in relation to the theocratic nation,
this day stands alone. And, of course, if the day was fixed by divine
prophecy, this would explain the complete absence of any other
official offer before this particular time.

Seventh, the *acts of our Lord* immediately following His entry
into the city only confirm the regal character of that event. If we
follow the order in Matthew, His initial act was to assert once more
His Lordship over the temple, from which He "cast out all them that
sold and bought in the temple, and overthrew the tables of the
moneychangers, and the seats of them that sold doves" (Matt. 21:12).
Mark adds another detail: He "would not suffer that any man
should carry any vessel through the temple" (11:16). This cleansing
is not to be identified with the earlier cleansing recorded in John 2:
13-17, as some determined harmonists have tried to do. The one
came at the beginning of our Lord's ministry and revealed His zeal
as the great Messianic *Prophet*. The second came at the close of
His ministry, and revealed His authority as the Messianic *King*.[48]

This cleansing of the temple can only be regarded as a great miracle,
as Jerome long ago asserted. If our Lord had been only a man, how
easily the traffickers could have overpowered and cast Him out! And
this miracle of cleansing was followed by other physical wonders.
Matthew says, "And the blind and the lame came to him in the
temple; and he healed them" (21:14). These miracles were *seen*,

---

[47] See *Daniel's Prophecy of the Seventy Weeks* by Alva J. McClain (7th ed.;
Grand Rapids: Zondervan Publishing House, 1940).
[48] So Lange, *Commentary on Matthew*, 12:12 ff., p. 377.

not only by His friends but also by His enemies, "the chief priests and scribes" (Matt. 21:15), who had concluded that they had no argument left against His deeds except to "destroy him" (Mark 11:18). Luke adds that "He was teaching[49] daily in the temple" (19:47). Thus for a brief season the Jewish temple became, in the words of Lange,[50] a "theocratical residence" of the Messianic King. And for this brief season, the people of Israel tasted some of the glorious blessing of the Millennial Kingdom: the Messianaic King personally present in His own temple (Mal. 3:1); the Word of the Lord going forth in instruction from Jerusalem (Isa. 2:2-3); the healing hand of the King upon all those suffering physical affliction (Isa. 35:4-6); the greedy shepherds of Israel cast out (Ezek. 34:1-10); the children crying hosannas in the temple (Ps. 8:1-2). These were some of the things the nation might have had without limitation or interruption if she had known the "time" of her "visitation" and the hearts of her people had been opened to receive the King. But this final taste of Messianic authority and compassion and miracle-working power was also the prophecy of a future and better day when Israel, with a contrite heart, will say, "Lo, this is our God; we have waited for him, and he will save us: . . . we have waited for him, we will be glad and rejoice in his salvation" (Isa. 25:9).

Eighth, the *weeping of the King* over His own city and nation should warn the reader against taking too seriously the unrestrained acclamation of the multitudes. For, as He well knew, the rulers were already set against Him and the forces were at work which would soon change the temper of the fickle crowd. And the King knew not only that He would die, but that He *must* die. This is the burden of His word to the Gentiles who came at this juncture, saying, "Sir, we would see Jesus." "Verily, verily, I say unto you," He replies, "Except a corn of wheat fall into the ground and die, it abideth alone: but if it die, it bringeth forth much fruit" (John 12:20-24). Certainly, with His illimitable and resistless power, as already abundantly evidenced, He could have established a kingdom on earth which would have brought unimaginable blessing to the world: the abolition of war, the healing of physical diseases, the correction of social evils, the solution of economic problems. But with all these temporal blessings sinful men would have been left without eternal life; and of all the sons of men, only one, Himself "a Son of man" (John 5:27,

[49] Greek imperfect tense.
[50] *Op. cit.,* p. 377.

ASV), would abide. Without His death on the cross, He could indeed have set up a kingdom, but thus He would abide "alone," the *solitary man* in the glory of an eternal heaven. But if He dies, there can be "much fruit" (John 12:24). He will bring "many sons unto glory" (Heb. 2:10). And thus, at His first coming, a decision was laid *upon man* whether or not he *then* would have a kingdom of righteousness established on earth. Surely, the weeping of the King underscores the reality of man's responsibility. If His rejection was determined of God in the sense of *irresistible divine causation,* if there was no genuine alternative left to Israel, then His tears have no meaning. But His lament shows that, looking at the matter from the standpoint of human responsibility, there was an alternative. The nation should have accepted her King. The historic fact that Israel did not receive Him, however, subtracts nothing from the reality of the offer and the divinely imposed obligation.

That the Apostle John was aware of the theological problem here, is evident from his record of the King's rejection (John 12:37-40). In verse 37 he asserts unqualifiedly the nation's responsibility: "But though he had done so many miracles before them, yet they believed not on him." Then, after quoting Isaiah in proof of God's fore-knowledge of Israel's unbelief, John turns to the side of God's sov-ereign determination: "Therefore they could not believe," he writes, "because that Isaiah said again, He hath blinded their eyes, . . . that they should not see . . . and be converted" (vss. 39-40). Here it should be observed that John does not indicate any philosophic theory by which we may succeed in reconciling the sovereignty of God with the responsibility of men; he simply accepts the two data as facts. And in this respect the Apostle follows the general method of Biblical revelation. This does not mean that we must make no effort to alleviate the intellectual uneasiness caused by the problem; but we may rest assured it will never be wholly solved by finite minds.[51]

Finally, the crucial importance of our Lord's historic triumphal entry into Jerusalem, with reference to Israel's immediate relation to the Mediatorial Kingdom of God, has been set forth in words more worthy than my own:

> In connection with the fate of all Israel, this hour may be named the
> decisive and irrevocable turning point. Assuredly we may, if we look at

[51] "Thus the real cause of Jewish unbelief, foretold by God, is not the divine foreseeing. This cause is, in the last analysis, the moral state of the people them-selves. This state it is which, when once established by the earlier unfaithfulness of Israel, necessarily implies the punishment of unbelief which must strike the people at the decisive moment, the judgment of hardening" (F. Godet, *op. cit.,* p. 235).

the same time at Jesus' words and tears (vss. 41, 42), regard this entry as a carefully prepared last attempt to preserve Israel as a people. Because Jerusalem contents itself today with the fleeting Hosannas, it has drawn upon itself the fulfilment of the judgment that its stones hereafter shall yet cry out: for the entry now gave to all opportunity to show their temper without disguise; the people now did not stand under the influence of the priests; no one's tongue was bound to silence by a command; it was the day which decided whether Jerusalem would become the blessed centre of all nations, or the terrible monument of retributive justice. What would have happened if Jerusalem had considered on this day the things which belonged unto her peace,—this is a question not capable of solution, and therefore also an idle one. Suffice it, since they now remained hidden from her eyes, the die was cast, and after the hen had vainly essayed to gather her brood together, the eagles, forty years after, stretch out not in vain their talons upon the carcass.[52]

8. *Following His triumphal entry, Christ speaks a new series of parables about the Kingdom; and after a final conflict with Israel's rulers, He utters His last lament and judgment over the city of Jerusalem.*

The view of the splendid capital, the knowledge of its crimes, the remembrance of the mercies of God towards it, the certainty that it might have been spared if it had received the prophets and Himself, the knowledge that it was about to put *Him*, their long expected Messiah, to death . . . affected His heart, and the triumphant King and Lord of Zion wept. —*Albert Barnes*[53]

During the brief time of His regal session in the temple, pursuing His ministry of cleansing, and teaching, and healing the sick, the religious rulers of the nation apparently made no attempt forcibly to put a stop to His activities or eject Him from the building (Luke 19:47-48). It is difficult not to feel that this very acquiescence speaks of a supernatural restraint. The best they could do, apparently, was to challenge verbally His authority to do what He had done: "By what authority doest thou these things? and who gave thee this authority?" (Matt. 21:23). His answer was a question of His own: "The baptism of John, whence was it? from heaven, or of men?" Realizing they were caught in a dilemma from which they could not escape, His enemies took refuge in the silence of wilful agnosticism: "We cannot tell," they answered. And Christ dealt with them in kind: "Neither tell I you by what authority I do these things" (Matt. 21:24-27). As a matter of fact, during His public ministry among them, they had often heard His regal claims and had seen a thousand signs of His divine authority. For such men, the time for argument had passed and the hour of judgment was at hand.

[52] J. J. Van Oosterzee, Lange's *Commentary on Luke*, p. 295, paragraph 6.
[53] Albert Barnes, *Notes* (25th ed., rev.; New York: Harper and Bros., 1861), on Luke 19:41-44.

a. *The New Series of Kingdom Parables*

It is significant that at this point our Lord again resorts largely to the parabolic method of teaching. In a new series of parables, at least seven in number, He drives home certain facts concerning His Messianic Kingdom. The first three, directed primarily against the ecclesiastical rulers who had challenged His divine authority (Matt. 21:45), are the parables of the two sons (Matt. 21:28-32), the wicked husbandmen (vss. 33-41), and the king's marriage feast (Matt. 22:1-14). The other four, given to His disciples (Matt. 24:3), were the parables of the budding fig tree (vss. 32-35 ff.), the faithful and unfaithful servants (vss. 43-51), the ten virgins (Matt. 25:1-13), and the talents (vss. 14-30).

It is also noteworthy that, with the possible exception of the first, these parables present a composite picture of the Kingdom as something definitely future, associated with a glorious advent of the King with great power; and that its establishment will be sudden, catastrophic, accompanied with the ordeal of Messianic judgment on the wicked and reward for the faithful.

Furthermore, this same idea, so prominent in the parables, is repeated and underscored in the Lord's direct teaching which immediately follows the series (Matt. 25:31-46). Here He unfolds in detail a picture of that Messianic judgment of living nations on earth which will take place "When the Son of man shall come in his glory" and He shall "sit upon the throne of his glory" (vs. 31). For those who hold to both the inspiration and intelligibility of Scripture, it should be clear that here we have no final judgment of the wicked dead, but a judgment of living nations; a judgment on earth, not in heaven; an assize convened at the beginning of the Millennial Kingdom of God, not at its close (cf. Rev. 20:1-15 and numerous texts already cited from Old Testament prophecy).

In the teaching of Christ, referred to above, there are indeed many details of interest and importance. But for the purposes of this study we need not be concerned with minutiae. The essential point, which cannot be reasonably disputed, is this: the Mediatorial Kingdom of Old Testament prophecy, which was announced in our Lord's early ministry as "at hand," was not established because of Jewish unbelief, and its arrival is now set definitely at the second advent of the King. Furthermore, instead of the fullness of regal blessings promised to the people of Israel, this nation must now suffer a period of judgments for its unbelief.

b. *The Final Conflict with Israel's Rulers*

The first three parables were so manifestly spoken against the rulers of Israel (Matt. 21:45), that spitefully they took counsel at once to "entangle him in his talk" (Matt. 22:15), hoping to create some semblance of a justifiable case against Him. But all the combined shrewdness of Herodians, Pharisees, and Sadducees came to nothing. So impressive and complete was His victory that "when the multitude heard this, they were astonished at his doctrine" (Matt. 22:33). And at this moment our Lord becomes the questioner. Cutting through the trivia and technicalities with which His enemies had been concerned (Matt. 22:17, 28), He drove straight to the very heart of the conflict: the divine character of the Messianic King whom He had claimed to be. His first question was, "What think ye of Christ? whose son is he?" And without hesitation they replied correctly according to the language of Old Testament prophecy, "The son of David" (Matt. 22:42; cf. Jer. 23:5). Then, referring to the 110th Psalm, Christ asks, "How then doth David in spirit call him Lord, saying, The LORD said unto my Lord, Sit thou on my right hand, till I make thine enemies thy footstool?" After this citation from their own Scripture, the Messianic character of which they made no attempt to deny, Christ poses the question which they dared not answer without admitting that God's Messianic King must be both *human* and *divine*: "If David then call him Lord, how is he his son?" After that, Matthew says, "No man was able to answer him a word" (22:41-46). Thus our Lord laid clearly before the rulers of Israel His claim of Messianic Deity, for which He would be put to death (Matt. 26:63-66).

The break with the ruling powers having now become irrevocable, our Lord turns to the "multitude" and His "disciples" for the purpose of publicly scourging the leaders of the nation in language which for severity has no parallel in the gospel records. By far the fullest account of His words on this occasion is found in Matthew (23: 1-36). Without discussing in detail this terrible indictment, a few points should be noted in relation to the Kingdom.

First, His indictment begins, strangely enough, with an unqualified recognition of the governmental authority of His enemies: "The scribes and Pharisees," He acknowledges, "sit in Moses' seat" (vs. 2). The astonishing nature of this admission can only be gauged by recalling that Moses was the first and the greatest of all the mediatorial rulers in the historical Theocratic Kingdom of Israel. Although that

Kingdom had ended with the captivity, and the chosen nation was now under the iron hand of Roman government, yet the shadow of regality still remained in the divine law of which the scribes and Pharisees were the teachers. And our Lord recognized it, even in the present evil leaders of the nation, saying, "All therefore whatsoever they bid you observe, that observe and do" — an acknowledgment which gathers impressiveness in the face of the awful disparity between their words and works, for "they say, and do not" (vs. 3).

Second, without minimizing in any respect the divine authority invested in the rulers of the nation, our Lord reminds the people that in His own person a greater than Moses has come. Therefore, all other authority must be regarded as subordinate to Him: "Neither be ye called masters: for one is your Master, even [the] Christ" (vs. 10). The Greek term *kathēgētai,* used nowhere else in the New Testament, is not the same as in verse 8 where the English word should be "teacher." Since He is "the Christ," He is not only their *teacher*: He is *kathēgētes,* the Leader and Master of Israel.[54]

Third, our Lord puts His finger unerringly upon the decisive character of the leaders' unbelief in relation to the establishment of the "kingdom of heaven." "But woe unto you, scribes and Pharisees, hypocrites! for ye shut up the kingdom of heaven against men: for ye neither go in yourselves, neither suffer ye them that are entering to go in" (vs. 13). While the principle here stated is applicable to all religious leaders in every age, it has peculiar force at this point in New Testament history of the Kingdom. For the unbelieving rejection of her Messianic King by the authorized leaders of Israel — an infection which finally spread throughout the nation — had for the time being effectually shut the door to the Kingdom offered by God through His Son upon earth. "The approaching kingdom of the Messiah is conceived of under the figure of a palace, the doors of which have been thrown open in order that men may enter. But such is the effect of the opposition offered to Christ by the scribes and Pharisees, that men withhold their belief from the Messiah who had appeared among them."[55] Accredited teachers of the nation, schooled in the predictions of the Kingdom by the prophets, fully aware of the miraculous signs which were the credentials of our Lord's Messiahship, these astute and intelligent men had turned their backs upon both the King and His Kingdom and were even then

[54] Cf. Alford's interesting discussion of Matt. 23:8-10, *op. cit.*
[55] H. A. W. Meyer, *op. cit., in loc.*

planning to destroy Him. Such was the awful hypocrisy denounced by our Lord with measured severity.

It must be observed here that, if the teaching of verse 13 were limited to the matter of personal salvation through Christ, it could hardly be true. For in this sense the Pharisees could shut no one out of the Kingdom of God. But they could and did, by their obstinate rejection of the Messianic King, shut both themselves and all the Israel of that generation out of His promised Kingdom, in the sense that its establishment is now, by the course of events, set at a second advent of the King.

Fourth, since the sins of a nation are cumulative like a river in flood moving toward its highest tide, even so the sins of Israel had been moving through the centuries to a consummation in a particular generation and at a particular time. Now at last that time had come, and that "generation" was standing before our Lord. They indeed had built and garnished the tombs of the martyred prophets, but by their actions they were showing themselves to be true "children" of their wayward "fathers" who had "killed the prophets" (vss. 29-31). And the stream of national iniquity was even now moving swiftly to its flood tide, as the leaders counseled together to kill the Messianic Prophet Himself. But even this will not be the end, for after His death and resurrection He will send to the nation other witnesses, and these the leaders of Israel will scourge in their synagogues, persecute from city to city, and kill (vs. 34). As a result, upon that generation of Israel will fall the corporate responsibility for "all the righteous blood shed upon the earth" from Abel to Zacharias (vs. 35). The mention of the place of Zacharias' murder, "between the temple and the altar," gives dreadful emphasis to the crime contemplated by Israel's leaders; for they were about to kill the "Prince of life" (Acts 3:15), who Himself was the Altar of Atonement (Heb. 13:10-12).

"All these things," Christ said, "shall come upon this generation" (Matt. 23:36). The Greek word here must not be taken in the sense of a *race*, but rather of the whole multitude of Israelites *living at the time*.[56] In this temporal sense, it is worthy of notice that the time from the crucifixion to the destruction of Jerusalem covered approximately one generation in length. Meyer rightly speaks of it as the "generation, which was destined to be overtaken by the destruction of Jerusalem. . . ."[57] This prophetic judgment uttered by our Lord

[56] Cf. J. H. Thayer, *Lexicon of the New Testament* (1889).
[57] H. A. W. Meyer, *op. cit., in loc.*

will give special significance to the place of the Kingdom in the Book of Acts which covers substantially this same time area of New Testament history.

The question might here be asked: In what sense could Israel be held responsible for the murder of Abel which took place long before there was any nation of Israel? And the answer of Ellicott has merit: "Men make the guilt of past ages their own, reproduce its atrocities, identify themselves with it; and so, what seems at first an arbitrary decree, visiting upon the children the sins of the fathers, becomes in such cases a righteous judgment." [58] But there is, I feel, a still more specific connection between crimes, such as the murder of Abel, and the responsibility of the generation which rejected the Messianic King. For the establishment of His Kingdom on earth would, according to Old Testament prophecy, put an end to all such crimes of violence and injustice. In that glad day the value of human life will have its long-delayed recognition: The King "shall redeem their soul from deceit and violence: and precious shall their blood be in his sight" (Ps. 72:14). "They shall not hurt nor destroy in all my holy mountain, saith the LORD" (Isa. 65:25). Viewed from this standpoint, Israel's sin in rejecting the Messianic King becomes a gigantic crime against all humanity, the *cause célèbre* of the ages. For it was not only the crimes of the past (Matt. 23:35), but also the crimes of the future (vs. 34), which Christ was now charging against the "generation" which rejected His rule: "All the righteous blood shed upon the earth" (vs. 35). What a fearful responsibility!

c. *The King's Final Lament over Jerusalem*

O Jerusalem, Jerusalem, thou that killest the prophets, and stonest them which are sent unto thee, how often would I have gathered thy children together, even as a hen gathereth her chickens under her wings, and ye would not! Behold, your house is left unto you desolate. For I say unto you, Ye shall not see me henceforth, till ye shall say, Blessed is he that cometh in the name of the Lord
—*Matt. 23:37-39*

In this brief and moving lament our Lord presents in summary the entire history of Israel, past and future, in relation to the Mediatorial Kingdom of God on earth. It is, in fact, a philosophy of all human history. The *God* of history is here, the eternal and incarnate Son, whose hand is always present in the affairs of men: "How often would I," He identifies Himself. The grand *purpose* of history is here: to gather sinners beneath the wings of God. The *tragedy* of history is here in the words: "Ye would not." By reason of the pre-

[58] C. J. Ellicott, *op. cit., in loc.*

cious but perilous gift of freedom, man is able to say No to God. But
the *triumph* of history is also here: for the nation which killed the
Prince of life will some day greet Him as the Blessed One who comes
"in the name of the Lord." But now, viewing the words of Christ in
their more specific and immediate reference to Israel, we shall consider several things.

First, it is no longer only the Pharisees and scribes, but *"Jerusalem"* and her "children," which are the objects of His concern.
This hallowed name not only pointed to the center of the ancient
Theocratic Kingdom in the highest flower of its historic glory, but
was a symbol of the total nation; for, as Lange observes, "All Israelites
were children of Jerusalem." This city which should have been a
blessing to all nations is now designated as the habitual[59] murderess
of the prophets and the stoner of the messengers of God (vs. 37).
And she was about to climax the long history of iniquity with the
murder of her own divine King.

Second, in the words, "How often would I have gathered thy chil
dren together, even as a hen gathereth her chickens under her wings,"
Christ reveals Himself as the God of Israel who, through the centuries of Old Testament history and to that present hour, had striven
for the good of the nation, and through Israel for the ultimate good
of all mankind. Alford agrees that "our Lord's words embrace the
whole time comprised in the historic survey of verse 35."[60]

The beautiful figure of the sheltering wings is often used in the
Old Testament of Jehovah's care: "He shall cover thee with his
feathers and under his wings shalt thou trust" (Ps. 91:4). And the
idea may have been associated with the cherubim of the tabernacle
which covered "the mercy seat with their wings" (Exod. 25:20). It
was there that God as the Protector of Israel was manifested in His
Glory and communed with His people. The ancient Rabbins often
used the figure of a bird's wings to picture the shelter of the Shekinah-Glory. Christ's use of the figure may, therefore, be intended to
remind Israel that He had come to offer once more in His own Person
the protecting divine Glory which had departed from the temple and
city when the Theocratic Kingdom ended with the Babylonian captivity. Lange speaks of the figure as something which "signifies that
He would have taken Jerusalem under the protection of His Messianic glory, if it had turned to Him in time."[61]

---

[59] Both Greek verbs are *present* in tense.
[60] Henry Alford, *op. cit., in loc.*
[61] J. P. Lange, *op. cit., in loc.,* footnote.

Third, the words "Ye would not" bear clear witness to the moral freedom and responsibility of the nation. What they did, in rejecting the King, they were free and bound morally *not* to do. Commenting on the clause, the learned Philip Schaff has said that these words "are important for the doctrine of the freedom and responsibility of man which must not be sacrificed to, but combined with, the opposite, though by no means contradictory doctrine of the absolute sovereignty and eternal decrees of God."[62] And he further quotes with approval the comment of Alford: "The tears of our Lord over the perverseness of Jerusalem are witnesses of the freedom of man's will to resist the grace of God."[62] This means, if words mean anything, that if Israel's rejection of the King was morally genuine, so also must the offer have been. And we must not overlook the tense chosen by our Lord in referring to Israel's decision: it is an *aorist,* showing that the act was regarded as past and done.

Fourth, the judgment of verse 38, "Behold, your house is left unto you desolate," must refer primarily to the *temple,*[63] for the lament of Matthew 23:37-39 is followed immediately by the statement, "And Jesus went out, and departed from the temple" (Matt. 24:1). But we must not exclude the city and the nation itself; for the temple was the center of the theocratic nation. In the historical kingdom the visible presence of Jehovah had been manifested in the temple. And from the precincts of the temple the Shekinah-Glory had gone forth in token of the end of that kingdom (Ezek. 9:3; 11:23). Now once again for a brief season, the Glory of God in the Person of the Messianic King had been present in the temple (Luke 19:47; John 12: 41). But the nation had rejected Him; and as He leaves this temple, it is no longer named "my house" (Matt. 21:13) but "your house" (Matt. 23:38). And by reason of His rejection and withdrawal, Israel's house is left "desolate." With a proper feeling for the historical importance of our Lord's word and action, Lange remarks, "The word marks the moment at which Jesus *leaves the temple,* and leaves it for a sign that it was abandoned by the Spirit of the theocracy."[64] A. T. Robertson speaks of it as "a tragic moment." The desolation, thus inaugurated by our Lord's judicial departure, will reach its dreadful climax in something named by Him "the abomination of desolation" (Matt. 24:15), when the Jewish temple will once more have a regal occupant — this time, Satan's own great pre-

[62] Quoted in Lange's *Commentary, op. cit.,* footnote on Matt. 23:37.
[63] So Calvin, Lange, Ewald, *et al.*
[64] J. P. Lange, *op. cit.,* on Matt. 23:38.

tender and usurper whose presence there will loose upon the nation its most terrible "time of trouble" (Matt. 24:21-22; II Thess. 2:3-4).

Fifth, the darkness of judgment in our Lord's lament is mercifully relieved by the light of divine hope. For the nation which is left "desolate" will some day acclaim the same rejected King with joyous cry, "Blessed is he that cometh in the name of the Lord" (Matt. 23:39). These words cannot refer to any other future time except the second advent of Christ and the conversion of Israel.[65] In this final and "exquisite" utterance of our Lord, therefore, we have the inspired refutation of the modern and popular theory that God is done with the *nation* of Israel. For the day will come when Israel shall "no more be termed Forsaken," and her land shall no more "be termed Desolate" (Isa. 62:4).

But between the Lord's historic abandonment of Israel's "house" and the glad day of His return, there will be an *interval* of time. Two conditions will characterize this interval: first, the Messianic King will be absent — "Ye shall not see me"; and, second, the desolations of Israel will continue without relief — "your house is left unto you desolate." The interval will end with the second advent of Messiah and the conversion of the nation — "till ye shall say, Blessed is he that cometh." In the guarded language of divine inspiration, however, the length of the interval is left wholly indeterminate. But there is no intimation that the end might not come within the lifetime of the generation to which He spoke: "Ye shall not see me . . . till ye shall say. . . ." (Matt. 23:38-39).

> 9. *In His last and longest eschatological discourse, our Lord now unfolds more fully the prophetic program of the end, revealing particularly the parenthesis of time and events which must intervene between His departure and the beginning of the end.*

It is of high significance that our Lord ends His prophetical office, immediately before His last suffering, with such a eschatological discourse. The course which our Savior's teaching has taken during His public life, shows the type of the natural course of development of Christian dogmatics. As He had appeared with the preaching of faith and conversion, so ought at all times the practical questions to come first. But as He did not leave the earth without having also disclosed the secrets of the future, so a Dogmatics which, in reference to the *eschata,* takes an indifferent or sceptical position, is in itself imperfect, and like a mutilated torso. It lies in the nature of the case that Christian eschatology, the more the course of time advances, must become less and less an unimportant appendix, and more and more a *locus primarius* of Christian doctrine. —*J. J. Van Oosterzee*[66]

---

[65] So Alford, Ellicott, *et al.* Stier says, "He who reads not this in the prophets, reads not yet the prophets aright."

[66] J. J. Van Oosterzee, Lange's *Commentary on Luke,* p. 326, paragraph 1.

It was Christ's prediction of judgment upon Israel's temple, doubtless, that aroused in the disciples their intense desire for information as to the nature and duration of this period of Israel's desolation which would end with the second advent of the King and the establishment of His Kingdom. This relationship becomes more impressive if the questions in Matthew 24:1-3 are read in immediate connection with the last three verses of chapter 23. It was in reply to the disciples' questions that our Lord uttered His greatest prophetic discourse. The records of this discourse are contained in chapters 24 and 25 of Matthew, in chapter 13 of Mark, and in chapter 21 of Luke. Although Matthew gives the fullest account, Luke has some highly important material not found in either of the other two Synoptics. In fact, without this material it is impossible for the interpreter to distinguish generally between what has now become history and what is still future.

The disciples' inquiry may be summed up in four questions: First, "When shall these things be?" (Matt. 24:3). Second, "What shall be the sign when these things are about to come to pass?" (Luke 21:7, ASV). Third, "What shall be the sign of thy coming?" (Matt. 24:3). Fourth, "What shall be the sign . . . of the end of the age?" (Matt. 24:3, lit.). The main events under consideration in these questions can be reduced to two: first, *the judgment upon Jerusalem* involving the destruction of the temple; second, *the return of Christ* to consummate the age. The problem of the interpreter now is to identify those portions of the entire discourse which deal with these two grand events respectively. Some have despaired of disentangling the two. Others have referred all to the destruction of the temple, in A.D. 70, making this event the second coming of Christ. The literary clue to this problem is given in the words of Luke 21:12-24, a passage which should be studied in its own context and also in comparison with the accounts of Matthew and Mark.

All three Synoptics begin the discourse similarly. There will come false Christs, wars and rumors of wars; nation shall rise against nation, and kingdom against kingdom; there will be famines and earthquakes. Luke alone adds pestilences, terrors, and signs from heaven (Matt. 24:4-8; Mark 13:5-8; Luke 21:8-11). All three accounts warn that the first appearance of these things does not mean the *end* of the age: the "end" is not "yet," or "immediately" (Luke 21:9, ASV). Matthew and Mark point out that these things are only the "beginning of sorrows" (Matt. 24:8, lit. "birth pangs"). They are the first pangs of a world which must be born anew by the establishment of Messiah's Kingdom (Matt. 19:28), and therefore are true signs of the *end*, not merely of the destruction of Jerusalem and its temple.

It is precisely at this point in our Lord's discourse, however, that Luke records a section which has no exact parallel in the other two Gospels. It is, in fact, a literary parenthesis inserted in Luke's account of coming events. This parenthetical section begins with the words, *"But before all these things"* (21:12, ASV), i.e., the things already referred to which will mark the beginning of the "end." The section ends with the words, *"And Jerusalem shall be trodden down of the Gentiles, until the times of the Gentiles be fulfilled"* (21:24). It should be obvious that in this section of Luke's account we have the answer of Christ to the disciples' question about the judgment of Jerusalem and the temple, for here He speaks especially of the events which will occupy the time from His departure to the destruction of the city in A.D. 70. As for that vast interval of time between A.D. 70 and the arrival of the "end," Christ has no comment except that Jerusalem will continue under the Gentile heel until the end of Gentile world supremacy. And just as Gentile world supremacy began with the end of the Old Testament Theocratic Kingdom, even so, according to the prophets, Gentile supremacy can only end with the restoration of the Kingdom to Israel at the glorious advent of her Messianic King. It is significant that while Luke speaks of desolations and tribulations as precursory to Jerusalem's destruction, he does not put in this connection either "the abomination of desolation" or the unparalleled "great tribulation" mentioned in Matthew and Mark; for *these* terrible experiences belong to the "end," not to the historical destruction of Jerusalem by Titus the Roman. The latter was only a shadow, not the fulfilment, of Christ's words concerning the "end."

If the student will now read the Lukan account, omitting the parenthesis in 21:12-24, it will become clear that verses 11 and 25 join perfectly in subject matter. To exhibit this literary continuity the verses are reproduced as follows: "And great earthquakes shall be in divers places, and famines, and pestilences; and fearful sights and great signs shall there be from heaven. . . . And there shall be signs in the sun, and in the moon, and in the stars; and upon the earth distress of nations, with perplexity; the sea and the waves roaring"; etc.

In summary, it may be said that all three Synoptics record the teaching of Christ about His second coming and the end of the age, but only Luke clearly identifies and records separately what Christ said specifically regarding the judgment about to fall upon Jerusalem in A.D. 70. This means that in Luke we have an account of signs which point to two different things respectively: first, the now historic destruction of Jerusalem, and, second, the future arrival of the "end." The attempts of harmonists to force a conformity between the material in Luke 21:12-24 and the material in Matthew and Mark, are based on similarity of language rather than that of subject matter; e.g., the warning to flee from Judaea into the mountains (Matt. 24:16; Mark 13:14; Luke 21:21). But this would be sound advice in any threatened siege of Jerusalem, whether in A.D. 70 or at the end of the age. Furthermore, it must not be overlooked that only Luke gives the panoramic reference to the "times of the Gentiles" which are conterminous with the subjection of Jerusalem to Gentile power. This should not be surprising, for careful students have noted that, of the three Synoptic writers, Luke (a Gentile) has the more universal outlook. And since divine inspiration is not a mechanical thing, but always chooses or fits the writer for his peculiar task, it is altogether appropriate that Luke should have noticed and recorded (as a parenthesis, both grammatical and chronological) the prophecy of our Lord which clearly anticipates the present Gentile age.

We must be careful, however, not to read into the words of Christ any hard and fast chronological scheme. For, in conformity with the general method of predictive prophecy, our Lord pictured together future events which would be outrolled separately in their historical fulfilment. This method is not something wholly arbitrary but has a gracious purpose. Within certain limits, it leaves room in history for the interplay of both divine sovereignty and human freedom. The future event is always certain, but the time element (with certain important exceptions) has elasticity. This is particularly true of the present church age. Thus, it should not be surprising to find interpreters confusing the destruction of Jerusalem with the end of the age. For, viewed from the standpoint of Jewish opportunity and responsibility, the siege of Jerusalem in A.D. 70 might have led directly to the end of the age, as we shall see in considering the history of the Book of Acts. This divinely ordained elasticity of time is the rock upon which, fortunately, all rigid chronological charts of *the present age* have been wrecked. But at the same time it has left open the door for Israel's access to divine forgiveness, and also for the Church's hope of the imminent coming of the Lord.

It has already been shown above that, once Israel had made her fateful decision against the Messianic offer, the arrival of the King- dom is set at the second and glorious advent of Christ. Therefore, as might be expected, our Lord's prediction of things to come reached its climax in His regal "coming in the clouds of heaven with power and great glory" (Matt. 24:30; Mark 13:26). Furthermore, the events of the endtime will not be interminably drawn out. Once they begin, the same "generation" of men will see their full accomplishment. "When ye see these things coming to pass. . . . This generation[67] shall not pass away, until all these things be accomplished" (Mark 13:29-30, ASV).

All three Synoptics unite in their testimony regarding the glorious advent of the "Son of man" as the climax of the end (Matt. 24:30; Mark 13:26; Luke 21:27); with the implication, of course, that the arrival of the King will bring the Kingdom. And Luke is careful to name specifically the "kingdom of God" in connection with the events of the end: "when ye see these things come to pass, know ye that the kingdom of God is nigh at hand" (21:31). In the parallel passages, Matthew (24:33) and Mark (13:29) write, "know that it is near, even at the doors." The subject of the verb here probably should be "He" instead of "it" (cf. ASV). But the dif- ference is of small consequence, since all prophecy agrees that it is the *glorious* coming of the King which will bring the Kingdom. The main point has to do with the futurity of the Kingdom and its coincidence in time with the glorious advent of Christ. How this point could be made clearer than in the words of Christ Him- self, as recorded by Luke 21:31, it is impossible to imagine. There is not much said by the commentators here about the meaning of the words, "The kingdom of God is nigh at hand." One writer dismisses the matter with this brief comment: "The consumma- tion of the kingdom is here meant, not the beginning." [68] But that

---

[67] Lange says, "*This generation* means the generation of those who know and discern these signs" (*op. cit.,* on Matthew 24:34).

[68] A. T. Robertson, *Word Pictures in New Testament,* 1930, *in loc.* The same writer inconsistently says that Mark 1:15, where substantially the same expression of *nearness* occurs, means the "arrival" of the Kingdom! To make such an expres- sion mean *beginning* in one place and *end* in another place, seems to indicate exe- gesis determined by theological prejudice.

is not what Luke wrote. It is not the Kingdom but the present age which will be consummated at the second advent of Christ. At that time the age of Gentile misrule will end, being supplanted by the glorious and perfect rule of our Lord Jesus Christ. The near at hand Kingdom, referred to in Luke 21:31, can be nothing but the inauguration of the *regnum gloriae* of the long-rejected Messiah of Israel.

Another distinctive feature of the Lukan account appears in 21:28: "And when these things begin to come to pass, then look up, and lift up your heads; for your redemption draweth nigh." For this passage, it is generally agreed, there is absolutely no parallel in either Matthew or Mark. Evidently in Luke 21:28 we have something different, both in subject matter and time, from verse 31, which does have a parallel in both Matthew 24:33 and Mark 13:29. This is a distinction of great importance. Luke 21:28 refers to the *beginning* of the signs predicted by our Lord; and in Luke these include signs both of the historic destruction of Jerusalem and also the end. But Luke 21:31 refers to their *completion,* as indicated clearly by its parallel in Matthew: "when ye shall see *all* these things" (24:33, italics supplied). Furthermore, there is a difference between the events signified: when the signs *"begin,"* the disciples are to "look up" because their "redemption draweth nigh" (Luke 21:28). But when *"all"* the signs have been seen, they are to understand that "the kingdom of God is nigh" (Luke 21:31; cf. Matt. 24:33).

Now the "redemption" of Luke 21:28 is not a synonym for the "kingdom of God," but refers to a very specific thing in connection with individual salvation. The Greek term is *apolutrosis* which occurs ten times in the New Testament; and, with the exception of Hebrews 11:35, always refers to personal Christian redemption. Sometimes it stands for a *present* redemption of the soul from sin (Rom. 3:24; Eph. 1:7); but in other places it describes a *future* redemption of the Christian's *body*. In this narrower sense, Paul says, we are "waiting for the adoption, to wit, the redemption of our body" (Rom. 8:23; cf. also Eph. 4:30). Now the "redemption" of Luke 21:28 cannot refer to the salvation of the soul from sin, for the men addressed were certainly already saved. It must therefore be a reference to the redemption of the "body," a doctrine which will be more fully developed in later New Testament writings.

This means that our Lord, in the record of Luke, distinguishes in time between the redemption of the Christian's body and the arrival of the Kingdom of God. Furthermore, He puts the "redemption" *first* as an event to be looked for from the moment that "the things" catalogued by Luke "begin" to come to pass (21:28). Now the very first of "these things" are described in Luke 21:12, "they shall lay hands on you, and persecute you, delivering you up to the synagogues, and into prisons, being brought before kings and rulers for my name's sake." And in the Book of Acts, also written by Luke, we have indisputably his historical record of the *beginning* of the things foretold by Christ. As the disciples began their post-Pentecostal testimony to the people of Israel, Luke writes, the rulers "laid hands on them, and put them in hold" (Acts 4:1-3). Thus, the language of the prediction and that of the beginning of its fulfilment are almost identical; and since both were recorded by Luke, it would be strange if he had not been wholly aware of this correspondence. At any rate, it is impossible to deny that Luke's historical account affirms that the things predicted by the Lord did "begin" almost immediately following the day of Pentecost.

The foregoing facts lead to certain highly important conclusions in the field of New Testament eschatology. First, the Kingdom will not arrive until men have witnessed *all* the signs described by our Lord. But, second, true believers may legitimately look for the "redemption" of their bodies at any time after the *beginning* of these things. Thus in Luke's account of our Lord's final prophetic discourse we have an intimation of the later Pauline eschatological order of events: first, a rapture of believers; second, a period of world-wide tribulation and judgment; third, the glorious appearing of Messiah; and, finally, the arrival of the Kingdom.

Furthermore, in Luke's account of Christ's words, a firm foundation was laid for the constant upward look on the part of the Church for the Lord's coming to redeem the bodies of His saints. And this is a very important consideration, both theologically and practically. Without this there could have been no blessed hope for the Church and her losses involved would have been incalculable. As Edersheim reminds us: "The peculiar attitude of the Church: with loins girt for work, since the time was short, and the Lord might come at any moment; with her hands busy; her mind faithful; her bearing self-denying and devoted; her heart full of loving expectancy; her face upturned toward the Sun that was so soon to rise; and her straining to catch the first notes of heaven's song of triumph — all this would have been lost." [69]

To summarize the chief points in the above discussion: the Kingdom will not come until *all* the things predicted by our Lord have come to pass; but the members of the Church, the royal family in the future Kingdom, could look for the "redemption" of their bodies at any moment after these things *began* to come to pass.

10. *The last hours of the King's ministry before His death are spent in intimate and loving fellowship with His disciples, during which He prepares them for the interval of His absence and the interregnum.*

> We enter now on a new section of our Gospel: the last communications of the Lord to His disciples, closing with His heart opened out to the Father about them. The entire drift is in all points and ways to lead His own into a true spiritual understanding of their new place before God the Father, in consequent contrast with that of Israel in the world . . . . He was going to His Father on high, and here reveals what He in that glory would do for them while here below . . . .   —*William Kelly*[70]

This final ministry was fulfilled in three events: first, the last supper; second, the farewell discourse; and, third, the final prayer — all restricted to His disciples alone.

a. The Last Supper with the Disciples

Whether or not this last supper was the Jewish Passover has been a matter of controversy in the Church since the latter part of the second century. If the meal mentioned by the Synoptics is the one described in John 13 (as many competent authorities hold),[71] then I agree with Alford's dictum regarding the latter: "It was not the ordinary passover of the Jews" because John's record "absolutely excludes such a supposition."[72] Furthermore, in what Bengel and Bruce call "the Prelude" to the last supper, recorded by Luke alone (22:14-18), Christ specifically mentions the Jewish Passover which was at hand and declares He will not eat it: "With desire I have desired to eat this passover with you before I suffer; for I say unto you, I shall not eat it,[73] until it be fulfilled in the kingdom of God"

---

[69] Alfred Edersheim, *op. cit.,* Vol. II, p. 451.

[70] William Kelly, *An Exposition of the Gospel of John* (2nd ed.; London: Alfred Holness, 1908), p. 263.

[71] A. T. Robertson, *Harmony of the Gospels* (New York: Geo. H. Doran, 1922), pp. 279-284.

[72] Henry Alford, *op. cit.,* on Matt. 26:17-19: See also Marcus Dods, *Expositors Bible* (New York: Geo. H. Doran, no date), Vol. II, p. 75 on John 13:1-17.

[73] ASV evidently omits *ouketi* from the Greek text, following Mss., Aleph, A, B, and L.

(vss. 15-16, ASV). But He certainly did eat a last supper, at which several things took place which are of significance in relation to the Kingdom.

First, at the last supper our Lord shows that the Kingdom was on His mind by the fact that He mentions it at least five times; twice during the prelude to the supper, and three times during the supper. The passages are as follows:

Luke 22:16 (ASV) — "I shall not eat it, until it be fulfilled in the kingdom of God."

Luke 22:18 — "I will not drink of the fruit of the vine, until the kingdom of God shall come."

Mark 14:25 — "I will drink no more of the fruit of the vine, until that day that I drink it new in the kingdom of God" (cf. the parallel in Matt. 26:29).

Luke 22:29 — "And I appoint unto you a kingdom, as my Father hath appointed unto me."

Luke 22:30 — "That ye may eat and drink at my table in my kingdom, and sit on thrones judging the twelve tribes of Israel."

Second, it is clear that all of these references place this Kingdom in the *future*. As to the *when* in the future, this question should be determined by the context which indicates that Christ had His eye upon that future day when His disciples would be enthroned with Him in glory, sitting at the table of good things in His future Kingdom,[74] and ruling over the twelve tribes of a restored Israel (Luke 22:30). Nothing short of this day can fulfill the total meaning of the above references to a coming Kingdom.

Third, it was at the last supper that our Lord instituted the eucharistic emblems of His atoning death (Luke 22:19-20); and Paul puts the communion of the bread and the cup definitely in the category of things to be observed by the Church during the interval between His death and His second coming: "For as often as ye eat this bread, and drink this cup, ye do shew the Lord's death till he come" (I Cor. 11:26). This emblematic service had a prophetic import, as Schaff has said: "It is also a foretaste and anticipation of the great Marriage Supper of the Lamb which He has prepared for His Church at His last advent, when all eucharistic controversies will cease forever."[75] And, as we have already shown,

[74] Alford finds the fulfilment of both verses 16 and 30 in the future "Marriage supper of the Lamb" (*op. cit.*, on Luke 22:16).
[75] In Lange's *Commentary*, *op. cit.*, on Matt. 26:29.

the coming of the Kingdom is set at the second coming of the Messianic King.

Fourth, it is only in the light of the promised enthronement of the disciples in a future Kingdom that we can understand the contention which arose at the last supper as to which of them should be the greatest (Luke 22:24). In the order of events, Robertson connects Luke 22:16 directly with verses 24-30.[76] Thus, our Lord's first mention of the "kingdom of God" became the immediate occasion for the "strife." In dealing with this disgraceful strife, Christ subtracts nothing from His earlier teaching about the Kingdom but rather reaffirms both its reality and the regal position of His own disciples within it (vss. 29-30). But He rebukes them for not seeing that distinctions of rank will be based on willingness to serve and suffer. In the aristocracy of the coming Kingdom there will be no place for self-seeking; but its pattern will be the King Himself who was among them as one who served (vss. 25-28).

Fifth, it was during the last supper that the Lord, in a striking passage recorded by Luke alone (22:35-36), sought to prepare His disciples for the changed conditions which would obtain between His departure and His return to establish the Kingdom. He begins by reminding them of the special care bestowed on them during their earlier ministry of proclaiming the Kingdom of heaven as at hand. "When I sent you without purse, and scrip, and shoes, lacked ye anything? And they said, Nothing" (vs. 35). Indeed, they told the truth! During the presence of the Messianic King, the disciples had surely tasted the "powers of the age to come" (Heb. 6:5, lit.), so far as physical blessing had been concerned. There is no record of any illness among them. For friends and relatives, healing was available without reserve (Matt. 8:14-16). Even death itself was no longer irreversible (Mark 5:35-43; John 11:1-47). If food and drink were lacking, the miracle-working power of the King was sufficient for the emergency (John 2:1-11; 6:1-15). For His disciples and Himself there was a supernatural immunity to the ordinary hazards of life (Matt. 14:24-33;Luke 4:28-30). Even such mundane things, as a need for tax money and the means of daily livelihood, were not beyond His interest and power (Matt. 17:24-27; Luke 5:2-9). By no process of "spiritualization" can these things be robbed of their physical reality.

So much for the past. "But now," Christ warns, things will be

---

[76] A. T. Robertson, *op. cit.*, p. 190.

different; "he that hath a purse, let him take it, and likewise a wallet; and he that hath none, let him sell his cloak, and buy a sword" (Luke 22:36, ASV). These are radical words from the lips of Christ, suggesting a radical change of conditions just at hand, and too little attention has been paid to their signification. What He had formerly commanded them *not* to take (Matt. 10:9-10), He now commands them to take! With an accurate sense of what was about to take place, Van Oosterzee has described the change between the past and the future:

> Then they had in no respect had want, no care had oppressed them; but now it was another time. So unacquainted are they as yet with that which tonight impends, that the Savior can bring to them in no other way a presentiment of it than by holding up to them the sharp contrast of *then* and *now*. He enjoins on them the direct opposite of that which He had then commanded them. Once the least care was superfluous, now the most anxious care was not too much.[77]

What our Lord here enjoins upon His disciples is simply the *duty of self-preservation* as the need may arise under the new conditions. They must now give thought to two things: first, the physical requirements of life, as indicated by a "purse" for money, and the "wallet"[78] for provisions; and, second, some measure of defense against external physical dangers, as indicated by the "sword." This certainly is no warrant for any disciple to devote his life exclusively to the accumulation of physical wealth, any more than to devote his life thus to military pursuits. As a matter of fact, where government exists, as Paul reminds us, the State takes charge of the "sword" (Rom. 13:4), so that the Christian is not left to defend himself. But where such protection does not exist the disciple is not to throw away his life recklessly and uselessly.

The changed situation would not mean a *sudden* end of all miracles. The Book of Acts will record many instances of great intrusions of divine power. The different ages of God's dealings with men are not always sharply divided with no transitional stage. But the announcement of Christ did mean, as we shall find, that the period of great *public* miracles would gradually close; that physical miracles of any sort would eventually become the *exception* rather than the rule; and that even these exceptional miracles would generally be hidden from an unbelieving world behind the veil of God's *providential* working. What needs to be emphasized, however, is that these conditions are not descriptive of the final age of human

---

[77] In Lange's *Commentary, op. cit.,* on Luke 22:36.
[78] Robertson calls it a "traveling or bread bag" (*Word Pictures in New Testament,* on Matt. 10:10).

history, but belong only to the *interim* before the coming of the Kingdom age.

Sixth, the words of Christ regarding Judas raise the theological problem of divine sovereignty versus human responsibility in relation to the Kingdom: "truly the Son of man goeth, as it was determined: but woe unto that man by whom he is betrayed" (Luke 22:22). The rejection of the regal "Son of man" and His Kingdom was no *chance* incident in the history of the world, for this matter was part of the counsels of the Eternal One. On the other hand, what Judas did in conspiracy with the leaders of Israel was something which morally the conspirators *ought not* to have done, and for which therefore they will be held personally responsible before the bar of God. Our Lord's terrible words, "good were it for that man if he had never been born" (Mark 14:21), underline this responsibility. But if the moral responsibility for rejecting the Messiah and His Kingdom was genuine, then so also the divine offer must have been genuine. To ignore these facts may allay somewhat our intellectual uneasiness, but we cannot thus be true to the reality of Biblical history.

b. The Farewell Discourse to the Disciples

The record of this discourse is found only in the Gospel of John. It begins at 13:31, immediately following the departure of Judas; and it continues through to the end of chapter 16, interrupted only by an occasional question from the disciples (cf. 13:36; 14:5, 8, 22; 16:17). The connection in thought between the final verses of chapter 13 and the opening verses of chapter 14 is too close to be ignored. As Godet has pointed out, "The division of the chapters here is very faulty."[79] The lofty language with which the Lord begins in 13:31 sets the tone of the entire discourse: "when he [Judas] was gone out, Jesus said, Now is the Son of man glorified, and God is glorified in him." It is interesting, and very precious, that this farewell discourse was spoken *only* to the Eleven. For what our Lord was about to say, both in the discourse and in the prayer which followed it, was intended for the ears of the saved alone. The discourse was probably spoken in the Upper Room.[80]

Although during the supper the Kingdom had been mentioned specifically at least five times, there is no reference at all to it in the much longer record of the farewell discourse which followed.

---

[79] F. Godet, *Commentary on John, in loc.*
[80] So Andrews, Meyer, Stier, Alford, Ellicott, *et al.*

This omission would be very strange if, as some claim, our present age is the period of the Messianic Kingdom. But if in His discourse to the Eleven He was preparing all His disciples for an *interim* between His departure and His return to establish the Kingdom, then His silence as to the latter becomes understandable. And this undoubtedly was the main purpose of the discourse.

The discourse begins with a clear reference to the period of time for which the Lord's instruction was particularly intended; and He mentions the specific events with which the period would begin and end (John 13:31-14:3). In general, it will be a period of time characterized by the *bodily absence* of the Messianic King, a prospect which already was troubling the hearts of the disciples. The period therefore will begin with His *departure*: "Little children, yet a little while I am with you," He said to them, and "I go to prepare a place for you" (John 13:33; 14:2). And the period will end with His *return*: "I will come again, and receive you unto myself; that where I am, there ye may be also" (John 14:3).

Now with reference to the Lord's promise to "come again," several things should be noticed. First, this coming will be a *bodily* return: the contrasting statements are, "If I go . . . I will come again," and they are tied together in the same context. If His departure was in bodily form, so also must be His return. This coming, therefore, must not be confused with the spiritual coming referred to later in the discourse (cf. 14:23). Second, the Lord's action described here in connection with His coming has to do only with those believers who live during the interval of His bodily absence. Subsequently there will be other great actions culminating in the establishment of His Kingdom over all nations. For the *parousia* of our Lord will cover a period of time and include a whole series of events.[81] The first of His acts will be the removal of the Church of the present age from the earth, an event which Paul will later describe in detail (I Thess. 4:13-18). Third, viewed from this standpoint, the second coming of the Lord is always an *impending* event. The tense of the verb rendered, "I will come," is a "futuristic present middle" which refers to "the second coming of Christ." [82] And the present tense here "indicates imminence," as Godet admits, though he misinterprets the passage.[83] Since

---

[81] Although he applies it too broadly at times, Alford has stated the *principle* correctly: "The coming again of the Lord is not one single act" (*op. cit.*, on John 14:3).
[82] A. T. Robertson, *Word Pictures in New Testament, in loc.*
[83] F. Godet, *op. cit., in loc.*

throughout the New Testament the saved of the present age are urged to an attitude of constant expectancy, it is only logical to find that the very first act in the Lord's *parousia* will concern *them*.

The main part of the farewell discourse is devoted to the life and activities of His disciples during the interval of time between His departure and His return. The outstanding features of this interval, the present age of His *ekklēsia* (Matt. 16:18), are described as follows:

First, the interval of His bodily absence will be a period when He will *manifest Himself* to His own in a spiritual way: "I will not leave you comfortless," He promises, "I will come to you" (John 14:18). That this coming is wholly spiritual in nature is clear from the explanation which follows. After the world can no longer see Him, the disciples will continue to see Him (vs. 19). In answer to the natural question of the disciples, "How is it that thou wilt manifest thyself unto us, and not unto the world?", He explains that this manifestation will be related to the Word of God: "If a man love me, he will keep my words; and my Father will love him, and we will come unto him, and make our abode with him" (vss. 22-23). This spiritual manifestation of Christ has been continuously accessible to all who hear His voice: "if any man hear my voice, and open the door, I will come in to him, and will sup with him, and he with me" (Rev. 3:20). During the entire age of His bodily absence, for those who obey His words, the promise holds good: "lo, I am with you alway, even unto the end of the age" (Matt. 28:20, lit.).

Second, the period of Christ's bodily absence will be a time of *special ministry by the Holy Spirit.* The large place given the Holy Spirit in Christ's farewell discourse has often been noted by students of the Word of God. In answer to our Lord's prayer, He will come to the disciples and abide forever with and in them (John 14:16-17). He will be their teacher, bringing to their remembrance the words of the absent Christ (vs. 26). He will testify of Christ (15:26), convicting the world of sin, righteousness, and judgment (16:8-11). He will speak to the eleven disciples of things which, before Christ's departure, they were not yet ready to hear; and also reveal "things to come" (vss. 12-14). The primary application of these promises was certainly fulfilled in the Spirit's guidance of those who would write the Scriptures of the New Testament, but the promise of His ministry is applicable to all believers of the present age during the absence of Christ. This does not mean, as some have wrongly assumed, that there could be no such ministry of the Spirit while Christ is once again bodily present on earth. This false notion has been wrongly based on the words, "If I go not away, the Comforter will not come" (John 16:7). But the first clause here refers to the *whole* of Christ's path back to the Father — His death, resurrection, and ascension. Without all this, the present special ministry of the Spirit in the Church would have been impossible. On the basis of Christ's finished work, the Spirit's ministry becomes possible, not only in the age of Christ's absence, but also during His bodily presence in the coming age of the Kingdom.

Third, the period of Christ's bodily absence is to be *a time of witnessing and fruit-bearing* by the disciples. "Ye also shall bear witness," He says, "because ye have been with me from the beginning" (John 15:27). The great convicting work of the Holy Spirit in the world will be wrought through those who believe: for this purpose, Christ said, "I will send him unto you" (John 16:7 with vss. 8-11). For this ministry, the disciples must be united spiritually with Christ, taught, guided, shown the things of Christ, and informed as to things to come. The result of this union and instruction by the Holy Spirit will be a life of fruit-bearing, as indicated in the beautiful parabolic section on the vine and the branches (15:1-8). The heart and summary of the matter is set forth in verse 16: "Ye have not chosen me, but I have chosen you, and ordained you, that ye should go and bring forth fruit, and that your fruit should remain." And this fruit-bearing ministry is connected with prayer: "that whatsoever ye shall ask of the Father in my name, he may give it you."

Fourth, we are not to forget that this period of Christ's absence, so glorious in many respects, is also *a time of humiliation, persecution, and suffering.* If the world hates them, the Lord's people are not to think it strange: "ye know that it hated me before it hated you." It is because they belong to Him and are "not of the world" that the world will hate them (John 15:18-19). When they are expelled from their places of worship, even put to death as an act of religious piety, they are not to let such experiences cause them to stumble, since they have been warned in advance (John 16:1-4). These things will not be easy to bear: they will often be weeping while the world rejoices; but eventually their sorrow shall be turned into joy (vss. 20-23), a possible reference to that coming "day" of the Church's deliverance at the Lord's coming.[84] All that He has said, therefore, is intended to give them His "peace" in the midst of suffering. And His final word is very comforting: "In the world ye shall have tribulation; but be of good cheer; I have overcome the world" (vs. 33).

How the tribulation and sufferings of "the present time" (Rom. 8:18) can be reconciled with the popular theory of a *present* reign of Christ with His saints, in a Messianic Kingdom allegedly established on earth at His first advent, is one of the mysteries of theological opinion.

c. The Final Prayer for the Disciples

This wonderful prayer occupies the whole of the 17th chapter of John's Gospel, a passage which has rightly been called the "Holy of Holies" of the Scriptures. Uttered immediately after His farewell discourse (cf. 16:33 with 17:1), it forms the high climax of our Lord's loving preparation of His own for the period of His absence from them. In this record we have the very door of heaven opened, as it were, and we hear a sample of that mediatorial intercession for us which is now being made without ceasing by the Eternal Son at His Father's Throne above. "Beyond that welcome door I know (and, oh, for more why should I care?) . . . Jesus is there." [85] An exposition of the prayer does not fall within the purview of this volume, but several things about it should be noticed which suggest that our present age is not the age of the Kingdom.

First, it is a prayer which is suited particularly to the present period of *Christ's absence*. Speaking of those given Him by the Father, He says, "While I was with them in the world, I kept them" (vs. 12). But a change is at hand: "now I am no more in the world." And so during the period of His absence, He commits them to the Father's care: "Holy Father, keep through thine own name those whom thou hast given me" (vs. 11). There is indicated here no bodily presence of Christ, such as will obtain in His future Kingdom.

Second, the prayer contemplates the disciples living in a *hostile world*, the objects of hatred because of their testimony and separated life: "I have given them thy word; and the world hath hated them, because they are not of the world, even as I am not of the world" (vs. 14). In these words we have a perfect description of the pres-

---

[84] So Henry Alford, *in loc.*
[85] For the complete poem, see *The High Priestly Prayer* by H. C. G. Moule (2nd impression; London: Religious Tract Society, 1908), pp. 221-222.

ent age of the Christian witness against the world, but utterly inappropriate if applied to that future glorious age when all nations will be enjoying the incomparable benefits of the reign of the Son of man with His glorified Bride.

Third, the prayer contemplates the disciples living and working in the environment of *the kingdom of Satan*. Hence, the petition of verse 15, "I pray not that thou shouldest take them from the world, but that thou shouldest keep them from the evil one" (ASV). It is not merely from "evil" in the abstract, that they are to be kept, but from that great "evil one"[86] himself, who is the "god of this age" (II Cor. 4:4, lit.) and the "prince of this world" (John 12:31). The whole world, in which the disciples must live, "lieth in the evil one" (I John 5:19, ASV). They may indeed feel his blows, but they are to be "preserved outside the awful circle of his spell and power."[87] Contrast this situation with that of the coming Kingdom: *Now* the disciples are kept from the evil one; *then* the evil one will be kept from them, and also from the whole world of nations for the duration of His Messianic reign (Rev. 20:1-6). With the saints glorified and ruling with Christ, with Satan bound and imprisoned, the need for the petition of John 17:15 will be happily past.

Fourth, while there is a sense in which the mediating work of the Son extends both backward and forward in the ages of time, the language here suggests that this prayer belongs primarily to *the Church of the present age,* the body and bride of Christ. No less than five times He prays for the *one-ness* of all who believe: "that they may be one, as we are" (vs. 11); "That they all may be one; as thou, Father, art in me, and I in thee" (vs. 21); "that they also may be one in us" (vs. 21); "that they may be one, even as we are one" (vs. 22); "that they may be made perfect in one" (vs. 23). This is no prayer for external church union, however desirable that may be to some. It is rather a prayer for the union of the disciples through the gift of a common spiritual life. And the prayer was answered on the Day of Pentecost when the Holy Spirit became that indwelling life of the Church, binding together the members of the body — "even as we are one," the Son says to the Father (vs. 22). There were people saved before Pentecost, and there will be multitudes saved after the Body of Christ is completed at His coming;

---

[86] So Meyer, Alford, Lange, *et al.* Vincent says, "This rendering is according to John's usage. See I John 2:13-14; 3:12; 5:18-19" (*op. cit., in loc.*).
[87] H. C. G. Moule, *op. cit.,* p. 141.

but the Church of the present age is a unique body in its glory and dignity and regal prerogatives.

Fifth, there is clearly an *exclusive* aspect to the intercessory prayer of Christ: "I pray not for the world," He says, "but for them which thou hast given me" (vs. 9). The prayer is striking for its omissions. Beyond the "world" in general which He specifically shuts out, there is no mention of the nation of Israel, nor of the Gentile nations, nor of the poor and afflicted, nor of the thousand and one heartbreaking problems of humanity with which the Messianic Kingdom of our Lord will be concerned. The prayer is wholly concerned with the preparation of a body which is to reign with Him in that future blessed Kingdom. For its members He prays: that they may behold the glory of the Son (vs. 24); that they may share in this glory (vs. 22); and that they may be with Him where He is (vs. 24).

> 11. *During the final indignities of the trials and crucifixion, our Lord with great clarity renews the regal claims of the Messianic office.*
>
> "So *Thou* art a king?" questions Pilate with ironical emphasis. "Thou sayest it," answers Jesus, with the accent of sublime self-assurance. And in the face of the *su* He emphasizes the *ego*. Not only, however, does *hoti* recognize the utterance of Pilate—it likewise acknowledges the correctness of his deduction; from the kingdom of Jesus thou rightly inferrest His kingly dignity, says Jesus. Hence we represent *hoti* by *yea*. —*John Peter Lange*[88]

One of the most striking facts about the career of our Lord upon earth is that during the death trials He continued calmly to press, more clearly than ever before, His claim to be the Mediatorial King of Old Testament prophecy. Before the Sanhedrin, before Pilate, His testimony is unwavering.

Consider, first, His examination by the Sanhedrin, where the charge was primarily *religious* in nature. Angered by His silence under accusation by false witnesses, the high priest placed Him under a solemn oath to answer whether or not He was "the Christ, the Son of God" (Matt. 26:63). While the law of the formal oath (Lev. 5:1) doubtless required our Lord to break His silence, there was something at issue greater than this, which was His identity as the Mediatorial King of Old Testament prophecy. And thus His answer to the high priest becomes memorable: *"Thou hast said"* (Matt. 26:64). This was not an evasion, as the ordinary English reader might suppose, but definitely "a Greek affirmative,"

---

[88] J. P. Lange, *op. cit.*, on John 18:37.

as A. T. Robertson has well said. Mark records it simply, *"I am"* (14:62). But the simple affirmation was not enough at a time like this. What is the evidence that His affirmation is true? It is found in what follows: "Hereafter shall ye see the Son of man sitting on the right hand of [the] power, and coming in the clouds of heaven" (Matt. 26:64). The unmistakable reference here was to a pair of the greatest Kingdom prophecies of the Old Testament, Psalm 110:1 and Daniel 7:13; and Christ applied them to Himself. Bruce has paraphrased in striking fashion the answer of the Lord to His Sanhedrin judges: "The time is coming when you and I shall change places; I then the Judge; you the prisoners at the bar." [89] The high priest, better schooled than some theologians, understood His regal claim, rent his clothing judicially, and called upon his fellow judges to pronounce Him "guilty of death" (Matt. 26:66). The action of the great Jewish Council, dramatic as it seemed under the circumstances, was only a tardy *judicial* ratification of a tragic decision which had already become a fact of history.

Let us come now to the examination before Pilate, the Roman governor. The charge here was *political,* and was so intended by the Jews who made it: "We found this fellow perverting the nation, and forbidding to give tribute to Caesar, saying that he himself is Christ a King" (Luke 23:2). Now, however contemptuous Pilate may have been toward the technicalities of Jewish religion, he could not ignore the political charge. Knowing this, the Jewish leaders were not slow to press their advantage: "If thou let this man go, thou art not Caesar's friend; whosoever maketh himself a king speaketh against Caesar" (John 19:12). There are some interpreters who argue that this charge was a *total* misrepresentation of the true nature of the Messianic Kingdom, and that our Lord's answer to Pilate proves that His Kingdom was wholly a "spiritual" matter, having no political or material implications whatsoever. It is passing strange that men have not seen the utter folly of trying to erect an adequate definition of our Lord's Kingdom based in large part on a brief conversation between Him and a cynical Roman governor who knew nothing about the Kingdom of God, and cared less.[90] But what are the facts? In the record

[89] A. B. Bruce, *Expositors Greek New Testament,* ed. *W. R. Nicoll* (London: Hodder and Stoughton, 1917), Vol. I. p. 320.

[90] The comment of E. R. Craven is to the point: Such a misinterpretation "supposes that our Lord whispered into the ear of a heathen . . . the great truth concerning His kingdom, which He had . . . *concealed* from His disciples . . . !" (In Lange's *Commentary, op. cit., Revelation of John,* p. 100).

of John's Gospel, the examination consists of three questions by Pilate and three responses on the part of Christ (18:33-38).

The first question was, "Art thou the King of the Jews?" (vs. 33). Our Lord's reply to this is a question of his own: "Sayest thou this thing of thyself, or did others tell it thee of me?" (vs. 34). The purpose of this question was not to gain information — Christ certainly knew the identity of His accusers — but rather by this means to clarify the exact meaning of Pilate's inquiry so that it could be answered intelligibly. If the source of the charge was Pilate, then it would be entirely *political* and nothing more. In that case the Lord's answer would be, No, I am not a king in that narrow sense of the term. But on the other hand, if Pilate is voicing a charge made by "others," that is, by the Jewish people, then the question is wholly different and must be answered differently. A charge of regal claims on the part of Jesus, if originated by the Jewish leaders, would carry with it all the implications of the Old Testament Mediatorial Kingdom and would have to be answered correspondingly.

We come now to the second question: "Am I a Jew? Thine own nation and the chief priests have delivered thee unto me; what hast thou done?" (vs. 35). Thus Pilate scornfully disclaims any and all responsibility for the charge, and the way is cleared for our Lord's reply to the original question. The first part of his reply is wholly negative: "My kingdom is not of this world" (vs. 36). The preposition is *ek,* indicating source or originating cause. His kingdom does not originate in the present cosmos or world system. As concrete evidence of this negative proposition, our Lord refers Pilate to the actual situation before his eyes: "if my kingdom were of this world, then would my servants[91] fight" (vs. 36). This was something that Pilate could understand: a "king" with no military support, and who actually had to be protected from physical violence on the part of his own subjects, could give no possible concern to the politically realistic Pilate.

This brings us to the third question of Pilate. He has satisfied himself that there is no political danger in the strange figure before him — a little later he will actually write over his head, "THIS IS THE KING OF THE JEWS" (Luke 23:38) — but just now he is mildly intrigued by the notion of a kingdom without any armed legions to support it; and so he asks of Jesus, "Art thou a

---

[91] The Greek word is rendered "officers" four times in the 18th chapter (vss. 3, 12, 18, 22).

king then?" (John 18:37). The answer of our Lord is without equivocation: "Thou sayest that I am a king," or, "Thou sayest it because I am a king." [92] Marcus Dods thinks we "must" render it, *"Thou art right, for a king I am."* [93] That this is the proper meaning is made certain by the words which follow: "To this end have I been born, and to this end am I come into the world, that I should bear witness unto the truth" (vs. 37, ASV). To this, Pilate has no answer, except to drop his cynical "What is truth?" (vs. 38) as he left the hall of judgment, tragically unaware that he had been in the presence of the King, who is the God of all truth.

Now to deduce from this brief exchange between Pilate and Jesus the sweeping proposition that the Messianic Kingdom is exclusively a kingdom of love and truth, which will never employ force in dealing with sinful men upon earth, is certainly theological conjecture at its worst. The Old Testament prophets had agreed that Messiah would rule over the nations "with a rod of iron" (Ps. 2:9), and this was confirmed by the King Himself in the days of His flesh (Luke 19:14, 27); but the force used will be that of divine omnipotence, not the force of human armies. In that remarkable vision of the coming of the King from heaven to establish His Kingdom on the earth, John says that "the armies which are in heaven followed him" (Rev. 19:11-14, ASV). Strange armies they are, bearing no weapons and striking no blows. For it is the "sharp sword" of the King Himself which strikes the enemy and wins the victory — "which sword proceeded out of his mouth" (19:21). That there is in the God of heaven a spiritual power, which can produce political and physical effects on earth, was clearly affirmed by our Lord in His final word to Pilate, "Thou couldest have no power at all against me, *except it were given thee from above*" (John 19:11, italics added). Is it necessary for us to argue as to the nature of this "power" which our Lord says had been "given" to Pilate "from above"? Surely, although divinely spiritual in origin, in its manifestation it was clearly *political* and nothing else. And the inference is compelling: If this power from above can make itself manifest on earth in the political career of a Pilate, on what ground of either reason or revelation can anyone deny the possibility of its greater exercise through the perfect Mediatorial King and His saints when He comes down to earth again?

Our Lord's consciousness of His own regal person and authority

[92] So Alford, Ellicott, Robertson, *et al.*
[93] *Expositors Greek New Testament, op. cit.,* Vol. I, p. 852.

never wavered, but only grew the stronger as He passed through the judgment of Calvary. Even there, suffering the agonies of crucifixion, He exercised the royal prerogatives which He claimed, by throwing open the doors of Paradise to a poor thief who prayed in his extremity, perhaps as only a Jew might have prayed, "Lord, remember me when thou comest into thy kingdom" (Luke 23:39-43).

12. *The problem of Jewish rejection of the King.*

In closing this part of the discussion, a question might well be raised: Why was the Lord Jesus Christ rejected by the nation of Israel when He offered Himself and the Kingdom for which they had long waited and prayed? I suggest at least six reasons, without pretending at all that these add up to a total answer: First, the high spiritual requirements our Lord laid down as essential for entrance into the Kingdom (Mark 1:15; Luke 18:15-17; John 3:3-5). Second, His refusal to establish a kingdom *merely* social and political in character (Luke 12:13-30; John 6:5-15). Third, His denunciation of the current religion with its traditionalism, legalism, and ritualism (Luke 11:37-54). Fourth, His scathing arraignment of the ruling classes (Matt. 23). Fifth, His association with and compassion for the outcasts of Israel (Matt. 9:10-13; Luke 15:1,2). Sixth, His exalted claims for Himself (John 5:16-18; 10:24-33; 18:37). This last, however, would have been no stumbling block if Christ had given them their own fleshly desires. The world will deify any leader who will give to the people enough "bread and circuses," while making no high moral and spiritual demands upon them. But they will reject the true God if He asks them to receive what they do not want.

In this connection we should not make the mistake of blaming all this on the ruling classes in Israel. Luke speaks of three classes of men whose voices were united in the demand for the rejection and death of the King; the *"rulers,"* the *"priests,"* and the *"people"* (Luke 23:13-23). It was, shall we say, a combination of civil, religious, and democratic authority. And the "people" here could not have been merely a "street mob," for it was the Passover season, and leading Jews from all over the known world were present in the city. The name of the Galilean Jesus had been on every lip. These happenings were not done in a corner (Acts 26:26).

One curious twist in the situation was that the "people" seemed to be sympathetic almost to the last moment (Luke 19:48-20:6; 20:19-26; 21:37-22:2). But suddenly the temper of the crowd changes. Matthew says that the chief priests and elders "persuaded the multitude" to ask Pilate for the release of Barabbas and the execution of Jesus (27:20). What arguments were used by these leaders, we are not told. But doubtless their arguments would have had something to do with the main charge laid before the Roman governor, and that was political, namely, that Jesus had forbidden the paying of tribute to Caesar, "saying that he himself is Christ a King" (Luke 23:2). Certainly the Jewish people here could have had no possible bias in favor of the Caesars; in fact, they would have welcomed with open arms *any* king who could deliver them from the tribute and bondage of Rome. And there had been a time when, impressed by our Lord's supernatural power, they had been ready to take Him by force and make Him king. But now they see Him, where He had never been before, apparently helpless in the hands of the Roman authorities. Does anyone suppose that the astute and highly intelligent Jewish leaders would fail to exploit the situation to their own advantage with the crowd? How easy now to point out the appalling incongruity before their eyes — the King of the Jews wearing a crown of thorns! Did the applause of the people, disappointed in their "hero," turn swiftly into vicious anger? If so, nothing could have been more plausible psychologically. History has shown more than once that the disappointment of the "people" can easily become a very terrible and violent thing.

PART FIVE

THE MEDIATORIAL KINGDOM IN ACTS, THE EPISTLES, AND THE APOCALYPSE

In passing from the Gospels, and especially the Synoptics, to the remaining writings of the New Testament, we are sensible at once of a great difference in the use made of this conception of the Kingdom of God. It is no longer the central and all-comprehending notion which it was in the popular teaching of Jesus, but sinks comparatively into the background, where it does not altogether disappear, and is employed, so far as retained, in an almost exclusively eschatological sense.   —*James Orr* [1]

[1] James Orr, "Kingdom of God," *Dictionary of the Bible,* ed. James Hastings (New York: Charles Scribner's Sons, 1901), Vol. II, p. 855.

PART FIVE

THE MEDIATORIAL KINGDOM IN ACTS, THE EPISTLES, AND THE APOCALYPSE

CHAPTER XXIV

THE MEDIATORIAL KINGDOM IN THE BOOK OF ACTS

The Jews had crucified the Messiah. But now, when vengeance swift and terrible might have been expected to fall upon that guilty people, Divine mercy held back the judgment and called them once again to repentance. The testimony was full and clear, and it was confirmed by a signal display of miraculous power . . . . During the forty years of Jeremiah's ministry the first destruction of Jerusalem was delayed. So now well-nigh forty years elapsed before the crash of that still more awful judgment which engulfed them [in A.D. 70].

—Sir Robert Anderson [1]

In approaching the Book of Acts the reader should keep in mind that the record here, like the Gospels which precede it in the canon of Scripture, consists primarily of *history*. Furthermore, it is evident from the writer's opening words that the historical events to be recounted are not only closely connected with preceding events but are actually a *continuation* of them. Luke begins with mention of "The former treatise" which he had written concerning "all that Jesus began both to do and teach" (1:1), an undoubted reference to the gospel record which bears his name. And if by these words he intends us to understand that the Book of Acts will continue the record of what our Lord had begun in the historical period covered by the Gospels, as many competent scholars maintain,[2] the reader should expect to find in this book a great deal about the Kingdom. For, during the days of His flesh Christ was engaged almost wholly in *teaching* about the Kingdom of Old Testament prophecy and in *doing* the predicted miraculous works which constituted His regal credentials as its Messianic King. Even His announcement of the Church, a new thing which is not identical with the Kingdom, was nevertheless made in close connection with the Kingdom (Matt. 16:18-19). We shall not be wrong, therefore, in looking for *both* the Kingdom and the Church in the literary

---

[1] Sir Robert Anderson, *The Silence of God* (11th ed.; Glasgow: Pickering and Inglis, no date), pp. 78, 82.

[2] So A. T. Robertson, Lechler in Lange, Alford, Bernard, Olshausen, *et al.* Cf. H. A. W. Meyer contra.

record of the Book of Acts. They are not present, however, in the same sense. The Church is present *historically,* having begun as a definite body of people on the day of Pentecost. But the Kingdom, although occupying a large place in apostolic preaching and teaching, is present only as an "eschatological" possibility, as James Orr has correctly indicated.

Actually, what we have in the Book of Acts is a record of events in a period of history which is *transitional* in certain important respects. Hence, while every portion of Holy Scripture is "profitable for doctrine," we shall find in Acts some events which are unique in their appointed time and place, never being intended to serve as a *permanent* norm for the Church of the present age. For example, the day of Pentecost has never been precisely duplicated, and all attempts to do so have resulted in nothing but spiritual disappointment and often disaster. The same is true of certain apostolic powers described in the historical record (cf. Acts 19:6-12).

1. *Christ's Post-Resurrection Ministry and the Kingdom*

The first eleven verses of Acts describe this ministry of our Lord. The parallel passages appear in chapter 28 of Matthew, chapter 16 of Mark, chapter 24 of Luke, and chapters 20-21 of John. Luke only, in the first-named passage, states the length of this ministry as "forty days" (Acts 1:3).

a. *The Disciples' Need for Further Teaching*

This problem is indicated in Luke 24:13-24. Concerning Jesus, after His death, two disciples had sadly said, "But we hoped that it was he who should redeem Israel" (vs. 21, ASV). More than once during the days of His flesh the Lord had told them that He "must" suffer and die and rise again (Matt. 16:21). But apparently they had failed to find any place for His death in the redemption of Israel. They could not harmonize Calvary with their hopes concerning the Mediatorial Kingdom of Messiah. And, according to Luke's account in Acts, the forty days of our Lord's post-resurrection ministry were designed to meet this particular need of the disciples in several ways.

(1) During this period of time Christ demonstrated to them the reality of His resurrection from the dead. In the words of Acts 1:3, "he shewed himself alive after his passion by many infallible proofs, being seen of them forty days." Some of these "proofs" are described

in detail by Luke in his "former treatise" (Luke 24:30-43). This testimony is confirmed by the other three gospel writers, and John adds that "many other signs truly did Jesus in the presence of his disciples, which are not written in this book; but these are written, that ye might believe that Jesus is the Christ" (John 20:30-31). And, as we shall see, these visual demonstrations were supported by appeals to the Old Testament prophetic Scriptures (Luke 24:44). Thus by sensible signs and Biblical testimony were the disciples convinced of the resurrection of Jesus, and so prepared for further instruction about the Kingdom.

(2) Luke says that during the forty days Christ was "speaking of the things pertaining to the kingdom of God" (Acts 1:3). And in his Gospel, where he elaborates somewhat more fully as to the content of our Lord's teaching on the subject, we learn that it included an exposition of the Old Testament testimony "concerning himself," with reference especially to His *suffering* and the subsequent *glory* (Luke 24:26-27, 46). In this teaching, the fact of His resurrection became the connecting link between the suffering and glory, solving the mystery of a Messiah who must die for His people and yet who also must reign over them gloriously in a coming Kingdom. It was this vital connection that gave to the resurrection so prominent a place in the doctrinal preaching of the early chapters of Acts.

(3) We are also told by Luke that before His ascension Christ gave certain "commandments unto the apostles whom he had chosen" (Acts 1:2). This unquestionably is a reference to the so-called "commissions" recorded in Matthew 28:18-20, Mark 16:15-18, Luke 24:46-49, John 21:15-17, and Acts 1:7-8. Having informed them concerning "the things pertaining to the kingdom of God," and also as to His own place in relation to that Kingdom, He now outlines a definite program of action to be followed by His disciples during the interregnum until He returns to establish the Kingdom.

In summary, therefore, we may say that the chief subject of our Lord's post-resurrection ministry was the "kingdom of God"; and the Biblical record contains no mention of the "Church" as such. This omission does not necessarily mean that the latter was not discussed at all (for it doubtless was); but it does mean that the Church must have occupied a wholly subordinate place in this period of Christ's teaching.

b. *The Content of the Post-Resurrection Commissions*

Certain differences which appear in the records may be explained by the fact that the commissions were given upon different occasions during the forty days. The various elements appear as follows:

(1) The disciples were commanded to bear witness concerning the Messianic King — "ye shall be witnesses unto me" (Acts 1:8).

(2) This witness would include the facts of His death and resurrection — that "it behoved Christ to suffer, and to rise from the dead" (Luke 24:46).

(3) In His name they were commissioned to preach "repentance and remission of sins . . . among all nations" (Luke 24:47); to "preach the gospel to every creature" (Mark 16:15); to "disciple all nations" (Matt. 28:19, lit.).

(4) In accomplishing this work the disciples were to follow a definite order of procedure: to Jerusalem first, then to all Judea, then to Samaria, and then to the uttermost part of the earth (Acts 1:8).

(5) Believers were to be fed (John 21:15-17), baptized, and taught to observe all that Christ had commanded the first disciples (Matt. 28:19-20).

(6) Unbelievers were to be warned of divine judgment: "he that believeth not shall be damned" (Mark 16:16).

(7) In the accomplishment of this work, they would be empowered by the Holy Spirit (Acts 1:8), and the spiritual presence of Christ would be with them to the end of the age (Matt. 28:20).

(8) If the latter part of Mark's Gospel be accepted as genuine (16:9-20),[3] then the witnessing would be accompanied by miraculous "signs" in confirmation of the message (vss. 17-18, 20), thus providing a continuation of the very things begun by our Lord in His preaching of the Kingdom during the days of His flesh.

It should be noticed that these Commissions do not abrogate our Lord's former teaching with reference to the Kingdom, nor do they contain anything inconsistent with that teaching. The disciples are to announce that the Messianic King is alive from the dead, that He has all power, that He is able to save from sin, and they are to induce men everywhere to prepare for the coming Kingdom. If there is anything new, it would be that whereas formerly the

---

[3] For the arguments pro and con, see the commentators and works on the text of the New Testament. Entirely apart from the textual problem, however, it cannot be denied that such miraculous "signs" did follow the proclamation of the Word, as recorded in the Book of Acts, especially in its earlier chapters.

witness was restricted to Israel (Matt. 10:5-6), now it is to be carried to all the nations. But the order of procedure indicates that Israel's priority still holds good (Acts 1:8).

c. *The Disciples' Question about the Kingdom*

When they therefore were come together, they asked of him, saying, Lord, wilt thou at this time restore again the kingdom to Israel?
—*Acts 1:6*

This meeting of verse 6 should not be confused with the assembling referred to in verse 4. It speaks rather of a final meeting, very probably on the day of our Lord's Ascension.[4] This means, of course, that the forty days of special instruction about the Kingdom were completed. And considering that their Teacher had been the Messianic King Himself, the risen Son of God, the disciples by this time should have been fairly well informed about the essential "things pertaining to the kingdom." Judged in the light of these facts, their final question on the subject should not be dismissed lightly as evidence of an "unspiritual" and "carnal" viewpoint, as some writers assume to do. Such treatment imputes not only inferior intelligence to the apostles but also, worse than that, incompetence to their Teacher. Regarded seriously, a number of important assumptions are latent in the question under discussion.

(1) The question assumes the restoration of a divine Kingdom which once existed. The Greek verb (*apokathistaneis*) means to restore something to its former place or state. Thayer says that in this text it means "restoration of dominion." And this dominion could be nothing else but the Theocratic Kingdom of Old Testament history, the Kingdom set up at Sinai and which ended at the Babylonian Captivity, an organized government on earth in which the nation of Israel held the central and sovereign place under God.

(2) The disciples' question also assumes that this Kingdom was not then established on earth. The tense of the verb is a *futuristic present*, indicating an expectation as yet unrealized. This accords with the final teaching of Christ before the time of the Cross as to the futurity of His Kingdom (Luke 21:31; 22:18, 30).

(3) The question also assumes that when the Kingdom is restored, Israel will once more possess the Kingdom in the sense of its meaning in Old Testament history and prophecy. The "Israel" here cannot be disassociated from the historical nation, the literal descend-

---

4 See H. Olshausen, *Biblical Commentary* (1st Am. ed., rev. after the 4th German ed. by A. L. Kendrick; New York: Sheldon, Blakeman and Co., 1857), Vol. III, p. 176.

ants of Abraham. This is the thought expressed in the excellent words of Lechler: "The kingdom which is the object of their hope, is a kingdom of Israel, a theocratic kingdom, deriving its existence and reality from the Messiah, and intended to give liberty, greatness and dominion to the people of Israel, who were at the time oppressed by a heavy yoke."[5]

(4) The disciples' question shows clearly that the one point upon which they lacked information was that of *time*. The emphasis on this point is more striking in the order of the Greek words: Lord, *at this time* wilt thou restore the kingdom to Israel? Evidently the apostles, schooled in the teaching of the Messianic King Himself, had heard nothing which would absolutely preclude the possibility of the establishment of the Kingdom in the near future of their own times.

d. *Christ's Reply to the Disciples' Question*

It is not for you to know the times or the seasons, which the Father hath put in his own power. But ye shall receive power, after that the Holy Ghost is come upon you: and ye shall be witnesses unto me both in Jerusalem, and in all Judaea, and in Samaria, and unto the uttermost part of the earth.   —*Acts 1 :7-8*

(1) In this reply to the disciples there is no rebuke nor correction for their general assumptions. If their ideas of the Kingdom had been totally wrong, certainly this was the time for Christ to have set them right, not only for their sakes but for ours also who would read the inspired record. If, because of her sins, God was now done forever with the historical nation of Israel; if all her divine covenants were now to be taken away and given to the Church; if the throne of David was now to be transferred from earth to heaven; if the glorious utterances of the prophets are only "beautiful dreams" never to be realized in the reign of Messiah in a Kingdom on earth where all war and disease and injustice shall have been abolished; if the sickly cast of platonic dualism is now to be thrown over great areas of Old Testament prediction in which the brightest aspirations of humanity are divinely validated — how simple it would have been for our Lord Jesus Christ to have set the apostles right in a single utterance. But there is no record of such an utterance at this crucial point. To say that the correction of their alleged "carnal" notions had to be left to the Holy Spirit, as some argue, proves too much. What then, if such were true, was the point of trying to teach them *anything* during the ministry of the

[5] G. V. Lechler, Lange's *Commentary on Acts,* tr. by C. F. Schaeffer (2nd German ed.; New York: Scribner's Sons, 1886), on Acts 1:6.

forty days *before* Pentecost? The Holy Spirit came on the day of Pentecost, not so much for the immediate purpose of giving the apostles *new* information about the Kingdom, but rather to give them "boldness" and "power" in preaching what they already knew (Acts 4:29-33). This is not to deny, of course, that the Spirit later did give new revelation to the chosen writers of New Testament Scripture.

Concerning the Lord's reply to His disciples' question about the "time" of the Kingdom, therefore, Lechler is wholly justified in saying that,

> As to the fact itself, the coming of the *Kingdom,* and as to Israel's privilege with respect to the latter, they entertained no doubt; and the Lord was so far from disapproving of such an expectation, that he rather confirmed it by declaring that the Father had fixed the times. Now we know that neither a period nor an epoch can be affirmed concerning an event which is only imaginary. Those interpreters have altogether mistaken the sense, who maintain that Jesus here entirely rejects the conceptions entertained by his apostles respecting the Messianic Kingdom, for this is by no means the case. He did not deny that either their expectation of the appearance on earth of his glorious Kingdom in its reality, or their hope of the glorious future which that Kingdom opened to the people of Israel, was well founded; he simply subdued their eager curiosity respecting the time . . . ." [6]

(2) Since the question of the disciples had concerned only the *time* of the Kingdom's establishment, so our Lord's reply deals pointedly with this matter: "It is not for you to know the times or the seasons." Now this is in perfect harmony with His previous recorded teaching, for the one factor about the future Kingdom left wholly and wisely unrevealed by the Lord was *chronological.* As to this, during the latter part of His ministry before the Cross, He had made clear at least three things: First, the Kingdom which had been rejected would be set up at a second advent of the King (Matt. 25:31-32). Second, the time of this second advent was to be left wholly unrevealed (Mark 13:32-33). Third, His second coming nevertheless was something to be looked for at every season, for the time might be long or short (Mark 13:34-37). And now, as He is about to leave them for His throne of grace in the heavens, if they are troubled about the Unknown Tomorrow, He assures them that it is in safe hands — within the Father's "own authority." [7]

(3) During the unrevealed time of the Interregnum, His apostles are to be occupied with a world-wide ministry of witnessing. It is easy to forget that, while the commission of verse 8 has an application to every believer of the present age, it was addressed in the

[6] G. V. Lechler, *ibid.,* on Acts 1:7.
[7] The Greek word is *exousia*, different from the "power" (*dunamis*) of verse 8.

first instance to "the apostles whom he had chosen" (Acts 1:2).
And although He had warned them to expect persecution, or even
death (John 16:1-4), there is no intimation in this final commission
to them that the task of witnessing might not be interrupted by the
coming of the Kingdom within the reach of their own generation.
It is completely unhistorical to read into the words of Acts 1:8 nineteen centuries of time. One of the reasons for leaving the time
span wholly unrevealed was, as we shall see, because another offer
of the King and His Kingdom was to be made to the nation of
Israel (Acts 3:19-21). And the silence of God as to the length
of the Interregnum left room for a genuine decision on the part
of the nation. To have revealed in advance any fixed chronology
would have turned the divine offer into a hollow mockery.

(4) The forty days of post-resurrection ministry closed with two
important and closely connected events. There was, first, our Lord's
visible ascension into heaven; and second, His promise of a similarly
visible second coming, given through the "two men . . . in white
apparel" as He was going up (Acts 1:9-11). Both the ascension
and its attendant promise were intended to give reassurance to the
disciples regarding Jesus and His relation to the expected future
Kingdom. The ascension, on the one hand, demonstrated the truth
of His claim to be the Messianic King; and the promise of a second
advent, on the other hand, reaffirmed the reality and certainty of
the future establishment of His Kingdom. These things were not
altogether new. In His trial before the Jewish Sanhedrin both of
these events had been predicted by our Lord and offered as the
forthcoming evidence of the righteousness of His Messianic claims.
Having been required under oath by the high priest to "tell us
whether thou be the Christ," He had answered, "Thou hast said"
(a clear affirmation in the Greek). And in support of the claim
He pointed to His session at the right hand of God and also to
His second coming, both to be demonstrated visibly: "Hereafter
shall ye see the Son of man sitting on the right hand of power,
and coming in the clouds of heaven" (Matt. 26:63-64).

(5) In this final promise of a second coming of the Messianic
King (Acts 1:11), the angelic messengers seem almost to exhaust
the resources of human language in declaring the reality and visibility of that grand event. The coming One will be "this same
Jesus [houtos, this very one], which is taken up." He will "so
[houtōs, in this way] come in like manner [hon tropon] as ye have

seen him go." This language grows in impressiveness when we recall that the great purpose of His second advent will be to establish the Kingdom on earth. If the coming of the King will be something fully tangible in the realm of sense experience, as affirmed by the angels, there remains no sound reason for denying the same reality to the Kingdom which He will bring. So the apostles understood, and so they taught.

2. The Day of Pentecost and the Kingdom

There can hardly be any reasonable doubt that on this historic day the building of Christ's *ekklēsia* began. No other date fits the data furnished by the New Testament. And this testimony has been so convincing that Dosker says without qualification, "The almost universal opinion among theologians and exegetes is this: that Pentecost marks *the founding of the Christian church as an institution.*"[8] But this very importance of the day of Pentecost to the Christian Church has tended to obscure its place in relation to the Mediatorial Kingdom of God. We shall consider now the origin of that day and the events which took place on its celebration as described in the second chapter of Acts.

a. The Origin and Nature of the Day

The day of Pentecost was a Jewish feast, the second of the three great annual festivals at which every male's attendance was required by law. These feasts are enumerated in Exodus 23:14-17, "Three times thou shalt keep a feast unto me in the year. . . . the feast of unleavened bread, . . . the feast of harvest, the firstfruits, . . . and the feast of ingathering, which is in the end of the year. . . . Three times in the year all thy males shall appear before the Lord GOD." The second of these, the Pentecostal Feast, derived its name from its observance on the fiftieth day, or seven weeks after the Paschal Feast (Lev. 23:16). Pentecost, then, was an integral part of the Law given by God at Sinai when the Theocratic Kingdom was there established. In fact, according to Jewish tradition, it commemorated the very day when the Law was given and the Kingdom established, as recorded in Exodus 19:1 ff. Furthermore, the importance of this feast was recognized in the period of highest glory reached in the historical kingdom: "Then Solomon offered burnt offerings unto the LORD. . . . on the solemn feasts, three times in the year, even

---

[8] Henry E. Dosker, "Pentecost," *International Standard Bible Encyclopedia* (Chicago: Howard-Severance, 1915), Vol. IV, p. 2318.

in the feast of unleavened bread, and in the feast of weeks [Pente-
cost], and in the feast of tabernacles" (II Chron. 8:12, 13).

The typical symbolism of these three great festivals of the Old
Testament Kingdom is fairly clear: The Paschal Feast pointed to
the redemption of His people by the blood of the Messianic King.
The Pentecostal Feast pointed to the ingathering of the firstfruits,
as represented by the *ekklēsia* begun on Pentecost, to be the royal
family in the coming Kingdom; and the Feast of Tabernacles still
points to that yet future day when the full harvest is realized in
the established Kingdom at the second advent of the King.

b. *The People Assembled on This Day of Pentecost*

Verse one says that "when the day of Pentecost was fully come,
they were all with one accord in one place." These were the first
believers, about "an hundred and twenty" (Acts 1:15), probably
including the eleven (vs. 13), to whom must be added Matthias
(vs. 26). So far as we know, the entire group were Israelites. As
they began to speak, a great audience came to hear what was being
said. This assembly was composed of "Jews, devout men, out of
every nation under heaven" (Acts 2:5). The various nations *from*
which they had come are named in verses 9-11. And besides the
"Jews" by birth, there were also "proselytes," i.e., Gentiles who had
been brought under the Covenant of Israel, as provided for in the
Mosaic Law of the Kingdom. That this great audience was wholly
Jewish, either by birth or by proselytism, is confirmed by the form
of Peter's address. In 2:14 Peter addresses them as "Ye men of
Judaea, and all ye that dwell at Jerusalem." Again in verse 22 he
speaks to them as "Ye men of Israel." In verse 29 it is "Men and
brethren," a customary form of address to Israelites (cf. 13:26; 23:1).
And, finally, the hearers are spoken of as "the house of Israel" (2:36).

c. *The Purpose of the Miracle of Tongues*

(1) The record of Luke indicates beyond question that the miracle
here consisted of a divine enabling to speak in various *existing* languages. In the fourteenth chapter of First Corinthians Paul describes
a spiritual gift wherein the recipient was enabled to speak in an
unknown language, which could be understood only with a corresponding miraculous gift of interpretation (I Cor. 14:2, 28). But
the Pentecostal gift required no such interpretation. When the
speaking began, Luke reports, the hearers were amazed because
"every man heard them speak in his own language" (Acts 2:6).

And they exclaimed, "How hear we every man in our own tongue, wherein we were born?" (vs. 8).

(2) The *purpose* of this gift of tongues was to bear a certain testimony to the nation of Israel. We have already seen that the assembly seems to have been wholly Jewish. To attend the Passover Feast, now fifty days past, Israelites from all parts of the ancient world were accustomed to come back to Jerusalem. According to Josephus, it was not unknown for above two million Jewish worshipers to be present for this feast. And this vast concourse of people would, of course, remain for the Pentecostal feast, the most popular of the three great annual festivals. Following Pentecost many of these foreign-born Jews would be leaving for their homes. That day, therefore, offered an unparalleled opportunity for presenting the facts concerning Jesus in His relation to the Kingdom of God to an audience which could carry the report to all areas of the ancient world where Jewish people were living. There seems to be a reference to this world-wide testimony in Romans 10:18 where Paul says about the Israel of his day, "Have they not heard? Yes, verily, their sound went into all the earth, and their words unto the ends of the world." And in the same context the apostle indicates that the report was generally rejected by the nation of Israel, referring to them as "a disobedient and gainsaying people" (Rom. 10:21). Yet a "remnant" did believe (Rom. 11:5); and the time will come when the nation itself will be restored to its ancient place of favor and supremacy (Rom. 11:11-26).

d. *The Testimony Given on Pentecost*

It is significant that, although there is no verbal record of what was actually said by the many who spoke in tongues, we do have such a record of the main address delivered by Peter who probably spoke in Greek which would be intelligible to most of the pilgrim Jews from various parts of the world.[9] This address, we may assume, included the important elements of the testimony delivered that day to the nation of Israel. And the apostle Peter, it should be recalled, was not only the first of the "living stones" to be built into our Lord's *ekklēsia* but also he had conferred upon him a certain authority in relation to "the Kingdom of heaven" (Matt. 16: 18-19). Let us now observe some of the significant elements in Peter's address on this signal occasion.

(1) Peter explains the miracle of tongues by quoting a passage

[9] So Ellicott, *Commentary on Acts, in loc.*

from Joel in which are listed certain events preceding the great "day of the LORD" which in Old Testament prophecy always ushers in the establishment of the Kingdom on earth (cf. Acts 2:16-21 with Joel 2:28-32). But nowhere does Peter say that all the elements of the prophecy were *fulfilled* on the day of Pentecost.[10] His very cautious language, "this is that which was spoken by the prophet Joel," points back to the one thing in which Peter was primarily interested, i.e., the testimony uttered under the Spirit's power on this occasion. This is confirmed by an interpolation inserted in the quotation from Joel. The last clause of Acts 2:18, "and they shall prophesy," is not found in Joel, either in Hebrew or Greek texts. It was inserted by the speaker, evidently to emphasize his point of interest, just as any preacher might so indicate in quoting an extended passage to present the Biblical context of a single point of interest. Peter is only saying that the miraculous testimony of Pentecost was something to be expected prior to the establishment of the Messianic Kingdom.

(2) Peter next reminds his Jewish hearers of the "miracles and wonders and signs," which had accompanied our Lord's original announcement of the Kingdom and had confirmed its truth (Acts 2:22). Here again the language is meticulously careful. Peter does not say, as we might expect, that these great miracles had been done by Jesus, but rather refers to them as works "which God did by him." Whether or not Jesus had performed miracles was not in dispute, for this could not be denied even by His enemies (Matt. 21:14-15). But, they argued, the source of His power was the devil (Matt. 12:22-26). And now Peter, speaking to the very men who had rejected Him and put Him to death, repeats the original claim of his Lord, namely, that the source of His miracle-working power was in *God*.

(3) In answer to the problem present in the Jewish mind, how a crucified man could be the Messianic King of Israel, Peter uses the resurrection of Jesus to show His identity and right to the throne of David (Acts 2:24-32). Both the death and resurrection of Messiah had been foreseen by David himself, and recorded in Old Testament Scripture (Ps. 16:8-11). That a Messiah out of the loins of David would some day sit on his historic throne, God had sworn with an oath (Ps. 132:11). And the crucified Jesus

10 G. V. Lechler, *op. cit., in loc.*

had proved His regal rights by rising from the dead, a fact to which Peter and all his company stood ready to bear witness (Acts 2:32).

(4) A second problem in the Jewish mind — Why, if Jesus is the Messiah, is He not *now* on earth ruling on David's throne? — Peter answers by referring his hearers to another great and well-known Kingdom prophecy, the 110th Psalm. From this passage he shows that the crucified and risen Messiah must first ascend into heaven for a session at God's right hand until His foes are brought into subjection by the coming of His Kingdom (Acts 2:33-35). That the throne in heaven, to which Christ ascended and where He now sits, cannot be equated with the throne of David, should need no argument, for the two are never so identified in Scripture (cf. Rev. 3:21). And Peter distinguishes between them in Acts 2:30 with 34. His address closes with the warning that the Jesus whom his hearers had killed has been made both "Lord and Christ" (vs. 36). These were solemn titles: *Kurios,* the Greek title generally used by the Jews themselves to translate the sacred name of Jehovah; and *Christos,* the Greek equivalent of the Hebrew "Messiah," the Anointed King.

e. *The Effect of the Pentecostal Testimony*

This can only be described as astonishing. The hearers, composed of multitudes who had joined in demanding the death of Jesus only a few days before, now are stricken in heart and cry, "What shall we do?" The answer of Peter is peculiarly suited to his Jewish audience. Every devout Jew *believed* in the true God and a coming Messianic King. What they needed to do was "repent" — *change their minds* — with reference to Jesus of Nazareth. Whereas they had denied Him, now they must acknowledge and confess Him to be God's Messiah, crucified, risen, ascended, and the coming King. And 3,000 Israelites did exactly that.

To all who truly experience a change of mind about Jesus, and who evidence this change by submitting to the rite of water baptism as authorized[11] by Him, Peter continues, there will come remission of sins and the gift of the Holy Spirit (Acts 2:38). The promise is extended to the hearers, to their children, and to all afar off (vs. 39). In this there is a definite echo of the promise in Joel

---

11 "In the name of Jesus Christ" (*epi* with the dative) is not a new formula for the rite of baptism, for our Lord had already given the proper formula in Matt. 28:19. Peter is only saying that the converts should be baptized *on the ground of* or *by the authority of* Christ's name. Cf. Mark 9:37 and the various grammars for this meaning. A similar meaning is found in Acts 3:6.

2:28 about "your sons and daughters," the great Kingdom prophecy with which Peter had begun. It is easy to miss the full significance of all this to the Jewish audience of that great day. But if Jesus was the Messianic King, as Peter had proven; and if there could be remission of sins extended even to the very Jews who were responsible for His death, as Peter had declared; then his hearers could have drawn only one conclusion, namely, that the restoration of the long-awaited Kingdom to Israel was still a possibility in their own generation.

That the Jewish converts did so conclude seems to be indicated by their immediate course of conduct. First, there is absolutely no record of any break with the Jewish temple worship, but on the contrary they continued *daily* with one accord "in the temple" (Acts 2:46) where, according to Old Testament prophecy, all worship would be centered in the future Kingdom (Isa. 56:7). Second, the attitude of these early Jewish believers toward property suggests the expectation of an imminent establishment of the Kingdom. The selling of their possessions and the sharing of the proceeds, was no adoption of a communistic policy. For what they did was wholly *voluntary* on every man's part (cf. Acts 4:34-5:4). Moreover, in the coming Kingdom, the prophets assign an important place for private property rights: "they shall sit every man under his vine and under his fig tree." And in these rights men will be fully secure: "none shall make them afraid" (Mic. 4:1-4). But every devout Jew knew that the Kingdom would begin on earth with a divine rectification of ancient wrongs: "the crooked shall be made straight" (Isa. 40:4). And of all wrongs upon earth, none are more complex and difficult of settlement than those arising out of the violation of property rights. Moreover, on the basis of Old Testament prophecy, the Israelites anticipated a restoration of the promised land on a grand and greatly enlarged scale (Gen. 15: 18-21); and in this restoration each tribe would be assigned an allotment (Ezek. 47-48). With an aroused expectation of the imminency of the divine Kingdom, in which there would be a divine rectification of historic maladjustments, it cannot be surprising that these Pentecostal converts did not attach very much value to *existing* possessions and property titles. To them, the Grand Jubilee of all the centuries seemed at hand.

Furthermore, these converts must have been encouraged in their expectation by the "wonders and signs" performed by the Apostles

(Acts 2:43). For these were signs of the Kingdom, as predicted in the ancient prophets, and which had marked the offer of the Kingdom by the Messiah during the period of the Gospels. These will be discussed more fully below.

It may seem somewhat surprising that in Luke's record of events which took place on Pentecost and immediately thereafter, as set forth in the second chapter of Acts, there is no mention of the Church by name. (The best authorities agree that the term in verse 47 of the King James Version is spurious.) This omission does not mean that the *ekklēsia* did not begin on the day of Pentecost, but only suggests that it did not yet occupy the center of the stage, as it came to do later when the apostolic offer of the King and His Kingdom once more was met with violent opposition on the part of the rulers of Israel, and which grew to a climax in the history of the Book of Acts.

3. The Official Reoffer of the Messiah and His Kingdom

The record of this important event is found in the third chapter of Acts, which furnishes the key to much contained in the entire book. Peter and John had gone to the Jewish temple for the regular hour of prayer (vs. 1). At the gate they were importuned for alms by a man lame from birth. In response, Peter commanded the man "in the name of Jesus Christ" to stand up and walk (vs. 6), and instantly he was wholly healed of his infirmity. It was a great *public* miracle, for the man was well known; even the rulers of Israel had to admit that "a notable miracle" had been done (Acts 4:15-16). The immediate result was the drawing of a great audience to the temple to see the healed man who was walking, leaping, and praising God (Acts 3:8-11). Like the gift of tongues on Pentecost, this miracle provided the audience and the pulpit for a divine proclamation to the people of Israel. As before, the address is delivered by Peter. It begins at verse 12 and extends to the end of the chapter.

a. What Peter says is directed to the *nation of Israel*, whom he addresses as "Ye men of Israel" (Acts 3:12), and "brethren" (vs. 17). His message comes from "The God of Abraham, and of Isaac, and of Jacob, the God of our fathers" (vs. 13); and in closing he reminds them they they "are the children of the prophets, and of the covenant which God made with our fathers" (vs. 25).

b. Peter ascribes the power of the miracle to the God of Israel who thus "hath glorified his Servant[12] Jesus" (Acts 3:13, ASV), an identification of Jesus with the great kingly Servant of Isaiah 40-53. He is also "the Holy One" and the "Just" One (vs. 14); the "Prince [author] of life" (vs. 15): the predicted "prophet" who would be "like unto" Moses (vs. 22).

c. This divine Messiah, sent to Israel, they had denied and killed; but God raised Him from the dead (Acts 3:13-15). Now Peter, speaking as the accredited messenger of God, tells the guilty nation that their denial and crucifixion of Messiah has not put them beyond the pale of mercy; nor has their sin lost for them another opportunity to receive the Kingdom. For their terrible crime was not only foreseen by the prophets, but God had actually overruled it for good, so that now their "sins may be blotted out" (vss. 17-19).

d. But Israel must meet the spiritual and moral demands which in every age are attached to the enjoyment of the blessings of the Mediatorial Kingdom. Just as in the record of that Kingdom of Old Testament history, and in the predictions of Old Testament prophecy, and in the announcements made by the Baptist and our Lord Himself — so now once more the demand comes to the chosen nation: They must "repent" and "turn again" (Acts 3:19, lit.). For the great social, economic, and political blessings of the Kingdom rest upon a spiritual foundation.

e. If Israel will meet these spiritual conditions, certain important things will follow: First, the terrible sins of this people can be blotted out. Second, they will enjoy "times of refreshing" from the presence of the Lord (Acts 3:19). Third, God will send Jesus, the Messianic King, who has been "appointed"[13] for them (vs. 20, ASV), and whose present session in heaven is only temporary (vs. 21). Fourth, the second coming of Christ will bring "the times of restitution of all things" which have been the main subject of all divine prophecy (vs. 21). It is highly significant that in the word "restitution" we have the noun form of a related Greek verb used by the disciples when they asked Christ when He would "restore" the Kingdom to Israel (1:6).[14] Thus, Peter is saying that the resto-

---

[12] The Greek term is *paida*, not *huios*.

[13] So read a majority of the most important Greek manuscripts. To the nation of Israel, first of all, belongs the Messianic King by divine appointment.

[14] The same verb was used by the Lord in affirming that Elijah would indeed come and "restore all things" (Matt. 17:11). Robertson says that as a medical term it means complete restoration to health. A related idea appears in the "regeneration" connected with the Kingdom by Christ in Matt.. 19:28. RSV renders the noun in Acts 3:21 "establishing" instead of "restitution."

ration of "all things" connected with the Kingdom, as described so fully by the Old Testament prophets, will arrive at the second advent of Messiah. And the nation of Israel must understand that, while the exact time of this grand event is unrevealed, its arrival at this particular stage of history is morally conditioned upon the repentance of the nation. Once more, therefore, an appalling responsibility was laid upon the shoulders of Israel. Although their adverse action in the face of this divine offer was fully known to God, still we dare not deny that the moral option was genuine, and that Israel had once again under God its opportunity to determine the immediate course of human history.

f. The reference to Moses in Acts 3:22-24 confirms the meaning and reality of the offer to Israel. Jesus is set forth here as the anti-typical realization of Moses' well-known prediction of the Messianic "prophet . . . like unto me" (vss. 22-23). Now among all the prophets of Old Testament history, Moses occupied an absolutely unique position. He was the first mediatorial ruler in the historical Kingdom of God on earth. Through Moses that Kingdom was established at Sinai, and its laws were given. And, unlike other prophets, the authority of Moses in his mediatorial rulership was almost absolute, as Korah and his fellow rebels found to their dismay. Even Moses, however, was subject to human frailty and mistakes. But since the Messianic Prophet will be perfect, His authority will be unqualified: Those who refuse to hear Him will be destroyed from among the people. All the prophets agree as to the nature of His authority in the coming "days" of the Kingdom (vs. 24): He will rule the world with a rod of iron (Ps. 2:9).

g. The address of Peter concludes by reminding the nation of Israel that by descent they are the primary objects of the prophetic utterances, and also of the blessings of the Abrahamic covenant which, as we have seen, are regal in character. Therefore, as the original offer of the Kingdom by the King was made to Israel *first* during the "days of his flesh," so now again, having been raised from the dead, He is offered "first" to the chosen nation for the purpose of turning them away from their iniquities (Acts 3:25-26). There is no other path to regal blessing.

Reflecting now upon the total content of Acts 3, it is hard to imagine how words could have made any plainer the historical reality of this reoffer of the King and His Kingdom to the nation of Israel. Some have objected that nowhere in the chapter does the term "kingdom" (*basileia*) occur. But this is pedantic argument. Surely, we should be able to recognize an idea when set forth in different semantic frames. And in Acts 3:19-21 we have something better than a term: actually, a *definition* of the Kingdom. As to *content*, it will bring "the times of restitution of all things, which God hath spoken by the mouth of all his holy prophets since the world began." As to *time*, it will come when God "shall send Jesus Christ" back from His present session in "heaven." And as to its *conditionality*, its coming is contingent upon the repentance and conversion of Israel.

During His earthly ministry our Lord had specifically foretold of such a reoffer. The prediction is recorded in Matthew 22:1-7, clothed in the form of a parable of "the kingdom of heaven," in which a certain king makes a marriage feast for his son (vs. 2). Two calls are sent out by the King, both addressed to a special group of people who had previously been invited, "them that were bidden" (vs. 3, perfect tense), a reference to the original and abiding call of this nation through Abraham to enjoy the blessings of the Messianic Kingdom, and renewed over and over again in the Old Testament. The *first* call of the parable was issued by our Lord through His disciples (Matt. 10:1-15; Luke 10:1-9), directed exclusively to the chosen nation; and it was officially rejected (Matt. 22:3). Then there was to be a *second* call announcing that the dinner is now "prepared" and "all things are ready" (vs. 4) — certainly a reference to our Lord's finished work of redemption at Calvary. Such a call could not have gone forth until after the Resurrection. But again the call is rejected, this time by actions which help to identify it in Biblical history: some Jews would turn away with contemptuous indifference, according to the parable, while others would mistreat and kill the messengers (vs 6). This points to the post-Pentecostal offer, as described in the Book of Acts, when the officials of Israel did exactly that. During the gospel period not an official disciple of Christ was killed by the Jews, but during the period of the Acts the terrible persecution and killing of the messengers began. And there is no *third* call for this generation of Israel, but judgment falls: the King sends forth his armies, destroys the murderers, and burns their city — a parabolic prediction of the awful destruction of Jerusalem in A.D. 70 (vs.7).

4. The Miracles of the Book of Acts

a. The Frequency of These Miracles

At least *thirty* specific miracles may be found in Luke's record of the Book of Acts, of which more than twenty are just as impressively spectacular as those listed in the four Gospels where Trench enumerates thirty-two. In this respect there is a striking similarity between these two periods of Biblical history.

But beyond the record of specific miracles there are in Acts at least *nine* general statements concerning the prevalence of miracles during this period. Two statements are made about the work of all the *apostles*: "Many wonders and signs were done by the apostles" (2:43); and "by the hands of the apostles were many signs and wonders wrought among the people" (5:12). One statement is concerned with the work of *Peter*: "they brought forth the sick into the streets, and laid them on beds and couches, that at the least the shadow of Peter passing by might overshadow some of them. . . . and they were healed every one" (5:15-16). One statement is about the ministry of *Stephen*: "And Stephen, full of grace and power, wrought great wonders and signs among the people" (6:8, ASV). Another statement is made about *Philip*: "the people with one accord gave heed unto those things which Philip spake, hearing and seeing the miracles which he did" (8:6). Two references are made to the joint work of *Paul* and *Barnabas*: "the Lord . . . granted signs and wonders to be done by their hands" (14:3); and, "Then all the multitude kept silence, and gave audience to Barnabas and Paul, declaring what miracles and wonders God had wrought among the Gentiles by them" (15:12). Finally, two statements are made about the work of *Paul alone*: "God wrought special miracles by the hands of Paul: so that from his body were brought unto the sick handkerchiefs or aprons, and the diseases departed from them, and the evil spirits went out of them" (19:11-12); and during his brief stay on the island of Melita "others also, which had diseases in the island, came, and were healed" (28:9).

In this record of the miracles of the Book of Acts there is a vast and rich field of study which deserves more attention than it has received in comparison with the gospel records.

b. The Nature of These Miracles

The most impressive aspect of these miracles is their *public character*. At least twenty of the thirty specific miracles were seen by witnesses, sometimes by great multitudes, as in the case of the miracle of tongues on Pentecost. The effect upon the beholders was to produce many converts and also to attract great crowds as the report was spread (5:12-16). Certain miracles within the circle of the church produced holy "boldness" and godly "fear" (4:30-31; 5:1-11). Some of the miracles were so spectacular and widely witnessed that even the most incorrigible opposers of the apostles could not deny their genuineness. Thus, concerning the lame man healed at the temple, the highly intelligent and astute members of the Jewish Sanhedrin admitted, "that indeed a notable miracle hath been done by them is manifest to all them that dwell in Jerusalem; and we cannot deny it" (4:15-16). As a matter of fact, the healed man was there "standing with" Peter and John before the eyes of the court, and the mouths of the judges were effectually shut: "they could say nothing against it" (4:14).

c. *The Classification of These Miracles*

The miracles of the Book of Acts are also impressive for their great *variety*, covering at least eleven different categories: first, the miracle of Christ's ascension (1:9-10); second, the outpouring of the Holy Spirit with its attendant phenomena (Acts 2:1-4; 10:44-46); third, healing of the diseased and infirm (3:1-10; 28:7-9); fourth, the casting out of demons (5:16; 16:16-18); fifth, raising the dead (9:36-42; 20:7-12); sixth, physical wonders (4:31; 8:39); seventh, miraculous deliverances (5:19-22; 16:26); eighth, immunity from ordinary hazards (27:23-26; 28:3-5); ninth, immediate judgment on opposers (5:1-11; 13:11); tenth, direct and tangible angelic ministry (12:7-8, 23); eleventh, miraculous visions and communications (9:3-6; 10:9-16).

d. *Earlier Biblical Parallels*

Obviously, in these miracles of the Book of Acts there are some striking correspondences with earlier Biblical records. Such correspondences may be found: first, in the supernatural events of the Old Testament historical Kingdom; second, in the numerous predictions made by the Old Testament prophets regarding a future Messianic Kingdom; and, third, in the miraculous deeds which attended the proclamation of that Kingdom by our Lord and His disciples in the period of the Gospels. For those who have studied the Biblical material presented in Parts II through IV of this volume, the evidences for the parallels will require no additional argument.

e. The Problem Raised by These Miracles

It is generally agreed by competent and unprejudiced observers that miracles similar in nature, variety, and number, are no longer evident among the Lord's people today; and furthermore, that such supernatural works did not persist beyond the apostolic period. Among Christian historians there is also general agreement that up until about A.D. 70 the record is clear. But the last part of the first century becomes obscure; and when the Church appears in the second century, the situation as regards the miraculous is so changed that we seem to be in another world. As one very able and devout historian has put the matter:

> The thirty years which followed . . . the destruction of Jerusalem are in truth the most obscure in the history of the Church. When we emerge in the second century we are, to a great extent, in a changed world. Apostolic authority lives no longer in the Christian community; apostolic miracles have passed; the Church has fairly begun her pilgrimage through "the waste of Time." As Dr. Arnold has finely said: "We stop at the last Epistle of St. Paul to Timothy with something of the same interest with which one pauses at the last hamlet of the cultivated valley, when there is nothing but moor beyond. It is the end, or all but the end, of our real knowledge of primitive Christianity; there we take our last distinct look around; further the mist hangs thick, and few and distorted are the objects which we can discern in the midst of it." We cannot doubt that there was a Divine purpose in thus marking off the age of inspiration and of miracles, by so broad and definite a boundary, from succeeding times.[15]

In the records of Acts and the Epistles there is evidence indicating a gradual change taking place during the approximately forty years between Pentecost and the destruction of Jerusalem. In the fifth chapter of Acts "every one" of the sick who were brought from various cities to Jerusalem "were healed" by the apostles (5:16). Twenty-five years later we find the greatest of all the apostles being denied his own earnest prayer for a well body (II Cor. 12:7-9). And as we near the end, we hear him advising Timothy to take a little wine for his "often infirmities" (I Tim. 5:23). Still later we learn that he has left another beloved worker "sick" at Miletum (II Tim. 4:20). In the early chapters of Acts no one witnessing concerning Christ dies, but as the opposition of Israel reaches its first crisis in the seventh chapter, Stephen is killed (vss. 54-59). A little later James dies by the sword of Herod (12:1-2). Although in the early pages of Acts Jerusalem is filled with miracles, after the martyrdom of Stephen there is never again any record of a public miracle in that city which was called "the

[15] Samuel G. Green, *Handbook of Church History* (3rd impression; London: Religious Tract Society, 1913), p. 22.

city of the great King." At the beginning and through the history
of the Acts there were special and miraculous gifts by which divine
revelation was channeled to men. These are named by Paul as the
gifts of "knowledge," "prophecy," and "tongues" (I Cor. 12:8-10;
but in the same context he warns that they will "cease" (I Cor.
13:8). The permanent things will be faith, hope, and love (vs. 13).

f. *The Purpose of the Miracles in the Book of Acts*

As men have studied the record of miracles in the Book of Acts,
in contrast with the situation of the present day, the question naturally arose as to the *reason* for this sharp and striking change.
To this question several answers have been proposed.

First, there are a few people who argue that such miracles are
still present in the life of the Christian community. Some of these
are sincere, doubtless, in their determination to see what they
wish to see; just as there are other people who are blind to the
things which they do not wish to see. These are problems for psy-
chological-rather than historical investigation. In this study we
are concerned with phenomena which are demonstrable publicly to
sense experience, and therefore susceptible of ordinary evidential
proof.

Second, there are others who admit realistically the present absence of the miraculous element which was prevalent during the
apostolic era. But, they argue, this is due to a declension in the
spirituality of the Lord's people; and a revival of apostolic faith
would also bring back a corresponding era of apostolic miracles.
To this it may be answered that there have been great spiritual revivals as well as great spiritual leaders in the later history of the
Church. But there have been no matching revivals of great public
miracles.

Third, others have argued that the purpose of miracles in the
apostolic era was to authenticate the truth of Christianity; that once
this had been done and the inspired record made, there remained
no further purpose to be served and therefore public miracles ceased.
But this argument seems to ignore the great miracles of the period
of the Gospels, entirely sufficient for purposes of authenticating the
general truth of Christianity for all time. And to say that their continuance was necessary only during the *initial* era of the Church,
would raise a further question: if useful then, why not also during
succeeding eras of the Church? Furthermore, this viewpoint unduly
narrows the divine purpose. The great public miracles of Biblical

history did indeed serve to authenticate divine revelation, but they also offered relief for desperate human problems and needs. And these needs did not cease with the end of the Book of Acts. With all our progress in the various fields of endeavor, and it has been very great, we still live in a world which is sick unto death, beset with all kinds of complex maladies. Our need for supernatural help has increased rather than lessened.

In the Scriptures great public exhibitions of miraculous divine power are invariably connected with the Mediatorial Kingdom of God. They are seen in that Kingdom when established at Sinai in Old Testament history, and did not wholly cease until it ended with the departure of the Shekinah-Glory (Isa. 37:36; 38:5-9). Such miracles also are recorded in the Old Testament predictions of a future re-establishment of the Kingdom under the reign of Messiah. They were also present when the Kingdom was announced as imminent during the period of the Gospels. And their continuance in the Book of Acts must be explained in the same way. They are the signs of the Kingdom, given primarily as a testimony to the nation of Israel, to whom in a peculiar sense that Kingdom belonged by divine covenant, and upon whose repentance depended its imminent establishment upon earth. This was the burden of the prophets as they spoke to Israel about the Kingdom (Isa. 35:1-7). The same thing was affirmed by our Lord in His earthly ministry to the chosen nation (Matt. 11:1-5). And it was reaffirmed by the apostles in their testimony to Israel throughout the Book of Acts (2:1-20, 43).

The Epistle to the Hebrews, written especially to Christian believers in the nation of Israel, makes specific mention of the great miracles during the period of Acts and indicates briefly their purpose and meaning. In chapter two the writer refers to the testimony "which at the first began to be spoken by the Lord"; and then says that the same message "was confirmed unto us by them that heard him" (2:3), a clear reference to the apostolic preaching in the Book of Acts. In connection with this latter testimony, the writer of Hebrews says, "God also bearing them witness, both with signs and wonders, and with divers miracles" (2:4). The three Greek terms here are quite generally used in the New Testament to describe miracles. *Dunamis* points to the source of the miracle: it is an act or display of divine "power." *Teras* describes the immediate effect it is intended to produce: it is a prodigy or "wonder." *Sēmeion* indicates the purpose of the miracle: it is a "sign" pointing to something beyond it.

In a later passage of crucial importance the writer of Hebrews again refers to the miraculous acts of divine power which had characterized the Acts period, this time using the Greek term *dunamis* and reminding the Jewish readers of that generation that they had "tasted . . . the powers of the age to come" (6:5, ASV). Here the miracles of Acts, although "tasted" by that generation, are clearly placed in the category of things which belong to a future "age." Now this "age to come" cannot be the Church age, because that had already begun on Pentecost and was even then running its course. Nor can the reference be to heaven or the eternal state, for then there will be no diseased to be healed or demons to be cast out.[16] The true meaning is "the age of the Messianic reign,"[17] which is to follow the Church age and will be ushered in at the second advent of Christ. The great miracles of Acts, then, are powers which really belong to the Millennial Kingdom. This suggests that their occasional and partial enjoyment by the generation living during the time of Acts, as also in the period of the Gospels, was intended to authenticate an offer of the Kingdom to Israel, a genuine offer although conditioned on the repentance of the nation. And it explains why, following the crises of Jewish rejection reached in Acts 28 and the destruction of Jerusalem, the age of great public miracles came to an end.[18]

This is not to say that there have been no miracles since that apostolic era; for the sovereign power of God is never limited by time or circumstance. But whatever miracles God may choose to work today are different in character. They are not great *public* exhibitions of divine power; not "signs" and "wonders," designed by their nature to compel belief. When miracles take place during the present era of the Church, as I am sure they do, they are generally veiled by the providential devices of God, thus permitting the wilful sceptic to attribute the miracle to causes which are secondary,

[16] M. R. Vincent, *Word Studies in New Testament* (New York: Scribner's Sons, 1924), *in loc.*

[17] W. F. Moulton, *Ellicott's Commentary* (Grand Rapids: Zondervan Publishing House, reprint, 1954), *in loc.*

[18] In an interesting passage, Geerhardus Vos seems to agree that there was some connection between the miracles during the period of Acts and the contemporary eschatological expectations: "The subsequent receding of this acute eschatological state has something to do with the gradual disappearance of the miraculous phenomena of the apostolic age" ("Eschatology of the New Testament," *I.S.B.E., op. cit.,* Vol. II, p. 980). But what the connection is he does not attempt to explain.

and often making it difficult, if not impossible, for the believer to "prove" its supernatural character.[19] This is in harmony with the chief characteristic of the life of the Church, which is *faith* in Christ in the sense of unlimited willingness to trust Him in all things. In the face of the inexplicable problems of human life, the mysteries of the divine will, the apparent inequalities of divine justice, and human perplexity under the sombre shadows of a silent heaven, the Church must "walk by faith, not by sight" (II Cor. 5:7). There is nothing inherently sinful about believing on the evidence of sense experience; but there is a special blessing for those who have believed without seeing (John 20:29), who, against the often adverse testimony of human experience, continue to believe and trust without reserve in Him who today is not visible, "Whom having not seen, ye love" (I Pet. 1:8). In the Church, God is preparing a special people, called out and tested in the crucible of adversity, who are destined to occupy the highest place of responsibility in the future Kingdom of Christ.

5. Jewish Opposition and Its Growth

The reaction of Israel here follows the same general pattern as in the period of the Gospels. The issue has not essentially changed: Is Jesus of Nazareth the Messiah of Old Testament prophecy? And this issue, it must not be forgotten, cannot be isolated from the question of the Kingdom; for the Messianic concept was primarily *regal* in nature. The hardening and progression of Jewish opposition moves through three rather definite stages, each culminating in a well-marked crisis: the first in the death of Stephen (ch. 7); the second in Paul's address at Antioch (ch. 13); and the third in his prolonged conference with the Jews at Rome (ch. 28).

a. *From Pentecost to Stephen's Martyrdom* (Acts 2-7)

It is noteworthy that, in the face of the great events of the day of Pentecost, there is no record of any serious opposition on the part of the Jewish leaders to the apostolic testimony. The public miracle of tongues provoked great wonder and perplexity, together with some ridicule. But when explained by Peter, supported by Old Testament prophecy, there was produced in the multitude a rather wide conviction that a terrible mistake had been made in

---

[19] On the entire problem see *The Silence of God* by the late Sir Robert Anderson, a work which upon its first publication was characterized by the New York Herald as "a book which has astounded Europe." (Reprint of the 11th English ed.; Grand Rapids: Kregel Publishing Co. 1952).

the rejection and crucifixion of Jesus. The immediate result was 3000 converts to belief in Him as the Messiah of Israel (Acts 2:37-41). And Luke adds that "fear came upon every soul" (vs. 43). Furthermore, the continuance of these converts in the temple as a central meeting place, "having favour with all the people," indicates that the new era began with no overt opposition (2:46-47). The Jewish leaders may have felt that with the death of Jesus they had effectively disposed of His Messianic claims. And although they had heard rumors of His resurrection, they doubtless had noted that during the days between the Passover and Pentecost the earlier excitement had apparently subsided, and had concluded that they now could afford to treat the movement tolerantly as only another Jewish sect which would quickly fade in popularity.

Luke's record of *official* persecution begins in Acts 4:1-3 where, after Peter's offer of the Kingdom on the condition of repentance, the apostles were arrested and held for examination, following which they were "threatened" and released (vss. 17-21). Later they were again imprisoned, but when set free by angelic intervention (5:18-19), they again resumed their testimony in the temple (vs. 25). Once more their ministry was halted by arrest by the authorities; and this time they were beaten and charged to speak no more in the name of Jesus (vs. 40). But even so, undaunted, they continued "every day, in the temple and at home," to preach "Jesus as the Christ" (vs. 42, ASV).

As a result of this bold and continued testimony there were many conversions. "The number of the men was about five thousand" (Acts 4:4). "And believers were the more added to the Lord, multitudes both of men and women" (5:14). Even "a great company of the priests were obedient to the faith" (6:7). This rapid increase in adherents raised an economic problem in caring for the needy among them and led directly to the first step in organization (6:1-5). Among the seven men appointed to deal with the problem was Stephen, a man whose impressive testimony brought an immediate collision with the Jewish authorities (6:8-14). His accusations against them as representatives of the nation, uttered during his examination, aroused such implacable rage that he was rushed out of the city and stoned to death without even the semblance of a judicial trial or verdict (7:51-59). The martyrdom of Stephen showed that the *intransigent* temper of the Jewish leaders had not been changed by the great events of Pentecost nor by the apostolic miracles and witness which followed. And it marked the end of the comparatively tranquil early days of the disciples in the city of Jerusalem.

b. *From Stephen's Death to Paul's Address at Antioch* (Acts 8-13)

The violent death of Stephen let loose "a great persecution" against the *ekklēsia* in Jerusalem, and its members were scattered throughout the areas of Judea and Samaria, "except the apostles" (8:1). The exception noted here by Luke, which is somewhat perplexing, may indicate the immense public prestige of the apostles by reason of their powerful preaching and mighty works. In this general persecution, which seems to have been the first systematic attempt to stamp out the testimony to the crucified Jesus as the Messiah, Saul of Tarsus became its most ardent and outstanding leader (8:1-3). But the preaching of the scattered disciples far outran the persecution, covering Samaria and reaching points south of Jerusalem (8:5-8, 25-26, 40).

It was during this persecution that the new movement won its most renowned convert in the person of Saul of Tarsus (9:1-20). The loss of this leader of the persecution must have been a staggering blow to the Jewish opposition. For when Saul changed sides in the battle and began at once to confound the Jews at Damascus by his preaching of Jesus, "proving that this is very Christ," Luke says that they "took counsel to kill him" (vss. 22-24). When he escaped over the wall in a basket and came to Jerusalem, the Jewish attitude was no better: "They went about to slay him" (vss. 25-29). The Jewish rulers evidently understood better than the church what they had lost and what the latter had gained in Saul of Tarsus. Actually, the disciples at Jerusalem were at first afraid of him (9:26), a genuine compliment to Saul's great ability and energy.

Following the departure of Paul from Jerusalem there was a brief respite from persecution: "Then had the churches rest throughout all Judaea and Galilee and Samaria" (Acts 9:31). While various factors may have contributed to this temporary condition of "rest," its connection in the Biblical record with the conversion of Saul has not received the attention it deserves.[20] For the time being, the Jewish persecution had lost its leading genius to the other side!

---

[20] The *men oun* with which verse 31 begins is Luke's way of gathering up historical connections.

Furthermore, Jewish hatred had been diverted to the person of Saul; and he had been spirited away from Jerusalem to Tarsus where he was beyond their reach. Also, the Jews at Jerusalem were occupied with troubles of their own in the attempt of the Roman Caligula to set up his image in the temple.

At this point in the historical record Luke inserts an account of the ministry of Peter, particularly in relation to Cornelius and his conversion, making clear that the Gentiles were not excluded from "repentance unto life" (Acts 9:32-11:18). It was in this connection that trouble appeared from a new source, this time within the Jewish section of the Church itself (11:1-3); and although settled for the time being (11:18), the problem continued to plague the Church throughout the ministry of Paul (Gal. 2:11-13; I Tim. 1:4-7).

The renewal of physical persecution, recorded in chapter 12 of Acts, although ostensibly begun by the Roman government as represented by Herod Agrippa, is nevertheless traced by Luke to the Jewish nation. The king began his campaign against the Church with cold-blooded efficiency — by killing off its leadership: first, James is killed; then Peter is arrested. And Herod did what he did from political motives: "because he saw it pleased the Jews" (vss. 1-3). John, third of the inner circle of apostles, would probably have been next; but the action was broken off by angelic intervention: Peter is delivered from prison, and the king is struck down by a fatal disease (vss. 7, 23).

While the testimony to Jesus as the Messiah was being carried to the many Jewish synagogues of the ancient world (Acts 13:5), Paul and Barnabas came in their itineration to "Antioch of Pisidia." There they immediately went to the Jewish synagogue on the Sabbath day, where, following the customary reading from the law and prophets, they were invited to speak (vss. 14-15). The address of Paul presented, first, a brief review of the Old Testament Theocratic Kingdom down to David through whose seed would come the covenanted Messianic Saviour of Israel (vss. 17-22); second, an affirmation that in Jesus is to be found the fulfilment of what had been written in Old Testament prophecies about the regal Messiah (vss. 23-37); and, third, an offer of forgiveness of sins, with a stern warning of judgment if they refuse (vss. 38-41). Such tremendous interest was aroused by the message that on the next Sabbath almost the entire city was assembled to hear the Word of God, the mixed audience consisting of Jews, proselytes, and Gentiles (vss. 42-44). Trouble immediately arose from "the Jews" who "spake against those things which were spoken by Paul, contradicting and blaspheming" (vs. 45).

The bold answer of Paul and Barnabas here indicates that another definite crisis has been reached in the matter of Jewish opposition: "It was necessary that the word of God should first have been spoken to you: but seeing ye put it from you, and judge yourselves unworthy of everlasting life, lo, we turn to the Gentiles" (13:46). And in support of their action, the speakers appeal to Jewish Scriptures, "For so hath the Lord commanded us, saying, I have set thee to be a light of the Gentiles, that thou shouldest be for salvation unto the ends of the earth" (vs. 47). The quotation is from Isaiah 49:6, a text set firmly in the context of a great Old Testament prophecy of the Messianic Kingdom. The question at Antioch, therefore, could not have been whether or not the Gentile church was now to supplant the nation of Israel on earth in the Messianic Kingdom, for the primacy of Israel had been established irrevocably in divine covenant and prediction. The question raised by the Antiochan Jews rather was whether the *Gentiles* could have any genuine share in the benefits of that Kingdom. And on this point also the prophets had been equally clear: while Messianic salvation is of the Jews and primarily for them, the Gentiles are not to be excluded. And in the case of both, the spiritual conditions are the same: they must "believe" that Jesus is the Messianic Saviour; and be justified by grace, not by law (vss. 38-39). According to the present offer to Israel, if the existing generation rejects the Grace of God in Jesus they will "perish" (vs. 41); but if any Gentiles accept, they will be saved. In any case, the outcome has been "ordained" of God (vs. 48), whose purposes are unchangeable and therefore cannot be frustrated by the stubborn actions of men.

It is to be noted that even after the Antiochan address the testimony in Jewish synagogues was continued (14:1). But Paul's stern warning that he is turning "to the Gentiles" did indicate that the trend of Jewish opposition was pointing once more to another lost opportunity in the long history of that nation in relation to the Mediatorial Kingdom of God on earth. The religious attitude of Israel toward the Gentile peoples indicated that they were far from ready spiritually to function as leaders in a re-established Theocratic Kingdom which would minister impartially for good to all nations upon the earth.

c. *From the Antiochan Address to the Conference at Rome* (*Acts* 14-28)

The Jewish opposition during this final period becomes massive and more intolerant. Its primary object is the Apostle Paul, whose ministry to the Gentiles and alleged neglect of the Mosaic ritual is made the basis of their complaint. Related to this was his progressive revelation of the nature of the *ekklēsia,* a point to be discussed below. But at bottom the *cause célèbre* was Paul's proclamation of Jesus as the Messiah of Israel. When Paul and his companions encountered persecution at the hands of Gentiles at Philippi (Acts 16) and Ephesus (Acts 19), the motive was basically economic: They "saw that the hope of their gains was gone" (16:19); and "our craft is in danger" (19:27). But the Jewish attack was invariably made on *religious* grounds. And the irony of its final manifestation is that the Jewish officials are the persecutors while the Roman officials are the protectors of the great apostle.

Immediately following Paul's address at Antioch the Jews at Iconium "stirred up the Gentiles" against his converts (Acts 14:2), and they united in an assault on Paul and Barnabas, attempting to stone them (vss. 4-5). When they fled to Lystra they were followed by Jews from Antioch and Iconium, who dragged Paul out of the city and stoned him, leaving him for dead (vs. 19). At Thessalonica, where Paul spent three Sabbaths in the synagogue proving from the Scriptures that Jesus was the Messiah, and where he made some converts, the unbelieving Jews stirred up a street mob which assaulted the house where he had stayed, renewing the old political charge of disloyalty to Caesar (17:1-9). At Corinth, when Paul again entered the Jewish synagogue to testify that Jesus is the Christ (18:5), the Jews met him with opposition and blasphemy; and once more he warns of coming judgment: "Your blood be upon your own heads; I am clean: from henceforth I will go unto the Gentiles" (vs. 6). With his converts, including Crispus, the ruler of the synagogue, Paul started meetings in a private home nearby (vss. 7-8). Evidently enraged because of his success, the Jews later conspired to bring Paul before Gallio's judgment seat, from which the cynical proconsul drove them with contempt, saying, "I will be no judge of such matters" (vss. 12-16). But they vented their spleen by beating Sosthenes, who had apparently succeeded Crispus and must have shown some sympathy for Paul (vs. 17). At any rate he appears among the saved (I Cor. 1:1). At Ephesus Paul spent three months in the synagogue "disputing and persuading the things concerning the kingdom of God"; but on account of Jewish opposition, he withdrew and conducted his work for two years in a school owned by Tyrannus, having immense success (19:8-10).

About this time Paul began to lay plans to go to Jerusalem (Acts 18:21; 19:21), although he was well aware of the peril of such a visit (20:22). Warned in advance by a prophet as to the outcome, his purpose did not waver: "I am ready," he replied, "to die at Jerusalem for the name of the Lord Jesus" (21:10-14). Upon his arrival at Jerusalem, by advice of the leaders of the church there, Paul made a last attempt to placate his Jewish enemies by conforming to a certain rite of purification in the temple (vss. 20-26).[21] But the attempt only made matters worse. When he was seen in the temple, "all the city was moved, "and he was dragged out and would have been beaten to death by the mob had it not been for the Roman captain whose soldiers rescued him with some difficulty because of the "violence of the people" (vss. 27-36). Paul's calm and measured speech to the Jews, given by permission of the Roman captain (21:39-22:21), was interrupted with a great cry of outrage: "Away with such a fellow from the earth; for it is not fit that he should live." And as they shouted, they "cast off their clothes, and threw dust into the air" (vss. 22-23).

Later, when permitted to appear before the Jewish Sanhedrin, Paul's opening sentence brought a blow upon his mouth by order of the high priest (23:2); and before the meeting ended, the captain felt it necessary to remove the apostle by force to keep him from being torn to pieces (vs. 10). The following day forty Jews bound themselves under a curse neither to eat nor drink until they had killed Paul; and with the knowledge and cooperation of the Jewish officials, a plot was made to carry out their lethal purpose (vss. 12-15). But again the apostle was given protection by Roman officers who, having learned of the plot and aware of the uncontrollable temper of the Jews, decided to remove him under military escort from Jerusalem to Caesarea in order to save his life (vss. 23-25). His defense there against the Jewish leaders before Felix accomplished nothing except to arouse in the governor the hope of

[21] For an able defense of Paul's action in joining in the temple ritual, see A. T. Robertson, "Paul, the Apostle," I.S.B.E., op. cit., Vol. IV, pp. 2285-6.

a bribe on behalf of the prisoner (24:26). And when two years later Felix was succeeded by Porcius Festus, the latter left Paul bound because he desired to "gain favor with the Jews" (24:27, ASV). The coming of Festus to Jerusalem was used by the Jewish leaders to request that Paul might be brought to Jerusalem, with the purpose of waylaying and killing him on the journey (25:3). But the governor countered by offering the accusers their day in court at Caesarea; and during the hearing, desiring to curry favor with the Jews, he asked Paul whether he would be willing to go to Jerusalem for trial. It was this query that led to Paul's historic appeal to Caesar (25:9-12). He was at last convinced that neither mercy nor justice could be had at Jerusalem, not even from the local Roman government there; and so he turned toward Rome, the most important center of non-Palestinian Jewry in the ancient world, there to make his final appeal to his kinsman according to the flesh.

But Festus, worldly politician that he was, began to entertain some misgivings about sending to Caesar a Roman citizen against whom nothing of any consequence had been proven. In fact, as he admitted, he was sending to Caesar a prisoner about whom he had nothing to write; a course of action which might turn out to be dangerous business for an aspiring governor. Therefore he requested King Agrippa to examine the prisoner for the purpose of finding, if possible, something which might justify his proposed action, rightly reasoning rather tardily that it would be "unreasonable to send a prisoner, and not withal to signify the crimes laid against him" (25:24-27). The conclusion of Agrippa, after the examination, was that "This man might have been set at liberty, if he had not appealed unto Caesar" (26:32). But the appeal having been made, there could now be no turning back. Thus began the long and dangerous journey which would bring the apostle to the capital of the ancient world, the place of his greatest ministry and also of his martyrdom.

d. *Paul's Conference with the Jews at Rome* (Acts 28)

Upon arrival at Rome the apostle was given the respect and privileges due an important political prisoner, being permitted "to dwell by himself with a soldier that kept him" (28:16).[22] In verse 30 we learn that this situation continued for two years

[22] The clause in verse 16, "the centurion delivered the prisoners to the captain of the guard," although probably not in the original Lukan text, nevertheless may represent a reliable tradition. Cf. the various textual authorities.

during which he lived "in his own hired house." This was a period when Christianity was regarded as a Jewish sect and hence one of the many religions tolerated by the Roman government. There is strong evidence for a second and later imprisonment when this attitude had completely changed. The ministry of Paul during these first two years began with an important conference.

(1) The apostle in the beginning addresses himself exclusively to Jews. Only three days after his arrival he "called the chief of the Jews together" (Acts 28:17). Since he was not free to go to them, he invited them to come to his own residence. And the fact that they came indicates not only their awareness of the important place occupied by Paul but also their deep interest in the Messianic issue. Evidently the decree of Claudius, banishing Jews from Rome (Acts 18:2),[23] had been allowed to lapse. And since Rome had been a great center of non-Palestinian Jewry (Acts 2:10), those meeting with Paul would include rulers of synagogues, wealthy traders, and even officials in the imperial court.

(2) Addressing the Jews as "Men and brethren," Paul emphatically denies any break with his nation: "I have committed nothing against the people, or customs of our fathers" (Acts 28:17). Israel, to Paul, was still *to lao* — *the* people. Furthermore, his appeal to Caesar was not for the purpose of bringing any accusation against the nation he still calls "my nation" (vs. 19), but only to protect his own life.

(3) If they should enquire as to the reason for his imprisonment, he desires them to understand that "for the hope of Israel I am bound with this chain" (Acts 28:20). This "hope" was a very specific thing, referred to in Acts four times (cf. 23:6; 24:15; 26:6-7). It involved (a) the hope of the coming of the Messianic Kingdom as set forth in Old Testament prophecy; (b) the hope of a resurrection of those Israelites who had died, to the end that they might participate in the Kingdom (cf. Ezek. 37:11-28).[24] As to this latter point, Paul had argued that the resurrection of Jesus should not be regarded as something "incredible" (Acts 26:6-9). The connection of the doctrine of resurrection with the Messianic Kingdom was the one thing which invalidated the Jewish objection to the crucified Jesus as the Messianic King. It is for this hope of the Kingdom and its attendant resurrection, the

---

[23] For an excellent discussion of this matter see Plumptre in Ellicott's *Commentary on Acts 18:2*.

[24] *Ibid.*, on Acts 28:20; also on 23:6 and 26:6-7.

apostle argues, that he stands in chains before the representatives of his nation.

(4) The interest aroused by their first meeting with Paul led to a later and larger meeting with the Roman Jews: "And when they had appointed him a day, there came many to him into his lodging"; and the meeting was prolonged "from morning till evening." The main subject of discussion was "the kingdom of God" and the relation of "Jesus" to that Kingdom, as set forth in the "law" and the "prophets" (Acts 28:23). The outcome of the meeting was inconclusive. Though "some believed" (vs. 24), there was no agreement among them, thus confirming in the mind of the apostle a feeling that, whether in Jerusalem or at Rome, the attitude of his nation had hardened into a fixed antagonism toward Jesus as the Messiah.

(5) Instead of a benediction, the meeting at Rome was closed with an imprecation (Acts 28:25-27). It is again the well-known prophecy of Isaiah, a passage quoted only upon the occasion of certain great adverse crises in the history of Israel. The *first* crisis came in the ministry of Isaiah when the rebellion of the nation was leading inexorably to the judgment of captivity and dispersion in which the Theocratic Kingdom on earth would end (Isa. 6:9-10). The *second* crisis came during the ministry of Christ when the attitude of Israel had made clear that He would be rejected by the nation (Matt. 13:13-15). The *third* crisis came when, following the official offer of the King in His triumphal entry, the nation's leaders prepared to kill Him (John 12:37-41). The *fourth* crisis came when the unyielding opposition of the nation toward a renewed offer of her Messianic King, now risen from the dead, had run its bitter course from Jerusalem to Rome. History was again repeating itself. And once more — this for the last time — the terrible words, uttered originally by Isaiah, later by the King Himself, then by the Apostle John, are heard from the lips of Paul (Acts 28:25-27) as he speaks to the people for whom he had "great heaviness and continual sorrow" in his heart (Rom. 9:2-3). It should not be overlooked that the words thus quoted in sharp crises of Israel's history are always heard in connection with the Mediatorial Kingdom of God. And they were spoken to Israel for the last time[25] shortly before Jerusalem fell in the awesome judgment of A.D. 70.

[25] Probably A.D. 61.

But these historical judgments upon the nation are never eternal or total. In the context of the original prophecy, Isaiah asks, "How long?" And the answer of God is not "forever," but *"until"* certain conditions are fulfilled. Furthermore, even the temporal judgment is partial, for the nation will be as "an oak, whose stock remaineth, when they are felled; so the holy seed is the stock thereof" (Isa. 6:11-13, ASV). Thus, in spite of her judgments, God has not cast away His people Israel. For there was, even in the day when Paul uttered the divine judgment upon the nation, "at this present time . . . a remnant according to the election of grace" (Rom. 11:1-5). And the "stock" of the tree spoken of by Isaiah (6:13) appears again in the "root" of Paul's "olive tree" which never dies (Rom. 11:15-27).

6. Preaching in the Apostolic Period of the Acts

Preaching during the period of Acts displays a twofold aspect: first, there was the proclamation of the *Kingdom* in established form as an impending possibility, contingent upon the attitude of Israel toward the King; and second, there was the testimony concerning the *Church,* begun on Pentecost, as the spiritual and royal nucleus of the coming Kingdom. This preaching was initially addressed exclusively to Jews. But as the tide of Jewish opposition grew, there was a change in emphasis. The period begins with the Kingdom in first place, the Church having almost no distinguishable separate identity. As the period progresses in time, the Church begins to assume a more prominent place, with a glory of its own, while the established Kingdom becomes more remote. Contemporaneously there is a shift from emphasis upon Jewish national primacy toward a universality in which national distinctions tend to disappear. Though the components of apostolic preaching are so closely related that one part cannot be wholly isolated, its subject matter appears to have had three distinct main emphases.

a. Concerning Jesus and the Way of Salvation

Believe on the Lord Jesus Christ, and thou shalt be saved.
—*Acts 16:31*

(1) It should need no argument to show that all apostolic preaching centered in the historic Person of "Jesus of Nazareth." He is the "Lord and Christ" of Old Testament prophecy (Acts 2:36); "the Holy One and the Just," the "Prince of life" (3:14-15); the great "prophet" like Moses (3:22-26); "the stone" of Israel, made

the "head of the corner," in whom alone there is salvation for men (4:11-12). He sits at the right hand of God as "a Prince and a Saviour" to give repentance and forgiveness to Israel (5:31). He is the suffering Messiah of Isaiah's prophecy (8:30-35), and also "the Son of God" (9:20). He is the regal "seed" of David (13:22-23), crucified and risen from the dead, through whom "all that believe are justified from all things," as opposed to the impotency of the law (13:39). He is the "man" by whom the world will be judged in righteousness (17:31), and the "God" who "purchased with his own blood" the Church (20:28). He is acknowledged and preached as the "Lord" of the Shekinah-Glory by Paul, converted Jewish scholar and Pharisee (22:6-11).

(2) In the preaching of the Acts period, the saving work of the Messianic Jesus was presented in three aspects. First, it was an individualistic and personal matter: "whosoever shall call upon the name of the Lord shall be saved" (2:21). Second, with reference to this personal salvation, there was no difference between Jew and Gentile (10:43-48). Third, in this personal redemption and salvation by the Messiah there was being laid a firm spiritual foundation for the promised Kingdom, as predicted in the prophets (3:19-21 with vs. 26).

(3) Thus we meet here one insuperable obstacle to the view which equates the Messianic Kingdom of Christ with His work as a personal Saviour of men. As to the latter, there is no difference between Jew and Gentile; each human soul must be saved in the same way of grace, and there are no national priorities. But in the established Kingdom on earth the nation of Israel will have the supremacy. To deny this distinction will involve us in either one or the other of two serious errors: if men are not all saved alike by the grace of God, then He has different ways of salvation; but if the nation of Israel is not to have priority in the Kingdom, then we must reject great areas of divine prophecy at its face value. In either case, the loss is theologically disastrous.

b. Concerning the Kingdom

Preaching the things concerning the kingdom of God.   —*Acts 8:12*

(1) The term "kingdom" (Grk. *basileia*) occurs eight times in Acts as referring to the divine rule. Seven times the phrase is "the kingdom of God" (1:3; 8:12; 14:22; 19:8; 20:25; 28:23, 31). Once the term stands alone without the name of Deity (1:6), but

here the definite article and the context put the meaning in the divine category beyond dispute. The invariable use of the phrase "kingdom of God," never "kingdom of heaven," suggests that, for the most part in this area of Biblical history, the teaching deals with the Kingdom in its more universal aspect, i.e., as including the Mediatorial Kingdom and the Church, both of which must be regarded as within the Kingdom of God. When *basileia* stands alone in the question of the disciples, "Dost that at this time restore the kingdom to Israel," the reference is clearly restricted to the Mediatorial Kingdom, for the *ekklēsia* had not yet begun.

(2) In the Book of Acts this "kingdom of God" appears as something future, the term being used, as James Orr has observed, "in an almost exclusively eschatological sense."[26] The Old Testament prophecies of the Messianic Kingdom, occasionally quoted by the apostles (cf. Acts 2:25-36; 3:22-26; 13:22-39), are used to show the *regal* rights of Jesus as the Messiah. But nowhere do the preachers ever assert that the Kingdom has been established. In passages about which there should be no dispute, this is a matter which belongs to the future when the King returns from heaven (cf. 1:6-11; 3:19-21; 15:13-16). The passage in 14:22, "we must through much tribulation enter into the kingdom of God," is sometimes used to prove a present Messianic Kingdom established on earth in the Church. But such a use would prove too much. The people to whom the text was addressed were "disciples" and therefore already within the "kingdom of God" in the broad sense of John 3:5. Such an entrance is by the new birth, not by "tribulation." But in the Old Testament prophetic picture of the coming Messianic Kingdom, as every intelligent Jew understood, a period of terrible tribulation always precedes its establishment on earth. And the disciples during the period of the Acts, pursuant with Peter's offer (3:19-21), were looking for the coming of that Kingdom. Therefore, the passage in 14:22 is in complete harmony with the historical situation and the progress of revelation. It is always true, of course, that all who would *reign* with Christ in His future Kingdom, must suffer with Him (II Tim. 2:12). But this is something else.

(3) The argument advanced by some, that since the apostles

[26] See Note 1, p. 386.

throughout the Acts period preached "the things concerning the kingdom of God" (19:8), therefore the Kingdom must have already been established, is not very good logic. Most of us preach and teach many things in the Christian faith which are not yet realized in experience. No sensible person would argue that because the apostles continually preached the resurrection of the dead, therefore, it must have already taken place. Those who pray intelligently, "Thy kingdom come," are those who will also speak a great deal about its future glories and benefits. And the preachers of the early apostolic era had an added incentive: they knew that the Kingdom, viewed in the light of the divine offer, was an imminent possibility in their generation.

(4) Those who admit a genuine offer of the Kingdom to Israel in the period of the Gospels, could have no logical reason for objecting to a similar offer in the Acts period. As a matter of fact, the justifiable reasons for such an offer in the latter period are greater than in the former. For the preaching in Acts proceeded on the basis of the death and resurrection of Messiah which had now become historic facts, thus providing the soteriological foundation without which there could have been no *enduring* Messianic Kingdom established on earth. And the former problem of a Messiah who dies and yet reigns gloriously had now been cleared up by the resurrection of Jesus. It would have been strange, therefore, if there had been no reoffer of the Kingdom following Pentecost, such as Luke records in the third chapter of Acts.

It may be asked how there could have been any genuine option for Israel during this period, since the destruction of Jerusalem had already been clearly predicted by our Lord as a judgment upon Jewish unbelief; and also that the people were to be scattered among all nations and Jerusalem trodden down until the times of the Gentiles be fulfilled (Luke 21:24). The answer is that every intelligent Jew understood from the prophets that a terrible time of tribulation would immediately precede the establishment of the Messianic Kingdom. Therefore, the fulfilment of our Lord's predictions could have ushered in the end, since the *time* element is always unrevealed. To read 1900 years of time into these predictions is to abandon the historical standpoint in our interpretation. And the early disciples were expecting the shock of tribulation, the imminency of the Church's separate rapture having not yet been clearly revealed as it would be later in the Pauline epistles.

c. *Concerning the Church*

> The church of God, which he hath purchased with his own blood.
> —*Acts* 20:28

(1) The Greek term *ekklēsia*, as referring to the Christian Church, occurs nineteen times in the Book of Acts. Regarding its distribution, if the spurious appearance in 2:47 be omitted, the term is found only once in the first seven chapters. The other eighteen are found in chapters 8-20. The remaining chapters are concerned mainly with the personal experiences of Paul on his journeys to Jerusalem and Rome, and therefore the absence of the term in this section has no significance.

(2) The historical question now is: How did the early disciples interpret the *ekklēsia?* In reply we may observe that the record provides no evidence that in the early days of the Church's existence its members were fully acquainted with its distinctive character as later revealed in the New Testament epistles. The early Church was wholly Jewish in membership; and the long usage of the term *ekklēsia* for the *qahal* or "congregation" of Israel would have naturally suggested a similar connotation. Furthermore, in our Lord's original prediction concerning His *"ekklēsia,"* He reveals only one general feature, i.e., its place of authority in relation to the future "kingdom of heaven" (Matt. 16:18-19). And since the disciples were looking for an early restoration of that Kingdom "to Israel," it should be clear that their hopes were centered on the Kingdom rather than on the *ekklēsia.* Of course, it would be hard to believe that during the forty days of His teaching the disciples "the things pertaining to the kingdom of God" (Acts 1:3), our Lord would have said nothing about the *ekklēsia.* But the record in the early chapters of Acts suggest strongly that the *ekklēsia* was then regarded as the saved Jewish "remnant" of Old Testament prophecy which would constitute the spiritual nucleus of the Messianic Kingdom. Certainly, in those early days, the Church was not in possession of the truth, later revealed, that it was destined to be a unique body as distinguished from all other bodies of the saved in all ages. This observation not only fits the historical situation but also harmonizes with the progress of revelation.

(3) The early emphasis upon the Kingdom helps to explain the rise of the Jewish-Gentile problem in the Apostolic Church. The

proposed explanations range widely, from Baur's theory of two versions of Christianity, the one Petrine and the other Pauline, down to the recent theory of two Churches, the one in Acts being Jewish and the other the universal body of Christ in the present age. The true explanation must be found in the transitional character of the period covered in the Book of Acts. Because of the reoffer of the Kingdom to Israel, the period begins with the Kingdom in the forefront. And while the prophets had made clear that the Gentile nations were to share in its benefits, the nation of Israel always held the place of priority. Therefore, it becomes understandable that the admission of Gentiles to the *ekklēsia* raised the problem of *how* they were to be received, if at all. Within the Church the problem moved toward a solution in co-ordination with two other movements: first, the growth of Jewish opposition to the offer of the Messianic Kingdom; and, second, the progress of revelation as to the unique nature of the *ekklēsia* begun on the day of Pentecost.

(4) The shift in preaching emphasis, from the Kingdom as an imminent possibility contingent on Israel's repentance, to the Church as a unique body of believers in which all racial and national distinctions disappear, helps to explain another curious phenomenon in the history of the Acts. Out of the 28 chapters of the book, no less than fifteen are concerned primarily with the work of the apostle Paul. And, as we have noted, the Jewish opposition very quickly centered upon this one man following his conversion. Now the reasons for this attitude were undoubtedly various. But Paul's distinctive view of the *ekklēsia* must not be overlooked. For it was through this apostle, as an instrument of divine inspiration, that God unveiled the lofty character of the *ekklēsia* begun on Pentecost. This is most fully developed in the Ephesian and Colossian Epistles, written shortly after A.D. 60 during his first imprisonment (cf. Acts 28:16, 30 with Eph. 4:1 and Col. 4:18). However, several years earlier the *core* of the same view had appeared in the First Corinthian Epistle, where the *ekklēsia* is presented as the one body of Christ in which there is no distinction between Jew and Gentile (12:12-13 ff.). Such a doctrine of the Church, possibly expressed still earlier in his oral ministry, would at least in part account for the bitter animosity of the Jews outside, and sometimes within, the churches. It was one thing to say that Gentiles might enter the *ekklēsia;*

it was something else to declare that within that body the Jew had no advantage or priority over the Gentile! And it is a striking fact that at the very time *Paul* was nearly torn to pieces by the Jews at Jerusalem, there was in that city a Christian church with James and its elders, all apparently enjoying immunity from Jewish persecution (Acts 21:17-19, 31).

(5) Historically, therefore, the theological barrier between Jew and Gentile was completely broken down when the opposition of Israel to our Lord's Kingdom was again moving to the crisis of divine judgment, and when contemporaneously the Pentecostal *ekklēsia* was being unveiled in the Pauline epistles as a unique body having a glory all its own. And, we may add, if there had been no reoffer of the Kingdom to Israel in the period of the Acts, the Jewish problem might easily have been clarified at the very beginning by an immediate full revelation of the nature of the Church begun on the day of Pentecost. The fact that it was delayed demands some explanation which is in harmony with both history and revelation.

7. *A Summary of the Acts Period*

In preaching and testimony the Acts period must be regarded as transitional, displaying characteristics which belong to both the Kingdom and the Church.

Just as in the period of the Gospels the Kingdom had been offered to the nation of Israel, even so during the history of Acts the Kingdom was again offered to Israel. In both periods the offer was authenticated by the same "signs and wonders" which, according to the prophets, belonged properly to such an offer. And its establishment, in both periods, was conditioned upon re-pentance and acceptance of Jesus as the Messiah on the part of the nation. Furthermore, in both periods there was Jewish opposition which moved to a crisis of rejection.

But parallel with this movement in Acts there was also the history of the Church which began on Pentecost as the spiritual nucleus of the coming Kingdom; and which, following the crisis of Jewish rejection of their Messianic King, was revealed as a unique body destined among the saved of all ages to occupy the highest place in the Kingdom of God. As the period of Acts ends, we pass from the time area of "signs and wonders" into an era characterized chiefly by the demand for unquestioning faith in the presence of a silent heaven as far as great *public* miracles are concerned.

The period opened with the triumphant sermon of Peter on Pentecost, followed almost at once by his official offer of the Kingdom made from the temple porch, both addressed to representatives of the nation of Israel assembled from all nations at the city of Jerusalem. The period moved to its close with the day-long appeal of Paul, now a prisoner in chains, addressed to the "chief of the Jews" assembled in the great Gentile metropolis of Rome. It was followed quickly by the "prison epistles" in which the unique glory of the *ekklēsia* was fully revealed. The end came in the destruction of Jerusalem and its temple in A.D. 70.

The Book of Acts, therefore, presents another one of those probationary periods ordained by divine grace for the nation of Israel. And like a similar period in Old Testament history, when Israel wandered in the wilderness, it lasted approximately one generation. This time, however, the nation failed to enter the promised "rest" of the Kingdom, not only at the beginning but also at the end of the probationary period.

Significantly, both in Old Testament prophecy and in our Lord's eschatological discourse, *the last landmark* before we enter the uncharted time of the present age, is the destruction of Jerusalem (Dan. 9:26; Luke 21:24). Beyond this now historical landmark looms only the beginning of the end. Between the destruction of Jerusalem and the Rapture of the Church (I Thess. 4:13-18), divine revelation indeed speaks of general conditions and tendencies, but there is no single *event* by which the Church may infallibly locate herself in the ocean of time.

The period covered by the Book of Acts, therefore, while a genuine segment of the present Church age, has nevertheless a character which differs markedly from that area of time following the destruction of Jerusalem. In this peculiar character we may find at least a partial explanation of the complexities of that Biblical history of the Church which by divine inspiration was recorded by "the beloved physician."

CHAPTER XXV

THE MEDIATORIAL KINGDOM IN THE EPISTLES

> There is no critically undisputed passage in the Scriptures which declares, or necessarily implies, even a *partial* establishment [of the Kingdom] in New Testament times. —*E. R. Craven*[1]

Among the 27 books of the New Testament, no less than 21 belong to the epistolary class. Since the epistles speak of both the *ekklēsia* and the *basileia*, their content should be briefly surveyed to find the place given to these two subjects, the general character of each, and how they are related.

1. *The Church in the Epistles*

a. The epistles were sent to churches or to members of churches, under various forms of address: to a church (I Cor. 1:2); to a group of churches (Gal. 1:2); to the whole body of saints in one church (Rom. 1:7) or those in all the churches (Jude 1:1); or to a person connected with a church (I Tim. 1:2-3). Apparent exceptions, e.g., "to the twelve tribes which are scattered abroad" (Jas. 1:1), and to the "sojourners of the Dispersion" (I Pet. 1:1, ASV), do not actually depart from the general rule; for the people addressed in these cases, as the letters show, are believers in Christ and therefore members of His *ekklēsia*. Even the letters enclosed within chapters 2 and 3 of Revelation are sent respectively to seven local churches. There is no epistle of the New Testament addressed to the saints in "the kingdom of heaven."

b. The frequent occurrence of the term *ekklēsia* in the epistles suggests that they are concerned chiefly with this particular body of the saved. The term appears only three times in the Gospels, doubtless in a prophetic sense (Matt. 16:18; 18:17); nineteen times in the Book of Acts; and sixty-seven times in the epistles. If the epistles included within the Apocalypse be added, the num-

---

[1] E. R. Craven, "Excursus on the Basileia," Lange's *Commentary on Revelation*, tr. by E. Moore, ed. by E. R. Craven (New York: Scribner's Sons, 1874), p. 95, paragraph 3.

ber would be eighty-seven times out of a total of one hundred and nine occurrences in the New Testament.

c. The epistles are concerned mainly with the career of the *ekklēsia* on earth in time. They date the beginning of the Church at the descent of the Holy Spirit on the day of Pentecost to baptize its members into the one body of Christ (I Cor. 12:13, ASV); and they place the completion of the Church at the second coming of Christ (I Thess. 4:13-18). Between these two events the life of the Church is regarded as an *interim* — "until the Lord come" (I Cor. 4:5; cf. 11:26; Phil. 1:6; I Tim. 6:14). For the Church, this interim is a time of humiliation (Phil. 3:21, ASV), testing (Jas. 1:12), trouble and persecution (II Cor. 4:8-9), suffering and groaning (Rom. 8:18-23), patient endurance (Jas. 5:7-11), refining and perfecting (Jas. 1:2-4), unceasing labor (I Cor. 3:8-15), agonizing conflict (I Tim. 6:12; II Tim. 4:7, Grk.), and unrelenting struggle toward a goal which lies beyond this age and world (Phil. 3:12-14). For the present, therefore, the members of the Church must in a peculiar sense walk by faith (II Cor. 5:7), live in hope (Rom. 8:24-25), endure hardship as good soldiers of Christ (II Tim. 2:3), not looking at the things which are seen but at the things not seen (II Cor. 4:18).

This general picture of the Church's career[2] on earth, as presented in the epistles, stands in sharp contrast with the prophetic picture of the Kingdom on earth, the latter appearing both in the Old Testament prophets and in the teaching of our Lord as a golden age of rest and blessing which is the goal of all human history under God.

2. *The Kingdom in the Epistles*

a. The word "kingdom" (*basileia*) is used eighteen times in the epistles as referring to the divine rule. In eight of these occurrences the expression is "kingdom of God" (Rom. 14:17; I Cor. 4:20; 6:9, 10; 15:50; Gal. 5:21; Col. 4:11; II Thess. 1:5). Seven times the Kingdom is specifically assigned to our Lord Jesus Christ (I Cor. 15:24; Eph. 5:5; Col. 1:13; II Tim. 4:1, 18; Heb. 1:8; II Pet. 1:11). The three other passages are I Thess. 2:12, Heb. 12:28, and Jas. 2:5.

b. Some of these passages assert specifically that the Kingdom belongs to the *future* rather than to the present age of the Church. The Apostle Paul brackets together in point of time the future

---

[2] The doctrine of the Church will be presented in another volume of this series.

"appearing" (*epiphaneia*) of Christ with "his kingdom" (II Tim. 4:1). Later in the same chapter he expresses his firm assurance that the Lord will preserve him unto his "heavenly kingdom" (vs. 18). This expression is not a synonym for heaven, but rather indicates that the long-awaited Messianic Kingdom will be "heavenly" in origin and character as contrasted with earthly kingdoms. It is the closest approximation to the familiar phrase "kingdom of heaven" so frequently used in Matthew's Gospel. Peter exhorts Christian believers to be diligent in walk and work so that they may have an abundant "entrance . . . into the everlasting kingdom of our Lord and Saviour Jesus Christ" (II Pet. 1:11). In these texts cited there can be no question about the futurity of the Kingdom.

c. The idea of *futurity* is also present in a number of passages which speak of the Kingdom as something which the members of the *ekklēsia* shall inherit (I Cor. 6:9, 10; 15:50; Gal. 5:21; Eph. 5:5; Jas. 2:5). The Apostle Paul not only sees this inheritance of the Kingdom in future time but definitely excludes it from the present age by placing it after the resurrection and rapture of the Church. "Now this I say, brethren, that flesh and blood cannot inherit the kingdom of God" (I Cor. 15:50). This view, of course, harmonizes with our Lord's eschatological picture of His Kingdom. He must first return from heaven in glory in order to sit on the "throne of his glory" (Matt. 25:31). Only then as the King will He say to the righteous, "Come, ye blessed of my Father, *inherit the kingdom* prepared for you from the foundation of the world" (vs. 34, italics added). The inheritance may indeed be sure to all groups of believers, whether in heaven or on earth, but its realization in experience must wait for the coming of the Lord.

d. The theory that Christ and the saints are now reigning in a present kingdom of God on earth, is specifically refuted by the Apostle Paul. Writing to the Corinthians, who had caused him so much trouble and anxiety, he speaks with great irony, "Now ye are full, now ye are rich, ye have reigned as kings without us." Then with one of those abrupt changes so characteristic in his letters, he speaks in a tone of tender yearning and love, "and I would to God ye did reign, that we also might reign with you" (I Cor. 4:8). For, to the apostle, that glorious prospect would mean an end of all hunger and thirst, reviling, persecution, defamation, uncertainty of dwelling-place, and danger of life itself (vss. 9-13). But since believers are not yet fit to reign, they must be careful to "judge nothing before the time, until the Lord come" (vs. 5). In the meantime, the present sufferings have a beneficent purpose in relation to the future Kingdom: "If we endure, we shall also reign with him" (II Tim. 2:12, ASV).

In support of the idea of a present Messianic reign of Christ over the nations, appeal is sometimes made to Romans 15:12, "There shall be a root of Jesse, and he that shall rise to reign over the Gentiles; in him shall the Gentiles trust." A study of the context, however, shows that Paul does not assert the present *fulfilment* of this prophecy. The passage begins as follows: "Now I say that Jesus Christ was a minister of the circumcision for the truth of God, to confirm the promises made unto the fathers" (vs. 8). Then the apostle cites four of these Old Testament promises (vss. 9-12). But nowhere in the passage are these promises said to have been *fulfilled* at the first advent of Christ. The verb is "confirm" (*bebaioō*).[3] And this our Lord did establishing firmly the Old Testament promises of a future Kingdom to Israel at their full face value, both by word and deeds. They cannot be invalidated, therefore, by any device of interpretation.

e. Of the remaining passages where *basileia* occurs, there is not one which grammatically cannot be interpreted consistently with the doctrine of a *future* Kingdom. And where there may be any question, the interpreter must always be guided by the clear doctrine taught in passages about which there is no uncertainty. To attempt any exhaustive exegesis of the texts listed below will not be necessary. It will be sufficient to show only the reasonable *possibility* of an interpretation in harmony with the idea of a future Kingdom.

Rom. 14:17. "*For the kingdom of God is not meat and drink; but righteousness, and peace, and joy in the Holy Ghost.*" The thought here fits a *future* Kingdom better than a present one. For surely in the present life no one can deny the importance of meat and drink; but so far as the Church is concerned in the future Kingdom, these things will be of no consequence. Therefore, since the Church is to reign in that Kingdom, its members should not judge or grieve one another in such matters here and now (cf. vss. 13-21). All disputes of this nature should be left for the "judgment seat of Christ" which will inaugurate His Kingdom upon earth (vs. 10).

[3] For the usage of the verb see Mark 16:20; I Cor. 1:6, 8; and Heb. 2:3.

I Cor. 4:20. *"For the kingdom of God is not in word, but in power."* Here we have, as Meyer points out, an assertion of the *causal basis* of the future Messianic Kingdom for which the early Christians were looking. It is characterized by "power" (*dunamis*) rather than boastful talk. The same Greek term is used to describe the great public miracles which, according to Hebrews 6:5, belong to "the age to come," i.e., the Kingdom age. To interpret I Corinthians 4:20 as a present kingdom of the saints would make Paul contradict what he had already written in verses five and eight.

I Cor. 15:24. *"Then cometh the end, when he shall have delivered up the kingdom to God, even the Father."* The time of this Kingdom may be ascertained from the main subject matter of the context, which is *resurrection.* Every man must be raised from the dead, we are told, but each in his own order: "Christ the firstfruits; then they that are Christ's, at his coming. Then cometh the end. . . ." (vss. 23-24, ASV).[4] This threefold order of resurrection fits the eschatological system of the New Testament; first, the resurrection of Christ Himself; second, the resurrection of His saints at the second advent (I Thess. 4:13-18); third, the resurrection of the unsaved at the "end" (cf. Rev. 20:11-15). Since the Kingdom is to be established at the second coming of Christ, and it is to be delivered up to the Father at the "end," the period of the Kingdom must be located in the future between the two resurrections, as also indicated clearly in Revelation 20.

Col. 1:13. *"Who hath delivered us from the power of darkness, and hath translated us into the kingdom of his dear Son."* The context here suggests that the action must be regarded as *de jure* rather than *de facto.* Believers have been "delivered . . . from the power of darkness," the apostle declares. Yet in another place he warns that we must still wrestle "against the rulers of the darkness of this world" (Eph. 6:12). Our translation into the Kingdom of Christ, therefore, must be similar to that act of God when He "raised us up together, and made us sit together in heavenly places in Christ Jesus" (Eph. 2:6). Although we are not yet *de facto* seated in the heavenlies, the thing is so certain that God can speak of it as already done. In the same sense, we have been (aorist tense) transferred *judicially* into the Kingdom of our Lord even before its establishment. Being what He is,

---

[4] On the passage see H. A. W. Meyer, *Commentary on Corinthians,* tr. of 5th ed. by D. G. Bannerman (New York: Funk and Wagnalls, 1884), p. 356.

God "calleth the things that are not, as though they were" (Rom. 4:17, ASV). Such at times is the language of divine inspiration.

Col. 4:11. *"These only are my fellowworkers unto the kingdom of God, which have been a comfort unto me."* The Greek preposition here is *eis,* and therefore the passage may be read in harmony with the idea of a future Kingdom, toward which as a glorious goal all the labors of the Church are directed.

I Thess. 2:12. *"That ye would walk worthy of God, who hath called you unto his kingdom and glory."* The language here is similar to other passages where believers are said to be called unto (*eis*) things not yet realized in Christian experience. Compare I Peter 5:10 — "God . . . hath called us unto his eternal glory."

II Thess. 1:5. *"That ye may be counted worthy of the kingdom of God, for which ye also suffer."* Compare the words of Christ in Luke 20:35 where some are "accounted worthy" of a *future* resurrection from among the dead. The Greek verb is the same.

Heb. 12:28, *"Wherefore, receiving a kingdom that cannot be shaken, let us have grace, whereby we may offer service well-pleasing to God"* (ASV). It is not unusual for Scripture, on behalf of believers, to assert *ownership* regarding certain blessings even before they are *possessed* in Christian experience. Compare I Corinthians 3:21-22 where "all things" are said to belong to the believer, yet among these things are some that are yet "to come." The ownership is legally certain, though the experience of possession may be future.

f. The term "throne" (*thronos*) as referring to a divine Kingdom, occurs four times in the Epistle to the Hebrews, and in no other epistle. In 8:1 and 12:2 the reference is clearly to the throne of God at whose right hand Jesus is now seated. In 4:16, where the expression is "the throne of grace," the meaning is not the throne of the Messianic Kingdom, but rather again the throne of *God* where today Jesus sits as High Priest to plead the cause of His own.[5] The passage in Hebrews 1:8 unquestionably refers to the eternal throne of Deity, which our Lord shares in His own right as "the Son" in the Universal Kingdom of God.[6] This position of divine sovereignty is presented by the writer of Hebrews as evidence of our Lord's infinite superiority over all

[5] So Alford, H. A. W. Meyer, *et al.*
[6] See Chap. IV, sec. 6 of this volume.

angelic beings (vss. 7-8). In verse nine it is His personal right-eousness as *Man* that is made the ground of His exaltation above all His "fellows."

3. *The Kingdom during the Present Church Age*

The question now may be raised as to whether or not there is *any* Biblical sense in which we could properly assert a *present* existence on earth of the Mediatorial Kingdom of God. In seek-ing an answer to this question, we should be willing to disavow in advance any differences based wholly on semantic considera-tions. Ideas are more important, of course, than strife about words. But on the other hand, it should be mutually agreed that a Biblical terminology is highly desirable, if for no other reason than in the interest of intelligent discussion. Above all, we should seek sincerely to understand each other in discussing these matters, always remembering that men may be correct in their ideas while faulty in their choice of terms.

a. *Some Necessary Distinctions*

(1) There is a sense, of course, in which Christ today rules in the Church. But the nature of this rule is very different from that of the Mediatorial Kingdom.

> It is as its Head that He rules over it [the Church], not as its King; for this latter title is never used of this relation. Nor is His rule over His Church legal and external, like that of an earthly king . . . The relation between Him, the Head, and the Church, His Body, is a living one, such as nowhere else exists, or can exist; His will is the law, not merely of its action, but of its life . . . . He rules in the Church through the law of a common life . . . .[7]

(2) It is also true that our Lord today, as always, rules in what I have called the Universal Kingdom of God, which is generally ad-ministered providentially (cf. Chap. IV). But this rule must be dis-tinguished from that direct and immediate rule which will charac-terize the future Mediatorial Kingdom.

> As Jehovah was absolute ruler alway over all nations, and yet was not the theocratic King of any till the election of Israel, so the Lord Jesus became the "Prince of the Kings of the earth" at His ascension, but does not yet stand in immediate kingly relations to any one peo-ple. His investiture with universal authority does not involve the in-stant possession and exercise of it . . . . Providentially He reigns over all nations, executing the Father's will, raising up and casting down kings . . . . He reigns, but He is invisible, and the world at large knows it not; the nations pay Him no conscious obedience.[8]

---

[7] S. J. Andrews, *God's Revelations of Himself to Men* (New York: Scribner's Sons, 1886), pp. 284-285.
[8] *Ibid.*, pp. 285-286.

(3) The reign of Christ in His Mediatorial Kingdom will be sharply different from both His control of the Church and His providential rule over the Universe.

> Had it been the purpose of God to set the Son at His ascension as the King of the nations, He would in some way have made His kingship so plain that the nations could not have been ignorant of it, and of the duty of allegiance and homage. There must, also, have been in every land those publicly invested with His authority to act as His representatives, and with power to give commands and to compel obedience . . . but [today] He does not appoint their princes, nor dictate their laws, nor is His hand seen in judgment.[9]

The confusion of the three aspects of our Lord's rule cited above leads to serious consequences. First, it makes the present age the period of the Mediatorial Kingdom. Second, it has the Church in its present imperfect state performing functions which can only be fulfilled when the body of Christ is complete and perfected. Third, it dissolves the divinely covenanted purpose in the nation of Israel. Fourth, it does not distinguish clearly the two offices of Christ as Priest and King. Fifth, it makes the present age of the Church the final period of historical redemption. Sixth, it seats mortal, sinful, and fallible men on the throne with the risen and glorified Christ. As to this last point, Andrews has well said, "To affirm that mortal and sinful men are already admitted to have part in His functions of universal rule, and are empowered by Him to govern the nations, is a proud and presumptuous antedating of the Kingdom. His kings must be first made like Him, immortal and incorruptible. When the earthly in them is changed into the heavenly, then can they exercise His heavenly authority."[10]

Theological confusion, especially in matters which have to do with the Church, will inevitably produce consequences which are of grave practical concern. The identification of the Kingdom with the Church has led historically to ecclesiastical policies and programs which, even when not positively evil, have been far removed from the original simplicity of the New Testament *ekklēsia*. It is easy to claim that in the "present kingdom of grace" the rule of the saints is wholly "spiritual," exerted only through moral principles and influence. But practically, once the Church becomes the Kingdom in any realistic theological sense, it is impossible to draw any clear line between principles and their implementation through political and social devices. For the logical implications of a present ecclesiastical *kingdom* are unmistakable, and historically have always

[9] *Ibid.*, pp. 286-287.
[10] *Ibid.*, p. 293. Cf. his entire chapter IV.

led in only one direction, i.e., political control of the state by the Church. The distances down this road travelled by various religious movements, and the forms of control which were developed, have been widely different. The difference is very great between the Roman Catholic system and modern Protestant efforts to control the state; also between the ecclesiastical rule of Calvin in Geneva and the fanaticism of Münster and the English "fifth-monarchy." But the basic assumption is always the same: The Church in some sense is the Kingdom, and therefore has a divine right to rule; or it is the business of the Church to "establish" fully the Kingdom of God among men. Thus the Church loses its "pilgrim" character and the sharp edge of its divinely commissioned "witness" is blunted. It becomes an *ekklēsia* which is not only in the world, but also *of* the world. It forgets that just as in the regeneration of the individual soul only God can effect the miracle, even so the "regeneration" of the world can only be wrought by the intrusion of regal power from on high (Matt. 19:28).

> Any attempt to establish the Kingdom of God here on earth leads to false enthusiasm and is a sign of sectarianism. Those who attempt it want to abolish the twofold character of the Church and thus avoid any possible cause of offence. The other mistake is to identify directly the earthly and empirical Church with the Kingdom of God, but that is to reduce the *ekklēsia* to the level of a synagogue, even if it is most loyally confessional and altogether bound to the sacraments. Here lies the danger of "High-Churchism" both in its Roman and in its Protestant garb. The Church is never *the Ultimate End* (to eschaton), but is always oriented toward *the Ultimate End*, the Kingdom of God itself.[11]

b. *The Present Relation of the Basileia to the Ekklēsia*

That there exists today a genuine relationship between the two cannot be successfully denied. Let us now attempt briefly to summarize this relationship:

(1) During the present Church age, from Pentecost to the second coming of Christ, the Mediatorial Kingdom must be said to be in *abeyance,* in the sense of its actual establishment on earth.

(2) In another sense, however, it might be said that the Mediatorial Kingdom does have a present *de jure* existence, even prior to its establishment. This is true, first, in the sense that God is today saving and preparing in the *ekklēsia* the members of the royal family who are destined to rule with Christ in the future established Kingdom; and, second, in the sense that, as those born into the royal family, we enter *judicially* into the Kingdom before its es-

[11] Professor K. E. Skydsgaard, "Kingdom of God and Church," tr. by Rev. B. Citron, *Scottish Journal of Theology,* Dec. 1951, p. 393.

tablishment, a divine action so remarkable that Paul speaks of it as a translation (Col. 1:13).

(3) It must be admitted also that the Church of the present age is enjoying many of the *spiritual* blessings which in the Old Testament were predicted in connection with the Messianic Kingdom of the future; e.g., pardon for sin (Isa. 55:4-7), justification through faith by means of imputed righteousness (Jer. 23:6), regeneration (Ezek. 36:24-38), and the coming of the Holy Spirit upon men (Joel 2:27-28). But some of these blessings have always been available to contrite sinners, as far back as Abel (Heb. 11:4) and Abraham (Rom. 4:3), long before the Kingdom appeared in Old Testament history. Furthermore, the presence of blessings which belong to one *aspect* of the Kingdom does not necessarily mean that the Kingdom is already established on earth. A king might be rejected by his nation, be driven from his own land by rebels, and during his absence from the throne he might extend amnesty to all who would cease their rebellion; but there could be no re-establishment of his kingdom until he had been restored to his own country and throne, once more exercising directly all his regal rights and functions.

There is an interesting parallel in the career of King David, great ancestor of our Lord Jesus Christ. When David was chosen of God and anointed as king of Israel (I Sam. 16:1, 13), he did not immediately occupy the throne. For a time he was actually a fugitive in the wilderness, pursued by Saul whose regal rights had been abrogated (I Sam. 15:28), and who therefore continued to hold the throne solely as a usurper. During this period several hundred men, in distress and debt, "gathered themselves" unto David and became his loyal followers (I Sam. 22:2). Later, when Saul's rule was ended by defeat and death, the kingdom of David was established over Israel, the event being definitely marked by services of anointing (II Sam. 2:4; 5:3). Similarly, at His first coming our Lord was exalted to be both Lord and Messianic King (Acts 2:36); but not until His second coming will He establish His Kingdom on earth as the rightful successor to the throne of His father David. In the interim He is gathering to Himself a body of people, distressed and debtors because of sin, who are destined to be associated with Him in the coming Kingdom. Upon them, from His present throne in the heavens, He is abundantly able to bestow certain of His regal blessings even before the arrival of the Kingdom.

(4) The fiction of a present "kingdom of heaven" established on

earth in the Church, has been lent some support by an incautious terminology sometimes used in defining the "mysteries of the kingdom of heaven" (Matt. 13:11). The parables of this chapter, it is said carelessly by some, describe the kingdom of heaven as now existing in "mystery form" during the Church age. Now it is true that these parables present certain *conditions* related to the Kingdom which are contemporaneous with the present age. But nowhere in Matthew 13 is the establishment of the Kingdom placed within this age. On the contrary, in two of these parables the setting up of the Kingdom is definitely placed at the end of the "age" (vss. 39 and 49 ASV, with 41-43). And it is to be noted that in each of these references, our Lord is speaking as the infallible interpreter of His own parable.

What is certain in the teaching of these difficult parables is that the present age, viewed from the standpoint of the Kingdom, is a time of *preparation*. During this period the Son of man is sowing seed (vs. 37), generating and developing a spiritual nucleus for the future Kingdom, a group called "sons of the kingdom" (vs. 38, ASV). At the same time He is permitting a parallel development of evil in the world under the leadership of Satan (vss. 38-39). It is the purpose of God to bring both to a "harvest," when the good and bad will be separated, and then to establish the Kingdom in power and righteousness (vss. 41-43, 49).[12]

---

[12] The absence in Matthew 13 of any mention of the *ekklēsia*, or of its pretribulation Rapture, is not strange; for such mention at this point would be completely unhistorical in the progress of divine revelation.

CHAPTER XXVI

THE MEDIATORIAL KINGDOM IN THE APOCALYPSE

It is only through this doctrine of the Kingdom that the Apocalypse can or will be understood and consistently interpreted. The reason for this lies in the simple fact that it announces the Coming and the events connected with the Advent of the Theocratic King. Now to enter fully into its spirit and appreciate its force, to form an adequate conception of the testimony of Jesus either as a whole or in its several aspects, there must of necessity be a *previous* acquaintance with the covenants and a correct *apprehension* of the burden of prophecy based on those covenants, resolving itself into the promised Kingdom.
—*George N. H. Peters*[1]

1. The last book of the Bible is pre-eminently *the Book of the Kingdom of God* in conflict with, and victory over, the kingdoms of this world. With this general viewpoint most commentators would agree, regardless of differences over principles and details of interpretation. It is closely supported by the terminology of the book: The word "throne" (*thronos*) occurs 41 times; of which 38 refer to the divine kingdom (1:4), 3 to the satanic kingdom (16:10, tr. "seat"). "Kingdom" (*basileia*) is found 7 times; referring 3 times to God's kingdom (1:9), and 4 times to the kingdom of evil (16:10). The term "crown" occurs 11 times: in 3 references representing *diadēma*; applied to Christ (19:12), to Satan (12:3), and to the beast (13:1): in 8 references representing *stephanos*; applied to Christian believers (2:10), to the rider on the white horse (6:2), to the demonic hosts (9:7), to Israel (12:1), and to the Son of man (14:14). "Reign" (*basileuō*) is used 7 times, always of the divine kingdom (5:10). "Power" (*exousia*), i.e., authority to rule, occurs 20 times, about evenly divided between the two opposing kingdoms (2:26; 13:4). "Rule" (*poimainō*) in the sense of shepherdly government is used 4 times, always of Christ's activity (19:15). As terms indicating a supreme function of government, the verb "judge" (*krinō*) occurs 8 times and the noun "judgment" (representing *krisis* and *krima*) 6 times; significantly in every instance applied to the divine government (6:10; 14:7). The word

[1] Geo. N. H. Peters, *The Theocratic Kingdom*, (New York: Funk and Wagnalls, 1884), Vol. III, p. 366.

"wrath" (representing *thumos,* 15:1; and *orgē,* 6:16) is used 15 times as indicating the expression or execution of the divine judgment, and once in the lower sense of Satanic anger (12:12).

2. The Apocalypse is also *the Book of the Second Coming of Christ.* After six verses of introductory material, the main body of the book opens with the glad announcement: "Behold, he cometh with clouds; and every eye shall see him" (1:7). And the final word from Christ Himself, uttered from His present throne of grace in heaven, is the promise, "Surely I come quickly"; to which John responds with the last prayer recorded in Scripture, "Even so, come, Lord Jesus" (22:20).[2] That the second advent and the Kingdom are brought together as the main subjects of the last book of Scripture, will occasion no surprise to those acquainted with divine revelation. For these two great eschatological events are inseparable as the goal of history, as we have already noted especially in the teaching of Christ Himself. The personal and glorious coming of Messiah will bring in the Kingdom, and without such a coming there can be no Messianic Kingdom. Between the two prayers, "Thy kingdom come" (Matt. 6:10) and "come, Lord Jesus" (Rev. 22:20), therefore, there is little difference as to their great objective, except perhaps that the latter represents the more mature thought in the progress of divine revelation.

3. The revelation of the Kingdom and its glorious King in the Apocalypse can only be apprehended in close connection with the Old Testament, especially its prophetic literature, and particularly the Book of Daniel. Although the Apocalypse contains no direct citation from the Old Testament, it is saturated with Old Testament phraseology. In the total of 404 verses, Westcott and Hort list about 265 which contain Old Testament language; and also about 550 references to Old Testament passages. "Nothing is more important for the understanding of our author's mental and literary processes than a close study of his use of Old Testament language."[3] An exposition which leans heavily upon the Old Testament, and

---

[2] See the discerning appraisal of Archbishop Trench: "What is the keynote to the whole Book? Surely it is 'Maranatha,' 'our Lord cometh' . . . . With this announcement the Book begins . . . with this it ends . . . and this is a constantly recurring note through it all . . . . We may say, indeed, that in some sort *ho erchomenos* is a proper name of our Lord" (*Epistles to the Churches,* p. 7). Also see Dusterdieck in *Meyer's Commentary on the Revelation,* p. 27: "The entire prophecy of the Apocalypse rests upon the fundamental thought of the *personal return of the Lord.*"

[3] Frank C. Porter, "Book of Revelation," *Dictionary of the Bible,* ed. James Hastings (New York: Scribner's Sons, 1902), Vol. IV, p. 254.

especially its prophetical writing, according to Hengstenberg, "is absolutely indispensable to a proper understanding of the Revelation."[4] And James Orr says, "Its precursor in the Old Testament is the Book of Daniel, with the symbolic visions and mystical numbers of which it stands in close affinity."[5] It may be laid down as a first principle, therefore, that no interpretation of the Revelation can be accepted which breaks with the thought of the Old Testament prophets.

4. Let us now approach the Book of Revelation from the standpoint of the general eschatological concepts of the Old Testament. If the prophets teach anything clearly, they teach that in the last times there will come, first, a period when God will pour out His judgments upon the world; also that following these judgments a Messianic Kingdom of God will be established on earth; and that this Kingdom will become universal in scope and be prolonged without end. Now these are precisely the general ideas of the Apocalypse, and they are stated in the same sequence. Passing over for a moment the introductory material dealing with the Giver of the revelation and the Churches which receive it (chs. 1-3), the book presents three general subjects: first, a period of divine judgments on the world (chs. 4-18); second, the coming of Christ to establish His Kingdom on earth (chs. 19-20); and third, an extension of this reign of Christ into the eternal Kingdom of God in the new heavens and earth (chs. 21-22. Cf. especially 22:3-5).

5. The clear and exact correspondence between the general ideas of the Old Testament prophets and the Book of Revelation is also supported by our Lord's final eschatological discourse as recorded in the Gospels. As to the events of the end-time: first, there is to be a period of unparalleled "tribulation" in the world (Matt. 24:21-26); second, this will be followed "immediately" by the glorious second advent of Messiah (Matt. 24:29-30), when He will establish His Kingdom over the nations (Matt. 25:31-34); and third, the judgments of this Kingdom will extend into the eternal state (Matt. 25:41, 46).

6. It also should be noted here that the Apocalypse preserves and further clarifies the same distinction between the Mediatorial Kingdom of Messiah and the Universal Kingdom of God, which we have

---

4 E. W. Hengstenberg, *Revelation of St. John*, (Edinburgh: T. and T. Clark, 1851), Vol. I. preface, p. VII.

5 James Orr, "Book of Revelation," *International Standard Bible Encyclopedia*, ed. James Orr (Chicago: Howard-Severance, 1915), Vol. IV, p. 2582.

already observed throughout the earlier Scriptures. In this final book John sees two kingdoms, each preceded by a throne of judgment. From the first of these thrones (4:2) issue the divine judgments which finally usher in the Mediatorial Kingdom of Christ on earth for a thousand years (20:6). From the second throne of judgment (20:11-15) issue those final judgments which prepare for the Universal Kingdom in its final form where the *one* eternal throne is that "of God and of the Lamb" (22:3-5).

These general correspondences running through the Scriptures are too evident to be ignored, as too often they have been. On the contrary, they should provide the surest guidance to the understanding of the Apocalypse in its revelation of "things to come." From this standpoint, the book may be examined under the following outline:

Introduction: The Revelation of Future Things and Its Present Blessing (1:1-3)

   I. The Churches to Which the Revelation Was Addressed (1:4-3:22)

  II. The Revelation of the Period of Pre-Kingdom Judgments (4:1-18:24)

 III. The Revelation of the Period of the Messianic Kingdom (19:1-20:15)

  IV. The Revelation of the Final Universal Kingdom of God (21:1-22:5)

Conclusion: Exhortations to the Churches in View of the Lord's Coming (22:6-21)

I. The Churches to Which the Revelation Was Addressed (Rev. 1:4-3:22)

All, then, are agreed that these seven Epistles, however primarily addressed to these seven Churches of Asia, were also written for the edification of the Universal Church; in the same way, that is, as St. Paul's Epistle to the Romans, or to Timothy, or St. James to the Dispersion, were written with this intention. The warnings, the incentives, the promises, the consolations, and, generally, the whole instruction in righteousness in these contained, are for everyone in all times, so far as they may meet the several cases and conditions of men; what Christ says to those here addressed He says to all in similar conditions. Thus far there can be no question.   —*Archbishop Trench*[6]

1. The entire Book of Revelation (as well as the individual letters of chapters 2-3) is addressed to seven churches: "John to the seven churches which are in Asia" (1:4). Later in the same chapter

---

[6] R. C. Trench, *Epistles to the Seven Churches* (6th ed.; London, 1897), pp. 234-235.

the geographical locations of these churches are named as Ephesus, Smyrna, Pergamos, Thyatira, Sardis, Philadelphia, and Laodicea (1:11), thus indicating their literality. Still later the same churches appear under the symbolism of seven golden candlesticks, which are identified by the divine Person in the vision thus: "the seven candlesticks which thou sawest are the seven churches" (1:20).

2. The Greek term used in Revelation to designate the seven bodies of believers is *ekklēsiai*. In the entire book the term occurs twenty times, always of the seven churches to which the book was addressed. Outside of the first three chapters, which are introductory in character, the word is found only once, in the closing epilogue which refers back to the original recipients of the Revelation (22:16). It is a striking fact that *ekklēsia* is never used in the main body of the book where the great eschatological events of the end are described (4:1-22:5). Furthermore, the Book of Revelation always employs *ekklēsia* in connection with the churches *on earth*; never with any body of the saved in heaven.

3. It should be noted also that all references to an *ekklēsia* in the Apocalypse apply only to *local churches*. The symbol is not *one candelabrum* with seven branches, but rather a group of seven separate lamp-stands[7] in the midst of which the Son of man walks (2:1). There is in this Book of Revelation no one true world-church on earth. The idea of any historical ecumenicity is totally absent. It is true that in chapter 19 the truly saved of the present age are presented as a "wife" at the marriage of the Lamb (vs. 7); but this scene is set "in heaven" (vs. 1), and the wife here is presented as having been perfected in character (vss. 7-8). Furthermore, she is not called an *ekklēsia*, a term which by the writer of Revelation is always reserved for local churches on earth composed of good and bad (cf. the description in chs. 2-3). The only genuine example of an ecumenical organization of religion on earth appears in the great harlot of chapter 17.

4. There is doubtless some symbolic meaning in the *number* of churches selected by the Spirit of God for description; and about this good men have differed widely. But the one thing upon which there seems to be general agreement is that "seven" here speaks of a *totality of characteristics*. In the seven churches we have both every kind of church and also every kind of member, which not only

---

[7] Plumptre says, "The Seer beholds not a lamp with seven branches, but seven distinct lamps" (*Epistles to the Seven Churches* [3rd ed., London: Hodder and Stoughton, 1884], p. 35).

existed on earth in John's generation but also will exist throughout all ecclesiastical history. In other words, we have in the seven selected local churches a composite picture of *all* local churches on earth at any particular time. The number *seven* can hardly be pressed here to signify some over-all visible organization of the churches. If there was some co-operative organization of this kind existing at this early stage of history, it is wholly ignored by the writer of Revelation. Each local church is treated as a unit, complete in itself and related directly thus to Christ for good or for bad. The term *ekklēsia* in Revelation is never used in the sense of the one true body of Christ, as used elsewhere in the New Testament (cf. Matt. 16:18; Eph. 1:22-23). Whether there may be found, in this number *seven*, some typical foreshadowing of seven successive eras of church history is a matter which I have come to regard with some reserve and caution for reasons which will be stated below. We are certain, however, that each separate epistle is what the Spirit saith to *all* the "churches" (cf. 1:4; 3:22).

5. It should be observed that all the churches of Revelation 2-3 are pictured as living under the sign, *Till He come*. There are five references to the coming of Christ. Three of these warn of judgment: to Ephesus He says, "Repent, and do the first works; or else I will come unto thee quickly, and will remove thy candlestick" (2:5); to Pergamos, "Repent; or else I will come unto thee quickly, and will fight against them with the sword of my mouth" (2:16); to Sardis, "If therefore thou shalt not watch, I will come on thee as a thief" (3:3). Twice our Lord speaks of His coming as an encouragement: to Thyatira, "But that which ye have already hold fast till I come" (2:25); and to Philadelphia, "Behold, I come quickly: hold that fast which thou hast, that no man take thy crown" (3:11).

In addition to these direct references, our Lord speaks encouragingly to the churches about things associated with His second coming. In 2:23 He refers to the day when He "will give unto every one of you according to your works." In 2:10 the faithful are promised "a crown of life." In 2:26-27 the overcomer is promised "authority over the nations" to rule them "with a rod of iron" (ASV). In 3:10 those who are steadfast have the promise of Christ that "I also will keep thee from the hour of trial, that hour which is to come upon the whole world, to try them that dwell upon the earth" (ASV). And in His final word to the faithful individuals of the rejected Laodicean church, our Lord offers the assurance of a place with Him on His throne (3:21).

This picture of the churches on earth points unmistakably to the *interim* between the ascension of Christ and His return to establish His Kingdom on earth. Always the regal rewards for the faithful and the Messianic throne of Christ are future, never present during the era of the churches on earth.

6. Furthermore, the picture of the career of the churches on earth is utterly incongruous with the theory of a Messianic Kingdom presently established on earth. Let any student read the record in chapters 2 and 3, so sorry in many respects; then compare the conditions there described with the idyllic conditions set forth by the prophets and our Lord in connection with the Mediatorial Kingdom; and by no device of fair interpretation can the two eras be equated as one. The conditions obtaining during the life of the churches on earth have been ably summed up by Seiss:

> Never, indeed, has there been a sowing of God on earth, but it has been oversown by Satan; or a growth for Christ, which the plantings of the wicked one did not mingle with and hinder . . . . The Church is not an exception, and never will be, as long as the present dispensation lasts. Even in its first and purest periods, as the Scriptural accounts attest, it was intermixed with what pertained not to it. There was a Judas among its apostles; an Ananias and a Simon Magus among its first converts; a Demas and a Diotrephes among its first public servants. And as long as it continues in this world, Christ will have His Antichrist, and the temple of God its men of sin. He who sets out to find a perfect Church, in which there are no unworthy elements and no disfigurations, proposes to himself a hopeless search. Go where he will, worship where he may, in any country, in any age, he will soon find tares among the wheat, sin mixing in with all earthly holiness; self-deceivers, hypocrites and unchristians in every assembly of saints; Satan insinuating himself into every gathering of the sons of God to present themselves before the Lord. No preaching, however pure; no discipline, however strict or prudent; no watchfulness, however searching and faithful, can ever make it different.[8]

So universal and persistent is this mixture of good and bad in the churches that in each case the final exhortation to hear and the promise of reward are addressed to individual members. In every one of the seven epistles the call is, "He that hath an ear, let *him* hear"; and the promise in every case is, "To *him* that overcometh" (italics supplied). Among the churches on earth to which the Revelation was addressed, there is not even one which the Lord could present as an *ekklēsia* "that overcometh."

7. If, as generally agreed, the seven churches of Revelation present symbolically a composite view of the professing church on

_____
[8] J. A. Seiss, *The Apocalypse*, 1865, Vol. I, pp. 178-179.

earth in human history, it becomes significant that absolutely *no chronology of the period appears in the picture.* Although found in different geographical locations, the seven churches are presented as existing *together in time*: they *are* in Asia, according to the writer. While of necessity there is a literary order, there is no hint of any temporal sequence. And this is as it should be, to conform with the historical interlude to which the *ekklēsiai* on earth belong. Since to the Church, from the day of its birth on Pentecost, the coming of the Lord is always imminent, obviously there could be no chronological chart of ecclesiastical history given in advance. This one fact stands opposed to any interpretation which finds in the seven churches of the Apocalypse any rigid prophetical system of successive church eras sufficiently well defined to read in advance of the history.[9] All such schemes applied to the present age raise an eschatological dilemma from which there is no escape except by erasing the sign, "Till He come," under which the churches must live in every moment of their existence upon earth. The logic of the matter is quite simple: If in the seven churches there was prophetically revealed the entire history of the Church in seven successive eras, and if these eras could be identified with certainty in advance of the history, then it is obvious that the coming of the Lord could not occur at any point short of the seventh era. On the other hand, if the eras could *not* thus be identified, then there was no such revelation.

This chronological blank is peculiar to the revelation of the career of the churches on earth. When we move from this section of the book (chs. 2-3) to the period of divine judgments (chs. 4-18) and the establishment of the Kingdom which follows (chs.

---

[9] For a brief but able account of such interpretations, and weighty arguments against them, the reader should consult the "Excursus" by Archbishop Trench in his *Epistles to the Seven Churches*, pp. 233-250. His conclusion is that "The multitude of dissertations, essays, books, which have been, and are still being written, in support of this scheme of interpretation, must remain a singular monument of wasted ingenuity and misapplied toil; and, in their entire failure to prove their point, of the disappointment which must result from a futile looking into Scripture for that which is not to be found there."

However, Trench's conclusion seems too sweepingly dogmatic. For the true explanation may be that in the seven churches of the Apocalypse the Holy Spirit did give a *latent* revelation of the Church's career on earth, but so obscure that it could not be clearly discerned until the last or Laodicean era had been reached. If so, it would be significant that only in modern times have many devout Bible students come to agree that there was such a revelation and that we are now living in the final era of the Church on earth. Such a method of revelation is not novel in Scripture; for the Second Advent of our Lord could not be certainly identified in Old Testament prophecy until the First Advent had been realized in history.

19-20), the case is entirely different. The chronology of the Judgment period is clearly based on a single measurement stated variously as 1260 days (12:6), 42 months (13:5), and three and a half years (12:14). Similarly, in the case of the Messianic Kingdom, the measurement is stated specifically as a "thousand years" (20:6). Whether or not these numbers are to be taken as stated, or only as symbolic, will be discussed later. The point here is that there is nothing of this character applied to the total career of the churches in Revelation.

II. THE REVELATION OF THE PERIOD OF PRE-KINGDOM JUDGMENTS (Rev. 4-18)

The great day of the LORD is near, it is near, and hasteth greatly, even the voice of the day of the LORD: the mighty man shall cry there bitterly. That day is a day of wrath, a day of trouble and distress, a day of wasteness and desolation, a day of darkness and gloominess, a day of clouds and thick darkness. A day of the trumpet and alarm against the fenced cities, and against the high towers. And I will bring distress upon men, that they shall walk like blind men, because they have sinned against the LORD: and their blood shall be poured out as dust, and their flesh as the dung. Neither their silver nor their gold shall be able to deliver them in the day of the LORD's wrath; . . .
—*Zephaniah* 1:14-18

Regardless of the numerous and wide differences of opinion as to details of interpretation, there should be no disagreement regarding at least three general features of this section of the Apocalypse: *First,* it presents a period of divine judgment and wrath poured out from heaven upon a world system which is opposed to God and His Christ (4:2; 6:15-17; 11:18; 14:7; 15:1, 4; 16:7; 17:1; 18:8-10). *Second,* these judgments appear in three series of seven each: seven seals (6:1-17; 8:1); seven trumpets (8:1-9:21; 11:15-19); and seven bowls or vials (15:1-16:21), the last vial being followed by a voice, saying, "It is done" (16:17). *Third,* within the entire period there appear some clear and striking correspondences with certain divine judgments predicted in the Old Testament and also by Christ Himself, as preparatory to the establishment of the Mediatorial Kingdom on earth. To avoid repetition, the earlier parallels will not always be cited in the following discussion. It is assumed that the material here will be read in connection with the relevant chapters under Parts III and IV.

1. *A Court of Judgment in Heaven (Rev. 4-5)*

Behold, a throne was set in heaven, and one sat on the throne.
—*Rev.* 4:2

This throne was the first object seen by John, following the transference of his viewpoint from earth to heaven (4:1-2). The glorious appearance of the throne and its occupant speaks definitely of Deity (4:3, 5). Other thrones, on which are seated twenty-four "elders" wearing golden "crowns" (4:4), are seen about the central throne, and surrounding all stand innumerable hosts of angels (5:11). In the "midst" of the divine throne there is seen One named "the Lion of the tribe of Juda, the Root of David," whose appearance is like a "Lamb" sacrificed (5:5-6). He receives from the hand of God a seven-sealed book (5:7), and as He breaks its seals, the judgments of God fall successively upon the world (6:1 ff.). These judgments continue through chapters 6-19, not ceasing until as King of kings our Lord has established His Messianic Kingdom over all the earth (ch. 20), a reign which issues finally in the universal and everlasting Kingdom of God (chs. 21-22).

Now all this is only an expansion of the main ideas in a vision of the prophet Daniel where in the brief space of six verses (7:9-14) may be found in epitomized form all the main divisions of the Book of Revelation from chapter 4 to 22:5. First, there is a divine judgment court set in heaven where the "Ancient of days" is enthroned in the midst of other thrones, all surrounded by myriads of angels (Dan. 7:9-10; cf. Rev. 4-5). Second, from this high court divine judgments fall upon the nations and the "beast" that leads them (Dan. 7:11-12; cf. Rev. 6-18). Third, the divine "Son of man" comes with the clouds of heaven and receives a Kingdom over all "people, nations, and languages" (Dan. 7:13-14a; cf. Rev. 19-20). Fourth, this Messianic Kingdom finally perpetuates itself in an "everlasting dominion" which shall never be destroyed (Dan. 7:14b; cf. Rev. 21-22).

The judicial character of the period is also indicated by certain *announcements made from heaven*. The action begins with the breaking of the first four seals accompanied by the voices of the four living creatures, each saying, "Come";[10] and the four horsemen begin their terrible ride (Rev. 6:1-8). The breaking of the sixth seal brings a judgment of such appalling nature that even the unbelieving world is moved to cry for some refuge "from the wrath of the Lamb: for the great day of his wrath is come" (6:12-17). In the brief interlude between the sounding of the fourth and fifth trumpets, another angel flies through the midst of heaven, crying, "Woe, woe, woe, to the inhabiters of the earth by reason of the other voices of the trumpet of the three angels, which are yet to

---

[10] The weight of textual evidence supports the omission of the words "*and see.*" The call is not addressed to John, but to the riders of the four horses.

sound!" (8:13). At the sounding of the seventh angel, the twenty-four elders worship God, saying, "Thou hast taken to thee thy great power, and hast reigned. And the nations were angry, and thy wrath is come" (11:17-18). At the very time that the satanic beast sweeps to world power, an angel flies in mid-heaven, calling upon all men to "Fear God, and give glory to him; for the hour of his judgment is come" (14:6-7). As the seven angels of the last series prepare to pour out their vials, John reports that these are "seven plagues, which are the last, for in them is finished the wrath of God" (15:1, ASV). And when the seventh angel has poured out his vial, a great voice comes from the throne in heaven, saying, "It is done" (16:17); thus indicating that with the judgments of this last vial — on the great harlot, on Babylon, and on the two beasts (chs. 17-19) — the judicial work of the period will be complete.

When all legitimate room is allowed for symbolical language, it is certainly not too much to say that there is no series of events in the known history of the world which might even approximately measure up to the gravity of the announcements recorded by the Apostle John in these chapters of the Apocalypse.

2. Rise of a Great World Conqueror

Behold a white horse: and he that sat on him had a bow; and a crown was given unto him: and he went forth conquering, and to conquer.   —Rev. 6:2

All the figures of this verse — the white horse, the bow, the crown — are symbols of victory, as Vincent has pointed out. Therefore, by many, the rider has been identified with Christ. But there are serious objections to this view. First, it would introduce confusion into the symbolism of the vision, where our Lord appears as the Lamb *in heaven* breaking the seal which releases the rider of the white horse *on earth*. Second, it makes Christ the leader of the infernal trio of war, famine, and death (6:4-8). Although He releases these dire horsemen in judgment on the world, it is wholly incongruous to place *Him* on earth in the vanguard of such a company. Third, such a view would introduce two glorious comings of Christ to earth: one at the beginning of the judgment period, and another at its close (19:11-16). Fourth, in the coming described in chapter 19, our Lord is named unmistakably as "Faithful and True" (vs. 11), "The Word of God" (vs. 13), "KING OF KINGS, AND LORD OF LORDS" (vs. 16). But in 6:2 no such identifying name is applied to the rider of the white horse.

Fifth, when Christ comes to the earth in glory, according to all Biblical testimony, He will come in His true character to bring peace, not war with all its terrible results, to a troubled world.

The similarities between the rider in 6:2 and the one in 19:11 are few and wholly external. These may be sufficiently accounted for by the fact that the antichrist, to whom so much space is given in the Apocalypse, is also a *pseudo*-christ who will present himself to humanity as the "man of the hour." Since, according to Old Testament prophecy (Dan. 7:8), the antichrist will begin his political career as a "little horn," it is reasonable to expect that some notice would be given to this important public event in John's visions of the future. To the objection that Christ is the true Conqueror, it may be answered that the path of the antichrist must also be marked with victories which will take him quickly to the position of absolute world power, as described in chapter 13.

This suggested identification of the rider in 6:1-2 helps to complete the great drama of the end-time judgments. The period begins with the divine Messiah in heaven, controlling the circumstances and events out of which the false messiah rises and rides to power on earth. And it ends with the true Messiah coming down from heaven personally to meet and defeat the false messiah in the earthly area of his satanic empire. Obviously, the political and military career of the latter must *begin* some place in history. World empires do not spring up suddenly without historical antecedents. It would be strange, therefore, if no hint were given of a beginning of the vast empire which appears in chapter thirteen under the undisputed reign of the beast (13:7). The rider on the white horse is the counterpart of the "little horn" of Daniel's vision. And in their respective Biblical contexts both are immediately related to the court of divine judgment "set" in heaven (Dan. 7:8-10 with Rev. 4:2 and 6:1-2).[11]

3. *World-wide War and Chaos (Rev. 6:3-8)*

Another horse that was red: . . . and lo a black horse: . . . and behold a pale horse . . . .
—*Rev. 6:4, 5, 8*

The grouping of the four horsemen here is historically sound. Warfare always brings in its train bloodshed, economic ruin, and death. Furthermore, the resulting demoralization and chaos pave

[11] A recent commentary, written by the liberal Thomas S. Kepler, makes the rider on the white horse an embodiment of the historical Roman Empire (*The Book of Revelation*, Oxford University Press, New York, 1957). This does not miss the mark too badly, for in Daniel's parallel prophecy the "little horn" rises out of the area of that empire and heads it in its final form.

the road for the "man on horseback," the strong leader who offers
fair hope to discouraged peoples. Given sufficient disorder, men will
pay almost any price for the restoration of order. And the judgments loosed by the breaking of the first four seals are severe and
far-reaching. The rider on the white horse goes forth in conquests
against which, for the time being, there is no successful opposition
(vs. 2). The rider on the red horse is given "a great sword" with
power to take peace "from the earth" (vs. 4). Death rides the pale
horse, followed by Hades, with power to kill "a fourth part of the
earth" (vs. 8).[12] And since in times of widespread warfare, especially
in modern times, the liberties of men are always restricted, it should
not be surprising to find religious persecution following in the train
of the four horsemen. Thus with the opening of the fifth seal, John
sees "under the altar the souls of them that were slain for the word
of God, and for the testimony which they held" (vs. 9).

Obviously these first five judgments will be externally *providential* in character. To the eyes of the world there will be nothing
demonstrably supernatural about them. The human race has always
suffered from conquerors, wars, famine, disease, and persecution.
If there is anything unusual in John's opening vision of the future, it
must be found in the magnitude by which these calamities will then
be measured. But in them there will be visually apparent nothing
to *convince* unbelievers that the hand of God, acting permissively,
is behind the ravaging afflictions which will then be sweeping the
entire world.

4. *Geological and Cosmic Disturbances (Rev. 6:12-17)*

> When he had opened the sixth seal . . . there was a great earthquake;
> and the sun became black . . . .   —*Rev. 6:12*

With the sixth seal, the *supernatural* nature of the judgments
becomes clearly manifest. On earth there is "a great earthquake"
(vs. 12); "every mountain and island were moved out of their
places" (vs. 14). Even the celestial areas are affected: the sun becomes "black" and the moon as "blood" (vs. 12); stars fall to the
earth (vs. 13); and the heaven departs as a scroll rolled together
(vs. 14).

This is doubtless the language of *appearance*, which is the literary
method generally of Biblical inspiration. But the phenomena here
described must involve the physical earth and some part of its surrounding universe. For those who accept the Biblical record of the
physical phenomena attending the death and resurrection of Christ

---

12 The Greek word rendered "death" in Rev. 6:8 doubtless refers to *pestilence.*
See ASV margin and usage in the Septuagint.

— the sun darkened, the earth quaking, the rocks rent, and the Roman soldiers stricken as dead men (Matt. 27:45, 51; 28:4) — there should be no hesitation to believe that similar phenomena will accompany the judgments which precede the second advent of Christ to establish His Kingdom.

To see in these cataclysmic happenings only certain political and military movements in ancient history,[13] ridiculously minor when compared to the magnitude of events even in our own times, is to ignore the impressive effect produced upon the world generally by the phenomena described in Revelation 6:15-17:

> And the kings of the earth, and the great men, and the rich men, and the chief captains, and the mighty men, and every bondman, and every free man, hid themselves in the dens and in the rocks of the mountains; And said to the mountains and rocks, Fall on us, and hide us from the face of him that sitteth on the throne, and from the wrath of the Lamb: For the great day of his wrath is come; and who shall be able to stand?

Caught in the terror of events wholly beyond their control, the collective estimate of mankind will be that the world is standing under the judgment of God: "For the great day of his wrath is come," men cry, "and who shall be able to stand?" (vs. 17). The reference is apparently to the well-known Old Testament "day of the Lord," also spoken of as "the great and the terrible day of the LORD" (Joel 2:31). The thought of Rev. 6:17 is almost identical with that of Joel 2:11, where the prophet writes, "The day of the LORD is great and very terrible; and who can abide it?" For several reasons, it will not do to argue that the cry of men in Revelation 6:17 represents a mistaken opinion, or that the events described do not necessarily indicate that the day of divine judgment has arrived. First, the divine author here lets the cry of mankind stand without any correction or modification. Second, the cry is in accord with the uniform testimony of chapters 6-18 as to the judicial character of the period. Third, if an objection be raised as to how men in general could have any prior knowledge about "the day of the Lord" and its judicial character, the answer is at hand: Before the opening of the sixth seal the martyrs of that time will have already borne their faithful testimony to "the Word of God" and died for its sake (6:9).

It should be noted here that in the great eschatological discourse of our Lord, there is an exact forecast of the judgments and their sequence under the first six seals of Revelation 6. First, He warned of false Christs (Matt. 24:5; Luke 21:8). Second, He predicted war-

---

[13] See Barnes on Revelation, p. 193, for a partial list of the various conflicting opinions, including his own identification of the sixth seal with the invasion of Rome by the Goths and Vandals!

fare on a world-wide scale (Luke 21:10). Third, He predicted famines and pestilences (Matt. 24:7). Fourth, He spoke of religious
persecution and martyrdom (Matt. 24:9). Fifth, He spoke of great
earthquakes and fearful sights from heaven (Luke 21:11). But
terrible as these future events would be, Christ warned, they will be
only the "beginning of sorrows" (Matt. 24:8); thus leaving room for
the other and greater sorrows to be more fully revealed by the visions
of John beyond the six seals.

5. A Double Series of Supernatural Judgments (Rev. 8-18)

> And I saw the seven angels which stood before God; and to them
> were given seven trumpets.   —Rev. 8:2
> And I saw another sign in heaven, great and marvellous, seven
> angels having the seven last plagues.   —Rev. 15:1

The opening of the seventh seal (8:1) introduces a second series
of seven judgments (chs. 8-14), and these are followed by a final
series of seven judgments (chs. 15-18). Both series are imposed
through angelic agency: the former series signified by the sounding
of trumpets; the last series by the pouring out of the vials. Throughout the visitation of these judgments, the supernatural manifestation
of the divine Hand becomes increasingly evident, until the train
of events is consummated by the entrance of the incarnate Son
once again into human history, this time not only visibly but also
in power and glory (ch. 19).

It seems best to regard the entire three series of sevens, together with
their respective members, as following each other in sequence. It
is true that occasional similarities appear between certain judgments
of the seals, trumpets, and vials: e.g., trumpets 2, 3, and 4, with
vials 2, 3, and 4 (8:8-12 and 16:3-8). But these similarities are
not sufficient to justify the *recapitulation* theory of interpretation. In
the first place, the differences are much greater and more numerous
than the similarities. Even where the *object* of judgment is the
same, the *effect* is totally different: At the fourth trumpet the sun
is partially darkened (8:12), but under the fourth vial the sun's
heat is greatly increased (16:8). Compare also the first trumpet
with the first vial (8:7, 16:2). Second, since the physical objects
of judgment are limited in number, any long sequence of judgments must to some extent fall upon the same objects.[14]

---

[14] For arguments against the allegorizing *recapitulation* interpretation, consult
Dusterdieck in Meyer's *Commentary on Revelation*. On page 269 he writes: "The
allegorizing commentators guess here and there without any foundation, because the
text throughout contains nothing allegorical." And on page 415 he argues that
there is "no basis whatever for the recapitulation-parallelism" scheme as applied
to the seals, trumpets, and vials.

Finally, the profound difference in these judgments is found in the degree of increasing severity as the several series run their course. Nothing could be more impressive than the contrast between what happens under the first seal and what happens under the last vial. The former releases an unnamed rider on a white horse who goes forth conquering and to conquer (6:1-2). The latter brings complete destruction upon the total world empire which he builds (chs. 17-18) and the doom of the conqueror himself (19:11-21). Between the beginning of the judgment period and its end, the storm of divine wrath falls upon the world with ever increasing intensity. For example, the first four seals bring judgment in events which are familiar to all men — war, famine, death. But the first four trumpets bring *extraordinary* events, clearly supernatural in character; yet thus far affecting only a third part of its objects. When the first four vials are poured out, however, the supernatural judgments are no longer partial but become *universal* in their effects upon the inhabitants of the earth. The sole exceptions concern small areas given special divine protection, e.g., the 144,000 of 7:3-8, and the woman of 12:13-17; both representing certain members of the nation of Israel. Outside of these there seems to be no exemption from the pre-Kingdom judgments.

6. *A Divine Testimony on Earth during the Pre-Kingdom Judgments (Rev. 11:3-12)*

I will give power unto my two witnesses.   —Rev. 11:3

In this testimony, the outstanding figures are the "two witnesses" to whose earthly career a large part of chapter 11 is devoted (vss. 3-12). As to their identity, one is most certainly Elijah who, according to Malachi and also Christ Himself, will appear with a special testimony preceding the glorious advent of the Messianic King (Mal. 4:5-6; Matt. 17:11).[15] The identity of the other witness is not clearly revealed in Scripture, but it is known that the Jews were expecting a second prophet with Elijah. In Matthew he is referred to as "Jeremiah, or one of the prophets" (16:14). In John 1:20-21 he is designated simply as "that" or "the" prophet, in distinction from the Messiah and the well-known Elijah. The origin of this Jewish expectation is found in Zechariah 4:3, 11-14, to which the symbolic description of Revelation 11:4 clearly points.

[15] Early church fathers, including Chrysostum, Jerome, and Augustine, taught that Elijah the Tishbite would appear personally before the second coming of Christ (cf. Philip Schaff in Lange's *Commentary on John* 1:21). In this view Ryle concurs.

The testimony of the two witnesses is quite evidently opposed to the "beast" from whose animosity, during the brief period of their earthly ministry, (vs. 3), they are supernaturally protected (vs. 5). In support of their message, they have power to smite the earth with various supernatural judgments (vs. 6). Having completed their testimony, the beast is permitted to overcome and kill them when he reaches the height of his world power (vs. 7). Three and a half days later they rise from the dead and ascend into heaven (vss. 11-12).

The effect of their testimony is very impressive, appearing very early in the Book of Revelation and probably accounting for the martyrs seen under the fifth seal (6:9). In chapter 7 the effect greatly expands, including 144,000 Israelites (vss. 3-8), and also "a great multitude, which no man could number, of all nations" (vss. 9-14). In chapter 12 John sees still another company of Israelites "which keep the commandments of God, and have the testimony of Jesus Christ" (vs. 17). In that awful day they will overcome "by the blood of the Lamb, and by the word of their testimony," being faithful unto death (vs. 11). Even in the final scene of divine judgment upon the world system of the "beast," the divine testimony is perpetuated in a "people" of God, who are called to "come out" before the hour of doom (18:4).

There is in chapter 4 a symbolic forecast of this divine testimony and its precious fruit on earth during the period of pre-Kingdom judgment. Concerning the judgment throne set in heaven, John says, "there was a rainbow round about the throne" (4:3), a symbol speaking clearly of bright hope for all who turn to God throughout the entire period.

Thus, in the judicial dealings of God with men, there is a definite progression which runs through the ages. During the present age, the period of the Church, the throne is a "throne of grace" with no mixture of penal judgment (Heb. 4:16); God is not today imputing unto men their trespasses in any formal or judicial sense (II Cor. 5:19). During the Kingdom age, including the judicial actions by which it will be established on earth, there will be a throne of judgment, but surrounded by a rainbow (Rev. 4:3), thus suggesting grace in the midst of judgment. But when we come to the eternal state, it is prefaced by a throne of pure judgment, a "great white throne" unrelieved by any color of hope; the subjects here being "the dead" for whom there can be no hope (Rev. 20:11-15).

7. The Chronology of the Pre-Kingdom Judgment Period

My two witnesses . . . shall prophesy a thousand two hundred and three-score days. —*Rev. 11:3*

Power was given unto him [the beast] to continue forty and two months. —*Rev. 13:5*

. . . for a time, and times, and half a time . . . —*Rev. 12:14*

It is a fact, open to all who read, that the Book of Revelation presents a definite chronology of the period of pre-Kingdom judgments; and this is based on a single unit of measurement stated variously as 1260 days (11:3; 12:6), 42 months (11:2; 13:5), and 3½ times (12:14), i.e., *years* (see Vincent, Thayer, Hengstenberg, *et al*). While it is true that certain numbers in the Book of Revelation may sometimes be employed in a symbolic sense (cf. the "seven Spirits" of 4:5), it would be hard to find any such meaning in the number 1260. That the figures here are intended to be understood literally seems clear from the fact that evidently the *same* period of persecution in Revelation has been designated in terms of days (12:6), months (13:5), and years (12:14). This one fact completely nullifies the year-day theory of prophetic interpretation. For the 1260 days here equal 42 months or 3½ years, and therefore certainly not *1260* years.

Furthermore, if we examine the context of chapters 11-13, we shall find not only one, but *two* periods to which this same unit of measure is applied. The first is the period of the two witnesses in conflict with the beast, stated as 1260 days, ending with their death at his hands (11:3, 7). A second period follows in which the beast, having now put down all opposition and reached the place of world power, is given "forty and two months" to continue his reign (13: 4-8). Adding together these two periods of the same length respectively, obviously the total time equals exactly *seven* prophetic years of 360 days each.

The terminus of this total period of seven years is marked beyond dispute in the Book of Revelation. Since the last half of the seven-year period measures the career of the beast as an absolute world ruler, the end must be found in his defeat and doom at the glorious coming of Christ as described in Revelation 19:11-21. The *beginning* of the seven-year period is not so clearly marked. But since in the Apocalypse this seven-year period is prominently concerned with the total public career of the beast (as also in Daniel 9:27), it is a reasonable assumption that the beginning is marked by the going forth of the rider on the white horse under the first seal (6:1-2).

Thus the chronological picture of pre-Kingdom judgment presents a well-articulated and appropriate whole. Upon a world which has rejected the true Messianic King at His first coming, God will loose a false messianic ruler (the "strong delusion" of II Thess. 2:9-11), who rises to world power in the space of three and a half years and who will wield his terrible power during a subsequent period of the same length. At the end of the total period of seven years, the false messiah will be defeated and destroyed by the second coming of the true Messianic King.

The facts stated above are in perfect harmony with Daniel's great prophecy of the Seventy Weeks. In chapter 9 a future "prince" out of the Roman Empire (vs. 26b) makes a "firm covenant" with Daniel's people for a period of "one week", i.e., one period of seven years (vs. 27, ASV). In the midst of this period he breaks with the people of Israel, stops their sacrificial system, and inaugurates a time of persecution lasting to the end of the week, obviously three and a half years. The same persecutor, the same persecuted people, and the same period of persecution, are referred to in Daniel 7:25 and Revelation 13:5-7; with which compare Daniel 12:1, 7.

The literality of these time-measures is now grounded in history. It is generally agreed by devout students of Biblical prophecy that the first sixty-nine "weeks" of Daniel's prophecy are "sevens" of *years,* and that they have been literally fulfilled by the first coming of Christ (9:25). But if the first sixty-nine sevens of years are literal years, then so also must be the last seven of years. That this last seven lies prophetically in the future has been established by the testimony of Christ Himself. The argument is as follows: both Daniel and our Lord spoke of something called "the abomination of desolation." Whatever this thing may be, it is certain that Daniel located it within the last "week" of his great prophecy (Dan. 9:27 with 12:11). It is equally certain that Christ placed it at "the end" of the present age in connection with the terrible "tribulation" immediately preceding His second coming in glory (cf. verses 15, 21, 29, and 30, in Matt. 24). Therefore, since our Lord has not yet come in glory, Daniel's final "week" of years must lie in the future. This is Christ's own interpretation, and should settle the matter.[16] It also harmonizes perfectly with the New Testament doctrine of the Church, because in this view her career on earth must be placed

---

[16] For the extended argument on this point, see *Daniel's Prophecy of the Seventy Weeks* by Alva J. McClain (7th ed.; Grand Rapids: Zondervan Publishing House, 1940), pp. 23-40.

between Daniel's sixty-ninth and seventieth weeks, an area for which there is no recorded chronology.

The tremendous events envisioned in and following the last week of Daniel's prophecy (9:25, 27), and subsequently developed more largely in Revelation 6-20, have never been certainly identified in any area of human history. This is evident from the utter confusion and disagreement among those who have tried to do so. Invariably, also, the chronology has to be forced into the mold of the year-day theory, and the events of history always fail to measure up to the predictions. If the rout of pagan hosts before the military forces of Constantine (Elliott), or the invasion of Rome by the Goths and Vandals (Barnes), can be called *The Great Day of God's Wrath* (under the sixth Seal, Rev. 6:17), then sinners can have nothing much to fear at the prospect of divine judgment.

It is sometimes argued that a period of only seven years is altogether too short to compass all the world-shaking convulsions of the end-time as set forth in Revelation 6-19. To this it may be answered that the very brevity of the time is proof of the mercy and grace of God. Speaking of these very days of the "great tribulation," our Lord said, "And except those days should be shortened, there should no flesh be saved: but for the elect's sake those days shall be shortened" (Matt. 24:21-22). And the elect here are those of the nation of Israel, for whom this will be the "time of Jacob's trouble" (Jer. 30:7), and of whom God had spoken through Isaiah: "In overflowing wrath I hid my face from thee for a moment; but with everlasting kindness will I have mercy on thee, saith Jehovah thy Redeemer" (54:8, ASV).

8. *The Place of Israel in the Period of Pre-Kingdom Judgments*
And the dragon was wroth with the woman.   —*Rev. 12:17*

In the Book of Revelation, the appearance of the last one of Daniel's seventy weeks of years, constituting the chronological frame of the period of pre-Kingdom judgments (chs. 6-19), is perfectly consistent with the purposes of God for the nation of Israel. For in the original prophecy, the angelic messenger said to Daniel that the entire "seventy weeks" were determined "upon thy people and upon thy holy city" (9:24). To this people belonged in a peculiar covenantal sense the future Messianic Kingdom. And although during the present age, because of her sinful rejection of the Messianic King, the nation of Israel has been set aside temporarily (Rom. 11:11-15), we should expect that this nation would once more appear

as the object of God's special concern when He prepares judicially
to establish on earth the long-expected Kingdom. In full accord
with this assumption, Israel does appear once more in her place
of national distinction during the period of judgments preparatory
for the Kingdom.

The evidence for this restored distinction is very clear in the
inspired record. Before the storm of supernatural judgments is
loosed upon the world, a company of 144,000 Israelites are pro-
tectively sealed as "the servants of our God" (Rev. 7:2-4; cf. 14:
1-5), definitely distinguished from the uncounted multitude from "all
nations" appearing in 7:9. Chapter 11 opens with a clear distinction between the people who worship in the "temple" and the "Gentiles" who tread underfoot "the holy city" (vss. 1-2). In the same
verses, John is told to "measure" the temple, the altar, and the
people who worship there — a symbolic action suggesting the resumption of divine possession. The testimony of God during this period
is directed primarily toward the nation of Israel; and the "two witnesses" (vs. 3) are certainly Jewish in origin (Mal. 4:5-6). Even
the plagues to be visited upon their enemies are reminiscent of former judgments associated with Elijah and Moses in the history of
Israel (Rev. 11:6). The whole of chapter 12 is concerned with a
"woman" who is unmistakably identified with the Israel of history
(cf. vs. 5). She is the special object of persecution by the beast, but
is divinely preserved throughout the terrible period of his reign (vss.
6, 14); although those of her seed who hold the "testimony of Jesus"
continue to be exposed to his wrath (vs. 17). All this persecution
of Israel, both past and future, is traced back to Satan himself (vs.
9). And in the final scene this conflict reaches even into the heavens
where Satan meets defeat at the hand of Michael (vss. 7-9), the
great angel to whom has been divinely assigned the protection of
the interests of Israel (Dan. 12:1).

Also certain features which appear in the *imagery* of this judgment period are historically associated with the nation of Israel.
Almost immediately following the measuring of Israel's temple on
earth (Rev. 11:1), the temple of God in heaven is opened and
there reappears "the ark of his covenant" (11:19, ASV). The seven
angels with the last seven pre-Kingdom judgments come out of
"the temple of the tabernacle of the testimony in heaven" (15:5,
ASV). And when the last vial is emptied, the announcement of
finished judgment issues from this same heavenly temple (16:17).

The Israel which appears within the frame of end-time events, as the object of God's special concern, is the Israel of Old Testament history. The symbolic description in chapter 12 is unmistakable; and in chapter 7 even the tribes are named. The attempts of spiritualizing interpreters to identify this Israel with the Church, and to find the fulfilment of the predictions of Revelation 12 and 13 in history, have not succeeded. The dictum of Dean Alford still remains unshaken: "I am . . . quite unable . . . to point out definitely any period in the history of this world's civil power which shall satisfy the 42 months of chapter 13:5. As far as I have seen, every such attempt hitherto has been characterized by signal failure."[17]

In fact, the premillennial view of the permanence of God's covenantal relation to the historic nation of Israel is today receiving strong support from unexpected sources. Dr. T. F. Torrance, professor of dogmatics at the University of Edinburgh, has recently written: "The historical particularity of Israel covenanted with God persists through the Christian era. God has not cast off His ancient people (Rom. 11:1 ff.); for the covenant with Israel as God's people remains in force, and cannot be 'spiritualized' and turned into some form alien to the stubborn historicity of its nature without calling in question the whole historical foundation of God's revelation in Old Testament and New Testament."[18] We welcome this unequivocal testimony as to the factual and permanent nature of Israel's historic relation to God, even though we may not concur in all the conclusions drawn by Dr. Torrance from the fact.

9. The Church during the Period of Pre-Kingdom Judgments

For God hath not appointed us to wrath.　　　—I Thess. 5:9

a. As stated above (point 2, p. 446), the term *ekklēsia* occurs frequently in the first three chapters of Revelation but not at all thereafter, except once in the epilogue, where the divine Author turns from the area of prediction to speak a final word of comfort and admonition to the "churches" to which the entire prophecy was addressed. From this usage it appears that in the Book of Revelation *ekklēsia* is reserved always to designate churches existing on *earth*. And it therefore becomes significant that during the judgments of chapters 4-19 the term is never once applied to any body of saved persons on earth, although several such bodies appear (cf. 7:1-8; 7:14, ASV; 12:11, 17; 13:7; 14:1-5; 18:4). This omission would be

---

[17] Henry Alford, *Commentary on Revelation*, Intro., Sec. V., Par. 30.
[18] T. F. Torrance, "The Israel of God," *Interpretation*, July, 1956, p. 317.

strange if, during the period described, there were any *ekklēsiai* remaining on the earth.

b. The lofty position of the Church in relation to the coming Kingdom would be seriously inconsistent with subjection to the terrible judgments which will prepare for its establishment. For the Church is the very "body" of the Messianic King (Eph. 1:23), a term of intimacy never applied to any other redeemed group of people. To the members of the Church is promised that they shall have a part in *judging* the world (I Cor. 6:2) and that they are "joint-heirs with Christ" (Rom. 8:17), destined to "reign" with Him (Luke 22:29-30; II Tim. 2:12). Also to the Church our Lord has assigned the high authority represented by the "keys of the kingdom of heaven" (Matt. 16:19); and against her "the gates of hell shall not prevail" (vs. 18). Now in sharp contrast to these assurances given to the Church, the Book of Revelation declares that "the beast that ascendeth out of the bottomless pit" (11:7) will make war against "the saints" on earth during his awful reign, and "overcome them" (13:7). Furthermore, this power of the beast will extend over "all kindreds, and tongues, and nations." We must not overlook, either, that this power of the beast to overcome the saints of that future time will be "given" by God Himself, thus setting it within the category of divine judgment. The verb "given" is used frequently throughout the book with this connotation. Now great as her sufferings have been at times in the past, nothing comparable to this can be found in the long history of the Church on earth. Such an idea would be excluded in advance by the fact that the present age of the Church is not in any eschatological sense the "great day" of divine wrath, as that future time will be (Rev. 6:16-17).

c. Opposed to the idea of the Church's exposure to this period of future judgment, there is also the specific promise of Revelation 3:10 — "Because thou didst keep the word of my patience, I also will keep thee from the hour of trial, that hour which is to come upon the whole world [lit., "inhabited earth"], to try them that dwell upon the earth" (ASV). While this promise was addressed initially to the *ekklēsia* at Philadelphia (vs. 7), it is also intended for the whole Church as symbolized by "the seven churches" (1:20), for the letter closes with a general call to "hear what the Spirit saith to the churches" (3:13).

As to the precise meaning of Rev. 3:10, the first thing to be noticed is *what* the Church is to be kept from: not from the ordinary trials of human life, but from a special hour (lit., "the" hour) of trial which is yet future and will fall upon the entire inhabited earth. Since "hour" in Scripture may refer to any specific expanse of time (cf. John 4:23), the particular "hour of trial," in its Biblical context, points definitely to the "hour of his [God's] judgment," as the period of Revelation 6 - 19 is designated in 14:7. The verb *tēreō* with the preposition *ek* in 3:10 seems to indicate the action of being *kept* out of rather than being *delivered* out of. And this idea is supported by the inspired record of what will happen during that awful "hour." Of all the temporal judgments of the period, the worst will be the suffering involved in the test of decision between Christ and the antichrist; and this will fall exclusively upon the saved, not upon the unsaved (13:15).

The notion that those who become believers on earth during the period of pre-Kingdom judgments will be divinely guarded *from* the afflictions entailed, in alleged fulfilment of the promise in Rev. 3: 10, is simply false to the record. In that hour the physical judgments will generally fall upon the saved and unsaved alike. But, excepting the 144,000 sealed Israelites, in the supreme "trial" those who choose Christ will be killed, while those who reject Him will live! Even the two great prophets of the hour, having borne their faithful witness for 1260 days, will at last suffer martyrdom and the diabolical indignities which attend it (11:7-10).

The promise of Revelation 3:10 is supported by other promises to the Church: "We shall be saved from wrath through him" (Rom. 5:9). "And to wait for his Son from heaven, . . . which delivered us from the wrath to come" (I Thess. 1:10). "For God hath not appointed us to wrath" (I Thess. 5:9). There is also the great promise of our Lord Himself, "He that heareth my word, and believeth him that sent me, hath eternal life, and cometh not into judgment, but hath passed out of death into life" (John 5:24, ASV); a passage which, according to Alford,[19] expressly negatives the notion that the Church can be made subject to the judgments associated with the Millennial Kingdom.

d. Although during the judgments described in chapters 4 - 19 there is no mention of any *ekklēsia* on earth, there are at least three references to *a body of saved people in heaven* during the period, and who are designated by terms which are applicable best

[19] Henry Alford, *Commentary on New Testament,* on Rev. 20:5.

to the Church of the present age. The references occur in chapters 19, 13, and 4-5, and will now be considered in this order.

(1) *The "wife" of the Lamb in Rev. 19:1-9*

The symbolical language here will not be strange to readers of the New Testament. The Apostle Paul has described the Church of the present age as the future wife of Christ. Thus he writes to the Church: "I have espoused you to one husband, that I may present you as a chaste virgin to Christ" (II Cor. 11:2). The same spiritual relationship and also the same future day of presentation is spoken of in Eph. 5:25-27, "Husbands, love your wives, even as Christ also loved the church, and gave himself for it; that he might sanctify and cleanse it. . . . That he might present it to himself a glorious church, . . . that it should be holy and without blemish."

To the Apostle John finally it was given in prophetic vision to behold the blessed consummation of this conjugal relationship between the Church and her Lord. He hears the voice of a great multitude saying, "The marriage of the Lamb is come, and his wife hath made herself ready" (Rev. 19:7). Another voice adds, "Blessed are they which are called unto the marriage supper of the Lamb" (vs. 9). Nothing could be more certain than that John and Paul are speaking of the same body of the saved and of the same eschatological event. But the point of immediate interest is that the entire scene of the marriage and its glorious supper is set by John *"in heaven"* (vs. 1), not upon the earth. In the order of events, therefore, John puts the Church in heaven before the glorious coming of Christ (19:11-16), and before the final and most terrible of the entire series of judgments preparatory to His establishment of the Kingdom on earth (19:17-21).

(2) *The "tabernacle" of God in Rev. 13:16*

In the 13th chapter of Revelation the beast "out of the sea" (vs. 1) appears at the height and fullness of his brief span of world power. The entire world of nations, politically and religiously, is at his feet. And with the exception of those "written in the book of life of the Lamb," all that dwell upon the earth shall worship him (vs. 8). At this point in his mad career, he opens his mouth in terrible "blasphemy against God, to blaspheme his name, and his tabernacle, and them that dwell in heaven" (vs. 6). Thus, according to the King James Version, the objects of the beast's blasphemy are *four*: God, His Name, His tabernacle, and certain ones who dwell in heaven. But the best Greek text reduces the number to *three* objects. The manuscript evidence overwhelmingly supports the omission of the conjunction *kai* ("and") in the final clause. The words "them that dwell in heaven," therefore, stand in apposition[20] to the preceding clause, and are exegetical in character, defining and identifying the "tabernacle" mentioned there. The "tabernacle" of Rev. 13:6, hence, cannot be heaven itself (as in Heb. 9:11), but is specifically defined as a body of personal beings who will be dwelling in heaven at this time during the career of the beast. The American Standard Version has well rendered the verse as follows: "And he opened his mouth for blasphemies against God, to blaspheme his name, and his tabernacle, *even* them that dwell in the heaven."

Who are these dwellers in heaven referred to as God's "tabernacle"? The Greek term used here, I think, points to the correct answer. It is *skēnē,* which means a tent, dwelling, abode, or habitation. In Scripture it is used variously: to designate the tabernacle of Old Testament history (Heb. 8:5); the celestial tabernacle (Heb. 8:2); the holy of holies (Heb. 9:3); and the bodily tabernacle of the soul (II Pet. 1:13-14). Although this term itself is not applied directly in the New Testament to the Church, the idea it represents is often connected with the Church. According to Paul, the Church is a "temple" [*naos*] of God (I Cor. 3:16-17); a "habitation [*katoikētērion*] of God" (Eph. 2:22); and the "body" (*soma*) of Christ (Col. 1:24). Herein is one of the unique glories of the Church: to be the corporate dwelling-place of God through the Spirit, beginning with the day of Pentecost and extending out into future ages without end. In the visions of the Apocalypse, then, the Church of the present age appears in its corporate capacity as the habitation (*skēnē*) of God already *in heaven* at the very time the antichrist reaches the height of his power *on earth.* And this point in time, the reader should recall, will arrive at exactly the middle of the entire period of seven years covered by the judgments of chapters 6-19, i.e., at the beginning of the beast's total power extending forty-two months (13:5).

This body of the saved in heaven, referred to as the "tabernacle" of God, must not be confused with "the great multitude" of Rev. 7:9-17; for, according to the divine identification, the latter are those who are seen coming (Grk. present tense) up out of "the great

---

[20] Alford's opinion, that "the apposition is strange" here, arises through his failure to recognize the true nature of this "tabernacle."

tribulation" of those terrible days (vs. 14, ASV), whereas the Church is to be kept out of that "hour of trial" (Rev. 3:10, ASV). Moreover, though both groups are redeemed through grace by the same Lord, the descriptions of their respective destinies are clearly different, as may be seen by comparing the account in Rev. 7:14-17 with New Testament predictions of the Church's regal future.

The question now may be raised as to what form the beast's blasphemy of God and the Church will take. Since to blaspheme is to speak impiously and injuriously of divine things, in what way will he speak? To this the inspired record gives no specific answer in the passage. But from the general teaching of Scripture there are some legitimate inferences which may be drawn. First, among all the redeemed, none have attracted a greater measure of satanic hatred than the Church which is the body and bride of Christ. For its members are destined to reign with Him in the highest level of His Kingdom, a comparable place once held by Satan himself. Second, when the satanic beast of the end-time reaches the height of his absolute earthly power, the Church will have been removed to heaven wholly beyond his malignancy. Third, this mysterious disappearance of millions of people from the earth bodily in "the twinkling of an eye" (I Cor. 15:51-52) will be a world-shaking event, something impossible to keep from public knowledge by any power or device of news control. Such an event, clearly miraculous in nature, will demand some plausible explanation on the part of the beast who will then be on the march toward political supremacy and seeking to attract to himself as world leader the admiration and confidence of all men. In this dangerous emergency, with his leadership at stake, what could be more reasonable than to find the beast resorting to the well-known technique of "the great lie," explaining perhaps to his followers that the vanished people were opposers of social progress, "apostles of discord" standing in the path of religious unity; and therefore they have been taken away by *divine judgment?* Perhaps this will be part of the "strong delusion" welcomed by the ungodly of that coming day (II Thess. 2:11). At any rate, a lying explanation of this kind would certainly satisfy the meaning of the "blasphemy" of Rev. 13:6, for it would malign both the character of God and also that of the true Church which today is the only light of the world and salt of the earth.

(3) The "four and twenty elders" in Rev. 4 and 5

The careful reader of these two chapters will already have noted that the atmosphere of the scene pictured here is *judicial* in character. The "throne" of 4:2, like the throne of 20:11, speaks of judgment; God as judge sits upon the throne. In His hand there is a seven-sealed book which no one can open except "the Lion of the tribe of Juda, the Root of David," who appears here as "a Lamb" bearing the marks of having been sacrificed (5:1-6). After an outburst of universal adoration and expectant joy the Lamb begins to break the seals of the book; and the judgments of God begin to fall successively upon the world (5:8-6:1). A very striking feature of this judgment scene is the presence of "four and twenty elders," sitting in a circle immediately surrounding the central throne, and who display at least four marks of identification.

First, they sit upon *"thrones"* (4:4, ASV). The term here (unfortunately rendered "seats" in the KJV) is the same as used of the judgment-seat of God. Thus the elders sit with God as assessors or associate judges in the judicial acts about to be inflicted upon the world. This means that they cannot represent angels, for the latter appear in Scripture always as servants, and never as *judges*.[21]

Second, the "four and twenty elders" are clothed in *"white raiment"* (vs. 4). Such raiment doubtless speaks of both regal splendor and moral character, a fitting symbol of the unimaginable glory for which the redeemed are even now being prepared.

Third, these elders wear on their heads *"crowns of gold"* (vs. 4). Both the crown and its costly substance represent the regal or reigning function at its highest level. While the ideas suggested by "thrones" and "crowns" respectively are not ordinarily wholly separable, yet in Scripture the "crown" seems to have the meaning of *executive* function, whereas the "throne" is reserved as a symbol of that aspect of rulership which appears in its *judicial* activity. Of the latter there is an excellent example in the promise of our Lord that His disciples are to "sit on *thrones judging*" (Luke 22:30, italics added).

Fourth, the twenty-four elders sing a *"new song"* (5:9-10). Although the four "living creatures" (ASV) join the elders in falling down before the Lamb in worship (vs. 8), it is significant that the song, the harps, and also the prayers of the saints, seem limited to the elders. Hengstenberg says dogmatically that the words of verse 8,

---

[21] E. W. Hengstenberg, *Revelation of St. John,* tr. by Patrick Fairbairn (Edinburgh: T. and T. Clark, 1851), Vol. I, p. 206.

"having every one," etc., refer to the elders only, not to the living creatures, rightly identifying the latter as cherubim (cf. Ezek. 10: 20).[22] Moreover, the Greek *hekastos,* rendered "every one" here, is masculine and therefore points back to "elders" with which it agrees in gender; whereas *zōa* (KJV "beasts") is neuter. By the very redemptive nature of the song which follows, the cherubim would be excluded, for angelic beings are not subjects of redemption. There is a textual problem, however, in connection with the pronouns of verses 9 and 10. On the basis of weighty manuscript evidence, the textual editors have properly changed the *"us"* and *"we"* in verse 10 (cf. KJV) to the third person "them" and "they" (cf. ASV). Then feeling it desirable to bring verse 9 into forced conformity with these changes, but finding no evidence of any alternative pronoun to the *"us"* there, a few editors[23] simply dropped the pronoun altogether, leaving the verb "redeemed" without any proper object. Not understanding the relation of these elders to the redeemed, they failed to see that there was no necessary conflict between a first personal pronoun in verse 9 and the third personal pronoun in verse 10. As Hengstenberg pointed out long ago,[24] the elders speak of *themselves with* the redeemed in verse 9, whereas in verse 10 they speak objectively of the Church *as its representatives,* which they are in chapters 4 and 5.

In summarizing the four marks of identification outlined above— the thrones, the white raiment, the golden crowns, and the redemption song — it may be said that among all the saved there is only one body in the universe of which *all* these things are true. Others may be redeemed, walk in white, even reign with Christ, but only the Church which is the body and bride of Christ will enjoy these special privileges and also sit with Him in judgment of the world (I Cor. 6:1-3; Rev. 3:21).

To this may be added the argument from the term itself. The elders are *presbuteroi.* It would be hard to imagine any symbol which could better represent the Church than a company of these *presbuteroi,* so familiar to the early Christians. They were in every congregation (Tit. 1:5). It was their proper business while on earth to represent the *ekklēsia* in various ways. If one of its members fell sick, he was instructed to send for the "elders" who would represent the Church in the solemn service prescribed by the Epistle of James

---

22 E. W. Hengstenberg, *ibid.,* pp. 238-239.
23 Tischendorf, Alford, Wordsworth, Lachmann.
24 E. W. Hengstenberg, *ibid.,* pp. 239-242.

(5:14-15). When Paul wished to discuss certain matters with the Ephesian Church, he sent for its "elders" as representatives of the congregation (Acts 20:17). Why should not a group of these well-known officers, therefore, serve appropriately in heaven as a symbol of the entire body of Christ? Furthermore, the fact that the elders were properly a *ruling* body on earth would add to their appropriateness as a symbol of the Church enthroned in heaven. The number chosen here, while of interest, is not of great consequence. It may be noted, however, that the number 24 is never used as a symbol in the Apocalypse apart from these "elders," suggesting the absolute uniqueness of the Church for which they stand.

It is an impressive fact that, in the long and bewildering history of attempts to interpret the symbols of the Apocalypse, there is hardly any instance of greater unanimity than with reference to that of the twenty-four elders. Among the well-known commentators who regard these elders as representative of the *Church* are Alford, Barnes, Benson, Binney, Carpenter, Clarke, Clemance, Book, Crafer, Crosby, Dusterdieck, Fausset, Girdlestone, Godet, Gray, Henry, Holden, Kuyper, Milligan, Plummer, Robertson, Scott, Sheppard, Simcox, Slight, Smith, Swete, Weidner. Vincent says, "The twenty four elders are usually taken to represent the one Church of Christ." And Hengstenberg declares, "That the elders are representatives of the church, there can be no question." [25]

The commentators named represent many eschatological viewpoints. They were not writing in support of any pretribulationist school of thought. As a matter of fact, they were in sharp disagreement with one another about much in the Book of Revelation. The reader grows weary trying to follow the ramifications of their different systems of interpretation. Some of them almost despair of reaching any safe conclusions about many things in the book. Furthermore, they do not all agree as to the precise nature and extent of the Church, nor as to its place in the divine plan of the ages. Yet in spite of these disagreements, they are united in the opinion that the twenty-four elders of chapters 4 and 5, enthroned in heaven, do represent the true Church of God! This interpretation, if adopted by premillennialists who believe the Book of Revelation presents an *intelligible* program, shuts out of court any eschatologi-

---

[25] For the quotations, documentation, and extended argument, see my address on "The Pretribulation Rapture and the Commentators," published in a symposium under the title, *Understanding the Times* (Grand Rapids: Zondervan Publishing House, 1956), pp. 198-207.

cal scheme which would leave the Church on earth during any part of the terrible judgments of the end-time described in chapters 6-19.

Regardless of the chronological arrangements which may be made of these judgments, whether some recapitulation or overlapping scheme be adopted, the opening action of chapters 4 and 5 simply cannot be pushed into the picture which follows in 6 to 19. There is a definite sequence here: No judgment falls until the first seal is broken; the first seal is not broken until the Lamb receives the sealed book; the Lamb does not take the book until the twenty-four elders are in heaven, enthroned and crowned. If the action in heaven described in chapters 4 and 5 does not precede the judgments of chapters 6 to 19, then no one can make any sense whatever out of the order of the events set forth in the last book of the Bible; and we may as well complain with Luther, "Even if it were a blessed thing to believe what is in it, no man knows what that is." But the very intensity of the labors of Christian scholars down through the centuries is the strongest witness to their rejection of such a verdict.

10. *Harbingers of the Coming Kingdom*

For reasons which will become apparent, I have reserved until now the discussion of certain matters recorded in chapters 5, 10, 11, and 12 of Revelation, which appear as the great pointers toward the coming Kingdom and its constitutive events as presented in 19: 11-20:15.

a. *The Sealed Book of Revelation 5.* In the magnificent scene of chapters 4 and 5 there is seen in the hand of God a "book written within and on the backside, sealed with seven seals" (5:1). The Lamb receives this book from the hand of God, and as He breaks its seals there fall upon the world with increasing severity the judgments of heaven. As to the nature of the book (lit. "roll"), Deismann showed some years ago, on the basis of archaeological evidence,[26] that it must be understood in the light of a similar document which appears in Jer. 32:6-15. This was not a book at all in the ordinary sense, but rather a *title-deed* written on both sides of a sheet of material, which was then rolled up and sealed, leaving the roll so that one copy would be outside and visible but the other copy hidden inside. In case of tampering or dispute, the breaking

[26] Adolph Deismann, "Treasures in Earthen Vessels," *The Biblical Review,* October, 1922.

of the seals would reveal the original copy and establish the lawful owner in his rights. Thus Biblically interpreted, the sealed document of Revelation 5 becomes a symbol of high importance; and the breaking of its seals by our Lord marks the first judicial assertion (in Revelation) of His regal rights, for the purpose of punishing and dispossessing the usurpers of His realm. In this sense, the breaking of the first seal becomes a strong harbinger of the impending Kingdom.

b. *The Angelic Action of Revelation 10.* Here a "mighty angel" comes down from heaven and sets his feet on land and sea (vss. 1-2), thus serving public notice of divine ownership. This meaning is confirmed by the angel's words: "there shall be delay no longer" (vs. 6, ASV); for in "the days of the voice of the seventh angel, . . . the mystery of God should be finished, as he hath declared to his servants the prophets" (vs. 7). The "mystery" here mentioned is closely connected with the "delay." If in the Old Testament there was one thing which to the prophets was mysterious about the eagerly expected Messianic Kingdom, it was the seeming long delay in its establishment. As an example of the acute distress felt in the presence of this mystery, let the student read the cry, "How long, LORD?" (Ps. 89:46), in the context of the entire psalm. So also the redeemed have felt down through the centuries as they have prayed, "Thy kingdom come." As the pledge that these prayers shall be answered we have the great angelic shout of chapter 10: There is to be no more long delay, for very shortly the mystery of a long-deferred kingdom will be finished. In fact, from this point in the chronology of the book, within the brief span of "forty and two months" (13:5), the satanic usurper will be fully dispossessed and the rightful King will arrive in power and glory.

c. *The Great Voices of Revelation 11.* As the seventh angel sounds his trumpet, these voices are heard saying, "The kingdom[27] of the world is become the kingdom of our Lord, and of his Christ; and he shall reign for ever and ever" (11:15, ASV). This is the *de jure* announcement of what in a short time will be made *de facto.* It is only a sovereign God who can speak like this: for He "calleth those things which be not as though they were" (Rom. 4:17). And it is an impressive exhibition of divine grace and sovereignty that the announcement is made at the precise moment when the beast

---

[27] The singular number here (supported by weighty Ms. evidence) points to the satanic unity of the world system of nations at the end-time.

reaches the height of his power on earth, with all opposition crushed (Rev. 12:7; 13:4-8). What an encouragement for the redeemed to know that there are no dark hours to God. Even when all seems to be lost, for those who have eyes to see, the Lord still sits upon His throne high and lifted up in the heavens; and the unfailing character of His Universal Kingdom guarantees that the Mediatorial Kingdom of His Son shall be established on earth, in spite of all satanic opposition.

The grand theme of these "voices in heaven" is now picked up by the twenty-four elders and expounded in larger detail: "We give thee thanks, O Lord God Almighty, which art, and wast, and art to come; because thou hast taken to thee thy great power, and hast reigned. And the nations were angry, and thy wrath is come, and the time of the dead, that they should be judged, and that thou shouldest give reward unto thy servants the prophets, and to the saints, and them that fear thy name, small and great; and shouldest destroy them which destroy the earth" (11:16-18).

First, we note that in this passage the high point is that God has now at last *"taken"* to Himself the great power which is His by right. This harmonizes with the angelic declaration in chapter 10 to the effect that there is to be "delay no longer" (10:6, ASV). The mystery of a silent heaven is now at last to be cleared away. The verb rendered "taken" is perfect in tense, indicating that this judicial act will have continuing results; which will appear in the exercise of God's "great power" through supernatural judgments and works, never again to be interrupted until the entire eschatological program is complete. This thought has an interesting confirmation in the omission of the clause "and art to come" from verse 17 by the large majority of Greek manuscripts. It occurs without question, and properly, in Revelation 1:4, 8, and 4:8. But it becomes inappropriate from 11:15 onward in the chain of events; for at this point in prophecy, God *has come judicially* in the sense of the special and immediate exercise of His regal power of judgment, which will not cease until the Mediatorial Kingdom of His Son is fully established over all the earth. It is significant in this connection that the similar futuristic clause of 16:5, "and shalt be," is also lacking in manuscript support (cf. ASV).

Second, the words "and hast reigned"[28] must not be interpreted to mean that the Mediatorial Kingdom has now been *fully* established

_____
[28] The tense is an *aorist*.

on earth, for this would contradict practically everything in the book from chapter 11 through 20. We have already seen that one of the important functions of the divine reign is that of *judging*. In this sense *only*, the reign of God has begun here, i.e., in the judicial acts which precede the events of chapter 20. And in accordance with this idea, we note that the entire passage of 11:15-19 is permeated with marks of such *judicial action*: God's "wrath" has come; the dead are to be "judged"; "rewards" are to be bestowed; the destroyers are to be destroyed; and the phenomena of verse 19 are all signs of divine judgment.

d. *The Great Voice of Revelation 12.* In this chapter there is war in heaven: Michael and his angels fighting against Satan and his angels; and the outcome is the casting of Satan out of heaven down to the earth. This action must lie in the future, because during the present age of the Church, its members must do battle spiritually against Satan and the hosts of his wicked spirits who are *now* "in the heavenly places" (Eph. 6:10-12, ASV). But in the action described in Revelation 12 Satan's liberty is reduced to the area of the earth; and when this takes place in harmony with divine prophecy, exactly forty-two months before the end (13:4-5), Satan will begin this restricted career on earth with "great wrath," knowing that he has but "a short time" (12:12) before his imprisonment in the "abyss" of Revelation 20:1 (ASV). This casting down of Satan is hailed with joy in heaven, and a great voice says, "Now is come the salvation, and the power, and the kingdom of our God, and the authority of his Christ: for the accuser of our brethren is cast down . . ." (12:10, ASV). This repeats substantially the announcement of 11:15-17 but adds an important idea: Just as God, who always has all power, *took* this power at a certain time (11:17) and began to use it in judicial preparation for the Kingdom, even so our Lord Jesus Christ, who was given all "authority" at His ascension (Matt. 28:18), now at this juncture in the divine record begins to exercise this authority in preparing judicially for His Kingdom soon to be established on the earth.

III. THE REVELATION OF THE PERIOD OF THE MILLENNIAL KINGDOM (Rev. 19:11-20:15)

It will have been long ago anticipated by the readers of this Commentary, that I cannot consent to distort its words from their plain sense and chronological place in the prophecy, on account of any considerations of difficulty, or any risk of abuses which the doctrine of the millennium may bring with it. Those who lived next to the Apostles, and the whole Church for 300 years, understood them in the plain literal sense: and it is a strange sight in these days to see expositors who are among the first in reverence of antiquity, complacently casting aside the most cogent instance of unanimity which primitive antiquity presents. As regards the text itself, no legitimate treatment of it will extort what is known as the spiritual interpretation now in fashion. If, in a passage where *two resurrections* are mentioned, where certain *souls lived* at the first, and the rest of the dead lived only at the end of a specified period after that first, — if in such a passage the first resurrection may be understood to mean *spiritual* rising with Christ, while the second means *literal* rising from the grave;—then there is an end to all significance in language, and Scripture is wiped out as a definite testimony to any thing. If the first resurrection is spiritual, then so is the second, which I suppose none will be hardy enough to maintain: but if the second is literal, then so is the first, which in common with the whole primitive Church and many of the best modern expositors, I do maintain, and receive as an article of faith and hope.   —*Henry Alford* [29]

There have been minor differences among premillennial interpreters with reference to some details of Revelation 20, but these are as nothing when compared to the confusion which reigns among postmillennial and amillennial writers who attempt to expound the chapter. One need only read the more recent literature of these schools to find that they seem to be a united family only in their unyielding scorn for the premillennial viewpoint and in their opinion that "the thousand years" are not a thousand years.

Although the twentieth chapter of Revelation holds a place of high importance in the eschatology of the Kingdom, it is inexcusable misrepresentation to allege, as some opponents have, that the weight of the premillennial view rests mainly upon that chapter. As already indicated earlier in this volume, the correct view of the Kingdom must represent an eschatology formulated from an examination of the *whole* of Old and New Testament prophecy; and its essential features can be established apart from Revelation 20.[30] If Biblical prophecy in general teaches anything clearly, it is that Messiah will come in great glory at the end of the present age to establish His Kingdom over all the earth; and this is the firm core of Premillennialism. The unique contributions of Revelation 20 are at least two: first, a *chronology* of the coming Kingdom; and, second, a concise

[29] Henry Alford, *New Testament for English Readers,* on "The Millennial Reign" in Rev. 20:4-6.
[30] "The millennial reign on earth does not rest on an isolated passage, but all Old Testament prophecy goes on the same view" (A. R. Fausset on Rev. 20:5, *Commentary,* Unabridged).

outline of constitutive events in their proper order, so clear that there should be no cause for misunderstanding.[31]

In approaching the events of Revelation 20, we should begin with the grand event described in chapter 19:11-21, for it is this glorious coming of Christ which gives meaning to all that follows. In fact, viewed from a literary standpoint, this last part of chapter 19 might well have been made the first part of chapter 20.

1. *The Arrival of the King* (Rev. 19:11-16)

> Behold, he cometh with clouds; and every eye shall see him.
> —*Rev. 1:7*

As to the *identity* of the central Person in Rev. 19:11-16 there can be no serious question, as there has been in the case of other figures which appear in earlier visions of the book. The *names* He bears are alone sufficient to put the matter beyond dispute: He is called "Faithful and True" (vs. 11). His name is called "The Word of God" (vs. 13). On His thigh there is the name, "KING OF KINGS, AND LORD OF LORDS" (vs. 16). Added to this glittering array, there is a name known only to Himself, an intimation of the mystery of Deity (vs. 12). His *appearance* also confirms His identity: His eyes are as a flame of fire, and many crowns are upon His head (vs. 12). He wears a vesture stained with blood; not His own, but that of the winepress of divine wrath (vs. 15), reminding us that His is the hand which loosed the divine judgments of chapters 6-19. His *activities* are in character: In righteousness He judges and makes war (vs. 11); descending from heaven, He leads the heavenly armies (vs. 14); with the sharp sword of His mouth, He comes to smite the nations and to rule them with a rod of iron· (vs. 15). All the rays of Biblical prophecy come into sharp focus here as they point to Jesus, the incarnate and glorified Son of God, and no other. For the last word from heaven just before His descent reminds the reader that "the testimony of Jesus is the spirit of prophecy" (vs. 10).

From the description in Rev. 19:11-16 it must be clear that, in the inauguration of His Mediatorial Kingdom on earth, our Lord will come down from heaven exactly as He declared He would:

---

[31] As the President of Faith Theological Seminary has written: "In earlier books of the Bible we have glimpses of phases of the Millennial Kingdom or of the return of Christ . . . . At the end of the Bible, in Revelation 19 and 20, a picture is given to gather them together and show their arrangement in the pattern of God's plan . . . . It is so clear that one marvels that anyone should misunderstand it" (Dr. Allan A. MacRae, an address published under the title "The Millennial Kingdom of Christ").

personally, visibly, gloriously, powerfully, and with hosts of angels (Matt. 24:26-30; 25:31). Included in the heavenly "armies" which attend Him, Alford insists, we should see the "glorified saints" of the Church. Whether this identification be correct or not, it is certain that these "saints" shall be with Him when He comes to reign (I Thess. 3:13). It would be inconceivable that the Lamb's "wife," after the blessed consummation of the marriage in heaven should ever again be separated from her glorious Bridegroom. The promise is that we shall "ever be with the Lord" (I Thess. 4:17). Today, during her life on earth, Christ is "with" the Church *spiritually:* "Lo, I am with you alway, even unto the end of the age" (Matt. 28:20). But when its membership is complete, the Church will be taken up from the earth by rapture and resurrection to be *personally* "with" her divine Head. And this conjugal relationship will be everlasting, never to be broken by divorce, nor marred by any separation.

2. The Defeat of the Beast (Rev. 19:17-21)

And the beast was taken.   *Rev. 19:20*

Throughout chapters 6-19, during the pre-Kingdom judgments upon the world, there is a definite progression in the gathering of the massive forces of evil. The pseudo-messiah of 6:2 rides swiftly to his goal of world political power, and then is revealed in his true character as the "beast" of 13:1-5. Following the consolidation of his power, the judgment of God is concentrated upon his "throne," and his kingdom is plunged into "darkness" (16:10). His immediate reaction is a move to gather his forces for a test of strength. With a show of superhuman "signs," he sets out to bring together the military resources of the kings of the entire world, for a rendezvous in the great plain of Esdraelon (16:16), scene of so many battles in ancient days.[32] There they now appear in Revelation 19 for the climactic judgment which will clear the way for the establishment of Christ's Kingdom on earth (19:17-21).

If the question be raised as to why this fateful gathering should take place in the land of Palestine, the obvious answer is that, according to the record of chapters 6-19, the only area of successful open resistance to the beast remaining on earth appears in the 144,000 protected by the divine seal (7:1-8); and these are *Israelites.* Furthermore, they are not only "on earth" (as Alford rightly

---

[32] On the "geographical" identification, see E. R. Craven in Lange's *Commentary, in loc.*

notes),[33] but more specifically, in the vision they appear on "Mount Sion" (14:1), and therefore are in the historic land of Israel. Except for these,[34] all other open opposition has been abolished by the beast. The two great witnesses have been killed (11:7). The apostate church has been utterly destroyed (17:16). What is left of the nation of Israel has been forced to take refuge in the wilderness (12:14). All others, whether Jew or Gentile, who rejected the mark of the beast have been martyred (13:15). Could anything be more reasonable, therefore, than to find the satanic dictator now, with his throne and kingdom shaking under the terrible judgment of the fifth vial (16:10), in this emergency turning his ominous attention toward that land and city where down through the times of divine revelation most of the troubles of Satan have been centered? Moreover, according to Old Testament prophecy, the hard core of resistance to the beast at the end will be Jewish, and centered in Jerusalem (cf. Zech. 12:1-9). And surely nothing could be more ironically appropriate than for God to permit the military assembly in Palestine in order that His final judgment might fall in the land[35] where a satanically inspired world once passed its judgment upon God's own Mediatorial King. Furthermore, there is divine propriety in the manner of judgment which will now put an end to Satan's long misrule upon earth. Whereas the previous judgments of Rev. 6-18 have been inflicted by our Lord from His place in heaven through *angelic* agency, the doom of the beast is reserved for the personal hand of the true King of kings. There will be no intermediate agent now, but He Himself will speak the word of execution (19:21).

Reading the record of Revelation 19:17-21, the question occurs as to how any rational earthly ruler could think to pit his strength against the King of kings. But this is only a piece of the greater

---

[33] Henry Alford on Rev. 14:3, *The Greek New Testament,* 4th ed., 1871.

[34] The reference to the 144,000 as "the first fruits unto God and to the Lamb" (14:4) cannot mean the first in *time* of all the redeemed in world history, for this would displace the saints of the Old Testament. In the context of Revelation, they are the "firstfruits" of the nation of Israel to be redeemed out of end-time judgments, to form the nucleus of the living nation on earth in the Millennial Kingdom. For they are divinely protected from physical harm and therefore do not die (7:3).

[35] The objection that Palestine offers no area of sufficient size to permit the assembling of the military forces of the world, although still being repeated monotonously, has been rendered wholly meaningless by recent developments in military weapons. At this writing, we are being reliably informed that as few as fifty H-bombs, carried by as many planes and exploded at strategic places, could effectively destroy the national existence of the Soviet Union, or any other comparable power.

mystery of the illimitable ambition of Satan himself, who from the beginning has not hesitated to match his strength and ingenuity against the omnipotence of Deity (Isa. 14:12-14). And the beast is *Satan's* king, energized and driven by him in his mad endeavors (Rev. 13:4). If we should need any closer evidence of the boundless ambition of even ordinary human beings, there is today an example before our eyes — in a government of men who in Russia have set out with the openly avowed policy of abolishing God from the universe. "If they do these things in a green tree, what shall be done in the dry?" (Luke 23:31). For sinful humanity, any large measure of success is always heady wine. And we should recall that the beast, at the apex of his power, will have accomplished in a brief space of time something unparalleled in human history: the building of a world empire above and beyond successful challenge by any human force on earth. "All the world wondered after the beast . . . saying, Who is like unto the beast? Who is able to make war with him?" (Rev. 13:3-4).

One remarkable feature of the final conflict is that the heavenly "armies" of our Lord bear no weapons and strike no blows. In all that vast assembly, only its regal Leader bears a sword. His vesture alone, not theirs, is stained with blood. Thus, we are told, the opposing armies "were slain by the sword of him that sat upon the horse, which sword proceeded out of his mouth" (Rev. 19:21). Now this would be utterly strange if the conflict were wholly a *spiritual* affair, such as that pictured in Ephesians 6:10-17. For in that case the saints would be obligated to put on the whole armor of God and fight against the "rulers of the darkness of this world." But the situation at the end is totally different: for this is a battle which, though basically between spiritual forces, nevertheless breaks out into the realm of "flesh and blood" so that even the fowls of heaven are filled with it (19:21). The cautious comment of Alford here is very much to the point: "*All* must not be thus spiritualized. For if so, what is this gathering? Why is His [Christ's] personal presence wanted for the victory?"[36]

The truth of the matter is that a *spiritual* cause may produce tangible effects which are physical in nature. The beast and his armies appear at the end-time in "flesh and blood," but our Lord will need no physical weapons to destroy them. He has only to speak the "Word" and they perish. Thus the hosts of Pharaoh perished

---

[36] Henry Alford, *ibid.*, *in loc.*

in the Red Sea; and the 185,000 soldiers of Sennacherib perished outside the walls of Jerusalem. So also Ananias and Sapphira died in the Early Church. These are historical facts of divine revelation which cannot be gainsaid; and they wholly invalidate all interpretations which assume that spiritual forces must never produce any but spiritual effects. If it is argued that such a holocaust of physical destruction as that pictured in Revelation 19 is wholly out of character for "the meek and lowly Jesus," the answer is that this same Jesus is none other than the Incarnation of that God whose destroying hand was made bare again and again in Old Testament history.

3. *The Binding of Satan* (Rev. 20:1-3)

And he laid hold on the dragon.   —*Rev. 20:2*

Having cast the "beast" and the "false prophet" alive into the lake of fire and having destroyed their deluded followers, the time has come to deal with that great evil spirit who is ultimately responsible for the delusion of the nations. For this purpose, now, an angel comes down from heaven, having the key of the bottomless pit, and a great chain in his hand. Of his action we read that "he laid hold on the dragon, that old serpent, which is the Devil, and Satan, and bound him a thousand years; and cast him into the bottomless pit, and shut him up, and set a seal upon him, that he should deceive the nations no more, till the thousand years should be fulfilled; and after that he must be loosed a little season" (20:1-3).

The language here is very specific: The object of the angel's action is the *dragon* of the Book of Revelation, the ancient *serpent* of Genesis, whose well-known names are the *Devil* and *Satan*. The angel lays "hold" on him, binds him, casts him into the abyss, shuts him up, seals the prison, and thus renders him powerless to deceive the nations for a period of a "thousand years." If this language does not mean that the immobilization of Satan is complete, so far as his deception of the nations (Grk. *ethnē*) is concerned, then there is no way to express the idea. And this binding of Satan, according to St. John's account, takes place at the coming of Christ in glory to establish His reign on earth for a thousand years. After making all legitimate allowance for possible figurative and symbolical terms, the central facts here are so clear that there should never have been any serious dispute about them. And this was the case during the first three hundred years of the Early Church. But since that time the passage (and the entire chapter) has been a battleground of theological conflict.

Of all the divine acts described in Revelation 20, none appears to be more reasonable than the binding and imprisonment of Satan. In the first place, if there is ever to be a Kingdom of God on earth, a reign characterized by the total absence of war and by rigid control of disease and death, it should be evident that in such a kingdom there can be no place left for the great deceiver of the nations, who is said to have not only the power of inflicting disease upon men (Job 2:7) but also the "power of death" itself (Heb. 2:14), to say nothing of his control over the demonic world (Matt. 12:22-26). To be sure, the vast powers of Satan have never been outside the permissive control of our sovereign God, but the continued exercise of such powers would be utterly incongruous within an established Kingdom of God on earth. This is suggested in the pattern of prayer where we are taught not only to pray, "Thy Kingdom come," but also "Deliver us from the evil one" (Matt. 6:10, 13, ASV). At the coming of our Lord these petitions will be answered, not only in part, but fully. In that wonderful day there will be no room left for the diabolical activities of "the prince of the power of the air, the spirit that *now* worketh in the children of disobedience" (Eph. 2:2, italics added). Satan shall be bound in such a way that he can deceive the nations "no more" till the thousand-year reign of Christ is done.

In the second place, such a binding of Satan for a thousand years will constitute a conclusive demonstration of man's personal responsibility for his own depravity. Although Satan has indeed been the originator of much of the evil of our fallen race, he cannot be charged with all of it. Yet the alibi of Eden — "The serpent beguiled me" — has never ceased to be the excuse offered by men for their sins. Our Lord struck at this alibi when, after enumerating a terrible catalogue of human iniquities, He declared that their source was "from within, out of the heart of men" (Mark 7:21-23). Yet men — even Christians — have been loathe to believe that this is altogether true. Through the ages of God's dealing with a fallen race, He has tested its members under many different conditions; and in every test, apart from the grace of God, man has always proven to be a failure.[37] But *sinful* men have never been given an

---

[37] To ridicule the idea of God testing sinful men under different conditions, as some anti-dispensationalists are fond of doing, only shows that the objectors have not read their Bibles carefully (cf. Deut. 8:2, etc.).

opportunity to "prove" what they will do in an environment from which the great deceiver of souls has been completely banished. The purpose here is not to acquaint *God* with something which He does not now know, but rather to prove to *men* themselves how desperately wicked they really are. The complete immobilization of Satan for a thousand years, therefore, will lay the basis for God's final argument against the popular doctrine of the inherent goodness of man when placed in the right kind of environment. It might be thought that all orthodox theologians would recognize the value of such a demonstration of the doctrine of total depravity, but such is not the case.

On the other hand, the binding of Satan will show under the rule of Christ the yet unrealized and vast possibilities of human life in physical existence on earth, even where sin still exists in a society composed of both regenerated and unregenerated men. For, great as the progress of the world has been in many ways, by all reasonable men it is generally agreed that things ought to be almost infinitely better than they are. What this binding of Satan by our Lord will mean to the world has been well stated by Fausset: "A mighty purification will be effected by Christ's coming. Though sin will not be abolished — for men will still be in the flesh (Isa. 65:20) — sin will no longer be a universal power, for the flesh is no longer seduced by Satan. He will not be, as now, 'the god and prince of the world'; nor will the world 'lie in the wicked one': the flesh will be evermore overcome. Christ will reign with His transfigured saints over men in the flesh (Auberlen). The nations in the millennium will be prepared for a higher state, as Adam in Paradise, supposing he had lived in an unfallen state."[38]

4. *The Thrones of Judgment* (Rev. 20:4)

> And I saw thrones, and they sat upon them, and judgment was given
> unto them.   —*Rev. 20:4*

It is not without significance that after the binding of Satan the very first scene shown to John was a plurality of "thrones." And in harmony with the general usage of this term in Revelation, judicial action is associated with these thrones: "judgment" is given to those who sit thus enthroned. This is as it should be. For here manifestly we have the actual beginning of the thousand-year Kingdom; and the activities of such a reign must begin with *judicial* action. Since this Kingdom will begin on earth with the actual situation

---

[38] A. R. Fausset, *ibid.*, on Revelation 20:3.

existing here as the coming of Christ finds it, there will be many crucial matters needing to be settled by such action without delay. Among these will be the determination of what nations and what persons will be permitted to enter that blessed age and enjoy its wonderful benefits; the adjudication of ancient wrongs; the solution of the immediate problems of a complex society; and the assignment of responsibilities within the divine government as it will exist among men. Even today, in spite of our limited knowledge, intelligent men can put their fingers upon a thousand things in government that should be changed. But at present always the getting of things changed is either almost infinitesimally slow or is accomplished by revolution which may leave the situation worse than it was before.

A question now arises: Who are the persons seated on the thrones seen by John? The passage does not *name* them. They cannot be angels, for judicial action is no part of their proper activity. Nor can these enthroned judges be the martyrs mentioned in the next clause of verse 4, as Beza and others have thought. Lange is right in saying that "The context also is against it. First, John saw the thrones and those who seated themselves upon them; and *then* the beheaded ones who revived and reigned with Christ";[39] but he overlooks the most important clue pointing to their true identification. This is a question which is best settled within the context of the Book of Revelation itself. The only persons who appear on thrones elsewhere in the book are the twenty-four elders of 4:4 and 11:16. And since the judges of chapter 20:4 are brought before us *unnamed*, as if readers were expected to know who they are, exegetical logic and good sense point back to the same persons. These were associated with the pre-Kingdom judgments of chapters 6-19 poured out from *heaven;* and what could be more reasonable than to find the same group associated with the judgments with which the Kingdom now begins on *earth?* As already indicated in the foregoing argument, these elders represent the Church of the present age, the Body and Bride of Christ. Only to this group of the saved is reserved the exalted assignment of judicial responsibilities in the Kingdom of our Lord. They are to act, under Him, as associate justices in the affairs of the Kingdom.

The *nature* of this judicial activity needs to be considered more precisely. Certainly, it cannot be the kind of judging which would weigh the secret thoughts and motives of men, and decide their

[39] See Lange, *in loc.*

eternal destinies. Only God can render such judgment, and the Father has committed all this to the Son (John 5:22). There are some things which Deity cannot share with finite beings, no matter how good and perfect they may be. The judgment assigned in Revelation 20:4, therefore, must be of the same nature as that promised in Luke 22:29-30 and I Corinthians 6:2; and these promises in their context must be limited to such matters as are appropriate to the abilities of the saints, then made perfect in goodness and wisdom; but who, we must never forget, still remain finite beings. What God can and may do in the perfecting of His Church, we must admit, passes beyond present human imagination (I Cor. 2:9); but we shall never become gods. There is a judging activity, however, of which men are capable even today, though very imperfectly. This consists in the investigation of facts, the interpretation of existing law, its application to specific cases, and the rendering of verdicts. Since throughout the Millennial Kingdom human life will continue with the possibilities of sin and error, though greatly restrained and controlled, it should be obvious that there will be need for such judicial activity then as well as now. But the immeasurable superiority of this millennial judging will be the absence of that prejudice and fallibility so characteristic of present human courts, even at their best. For, in that glad day, there will be no weariness, no disease, no weakening of the faculties of the mind by reason of age, and no sinful inclinations to cloud the pure judgments which will be issued by the perfected members of the Church. And each of the judges, we must not forget, will then be fully possessed and indwelt without hindrance by the Holy Spirit of God, who is "the spirit of wisdom and understanding, the spirit of counsel and might, the spirit of knowledge and the fear of the Lord" (Isa. 11:2). Then at last justice will "roll down as waters, and righteousness as a mighty stream" upon a world where too often at present judgment has been turned into "wormwood."

5. *The Resurrection of Martyred Saints* (Rev. 20:4, 5, ASV)

And I saw the souls of them that had been beheaded for the testimony of Jesus, and for the word of God, and such as worshipped not the beast, neither his image, and received not the mark upon their forehead and upon their hand; and they lived, and reigned with Christ a thousand years. The rest of the dead lived not until the thousand years should be finished. This is the first resurrection.
—*Rev. 20:4-5, ASV*

a. The term "souls" (*psuchai*) here seems clearly to mean souls that had been *disembodied physically*. And thus it was understood by the Early Church Fathers generally. In fact, it is in the highest degree improbable that any other view would ever have been proposed except for the rise of philosophic antagonism toward a premillennial resurrection of saints. Since that time a vast amount of ingenuity has been expended in trying to spiritualize everything possible in the context.[40] In support of the idea of *disembodied* "souls," the following facts should be noted:

First, the writer of Revelation is very precise in his language, distinguishing carefully between the *persons* who had suffered decapitation and their "souls" which survived the terrible ordeal. John does not say that he saw "souls" that had been beheaded, but that he saw the souls of *"them"* that had been thus executed. There is no confusion here whatever, except in the minds of interpreters who for various reasons hesitate to accept the record at its normal value.

Second, while it is true that the Greek *psuchē* may sometimes be rendered in the sense of physical "life" (cf. Acts 20:10), even in the majority of such cases the idea of "soul" as a metaphysical entity cannot be excluded. For in the Bible it is the presence of this metaphysical entity that maintains man's physical life: "the body without the spirit is dead" (Jas. 2:26).[41] When Paul reassuringly said concerning the young man who fell out of the window, "His life [*psuchē*] is in him" (Acts 20:10), the passage could just as properly have been translated, "His *soul* is in him." Furthermore, the Bible more than once uses the term *psuchē* to distinguish sharply between physical and metaphysical existence. "Fear not them which kill the body, and are not able to kill the soul (*psuchē*)," Jesus warned, "but rather fear him who is able to destroy both soul and body in hell" (Matt. 10:28).

Third, in the context of the Apocalypse, this vision of "souls" in 20:4 should recall to our minds at once the similar vision under the fifth seal (6:9-11) where we find the *first* of the honored company of martyrs during the sore afflictions of chapters 6-19. Then follows the vision of 7:9-17 which reveals how *vast* the number

---

40 As an example, the reader is referred to a recent book under the title of *Revelation Twenty* by J. Marcellus Kik (Philadelphia: Presbyterian and Reformed Pub. Co., 1955). He attempts to show that *psuchē* in the New Testament generally means "life"; then translates the term in Rev. 20:4 by the noun "lives"; and finally paraphrases it as "victorious lives," thus substituting a *moral* meaning for the original metaphysical idea. By this devious process, the *psuchē* of Rev. 20:4 becomes *a way of living!*

41 The problem of Dichotomy versus Trichotomy does not impair the argument.

will be — "a great multitude." And the vision of 20:4 presents the *completed* company at the end of the beast's reign. The language of St. John is exactly the same at the beginning as at the end: In each place he tells us that he "saw" the "souls" of people who had been killed (6:9; 20:4).

Fourth, to argue that the soul, as an immaterial element of man's person, is wholly intangible is to yield overmuch to philosophic notions. In the Word of God, the soul is very real; certainly not altogether outside the realm of possible tangibility. Our Lord taught this clearly in His remarkable story of the rich man and Lazarus (Luke 16:19-31). The language of this passage is strikingly similar to that in Rev. 6:9-11, where the *souls* in heaven are not only seen by St. John but themselves see, hear, speak, are at rest, and are concerned with what is happening on earth. Furthermore, these souls are comforted with the divine assurance that justice in their cases will be done, but they must wait until the full number of the martyrs out of "the great tribulation" is complete. Such language cannot be materialized into mere physical blood crying out from the ground (as Hengstenberg) or dissolved into "victorious lives" (as Kik). For if the souls of the rich man and Lazarus were literal, there is no sound reason for doubting the reality of the martyred souls seen in Revelation 6:9-11; and if these are real, so also are the souls in Revelation 20:4.

Fifth, there is a definite sequence indicated by John's use of the verbs "saw" and "beheaded." He did not see the souls as they were being killed; but saw them (aorist tense) after they had been beheaded (perfect tense); suggesting that the intermediate state into which the souls had been introduced by the act of beheading still existed when John saw them.

b. Concerning these disembodied souls, John says that *"they lived and reigned" with Christ!* Here instead of following the clear thought connection of the context, the opposers of a premillennial resurrection of saints have expended much labor and ingenuity in efforts to show that the verb rendered "lived" does not refer to a resurrection of the body, but rather to the giving of *spiritual* life. According to their argument, the souls here are *regenerated* instead of resurrected. Against this view the following facts are presented:

First, although the verb *zaō* is used of both physical and spiritual life, the context of Revelation 20:4 is decisive in favor of the former. That the beheading in the passage is literal and physical not many have had the hardihood to deny, though they cannot agree among themselves as to just where and when it takes place. Upon this one admission of literality their entire case goes to pieces. For, if the people involved were beheaded *physically*, and then lived again, common sense would suggest that they received back the same category of life that had been lost.

Second, to argue that the life here is the kind of life received by the sinner in regeneration, is to introduce theological confusion into the passage. For the people who "lived" are the same people who had earlier lost their lives "for the witness of Jesus, and for the word of God" (vs. 4). Thus we would reach the absurdity of having souls being regenerated *after*[42] they had been beheaded for their faithfulness to Christ! If the verb "lived" in Revelation 20:4 means that these souls were made alive *spiritually*, then it follows that they must have been *dead* spiritually until that time. But how could unregenerated people have been faithful in their witness to Jesus, as the passage declares that they were?

6. *The First Resurrection* (Rev. 20:5)

In 20:5 the writer of Revelation specifically identifies the kind of life referred to by the words "they lived" in verse 4. "This," he says, "is the first resurrection." Such a clear definition should be enough to settle the question. But again there has been prodigious labor expended in attempts to show that the term "resurrection" (*anastasis*) here refers to regeneration. Against these attempts the following may be said:

a. In spite of all that has been written on the point, no one has ever produced a single indisputable instance in the New Testament where the Greek *anastasis* is ever applied to man's soul, or an instance where the new birth is ever called a "resurrection." This would be strange if the terms were ever regarded as interchangeable. The very etymology of the Greek term suggests the idea of the standing up again of a body which has been laid down in the grave. Such an idea would be wholly incongruous when applied to the soul or spirit.

b. Those who try to change the "first resurrection" of Rev. 20:5 into spiritual regeneration generally use the great passage of John 5:24-25 as a point of departure. This deserves some attention. The

---

42 Mr. Kik argues rather curiously that, because of the frequent use of the *aorist* verb forms in 20:4, therefore the actions in that verse must take place at the *same* time. But he strangely makes no mention of the *perfect* tense verb for "beheaded" (*Revelation Twenty*, p. 52).

first resurrection, it is alleged, is found in verse 25: "The hour is coming, and now is, when the dead shall hear the voice of the Son of God: and they that hear shall live." Now this is admittedly a clear reference to spiritual regeneration; but it is to be noted that our Lord is careful *not* to call it a "resurrection." Not only so, but He moves from the subject of spiritual life in verses 24-25 to the specific subject of physical life in verses 28-29, and only the latter is called "resurrection" (*anastasis*). Moreover, only those who are the recipients of resurrection are said to "come forth" from "*the graves,*" as we might naturally expect.

Still further, in John 5:25-28 our Lord lays an exegetical foundation for the two resurrections of Revelation 20, by affirming that the saved will come forth unto "the resurrection of life" and the unsaved to "the resurrection of judgment" (John 5:29, ASV). And the order is correct: first, the saved; then, the unsaved. Finally, Christ distinguishes in *time* definitely between His work of regeneration and His work of resurrection. As to the time of the former work he says, "The hour is coming, and now is" (vs. 25). But of the work of resurrection he says only, "The hour is coming" (vs. 28), a clear reference to an eschatological "hour." Thus the work of regeneration proceeds during the present hour — "*now,*" and also during an "hour" which is "*coming*"; i.e., the eschatological hour. But the work of resurrection is reserved wholly for the eschatological hour. It should be obvious that since the present "hour" of regeneration has already lasted 1900 years, there is no reason why the future hour may not last for a "thousand years," beginning with the resurrection of the saved and ending with the resurrection of the unsaved, as Revelation 20 states the order. Thus our Lord outlined the framework of a future age characterized by two divine works: first, the work of *spiritual* regeneration; and second, the work of *bodily* resurrection. The details are filled in by the Old Testament prophets and the Book of Revelation. The age will begin with the resurrection of the saints of past ages, and it will end with the resurrection of the unsaved. During the same age multitudes will be saved by the work of *regeneration,* and for these, apparently, there will be no physical death.

c. Returning now to the record in Revelation 20, we should observe the precise language with which the two resurrections are described. Certain people who had been *beheaded* are said to "*live,*" and this is defined as "the first resurrection." As for the rest of the dead, John says, they "lived not again until the thousand years were finished" (vs. 4-5). At the end of the thousand years, in the divine record, the resurrection of these "dead" is described in detail. If these two resurrections are not of the same *bodily* character, then language is of no value in conveying ideas, and we might well join in the dictum of Dean Alford as expressed on the point at issue: "If, in a passage where *two resurrections* are mentioned, where certain *souls lived* at the first, and the rest of the *dead lived* only at the end of a specified period after that first, — if in such a passage the first resurrection may be understood to mean *spiritual* rising with Christ, while the second means *literal* rising from the grave; — then there is an end to all significance in language, and Scripture is wiped out as a definite testimony to anything."[43]

d. The words, "This is the first resurrection," do not mean that this resurrection is confined to the "beheaded" martyrs of verse 4. For, in the Biblical record, the Church of the present age, the bride of Christ, has already appeared in her glorified state in heaven (19:1-9). And the two witnesses of chapter 11 were resurrected almost immediately following their death (11:11-12). As a matter of fact, there are various classes of saved people who will have a part in this "first resurrection." But the martyrs of the judgment period of chapters 6-19 constitute the *last* of these classes. When these martyrs "live" again, the Holy Spirit writes *finis* to this blessed resurrection with the pronouncement — "This is the first resurrection" (20:5). In the excellent comment of Lange: "With these words the Seer constitutes that entire resurrection-process which begins with the Parousia of Christ, a distinct dogmatical conception."[44]

It is significant that when the record moves from the resurrection of the martyred saints of verses 4-5 to the material in verse 6, the writer seems to broaden the scope of the first resurrection. It is no longer a specific class under consideration (the "beheaded ones"), but the statement becomes very general: "Blessed and holy is he that hath part in the first resurrection: on such the second death hath no power" (vs. 6). There is room left here for all the various groups of the saved, from the "church of the firstborn" (Heb. 12:23) down to the last martyr of the end-time.

e. The doctrine of a special resurrection for the redeemed, as taught in Revelation 20 is not something new, but is in harmony

---

[43] For the full quotation see pp. 475-476.
[44] J. P. Lange, *Revelation of St. John, in loc.*

with the general tenor of all previous divine revelation regarding the Mediatorial Kingdom. In the Old Testament, while the resurrection of the unrighteous is taught by implication, it is the resurrection of the righteous which is emphasized in such passages as Isaiah 25:8, 26:19, Ezekiel 37:1-14, Daniel 12:2, and Hosea 13:14. There was a sound reason for this. The Mediatorial Kingdom of history was on earth, not a kingdom in some far-off heaven. When this Kingdom came to an end, the prophets spoke of its future restoration in splendor and glory; and again it was to be on earth, with its center at Jerusalem in the land of Palestine. To have a part in that coming Kingdom was the deepest longing of every devout Israelite, to whom, therefore, physical death was a very terrible thing, for it seemed to interpose a formidable barrier to his participation in the coming Kingdom. The inspired answer to this distressing problem, in the prophets, was the doctrine of a resurrection for the righteous: "Thy dead men shall live," Isaiah writes, "Awake and sing, ye that dwell in dust" (26:19). And Ezekiel, writing in the midst of the captives who said, "Our hope is lost; we are clean cut off," speaks thus for Jehovah, "Ye shall know that I am Jehovah, when I have opened your graves, . . . O my people. And I will put my Spirit in you, and ye shall live, and I will place you in your own land" (37:11, 13-14, ASV).

In the New Testament it was this of which the Apostle Paul spoke to his people as "the hope and resurrection of the dead" (Acts 23:6; cf. 24:21, 26:6-8). Our Lord referred to the same event as a special resurrection in which only those would participate who are "sons of God, being sons of the resurrection" (Luke 20:35-36, ASV); and in another place He speaks of it as "the resurrection of the just" (Luke 14:14). To have a part in this resurrection was so great a prize, according to the Apostle Paul, that he could afford to lose everything in its attainment; and actually count the loss as nothing (Phil. 3:8-11). In the light of this well-attested Biblical doctrine, it would be passing strange if nothing were said about it in the Apocalypse which is pre-eminently the New Testament book of the coming Kingdom.

7. *The Mediatorial Reign* (Rev. 20:2-7)

a. *The Measure of Time*

This is stated as "a thousand years," and the expression occurs six times in Revelation 20:2-6, once in every verse, thus indicating its importance. But this repetition is not merely tautological, for in each recurrence the expression is connected with a distinctive idea: First, Satan is bound for a thousand years (vs. 2). Second, the nations will not be deceived for a thousand years (vs. 3). Third, the martyred saints reign with Christ for a thousand years (vs. 4). Fourth, the rest of the dead live not again till the thousand years are finished (vs. 5). Fifth, *all* who have part in the first resurrection will be priests of God and reign with Christ a thousand years (vs. 6). Sixth, Satan will be loosed after the thousand years (vs. 7).

The measure thus repeated seems clearly to refer to a single unit of time. One writer of the modern postmillennial school says dogmatically that the "thousand years" of verses 1-3 refers to a future period on *earth*, while the "thousand years" of verses 4-6 refers to the intermediate state of the righteous souls between death and resurrection.[45] But no sufficient reasons are given for this radical theory. Obviously, this would make the second "thousand years" chronologically meaningless, for the time would be different for every one who dies, except for those who happen to die at the same time! Furthermore, to allege two different periods of a thousand years, referring to two totally different modes of existence, would destroy the literary unity of the passage which begins with the binding of Satan for a "thousand years" (vs. 2) and ends with his loosing after the thousand years (vs. 7). This is to say nothing about the unbiblical notion of disembodied "souls" reigning with Christ *before* their resurrection and glorification.

Most postmillennial and amillennial attacks upon the doctrine of a Millennial Kingdom, to be established at the second advent of Christ, begin with a denial of the *literality* of "the thousand years." All agree in giving to this figure a symbolic meaning, but they disagree over whether or not the idea of *time* is totally excluded. To some (as Warfield) the figure simply represents an inconceivable idea. To others the time element is genuinely present: the *years* are literal, but not the *sum* of a thousand![46] This admission of a literal period of time, though the length is unknown, is fatal to the entire scheme. For if the period can be measured in literal years at all, we might just as well (and more wisely) accept the figure given by St. John.

45 Loraine Boettner, *The Millennium* (Philadelphia: The Presbyterian and Reformed Pub. Co., 1958), p. 66.
46 To postmillennialist J. Marcellus Kik, and also to amillennialist Floyd E. Hamilton, the "thousand years" extend from the first coming of Christ to His second coming. To postmillennialist Loraine Boettner the period will not be less than a thousand years but probably much *longer*.

All this leads to the observation that the figure as stated in the inspired record is patently not an unreasonable figure, else a vigorous critic of the premillennial view could hardly admit that the time would be "probably not less than a literal thousand years . . . a definitely limited period."[47] Since the Kingdom of Christ is to be set in the context of human history, its length might well bear some relevance to what is known about that history. Viewed from this standpoint, the figure of a "thousand" sounds more reasonable than two hundred thousand or other speculative guesses of the anti-literalists. It may be recalled that in early Biblical history some of the patriarchs approached a millennium of years in their ages, and Isaiah declares of the righteous in the coming Kingdom that there shall be no more "an old man that hath not filled his days" (65:20). Furthermore, the Theocratic Kingdom of Old Testament history endured from Moses to the Captivity, a period of somewhat less than a thousand years. Thus, the figure set by St. John seems to make good sense. Why, then, should we tamper with it?

In chapters 4-20 of the Book of Revelation there are at least twenty-five references to measures of time. Of these, only two *require* what is called a "figurative" treatment: the "day of his wrath" (6:17), and "the hour of his judgment" (15:7)[48] Such a usage of "day" and "hour" as referring to some period of time, whether long or short, is so common that it needs no discussion. But even in such cases the total time may be quite definite: thus we may speak of Hitler's "day," and we know exactly how long it lasted. The other twenty-three references to time may be divided into three classes:

First, there are seven references to the seventieth week of Daniel's prophecy and its two main divisions (Dan. 9:27); stated variously as 1260 days (11:3, 12:6), 42 months (11:2, 13:5), and 3½ years (12:14). The "short time" of 12:12 clearly refers to the 42 months of 13:5, while the "little season" of 6:11 seems to cover both halves of the entire seven-year period. Now the literality of these stated figures is grounded in history, for the first 69 weeks of years in Daniel's prophecy have been fulfilled exactly by the first coming of Christ. If not, then He is not the Messiah. We have a right to

[47] Loraine Boettner, *ibid.,* p. 64.
[48] "The Lord's day" of 1:10 may also belong in this category, as I am inclined to believe; but it is also possible to interpret the reference as a literal day of an ordinary week.

expect, therefore, a similar literal fulfilment of the seventieth week of years.

Second, there are the six references to the "thousand years" in Rev. 20:1-7. Since this measure of time is applied to the Kingdom which follows immediately the literal seven-year period of pre-Kingdom judgments, there is a strong presumption of literality as to the thousand-year measure. And any other viewpoint should be rejected unless based on Biblical reasons which are clear and indisputable. No such reasons have ever been produced, though brilliant minds have been struggling to do so for considerably more than a thousand years. Calvin, who rejected the idea of literality, was wiser in dismissing the matter *without* argument.

Third, the other ten references to time may be classed as miscellaneous: the "half an hour" of 8:1; the "five months" of 9:5; the "days" of the voice of the seventh angel of 10:7; the "three days and an half" of 11:9, 11; the "same hour" of 11:13; the "one hour" of 17:12 and 18:19; and the "one day" of 18:8. In fact, great precision in chronology is strongly suggested by the reference in 9:15 where we learn that the four angels were loosed that had been prepared for the *"hour"* and *"day"* and *"month"* and *"year."* It will have been observed by careful readers that each of these miscellaneous references represents a subdivision of the seven-year period of pre-Kingdom judgments, lending further weight to the presumption of literality. For, if the total time is literal, so also are its subdivisions.

In the thousand years of Revelation 20:1-7, then, we have set forth the *precise* length of the Mediatorial Kingdom, which earlier had been stated indefinitely in Old Testament prophecy. The outstanding parallel passage appears in Isaiah 24:21-23. In this chapter the prophet presents a picture of the judgments of God upon the world in preparation for His "reign in Mount Zion, and in Jerusalem" (vs. 23). At the close of these judgments, He gathers "the high ones that are on high" (Satan and his angels) and "the kings of the earth" (cf. Rev. 19:19), shutting them up "as prisoners . . . in the pit" (Isa. 24:21-22). Then the prophet says, "After many days shall they be punished" (vs. 22, ASV margin). The *many days* here correspond to the thousand-year reign of Revelation 20, which begins with the defeat of the earthly kings and the binding of Satan, and ends with the final judgment upon them.[49]

---

[49] For other Old Testament parallels, see *The Thousand Years in Both Testaments* by Nathaniel West, 1880.

In arguing for the literality of the time-measures generally in the Book of Revelation, we do not deny that, in at least some cases, there may be also a symbolical meaning. But such meanings are strengthened by the literal and factual foundation. There is endless room for exploration in the symbolism of Biblical numbers. What we must regard as reprehensible is the assumption, too often manifested by the anti-premillennialists, that the admission of a symbolical meaning automatically shuts out of court any possible literality in Biblical numbers. As an argument against literality in the numbers in Revelation, the reference to "the seven Spirits of God" is often cited (Rev. 1:4, 3:1, 4:5), the assumption being that, since there is only *one* Spirit of God, the number here cannot be literal. And with this one example, some writers feel they have demolished the literality of all numbers in the Apocalypse. But here, it should be noted, the expression cited is not itself the symbol but is rather the divine *interpretation* of a symbol. What John saw was the symbol — "seven lamps of fire." And the symbol was literal. John actually saw the lamps of fire, and he saw *seven* of them, not eight or some indefinite number. Furthermore, when the inspired record declares that "the seven lamps" are "the seven Spirits of God," it must be remembered that according to New Testament usage the Spirit of God may be mentioned when the reference is to His *work* or *gifts* rather than to His Person. The placing of the seven Spirits "before the throne" (4:5) clearly suggests the activity of ministration. Thus, while the number *seven* doubtless bears the symbolical meaning of unity and perfection, there is no reason for dogmatically denying the possibility of a reference to a literal *seven* of spiritual activities. The burden of proof rests upon those who deny this as a possibility.

In concluding our discussion of "the thousand years," we should observe that the mediatorial reign of *Christ* is not limited to this precise measure of time. The record specifically states that this measure applies to the reign of the *saints:* "they . . . shall reign with him a thousand years" (20:6). In a very real sense, the mediatorial reign of Christ Himself may be said to begin *de jure* with His judicial work from heaven, as suggested by the announcement in 11:15 — "The kingdoms of this world are become the kingdoms of our Lord, and of his Christ." And not only so, but His mediatorial reign extends beyond the end of the thousand years. "For he must reign," Paul writes, "till he hath put all enemies under his feet.

The last enemy that shall be destroyed is death" (I Cor. 15:25-26).
And the destruction of death is beyond the end of the thousand
years (Rev. 20:7, 14).

b. *Nature of the Millennial Reign*

One of the current arguments against the literality of the Kingdom, as described in Revelation 20, is that so little space is given to
it there. Of course, if such an argument has any validity at all, it
could be brought against the doctrine of any sort of a kingdom,
whether spiritual or otherwise. But all such arguments ignore what
has been called the principle of "parsimony" in Scripture. The Old
Testament prophets had described this future Mediatorial Kingdom
in great detail, and for those acquainted with the Old Testament
there would be no need for any profuse repetition of what was already
revealed. The Book of Revelation, as rightly observed by scholars of
every school of thought, is saturated with Old Testament ideas and
expressions and therefore can be approached only through the Old
Testament. For those who use this approach, obviously, there would
be no need for detailed repetition. This entirely reasonable assumption appears in the teaching and ministry of Christ. If men went
wrong in their ideas of the Kingdom, He pointed to the source of
their error: "Ye do err, not knowing the scriptures" (Matt. 22:29).
And the Scriptures here, it is sometimes forgotten, are those of the
Old Testament. Furthermore, the men to whom the Lord spoke
were the scholars of His day, men who had a thorough *formal* knowledge of the Old Testament, but who rejected in part what the
prophets clearly taught. Similarly, as pointed out earlier in this
volume, those today who are belligerently opposed to the idea of
a literal Kingdom of Christ on earth are the scholars who either largely
ignore the Old Testament or else dissolve in the acid of their "spiritualization" those prophetic elements which are repugnant to them.

By such men, it has also been argued that it is wholly incongruous for the Book of Revelation (according to our premillennial
view) to give fourteen chapters (6-19) to the pre-Kingdom judgments extending over a short period of *seven* years, while only one
chapter (20) is given to the Kingdom itself which lasts for a thousand years.[50] To this it might be replied that God Himself calls
the judgment period "a little season" and "a short time" (Rev. 6:11,
12:12); and we should be grateful that in the mercy of God this is

---

[50] Cf. Loraine Boettner, *ibid.*, pp. 201-202.

so. But it is also a fact that Scripture generally gives more space to its warnings of judgment than to its descriptions of the joys of heaven. And this is wholly reasonable. On our highways, men do not ordinarily put up signs telling the traveler that "This is a safe road"; but for the most part all such signs are those of *caution* and *danger*. The world in which we live is one of sin and hazard and death. Some day all this will be ended, but until that day we should be thankful for the abundance of warnings concerning wrath and judgment to come.

But the twentieth chapter of Revelation is not entirely silent as to the nature of the millennial government. In general, it is characterized by three expressions: First, we are told that "judgment" (*krima*) will be given to the enthroned saints (20:4). Second, we learn that all who have part in the first resurrection shall be "priests" (*hiereis*) of God (vs. 6). And, third, the same verse declares that they shall "reign" (*basileusousin*) with Christ. Thus the governing activities of the coming Kingdom, as indicated by these terms, will be judicial, sacerdotal, and regal. It would be impossible, of course, to conceive of any kind of genuine government, whether human or divine, without the judging and ruling functions. But, to some, the *sacerdotal* idea is thought to be theologically incongruous. This objection seems to be based in part upon the ·*present* desirability of complete separation of church and state. In the coming Kingdom, however, this rather illogical separation will disappear. Under the personal rule of Christ, the firm union of church and state will not only be safe; it will be the highest possible good. The resumption of the priestly function, as a proper activity of government, will not modify in any sense the absoluteness of the exclusive priesthood of our Lord. For the priesthood of the members of the body of Christ even today, as also in the coming Kingdom, is only an activity of limited priestly service,[51] such as is appropriate to saved sinners. We do not mediate between men and God. Hence, there can be no possible objection to its continuance in the Kingdom, for then the priestly service will be rendered by perfected saints, no longer marred by sinful inclinations and infirmity.

The governing function in the coming Kingdom is described somewhat more fully in Rev. 19:15 where, concerning the descending King, John says: "And out of his mouth goeth a sharp sword, that with it he should smite the nations: and he shall rule them

---

[51] Cf. the Greek verb *latreuō* in Rom. 1:9.

with a rod of iron; and he treadeth the winepress of the fierceness and wrath of Almighty God." Such a rule on the part of a just and merciful God, it might be supposed, would be most welcome to all who are troubled with the terrible inequities of human history and the appalling problems current in our times. But here again the anti-premillennialists have labored hard to modify the force of the language of this passage. For example, Hamilton[52] devotes considerable space in an attempt to show that the verb *poimainō* refers to the tender care of a shepherd rather than to a "rod-of-iron" rule over the nations.

It is true that the Greek *poimainō*, rendered "rule" in 19:15, has the general meaning of *shepherdly* rule. But this meaning implies, rather than cancels, the factor of severity in the rule of Christ over those who will believe during the thousand-year reign. The idea of severity runs through the context of the entire verse: there is here a "sharp sword" as well as a "rod of iron"; and in His rule our Lord "smites" the nations and "treadeth" the winepress of divine wrath. These are verbs which cannot be emptied of their severity.

Even in the Church of our present age, which by some is alleged to be the established kingdom of Christ on earth, our Lord often lays the rod of severe and deserved chastisement on His people, resulting sometimes in the ordeal of physical death (I Cor. 11:29-32). But such severity is always for our ultimate good — "that we should not be condemned with the world." Furthermore, there is operative even today a *providential* rule of God over the nations, in the exercise of which He sometimes "smites" the nations with great severity without utterly destroying them.

In fact, the shepherdly rule of God is always both severe and tender: lovingkindness toward all who yield to His perfect Will, but chastisement for those who stray from the path of righteousness, and destruction for those who are incorrigibly rebellious. And in the coming Mediatorial Kingdom of Christ this rule will be direct and immediate, no longer veiled in obscurity nor subject to the time-lag which so often now characterizes the working of the divine providential control. In that future Kingdom of Messiah there will be a perfect balance between tenderness and severity. As seen by Isaiah, He will rule with a "strong hand," but He also shall "gather the lambs . . . and carry them in his bosom" (40:10-11).

If in Revelation 20 the nature of the Mediatorial Kingdom is de-

[52] Floyd E. Hamilton, *The Basis of Millennial Faith*, 1942, pp. 83-90.

scribed very briefly and only in general terms, it should be observed that within this terminology ample room is left for all the profusion of detail set forth in the Old Testament prophetic picture of that Kingdom; and not a single element or aspect is canceled by either direct denial or implication. Hence, we cannot be wrong in following the Apostle Peter who said that at the second advent of Christ there would be ushered in an age described as "the times of restitution of all things, which God hath spoken by the mouth of all his holy prophets since the world began" (Acts 3:20-21).

c. *Some Problems and Objections*

Objections to the premillennial view of the Kingdom have at times become so absurd and puerile that they deserve no answer at all. But for the sake of sincere seekers who may have been troubled by specious argument, at least a few of these alleged problems should be mentioned.

(1) Some people have been genuinely concerned about the *problem of sin* in an otherwise perfect Kingdom of God in human life. And, of course, Scripture makes it very clear that sin will be present during the Millennial Kingdom. The fact that Satan must be bound so that he cannot deceive the nations during the age of the Kingdom (Rev. 20:3) shows that in the people of that age there will remain the inclination to respond to satanic temptation. And the prediction that a great multitude will thus respond as soon as Satan is loosed (20:7-8) only confirms the existence of a sinful human nature. But this melancholy fact should not trouble the opposers of Premillennialism who believe in a *present* Kingdom of God on earth. Why should the presence of sin be regarded as an insuperable objection to a future Kingdom of God, if it can be reconciled with a present kingdom? Furthermore, the problem of sin in the coming Kingdom will be greatly alleviated by the binding of Satan and an immediate divine control over all overt acts of rebellion against the laws of the Kingdom. As to those who argue that human sin should be conquered by the "Gospel," not by divine *force,* we may ask whether they would be willing to dispense with the physical restraint of civil government *today,* poor as it often is. If the "sword" of civil rulers, who are called ministers of God (Rom. 13:4), is not inconsistent with the present providential Kingdom of God, why should force be thought out of place in the future Mediatorial Kingdom of Christ?

As to this problem of sin in the Millennium, there is a very striking parallelism between the "regeneration" of the individual person (Tit. 3:5) and what our Lord called the "regeneration" of human society in the Millennial Kingdom (Matt. 19:28). In each there takes place a radical and tremendous miracle: in the one case an absolutely new divine control enters the human personality; and likewise a new intrusion of supernatural control will come into the area of human affairs. In each case, there is left a sinful element which requires constant control. Yet in each case this situation is not the final state. For just as the old nature of the individual believer will at last be destroyed, even so after the thousand years will the Kingdom be purged of all that needs to be held in restraint by immediate divine control. Thus the future regeneration of society will recapitulate the present regeneration of the individual. Neither grows gradually into a new birth; but each begins and ends with a distinct "crisis" experience supernatural in character.

(2) It has also been objected that the *bodily* presence of Christ ruling on earth in the Kingdom would be much inferior to His *spiritual* presence as now manifested in every place. Such an objection is based on both bad theology and bad logic. Why should it be assumed that the world could not enjoy the presence of Christ bodily and spiritually at the same time? If our Lord can be present bodily in *heaven* today while at the same time He is manifesting Himself wherever two or three are gathered in His name, why could He not during the millennial reign be present bodily in *Jerusalem,* while at the same time manifesting Himself spiritually wherever men call upon Him? Or is heaven only a state of mind, and not a definite *place?*

This same objection has sometimes been pressed to ridiculous lengths: if Christ and His saints are to be present bodily ruling in the coming Kingdom, where would they live! The answer is, of course, in *heaven.* The residence of the saints in heaven while ruling on earth, actually, is much less of a problem than that of a business man whose office is in a city while his residence is in the suburbs. One wonders at times how foolish the objectors can get. Have they learned nothing about the powers of a resurrection body, as set forth in the Bible, with its immeasurable superiority over both space and time?

The appearance of Christ among the people of the Millennial Age will have a very practical effect. Intellectual belief in the existence of God will then no longer rest wholly on difficult and tenuous philosophic arguments. Christian evidences will no longer be largely dependent on the process of sifting and appraising historical testimony. The personal and visible presence of the glorified Son of God will constitute the supreme Christian apologetic, immediately accessible to all men. It has sometimes been argued that, since genuine belief cannot be produced by sense experience (Matt. 16:17), the visible presence of Christ could have no spiritual value. But this is an illogical deduction from a valid principle. It might just as well be argued that, since faith cannot be produced by any weight of historical evidence, therefore the latter has no spiritual value. The truth is that both historical evidence and sense experience may be *channels,* though not sources, of Christian faith.

To discount wholly the value of sense experience in matters of faith is to forget the original testimony of the apostles. In his great apologetic recorded in First Corinthians 15:3-8, Paul attaches great weight to the historical fact that the risen Christ had been *"seen"* by Cephas, by the twelve, by himself, and by over five hundred brethren at the same time. If these visible "appearances" of the risen Saviour had such a high value in the apostolic era, why should we deprecate similar appearances during the millennial age; with the added advantage that then the visibility will be made readily accessible to all — for "every eye shall see Him" (Rev. 1:7). Certainly in the Millennium, as also today, the testimony of sense experience alone cannot produce the response of Christian faith. But under God it has its value, as our Lord graciously recognized in the case of Thomas (John 20:24-31).

(3) The mingling of Christ and His glorified saints with people still in the flesh on earth, by some, has been regarded as an incongruity. This has even been called, almost impiously, a "mongrel mixture." On this point, we can give no better answer than to point to the post-resurrection ministry of our Lord among His disciples, teaching them personally for the space of forty days (Acts 1:3), and even eating with them (Luke 24:43). Can it be a mere coincidence that the main subject of His teaching, while thus "mingling" with the disciples, was "the Kingdom of God?" If there was no pedagogical value in His bodily presence, why was not all this important instruction given *spiritually* after He had returned to heaven? While we should thank God every day for the spiritual presence and teaching of Christ, surely the addition of His bodily presence will be something of very precious value.

This objection at times has been based on unfair assumptions. Boettner, for example, thinks that for the saints to "return to earthly life and earthly conditions would be, literally and figuratively, a great 'come-down.'" And he feels that he would rather at death go to heaven than to suffer such a "come-down."[53] Well, of course, no intelligent premillennialist ever taught that glorified saints would return to "earthly life and earthly conditions." As for the alleged "come-down," even if some things on earth might not be wholly to our liking, we cannot forget that our Lord once "came down" into a disagreeable world to extend help to sinners. And many a missionary since that time has been willing to "come down" in the scale of human comfort in order to relieve the spiritual and physical ills of humanity. Why should anyone suppose that the saints, once glorified, will become callous to the desperate needs of the world? Especially, since in that day the relief they will be able to bring can be ministered many times more effectively, and with no physical weakness or discomfort to themselves. Can anyone suppose that the great missionaries of the past, many of whom died at the beginning of their work, would be unwilling, once glorified, to resume their beloved ministry, as our Lord resumed His ministry following His resurrection? Will the sheer joy of helping needy people be lost when we get to heaven? If the saints can today minister to the various needs of the world without fear of contamination, surely it will not be impossible in the more perfect millennial age.

(4) Another oft repeated objection to a literal reign of Christ and His saints over the nations is that this would be a "carnal" reign. A recent book, criticizing the premillennial view, puts the matter like this: "The kingship of the believer does not require a literal throne with a subject people under him. His reign is spiritual. He reigns over the devil, the flesh, and the world. Even death is subject to him. This is a much superior reign than is generally conceived. Yet people seem to be fascinated by the lesser and carnal type of reign."[54] To this argument it may be replied, first, that all premillenialists rejoice in the spiritual victory the Christian has now in Christ over the world, the flesh, and the devil. The implied dilemma is wholly false, for the difference here is not over what is affirmed, but rather in what the objector *denies*. As to his charge that a *literal* reign of Christ with His saints over the nations would

53 Loraine Boettner, *ibid.*, p. 80.
54 J. Marcellus Kik, *ibid.*, pp. 46-47.

be a *carnal* reign, I feel that his language is certainly careless, if not irreverent. For if our Lord can today exercise a literal but providential control over the nations in the Universal Kingdom of God, as He does, why should His literal but more direct control in the Millennial Kingdom be stigmatized as "carnal"?

In pursuing his illogical argument against the literality of the millennial reign, Mr. Kik arrives at an inconsistency so glaring that one wonders how he could have failed to see it. As already stated above, he believes that we are *now* living in the Millennium, and that the saints are *now* reigning with Christ. The promise of Christ to His disciples, that they would "sit on twelve thrones, judging the twelve tribes of Israel," is *now* being fulfilled, according to Mr. Kik, by the saints ruling the church. If we ask how the saints are reigning in the church, he answers that this in part is by church *discipline* (p. 45)! Thus we come at last to something very *literal;* as the late Dr. J. Gresham Machen, and others, could have personally testified. Doubtless Mr. Kik would say that the exercise of church discipline should be a *spiritual* matter; to which we heartily agree, and also point out that if church discipline can be exercised today both literally and spiritually, the same thing can be true about the reign of the saints in the coming Millennium.

As to the term "carnal," used so frequently by the objectors in an epithetical manner: if it can be applied properly to anything, certainly it would more fitly describe their alleged *present* millennial "reign" of the saints in church discipline than the premillennial view of the saints' future reign. For now, all too often, the wrong people are thrown out of the church, while the wrong people are left in; and the judges themselves need to be judged. Also, as Paul once pointed out, it is often hard to find even one man today who is wise enough to settle the ordinary disputes within the church (I Cor. 6:1-7). Actually, if the term is to be used at all, it is Mr. Kik's view of the saints' so-called present "reign" in the church that deserves the term "carnal."[55] There will be no such carnality when the perfected and glorified saints reign in the future Kingdom of Christ.

In his attempts to vindicate the *spirituality* of his own view, and also fasten the charge of *carnality* upon his opponents, Mr. Kik lists the many great spiritual blessings *now* enjoyed by the saved: Christ is our Saviour; God is our Father; the Holy Spirit is our

---

[55] See St. Paul's application of the term to the Corinthians (I Cor. 3:3).

Comforter; we are members of the Bride of Christ; we have security
from all possible enemies. Then he asks, What more could we desire? And he wonders whether perhaps we may not be hankering
after *carnal* things — more money, less physical discomfort.[56] Well,
the answer to this is that, like Mr. Kik, we thank God every day
for what we have right now by the grace of our Lord Jesus Christ.
But, with the Apostle Peter, we are also looking for even more of
the exhaustless grace of God which is to be brought at the "revelation of Jesus Christ" (I Pet. 1:13) to establish His Kingdom over
all the earth. We admit that we are concerned about the problems
of physical existence. We think that the Church right now could
well manifest more of the compassion of Christ about these things.
We would like to see an *end* of the terrible diseases of mankind,
an *end* of the deadly peril of another world war, and *complete*
economic justice for all men. Furthermore, we would like to see the
Good News of Christ carried *fully* to every human soul without
delay. And this takes both material wealth and physical stamina,
even in Mr. Kik's present-day millennium.

It may be argued, of course, that the Church should be working
at these problems right now, and not waiting with folded arms for
the coming of a future kingdom. To this we agree; and we thank
God for the souls already saved, and for the influence of the Gospel
toward the solution of economic problems and relief of human suffering. But the problems are so vast in number and size, the
wheels of progress turn so slowly, and the reverses often so disastrous, that we find ourselves longing for another intrusion of supernatural help from above, greater and more prolonged than any
such intrusion in past history, to reinforce the present efforts of His
people. Moreover, we believe that such help from above has been
promised in the Word of God; and that in looking for its coming
we shall be made better servants of His, and more faithful in all
that we do before the arrival of His Kingdom. The intelligent
Christian does not serve God because he is afraid the world will
go to pot without his efforts, but out of love and obedience to a
Saviour who gave Himself that we might be saved.

The prejudice against such divine help from above, strange to
say, has been stubborn, unreasonable, and not a little childish.
Many years ago I sat in a seminar which was discussing some of
the problems of society. The professor in charge had said that if

---

[56] J. Marcellus Kik, *ibid.*, p. 30.

only two goals would be reached — the abolition of war and the attainment of social justice — the world could enjoy a virtual millennium. He was a bit surprised at my suggestion that these identical goals are named in Biblical prophecy, to be realized fully in the Kingdom which is to be established supernaturally at the coming of Christ. But his rejoinder was that such a way of solving human problems would not be a good thing at all; that men should and must solve their own problems. When I asked whether he might not welcome a little supernatural help from above, he remained unshaken in his position.

Of course, logically, if it is always best for us to solve our own problems, we should kill off all our geniuses, for these rare individuals have solved hundreds of problems completely beyond the ability of the vast majority of the human race. (And the argument is strengthened by the fact that Christ is no alien to our race, but became true man by His virgin birth, and still so remains). But the rather petulant prejudice against supernatural help from above has no logic. It recalls the remark of Robert Louis Stevenson who, when he was told of the death of Matthew Arnold, said, "That's too bad. He won't like God." Or the "propaganda" advertisement appearing in a radical socialist publication: "WANTED — A new social order; a new sense of economic justice, a new approach to the problem of war, and a new political system. *No gods need apply.*" Or the erection of a placard by a certain French king which read: "All miracles in this place are forbidden."

A measure of this secular foolishness seems to have rubbed off on some of our present-day theologians. They are willing to let God work miracles in what they call the spiritual realm, but in other realms they have posted their "no miracle" signs all over the place. We need to be taught again and again that our fallen human nature deeply resents the truth that there are some things wholly beyond our power to do, and which only God can supernaturally accomplish. Men may indeed *improve* themselves and society in many ways; but just as the regeneration of the human soul is a miracle from above, so also is the regeneration of society. "With men this is impossible." This is not a philosophy of quietism, but only a realistic recognition of human limitations in a sinful world. The hope of supernatural reinforcement from above, instead of stultifying Christian effort, should give us new encouragement because we know that *"The morning cometh."* The eschatological motive has been a tremendous force in the history of human progress; and recently is being given more of the attention that it deserves, even by liberal writers.[57]

(5) The employment of *force*, it has been objected by some theologians, would be wholly inappropriate in any future Kingdom of God. They argue that the divine reign should be "spiritual" in character, a rule of *love* through the Gospel. To this we may reply that what *ought* to be is often not the same as what actually *is*. In a sinful race, the ideal is one thing; the realistic possibilities are often something else. As an example of this clash of opinion, we have, on the one hand, a very influential, liberal, religious publication declaring that no peace in the world can be "based on force"; while, on the other hand, a great secular magazine argues that "America's strength (militarily) is the last, best hope of peace on earth." The truth lies somewhere in between these two extremes. The power of love is great beyond imagination, but even love has its limitations in a sinful world where freedom of will exists. If this were not so, we might safely dispense with civil government as the world advances. Actually, however, the progress of civilization only increases the size and complexity of government. More than that, if love conquers all, hell itself might be abolished at last. The present need for human government, and the everlasting character of hell, constitute the best answer to those who feel that the employment of *force* is unworthy of the Kingdom of God.

In discussing the matter of human government, a recent writer has stated realistically the problem as follows:

> The science of morals is concerned with things as they ought to be. The science of law is concerned with things as they are supposed to be. The science of politics is concerned with things as they are . . . . You cannot make governments out of moral aspirations. Every revolution begins as an idea, but it ends as a fact. Absolute power (like every sort of power) can be yielded, of course, but it cannot be conferred. It can only be taken and kept.[58]

This very blunt appraisal of the problem of power among human governments is not inapplicable to the divine government. It should remind us that when the Kingdom of Christ arrives, it will not come by a majority vote of the people, *nor* as a result of international agreements. It will rather be a supernatural action of divine sovereignty, resulting in the glad cry, "We give thee thanks, O Lord

[57] See Ray C. Petry, *Christian Eschatology and Social Thought* (New York: Abingdon Press, 1956).

[58] F. Lyman Windolph, "Wanted: A Sovereign," *The American Scholar*, No. 2, 1947, p. 161.

God Almighty . . . because thou hast taken to thee thy great power, and hast reigned" (Rev. 11:17).

IV. THE REVELATION OF THE FINAL UNIVERSAL KINGDOM OF GOD (Rev. 20:7-22:5)

The remaining two chapters [of Rev.] describe the eternal and consummated kingdom of God on the new earth. As the world of nations is pervaded by Divine influence in the millennium, so that of *nature* shall be, not annihilated, but transfigured, in the subsequent eternal state. The earth was cursed for man, but is redeemed by the second Adam. *Now* is the Church; in the millennium shall be the kingdom; after that shall be the new world wherein God shall be all in all . . . God's works are progressive. The millennium in which sin and death are much restricted, is the transition state from the old to the new earth. The millennium is the age of regeneration. The final age shall be wholly free from sin and death.   —*A. R. Fausset*[59]

By some interpreters, the New Jerusalem of chapter 21 has been assigned to the Millennial Kingdom of chapter 20. But this view must be rejected for various good reasons: First, it would seriously violate the literary order of the book, by reverting to a description of the Millennium after what is admittedly an account of the last Judgment in 20:11-15, which follows the Millennial Kingdom. Second, in the new condition described by chapter 21 there is neither sin nor death, but in the Millennium both are present. Third, in the language of 20:1-22:5 there is a constantly recurring note of eternal *finality* which would be entirely inappropriate for the Millennial Kingdom which is transitional in character — "a thousand years" in length. As to the *order* of events, the conclusion of Alford is sound: "The whole of the things described in the remaining portion of the book (21:1-22:5) is subsequent to the general judgment, and descriptive of the consummation of the triumph and bliss of Christ's people with Him in the eternal Kingdom of God."[60]

No attempt will be made here to treat in detail the impressive visions described in the final section of Revelation. The material belongs to the field of General Eschatology to which I hope to devote a later volume. It will be sufficient, with reference to the Kingdom, to note only the *final* character of the things now before us. For these things not only belong to the category of "last things"; they mark the *end* of the category. The keynote of the section might well be stated in the words of St. Paul — "Then cometh the end" (I Cor. 15:24).

---

[59] A. R. Fausset, *ibid.*, p. 724.
[60] Henry Alford, *ibid.*, on Rev. 21:1.

1. *The Final Rebellion* (Rev. 20:7-10)

Fire came down . . . and devoured them.   —*Rev 20:9*

This rebellion of Satan and his deluded followers is not part of the Millennial Kingdom, but follows it. As John describes the tragic event, it does not come until "the thousand years are expired" (vs. 7). Then for a brief season the divine restraint will be relaxed for the purpose of providing one last and supreme demonstration of the appalling wickedness of the unregenerated human heart. How such a rebellion could spring up, following a kingdom which began with a society of regenerated people, should be no mystery. For regenerated parents are no guarantee of regenerated progeny, as we should have learned long ago. If the number who respond to the satanic leadership seems disappointingly large — "as the sand of the sea" — we must remember that under the millennial control of disease and death, the human race will greatly multiply. Moreover, the large number of the unsaved is always balanced by the promise made to Abraham — "I will multiply thy seed as the stars of heaven, and as the sand which is upon the sea shore" (Gen. 22:17). And the saved in every age, in a sense, are Abraham's seed (Gal. 3:29). When John describes the objective of the satanic attack as "the camp of the saints," there is no necessary implication that all the millennial saints are shut up in Jerusalem.[61] It only means that Satan recognizes, as we might expect, that here in "the beloved city" is the center or "citadel" (*parembolē*; cf. Acts 21:34) of the millennial government. The rebellion ends in judgment, not in a battle. Though Satan gathers the rebels "to battle," there is no battle. The end is by the fire of divine *execution*.

2. *The Final Judgment* (Rev. 20:11-15)

I saw a great white throne.   —*Rev. 20:11*

a. The *Judge* here must be our Lord Jesus Christ. To Him alone, according to His own claims, has been committed "all judgment": "the Father judgeth no man" (John 5:22). And for this immense adjudication our Lord is perfectly fitted; for He not only has the requisite divine ability, but He alone of the Persons of the Godhead has had a personal experience of human life, being not only Son of God but also "Son of man" (John 5:27).

b. The *purpose* of this judgment is not to determine who is to be lost or saved. This is a matter which must be settled before death. In this respect, all men are always living in a day of judgment, a time

---

[61] See Loraine Boettner's unfair caricature, *ibid.*, p. 71.

when by the grace of God personal destiny is determined by human decision. As our Lord once said, "He that believeth on him is not judged: he that believeth not hath been judged already, because he hath not believed on the name of the only begotten Son of God" (John 3:18, ASV). The purpose of final judgment is to exhibit the character of the judged and award to them "according to their works."

c. The *subjects* of this judgment are named in the passage as "the dead" (Rev. 20:12). And since they are to be judged "according to their works" (vss. 12-13), the implication points strongly to a class of people who are dead spiritually as well as physically. "By works of law shall no flesh be justified in his sight" (Rom. 3:20, ASV margin). For the saved, on the other hand, there can be no such judgment, because their judgment with reference to sin took place at Calvary. It is a very solemn fact, of course, that the believer's *works* must be brought into judgment for reward or loss (I Cor. 3:12-15), but this will have taken place at some point between the Rapture of the Church and the establishment of the Millenial Kingdom; and it will have nothing to do with salvation. Furthermore, since all those saved before the Millennial Kingdom will have a part in the "first resurrection," and during the Millennium none of the saved will die, there appears to be no reason for any resurrection for saved people afterwards. If there are any of the saved in this final resurrection, nothing at all is said about their destination, whereas that of the unsaved is specifically stated (Rev. 20:15).

d. The *books* mentioned must include at least the written Word of God and the divine record of human deeds. In the latter perhaps there will be other books; such as the book of *memory;* and the book of the *universe* where, it has been suggested by some, there could be found a physical recording of the image of every act committed and the sound of every word uttered from the beginning of the world. As to the "book of life" which appears here, this seems to be definitely set apart from the books out of which the dead are to be judged according to their works. It is not one of "the books," but "another book." Its purpose is to testify silently, by its omissions, against those who had rejected the mercy of God. Significantly, there is here no book of death, for while men are elected to salvation, none are elected to damnation. It is their own choice, not God's, that brings them at last into the place of doom.

e. The *outcome* of this judgment is eternal perdition in the lake of fire (vss. 14-15). No other destination is even mentioned in the context of the passage. If any are saved out of this judgment and ushered into heaven, strangely nothing is said about them. Such an idea seems to be excluded by the opening words of the passage: the Judge sits on a "great white throne" (vs. 11). Encircling this throne there is no "rainbow" of bright hope, as in the case of the pre-Kingdom judgment throne (4:3), bringing salvation to an innumerable multitude (7:9-14). But the color of the final judgment throne is the ineffable whiteness of absolute holiness and justice, unrelieved by any semblance of grace. At this solemn adjudication the matter of rebellion and discord in the universe receives its final disposition in preparation for the Kingdom in which God will be "all in all."

3. *The Final Universe* (Rev. 21:1)

A new heaven, and a new earth.   —*Rev. 21:1*

The "heaven" and "earth" here undoubtedly refer to the *physical* universe. The "first" or original universe passes away, and is replaced by a "new" universe. This does not necessarily mean the annihilation of our present world of matter; for the Greek *kainos* may mean new in *character* rather than in substance. The same term is used of the regenerated believer: he becomes a "new creation" (II Cor. 5:17, ASV) in a crisis which does not annihilate the personal entity but transforms it. So in the final change of the physical universe, it does not lose its identity, but will pass away as to its "outward and recognizable form" and be renewed in a "fresh and more glorious one."[62]

The method of renewal, according to Peter, will be by fire: "the heavens shall pass away with a great noise, and the elements shall melt with fervent heat, the earth also and the works that are therein shall be burned up." And out of this divinely wrought dissolution will come "new heavens and a new earth, wherein dwelleth righteousness" (II Pet. 3:10-13). Peter's language here clearly distinguishes between the physical universe and the righteous order of things which will dwell there. And the transformation by fire applies to the former.

Modern research is teaching us more and more about the wonders of *physical* substance. It is no longer regarded as the dead and mechanistic thing postulated by an obsolete science. The possibili-

[62] Henry Alford, *ibid.,* on Rev. 21:1.

ties existing in a clod of earth are beyond human imagination. And what God can do with our present universe, in preparation for His eternal Kingdom, can only be guessed at. Yet perhaps we have a suggestion in the nature of the resurrection body of the saved where corruptible matter by the energizing power of the Spirit takes on a wondrous character, being made glorious, powerful, and imperishable (I Cor. 15:42-44). Our present physical universe, with all its marvels, is nevertheless now a realm characterized by transience, decay, and death. Even the millennial state, with these liabilities under far-reaching divine control, will fall short of the ideal world. "We, according to his promise, look for new heavens and a new earth" (II Pet. 3:13).

4. The Final City (Rev. 21:2, 9-22:5)

That great city, the holy Jerusalem.   —Rev. 21:10

It is interesting to observe that, while the account of the new universe is confined to a single verse, no less than twenty-five verses are used to describe its great city in detail. The record speaks of its "glory" (vs. 11), its "gates" (vss. 12-13, 21, 25), its "wall" (vss. 14, 18), its "measure" (vss. 15-17), its "foundations" (vss. 19-20), its "street" (vs. 21), its "temple" (vs. 22), its "light" (vs. 23), its "nations" (vs. 24), its "river" (22:1), its wondrous "tree" (vs. 2), and its "throne" (vs. 3).

The name of the city, as in common usage, refers to both the structure and those who dwell there. According to the angelic word, the "holy Jerusalem" is "the bride, the Lamb's wife" (21:9-10). The members of the Church will be its honored citizens (Phil. 3:20, ASV). But the saved of all ages will have free access to its glories and benefits (Rev. 21:24-26).

Although the details of its description suggest many very precious symbolical meanings, we must not lose sight of the *literality* of the city. For it is a *place*, "prepared" by the Lord of glory Himself (Rev. 21:2; John 14:1-3). Surely, it would be foolish to argue that, because in the Holy Communion service its symbolism is the thing of highest importance, therefore it is of no consequence whether or not we have a literal bread and a literal cup. If the King of the New Jerusalem and also its inhabitants are literal, there is no reason for balking at the literality of the city itself. While some details of its structure may not be fully understood, none of them are wholly outside the realm of sober possibility. If there were twelve apostles and twelve tribes of Israel, why should not the new Jerusalem have its twelve foundations and twelve gates, bearing these historic names? (Rev. 21:12-14). These details have an anchor in the facts of history.

The dimensions of the New Jerusalem are admittedly gigantic — "twelve thousand furlongs" in breadth, and length, and height (vs. 16). Even if we interpret this language as indicating the shape of a perfect cube, however, the concept is not inconceivable. In this case, its lines and equal dimensions would suggest that exquisite simplicity toward which modern architecture is moving. But on the other hand, as it may be, if the height of the city refers to the *eminence* upon which the city is set (possibly formed by the twelve foundations arranged in pyramid fashion), then again the literal concept would be one of great architectural splendor. The 144-cubit wall seems to harmonize better with this interpretation of the city's dimensions. What a sight such a city would be, gradually rising toward the sky by the great step-backs of its twelve-jeweled foundations. It is true that this concept would be totally out of proportion with the dimensions of our present earth. But there is to be a "new earth." And if the earth is to be made the eternal dwelling place of Christ and His redeemed people, as the passage suggests, then the earth will become the center of all things. Surely there would be a divine fitness in this, for here the great drama of sin and redemption will have been played out before an awed universe. And in that case, doubtless, the new earth will be so constituted, both as to size and glory, that it will harmonize perfectly with its eternal city.

5. *The Final Kingdom*

They shall reign for ever and ever.   —*Rev. 22:5*

a. When the last enemy of God has been put down by our Lord acting as Mediatorial King, the purpose of His Mediatorial Kingdom will have been fulfilled. As the Apostle Paul wrote, "He must reign, till he hath put all enemies under his feet" (I Cor. 15:25). This point in the history of the government of God will have been reached when death itself comes to an end, for "the last enemy that shall be destroyed is death" (I Cor. 15:26). And this point is clearly indicated in Revelation 20:14 where we are told that "death" is cast into the lake of fire. With the end of this "last enemy" there can be no more any intermediate state; therefore "Hades" also is abolished. In the inspired record, the destruction of death and Hades appears as the last act of our Lord in preparation for the new and eternal world.

As we pass from chapter 20 into chapter 21 of the Apocalypse, therefore, we stand at the junction point between two worlds and between two kingdoms. It is the end of the "first" or "natural" order of things, and the beginning of the final order of things. Here also the Mediatorial Kingdom of our Lord ends, not by abolition, but by its mergence into the Universal Kingdom of God. Thus it is perpetuated forever, no longer as a separate entity, but in indissoluble union with the original Kingdom of God from which it sprang. What will happen is succinctly described in St. Paul's classic passage on the subject: "Then cometh the end, when he shall have delivered up the kingdom to God, even the Father; when he shall have put down all rule and all authority and power. . . . And when all things shall be subdued unto him, then shall the Son also himself be subject unto him that put all things under him, that God may be all in all" (I Cor. 15:24, 28). This does not mean the end of our Lord's regal activity, but rather that from here onward in the unity of the Godhead He reigns with the Father as the eternal Son. There are no longer two thrones: one His Messianic throne and the other the Father's throne, as our Lord indicated in Revelation 3:21. In the final Kingdom there is but one throne, and it is "the throne of God and of the Lamb" (22:3).

b. The changed conditions in this final Kingdom will be very wonderful and far-reaching. But, in general, it should be observed that there is no *absolute* break with the former world, as in the Platonic postulate. The Mediatorial Kingdom of our Lord will constitute the glorious consummating era of the first order of things and will serve as the divine *bridge* between the temporal order and the eternal order. As Lange has well said, "The Apocalypse alone sets forth the true mediation of the last metamorphosis of the old world, in the Millennial Kingdom."[63] When in the record of Revelation 21:5 the voice from heaven announces, "Behold, I make all things new," we must not suppose that our world will then lose its identity, but rather that in its reconstituted form, it will begin to exist under new and perfect conditions. Two of these conditions may be stated as follows:

First, of all these changed conditions, perhaps the greatest is that at last "the tabernacle of God is with men, and he will dwell with them, and they shall be his people, and God himself shall be with them, and be their God" (Rev. 21:3). Even during the glorious

[63] Lange, *Revelation*, p. 363.

millennial reign of Christ with His Church on earth, their actual
residence will be in heaven. But in the eternal Kingdom heaven
comes down to earth; God dwells with men! At last the long history of temporary theophanies will be done. In the face of Jesus
Christ men at last will see the face of God with no hindrance of
circumstance or interruption of temporality.

Second, in this final Kingdom of God some of the most familiar
things of the present life will be missing: "There shall be no more
death, neither sorrow, nor crying, neither shall there be any more
pain: for the former things are passed away" (21:4). And in such
a world, of course, there can be no sin; for sin is the cause of all
tears, all pain, and all death. Thus, we read, that in this new order of
things with its glorious city, there will be no place for the "unbelieving" and sinners (21:8). "There shall in no wise enter into it
anything that defileth, neither whatsoever worketh abomination, or
maketh a lie" (21:27). The description closes on a somber note:
All the unsaved are shut "without" the city (22:15), and for such
there is no remedy (22:11).

c. As the divinely given visions of the future Kingdom come to
an end in 22:5, our Lord Jesus Christ Himself speaks from heaven
historically in a final word to "the churches" (22:16). And He
identifies Himself here as "the bright and morning star"; for while
during the life of the churches on earth it is night, not day, the
morning is always "at hand" (Rom. 13:12). In His message we
note two important things:

First, as an antidote to any possible hesitation (often unspoken)
to believe all the wondrous revelation of this book of the Kingdom,
we are given His own gracious assurance: "These sayings are faithful and true" (22:6). And in the face of this divine validation, all our
doubts must wither away and die. For the very name of the Speaker
is "Faithful and True" (19:11); and therefore of all He has spoken
nothing can possibly fail.

Second, to "the churches" on earth, He gives a thrice-repeated
reminder of something which must never be forgotten; for it will
give courage in the hour of battle, strength in the hour of weakness,
and hope in the hour of despair. Let us hear Him as He speaks:

> "Behold, I come quickly" (vs. 7)
> "Behold, I come quickly" (vs. 12)
> "Surely, I come quickly" (vs. 21)

Thus, in His last historic word from heaven, our Lord writes once more over the portals of the Church that "Blessed Hope" under which she must live and labor during every moment of her existence upon the earth. And if we are wise in the simplicity of the Word of God, we shall respond in the words of the "beloved disciple," who heard and recorded the message:

"Even so, come, Lord Jesus" (vs. 20).

APPENDIX

Chapter XXVII

THE "SPIRITUALITY" OF THE KINGDOM

In the field of inductive logic there is a class of fallacies which arise through the careless use of language. Bacon named them "Idols of the Marketplace." Nothing could be more profitless than discussion without some prior agreement as to the meaning of important terms. To try to win an argument where terms are not mutually understood is like trying, as Locke has reminded us, "to dispossess a vagrant of his habitation who has no settled abode."[1]

Current discussions of the Kingdom of God involve the use of certain terms which often carry different meanings when used by different writers. Sometimes a single writer will use the same term in more than one sense or use different terms to convey the same idea. Such terms are "establish," "earthly," "heavenly," "carnal," "force," "conditional," "certainty," "postponement," "abeyance," etc. But most abused of all is the term "spiritual."

No other word in the vocabulary of the doctrine of the Kingdom has been the occasion of more misunderstanding and useless argument. A great deal of this confusion, in my opinion, has been due to the influence of Platonic philosophy in the field of Christian theology. Many a preacher, who may have never read a single sentence from Plato, has been more or less, perhaps unconsciously, under the sway of the rigid metaphysical dualism of this philosopher. To such men, the premillennial doctrine of a divine Kingdom established on earth, having political and physical aspects, seems to be sheer materialism. Yet their own theological views may involve some very serious practical inconsistencies. It has been said, with some justification, that a man's life and actions are the surest guide to his actual beliefs.

A parable will illustrate the point: During a church banquet a group of preachers were discussing the nature of the Kingdom of God. One expressed his adherence to the premillennial view of a

[1] "Essay Concerning Human Understanding," Book III, Chap. X.

literal kingdom to be established on earth among men. To this a rather belligerent two-hundred-pound preacher snorted, "Ridiculous! Such an idea is nothing but materialism." When asked to state his own view, he replied, "The Kingdom is a *spiritual* matter. The Kingdom of God has *already* been established, and is *within you.* Don't you gentlemen know that the Kingdom is not eating and drinking, but righteousness and peace and joy in the Holy Ghost?" And then the speaker reached hungrily across the table and speared another enormous piece of fried chicken! Nobody tried to answer him. As a matter of fact, no answer was necessary; he had answered his own argument. As the French would say, "He was hoist with his own petard." At the risk of being thought tiresome, let me recite the obvious conclusion: If the Kingdom of God can exist now on earth in a two-hundred-pound preacher full of fried chicken, without any reprehensible materialistic connotations, perhaps it could also exist in the same way among men on earth who will at times be eating and drinking under more perfect conditions in a future millennial kingdom.

But let us get back to a more serious side of the argument. Of course, the Kingdom of God is primarily a spiritual kingdom, always, and wherever it exists. But a spiritual kingdom, in Biblical parlance, *can manifest itself and produce tangible effects in a physical world;* or to be more precise, *in the world of sense experience.* If it cannot, I would see no practical value in having it here and now. But strangely enough, some of the very men who are so scornful of the alleged "materialism" of a millennial kingdom, are the most insistent that the Church *today* must make effective in society what they call the social and moral ideals of the present kingdom of God. Thus, it is our duty to vote the right ticket politically, give to the Red Cross, help the Boy Scouts, support the United Nations, endow hospitals, etc. But if a "spiritual" kingdom can and should produce such effects at the present time through the very imperfect agency of sinful men, why cannot the same thing be true in larger measure in the coming age when the rule of God will be mediated more perfectly and powerfully through the Eternal Son personally present among men as the Mediatorial King? In other words, if there can be a divine kingdom functioning here and now in the realm of sense experience without the taint of "materialism," what is wrong with the same thing in the future? Any denial of such a possibility, on alleged rational grounds, would at last plunge us back philosophically into the hopeless dilemma of Platonic dualism, which is still the curse of much that is called Christian thinking in the field of eschatology. Such a metaphysical dualism in Christian theology is today "obsolete" and "naive."[2] The conventional sneer at what has been called the "materialistic and carnal kingdom" of Premillennialism, in my judgment, has lost much of its force. What the opponents of the premillennial view of the Kingdom must now do, to win the argument on logical grounds, is to show that our Lord will never return bodily to earth in glory, personally and visibly.

The reasoning of such men at times seems very curious. If physicians conquer diseases, if scientists eliminate certain physical hazards, if by social legislation governments improve the quality of human existence, if wise statesmen succeed in preventing a war, etc., — these things are often cited as evidence of the progress of a present Kingdom of God. But if the Lord Jesus Christ Himself returns to earth in person to accomplish these same things, more perfectly and universally, then we are told that such a kingdom would be "carnal."

It should hardly be necessary to point out that, in the Word of God, it is nothing new to find a *spiritual cause* producing tangible effects in the area of sense experience. On this point, the personal testimony of the late Ananias and his wife Sapphira would be very impressive. These two people lived in the very beginning of that historical era when, as it is claimed by some, God established a "spiritual kingdom" among men. But they learned by bitter experience that a *spiritual* force can operate in the *physical* world of nature. Berkhof, in criticizing the idea that God will use force in the establishing of His kingdom, seems to feel that there is something utterly incongruous between spiritual power and physical effects, and that any such effects in the material world cannot be due to the power of God's Spirit.[3] But Ananias and his wife certainly died a sudden *physical* death because they had lied to the Holy Ghost. As to the question of whether a display of "force" could have any salutory results in the Kingdom of God, which Berkhof seems to doubt, Luke is careful to describe the effect of the death of Ananias and Sapphira thus: "And great fear came

---

[2] Burton Scott Easton, *International Standard Bible Encyclopedia* (Chicago: Howard-Severance, 1915), Vol. IV, p. 2565.
[3] L. Berkhof, *The Kingdom of God* (Grand Rapids: Eerdmans Publishing Co., 1951), p. 174.

upon all the church, and upon as many as heard these things"
(Acts 5:11).

The notion that a spiritual kingdom can have no immediate relation to considerations which are the stuff of physical existence, is
one of the strangest idols ever constructed in the cave of the human
mind. God is spirit; and wherever His power breaks supernaturally
into the system of nature, the cause may properly be called "spiritual," whatever the effect may be; whether the healing of a disease,
the raising of a dead body, the regeneration of a sinner, or the setting up of a political state on the earth. The kingdom established
at Sinai was not an earthly kingdom, although it was on the earth.
Actually, it was a spiritual kingdom which came down from heaven
historically into the world of physical existence and operated there
by the supernatural agency of God Himself. If we hold fast this
truth, we shall have less difficulty dealing with philosophically inclined theologians who seem to feel that there is something degrading about the idea of a spiritual kingdom established on earth
in control of human affairs within the realm of sense experience.

One thing in this connection that seems to disturb some theologians is the thought of a kingdom in which the glorified Christ with
His risen saints will be mingling with men of flesh and blood on
the earth. To illustrate this point, I quote from Berkhof's final
paragraph in his book on *The Kingdom of God*. The author first
states the premillennial view as follows: "Jesus Christ, the glorified
Lord, will be seated upon the throne at Jerusalem. And the risen
and immortal saints will reign with him 'the thousand years.' And
besides these there will be also men in the flesh, both of the Jewish
and of other nations, some converted and others unconverted. They
will all share in the glory of the Kingdom, and all enjoy the open
vision of Jesus Christ." Then with considerable indignation Berkhof exclaims, "With Brown we too would call out, 'What a mongrel state of things is this! What an abhorred mixture of things
totally inconsistent with each other.' This representation is not
warranted by Scripture and grates upon our Christian sensibility.
Beet truly says: 'We cannot conceive mingled together on the same
planet some who have yet to die and others who have passed through
death and will die no more. Such confusion of the present age with
the age to come is in the last degree unlikely'" (p. 176).

Here we have a prime example of the influence of philosophic
dualism in Christian theology. If Plato were living today, giving

a series of lectures on the millennial question, he might very well employ the exact language of Berkhof, Brown, Beet, *et al.* Certainly in his philosophical sensitive soul he would regard with abhorrence the idea of a spiritual kingdom having any genuine and worth-while relation to the world of sense experience. But the writers of Holy Scripture are not bound by any such philosophical prejudices. While they recognized the reality of mind and matter, of spirit and body, to them there was not only one *God* but also one *world*. And in this universe of God there is no unbridgeable chasm between that which is physical and that which is spiritual. In the Garden of Eden, God who is spirit walks and talks with man made of the dust of the ground (Gen. 3:8-10). The Lord Himself with two angels is entertained in the tent of Abraham (Gen. 18). To Moses the Lord spoke face to face, "as a man speaketh unto his friend" (Exod. 33:11). But the incarnation of the eternal Son in a body of flesh and blood is the supreme demonstration that there is no inherent or necessary antagonism between matter and spirit. This is to say nothing of the risen Christ appearing over and over to men and women in the flesh, mingling with them, eating with them, and teaching them for the space of forty days.

The entire history of divine revelation bears no uncertain witness that the penetration of "spirit" into the physical realm of nature is never regarded as something strange, abnormal, or incongruous. It is true that human sin has introduced a limiting factor into the situation. Man did lose his personal fellowship with God. But sin itself at bottom is a *spiritual* problem. While its effects are most apparent in the physical realm, matter is not an evil in itself. The ancient error of Gnosticism has been universally rejected by orthodox theologians, yet its baneful shadow still hangs over certain areas of eschatology. This alleged abhorrence at the thought of any intermingling of the "spiritual" and the "material" in a future millennial kingdom is not necessarily a normal reaction of the human reason. It is rather what the psychologists have called a "learned reaction." The Apostle Paul, well schooled in the philosophies of his day, solemnly warned against this danger: "Beware lest any man spoil you through [his] philosophy and vain deceit, after the tradition of men, . . . and not after Christ" (Col. 2:8). And the next verse makes it clear that the warning had to do with a false dualism, which would later develop into the historic school of Gnosticism, but which already was present in Paul's day: "For in him [Christ] dwelleth all the fulness of the Godhead bodily [*somatikos*]." The incarnate Son of God, in whose body both deity and humanity dwelt together in perfect union, is still the most complete answer to all gnostic tendencies, whether ancient or modern.

It is only fair to say that Dr. Berkhof, from whose scholarly book I have quoted above, recognizes that "spiritual" and "material" blessings can dwell together in the *final* stage of the Kingdom without any necessary incongruity or discord. In fact, in generous vein, he concedes that the premillennial view of the Kingdom has done some service as an antidote to a "one-sided spiritual conception of the Kingdom." He says that Premillennialism "reminds us of the fact that the Kingdom of God is something more than the purely spiritual invisible reign of God in the hearts of men; and that in the future it will find expression also in a visible external organization. It corrects the mistaken idea that the Kingdom consists only in spiritual gifts and spiritual graces, and teaches us to look with confidence for a material creation of resplendent beauty. In view of the prophetic utterances to which it directs our attention, the erroneous impression that the future Kingdom will offer enjoyments only to the soul, is swept away by the glad assurances that it will afford rich and varied material blessings as well" (p. 158). I doubt whether any premillennialist could have written any finer words on the point at issue. They prove that Dr. Berkhof is not basically a Platonist in his philosophy. If I understand him rightly, Berkhof has no serious objection to the mingling of spiritual and material blessings in the final and eternal state. But he rejects the idea of such a mingling of things in a Millennial Kingdom *this side of the eternal state.*

While space does not permit any full discussion of the Biblical meaning of the Greek adjective *pneumatikos,* at least something should be said about its general usage. It occurs twenty-six times in the New Testament, twice in adverbial form. In itself the term does not necessarily connote something morally good — in Ephesians 6:12 the demonic hosts are called *pneumatika.* Nor does the term necessarily exclude the idea of physical substance — in First Corinthians 15:44 the resurrection body of the Christian is named a *soma pneumatikon.* With reference to the things of God, which is its general connection, the meaning of *pneumatikos* is something *"emanating from the Divine Spirit, or exhibiting its effects and so its character";* that is, something *"produced by the sole power of*

God Himself without natural instrumentality, supernatural."[4] Therefore, the term may be used to designate a divine origin or *cause,*
and also to describe the *effects* produced by such a cause *in any
realm whatsoever,* whether physical or metaphysical. If we hold fast
to this general idea we cannot slip into unnecessarily narrow definitions. Consider, as an excellent example of the broad New Testament use of the term, the text in First Corinthians 10:3 where
Paul affirms that the Israelites "did all eat the same spiritual food."
What was this food? Well, the Old Testament record seems perfectly clear; but let A. T. Robertson answer: "The reference is to
the manna which is termed 'spiritual' by reason of its supernatural
character."[5] Now all sorts of explanations have been offered as to
the identity of this strange food which Israel ate for forty years
in the wilderness, but no reputable scholar ever suggested that it
was not a *physical* substance. The people ground it in mills, beat
it in mortars, baked or boiled it; it had a certain appearance and
its taste was described; if kept too long it even bred worms! (Exod.
16 and Num. 11). Yet the Apostle Paul, guided by the Holy Spirit,
says this manna was spiritual food. Meyer, commenting on Paul's
statement, well says, "It was, although material in itself . . . a food
of supernatural, divine, and spiritual origin."[6]

It is true that occasionally the New Testament uses "spiritual"
as a contrasting term to that which is either "natural" or "carnal."
Thus Paul speaks of the "first man Adam" as "natural [*psuchikon*],"
and the "last Adam" as "spiritual"; but the contrast here does not
exclude the factor of materiality, for both Adam and Christ had
bodies of flesh (I Cor. 15:45-46). In verse 44 Paul applies the
same contrasting terms to the two bodies: the present body is
psuchikon, while the resurrection body will be *pneumatikon.* But here
again the idea of materiality is not excluded, for the resurrection
body of Christ had "flesh and bones" (Luke 24:39). The real contrast is between the respective energizing principles of the two. Even
where the contrast is between "spiritual things" and "carnal [*psuchikon*] things" (I Cor. 9:11), it is not invidious. For both classes of
things here are good, originating with God who is the Creator of
all; although, of course, the one is superior to the other.

In the Old Testament, spirit and matter are never absolutely op-

[4] Thayer, *Lexicon of the New Testament,* p. 523, 3.a.
[5] *Word Pictures in the New Testament* (New York: Harper and Bros., 1930),
Vol. IV, p. 151.
[6] *Commentary on the New Testament, in loc.*

posed to each other. The Spirit of God comes upon men to work wonders in a physical context: upon Bezaleel to give craftsmanship in metal and wood (Exod. 31:1-5); upon the judges to give skill in military affairs (Judg. 6:34); upon Samson to bestow great physical strength (Judg. 15:14). Even in the much quoted passage from Zechariah — "Not by might, nor by power, but by my spirit" — the physical factor is present. For the tasks to be accomplished here were the rebuilding of the temple and the overcoming of foes who were obstructing the work (cf. Zech. 4:6, 9 with Ezra 4:1-4).

CHAPTER XXVIII

A PREMILLENNIAL PHILOSOPHY OF HISTORY

Christianity is not a philosophy. But Christianity has a philosophy — the best and the brightest of all philosophies. In fact, it will be the *final* philosophy, not only because it is founded upon divine revelation but also because it does justice to all points of view which have any value. Most philosophies are very narrow, often based upon only one aspect of reality. In the very rich variety of the world, the average philosopher may select one segment of reality which seems most impressive to him, and then proceed to explain the universe in terms of that one thing, which then becomes the "type-phenomenon" of his system. Thus one man is impressed by the fact of mind and he becomes an idealist. Another is intrigued by the wonders of matter and he becomes a materialist. In Christian philosophy both mind and matter are recognized as worth-while realities, each being given its proper place and function in the Kingdom of God.

Hence, an adequate philosophy should have at least three marks: First, it should be able to give due recognition to every aspect of reality, excluding none. Second, it should fit into a rational scheme of thought; that is, it should make sense. Third, it should have beneficial practical effects here and now. I am not a pragmatist, but they have a point. Their great mistake was to exalt this point into a theory of truth. Things are not true because they work; they work because they are true.

Now the Bible divides all human existence into two stages or kinds: With respect to their *nature* the one is called "natural," the other "spiritual" (I Cor. 15:46). As to their *context* the first is called "earthy," the second "heavenly" (I Cor. 15:48). As to their *duration* the first is called "temporal," the second "eternal" (II Cor. 4:18). As to their *time relationship* the one is described as "the life that now is," and the other as "that which is to come" (I Tim. 4:8).

Toward this present life on earth, there have been two extreme

527

attitudes: Some have wrongly regarded this life as the only thing worth-while, scoffing at the idea of anything higher and beyond. Thus, according to the consistent Marxians, there is no substance to the promise of "Pie in the sky, By and by." Others, also wrongly, have scorned the present life as of small or no account, even arguing that salvation consists in getting loose from it altogether. On this philosophic road, at various stages, were the Hindu religionists, the monastics of the middle ages; even Plato, and a few theologians who should have known better. Over against these one-sided emphases, the Bible, with its unerring philosophic balance, recognizes certain genuine values in both the present life and that which is to come. Life on the present earthly stage is, of course, not the best; *but it is "good"* (Gen. 1:31). The Bible writers are never hard put, as Plato was, to explain how the eternal world of spirit ever became entangled in the web of physical existence.

Now it should be obvious, of course, that history can deal only with the present life, that which is temporal. History can have nothing to do with the world to come, which is eternal. Likewise, any genuine philosophy of history must be subject to the same limitations. Such a philosophy, if it lays claim to any truth, must give some rational account of the life which now is.

Let us inquire now very briefly into the answers on this point which appear in certain types of theology. Classical postmillenarianism had plenty of defects, but it did make a serious attempt to deal with human history. The same thing was true of the liberalism of the last generation. Both had a goal in human history, more or less clearly defined. God was making progress, slowly at times, but surely. Science also, although not too sure about God, had its own philosophy of progress toward a goal. This optimistic theory of human progress had much its own way for the half century ending in 1914. After that the foundations were badly shaken; prop after prop went down, until today the theory is under attack from every side. Devout postmillenarianism has but few champions. Liberalism is hard put to defend itself against new enemies. Some of the greatest names in science are feeling a pessimistic "guilt" which is almost pathological.

In the midst of this debacle a new and powerful school of theology has arisen, laying claim to some of the most brilliant minds of our generation. This is the "Theology of Crisis" of Barth and Brunner, to which the so-called "Christian Realism" of such men as John C. Bennett and Reinhold Niebuhr is closely related. Their ideas have been developed largely under the influence of the Danish Kierkegaard. To the great consternation of liberalism, these men and their followers are taking refuge in pessimism so far as human history is concerned. According to their expressed views, the Kingdom of God has little, if any, relation to the present world and human history. The Kingdom to them is wholly "eschatological." But by this term the theologians of crisis do not mean what is meant ordinarily. In the Bible, eschatological events are found *in* the end of human history. But the "eschatology" of Barth is both *above* and *beyond* history, having little or no vital relation to history. Dr. Berkhof has written a very valuable summary and critical evaluation of this new "eschatology." [7]

What Berkhof fails to see, it seems to me, is that his own amillennial school of thought is in some measure "tarred with the same brush," at least in its doctrine of the established Kingdom of God. According to this view, both good and evil continue in their development side by side through human history. Then will come catastrophe and the crisis of divine judgment, not for the purpose of setting up a divine kingdom in history, but after the close of history. Our only hope is in a new world which is beyond history. Thus history becomes the preparatory "vestibule" of eternity, and not a very rational vestibule at that. It is a narrow corridor, cramped and dark, a kind of "waiting room," leading nowhere *within* the historical process, but only fit to be abandoned at last for an ideal existence on another plane. Such a view of history seems unduly pessimistic, in the light of Biblical revelation. While we who are premillennial in theology cannot, of course, accept the liberal illusion of human progress and its "profound satisfaction with human goodness," [8] we must nevertheless reject likewise the "historical" despair of the theology of crisis.

What then can we learn from past history that we may be able to infer something reliable about what to expect in the future? Well, if there is anything crystal-clear in Biblical history, it is that the existence of our sinful race falls into periods of time (call them *eras, ages, dispensations*, or whatever you will), and that each age represents an advance over the preceding age, when looked at from the standpoint of what God is giving and doing for man. It is true

[7] L. Berkhof, *op. cit.*, pp. 114-31.
[8] J. Gresham Machen, quoted by Ned B. Stonehouse in *J. Gresham Machen, A Biographical Memoir*. p. 302.

that sinful man is always failing; but where sin abounded, grace did much more abound. Thus to the old question, "Is the world getting better or worse?" from one standpoint we might answer, "The *age* is getting worse, but the course of history by the grace of God is moving forward."

On the basis of this law of divine progress in ages past, therefore, we may legitimately argue that "the life which now is" should have some proper goal. It ought to go some place. And it should not be finally adjudicated and brought to an end until all its known possibilities have been fulfilled within the admitted limits imposed by that which is finite and sinful. Let me try to make this point very clear. Forgetting for the moment what has been accomplished in the natural world by those great intrusions of supernatural power in the course of history, and confining our attention wholly to what man under God has done, we know that *some* physical diseases have been conquered, *some* wars have been prevented, *some* hazards to life and safety have been eliminated, *some* years have been added to the brief span of human life, *some* social and political evils have been corrected. If this be so, why then should there not be an age when *all* wars will be stopped, *all* diseases cured, *all* the injustices of government rooted out, and a *full* measure of years added to human life? Why should there not be an age in which all such unrealized and worth-while dreams of humanity will at last come true on earth? If there be a God in heaven, if the life which He created on the earth is worth-while, and not something evil *per se,* then there ought to be in history some worthy consummation of its long and arduous course.

It is just there that we must part company with any theological school which dogmatically asserts that there will never be such a "Golden Age" upon earth in history, which argues that for the present we must be satisfied with a mere pittance of progress in such matters, that the world which now is must continue with its terrible needs, its tragic handicaps, struggles, and problems, to the very end. And then God will suddenly write a catastrophic finis to the whole of it, abolish human existence on its first and natural plane, and thrust us all, both saved and unsaved, out into the eternal state.

I am quite well aware of the peril of basing eschatology on philosophic considerations. The Word of God alone must be our base of authority. But where Biblical interpretation may be in question, surely the right view should display clearer marks of rationality than the wrong one. And such a philosophy of history, as I have been describing, seems to me to be utterly irrational. Remembering that history has only to do with the life that now is, such a philosophy of history has no proper goal. To borrow a figure once used by the late President E. Y. Mullins[9] in another connection, it is like a man building a great staircase. Step by step he sets it up, laboring wearily, often suffering painful reverses because of tragic hazards and poor materials. And now at last it is finished. But lo, it is a stairway that goes no place! It is just a staircase, and nothing more. Or to vary the figure, history becomes a loaded gun which, when the trigger is pulled, fires a blank cartridge! Such a philosophy of history not only flies in the face of the clear statements of Scripture, but also runs contrary to the reason of man in his finest moments and aspirations.

The premillennial philosophy of history makes sense. It lays a Biblical and rational basis for a truly optimistic view of human history. Furthermore, rightly apprehended, it has practical effects. It says that life here and now, in spite of the tragedy of sin, is nevertheless something worth-while; and therefore all efforts to make it better are also worth-while. All the true values of human life will be preserved and carried over into the coming kingdom; nothing worth-while will be lost. Furthermore, we are encouraged in the midst of opposition and reverses by the assurance that help is on the way, help from above, supernatural help — "Give the king thy judgments, O God. . . . In his days shall the righteous flourish. . . . all nations shall call him blessed" (Ps. 72:1, 7, 17).

This brief discussion may well be closed with the impressive words of a great Jewish-Christian scholar:

> Is not such a consummation of history a necessary postulate of our thought? Would we not expect such a transition period between the present and the ultimate everlasting condition? As we have seen in the past a succession of developments, of which *man* is the highest, is there not to be the reign of the *Son of Man*, and a sphere in accordance with His character and glory? Is there to be always the contrast between heaven and earth, the ideal and the actual? Is the history of the world, which began with miracle, and a period of constant manifestation of the higher world unto the children of men, not to terminate in a similar age of heavenly influence and blessedness? Is earth simply a failure, abandoned by God to the power of the enemy, the scene of divine judgment, and not the scene of the vindication and triumph of righteousness? Is not Jesus the Son of Man, the Christ who shall reign on earth? We believe that He will come, and with Him the Kingdom, and with the Kingdom the fulfilment of the prayer, "Thy will be done on earth as it is in heaven." [10]

[9] *Christianity at the Crossroads*, 1924, p. 111.
[10] Adolf Saphir, *The Lord's Prayer*, pp. 207-208.

INDEX OF SUBJECTS

533

INDEX OF AUTHORS

INDEX OF TITLES

INDEX OF SCRIPTURE

545